GREAT EUROPEANS

GREAT EUROPEANS

BUILDERS OF WESTERN CIVILIZATION

Edited by
JOHN CANNING

A CENTURY BOOK
published by
SOUVENIR PRESS

ISBN 0 285 62092 4

FIRST PUBLISHED: 1973

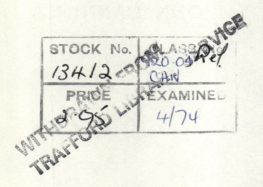
PRINTED IN GREAT BRITAIN BY
C. TINLING & CO. LTD., LONDON AND PRESCOT

CONTENTS

CONTENTS

ILLUSTRATIONS

ILLUSTRATIONS

Introduction

IT IS APPROPRIATE to salute British entry into the European community by identifying, and by assessing the significance of, some of those who are likely to be included in everybody's list of European Immortals, people who fought for the idea and ideal of Europe or at least for a Europe *des patries*, or who enriched or enhanced its diverse cultures.

It is legitimate to start with Charlemagne and Gregory VII. Each emerged to leadership in his own distinctive way; each had a sense of divine mission; each was the heir of Rome and of that idea of unity of which—despite the centuries of anarchy from the fourth to the eighth century—the material evidence was still visible and serviceable in Roman roads and Roman laws. Moreover, Charlemagne was not only politically skilful but devout. The idea of Europe had its origins as much in Christianity as in the heritage of Rome; the Church for almost a millennium was the embodiment of the idea of unity; it provided emperors and kings with their major officials, and was the vehicle through which the knowledge and learning of the past was preserved. The idea of Europe is then Christian as well as Roman.

Any survey of great Europeans shows the richness and diversity of European culture. It demonstrates also the persistence of the British-European relationship and how false are the ideas of British cultural or political isolation. Eight of the names here are British, from Shakespeare to Churchill. At each successful climacteric in British history the island has been invaded from Europe—successfully in 55 B.C. (and it remained European for the next four centuries), successfully by the Angles and Saxons and Danes (and it was for a century or more part of a North European empire), successfully by conquest in 1066 and 1485, and successfully and by invitation in 1688 and 1714. Some of the unsuccessful invasions have of course been as important as the successful—1715, 1745, 1805, 1940—but they should not blind us to the ease and regularity of the fact of invasion and to the fact that for many centuries Britain was totally involved in European affairs. That involvement even took the shape of an Anglo-French kingdom; and a sense of nationalism would have been incomprehensible to the Normans and Angevins. As Professor Richard Southern has demonstrated, the links were as tight economically as they were in language and culture. As he has said, what might be

9

called a Common Market "stretched from Yorkshire through the industrial towns of Flanders and the fairs of Champagne to the great towns of Italy and the ports on every shore of the Mediterranean".

Yet what also emerges from these pieces is that Europe has developed not by denying nationalism but from the fruitful clash of national cultures. One of the striking themes in the book is the clear line of intense national identity that links Joan of Arc through Louis XIV and Napoleon to Charles de Gaulle. There is an equally distinctive British—or is it English?—emphasis. However strong these ties of the local *pays* throughout European history, scholars have moved around Europe in peace and in war without benefit of passports and have been perhaps the real creators of the idea of Europe. This has been true from the time of Erasmus to our own day. And all the scholars and philosophers described here have been not only devotees of the idea of Europe, and at ease in any part of it, but believers also in the ultimate triumph of reason. For central to its story is not just the legacy of Rome and of the Christian faith, but of a matching faith in reason and education, in scepticism and tolerance, of which Erasmus and Montaigne are perhaps the pre-eminent examples.

Moreover, as the chapters on Dante and Aquinas, Lorenzo and Leonardo bring out, the legacy goes back not just to Rome with its sense of order and balance but to that spirit of enquiry enshrined throughout the Middle Ages in respect for Aristotle, and captured during the Renaissance by the rediscovery of Plato. Many of these men, not least Erasmus, would have been at home in our own world, perhaps more than in their own. Some of the men recorded here were in the best sense of the phrase Men for all Seasons; they came to their roles in history by many paths and some of the greatest of them (William the Conqueror, Leonardo, and Erasmus) were illegitimate; but central to all of them, whether politicians or soldiers or writers, was a faith in the power of the human mind and a quest for order and for improvement. The logical result of this process was a European Community, long though it has taken to reach it. For this reason, as well as for the intrinsic interest of their biographies, this volume is a tract for our times.

Esmond Wright

Editor's Note

FOR CENTURIES Europeans have felt vaguely that they were embraced by a common heritage; yet regional differences and national rivalries have been so strong as often to blur and obscure this sense of cohesiveness. Now, suddenly, over a great area and a vast population Europe has become self-conscious, dramatically aware of itself as never before as the inheritor of a great and distinctive civilization; a civilization, moreover, so dynamic as to have had a profound influence in every other Continent of the world.

The advent of the enlarged European Community means inevitably that national pantheons will have to be expanded to include those great figures who have most helped to create the European ethos. My aim in this book has been to present the lives and works of some of these people.

The forty-three men and one woman selected can represent only a small proportion of the number of significant people; and the choice—because a personal one—may seem perhaps somewhat arbitrary. I hope the reader will at any rate agree with a majority of the inclusions.

The categories into which the personalities fall are about as varied as "great" lives can be. Moralists, philosophers, statesmen, revolutionaries, kings, inventors, poets, dramatists, novelists, scholars, soldiers, painters, scientists, reformers; there is also one Pope and one musician. But many of them cannot be contained within a single category: thus Goethe is poet, dramatist, novelist and scientist; Leonardo is painter, sculptor, poet, musician, scientist and engineer. Churchill and De Gaulle are not only soldiers and statesmen, but men-of-letters; and Newton, Darwin and Einstein are not only scientists, but inventors of scientific systems. It is often the nature of genius to be protean, but is the European variety perhaps more exotically hydra-headed than most?

However that may be, I shall be more than satisfied if this book can do a little towards increasing awareness of the immense significance of the European achievement.

John Canning

CHARLEMAGNE
(742–814)

CHARLES, the elder son of Pippin, the King of the Franks, was born in 742 or thereabouts. Little is known about his boyhood, except that at the end of 753 he was sent by his father to meet the Pope, and that he was anointed by him at Saint-Denis. In 761 he accompanied his father in a military expedition into Aquitaine. In 768 Pippin died and his kingdom was divided between his two sons, Charles and Carloman. Three years later Carloman died, and the whole inheritance was Charles's. Reigning for what was an unprecedented length of time, until his death in 814, Charles the Great, or Charlemagne, as he is known, united the Christian peoples of Western Europe under his rule and was seen as the restorer of the Roman Empire in Europe.

From the third century Roman rule and civilization had begun to disintegrate. Gaul and Italy had been subjected to barbarian invasions, and successive emperors had attempted to meet the danger by allying with the invaders. By the fifth century the Roman Empire in the west had ceased to exist, and the Roman world was divided among many different tribes. Notable amongst them were the Franks, who established themselves in a kingdom between the Somme and the Loire. Under Clovis, from 481 to 511 the Franks established their capital in Paris, and then advanced towards the Pyrenees and across the Rhine.

However, with the death of Clovis, the kingdom fell apart and four clear regions were established. There was Neustria, from the Loire to the Meuse; Austrasia, a Frankish region which stretched across the Rhine; the kingdom of the Burgundians; and to the south-west, Aquitaine. Clovis's successors were famed for their purposeless civil wars and for their ineffectiveness as rulers. Known as the Merovingian dynasty, it was said that in this period nothing was left the king except the name of king. Nevertheless, for nearly three hundred unstable years this dynasty persisted, until at the beginning of the eighth century a new dynasty, the Arnulfians (called after St Arnulph, Bishop of Metz), or Carolingians, came to the fore. In particular it was Charles Martel, or Charles the Hammer, descended from powerful families in Austrasia, who asserted himself and set about unifying the now divided and anarchical kingdom of the Franks. This was all the more urgent since there was the danger of foreign tribes, particularly the Moors who had conquered Spain, advancing across the Pyrenees.

In 717 Charles Martel set about joining together Austrasia and Neustria and subduing Aquitaine and other regions. In 732 or 733 he defeated the invading Moors at Poitiers. He appeared therefore as the Champion of Christianity and the ally of the Papacy. His death in 741 was followed by more dynastic confusion, but by 754 his son Pepin the Short was installed as the head of the official dynasty, ruling over the whole of the kingdom of the Franks and much of Italy. Thus Charlemagne followed both his grandfather and his father in a continued attempt to unite the Franks and to make government effective.

As a man, Charlemagne probably differed little from his predecessors. He was exceptional only in his energy and in his determination. He was certainly a tall man, all the more so because the average height then was quite small. He was said to be fair and handsome, simply dressed except on great ceremonial occasions. His language was normally that of the Frankish dialect as it was spoken west of Cologne, and he also knew Latin quite well. The royal court was frequently on the move, and the king lived the open-air life of a medieval monarch, spending much time on military campaigns, hunting or visiting his domains. But he showed that his preferred residences were in the north and east of the Frankish kingdom. There was Herstal, which was on the Meuse, north-east of Liège; there was Worms on the middle Rhine; eventually there was Aachen, near to the hunting-grounds of the Ardennes hills. Charlemagne liked to celebrate the great occasions of the Christian year in these residences, surrounding himself with his court, that is to say his family, his friends, advisers, magnates, churchmen, scholars, warriors, women, minstrels and entertainers of all sorts, together with visitors, foreign ambassadors, travellers and others. All contemporaries were agreed that Charlemagne was the dominant figure in these gatherings, and that where he was lay the centre of the court and of the kingdom. There was no fixed capital. It was Charlemagne who was seen as the shining centre of his realm.

It is certain that when his brother Carloman died in 771, Charlemagne moved swiftly and skilfully in order to ensure that the inheritance went to him rather than to his nephews. This meant that without fighting Charlemagne had achieved great authority over a vast area, and he ruled over Austrasia, Neustria, Aquitaine, as well as Burgundy, Provence, Alsace and regions still further east. The next year, fulfilling the customary expectation that the king should lead his warriors on expeditions, he took his army into Saxon territory where they pillaged and looted, and received the submission of several tribes. In 773 Charlemagne, having been appealed to by the Pope, led a Frankish army into Italy and forced the Lombards to accept his authority.

Neither the successes against the Saxons nor against the Lombards were permanent and new campaigns had to be fought, but Charlemagne's successes were renewed. A more spectacular expedition was launched in 778 when Charlemagne took his army across the Pyrenees and gained the submission of Saragossa, only to find his forces badly mauled when they returned across the mountains. This reverse was followed by other crises, when various nobles rebelled against Charlemagne, when he was attacked militarily both in Saxony and in Spain, and when successive bad harvests made living conditions intolerable.

Nevertheless Charlemagne survived. The force of his personality impressed everyone; he was tireless in organizing campaigns; he could be ruthless in punishing enemies; he sent his forces into the eastern Alps and the Danube basin, encountering the Slavs, and he sent his forces westwards seeking to subdue the rebellious Bretons in the Armorican peninsula. Even to contemporaries he had changed from being the leader of a warrior band and a victor in battle to being the glory of Europe, the father of the continent, a monarch superior to all other rulers in goodness and as a dispenser of justice. His authority stretched from Saxony and the Baltic in the north, to Navarre and to the Papal States in the south, from a somewhat rebellious Britanny in the west to Carinthia and Pannonia in the east. When in 794 Charlemagne began building his royal residence at Aachen, with a great chapel in which the throne looked down on the main altar, then it has been suggested that Charlemagne was conscious of himself as the head of the world and was making Aachen into a second Rome. At all events it is likely that Charlemagne had for some time been considering that he should be definitively consecrated by the Pope as Emperor.

In 800, after having successfully supported Pope Leo in a dispute where a number of bishops and Roman citizens had been seeking to have him tried in court for various offences, Charlemagne went south. With a great and impressive following Charlemagne approached Rome, and the Pope did him the great honour of coming twelve miles out of Rome in order to meet him. After having demonstrated his authority by bringing together all the notables of Church and city who had been concerned with the Pope's alleged misconduct, so that the Pope should publicly declare his innocence, it was then that he was offered the supposedly vacant Imperial dignity. On 25 December, after the third mass of Christmas, the Pope placed the crown upon his head and those present acclaimed Charles as the Emperor. From this time his name appeared before that of the Pope on documents, and his name appeared on papal coins. It seemed the climax of his reign.

Much of Charlemagne's success is attributable to the work both of his grandfather and father. Pippin the Short had been particularly concerned with re-establishing the king's power, since although no-one ever doubted the importance of the king both as a political and a religious figure, his actual authority was often flouted. It was the local officials, the counts who governed the towns and the provinces, and who had the right to appoint lesser officers in their regions, who tended to have real power. Therefore if there was to be strong and stable government, then it was necessary to control these. At first Charlemagne sought to appoint Frankish noblemen whom he could trust, and tried to prevent the office from becoming hereditary. He tried to prevent any one magnate from accumulating too much power, and he never wanted to give more than one county to any particular magnate. Within the county (which often coincided with a bishopric) Charlemagne created a group of professional judges whose job it was to advise the count on judicial matters; the count was not allowed to have the only court, but his auxiliaries were also enabled to have courts. In these ways the king hoped to prevent too much accumulation of power in the hands of any one official.

But as the Empire expanded it became increasingly difficult for this control to remain effective. It was not always possible for a Frankish count to be appointed, particularly if there already existed a powerful local magnate with whom the population had strong ties. For political reasons it was sometimes necessary for one man to receive royal favours, and it was natural that he would expect that his authority and power could eventually be inherited by his son. It was not always practical for the king to interfere, and in any case constant interference with his subjects was not thought worthy of a Christian ruler. Then there were the frontier districts where local commanders (often given the rank of marquises) had to have a great deal of authority, and although Charlemagne made use of these officials to control the counts, he was aware of the dangers of creating an over-powerful class of subject.

Therefore a new form of royal control was tried out. It was that special envoys sent out by the king, the *missi dominici*, were to act as royal agents in the provinces. By their very nature they acted without intermediary and took the place of the king as if he had been personally present. Their job was to hear complaints and to enquire into abuses, to inspect accounts, supervise the administration and make pronouncements on the law. As time went by an increasing number of these officials was appointed, often to carry out special tasks.

At the same time as these means were used to ensure that local officials were controlled by the central government, the central government itself had to become more efficient. The court was organized with permanent officers entrusted with specific tasks which could be carried out, if necessary, in the king's absence. The administration of customs dues, tolls and market dues was made more efficient, since this formed the chief indirect source of income. Charlemagne continued his father's custom of placing the name and monogram of the king on coins, and established standard values for currency. A single mint at Aachen was responsible for the production of coins throughout the Empire, and also provided a source of revenue. In addition the custom whereby the king was entitled to a series of voluntary "gifts" was tightened up so as to become a regular obligation.

But power was not simply a matter of organization. It was also a religious matter. Both Pippin and Charlemagne had been consecrated, and they were kings by heredity and by consecration. Thus the kingship was an expression of divine will. Charlemagne made a further change by insisting upon an oath of personal fidelity from his subjects; whenever his authority was in danger he resorted to this oath of fidelity, and those who ran away in order to avoid taking the oath were threatened with punishment. In this way the king's authority was dependent both upon God's will and upon a man-to-man contract. Charlemagne was a king in the Biblical tradition and was compared to David and Solomon.

Although, as has been shown, the Carolingian Empire possessed many of the characteristics of the modern state, it was not thought of as a state. It was rather a collection of peoples who were ruled over by a divinely-chosen man. If, amongst the more highly born and educated officials the existence of this Empire caused them to forget something of their provincialism, any sense of Europe which they possessed could only be Christian. It was Christianity which was a most important factor in creating unity. It was the Church which provided the king with his most effective assistants in government, and it was in the Church that the educated men were to be found who were most influential in every sort of development.

Charlemagne was a devout man. As has been shown he ruled as a divinely-chosen ruler. He was able to preach, as though he were a priest, and he was able to exhort his subjects to lead a good life, and to punish them if they did not do so. He could act as an authority on matters of faith, he could preside over religious meetings and he could summon a synod of bishops. It was part of his power to be able to appoint men as bishops, and his superiority in this respect was shown in the title which he was sometimes given as "bishop of bishops". He succeeded in establishing a hierarchy amongst archbishops and bishops so that he was able to control the Church in his own interests and use it as a source of patronage and an important mechanism in the system whereby the Empire was ruled.

The main part of spiritual life was to be found in monasticism which was developing in these years. It was towards the end of the seventh century that monasteries ceased to be the highly spiritual organizations which were associated with St Columba and began to apply the rule of St Benedict. Charlemagne wanted the monasteries to be organized according to some coherent system, and he encouraged monasteries to live according to some particular rule. Once the rule had been established then he insisted, whenever it was possible for him to intervene personally, that the rules should be observed. The vagrancy of the monks, the anarchy caused by the great variety of orders and customs, and the uncertainties arising from the existence of many different rules, were anathema to him. He would have liked the rule of St Benedict to be general throughout the west; he wanted to use the monks as missionaries in the newly conquered and un-Christian regions of Saxony and the Slav countries; in short he hoped that organized monasticism would be one of the props of his government.

There was also the question of education and of culture. During the first half of the eighth century many of the centres of learning had been destroyed in the wars, and by the time of Charlemagne it was only in the isolated monasteries that manuscripts were read and copied. It became rare to find a layman who could sign his name. Charlemagne attempted to organize a renaissance. He collected scholars around him at his court, and he sought out scholars from foreign countries such as Italy and England where learning still existed. He gave instructions to bishops and to abbots that both dioceses and monasteries should provide education for those who were capable of receiving it. Schools were to be re-opened in Gaul and to be founded in Germany. In churches the divine service should be properly conducted, the Gregorian chant should be correctly sung, the monks and clerics should be educated. He encouraged the collection of books; he asked that corrupted texts should be amended and that Latin should always be correctly written; he urged that commentaries should be made on the ancient books.

The result was, as one contemporary put it, "Scholars are so greatly in debt to Charles that they will remember him always". Some schools became famous. Certain methods of instruction became well established. A number of scholars from different countries flourished under Charlemagne's encouragement and patronage, such as Alcuin who was Anglo-Saxon, Paul the Deacon who was Lombard, Angilbert who was Frankish, and Theodulf of Orleans who was Visigoth. Much of the learning was devoted to the study and interpretation of ancient texts, with a view to establishing correct usage and belief in religious matters. Once again Charlemagne had a practical aim in mind and saw the need for laws and organization. In Charlemagne's administration writing, and the written word, played a vital part, and this was a sharp contrast to his immediate predecessors.

It was not only in learning that there was a cultural renaissance under Charlemagne. The king himself was interested in architecture, and directly influenced a number of buildings. These were magnificently decorated, either with precious metals or with mosaics. Painting developed and the art of fresco was revived, and it seems that stained-glass windows were also used. All this supposes wealth, and it is noticeable that in this period the aristocracy of the Franks becomes more important and more distinguishable from other parts of society. They were scattered throughout the Empire and often the recipients of large gifts of land from the king. Sometimes a single family could dispose of the revenues of several bishoprics or abbeys, and regarded these possessions as their hereditary right.

The great mass of the population were peasants, and although there must have been many regional differences, there was a rough economic and social unity throughout the Empire. Briefly speaking there were two classes of peasants: there were the free peasants who were either small-holders or tenants, but who could always abandon their holding, and there were the *servi*. Perhaps the way of life of the free peasants did not differ much from the *servi*, but there was a difference of situation. Slaves continued to exist, although their numbers were declining, just as the conditions for their recruitment had changed. However, the *servi*, or vassals, lived in a variety of conditions, but they were always bound to some lord whilst retaining the ownership of their possessions and remaining masters of themselves. All this meant that there were men who owed allegiance not so much to the king or to the law, as to their lord. It meant too that society was becoming organized in terms of a hierarchy, with various bonds between man and man which could become more important than the bond between king and people.

In spite of the fact that the old Roman roads had been neglected, and that agricultural surplus was normally slight, it does seem that there was growing trade in this period. There were many fairs; there were towns such as Paris, Tours, Avignon, Cologne, Metz and Milan, where the growing populations were dependent upon local movements of food supplies; in spite of the existence of pirates, there was a great deal of trade between continental Europe and Scandinavia on the one hand, and between Europe and the East on the other. The traditional trade routes remained open and presented another manner in which wealth could be acquired, at a time when wealth often appeared to be the true source of power.

Thus over a wide area of Europe there was unity. Only at the frontiers were there wars. Within the Empire there was peace and, generally speaking, obedience to the Emperor's orders. The whole population was Christian, governed by a single prince attempting to create a uniform system of laws. Western Europe had a power centre, stretching across France and Germany.

But what was to happen after the death of Charlemagne? From 806 onwards Charlemagne began to prepare for the succession, showing that his concept of unity was not as great as some people have imagined. The Frankish kingdom, like all Germanic kingdoms, was the property of the reigning monarch and had to be shared among his heirs. He arranged that Italy and Aquitaine were to go to two of his sons, whilst Francia and Aachen would be the kingdom of his eldest son. The deaths of two of these sons before Charlemagne's own death prevented this division from taking place, and in 813 Louis was declared heir to the whole state, except for the kingdom of Italy. But Charlemagne's silence over the question of the unity of the Empire was important, because after his death there were many pressures which caused it to disintegrate.

Some historians have felt that the signs of disintegration were already present even when Charlemagne was still alive. After 800 Charlemagne was active in many instructions urging that the laws must be revised, that churches must not be neglected and that violence must be avoided. This, it has been argued, shows not only his continued energy, but the continuation of problems within his realm. The device of the *missi dominici* was only a stopgap; their influence could only be temporary. There had been many concessions to the nobility, who had grown in wealth and power, and it was normal that they were forming particular clans with special interests. The Church was becoming increasingly important, and the episcopate was capable of becoming powerful enough to challenge the secular authority of the king. Above all the Empire was so large that only a man with exceptional ability and with an unusual reputation could have the energy and vision to govern such a vast territory. From the north were coming the Viking invaders, and a contemporary chronicler records Charlemagne in tears when he saw a Viking ship since he foresaw the fate of many of his people.

In January, 814, he suffered an attack of fever and died within a few days. He was buried at Aachen, and over his tomb was placed an inscription saying:

> "Beneath this tomb lies the body of Charles, the great and orthodox Emperor who nobly increased the kingdom of the Franks and who reigned prosperously for forty-seven years."

It has been argued that Charlemagne was neither a great leader in war nor a great lawgiver. It has many times been pointed out that the Empire which he had created was doomed to disappear, and that the dynasty which had come to power began to be dispossessed during the ninth century. But features of the Empire persisted. There was the principle of the monarch, ruling the state as though it were his private domain and as though he were the fount of justice; there was too the principle of the monarch's power being limited by custom and by the advice of councillors and assemblies. The Church was made into a hierarchical institution and given a rôle to play in the state. The aristocracy was able to acquire a position in society so that the rule of the seigneurs was to become all-important. The Carolingian renaissance of learning and culture was to be outstanding for the Middle Ages, and through them to the modern period. Thus there was created a way of thinking which was common to the whole of Europe; the emergence of the succession-states and of political disunity was very far from causing anarchy; the memories of Carolingian greatness and authority were to live on for centuries to come.

HILDEBRAND: POPE GREGORY VII
(*c.* 1020–1085)

THERE are rare or privileged human beings who give their name to an age or an era. Napoleon was one, Queen Victoria, for rather dissimilar reasons, was another. A third, perhaps, was the subject of this brief biography. Like many great leaders, Hildebrand's origins were obscure. He was born possibly at Soana, certainly in Tuscany, somewhere between AD 1020 and 1025. He became a Benedictine monk, probably belonging to a house of his order on the Aventine Hill in Rome. The certainties multiply from Cluny where he spent part of his early life. Cluniac formation, added to native character and talents, made at least some advance in the Church inevitable.

Hildebrand began public life in the service of Gregory VI, eventually becoming his chaplain. He was soon to see his master's title to the papacy challenged by the Emperor Henry III. More than that, he had to stand by while Gregory was deposed by the Emperor and the Synod of Sutri in 1046 on alleged charges of simony. This prepared the way for the election of a German Pope, Clement II, who was intended to rule Italy virtually as the Emperor's local Pasha. Hildebrand stood faithfully by the deposed Gregory, and accompanied him into his German exile. There Gregory died in 1047, after an effective reign of less than two years. Leo IX, elected to the papacy in 1049, took Hildebrand back to Rome with him. The zeal, intellectual stature and, above all, loyalty of the man who became treasurer of the Roman Church made advance to further positions of trust a foregone conclusion. In 1054 Hildebrand presided as papal legate over the Synod of Tours which dealt with Berengarius.

By this time, Hildebrand's influence was considerable enough to sway papal elections. He had much to do with the election of Nicholas II in 1058, and of Alexander II in 1061. He came fully into his own when he was himself elected to the vacant chair in 1073 by popular acclamation, a procedure which played havoc, incidentally, with the formal rules for election laid down as recently as 1059. This unusual beginning was a fitting prelude to the career of a Pope who would change a good many rules, and dig the entrance of the main channel in which papal history was to run throughout the Middle Ages.

Hildebrand accepted certain basic principles with the truth-finding and simplifying capacity of authentic genius. He applied them logically and vigorously to practical situations as they arose. He saw the Church as a visible, external society with a right and duty received direct from God to preach the Gospel. This was a corpus of very definite truth, not an amorphous compound of vague platitudes and platitudinous uncertainties. From this conviction inevitably sprang a profound regard for law, and for the Church as a visible law-making society—much as the state was a law-making society, though in a different sphere.

Fortunately, the method and doctrine of this great Pope can be closely and accurately studied in its original application since the papal register, or record of copies of letters sent out, is preserved almost in its entirety. Indeed, it is the first of its kind to be so preserved. Still surviving in the register is his so-called *Dictatus papae*, a list of twenty-seven chapter-headings indicating a collection of canons on Church laws, now unfortunately lost. What survives amounts to a formulation of legal principle which was developed and enlarged, presumably, in an original text no longer extant. Even in this truncated state the *Dictatus* gives a clear picture of the guiding principles adopted by Gregory in the field of canon law.

Pope Gregory expected obedience from the Christian world; but he endeavoured to turn the higher clergy into people who get obedience because they are respected. He could not be unaware that the alternative to the papacy was an anointed priest-king into which the Emperor in other historical circumstances might have evolved. The seeds of such a possible growth were there. The Holy Roman Empire had been derived from the Empire of the Caesars, with precisely this aura of divinization. There was also the tradition of the age of Constantine. In return first for toleration of Christianity, and then establishing it as the official religion of the Empire, the Emperor had undoubtedly received in gratitude an ill-defined but extensive influence in Church affairs. If the Pope, and for that matter his bishops, were to convince the world of their superior moral rôle, and defeat the pretensions of the Emperor, they must first of all be morally superior. With this in mind, no doubt, clerical celibacy as the inner prerequisite and outward symbol of men completely dedicated was insisted on in synods of 1074 and 1075. It was a high and dangerous ideal, but Gregory himself had a good head for heights, and cared nothing for danger. If this were not so, he would in any case have taken care to avoid election to the papacy in that day and age. He was also one man who might convince everybody that the Church was disinterested in matters material, observing only spiritual criteria in making appointments. At all events, he carried the same assemblies into renewing decrees against simony.

Nobler spirits were one with the Pope, and agreed with what he was trying to do. But inevitably, there were those in Church as well as State who could well be content with an ideal much less demanding. There was a good deal of opposition, especially to the insistence on a celibate clergy, although by this time the practice had long centuries of Christian tradition behind it. Some of the strongest opposition to this aspect of Gregorian reform came from France and Germany. Backed by the older tradition, however, as well as the Pope, the Roman synod of 1078 threatened to suspend bishops who allowed their clergy to marry.

Special envoys were dispatched with something like system to make sure that the Roman decrees were everywhere enforced in Western Christendom. These papal legates were, in fact, the origin of the legatine system which was to become so significant in the centuries ahead, and of whom the last, as far as England was effectively concerned, were appointed to deal with the annulment of Henry VIII's marriage to Catherine of Aragon. Gregory VII now insisted that newly elected bishops took an oath of obedience to the Holy See. The visit of bishops to Rome from time to time began to acquire the force of customary obligation.

With a strongly centralized papacy thus established, a weighty counterpoise was provided to balance and at the same time emphasize the secular nature and duties of the Empire. In this way it was prevented from becoming, if it ever really threatened to become, a universal dictatorship in the field of faith and morals as well as in politics and feudal allegiance. Nevertheless, a complete separation of soul and body can only mean death, and harmony had to continue between these partners if Christendom were to survive. But there are few things more inharmonious than a struggle to maintain harmony, and Gregory's relations with the Empire from this time on proved no exception. Pope Alexander II's (1061–73) excommunication of five of Henry IV's Councillors had suggested how readily dialogue between Pope and Emperor might turn into a shouting match or worse.

The struggle between the two main forces of Christendom came to turn principally about the question as to who ultimately should appoint and control bishops. This battlefield in which conflict continued to develop between the spiritual and secular principles became known as the investiture struggle. Until shortly before the reign of Gregory VII, lay lords and princes had been steadily encroaching on bishoprics, abbacies, and the lands and revenues that went with them. Prelates were invested with their office and temporalities by the kind of external ritual which meant much if not everything to the medieval mind. While a bishop could receive the temporalities of his see as from a feudal lord, could he also receive his ring and crozier—the outward and visible sign of jurisdiction—in this way?

During the first half of the tenth century, Popes were too weak or indifferent to notice what was happening; or if they did, to dare challenge it. Indeed, at least one thinker, Thietmar of Merseburg, had upheld the temporal sovereign as God's representative on earth, and therefore having every right to confer on his subjects every symbol of their derivative jurisdiction. A man of Gregory VII's temperament could not be expected to accept this. Indeed, from the middle of the eleventh century, the Cluniac reformers had already indicated the trend of forward-looking, Christian thinking which Hildebrand could be trusted to follow enthusiastically. The ring and staff symbolized the episcopal function as such, and could not be conferred by laymen. This lay at the heart of the so-called investiture controversy: a struggle less about things than about principles: a war of words, but going beyond symbols.

Despite repeated papal condemnation of lay investiture, the Emperor Henry IV continued to make his own appointments not only in Germany, but also in Milan, Spoleto and Fermo where he invested bishops and abbots with their office. Henry himself, at least in the beginning of Gregory's pontificate, freely admitted this as a fault. The Emperor wrote to the Pope in 1073 a letter which we may read in the Latin of the *Acta Conciliorum*, published in Paris in the year 1714 from the original Roman register. Henry asked the Pope's pardon for his transgressions. "Not only have we invaded ecclesiastical interests (*res*), but it is true that we have acted unworthily, embittering the situation with the gall of simony. Not coming in by the gate but entering another way, we have sold the very churches, and not defended them as we should have done." He continues: "And now because we cannot put the churches right on our own without your authority, on these and, indeed, all our affairs we ardently ask for your assistance and also advice. Your command shall be most carefully observed in all things." He then pleaded that the particular situation in Milan be put right.

Perhaps it was this apparent willingness to acknowledge his faults and put his own house in order rather than the Church, that moved Gregory to stronger measures when Henry's further acts belied the good intentions put on paper. When the Emperor made it clear that he would only respond to strong measures, he found a Pope who also dared to be strong. But Gregory was not unconciliatory or harsh by nature. Soon after he became Pope, he wrote to Count Guy of Imola to allay discord between Archbishop Guibert of Ravenna and the citizens of Imola, who were being disturbed in their loyalty to the Roman See. The Count is asked to take their part and the Pope's until such time as legates arrive from Gregory himself to resolve the tension. Meanwhile, he has heard that "our confrère Guibert" has tried to withdraw the Imolese from their allegiance to the Holy See "contrary to the honour of Saint Peter to whom (*cui*) they swore fidelity". The Pope continues: "Truly, this relation surprised us all the more since we formerly witnessed in him fraternal charity and sacerdotal integrity of a kind to exclude, with little room for doubt, any causes of suspicion in him. Nor can we believe that so prudent a man has so far forgotten either the nature or the dignity of his office that he who himself swore fidelity to the Prince of the Apostles would now be so regardless of his peril as to draw others, who did no less than he, into perjury by demanding oaths of loyalty from them (*sacramenta*)."

This is the writing of an intelligent diplomat not of a headstrong firebrand. We need not suppose that Gregory acted out of character when at length he began to take serious issue with Emperor Henry.

Gregory sent a letter of sharp protest to the Emperor in December, 1075. The latter's answer to this was to convoke a diet at Worms in January, 1076. The twenty-six bishops there assembled obligingly upheld Henry. Not content with denouncing the "monk Hildebrand's" conduct, they went on to declare the Pope deposed. Gregory did not retaliate by attempting to dethrone the Emperor—this would have been a very questionable step for one with Hildebrand's knowledge of, and respect for, the law. However, in the Lenten synod of 1076, he excommunicated Henry and forbade him to exercise his royal office. It was a form of suspension analogous to the papal mode of proceeding with recalcitrant bishops. Bishops who had recently supported Henry were also either suspended or excommunicated. The Emperor's subjects were absolved from their oaths of allegiance, and further ordered not to obey imperial commands.

In a letter addressed to all the faithful in 1076, the first document, it seems, in the fourth volume of the register for his reign, Hildebrand justified himself while reminding the faithful of their duty where Henry was concerned, namely, "to snatch him from the hand of Satan and rouse him to true repentance". The faithful were well aware "how long Holy Church had put up with the unheard of transgressions and multifarious offences of the King, who was also a Christian—would he were!—and their own ruler".

Gregory insisted on the purity of his motives with quotations from the prophets Ezechiel and Jeremias: " 'If you do not bring home his wickedness to the wicked man, I shall hold you responsible for his soul!' " And, " 'Cursed is the man who withholds his sword from shedding blood',' " meaning the word of correction from those who live wickedly. . . . "God is our witness that no worldly respect or motive of convenience urges us to rebuke wicked princes and impious priests. . . . It is better that we should submit to death from tyrants, if need be, than by our silence, human respect or love of the quiet life consent to the overthrow of Christian law." Gregory's sincerity cannot be doubted. If he was unwise, it is difficult to see what else the circumstances of the time allowed him.

Something like a medieval Cuba crisis now developed. The irresistible seemed to be meeting the immovable. But it was the Emperor who eventually gave way. Before long he found himself obliged to seek absolution from the Pope. This took place in the famous scene at Canossa at the end of January, 1077. The drama of Canossa has been more than once dramatically described. The central event has been at least once painted and many times printed so that schoolchildren remain with the image of a tyrant Pope who waits warmly clad and gloating in his palace while a foolish and superstitious king waits ridiculously on his pleasure in the snow.

Reality, as always, is more sober than romantic imagination. But the reality, as far as we know it, in this case remains picturesque enough. It was an exceptionally severe winter when Henry made his way to Rome over the Alps. As Horace Mann described it: " 'Often had the men of his party to crawl down some steep declivity on their hands and knees, or to be carried on the backs of their guides, while the peasants lowered the queen with her child and female attendants wrapped up in the skins of oxen." Against this picture, which can only arouse our sympathy, the same authority is fair enough to remind us: "No sooner was it noised abroad that the German King had crossed the Alps than all the numerous foes of the papacy and reform. . . . rejoiced. Believing that he had come to humiliate their foe, evil-living bishops and nobles flocked to him with their retainers."

The Pope was in no hurry to absolve Henry; but he was not kept waiting in the cold, literally and metaphorically, out of hardness of heart or mere desire for petty revenge. Gregory was too large a man for contrivances as small as this. "The fact was that the action of Henry had placed Gregory in a most awkward position. To absolve him without the knowledge of the German princes would not be fair to them, and yet not to absolve him would seem harsh." In the end Hildebrand relented, allowing human rather than political considerations to prevail. Neither Pope nor Emperor gained much in the long run from this reconciliation, though Henry suffered the consequences first.

The Emperor's difficulties entered a new phase when the German princes elected a rival, Rudolf of Swabia, as their ruler on 15 March, 1077. This step won no approval from Gregory: still less the violent civil war in Germany which raged for the next three years. Gregory did his best to reconcile the contending parties by arranging a *colloquium,* or parley, between the two sides: but in vain. In the end, the Pope decided to improve the chances of peace and settlement in Germany by giving one side a clear moral advantage. In 1080 he again excommunicated Henry, at the same time deposing him as king not only of Germany but also of Italy. Rudolf of Swabia was now formally recognized as Henry's legitimate successor.

The most effective kinds of revolution are those which most closely follow lines of evolution. In Gregory's excommunication and deposition of a ruling monarch there was sufficient revolution to prompt a loyal supporter, Bishop Hermann of Metz, to ask him by what right he did these things. Gregory could reply in effect that he had done nothing more than the power implicit in the Christian tradition so far received in the West enabled him to do. Indeed, he had acted precisely as the unique situation which had arisen called on him to do. There were two powers in Christendom, the secular and the temporal; and in the ideal course of events there was no conflict between them since the secular power ruled according to the principles laid down and accepted by the spiritual. Both principles proceeded ultimately from God so that conflict was theoretically impossible. But what if in practice the temporal power betrayed its trust, and began to rule without reference to the spiritual? Any third tribunal was inconceivable. In such unfortunate circumstances it was the duty of the spiritual power to assert its superior authority boldly; and reduce, if necessary, even recalcitrant kings and emperors to Christian order. For Gregory, the Petrine power to bind and loose had become the ultimate principle in human jurisdiction.

Undeniably, there was logic in all this, and possibly a dash of something even more sublime. All the same, his claim to a universal regimen over the whole of Christendom, including its temporal as well as its spiritual aspects, indicated an extremely bold practical step in evolution. Different historical circumstances might well have delayed definition of the principle of subordination of everything else in a Christian, even a king, to the spiritual ideal, and therefore to the Pope as its visible expression. As the inheritor of the promises made by Christ to Peter, the Pope determined ultimately how the spiritual ideal should apply in any particular generation. The basic fact for Christians was that Christendom was ultimately a moral and religious order, not political. Therefore the spiritual head, not the temporal, had the last word in defining relations between the two aspects of the one society. It was one thing, of course, to define the papal supremacy theoretically in this way. The crucial historical question was to what extent and how long the Church could insist on its essential independence of the secular power in practice. In the long run, and indeed the short term, even a man of Gregory's capacity could fail.

Henry reacted to his own deposition in 1080 by getting the Synod of Brixen to depose Gregory the same year. Clement III was then elected as anti-Pope. Not until 1084, however, did Clement begin to rule effectively with the power of Henry behind him. In that year, thirteen cardinals defected from Gregory, and he was obliged to take refuge in the Emperor Hadrian's tomb, baptized in the middle ages as Castel Sant' Angelo. He was rescued by Robert Guiscard, the Norman. Not for the first time in history, the behaviour of the liberators was such as to make the Romans ask themselves what they were being liberated from. In the event, they brought about their own liberation from Guiscard, who withdrew to Salerno taking Gregory with him. The Pope died on 25 May, 1085, worn out in spirit and body, but not broken in faith and hope. He did not receive his final vindication quickly even from the Church. Not until some five hundred years later was he canonized by Paul V.

The struggle with the Empire was the principal characteristic of Gregory's pontificate, but it by no means filled the whole of his attention. His preoccupation was to establish a Christendom that was close-knit and uniform, not for the sake of uniformity but in order to produce the strength moral and even physical, required for continual existence to say nothing of growth in an age that was very rough, and also ready, at least with its fist. With this in mind Gregory corresponded on a scale large for his day with European princes and rulers, including those on the frontiers of the Church, as it were, in England, Poland and Denmark.

In our own day, we have seen the Anglican primate go very cheerfully to Rome, and find there a welcome more than ordinarily kind. It is ironical to find Hildebrand rebuking a "Cantuar" of his own day for showing much reluctance over a Roman visit. Gregory wrote to Lanfranc in 1081: "We have often invited your fraternity to come to Rome. . . . Up to now, as it seems, either from pride or negligence you have put it off; for you offer no canonical reason by way of excuse. The irksomeness or difficulty of the journey cannot sufficiently excuse you. For it is well-known that many who live far off, even those who are infirm and ailing in body, indeed, scarcely able to rise from their beds, have still managed to hasten in their litters to the hearth of the apostle out of love for Saint Peter." The letter ended by warning him that if he did not come to Rome by the feast of All Saints, 1 November, he must consider himself suspended from his episcopal functions.

A letter written later the same year, however, indicates not only a less strained relationship between Pope and archbishop, but also the extraordinary nature of some of the problems which only a united Christendom could be strong enough to solve. Lanfranc was urged to tackle vigorously more serious forms of moral delinquency, "and among the rest, and more than the rest, that grave evil we have heard of among the Scots (*de Scotis*), namely that a great many of them not only desert their wives but actually sell them. Stop this at all costs. We wish it to proceed from our apostolic authority that wherever this occurs, not only in Scotland but anywhere else in the island of the English (*Anglorum insula*), you extirpate it without delay. . . ."

Hildebrand was keenly aware of the blow to Christian unity dealt by the eastern schism. He wrote to Abbot Hugh of Cluny in 1075: "I wish I could enable you to understand fully how burdened I am with sorrow; how worn out by the new labour which every day brings me, growing as it does to cause yet more sorrow. Your paternal sympathy would then warm towards me and match my grief. . . . Often have I asked the Lord either to take me out of this life or else to bring relief through me to our common mother. But He has not yet seen fit to bring me out of great tribulation; nor has my life done the good I hoped for on behalf of this mother of ours in whose service I am chained. A vast grief and pervading sorrow hems me in on every side. For the eastern church, moved by the devil, has defected from Catholic faith; and in her members the ancient enemy has dealt a mortal blow to Christians everywhere." Although it was scarcely beyond the planning stage, a crusade against the Seljuk Turks was seen as part of the counter-measures needed to heal the breach.

By way of further contribution to his strategy of consolidation, Gregory introduced the Roman Mass rite into Spain. This bid fair eventually to replace the local Mozarabic rite completely. He also established Ember Days for fasting to be observed throughout the Latin Church. Realizing the importance of a sound ascetical foundation for the Church of his ideal, Gregory was at least instrumental in promoting the Carthusian reform begun by Bruno of Cologne. In 1084 Bruno set up his first community at Grenoble. His work was a reminder that the true power of the Church lay always in the sword of the spirit and the point of the pen rather than in material weapons: even those wielded by friends and allies.

Our own age, preoccupied with problems of authority, and at least in the west, increasingly critical of it, finds it hard to appreciate a man like Gregory VII. Not only did Gregory wield authority; he wielded it in a sphere where most people in our own English-speaking world would now think its exercise irrelevant if not audacious, namely religion. Nevertheless, setting aside the problem of truth in all this, Hildebrand's attitude had a certain

As Europe emerged from the mists of the Dark Ages there emerged, too, the immensely impressive figure of Charles the Great, or Charlemagne, to give him the style by which he is universally known. The Holy Roman Empire that he founded withstood the strains and stresses of a thousand years. His realm extended from the Pyrenees to the Baltic, from the Channel shore facing the isles of Britain to the Adriatic—very much the same vast area of Western Europe that became the homeland of the European Community of our own day.

Right: a Renaissance conception of his appearance drawn by Dürer.

Below: a sculpture from his shrine in Aachen cathedral, showing him dedicating the original church to the Virgin Mary.

The victory at Hastings in 1066 that won for Duke William of Normandy the title of William the Conqueror was of most momentous importance, involving as it did the association of England with the destinies of Europe. The portrait (*left*) of the Conqueror is one of the sculptured glories of Wells cathedral; while (*below*) is a scene from the Bayeux Tapestry, the contemporary record of the events leading up to and during the Norman invasion. The episode illustrated shows William seated in his camp, listening to the report of King Harold's movements brought him by one of his scouts.

significance, paradoxical as it might seem, in the development of liberty.

From present-day examples in the east, we can appreciate the danger of a state becoming almighty; of dictatorship without any kind of curb or contradiction even when it presumes to lay down the law on ethics and religion—or no religion. This might have been the fate of the whole of Western Europe but for men like Gregory VII who, in the middle ages, reminded the world that might is not right unless it is allied with justice. In any case, whatever might be said for a purely secular ideal of society in a later age, it would have been an anachronism in the eleventh century.

Henry IV himself embodied nobody's ideal. The cautious and scholarly pages of Walter Ullmann, for example, make it clear that Henry was thoroughly untrustworthy, and on at least one occasion resorted to forgery to gain his end. For such a man to have prevailed against Hildebrand would have been almost pure tragedy. Not that Gregory could transmit to his immediate posterity any concrete fruits of victory. He had, however, offered a precedent to guide future development. True, there was always a seamy side to politics, ecclesiastical not excluded, but Gregory VII reminded his contemporaries that this aspect was always something to be striven against and not passively accepted. He kept alive an ideal of justice and law, even if he could not always ensure that they were respected in fact. His example was important in a world which always tended to put its deepest faith in blood and iron—and, of course, gold.

WILLIAM THE CONQUEROR

(*c.* 1028–1087)

TO INCLUDE William the Conqueror among a group of "Great Europeans" may well appear a rash undertaking since he had little, if any, concern with Europe as it might be visualized to-day. Yet the spectacular career of this bastard boy, who in the eleventh century so perilously fought his way to the pinnacles of power, not only impressed his contemporaries, but left an abiding legacy to his posterity.

He entered, for instance, most deeply into the national consciousness of the kingdom which he conquered, and throughout the centuries few of the great political or religious controversies which have vexed England were debated without some reference to this medieval ruler who came to the country from Normandy. The posthumous career of William the Conqueror is in fact one of the curiosities of English literature. Generations of scholars have been led into a war of learned words about his policy, and stories about him, true and false, have become part of the currency of conversation. He is, in fact, the most familiar of all England's medieval kings. Evidently, he not only bestrode his own generation, but he cast his shadow also over a remote future.

So much has been written about William the Conqueror that it may be well to recall in the briefest possible way some of the indisputable facts of his extraordinary life. He was the illegitimate son of Robert I, Duke of Normandy, by Herleve, a girl of Falaise. In 1035 he succeeded, when a child some seven years old, to the rule of this anarchic province. He passed his boyhood in peril, and between 1046 and 1054 he waged, without intermission, a war for personal survival.

In 1066, as we all know, he invaded England, won the battle of Hastings, and became King of the English. And during his reign over England some very remarkable things happened. A new aristocracy consisting mainly of William's greater Norman followers was established in England, and during the same period the Church in England underwent a drastic reorganization. All this, moreover, took place at the same time as William himself was engaged continuously in defending his realm of Normandy and England from attacks from France and from Scandinavia—attacks which reached their climax during the last eighteen months of his life. And during those same eighteen months King William planned the Domesday Survey which is the greatest monument to his administration. He died in September, 1087, within sound of the church bells of Rouen.

Now, this career, however briefly summarized, must be regarded as one of the most astonishing in history, and it is small wonder that William has always attracted the attention of historians both for what he was and what he did. There he remains, a gaunt and massive figure, dominant and unlovable, but withal something of an enigma: brutal in war and avaricious in peace, a conscientious husband and father, personally pious, and notoriously continent, a man always to fear and often to admire.

A great warrior and a great constructive statesman, he stands foresquare in the foreground of his own tumultuous age. But he might well be regarded as alien to our own. None the less there are some surprising analogies to be drawn between the eleventh and the twentieth centuries. After all, William himself gave a new turn to the problem of what should be the connection between England and Europe—a problem which is to-day so strenuously debated. And many other issues before eleventh century Europe are still with us. The control of the Mediterranean, the cleavage between East and West, the defence of "European civilization" against the assaults of alien ideologies—all these are topics which have not noticeably diminished in interest over the years. But all of them posed problems which were of deep concern to William's contemporaries, and none of them were unaffected by what he accomplished.

If, however, the impact of the career of William the Conqueror is to be correctly assessed, it is necessary to glance however swiftly at the province from which he came. Normandy is the Viking province of Gaul, but the European implications of Norman action in William's time bore little relation to the pagan traditions of the Viking past. The earlier settlers from Scandinavia in the valley of the Lower Seine had always been a minority among the population of that region, and they had been rapidly absorbed into the Latin and Christian culture of France. At the same time, the boundaries of the Norman Duchy had been made to conform to those of the ancient ecclesiastical province of Rouen, and the increasing distinction of that province within the European Church took place concurrently with the development of Norman power.

A province which in Duke William's time could boast of Herluin of Le Bec, of John of Fécamp, of Maurilius of Rouen, of Lanfranc, and the young Saint Anselm was assuredly not to be ignored by Christendom at large. The transition had been gradually made, but the resulting contrast was absolute. Indeed, the transformation of the province which at the beginning of the tenth century had been ruled by Rolf the Viking into the state which confronted England in 1066 is one of the most remarkable in history. The Normans who in the time of William the Conqueror were so strangely to influence the fate of Europe were vociferously Christian in their political propaganda, and self-consciously French in their language, in their feudal organization, and in their political ideas.

It is natural for an Englishman to select 1066 as the cardinal date in Norman history, and although this can only be done with some qualification, he has good reasons for his choice. Hastings was the most influential battle ever fought in England, and Domesday Book which twenty years later recorded the Norman settlement was the most important administrative record ever compiled in any medieval kingdom. It is moreover with a sure sense of historical perspective that the English have agreed to start their long series of numbered Kings and Queens from William the Conqueror, for certainly his advent gave a new orientation to English development.

Whether the Norman Conquest was, or was not, a "good thing" for England is endlessly (and tediously) debated, and usually in terms which bear little relation to the conditions of the eleventh century. There can however be no doubt that the Conquest deflected the destinies of England away from the Scandinavian north and towards the Latin West. In this respect the defeat of Harold Hardraada of Norway at Stamford Bridge near York on 25 September, 1066, was almost as significant as the defeat of Harold Godwineson of Wessex near Hastings nineteen days later.

After William's final triumph, and his coronation as King of the English in Westminster Abbey on the following Christmas Day, England was to be brought progressively, more closely than ever before since Roman times, into the political system of Europe. The momentous results which this would eventually entail were, however, only slowly to be revealed. The Norman Conquest of England was assured by William the Conqueror. But its consequences for Britain would not be fulfilled until after his death, and its consequences for Europe would not be disclosed until the twelfth century was well advanced.

Then, however, it was made clear that the work of William the Conqueror, and of his royal successors in England, was an essential part of a larger movement of Norman action which affected the whole of Europe. By the fourth decade of the twelfth century the Normans had come to control, from London and Palermo, the two wealthiest and best organized kingdoms of western Europe. And the Norman efforts which had created these two realms must surely be regarded as belonging in some sense to a single enterprise. The battle of Hastings was fought only five years before the Normans captured Bari and ended the Byzantine administration in southern Italy; and in the very next year (1072), while William the Conqueror was carrying his authority into Scotland, the Normans wrested the great city of Palermo from the Saracens. The Norman conquest of England and the Norman conquest of Apulia, Calabria and Sicily were, moreover, made by men of the same feudal families such as Beaumont, Crispin, Grandmesnil, Montgomery and the like—men who were conscious of their close inter-relationship, and conscious also of their common interests.

It was in short a correlated endeavour which before the death of William the Conqueror had created a self-conscious Norman world that stretched from Abernethy to Taormina. Odo, Bishop of Bayeux and Earl of Kent, Geoffrey, Bishop of Coutances, who held wide lands in England, both received gifts from their relatives in Italy for the embellishment of their cathedrals at home, and the Norman masters of Normandy and England were proudly familiar with the successes achieved by their brothers and cousins on the shores of the Mediterranean. The same sentiments were evidently also felt by William the Conqueror himself who, it is said, was wont to refresh his courage by reflecting on the valour displayed by Robert Guiscard, the Norman leader in the south. And when in 1087 the Norman King of the English came to die, the news was carried with phenomenal speed across the Alps, and was received with concern, and with some dismay, by the Normans in Italy.

The achievement of William the Conqueror must thus be appraised in connection with a widespread expansion of Norman power which was to promote the political strength of the Latin West. And this was effected at a time when Latin Christendom, like Western Europe to-day, felt itself dangerously confronted by hostile systems of morals and belief backed by political powers of truly formidable size and strength. Until at least 1087, Islam was apparently stronger, certainly more wealthy, and demonstrably more "cultured" than Christendom, which, then as now, appeared to some to be decadent and demoralized.

In 1066, the Moslem world extended from Baghdad over much of Asia, over Egypt and the whole North African littoral, over Sicily and over three-quarters of Spain. Nor was the tide receding. Recently much of Asia Minor and of Syria had been lost. To Latin Christendom, restricted and divided, in the middle of the eleventh century the Moslem flood must have seemed menacing and still insurgent, while the defences of Christendom appeared lamentably weak. It is true that during most of the eleventh century the relations between the Cross and the Crescent could be aptly described in terms of a "cold war", but there was no doubt that until its close Latin Christendom felt itself lethally menaced by a militant social order ethically alien to itself.

Nevertheless, in face of formidable dangers, Western Europe during these decades attained a new sense of unity and a new access of power. Many explanations have been given for this. In the first place demographic and economic factors operating about this time are cited to account for what then took place. Stress is now laid, both by Marxist historians and by their opponents, on the growth of population which is alleged to have begun in the West during the latter half of the eleventh century, on technological advances which were then achieved in agricultural practice, and on the developing mercantile activities of the nascent communities in the towns. Other commentators would emphasize the political significance of the reforming movement in the Church which was being directed by the Papacy and notably by Pope Gregory VII (1073–1085) and by his successors. The Popes of this age, it is said, did little less than make Latin Christendom for the first time vividly aware of its own identity. Undoubtedly there is some truth in all these ideas. But another suggestion must be added to them. Attention must be called to the shift in the balance of European power consequent upon the formation of the great Norman dominions in the north and south of Europe.

Western Europe was made thereby not only stronger, but more unified in its military purpose. It was now not only able, but also eager, to take at long last the offensive against Islam. And to this change of temper also the Normans contributed. The development of Norman power by William the Conqueror would fortify western

Christendom, and the contemporary conquest of Sicily by the Normans, though undertaken for many diverse motives, was in the event an outstanding triumph of the Cross over the Crescent.

It is small wonder, therefore, that the Normans who had often exploited the notion of the Holy War for their own propaganda purposes should take a prominent part in initiating the Crusades. In 1096 of the eight chief leaders in the First Crusade, four were Normans. One of the most important contingents was led by a son of William the Conqueror. And before the eleventh century had closed the strongest of the Latin states in Syria had been founded at Antioch by the Normans.

The career of William the Conqueror thus formed part of a far-flung effort of Norman endeavour. The basic consequence of what he achieved was however that through him there was established, under a Norman Duke who was also King of the English, a conjoint Norman dominion stretching across the Channel, and politically united under a single rule. The very powerful state which was thus created inevitably became almost at once a major factor in European politics. For it was not only Normandy and England that were involved. Already before he came to England, William had obtained control over the countries of Ponthieu and Boulogne, and during the three years before the Norman invasion of England his power had been yet further extended. In 1063 he captured Le Mans and became effective master of Maine, and from 1064 onwards he could exercise power over much of Brittany. The political situation in northern France was thus being radically changed. In all the wide region from Boulogne to Vannes, from Cherbourg to Mantes, Norman influence was becoming dominant.

And now after 1066 the Duke of Normandy could claim all the power which in the past had belonged to any English sovereign, and these included larger, if undefined, claims to overlordship both in Wales and Scotland. These claims William would strongly assert. In his time the Norman advance into Wales was begun under the great marcher Earls whom he established at Chester, Shrewsbury and Hereford, and at the end of his life it was said that he was even contemplating the conquest of Ireland. In Scotland the progress of Norman power was even more notable. Malcolm Canmore, the Scottish King, acknowledged himself as in some sense William's vassal, and later rulers of Scotland were to accept the same dependence on the Conqueror's sons William II and Henry I. The final results of the Conqueror's career would thus be of revolutionary importance to northern Europe. In place of a congerie of French fiefs, some under Norman hegemony, there would be established a great Anglo-Norman realm whose power would extend over much of northern France, and stretch directly over all of England, and indirectly over most of Britain.

It was obviously of vital consequence to Europe as a whole that despite difficulties and reverses the unity of the scattered realm that was founded by William the Conqueror was to survive during the seventy years which followed his death. Despite the ineptitude of the Conqueror's eldest son, the Anglo-Norman realm waxed in strength during the reign of William II (1087–1100); and Henry I (1100–1135) was actually a more powerful ruler than his father. Even the civil war which followed Henry I's death hardly affected this progress.

The so-called "Angevin Empire" to which King Henry II, Duke of Normandy and Count of Anjou, succeeded in 1154 was essentially the great Anglo-Norman state which had been formed by William the Conqueror and defended by his successors, and to this there was now added the extensive county of Aquitaine. Indeed, this dominion now comprised more of France than was ruled by the Capetian Kings at Paris. Under the governance of men, who, like William the Conqueror, were also Kings of the English this vast imperial state stretched from the Tweed to the Pyrenees, and its authority was felt also in Wales, in Scotland and in Ireland.

Moreover, this imperial realm was always regarded by its rulers as a unity. It is misleading to intrude notions derived from modern nationalism into the policy of these Kings, or to criticize them for spending so much of their time outside England. They expended their energies naturally and profitably in this way in order to maintain the totality of their inheritance. They were not national figures. They were European rulers, and they were moreover among the most powerful monarchs of their age. The dominion founded by William the Conqueror and developed by his successors had in short come to dominate the political structure of Western Europe.

The results of these developments, as they affected both England and Europe, were moreover not only political. They were also economic. The continental connection of the Norman Kings affected almost every aspect of English government in the twelfth century, but economically the links between England and Europe became at that time almost as close. Western Europe, remarks

Professor Southern, emerged during these years as "a single powerful and aggressive economic system" and of that system England was part. Indeed what might be called a "common market" "stretched from Yorkshire through the industrial towns of Flanders and the fairs of Champagne to the great towns of Italy and the ports on every shore of the Mediterranean".

Such it would appear were among the consequences of the work of William the Conqueror and his sons. And it only needs to be added that the sea ports on every shore of the Mediterranean and the trade between them came during the same years under increasing influence from the Normans of the South. The best sea route from Genoa and Pisa to the Adriatic lay through the straits of Messina, and all the commerce directed from Spain, and from the ports of Algeria towards Egypt and Syria, or towards the terminal points of the great Asiatic trade routes had to pass through the narrows of the Mediterranean, which during this period were coming more and more under the control of fleets based upon Norman Sicily which in its turn was not unconscious of its filiations with Norman England.

The drift in the balance of power westward across the Rhine and southward across the Alps, of which the Anglo-Norman realm was a product and a partial cause, was also reflected in the flowering of an individual western culture. To this the name "twelfth-century renaissance" has been aptly given. This renaissance, which took almost as many forms as that of the fifteenth and sixteenth centuries, has been described with some justice as marking an epoch in European civilization. If this should be considered an exaggeration, it is certain that during these decades what may be called the Romance-speaking lands attained a dominance in European art and letters. It is surely remarkable that the most notable achievements of this great age, the poetry of the Troubadours, the development of medieval humanism, the beginnings of scholastic theology, the new learning and the new Universities in which it was to be housed, all came from a world which was centred on a France from which the Normans came—a world which also included the Italy which the Normans had helped to transform, and the England which had been conquered and settled by William the Conqueror and his sons.

The matter was to prove of such importance to the future that it deserves some illustration. Thus, as the twelfth century advanced, the new philosophical and classical scholarship came rapidly to be centred in northern France, and particularly in the episcopal schools of Chartres and Paris. The names of William of Conches and Thierry of Chartres for example come to mind in this connection, whilst the development of the new theology was foreshadowed in the work of Abelard, Peter Lombard and Hugh of St. Victor.

Legal studies tended at the same time to be prosecuted with the greatest vigour in Italy. The same concentration of scholarship in the West could be seen in the rise in this period of the medieval universities. This process was adumbrated in the medical school of Salerno, which at the outset was dominated by Bishop Alfanus who co-operated in some measure with the Norman, Robert Guiscard. But the real archetypal universities of the Middle Ages are Bologna, which concentrated on law, and Paris, which devoted its intense activities to humanism and theology.

By the middle of the twelfth century there was scarcely a single eminent scholar in Latin Europe who had not in some way been associated either with Chartres or Bologna or more particularly with Paris. In short, by increasing the political strength of the West, the Norman Conquest had contributed in some measure to the growth of an individual western culture.

For the same reasons the achievement of William the Conqueror meant that England would be brought into closer contact with Western Europe just at the time when Latin Christendom was entering on a cultural revival. The new learning came to England in the wake of the two archbishops of Canterbury, Lanfranc and Anselm, whom the Normans brought from Italy by way of the abbey of Le Bec, and henceforth the scholarly and artistic activities of England were gradually to be made part of an endeavour which was common to the whole of the West.

During the century which followed the Conqueror's death in 1087, with rare exceptions, whatever was thought or written in England was thought and written in Latin, and Romanesque architecture would find perhaps its finest expression at Durham. English scholars in their turn, while retaining their own sense of patriotism, drew their inspiration chiefly from abroad. Adelard of Bath, for example, who was characteristic of the early twelfth century, migrated to France as a young man to study at Laon and Tours, and he dedicated one of his books to William, Bishop of Syracuse, who was himself probably a Norman. Somewhat later England gave to Europe in John of Salisbury one of the most complete exponents of twelfth-century humanism. But the learning of John of Salisbury was acquired under masters of the school of Chartres, and he boasted that he had crossed the Alps no less than ten times.

John of Salisbury belongs to the latter half of the twelfth century. But neither his career nor the English conditions it reflects would have been possible apart from the conquest of England by William the Conqueror. Of course, there had here been loss as well as gain, in as much as irreparable damage had been inflicted on an earlier English vernacular culture. But it remains true that one of the results of the William's conquest was that England was brought into the main stream of European cultural development. Thus was it that she would make her own contribution to those great movements in scholarship, in architecture, and in education which were to be characteristic of Western Europe at the peak of its medieval achievement.

Care must assuredly be taken not to exaggerate the part played by the Normans between 1066 and 1154 in the making of medieval Europe, and, in particular, it is only with caution that one can associate the work of William the Conqueror with developments in which he would have had little personal interest, and which in fact only reached fruition at a later date. Nevertheless, it would be hard to deny that during the century which followed his death, and partly owing to what he achieved, Western Europe became progressively more conscious of its own individuality, and that its peoples— the English among them—then began to develop a new pride in shared ambitions and a new sense of common purpose.

William the Conqueror was a great king, and he dominated his own age. Was he also a "great European"? Certainly, the future history of Europe, and the part that would be played by England within it, were both profoundly modified by his acts.

SAINT THOMAS AQUINAS
(*c.* 1225–1274)

A BUILT-IN hazard of any system of thought that claims to possess truth in a special way is a tendency to underestimate truths discovered and developed in other systems. Concerned to preserve its own heritage incorrupt, it will often see corruption not only where others proffer different truths, but even when they express the same truths differently. The Catholic Church is not immune from this danger, however divine may be the guidance it claims to have led it down the centuries.

Whether we regard it as a proof of divine guidance or merely extraordinary human wisdom, it remains a fact that men and women of genius in the course of its history have prevented the mainstream of Catholic teaching from remaining in too narrow a channel or too shallow a bed. Saint Thomas Aquinas was one of those who reminded the Church of his own day, and for many a day after, that its proper sphere is truth, meaning every kind of truth that affects the ultimate end towards which man is striving.

He performed his task so brilliantly that a Pope some six centuries after his death could proclaim his system of thought to be the standard by which Catholic theology and philosophy should generally be measured. Although a hundred years later still, the Catholic Church finds itself once again in a time of questing, self-examination and self-criticism the influence of St Thomas has not lost its fascination and even dominance.

Thomas was to become known as the Angelic Doctor, but the turbulent middle ages in which he was born were scarcely reminiscent of angels. Nevertheless, in his background there was faith, and a kind of piety, albeit highly flavoured by the roughness of the times. One sister, Marotta, became abbess of the Benedictine convent of Santa Maria di Capua, but three others, more typically, married into families of the local nobility of the kind from which Thomas himself was sprung. A fifth sister was killed by lightning. Most of the violent death in the family, however, came from war. Of three elder brothers, two at least left a name behind them as soldiers, thus

44

imitating their father, Landolfo of Aquinas. Moreover, they served most of the time, not the Popes but the Hohenstaufen Emperor Frederick II.

For a large part of his life the Emperor was in conflict with the troops loyal to Popes Honorius III and Gregory IX. However, the attitude of Landolfo's family was due not so much to anti-papal feeling as to the fact that the family castle at Roccasecca, near Monte Cassino, was situated in that part of the kingdom of Sicily which lay on the Italian mainland next to the papal states. Landolfo thus owed feudal allegiance to Frederick.

It was at Roccasecca that Thomas was born about 1225. In 1231—there was no real inconsistency in this—he was offered to the great Benedictine abbey, rather as Samuel was offered to Eli to serve the Jewish Temple. Doubtless, his parents hoped that he would become a monk and eventually abbot of the monastery, as became his blood and family. Piety could live with ambition.

The motto of the Benedictine Order is *Pax*, but Monte Cassino, for all its monks and scholars was not always a haven of scholarly peace. In the thirteenth century, as in the twentieth, it could be overwhelmed by secular politics. In 1239, Emperor Frederick, enraged by a second papal excommunication, boldly occupied the monastery as a fortress, and sent all the foreign monks packing. All this in the event worked for the good of young Thomas. The abbot sent him, with other "oblates", to Naples to continue his studies in the larger atmosphere of the university, taking as his residence one of the two Benedictine houses in the city.

Finest minds learn best in the hardest school. Thomas Aquinas gathered strength as he learned to rise above his age and environment. At Naples he was introduced to Aristotle's thought, and the translated commentaries on it of the Arab Averroes. Not content with the new intellectual challenge, Aquinas decided by 1244 to accept another of an ascetical kind. The Order of Friars Preachers, founded by the Spaniard, Dominic de Guzman, in 1215, was still in its first enthusiasm. Vowed to evangelical poverty and service to the Church, its curriculum included study, preaching and lecturing, but without any hope of reward in the shape of ecclesiastical preferment.

Thomas came increasingly under its influence while in Naples, and eventually received the mendicant habit at the priory of San Domenico in April, 1244. Almost immediately afterwards, he set out for Rome. But he was directed less by piety than by the intention of his superiors in the Order to spare him an embarrassing encounter with his own family on the subject of his new vocation. Their foresight was justified. All the same, it proved inadequate to prevent the meeting.

Thomas now underwent what was probably the severest test of his whole life. Disappointed by their son's choice—it meant turning his back on honour and promotion in the Church—his parents, and particularly his mother, Donna Teodora, determined to make Thomas see reason—their kind of reason. His elder brother, Rinaldo, was warned of what was afoot. Camped at Terni, he was able to intercept young Thomas on the road to Bologna, and forcibly oblige him to return to Roccasecca. Donna Teodora made every effort short of violence to get her son to abandon the Dominicans. But the stuff of the parents was in the child. Thomas prevailed in his own kind of warfare; even so his farewell to arms was hardly the prelude to peace. At all events, in 1245, he was allowed to return to the Dominicans. It proved much to his advantage that he learned thus early to concentrate on his studies and vocation amid turbulent surroundings.

In 1252, Thomas faced a new kind of turbulence and a new stage in his career. His studies had taken him to Cologne and Paris. While in Cologne, from 1248 to 1252, Thomas had worked under Albert, and was ordained priest, although still very young. In spite of his youth, he was now sent on to Paris to lecture under Elias Brunet de Bergerac who occupied the chair reserved for foreign Dominicans. Another chair was reserved for French members of the Order. When Thomas began his career as university lecturer, a certain resistance to the mendicant order was becoming articulate in the city. Undeterred, the young friar began to read the "Sentences" of Peter Lombard to his students at the university, and to produce scholarly works of theology and controversy.

Thomas was, in fact, preparing for a second Dominican chair at the university, and the thought was much disliked by some. The mendicants—Franciscans and Dominicans—were still recent enough to be for many an undesirable innovation. Their competition was keenly resented. Even the university, hankering excessively after the quiet life, perhaps, now turned against him. The papacy itself, nonplussed by the virulence of the opposition, was persuaded for a time that the mendicants were all their enemies claimed. On 21 November, 1254, Innocent IV revoked all mendicant privileges. His successor, Alexander IV, however, promptly restored them. He also directed the Paris university to grant Aquinas a formal licence to teach. While Thomas gave his first official lecture, the soldiers of King Louis IX stood ready to protect him and his audience from the hostile mob outside.

Although Thomas, and for that matter, Bonaventure, the great Franciscan, continued to lecture in the colleges of their respective orders, the university refused to grant them any official status. Eventually, Pope Alexander ordered the university directly to admit Friars Preachers and Friars Minors to its membership. This was not done in a merely general way, but Aquinas and Bonaventure were personally named to be admitted officially as doctors of theology. Nevertheless, the formal ceremony of admission was delayed by some months. Even then the bishops and most of the secular clerics in the university made themselves conspicuous by their absence.

The warrior ancestry stood Thomas in good stead. Earlier experience of striving for his vision even against his family made it that much easier to strive against those who were rather less than related flesh and blood. In any case, the continuing opposition, ruthlessly critical, at least obliged him to clarify his ideas. The ground was thus carefully prepared for what was to prove the work of a lifetime, and for many a lifetime.

Now a "master", Thomas spent the next three years in the Paris professorship lecturing "between the hours of Prime and Tierce" on the Bible and its doctrine. This occupied all his working days. In the afternoon he dealt with *questiones disputatae*. From time to time he also functioned as special preacher for the university. It was in connection with his postmeridian activities that he produced the important treatise *De Veritate*. By the end of his time in Paris, he was directing a secretarial staff to do his transcribing and note-taking, whilst a fellow Dominican acted as secretary and confessor, guide, philosopher and friend. Amongst those whom Thomas was training for the next generation was the English Dominican, William of Alton, a Southampton man, who succeeded Thomas as "regent master" when he left Paris in 1259.

Thomas proceeded immediately to Valenciennes to take part in the general chapter held in June. There Thomas was appointed to a special commission of studies for his Order, together with four other Paris masters. They included his old mentor, Albert the Great. Thus Aquinas helped to shape the first Dominican *ratio studiorum*, or syllabus of studies, to guide the formation of young men becoming Friars Preachers. After Valenciennes, Aquinas returned to Italy the same year, 1259. Reginald of Piperno was now assigned to him by his Order as permanent *socius*, or companion.

Thomas's movements, dates of residence and appointments in Italy after his return from Paris and until 1268 cannot be completely listed with certainty. It is known that in 1260 he was made a preacher-general in his own province—the Roman Province. This would presuppose what is confirmed elsewhere that his relations with the Popes, more specifically Urban IV and Clement IV, were good. He was also in charge of a *studium* in the priory of Santa Sabina on the Aventine Hill in 1265. It is also likely that he taught at different times in Anagni, Orvieto and Viterbo.

The overall picture is that of a man much in demand and enjoying the trust not only of his fellow Dominicans, but also of the hierarchy, especially the Pope. On the road often, he stayed in no place very long, and the kaleidoscopic business of Church and Order left him no leisure. All the same, his energies were primarily those of a scholar, and the time spent travelling was not allowed to interfere harmfully with his thinking and writing.

Truly great work, at least in the literary or philosophical sphere. is usually the end-product of a life's endeavour before decline sets in. So with Thomas. But there were many works on the way. An important preliminary work, the *Summa contra Gentiles*, was calculated to make Christianity persuasive to cultivated Mohammedans and Jews. This was begun in Paris, and continued in Italy, in spite of the heavy pressure of his other engagements. Aquinas's work, in fact, resembled one of the great contemporary cathedrals in the new and daring style of early gothic. Built slowly over the years, the general style indicated the final form. But there was much alteration from the original plan and improvisation freshly inspired along the way. The various works and studies of his lifetime resembled chapels and cloisters, set apart from the main building but not disconnected, and helping to provide a whole that was decidedly complex but, in the main, consistent.

The great plan to put the whole of Christian teaching into one work was probably launched in Rome in 1265, In the next three or four years he managed to complete the first part of this *Summa Theologica*. The author aimed not only to expound positive Christianity, but also to deal with nearly every objection conceivable in his own age and all preceding. He was much assisted by the more accurate translations of Aristotle direct from the Greek which were becoming available. Indeed, Aquinas himself was a main factor in this. Fortunately, he was encouraged by Urban IV, who had been in the east himself before his elevation to the papacy. Thomas's principal assistant as translator was William of Moerbeke, a Flemish Dominican who knew Greece from first-hand experience. He later became Archbishop of Corinth. Nevertheless, Aquinas was not to be allowed to settle for long in the congenial and sympathetic atmosphere of the Roman Province. The circumstances which led to another journey northwards are not known. Certain it is, however, that by May, 1269, Aquinas was back in Paris. He arrived some time before the end of the school year which seems to imply haste for a purpose. Thomas must have known he was returning to a battlefield, but could scarcely have foreseen that he was entering on his toughest field of conflict to date.

To many at that time the solid teaching of the Church seemed to be melting into fiery nothingness in the great crucible of medieval thought which was Paris. Rival systems fought not merely for their own survival, but identified themselves with Catholic truth as such, and saw their own survival or eclipse as one involving the whole Church. This kind of contest was bound to be bitter. The rise of Latin Averroism, with the characteristic twist given it by Siger of Brabant, struggled with the safer and more traditional teaching that went by the name of Augustinianism. Thomas was himself at variance with Siger, but the chief bitterness arose in his conflict with the traditionalists. The Augustinian outlook was defended with competence and originality by the Franciscan, Bonaventure. He also would receive in due course the crowning compliment of canonization. Meanwhile, Bonaventure himself did not attack Thomas personally or his system. Some of the Franciscans did. The bitterest opponent of these years and for many years, however, was William of Saint Amour, a man determined to secure once and for all the overthrow of what he took to be heretical innovation.

"William of Holy Love" had begun his opposition to the mendicants at least as early as the 1250s. In a Latin work on the subject of Antichrist and his ministers, he had discovered, as he believed, no less than thirty-one heresies in a Franciscan book published in 1254. This led him to declare that the mendicants, far from being the latest wave of reformers in the Church, were merely those precursors of Antichrist foretold by Joachim of Calabria, a

Cistercian mystic who had flourished in the second half of the twelfth century.

William had been in the forefront of the opposition to the mendicants during Aquinas's first professorship in Paris. Thomas was better established and known by 1269, so that the antagonism between William and himself became appreciably more pronounced during the Dominican's second professorship. Especially so since shortly before Aquinas's second visit to Paris William published an encyclopedic work which amounted to a crushing onslaught on the whole mendicant position: a kind of *summa diabolica*, in its negative aspect, of all the errors which William believed to reside in the teaching of the friars.

It would be tedious to recount in detail the battle of the books which now began. But to them that believe, said Saint Paul, all things work together for good. If Aquinas's opponents had been less thorough, the Dominican himself, for all his natural endowment, might have been tempted to produce something less than what was to be the crowning work of his life. As it was, patiently and methodically, Thomas went on drawing grist from what most would regard as barren controversy for the relentlessly turning mill of truth within him. Between the upper and nether grindstone of debate, the *Summa Theologica* was being finely ground out.

For the writing itself Thomas adopted a style more akin to lecture notes than to literature. This left no room for misunderstanding or impatience as he set down cold solutions to the burning philosophical and theological problems of his faith. The *Summa* is written with scientific terseness and economy that sound dry even in sympathetic translation. The authentic thrill comes from the sustained argument and masterly unfolding of his many themes. He deals with well over five hundred "questions" each of which is divided and analysed into a varying number of subsidiary "articles". Thus thousands of topics are covered in this theological encyclopedia.

The objective and unemotional quality of the work gives it a scope which can be appreciated by those who do not believe, or at most hope one day to find faith. Like the *Upanishads*, Plato's *Republic* and the *Koran*, the work is significant as a monument to the human spirit as such, whatever faith may teach further as to inner content. Aquinas proceeds from what all men accept to what most men accept, and from thence to what Christians alone believe. He progresses by logical if not always easy stages.

The first part deals with God and creation; God as spirit and in Himself, before he is considered as Trinity. The second part deals with man; man as he is in himself, then in his relationship to God, and finally in his relationship with God by the grace of Christian revelation. The third part sets out to deal with Christ as the Son of God, and the Sacraments of the Church. Not all will follow him as far as this with faith, but most will follow with interest if not fascination.

As a sample of his reasoning, we may consider his treatment of the problem, "whether the fellowship of friends is necessary for happiness" (*Prima Secundae*, 4th question, 8th Article). He sets out first, three objections to prove that friends are necessary for happiness. One quotes Boethius on Seneca, who believed that delight in possessing some good depends on someone to share it with. Countering these, Aquinas quotes scripture (Wisdom 7, vs 11) "All good things come to me together with her", that is, divine wisdom. Since divine wisdom comes from contemplating God alone, nothing else is necessary for happiness. Aquinas now gives his own view in the "corpus" or body of the article. His first care is to distinguish terms and ideas carefully. "It all depends on what you mean by...." as Dr C. E. M. Joad used to say, imitating consciously or unconsciously the methodical approach of the scholastics. In this case, if we refer to "the happiness of this life", then a happy man needs friends so that he can do good to them, see them doing good, and enlist their help for his own doing of good. Aquinas quotes Aristotle's *Ethics* (IX.9) in support of this. If we are thinking of happiness in the after life, however, then the fellowship of friends is not essential since a man will find entire happiness in God himself. Nevertheless Aquinas adds to this the further idea of Saint Augustine that the blessed in heaven know not only God but one another. They rejoice in God and in one another's company. Aquinas then returns to the three objections stated at the beginning, giving the principles which answer them. Boethius, for example, is answered by pointing out that in God man has a sufficiency of every good, so that the only sharing strictly necessary for happiness would be what God shares with him.

Nor was the *Summa* by any means the only work of the last years. Some eighteen important contributions to theology, including six or seven *quodlibets*, or "occasional questions", were produced before Thomas left Paris.

It cannot be said that all of Thomas's works showed the un-ruffled serenity or used the unemotional language of the *Summa*. Nevertheless, Aquinas compared with his enemies, was mild to a fault. While in Paris for the second time, he composed a pamphlet, "Against the Pestiferous Doctrine of Those who Dissuade Youths from Following a Religious Vocation". But the nearest he ever came to the vitriolic seems to have been in his admittedly polemical, "About the Eternity of the World against the *Murmurantes*", the latter being those who complained that the Aristotelian concept of the creation of the world from all eternity involved philosophical contradiction. In this work, Thomas allowed himself to speak scornfully of those who assumed too easily that they possessed the monopoly of truth and wisdom in their pronouncements on such matters.

Thomas left Paris for the last time soon after Easter, 1272. By mid-year he was in Florence for a Dominican general chapter, or congress of principal superiors and leading spirits. It was on this occasion that he was commissioned to establish a *studium generale*, or study centre of philosophy and theology, in Naples. There in the convent of San Domenico Maggiore he lectured and conducted scholastic disputations. It is not certain that he had any official connection with the neighbouring university, although Charles I of Anjou, King of Sicily, was anxious to revive that institution; and as a patron of the Dominicans, may well have been pleased to see Thomas share his time between the two institutions of learning. Thomas wrote less in these years, but this still amounted to a significant output. He also found time in 1273 to preach a course of Lenten sermons in the city.

The last two years of his life were, by his own standard, years of diminished activity. By the standards of any lesser man, his energies were still tireless. Apart from lectures, sermons and various minor compositions, there were commentaries on various works of his beloved Aristotle; and above all, progress on the third and last part of the *Summa*. He managed to complete the treatise on the Incarnation of the Second Person of the Blessed Trinity, and further sections dealing with the Sacraments in general, and with Baptism and Holy Eucharist in particular. Even by this time, however, he was not considered beyond criticism. To become known is not always to become accepted. Whatever the judgment of posterity, in Thomas's own day most of the admiration still lay in the future. Some contemporaries considered him fortunate that he was not condemned by the Church in his own lifetime, more especially since certain of the conclusions of the Averroists were condemned by the Bishop of Paris in 1270. Aquinas's system was not touched; but even Bonaventure, leading the Augustinians, saw the move as a condemnation of any attempt to baptize the ideas of Aristotle. True to himself, and his inner light, Thomas struggled on with the *Summa:* until the day when, quite unexpectedly, the light became so bright that Thomas could not see to continue.

The decision to abandon further writing was taken after saying Mass on 6 December, 1273, the feast of Saint Nicholas, and in a chapel dedicated to the saint. It seems beyond doubt that Thomas Aquinas, who had relied all his life on reason enlightened by faith, enjoyed an experience which went beyond either. It was as if an amateur, seeing the work of a gifted artist, were to throw away his own brushes; not from despair, but from a simple realization that he could no longer compete. Aquinas now passed a comment on his own achievement which no alien critic could have surpassed in contempt or cruelty. He compared his life's work in the light of his vision to so much straw. This admission was wrung from him by Reginald, still his faithful amanuensis and companion. Nothing now seemed worth doing save to await the end and final revelation. It came soon.

Thomas was summoned to take part in the second Council of Lyons, a council whose object must have been dear to his heart since it was mainly concerned with the reconciliation of the Greek and Latin Churches. His own participation in it was not to be. He was not yet fifty years old, but the indications are that Aquinas was already physically exhausted; a ready prey for any disease that cared to attack with determination. One did. He fell fatally ill not long after he had set out on the road to Lyons. His first resting place was the castle of Maenza, near Terracina; but typically, when he realized he was nearing his last, he had himself moved to the neighbouring Cistercian abbey of Fossanuova, still a place of pilgrimage in the twentieth century. There he died on 7 March, 1274. The faithful Reginald of Piperno stayed long enough to preach at Thomas's funeral at Fossanuova before hastening back to Naples. In that city he went on to serve the memory as he had served the man.

The Church realized fairly quickly what it had lost by Thomas's death and gained by his lifetime's work. His body was scarcely entombed before men began to claim extraordinary favours at his intercession. Surprisingly, but not inappropriately, the first important reaction in his favour came from Paris. As early as May, 1274, the arts faculty requested the Dominican Order to send his body back to the university. Not that his teaching was by any means as yet fully accepted or generally recognized there or anywhere else. In England there was much opposition, especially at Oxford, to the ideas he had defended for a lifetime. Nevertheless, his stature came to be increasingly recognized with the passage of time and the growing enthusiasm of his fellow Dominicans.

Not quite half a century had elapsed since his death when the Church set her own indestructible seal on his memory. He was canonized in 1323. In 1567, Pius V declared him a Doctor of the Church, and his reputation has grown steadily over the centuries. Further vindication of Saint Thomas Aquinas came in the nineteenth century and subsequently, when a series of Popes beginning with Leo XIII, and not ending with Pius XII, elevated Thomism above all rival systems of scholastic philosophy. It became for Catholics the preferred vehicle to explain, in so far as they can be explained in human terms, the mysteries of Christian faith. Even now it is difficult to conceive of a time when Thomism will be discarded, or when another system will establish itself as a more comprehensive vehicle for the rational exposition of the tenets of Catholic faith.

Whether we accept or admire this system or not, it can scarcely be denied that Thomism contributed powerfully to the European spirit by helping to impart tremendous self-confidence to its intellectual and spiritual achievement. It assisted in moulding an ethos which distinguished European culture from the rest of the world for a matter of centuries. Indeed, it was still powerful enough in the age of discovery to carry Catholic Europe to the New World and the Far East and leave behind an indelible mark on even newer ages of political and cultural emancipation.

DANTE
(1265–1321)

DANTE ALIGHIERI was born in Florence in May, 1265 (the exact date is not known), of a family of noble extraction but reduced circumstances. His father was variously described as a lawyer or small tradesman, and the poet's baptized Christian name of Durante was later compressed to Dante.

Little is known of the early life of "that singular splendour of the Italian race", as Dante's first biographer, Boccaccio, called him, and a great deal of what has been written about him down the ages is conjecture. A certain amount of fact emerges from his own works, which contained much autobiographical material. In particular, his *Vita Nuova* includes the circumstances of his first celebrated glimpse of Beatrice, when both were nine years of age. This girl, believed to be Beatrice Portinari (even this is uncertain, although the facts and dates clearly fit), was to Dante never to become more than a far-off star, an ideal, rather than a known, human woman (indeed some commentators have doubted her real existence); and after an early marriage to Simone d'Bardi Beatrice Portinari was to die young, in her twenty-fourth year. But her name was to transform Dante's poetry and life, and echo down the ages as a legend from which many subsequent romantic writers were to draw inspiration.

The *Vita Nuova* and later the *Divina Commedia* represent, above all, Dante's contrasted springs of genius, and his influence on all periods down to our own. In spite of the wide ranges of subject encompassed by the two very different works, Beatrice remains the continuing link, emerging in the last part of the *Divine Comedy*, the *Paradiso*, as Dante's beatific spirit and guide. Thus Dante fulfilled his vow on her death, which left him profoundly shattered, "to say of Beatrice that which never yet was said of any woman".

In a sense this platonic romance, for all the obvious personal feeling behind its inspiration, was in the chivalric medieval tradition, established in earlier romances and by the troubadour poets of Provence, whose influence on Dante and many subsequent writers was profound. Historically, Dante was a figure of his time, and although he was sometimes said to be a precursor of the Renaissance, two hundred years later, this was only in the sense of artistic, not true philosophical and mental, affinity.

His teacher was Brunetto Latini, who in the words of the distinguished modern Italian scholar, Michele Barbi, in his *Life of Dante*, "first set the Florentines to governing the commonwealth according to sound policy". It was a school which prepared the citizen for civil life, and it was from Latini according to Dante himself, that he learned "how a man becomes eternal". It was also from him, as well as through his own family's traditional political affiliations, that he derived the ideas of government that were to inspire much of his work, such as *De Monarchia*, and eventually lead to the long exile which, again in Barbi's words, "widened Dante's horizon and made, out of a Florentine, a citizen of Italy".

Florence at the time of Dante's birth was divided into two factions, Guelph and Ghibelline. Dante's family was Guelph, the party of the lesser nobility and artisans; the Ghibelline embraced the feudal aristocracy. Both by his family and marriage Dante was drawn to the Guelph faction, although he moved to the moderate or "White" side of its "Black" and "White" divisions and in fact ultimately leant towards the Ghibelline side.

Nevertheless, although Florentine politics were to help form his mind and ideas, his early study was Latin poetry and rhetoric, learned with Latini and probably also at Bologna. Virgil, he was to declare in the *Inferno*, was the source of the "beautiful style" that made him famous. Cicero and Aristotle were other profound influences on his work until his death. After 1290 he became so deeply interested in philosophy that, in his own words, "the love of her drove away and destroyed every other thought". His study was so intense that it seriously impaired his eyesight. As Beatrice died in 1290 we may take it that the philosophic fervour was in some sense a drug of forgetfulness. Yet Dante, in fact, never did forget his loss; he merely absorbed the romantic impulse alongside the philosophy, drawing poetic inspiration from both. He married, some years later, Geurma di Manetto Donati, a high-born lady to whom he seems to have been betrothed long before, but the union is taken to have been an unsatisfactory one.

Before this he had, in 1289, taken part in the battle of Campaldino as a mounted soldier in the cavalry. This was the battle in which the Florentines and their Guelph allies defeated the Ghibelline league. Italy was torn and fragmented by internal wars, and

Florence itself was undergoing social change, both factors influencing Dante to an interest in public as well as artistic affairs.

From 1 November, 1295, to 30 April, 1296, he served on the special council of the people, and from May to September, 1296, was one of the Council of the Hundred, dealing with finances. In 1300, at thirty-five years old, he reached the highest point of his municipal career as one of the six priors of Florence, and asserted his own impartiality and moderation by procuring the banishment of the extremist leaders of both parties, Guelph and Ghibelline alike, who were involving Florence in internal strife. The office did not last long, but in October, 1301, when Charles of Valois (nominally invading Italy as a peacemaker) approached the city, he was sent on an embassy to Rome to appeal to the Pope, Boniface VIII. The Pope supported Charles who nevertheless sided with the "Black", or Right Wing, Guelph party, and after three days of street fighting in Florence was victorious. In January, 1302, Dante and others were banished, a sentence later hardened to the threat of burning if they ever returned or were caught.

Fortunately Dante was still in Rome, and from thereon he remained in wandering exile. He is said by some to have spent some time between 1307–1309 in Paris, where the university at that time led the world in the study of theology. Less likely is a theory that he also visited England and lived for a period at Oxford.

He never became wholly reconciled to his banishment and fervently espoused the cause of the German Henry VII when he was elected Emperor in 1308. To Dante's mind the Holy Roman Empire was the answer to Florentine and Italian strife, and Henry VII, in invading Italy, became the focus of his dream of a supreme ruler and universal empire, the only agency which could, he believed, transcend individual interests. It also implied his support of the Emperor against the Pope.

It was a part of his theory that papal authority should extend only to religious matters and that the secular remained the sole province of the Emperor. The papacy, he maintained, was itself degenerate and corrupt, mishandling its material resources and neglecting the poor, yet the Empire was necessary to the welfare of the world: God's gift to the people of Rome and independent of the supreme religious authority. In this sense Dante did not look on the German Emperor as a foreign invader—as the Florentines certainly did—and although his presentation of the whole theory of unification seems alien to us today, seen in the light of his time it was grounded on a genuine concern to end internal war and massacre, and unite Italy. It was a forerunner of Italian dreams of unification down to the time of Garibaldi, although the methods were to change with the periods.

Dante published these political theories in *De Monarchia* and clung to his strong antipathy to papal dominance as late as the Purgatory section of the *Divine Comedy*. "Time was", he wrote, "when Rome had two suns that showed to men the one and the other path, that of the world and that of God. Now one has extinguished the other: and the sword is united with the pastoral staff; and thus joined, of very necessity they go ill."

The unexpected death of Henry VII in 1313 was a blow to Dante's vision, but when in 1315 the Florence commune granted a form of amnesty to its political exiles, on condition that the exiles paid a fine and retracted their errors, he indignantly refused in characteristic terms of wounded pride: "Is this the glorious recall whereby Dante Alighieri is summoned after suffering well-nigh fifteen years of exile? Is this the reward of innocence manifest to all the world, of unbroken sweat and toil in study?" As a result he was condemned to death on 6 November. His sons (said to number six) were included in his disgrace but they were now in exile with him, as was also their one sister Beatrice, who became a nun: Dante's wife did not share their exile.

The exact details of the last eight years of Dante's life are not known, nor for certain where he spent them, but he found a final haven in Ravenna in about 1316. He may have held a professorship here, and certainly instructed visiting scholars in the poetic art, while finishing off his own *Divine Comedy*. In August, 1321, he was one of an embassy sent by Guido Novello da Polenta, the Lord of Ravenna and one of Dante's pupils, to try to avert an attack upon Ravenna by the Doge of Venice and others. Soon after his return he died at Ravenna in Sepetember, 1321. He was buried there with great honour, in a stone tomb that is still in existence.

Boccaccio left a description of him, saying he was of medium height with a long face, aquiline nose and black curly hair, and "he seemed always melancholy and thoughtful". The portraits of him are not, though, completely reliable. The melancholy had a cause, but seems also natural to the cast of his mind, for although the *Divine Comedy* has elements of what today we would call "black comedy", its Inferno is basically sombre, and the brightness in

Dante's works is too mystical and transcendent to suggest human joy. "Stern" is the epithet most commonly used by commentators of his aspect and moralizing in the *Divine Comedy*, as he travels through the regions of Hades, Purgatory and Paradise, compassionate on occasion but without ever losing the severity of moral judgment. This was based on total belief in the doctrine of the Church of his time, and the essential justice of the tortures inflicted by God on the sinner.

It is not surprising that Dante's reputation in other countries has fluctuated violently with the theological outlook of the era; that it should have been low in the eighteenth century, the age of enlightenment and reason, and once again flourished in the more puritanically orthodox Victorian age, only to descend again in our own time, when the permissive society reads Dante hardly at all.

Yet these judgments are emotional rather than scholastic and stem partly from one of Dante's major achievements as a poet. This was his dispensing with Latin (in which, however, *De Monarchio*, was written) in favour of Italian, which he raised to new heights of poetic expression. In a sense he is said virtually to have "made" the Italian language: "This shall be the new light, the new sun", he wrote. But his use of the vernacular necessarily limited the appreciation of those readers to whom the language was not known. Latin was at the time the universal scholastic language and even today knowledge of Italian and its subtleties is not wide enough to make Dante's full flavour easily accessible. Translations have been innumerable, but as with Shakespeare they are no substitute for the original.

Dante, who was also devoted to the arts of music and painting, was a musician with words; yet the music escapes many. Perhaps this is one reason why the English poets he most captivated were the romantic ones of the early nineteenth century: Byron (who lived for a time in Ravenna), Keats and Shelley, all of whom resided in Italy and learned to read Dante in the original.

The first work of what has been called his "trilogy", the *Vita Nuova*, the "new" or "early" life, deals autobiographically with his infatuation with Beatrice, and experience of other loves only to return to her as the platonic ideal. It was an "ideal of human perfection", a new concept of love and art, with what the author called "new rhymes". Love was a virtue inspiring man to good actions; thus even when Dante turned to philosophic study and politics, he continued to write of love as, in Barbi's words, "a source of instruction . . . a phase of learning".

In the second of the great trilogy (though they were not deliberately conceived as such), *Convivio*, Dante names Aristotle the "teacher and leader of human reason", and also draws on the Commentaries of St. Thomas, and the Confessions of St. Augustine, De Meteoris, Albertus Magnus and others. It shows a contempt for rulers who fail to acquire wisdom for their office, or to take the good advice of wiser men. Reason, says Dante, draws man close to God; a concept not totally alien to Thomas Paine's *The Age of Reason*, an antibiblical but deist book of almost five hundred years later, although it was opposite to the concept of reason held by other more atheistic and sceptic philosophers of the eighteenth century (Voltaire was more virulently antagonistic to Dante than even to Shakespeare).

Dante, nevertheless, was an advocate of the reform of Church management, not of its basic doctrine; a fact which has made his third and greatest work of the trilogy, the *Divine Comedy*, peculiarly susceptible to the religious outlook of succeeding periods. Dante designed the work, which took him some ten years, in three canticles (Inferno, Purgatory, Paradise), each in thirty-three cantos. The three canticles have almost the same number of lines, and each canticle ends with the word "stars". Its metrical device was the chain-linked *terza rima*. "Such facts are external," as Barbi wrote, "but noteworthy, evidence of a most felicitous and powerful genius that could combine the most sublime and burning inspiration with rigorous meditation and minute craftsmanship of form."

The *Inferno* in fact blends biblical and mythological traditions, but although Dante sometimes questions the justice of divine punishment of the sinner he always submits in the end to the orthodox assumption that God's will is final and best. The fact that the Roman Church's own conception of God's will, and of Hell, Purgatory and Limbo, might be wrong, and wholly imaginary, does not occur to him. Yet the doctrinal submission is an ambiguity; for Dante certainly uses his imagination in the whole account of his travels through these regions of suffering, repentance and transfiguration.

His own moral "sternness", already referred to, perhaps supports his orthodoxy, very alien to more modern systems of morality. For Hell and Purgatory to Dante were not myths, and he enhances their actuality by peopling them with famous human beings of all periods, including the most recent celebrated dead. In the *Inferno* particularly, with its demons tormenting the damned for ever without hope, he uses not only moral censure and the more high-minded forms of poetry, but a coarse and colloquial invective that has shaken many commentators living in more refined or squeamish civilizations. He does not draw the line at revolting scenes and images, far alien for instance to the Miltonic *Paradise Lost*, with its noble image of a fallen Lucifer. Dante's conception is medieval, much like the gargoyles on early Gothic architecture.

Dante nevertheless draws levels of ascent from deepest Hades to the final glory of the Paradise, according to the levels of the styles of sin. In the Purgatory—the cleansing region of non-eternal punishments—and Limbo, with its "sorrow without pain" (*duol senza martiri*), his compassion is often shown (in this aspect of Limbo he followed Aquinas). He notably questions the justice of the condition of faultless heathen men, "born on the banks of the Indus" and therefore through no fault of their own condemned for lack of baptism or knowledge of Christ; but again, as in the Book of Job, he comes up with the answer that it is presumptuous to question God and his justice. "He seems", wrote the notable English Dante scholar, the Rev. Edward Moore, "like a bird vainly beating its wings against the bars of its cage".

The levels of condemnation for certain crimes suggested by Dante seem often personal and arbitrary. Of crimes of violence and fraud, he stigmatizes the latter as far the worse, perhaps to some degree reflecting his own rigid standards of incorruptibility in Church and State. Sexual perversion shares the same level of punishment with usury, there being perhaps a curious link in the medieval mind, for usury was considered a crime "against nature". Dante has no sympathy with the sin, but as the homosexual group includes some of the greatest names in philosophic and artistic history, including his own loved and admired teacher, Brunetto Latini, he is again torn here by pity and concern: indeed too much so for some commentators until very recent times.

Another inventive attribute is the devising of punishments in some way appropriate to the crime: Gluttony is punished by eternal hunger and thirst, Anger is blinded by dense smoke, the sin of *Accidia* (loosely interpreted as Spiritual Sloth, i.e. lack of church-going and observation of its tenets) is expiated by a state of perpetual motion, without rest. W. S. Gilbert, well grounded in the classics, may well have been echoing Dante when he wrote the Mikado's song on the theme "to make the punishment fit the crime" in his comic opera *The Mikado*.

One characteristic of the real-life figures in the *Divine Comedy* is that they retain their original human responses and emotions, which are fired anew by the presence of this visitor from the world they have left. Dante's presence is a stimulus to memory and emotion—even the more savage emotions of the denizens of Hell—and many in Purgatory ask for the prayers of their living families or request that Dante should take back news of them, and their hopes of ultimate salvation. The whole concept is, in some ways, a curious foreshadowing of the functions of the Spiritualistic medium. Some, like Francesca in the famous Paolo and Francesca episode, still attempt to justify their original sin. It is not for nothing that the *Divine Comedy* has been called a great *dramatic* work, and Dante essentially a *dramatic* writer.

It is in Purgatory and Paradise that Dante's more lyrical vein becomes prominent. In Purgatory there is hope, and an atmosphere of the "gentle blue of orient sapphire". There are discourses on art and artists, widening Dante's own intellectual understanding of poetry, and the theme of sin dragging down the soul is sustained by its rise to Paradise. In Purgatory, as Edward Moore writes, "as sin after sin is removed, the soul, by a sort of natural buoyancy, rises upwards to return to God". It would otherwise, as Dante himself points out, be as unnatural as that "a living flame should lie passive on the ground" (*come a terra quete in foco vivo*). Thus we have paralleled the upward movement of Dante himself to Paradise, with its "great variety of tender blossoms", and what is virtually "the canticle of Beatrice", who guides the poet among the spirits of those he most loved and admired, yet who even in their various heavens retain the realities of human character. The poem is a study of man's free will, and the *Paradiso* culminates, in Barbi's phrase, in "a statement in lyric yet epic terms of the highest achievements of humanity".

One of the features of Dante's work is, in Moore's words, his "minute attention to all the details and accessories". In spite of the vastness of the subject and imagined terrain, there is a marked lack of inconsistencies. Technique, in fact, is always in control of imagination. These technical and poetical skills have helped Dante's work to survive the changes of time.

Sometime between the *Convivio* and *Divine Comedy* Dante created *De Monarchia*, and the later and greater work absorbed much of its political reasoning. *De Monarchia* had noted that Man has a corruptible and an incorruptible nature, and the *Divine Comedy* traces these spiritual characteristics through all the levels of the after life, while retaining the poet's fierce condemnation of the church's own corruptions, and passionate belief in the division, in the State, of the secular and theological. This, to Dante, was the divine plan; his Emperor was invested with the authority of God. It is this, politically and religiously, that divides him from our own society, as it divided him even in his own time from the Florentines, struggling to retain a republican identity. Yet the Divine Right of Kings permeated monarchical thought for long after Dante, and his vision of Hell remained largely current in Christian teaching near to our own time.

Although these were Dante's principal works there were others, including the *De Vulgari Eloquio*, a study of language, and the *Epistles*, addressed to statesmen, both written in Latin. A collection of shorter poems, *canzoni*, and sonnets are preserved under the title of *Canzoniere*. For long the authenticity of a very late work, believed to have been given as a lecture in Ravenna in 1320— *Quaestio de Aqua et Terra*—was strongly questioned, but Moore, Barbi and others have more recently accepted it as almost certainly by Dante. It is a questioning of the medieval assumption that of the four then recognized elements—earth, water, air and fire—water in fact lay concentrically "above" the earth. It was first discovered and published in 1508, but its scientific reasoning and detail are so meticulously medieval and Dantean that it is no longer thought possible that it could have been a forgery of two hundred years later.

Dante's greatness as a poet was quickly recognized in his own age, and even before the invention of printing his works existed in many manuscript copies. To Boccaccio, in the second half of the fourteenth century, was given the task of lecturing on the *Commedia* in church, and he produced a beautiful edition of the poet's works, making several copies in his own hand. The *Comedy* was later one of the first printed works to become widely known.

Dante's influence was widespread. In France Jean Lemaire de Belges (1473–c.1525) found him a revelation and his imitation of his *terza rima*—under the name of the *tercet*—influenced French poetry until the sixteenth century, and again, after a two hundred year gap, much later. In England Milton "rejoiced when he came in contact with Dante and Petrarch". In eighteenth and nineteenth century Germany, in particular, itself in the throes of a renaissance of literature and art, the study of and commentaries on Dante were extensive. The Dante fervour spread to England and America, where Longfellow was among prominent Dante admirers. His influence on the English romantic poets has already been mentioned; specifically one must cite Keats's sonnet, *A Dream, after reading Dante's episode of Paolo and Francesca*.

> As Hermes once took to his feathers light,
>   When lulled Argus, baffled, swoon'd and slept,
> So on a Delphic reed, my idle spright,
>   So play'd, so charm'd, so conquer'd, so bereft
> The dragon-world of all its hundred eyes;
>   And seeing it asleep, so fled away,
>
> Not to pure Ida with its snow-cold skies,
>   Nor unto Tempe, where Jove grieved a day;
> But to that second circle of sad Hell,
>   Where in the gust, the whirlwind, and the flaw
> Of rain and hail-stones, lovers need not tell
>   Their sorrows,—pale were the sweet lips I saw,
> Pale were the lips I kiss'd, and fair the form
>   I floated with, about that melancholy storm.

Shelley's idealization of Emilia Viviani in *Epipsychidion* was a conscious imitation of Dante's *Vita Nuova*; and Byron's constant references, particularly in *Childe Harold* and *Don Juan*, where his treatment of war and nature sometimes conjures up the death and madness images of Dante's Inferno. The fact that Shelley, the professed atheist with an appalled repulsion to hell-fire and the revengeful God of the Bible, should have been entranced with Dante as a poet is alone testimony to Dante's genius, and its power to rise above the orthodox religious ideas which he shared with his period.

Art, almost more than literature, has been deeply impregnated with the visions of Dante. Raphael in his *Parnassus*, at the Vatican, showed the figures of Homer, Virgil and Dante. Flaxman in 1807 illustrated the Paolo and Francesca passage, as did Fuseli, Blake and Dante Gabriel Rossetti. Rossetti's father was a Dante scholar and through him influences of the poet penetrated the Pre-Raphaelite movement of the 1880's in England.

Late in life William Blake, perhaps the greatest visionary since Dante, was commissioned by Flaxman to illustrate the *Divine*

Of all the medieval Popes, none was more vigorously assertive of Papal claims to sovereignty, both spiritual and temporal, than Hildebrand, who reigned as Gregory VII from 1073 until his death in 1085. On the right is Raphael's superb representation of the Pontiff that is among the artistic treasures of the Vatican.

Where Hildebrand sought political aggrandizement, St Thomas Aquinas was concerned with the establishment of Catholic doctrine in the hearts and minds of men. His writings exercised an immense influence, which still continues through his *Summa Theologica*. This fresco in a church at Florence shows, on the left, St Dominic; and, on the right, St Thomas Aquinas confuting heretics out of the sacred books.

No woman in European history holds a place of such high honour as Joan of Arc, the French peasant girl who listened to "voices" that came to her as she worked in the fields, and, guided by what they told her, put fresh spirit into a defeated army and despairing king, and fought the invading English to a standstill. This painting by Ingres, in the Louvre, shows her on her day of triumph, when Charles VII was crowned king in Reims cathedral. This is grandly conceived; but more appealing, and far more authentic, is the little sketch (*below*) on the margin of a manuscript in the French National Archives at Paris, done by some scribe who, while taking note of the details of the raising of the siege of Orleans, had Joan in the flesh before him.

May· MCCCCXXIX·

Comedy, and learned Italian, with remarkable quickness, in order to read it in the original language. John Palmer, in 1824, found Blake in bed with a scalded foot, "like a dying Michelangelo. Thus and there was he making in the leaves of a great book (folio) the sublimest designs from his (not superior) Dante". Blake produced over one hundred watercolours, although only seven were actually engraved at the time of his death. The pictorial influence went on right through Flaxman and Doré to contemporary ballet, when Frederick Ashton, in 1940, under the emotional impact of the Second World War, choreographed *Dante Sonata* with the illustrations of these artists in mind.

Similarly the influence penetrated into the modern German theatre, when Peter Weiss described his play *The Investigation* as an "Oratorio in 11 Cantos", deliberately evocative of Dante. Produced or publicly read simultaneously in three countries (East and West Germany and England) on 19 October, 1965, it was a dramatic compression of the Nuremberg trials which followed the Second World War. Even Dante's political creed had later repercussions; as Edward Moore percipiently noted: "In the sphere of practical politics, some such dream as that of Dante seems to have possessed for years the brain of Philip II of Spain. He hoped to become the political head of Catholic Christendom, working harmoniously with the Pope as its spiritual head."

From Machiavelli down to Mussolini some elements of Dante's view of the function of an Italian head of state lived on.

Dante survived the ferocious condemnation of Voltaire, Goethe and Goldsmith in their respective countries, for his genius is not just a matter of orthodox theology, but something that of its own volatility and poetic inspiration lives on to speak to new ages quite out of tune with its basic Catholic assumptions, and even its platonic romantic ideal.

JOHANN GUTENBERG
(*c.* 1398–1468)

A WORLD without daily newspapers, weekly or monthly magazines, children's comics or best-sellers; without telephone-directories, standard income-tax and census forms or advertising "literature"; without the institutions that lie behind these and similar aspects of our everyday existence, without public libraries in every town, the books to stock them and a mass-readership to keep them busy; without efficient record and reference systems in business, government and industry or speedy and effective communications at national and international levels; a world in brief without the universal literacy and education that have brought these and a host of related phenomena to pass—such a world is difficult for us to conceive.

Yet it is a thumbnail sketch of ancient and medieval societies down to the middle of the fifteenth century. For that is the great watershed dividing the civilizations where everything had to be laboriously written and copied by hand from the modern world of mechanical printing.

That one simple invention—printing by movable type—traditionally attributed to a virtually anonymous citizen of Mainz in West Germany, Johann Gutenberg, has been crucial to the whole development of Western civilization as we know it today. Indeed there has been no more profound invention in man's whole history on this planet, apart from the primeval discovery of the wheel. It is also something of which Europe can be uniquely proud, which Europe and a native European truly bequeathed to the whole globe. For only in comparatively recent times has the art of printing encompassed the world; even the Chinese, who discovered it independently for themselves long before Gutenberg, waited for much later, Western stimulus before realizing its potential to the full, concealed until recently by the ideogrammatic, non-alphabetical nature of their writing-system.

Astonishingly simple and self-evident, like all great ideas, it seems incredible that no-one should have thought of the secret before, that it took some three millenia of literate human society to work out. The Sumerians had a form of writing; the Egyptians, Phoenicians and Greeks invented increasingly sophisticated varieties of alphabet. The Egyptians devised an elaborate process for making "paper", hammering together overlapping and cross-laid strips of moistened papyrus. The Asiatic Greeks of what is now Turkey pioneered the widespread commercial use of its ancient successor, animal skin with the hair rubbed off—vellum or "parchment" (the word ultimately derives through the Italian *pergamento* from the name of their city, Pergamum). Parchment held sway until the days of Marco Polo when the knowledge of Chinese paper-making travelled along the trade-routes from Asia to the West and paper rapidly established itself as the cheaper commodity in thirteenth and fourteenth century Europe.

The Jews long before the birth of Christ were probably the first to fold sheets of written material into units or quires and sew them together to make a book instead of glueing them edge to edge in a great long roll—an idea the Christians borrowed, transmitted and popularized in Western Christendom (if Christianity had not triumphed in Europe we might still be reading in long strips, as the sheets roll uncut off our modern rotary presses). But these and all other nations and peoples before the 1430s or 1440s knew no other method of recording and publicizing facts and figures—and more important, *ideas*—than the painfully slow use of the pen by one man, making single copies, one at a time, each with its uncertain quota of inaccuracies and mistakes. No two copies were ever identical and the reader was always at the mercy of the handwriting of the individual scribe.

No wonder so few could read or write and showed so little interest in the small number of manuscripts in very limited circulation. Books were a luxury item for the Church and the rich.

The invention of printing changed all this. It astronomically increased the speed and accuracy of book-production. A contemporary scribe bitterly complained that the mechanical press could produce as much in a day as he could write in a year. More important it also released the written word from its comparatively local prison, making the international dissemination of literature and ideas free and easy in a way unsurpassed until the telephone, radio and television did the same, and more, for the spoken word. As a contemporary noted, this time with pride:

"Printing is the art of arts, the science of sciences, . . . illuminating the world. For its infinite virtue is that books found in Athens or Paris or any of the world's centres of learning or monastic and cathedral libraries may now be spread abroad to all races, peoples and nations everywhere."

When dictators muzzle the Press and impose censorship among their earliest actions, they assert in another way the profound significance of Gutenberg's achievement.

The stumbling-block for so long to his discovery was the very nature of Western writing, the 25 or 26 letters of different shapes and sizes, everlastingly repeated in different combinations in the sequence of words and sentences on the page. A man might imitate the example of a stone-mason and carefully carve words in relief on wood or incise them on a metal-plate, ink the surface and block-print a number of copies. But this block-printing takes even longer than copying with a pen, and it would take a man years to produce one copy of the Bible. Similarly it was no use devising a method based on whole words as separate units. There are too many words in a language to be economically produced and stocked in wood or metal, let alone the problem of keeping duplicates of the more recurrent ones.

Medieval Europe was also a collection of two-language cultures, Latin and the local national tongue or dialect; every printer would need a double vocabulary stock, and only the Latin would be of much use for printing works written by the people or nation next door. The inventor of a really practical and economic method of printing was therefore driven to the single letter as his fundamental working unit; only 20-odd units, sufficiently reduplicated, would enable him to construct any word or book in Latin or his native tongue or any European vernacular except Greek (which was anyway virtually unknown in medieval Western Europe until the fifteenth century). The same stock of letters could also be used time and again to produce different books.

The *movable* letter or type is the essence of the matter, and this is what Gutenberg discovered, a method of neatly producing thousands of handy copies of the individual letters of the alphabet, using metal for maximum durability. Book-binders and paper-makers were already using an efficient screw-press; no genius was required either to adapt this to hold a shallow tray containing the metal letters made up into words and arranged in lines and columns, or to spread the ink and lay the sheet of vellum or paper on top.

Gutenberg's invention had little or nothing to do with the construction of the actual printing-press, or the manufacture of paper or ink, or their effective conjunction in the press. What Gutenberg appears to have been the first to invent was an efficient little hand-mould for casting letters in metal. It sounds childishly simple, but it does presuppose three conditions which came together in sufficiently critical form for the first time in the world only in fifteenth-century Germany: the ready availability of a cheap, easily-worked metal; a technology with an advanced knowledge of metal-working; and a society literate enough to be bursting the current manuscript-market at the seams, so that mechanical printing with Gutenberg's movable letters was an economically viable proposition, not some idiosyncratic "scientific" invention like Leonardo da Vinci's parachute or submarine.

Gutenberg had to be a craftsman and metal-worker. If we knew nothing else about the inventor of printing, this much would be clear. Unfortunately little is known about the details of his life and career, and this is surrounded by doubt and controversy, complicated by the forging of various documents over the last two hundred years. Indeed, there is no unequivocal proof that he and not some contemporary was the actual inventor of the vital typefounder's mould. The earliest surviving examples of printing, including the famous 42-line "Gutenberg" Bible—probably the first full-scale book ever printed from movable type—and its successor, the 36-line Bible, carry no imprint recording the name of the printer, place of publication or date.

The earliest actually dated piece of printing, a Papal Indulgence of 1454, is naturally anonymous, and the first book complete with date and name of printer, the Mainz Psalter of 1457, was published by Gutenberg's erstwhile foreman, Peter Schoeffer of Gernsheim, and Gutenberg's former backer and *bête-noir* (or so it seems), Schoeffer's father-in-law, Johann Fust of Mainz. The evidence is all indirect and circumstantial, the most convincing perhaps being a short poem printed at the end of one of Schoeffer's books, dated 1468, in which "the two Johns of Mainz" i.e. Gutenberg and Fust are acclaimed as "the first printers", and a number of other fifteenth-century references which credit Gutenberg with the discovery. There is certainly no known claimant who has a better case to offer for that momentous step which took place in Mainz or Strasbourg sometime between *c.*1440 and 1455.

His mother's name was Gensfleisch so he belonged to one of the

ancient patrician families of Mainz, an important archbishopric at
the confluence of the Rhine and the Main and one of the foremost
centres in medieval Europe of the gold- and silver-smith industry.
His father worked in the local ecclesiastical mint, so Gutenberg
grew up in a home and a city surrounded by the craft and apparatus
of the metal-worker.

In 1411 political and commercial squabbling in Mainz led for a
time to the exile of a number of leading citizens and artisans,
including Gutenberg's father, and in 1428 many patrician families
abandoned Mainz when the local workers' guilds (fore-runners of
our trade unions) successfully challenged their prestige and
authority and deprived them of their hereditary rights and civic
privileges. Gutenberg probably left Mainz on this occasion to settle
one hundred miles further up the Rhine at Strasbourg, apparently
not returning to Mainz in the general amnesty declared in 1430—
the first appearance of Gutenberg's name in an extant historical
document. He will then have been in his late twenties or early
thirties.

In the 1430s he may have been involved in four different lawsuits in Strasbourg, and if lawsuits seem to litter Gutenberg's life
like marker-buoys—or shipwrecks—this is not because Gutenberg
was an unusually contentious, unpleasant or unlucky person.
Legal documents have a high survival rate in that most destructive
of processes, the march of time, and people went to law in medieval
Europe with the same relative frequency and for the same general
reasons that people often write to today's newspapers—to air
grievances and let off steam.

In Gutenberg's case a number of the lawsuits are almost certainly
apocryphal, later fictions circulated either to discredit his name or
support the claims of either Mainz or Strasbourg as the birthplace
of printing. The first lawsuit of 1434 is typical. The town-clerk of
Mainz, so the story goes, visited Strasbourg, only to be clapped into
prison by Gutenberg as security in an action he then brought
against Mainz city-council for failing to pay him some annuity. A
disgruntled Gutenberg, however, was forced not only to let the
town-clerk go, but also to renounce all claim to the money, thus
widening still further the breach between him and his native city.

No original record of this case has survived and suspicions are
aroused by its first appearance, significantly, in Strasbourg in the
middle of the eighteenth century, when the local inhabitants began
a fervent campaign lasting over a hundred and fifty years to

suggest that Gutenberg's disaffection with Mainz remained long after his original departure and that he invented printing at Strasbourg. The lawsuit of 1434 has all the trappings of a Strasbourg myth; we have only the word of an eighteenth-century Strasbourg archivist that he found it in the records.

Similarly Gutenberg is said to have been sued for breach-of-promise in 1436 by a girl of the Strasbourg nobility—she lost the action, and then for insulting a local cobbler who had given evidence for the prosecution. The cobbler won, which cost Gutenberg some £25. These stories have a strong flavour of Mainz rejoinders to the rival city's "Gutenberg" claims, and there is no doubt that two successive professors and librarians at Mainz between *c.*1750 and 1825 went to the lengths of actually forging several "fifteenth-century" documents, including a "letter" from Gutenberg to a non-existent sister unimaginatively called Bertha.

So too with the fourth and very much more important lawsuit of 1439, one of the two lawsuits which seem to involve Gutenberg's great invention directly. It concerned a partnership-contract with one of his apprentice-craftsmen, a Strasburger called Dritzehn, drawn up in 1438 just before Dritzehn died. Originally they planned to cash in on the imminent (or so they thought) great pilgrimage to Aachen, mass-producing cheap looking-glasses and mirrors. But they had miscalculated the year, so Gutenberg formally agreed to spend the interval instructing Dritzehn in "certain other of his arts hitherto concealed", promising substantial compensation to his heirs if Dritzehn died, but specifically excluding them from any normal rights of partnership-succession. Also the equipment they used, any "manufactured stock" and "the art" itself were to remain Gutenberg's property.

Dritzehn put up more than a thousand pounds towards this new venture and further money was borrowed. Lead and other metals were bought, together with a book-binder's press, certain "forms" (probably typepunches, as already used by book-binders for tooling titles), and a goldsmith supplied at considerable expense "materials exclusively concerned with printing", which probably means no more than gold-leaf for illuminating capitals. The details and phraseology are infuriatingly vague, but intentionally so, as trade-secrets are a problem in a society that lacks laws of patent.

When Dritzehn died his heirs challenged the contract, demanding a share in the business and its secrets, and Gutenberg took the matter to court—having already made sure that all "forms" in the workshop (this time perhaps meaning actual type) had been melted down, the press locked away, a certain four-piece object (the crucial type-mould?) unscrewed and the innocuous-looking, uninformative pieces slipped among the general litter of the workshop. Gutenberg won the action and remained master of his secret art, possibly continuing the work or experiments. It is naturally tempting to suppose that mechanical printing was the "art" in question and that printing was perhaps invented at Strasbourg during the late 1430's, but once again the information about this contract and the lawsuit derives not from contemporary legal records but transcripts of much later date which may be spurious, and no printed matter survives from Strasbourg or elsewhere that can be dated as early as this.

Gutenberg was resident in Strasbourg until March, 1444, when his name appears for the last time in the tax register there. Four years later he is on record at Mainz again borrowing about £250 from a relative. There is no clue as to his whereabouts or activities during this four-year gap, which unfortunately coincides with the approximate date of perhaps the earliest surviving fragments of mechanical printing. It also coincides with a note preserved in the archives of Avignon in France that a goldsmith from Prague named Procopius Waldfoghel stayed there between 1444 and 1446 and taught "artificial writing"—a tantalizing hint that Gutenberg was not the only man at least working on the problem of printing, that it was a lively contemporary issue.

But having borrowed £250 in October, 1448, Gutenberg proceeded within a year or two to borrow about £1,500 at 6 per cent interest from a Mainz lawyer, and at this point the ground becomes firmer, and we approach as close to the birth of printing, as far as Gutenberg is concerned, as may ever be possible. The lawyer's name was Johann Fust, one of the *nouveaux riches* at Mainz who had risen to prominence and success in the vacuum created by the overthrow and departure of noble families like the Gutenbergs in the 1420's. After the initial loan, for "work on his apparatus and equipment" and the further promise of some £500 annually for expenses, Gutenberg found it necessary within two years, in c.1452–3, to approach Fust again for a second £1,500, without having yet repaid any of the original loan or even the interest. Fust reluctantly agreed, but the interest was trebled and he demanded to become a sleeping-partner in "the work of the books"—the key phrase. Gutenberg continued operations till the autumn of 1455 when Fust took him to court. Gutenberg had still not paid a penny of either interest or capital, and since Fust himself had borrowed and now almost repaid the sums involved "among Christians and Jews alike" he was now personally some £5,000 out of pocket.

The court's judgement, couched in obscure German legal terminology, seems to have required Gutenberg's repayment of any surplus capital or expenses "not devoted to their common profit" plus the total accumulated interest on both loans. This proved impossible, so Fust took possession of Gutenberg's goods and chattels *in lieu*, including his "apparatus" and stock, and opened up business himself, appointing one of Gutenberg's workmen, Peter Schoeffer of Gernsheim, as technical production manager. It was the formation of the first successful publishing company with a subsequent list of impressive titles to its name, almost certainly beginning with the completion and publication of the "first" book, the 42-line "Gutenberg" Bible, a massive two-volume edition of 643 leaves (1,286 pages in our reckoning) measuring at least $16 \times 11\frac{1}{2}$ inches, of which perhaps two hundred copies were printed.

This book must have been in an advanced state of preparation when Gutenberg was declared bankrupt. Although undated and unsigned, microscopic study of the print itself shows it to be the earliest of the books printed at or near Mainz from the same or similar sets of type; and of the 48 known surviving copies (21 are perfect, 10 contain only one volume or less, and one now exists as 588 widely scattered sheets after it was broken up for sale by a speculative American dealer in the 1920's), one was signed and dated by its binder and rubricator, a local Mainz church-warden, who finished one volume on 15 August and the other on 24 August, 1456.

No precise figures are available, but even the most optimistic calculations about productivity cannot convincingly make the Fust-Schoeffer press start the 42-line Bible from scratch in November, 1455, after the lawsuit, and produce complete copies in any significant number nine months later, remembering that the full quota of each two leaves or four pages had to be printed before moving on to the next sheet. Still less, of course, is it possible for Fust and Schoeffer to have "invented" or even perfected the art of printing within the same vital gestation period. Most important of all, the signed copy of the Bible still exists, the bookbinder's note itself is not a forgery and has not been tampered with, and above all we possess the original document of Fust's formal deposition for the lawsuit, which outlines the history of his business relations with Gutenberg over the previous five years and summarizes the decision of the court. The document is even vaguer about the "apparatus" and "work" than the transcript of the Dritzehn affair and for the same reasons, but no doubts can be cast on its authenticity.

Whatever the exact details it seems clear that Gutenberg had mastered the art of printing between *c.*1450 and 1455 at the latest, backed by Fust's two loans and allowances, and that the main credit for the 42-line Bible belongs to the man who expended most of the real labour on its conception and production. It also begins to look as if the Fust-Gutenberg lawsuit was an astute medieval take-over bid by the business-minded Fust. The timing was perfect. Judging by later events Gutenberg stood poised, about to launch on the world the fruits of years of experiment and work and reap a golden harvest, enough certainly to satisfy Fust's only legal claim on the venture, the repayment of his loan and common share in the profits of "the books". There was obviously no love lost between the two—there rarely is in such circumstances—and Gutenberg would doubtless cut loose the moment he could. With an eye firmly on future expanding markets and himself as sole beneficiary, the canny, successful lawyer foreclosed on Gutenberg and demanded his money, the latter perhaps too busy or excited or plain unbusinesslike to realize what was really going on.

So the Fust-Schoeffer combine reaped the golden harvest of the 42-line Bible and at least four other substantial works, including the two Mainz Psalters of 1457 and 1459—two of the most beautiful books that have ever been printed, with their immaculately designed type and lay-out, the sheer quality and precision of the printing, and the richness of their ornamentation. If it is a sad reflection on history and human nature that a squalid tale of commercial exploitation invests these wonderful works and the almost as elegant 42-line Bible, that a sharp-minded unscrupulous businessman ruthlessly made himself master of what has been well described as "man's most pregnant mechanical invention since the wheel" at the expense of its artist- and craftsman-inventor, and if there is also little comfort in the knowledge that this was not the first nor the last time such a story can be told, then history, even in the popular imagination, has vindicated Gutenberg in some respects—he is generally known as "the inventor" of printing, the

42-line Bible is popularly described by his name, and there are cogent reasons for believing that the later, magnificent Mainz Psalters, for all their Fust-Schoeffer company imprint, were Gutenberg's brain-child, the main original object of his loans from Fust, his first-love and all-consuming passion.

And while it is sad to glimpse Gutenberg, desperately struggling to set himself up once again, with little or no equipment, no money and no credit, there is consolation in the fact that Fust and Schoeffer were unable to monopolize such an explosive mystery for any length of time. The secret was soon out—with six separate presses and their total complement of workmen concurrently printing the final stages of the 42-line Bible, this is not surprising. Too many people had to be in the know, and the world was too expectant.

Within ten years there were major independent presses in Bamberg, Strasbourg and Cologne, with a host of smaller, less permanent, less professional concerns elsewhere in Germany. At least two German craftsmen, Conrad Sweynheym and Arnold Pannartz, had also emigrated to the rich pastures of Italy, the home of Renaissance humanism, and founded Italy's first press in a Benedictine abbey at Subiaco, near Rome, before the end of 1464— Sweynheym being a native of Mainz who almost certainly learnt his trade from either Gutenberg or Schoeffer. Another ten years and Europe was ablaze with the invention from end to end. Such mighty concepts know no frontiers and Europe welcomed it with a solid, united front.

Switzerland had presses by c.1468, France by 1470, Spain and the Netherlands by 1472. The knowledge spread as fast as medieval communications and local business interests permitted, and finally entered Britain in 1476. Then, as now, Britain was among the last to appreciate the benefits of joining the European community, but in the end William Caxton returned from Belgium—another ironic coincidence—where he had already practised as a printer, and produced the earliest example of the art on English soil, a Letter of Indulgence on behalf of the Abbot of Abingdon, dated 13 December, 1476.

A mere twenty years separate the "Gutenberg" Bible and the establishment of presses throughout the length and breadth of Europe. By the year 1500 over a thousand different presses were operating in 238 European towns and cities, and some 20 million copies of nearly 50,000 different books and editions were in circulation, probably more than had ever been written by hand since the dawn of civilization. Within 250 years of Caxton, over 120,000 editions, totalling some 60 million individual copies had been printed in English alone. Such vast figures are difficult to grasp and their significance may seem to diminish when compared directly with the 20 million monthly circulation of the *Reader's Digest*, say, in the U.S.A. and Canada, or the 300 million school text-books alone printed in the U.S.S.R. in 1968. But relatively speaking the spread of mechanical printing in the 50 years after its advent is an astonishing phenomenon, without parallel in human history. It is as though every nation of the world had manufactured aircraft within five years of the Wright brothers, or harnessed their own nuclear power within three years of Hiroshima—and like these two achievements of the mind, the invention of printing was also quick to fulfil its immense potential for human good and evil.

It is not known for certain what happened to Gutenberg after his dispossession by Fust. He seems to have remained at Mainz for a time, since his name appears as witness on behalf of a relative there in a document dated 21 June, 1457. The same year, if we can trust the report of an eighteenth-century Strasbourg official, was the last in which he or his guarantor paid the regulation annual instalment of interest on a loan from the Chapter of St Thomas at Mainz fifteen years previously. The same dubious source still more suspiciously says that later Chapter accounts mentioned sums of money spent in an unsuccessful attempt to have both Gutenberg and his guarantor arrested. But if he had not already left Mainz, he almost certainly joined the mass exodus of eight hundred inhabitants after Count Adolphus of Nassau asserted his claims to the archbishopric by attacking and sacking the city in October, 1462. This event also ruined the printing industry in Mainz for about four years: Fust and Schoeffer took refuge with their stock in Paris, where Fust died in 1466—the Latinized version of his name and distorted machinations of his career possibly living on to contribute something to the legend of *the* Faustus: Sweynheym departed for Italy; others reopened business closer to home, assisting the spread of the new art throughout Germany. Gutenberg may have been one of the latter and helped two brothers of the name of Bechtermuenze set up business in nearby Elfeld.

In January, 1465, however, Count Adolphus, now securely enthroned as Archbishop of Mainz, formally appointed Gutenberg as a "gentleman of his court" with an appropriate salary, annual allowances of food and clothing and exemption from all civic dues and taxes, the declared reason being "the grateful and willing services rendered, which he may and will render hereafter". Perhaps Gutenberg had supported the Archbishop's cause in 1462 and not been expelled from Mainz after all. It would be nicer to think that the Archbishop was paying timely tribute to the most important citizen ever to be born and bred in Mainz and one of the most significant Europeans, if not human beings, of all time. It was almost too late; Gutenberg died three years later, on 3 February, 1468.

And what, after all, did his great invention amount to? A piece of equipment, designed to fit comfortably in the grasp of one hand, in use and substantially unchanged to this day—the typefounder's mould. In essence it is the two halves of a small rectangular box of cast-iron or steel, open top and bottom, but hinged at the lower end. Inside the hinge is a slot where the matrix is inserted, a flat slip of metal on which the impression of a single letter is stamped with an engraved punch. With the matrix in position, the hollow box is filled with molten metal—an alloy of lead, tin and antimony was early discovered to combine a low melting-point with maximum durability. A minute or two to harden, the fingers meanwhile protected from the heat by the thick pads of wood enclosing the box, a quick shake, and out falls a stick of metal with a letter in high relief at one end—a piece of printer's type. Repeat the procedure with the same or similar matrices and the basic essentials of the printing industry can be manufactured in a day.

The first inventor also incorporated the refinement which allows for the different width of letters like i and w—two precision-made slides that snugly fit inside the hollow cavity and adjust the space to the required degree. This was perhaps the most difficult part of the invention, but the inventor of printing was too much of an artist to let the narrowly practical override wider, purely aesthetic considerations.

Elegantly simple in itself, the typefounder's mould from the start led to books that were both useful and majestically beautiful. Human experience knows of no finer combination of virtues.

JOAN OF ARC

(*c.* 1412–1431)

OF ALL the men and women who have, in various ways, expressed the spirit of Europe, Joan of Arc is for many people the most touching.

She was born at the beginning of the fifteenth century when France, already exhausted by the first half of the Hundred Years' War with England, was torn by fierce strife between the feudal nobles, and when her king, Charles VI, was mad. In her childhood, Henry V of England renewed the English invasion, and in 1420 was invited to Paris by Queen Isabeau and the Duke of Burgundy to marry the Royal Princess, Catherine, and to succeed the mad king when he died.

The surviving son of Charles VI, the Dauphin, supported by the Orleanist faction known as the Armagnacs, had seen his armies everywhere defeated by the English and Burgundians. He had taken refuge in central France and was known as the King of Bourges. His mother had spread the rumour that he was illegitimate. Henry V of England died, in 1422, two months before the mad King of France. His son, Henry VI, a babe of nine months, was proclaimed King of France. The able Regent of France, the Duke of Bedford, began, in 1428, the methodical conquest of the kingdom. He crossed the Loire, and besieged the key city of Orleans. Much of the French countryside was desolate, and people were living in caves and even practising cannibalism.

"There is heard no more in France La Doulce the sound of the cock and hen", wrote a chronicler of the time. Even the farm animals would run for shelter when they heard the church bells ringing, it was said. The feudal nobles employed bands of mercenaries—Swiss, German and Scots—and these men lived off the land. There was comparative safety only in the towns with their moats and fortifications. But the towns depended for their protection on the English, or on local Burgundian or Armagnac chieftains. Even the church was divided, for there were two Popes—one in Rome and one in Avignon.

Joan was the daughter—one of a family of five—of Jacques d'Arc of Domrémy, a small village in Lorraine which with a few other villages depended on the town of Vaucouleurs. It was an Armagnac region, though surrounded by Burgundian territory. Although by no means one of the devastated parts of France, the inhabitants were constantly troubled by mercenaries and Burgundians; and in 1428 the inhabitants of Domrémy had to leave their village for some months whilst it was occupied and looted.

Joan was asked at her trial at Rouen whether there were any Burgundians or friends of the English in her village, and she answered, "I knew of no one, and if I had I would have smashed his face—if God had permitted". Joan had visions and heard voices telling her to go to the aid of the Dauphin, to raise the siege of Orleans, and to take the Dauphin to Reims and have him crowned and anointed as king. Miraculously she went to Chinon, where the Dauphin held court, was listened to by him and, with the Dauphin's best fighting men, raised the siege of Orleans, winning victories over the English, capturing Talbot, one of England's best soldiers, and then conducting the Dauphin to be crowned at Reims. She stood by him during the ceremony, holding her furled white flag. She urged the Dauphin, now veritably the King, to march on Paris, a Burgundian stronghold. He listened to courtiers who feared Joan, and would not do so.

Her voices now told her that it was God's will that she should be captured by the enemy. Not long afterwards she was taken prisoner at Compiègne and handed over to the English. She was tried at Rouen by a Church court, headed by the Bishop of Beauvais, for being a heretic and a witch. Found guilty, she was pardoned after she had made a submission. She was the prisoner, however, of the English who had bought her from her captors at Compiègne; and having been induced by her guards to put on her male clothing—which she had been forbidden to do by the ecclesiastical court—she was considered to have relapsed, and was burnt at the stake at Rouen. She had arrived at Chinon in the Spring of 1429, and she perished in the market place of Rouen in May, 1431.

Such are the bare facts, and yet there is certainly a good deal that can be called mysterious about Joan of Arc's life, and this element crops up constantly.

Joan of Arc's birth date is not known exactly; but it was probably during the year 1412. The events of her career, from the time when the governor of Vaucouleurs, Robert de Baudricourt, sent her to the Dauphin at Chinon, were attested by hundreds of witnesses of all social conditions at the Trial of Rehabilitation held in 1456 on the orders of the Pope and the King of France. The Trial is one of the most remarkable of historical documents. Regine Pernoud has said that a greater body of contemporary evidence exists about the acts of Joan of Arc and the impressions she made on those who knew her than about any other figure of the fifteenth century. The visions and voices which directed her will be understood differently by Christians and non-believers; George Bernard Shaw wrote, aptly, in the preface of his play, *Saint Joan*, that whilst criminal lunatics see visions and act on voices, so also did Socrates, Luther, Swedenborg, Blake, St. Francis and Joan. And, adds Shaw, if Joan of Arc was mad so was all medieval Christianity.

Some romantic writers of the nineteenth century have portrayed Joan as a poor peasant or an innocent shepherdess, thus making it hard to see how such a person could have led the Dauphin's armies to victory or stood up to her judges, as she did, in the trial of condemnation at Rouen. Joan's father was a farmer of some importance; and her mother, who came with her family to Reims when the Dauphin was crowned, was a woman of strong character and intelligence. Joan was a normal child who impressed people also by her strength of character as well as by physical hardihood. As she once said of herself, she understood the management of houses better than most women. At the Dauphin's court she never showed any sign of social inferiority. She was good looking in a boyish way, but she did not arouse sexual feelings as a rule. The d'Arc family were by no means ignorant of what was happening in France; and they had plenty of ways of knowing the situation from refugees and passing soldiers. The idea that Joan was a naïve young creature can be ruled out. She was, on the contrary, and in spite of a lack of formal education, rather imperious and self-confident and able to express her thoughts with devastating clarity.

She had begun to hear voices when she was thirteen—the first time when, lying by a stream, someone had told her she was wanted in the house. She went there and found she had not been sent for; as she dawdled about in the garden she was aware of a strong light near her, and then of a voice speaking to her out of the light, "*Tres bien et bellement*". But she was frightened, although the voice only told her that she was a good child and must always be devout and obedient. The voices were to come usually when Joan was in the woods, or when the church bells were ringing in the evening. She lost her fear and began to love them. As she grew older the voices, one of which she began to know as that of St Michael, the Archangel, and others as those of St Catherine and St Margaret, told her she had work to do for God, and this was to help the Dauphin, to serve him as a soldier and leader of soldiers. They had gradually given her more specific instructions: she was to go to Chinon and relieve Orleans from siege by the English, and after that she was to have the Dauphin crowned and anointed at Reims.

The effect on her of these voices was not to unbalance her—she remained what she had been before, a rather rough and imperious young woman full of good sense. She only talked when necessary about the voices which gave her, as it were, her marching orders.

When she went for the second time to ask Robert de Baudricourt to send her to Chinon to help the Dauphin, she had informed him of something he had only just learnt, that the Dauphin's troops had suffered another defeat in front of Orleans. She had made the same request to the governor before, and then he had threatened to have her whipped if she did not return to her father. He was obviously amazed at her persistence and, of course, he may well have thought that things were so grave that one might as well try anything. At all events, Joan eventually convinced him, and in this she was helped by a feeling that had got about in the town that she was an inspired woman.

When Baudricourt agreed to send her to the Dauphin the citizens of Vaucouleurs bought her a horse. She was also assisted financially by two young soldiers of good family who were convinced that there was something in this rather impudent and mannish young woman (seventeen was older then than it is now). She had told them about the heavenly voices which had said she was to go to the Dauphin, and to relieve the city of Orleans, and to have him crowned King, at Reims. "I would rather be at my mother's side", Joan had said to them, "for these things do not belong to my station; but it is necessary that I should do these things since God commands it". De Baudricourt gave her a sword and an escort which included the two young men; and she went to Chinon dressed as a page. Throughout the rest of her life—except for the brief moment when she submitted at the Rouen trial—she dressed in men's clothes. How else, she had asked, could she live among soldiers and fight in battle?

It was her confidence in her voices, combined with her artful simplicity and matter-of-fact manner, that impressed the Dauphin Charles when she arrived at Chinon in February, 1429, after a long and dangerous journey through Burgundian territory. To test her alleged powers, Charles hid himself among his courtiers, but she spotted him at once and knelt down before him. The Dauphin, a young man of twenty-six was a lover of luxury, like most of the Valois kings, and not fond of exertion or danger. He was easily influenced, and although the Duke of Alençon, a fiery young man who was to welcome Joan of Arc, and other stalwarts of a like mind had some power over him, he also easily yielded to the soft, interested courtiers and politicians such as the Duke de la Tremoille, who were all for caution and for seeking agreement with the Duke of Burgundy.

Charles was only energetic by fits and starts. After his crowning at Reims, he began to find Joan's intensity, and the Duke of Alençon's desire to continue the war with increasing vigour, too much for him. He ennobled Joan's family and exempted the village of Domremy from all taxation. But he did nothing to rescue her from captivity. Afterwards, it is true, he organized the great Trial of Rehabilitation and proved a good king, in part because his love for a mistress, Agnes Sorel, awoke his energies. He became known in history as Charles the Well Served.

After his first talks with Joan he appeared radiant. She told him what God had ordered her to do; and what, no doubt, above all gladdened him was her unquestioning faith—which he took to be an indication of what the people of France were thinking—that he was the only legitimate King of France. The stories spread by his mother, Queen Isabeau, that he was illegitimate, must often have troubled him. Joan was, he thought at once, a messenger of God. He ordered lodgement for her in his palace. The Duke of Alençon also considered her as something more than a useful mascot who might, with proper presentation, galvanize his troops. He at once instructed Joan in horsemanship, at which she was already practised, and in fighting with lance and sword.

The Dauphin, however, had some second thoughts. Supposing Joan's magic derived not from God, but from the Devil? He had her examined at Poitiers by priests and lawyers who, finally, accepted her visions as those sent by God for the salvation of France. Then, as testified by witnesses at the Trial of Rehabilitation and notably by Jean d'Aulon, who was attached by Charles to

Joan's household; "Joan was put into the hands of the Queen's mother, Yolande of Sicily, and of certain ladies by whom Joan was seen and examined in the secret parts of her body. After they had looked, a report was made by Queen Yolande to Charles that Joan was a pure and entire maid in whom appeared no corruption". Joan, it is said, wept with shame during these proceedings.

On 27 April, 1429, a newly raised army with Joan of Arc at its head and containing some of the best of the Dauphin's captains, left Blois to relieve Orleans. Joan's banner was of stiff white silk, with, painted on it by a Scot who lived in Blois, Christ bearing the world in his hands between two angels surrounded by lilies. After the examination in Poiters, Charles had decided to play the card "The Maid" thoroughly. Joan described herself as "War Chief" in a message she had sent to the English leaders—the Duke of Bedford, the Earl of Suffolk and the redoubtable soldier, Sir John Talbot. The message called on them to leave Orleans at once, and also to depart from France, "And believe that the King of Heaven will send greater strength to the Maid than you will be able to bring up against her".

News about a mysterious Maid who had been sent by God to the Dauphin had reached Orleans long before Joan had set out. The city had been partially besieged for seven months, and completely cut off from the Dauphin's zone by forts south of the Loire. It was crowded with refugees from the countryside and there had been plague inside the walls. Morale had ebbed at times, but the city had as its commander a stalwart leader in Dunois, the Bastard of Orleans. Everybody, at that time, believed in God, and in a God who would on occasion intervene directly in human affairs. The people of Orleans felt that only a miracle could save them; and here, in Joan, might be that very miracle.

Fortunately, the English had been slow in organizing the siege, and their fortifications only surrounded about half of the sprawling city. In skirmishes around Orleans they had always been victorious, and they counted on hunger and disease to bring the city into their hands.

The Duke of Bedford was unsure about the wisdom of a siege. It was expensive and not good for the morale of his troops—he would have preferred a number of small battles. Also he was no longer sure about the attitude of the Duke of Burgundy, who showed some signs of being willing to talk to the Dauphin. He, like the Dauphin, though for different reasons, preferred a fairly quiet war. Many of the French nobles and captains were prepared to fight hard, and believed in Joan. But others were anxious that this new army should be used rather as a bargaining counter with Burgundy in the future, and should not be wasted by being used to fight seriously.

As soon as the French arrived near the English forts on the Loire, there was a long debate about whether these forts should be stormed at once or whether there should be a period of waiting. The sheep, pigs and oxen which followed the army were embarked in barges into Orleans, the English in the forts contenting themselves with shouting insults. Joan had her way about a full-scale relief of the city. She herself, with Dunois, entered Orleans on 29 April and was greeted with enthusiasm by the people. When, riding through the streets that evening, her pennant was set on fire by a torch, people noticed that the Maid crushed out the flame with her bare hands as an old campaigner would do. She inspired confidence and enthusiasm.

Fighting for the forts lasted, with varying fortunes, in which twice at least Joan successfully rallied her repulsed soldiers, until 8 May. The English had fought fiercely, and the moats outside the forts were full of dead. But the tide of war had changed. It was the French who now fought with the desperate confidence of the English at Agincourt. On Sunday, 8 May, Talbot drew up his forces in a great meadow by the Loire. Joan, twice slightly wounded and suffering a little under her armour, heard mass in the open field. Dunois and La Hire were in favour of an immediate charge on the English. For once Joan said "no". It was not God's will to fight on a Sunday except in self-defence. Then a strange thing happened. The English army marched away from Orleans, seen off by French cavalry. The siege was over.

Bedford admitted that the presence of Joan had not only discomfited the defenders of the forts blockading Orleans, but "withdrew courage from the remnant in marvellous wise". Joan, for the English, was a sorcerer, a limb of the Devil, and for good measure, a whore.

The Dauphin, who welcomed Joan at Tours, was grateful; but he felt that no great haste ought to be made to go to Reims—he still listened to the temporizers. Joan was first to clear the English out of France south of the Loire. In a single week in June the French led by Joan and the Duke of Alençon, had captured Jargeau, and Beaugency, and then won, in the open field, the battle of Patay at which Talbot himself was taken prisoner. Reluctantly Charles, with an army of twelve thousand men, crossed the Loire and advanced on Reims, capturing the city of Troyes on the way. On 17 July the Dauphin was crowned and anointed and so, in the eyes even of those who had sided with England and Burgundy, Henry VI of England could no longer be deemed the legitimate King of France.

Joan's mission, that which had been ordered by her voices, was over, and she asked Charles to be allowed to return home with her parents, who had come to Reims. Charles's mind was constantly changing. He was tired of being ordered about in the name of God by Joan, and wanted to be back in peace at Chinon. Yet when Joan asked to be sent home, he said "no". He allowed Joan and the Duke of Alençon to do, then, the most obvious thing—to march on Paris. But the Royal army remained aloof from the attack which, therefore, was not more than a series of small-scale attempts to enter the city, during one of which Joan was again slightly wounded. The Parisians themselves were divided; and the working class was under the influence of the University, which was still anti-Armagnac. Nine months followed in which Joan fretted, without guidance, in the Dauphin's court where increasingly the Duke de la Tremoille and those who disliked her were becoming more powerful. They laughed at her child-like fondness for fine clothes. One of her hostesses at Bourges said of her, "She was very simple, knowing almost nothing except in affairs of war".

Joan and her companions captured a number of towns during this time. One of them was Melun, near Paris, taken in April, 1430. Whilst the church bells were ringing for victory Joan, standing by the moat of Melun, was aware of the warmth and the light of her voices. St Catherine and St Margaret told her that she was to be taken prisoner before the month of May was out. On 23 May, Joan, inside the Armagnac town of Compiègne besieged by the Burgundians, led a sortie with her customary dash. She was captured, the draw-bridge having been raised when enemy troops got behind her. She was sold to the English for ten thousand gold francs. It was possible that the Duke of Burgundy, wavering about the English alliance, would have allowed her to be ransomed. But King Charles made no offer. Nor was there any attempt to rescue her, and she often listened in vain in her dungeon in Rouen for the thudding hooves of a rescuing force.

The Trial of Condemnation was held by a Church Court composed of 75 French ecclesiastic dignitaries or members of the

University and headed by Pierre Cauchon, the Bishop of Beauvais. But Joan was not in a Church prison, but an English one, and Rouen was strongly held by English troops. The English were determined to execute her; it might, they felt, be a psychological blow to the hopes raised by the Dauphin's crowning at Reims. The Court questioned her for five months. She was, inevitably, found guilty of heresy and many minor crimes, and was condemned to life imprisonment in a women's gaol. But, after the verdict, her brutal guards took away her woman's clothing which she wore after the verdict as a sign of penitence, and forced her to put on her old page's costume. This disobedience enabled Cauchon to hand her over at once to the English, who on 24 May, 1431, a year after her capture, dragged her to the stake in the market place. The last living image of this girl—still not twenty years old—is that of her hoisted on a high plaster platform bound with chains to a stake, wearing a high-pointed dunce's cap bearing the words "Heretic Relapsed Apostate". A Dominican prior held a crucifix in front of her eyes until the executioner had lit the pyre and he had to jump down. Oil was poured on the flames and Joan, in her death agony, was hidden from the crowds. Afterwards, as was customary, the flames were beaten down and the charred body was exhibited. Her heart and liver were thrown into the Seine.

Why is Joan of Arc to be numbered among the great Europeans? The people of France, some in her life-time, thought of her as a Saint; and the Church, some five hundred years after her death, made her one. But that, and the question of her voices and divine guidance is, if not irrelevant, not enough to secure her a place in history. A few historians still consider that she was more of a mascot than a military leader. But these chose to ignore the testimonies at the Trial of Rehabilitation which indicate that she had uncommon gifts. In the numerous battles or sieges in her short life, she showed herself a thorough realist, and several times, notably at Orleans, had the insight to know that if you can hold on long enough the enemy will give way.

Yet even this matter of military genius is irrelevant compared with the fact that her coming to Chinon, her convincing the Dauphin of her mission, changed the character of the war. The Dauphin's armies fought with a new confidence and won great victories, and probably France would have been liberated sooner had King Charles been a man of greater energy. After Joan and her victories, those Frenchmen who had not objected to the union of France and

England under Henry V or VI felt the uneasy stirrings of patriotism. It took many years after 1431—over twenty in fact—before the English were finally driven from all France except Calais; and longer still before Burgundy and the vassal territory of Flanders ceased to menace the King of France. But Joan began the process. Her words, "Frenchmen, divided Frenchmen, pardon each other with all your hearts", symbolized the end of the local loyalties to duke or baron, though it took some time still to die, and the rebirth of the idea of the nation. The nation-state is, of course, the most powerful moulding force of European history. And Napoleon Bonaparte said of her that her career proved that there is no miracle which the French genius cannot perform when national independence is threatened. Raymond Poincaré said she invented the idea of patriotism before it existed.

But having recognized Joan of Arc as the inspirer of French national feeling, it seems likely that, as France was painfully reunited by the work of many able men after Joan's death, this national feeling would have come about in any event. Joan's abiding hold on the human imagination comes from her story, from the day in the garden at Domrémy when she first heard her voices until a few years later when she was dragged, grey-faced, to the stake. It is a story firmly based, as to the principal acts, on facts, but it contains so many mysterious elements that writers and scholars throughout Europe have presented different interpretations of her. The man who made the first film of Joan of Arc, Robert Bresson, when asked if his work would contain a new explanation of Joan answered: "One does not explain greatness, one tries to attune oneself to it." This greatness she showed when riding to battle, and above all in the terrible months of her martyrdom.

LORENZO DE' MEDICI
(1449-1492)

ANCIENT Egypt in the days of Rameses II, Periclean Athens, Augustan Rome, Carolingian France and eighteenth-century Versailles—ages acclaimed for the interaction of their material and cultural *richesse*, when high prosperity joyfully lavished its financial favours on art and architecture, philosophy and learning, on the adornment and satisfaction of man's aesthetic, spiritual and intellectual needs as against the grosser comforts of the body or baser emotions of the soul, avarice, ambition, naked power. High among these pinnacles of human civilization stands the city of Florence in the fifteenth century, the cradle of the Italian Renaissance and European humanism.

It is also normal in such ages for a single individual to become a central focus in the eyes of contemporaries and posterity alike. In the case of Florence that figure is Lorenzo de' Medici, the man who made the eyes of Europe fix upon his city and be dazzled by the lustre he and his family shed with such proud and specific intent. His contemporaries justly proclaimed him Lorenzo the Magnificent, *Figlio del Sole* (Son of the Sun).

He was the most illustrious member of the Medici family, a name writ large in European history and of a rare cosmopolitanism in its own day. Just before Lorenzo achieved his majority, it had been granted a unique international distinction for services rendered, the literal crowning of its coat of arms with the royal fleur-de-lis of France, granted by Louis XI, visible proof that the Medici, and the Florence they controlled for some seventy-five years till Lorenzo's death in 1492, could see with visionary clarity beyond provincial and even national boundaries to that higher community of the European mind. Lorenzo's own marriage-engagement was celebrated not in local Florentine or even Italian custom, but took the form of a French tourney, a spectacle new to the city, in which Lorenzo himself triumphed over all-comers in the genuine bravura of his jousting artistry and horsemanship. And it was Lorenzo's great-granddaughter who provided France with one of her noblest and most famous queens and queen-mothers, Catherine de' Medici, wife of Henry II.

The Medici compelled international admiration, affection and respect, and Lorenzo's role in their unfolding majesty is crucial, for he emerges from the solid security of the foundations established by his grandfather and great-grandfather to arch with supreme confidence and daring, upwards and out, building a human monument to himself, his family, his city and to Europe of staggering proportion and noble grandeur.

Situated roughly halfway between Rome and Milan, at the heart of the ancient homeland of that mysterious and sensitive people the Etruscans, Florence had been founded according to later legend by Julius Caesar after his destruction of Fiesole in the hills above its site. The verdant delights of the region, watered by the Arno, gave it the name Fiora (Flower City) or Fiorenza in the more affectionate local dialect. After Charlemagne was crowned in Rome monarch of the Holy Roman Empire on 25 December, A.D. 800, effective control of Italy became the subject of a long "cold war" between the imperial overlords and the Papacy, reaching its climax in the twelfth and thirteenth centuries. As part of its sustained campaign to make imperial authority merely nominal in Italy, the papal states to the south and east of Florence encouraged elsewhere the emergence of independent communities and separate townships too small to threaten their own united territories and supremacy. Florence had been given her opportunity and she began to capitalize on the prosperous advantages of her position—the dominant frontier community in the conflict between Church and State, the tough little buffer between Rome and the rising power of Milan, the tenacious middle-man on the commercial land-routes between north and south.

In 1172 a new city wall enclosed more than twice the area of its predecessor of a century before, and this in turn was replaced between 1284 and 1333 by another that more than trebled the limits of 1172. By 1300 Florence had a population of nearly 100,000. By 1400 it was the solid master of three-quarters of Tuscany, with only Siena stubbornly resisting its command of the whole. Masters of "the economic no-man's land where people have lived on their wits or on the strength of their right arms from time out of mind", the Florentines stood on the threshold of the Medici miracle. Their tenacity and independence tested hard and long, their confidence whetted and assured, they enjoyed an economic and commercial strength that had the whole weight of Europe behind it. Under Florentine direction, imported English wool fed a cloth-trade that was exported to be the envy and joy of every European community and nation: its silk and leather-ware, the craft-work of its gold- and silver-smiths were prized in every European market.

As early as the middle of the thirteenth century the city's eponymous gold coin, the florin, was the most stable currency in Europe, the preferred medium of major international trade and commerce. In the fifteenth century, like today (but in a different sense), it was true to say that "Florence is not Italy, but more than most cities she can claim to represent Europe". And fifteenth-century Florence, attaining its apotheosis under Lorenzo the Magnificent, is the age of the Medici.

His story then is not of himself alone but the climax of a family trilogy, starting some thirty years before his birth, when the first founder of the Medici fortunes, Lorenzo's great-grandfather Giovanni, spent the last ten flourishing years of his life as one of the most influential men in Florence. Money of course and the astute exploitation of commercial and political opportunities brought him to the fore soon after the leading member of the current ruling oligarchy died in 1417. The Medici succeeded the Albizzi, and when Giovanni died in 1429 his son Cosimo inherited a vast financial empire and the political potential that went with it. He now headed the largest and most prosperous merchant-bank in the city, topping nearly a hundred competitors and rivals, already boasting branches in no less than sixteen of Europe's capitals, and a personal fortune well in excess of a million pounds.

But Giovanni had been more than just a highly successful financier and local dignitary, and here too he established an historical pattern for his descendants. The great architect Brunelleschi had been commissioned to design and build a charitable institution for the poor and needy, the Foundling Hospital, and to rebuild San Lorenzo as a church worthy of a family chapel for the Medici: charitable deeds, then, which also usefully happened to promote and maintain popular esteem, and patronage of the arts to the united glory of family and city. It was all to become a humane, civilized and characteristically Medicean application of the profits of hard-headed financial dealings.

With long-term insight, Giovanni also staked the family's political future and dominance on a series of measures designed to secure the support of the populace, hitting hard the purses and pride of the aristocratic families and wealthy capitalists of his own class. These measures included a reduction in the salt-tax (the medieval equivalent of contemporary taxes on alcohol and tobacco), a pacifist foreign policy (war has always made the rich still richer and killed off the people), and most hazardous of all, replacement of the old poll or income tax by a flat $1\frac{1}{2}$ per cent tax on capital and public inspection of official tax returns. The opposition of his own class to these measures was intense for a time, but the gamble paid handsome dividends in the end. The family won the hearts and political backing of the bulk of the citizen-body for more than a generation; beneath its aristocratic veneer Florence was still a republic and a fiercely jealous defender of its democratic processes of government.

Giovanni took the family the first great strides forward. His son Cosimo spent the next thirty-five years (he died when Lorenzo was a highly impressionable fifteen) consolidating the advances already made and displaying even greater subtlety and courage than his father in increasing the family's fortunes and prestige. Within a year of his father's death he had instituted work on the construction and decoration of a new church, San Marco, and furthered his father's rebuilding of San Lorenzo. But it was in the middle 1430's that he triumphantly survived and then turned to great advantage a storm that at first threatened the extinction of the Medici and all its deeds—a conspiracy by their old enemies and rivals, the Albizzi. They struck in 1433 and the Medici, after four days of wavering debate by the Council and a substantial bribe to prevent a more drastic sentence, were banished from the city for ten years.

It was a short-lived defeat and exile. Within a twelvemonth the Albizzi had been ousted and the Medici returned to a tumultuous welcome, a posthumous vindication of Giovanni's appeals to the people and the spur to decisive action that made Cosimo an even greater family legend than his father and the most significant of all influences on his grandson Lorenzo. For Lorenzo in turn had to face a worse challenge to the authority of the Medici, and he had learnt well the lessons of Cosimo's example, a judiciously subtle mixture of direct and indirect counter-measures and safeguards. Many of the Albizzi and their supporters were hunted down and butchered with Cosimo at first unable—or studiously unwilling—to curb the violence of his partisans. But as the initial fury subsided he took firmer control and master-minded the long-term measures that prevented the recurrence of a serious threat for nearly fifty years. First a witch-hunt, leading to the exile of scores of real or suspected rivals with unusually long periods of sentence and no remission. Then a short spell as *gonfaloniere*, the Minister of Justice and Chief Minister of State. Then the most powerful and significant move of all, withdrawal from public office, but appointment of the Medici as permanent bankers to the government and himself as private confidential adviser to the Republic.

Cosimo thus contrived a complete hold on internal and external affairs of any moment, but from a discreet and unobtrusive stance which was both a protection and a source of diplomatic strength. Without this foretaste of indirect Medici government the Florentines would never have brooked Lorenzo's later, more open rule. Cosimo also introduced a revised version of his father's $1\frac{1}{2}$ per cent tax on capital, replacing the flat levy with a sliding scale dependent on income, with an all-important clause which provided for his own arbitrary assessment of taxes "in cases of difficulty or dispute". His friends and allies found it a gently profitable arrangement, his opponents delicately suffered. It has been well said that Cosimo wielded his tax reform "as a defensive and offensive weapon more deadly than daggers". What a marvellous study in the diplomatic exercise of power for the heady young Lorenzo to dwell on, a masterly example of self-effacing control of government, an effective tyranny without raising a suggestion of that dreaded title.

Florence enjoyed thirty years of harmonious existence from 1434 when the Medici returned from exile, to Cosimo's death in 1464. Personal advantage and profit was always tempered by wise thought for the general welfare of the state. Again he was a model for Lorenzo in his bold innovations in foreign policy and tenacious resistance to outside pressures. Florence and Venice had been traditional allies, particularly against Milan under the Visconti (but for the sudden death of the reigning Visconti in 1402, Florence would have limped through the fifteenth century, an insignificant crippled satellite of Milan, and there would have been no Florentine enlightenment). Cosimo adopted a different tack. A young *condottiere* or free-booting soldier of fortune, Francesco Sforza, was unilaterally supplied with money and arms and his successful removal of the Visconti sealed a lasting alliance between a new Sforzesci Milan and Medici Florence. Venice not only lost a friend; she also saw the ranks of her enemies doubled by the same stroke.

A natural resentment and fear drove her into the arms of Naples and a projected war on Florence. But Cosimo's resources were not merely political and speculative; his money worked hard far outside the walls of Florence. He only had to call in Medici bank-loans, and Venice and Naples found themselves unable to support an army worth putting in the field. Their rage and determination crumbled, and Florence and the Medici were even more securely enthroned. Another source of inspiration for Lorenzo's later conduct.

A most significant prize came Cosimo's way at about the same time. The Rome branch of the Medici bank was appointed official administrator of the papal finances. All the taxes, revenues, loans, salaries, donations and dues of the Church of Rome now passed at some stage through the hands of the Medici. The financial gains were immense, the associated power and influence profounder still. Characteristically this coup was won not by tense sessions behind closed doors or cut-throat, behind-the-scene intrigues; it was the unexpected offshoot of the Medici interest in the arts and Cosimo's particular love of learning. He was a passionate book-collector who appointed special agents to roam Europe for manuscripts to grace his library; he also liked to share his enthusiasm for books with others, and the Bishop of Bologna was generously supplied with loans to improve his own collection. In return the Bishop not only catalogued Cosimo's library for him, but later as Pope Nicholas V more than repaid his private debt with the award of the bank concession to the Medici.

On another occasion a rare and much-famed edition of Livy in Cosimo's library was the bribe that prevented a war with Naples, whose king had long envied it. In twenty-five years Cosimo is reputed to have spent over half a million gold florins on books alone, more than twice the annual revenue of the city, but it was money well spent. Even in their purely cultural pursuits, as Lorenzo amply observed, the Medici found power and profit, so firmly was their star in the ascendant.

At the time of Lorenzo's birth in 1449, work was well-advanced on the great town-house in the *via Larga*, the Palazzo Medici-Riccardi. Donatello, the greatest sculptor then in Italy, produced his *Judith and Holofernes* to grace its courtyard fountain and Cosimo arranged the payment of a weekly retainer for first call on his services thereafter. When Lorenzo was about ten years old, Cosimo was also responsible for the commission that brought Benozzo

Gozzoli to decorate the chapel walls of the *palazzo* in 1459–60 with his famous *Journey of the Magi*, the three resplendent riders leading the procession being portraits of Cosimo, his son Piero, and prominently isolated in front, the figure of principal attention and splendour, and looking much older than his years, his grandson Lorenzo.

At about the same time he managed to secure the services of that most talented young scholar and philosopher, Marsilio Ficino, to take up residence in his household as private tutor and friend of the young Lorenzo. He already sensed, as Gozzoli's fresco also intimates, that the future of the Medici lay in the hands not of his own, less accomplished sons, but in the volatile genius of his sparkling grandson. It was a remarkable combination—the wordly-wise, urbane grandfather, a real patriarch, taking the youngster under his special charge (the whole family naturally lived under the same roof) guiding, and grooming him from the labyrinthine depths of his practical experience.

When Cosimo died in 1464, the sorrowing citizens of Florence testified their support and affection for the man who had given them peace and stability for over thirty years, inscribing the words *Pater Patriae* (Father of his Country) on his tombstone, an honorific title derived from their beloved Classical antiquity, with all the associations of their beloved Cicero. It was a most potent stimulus and challenge to his heirs.

Cosimo had two legitimate sons. One had a touch of the Medici genius, but died before his father. The second, Lorenzo's father Piero, was a congenital invalid who as a young man had contracted the family disease, gout—Lorenzo was also to fall a victim to it in later life—and was consequently nicknamed *il Gottoso* (the Gouty). In fact he was far from stupid or incompetent, but he lacked the *finesse* and wary instincts of his father and grandfather, and had none of the young Lorenzo's daring and panache. Treacherous advisers persuaded him to speculate in land and real estate, and the Medici bank began to suffer a series of disastrous losses and saw many of its faithful share-holders and clients brought to the verge of bankruptcy and ruin. But his enemies overplayed their hand and Piero managed to salvage the situation, surviving a badly planned attempt on his life, using both bribes and threats in the nick of time to win over many of the opposing faction and securing the twenty-year exile of its more intransigent leaders.

He even brought Florence safely through a war against the

united forces of Venice, Ferrara, Pesaro, Faenza and Forli, led by one of the most famous Renaissance *condottieri*, Bartolommeo Colleoni. In contrast to Cosimo's long and stable rule, Piero's was a short and stormy voyage of five years. He died in November, 1469, leaving the huge Medici enterprise and its meteoric rise over the last half-century on the shoulders of a youngster of twenty. Lorenzo de' Medici now steps forward into history in his own right, the weight of a dynasty pressing urgently from behind.

Born to such great favour and fortune and endowed with all the advantages of birth, family pre-eminence and his own brilliant temperament, Lorenzo was still youthfully reluctant to don the proffered mantle of greatness—or was it perhaps a shrewd mock-diffidence that made him later write:

"Two days after my father died, although I, Lorenzo, was very young, scarce in my twenty-first year, the city-fathers and chief ministers of state came to our *palazzo* to offer their condolences and invite me to take under my charge the affairs of the city and our Republic as my father, grandfather and great-grandfather before him had done. My youthful instincts were against acceptance of their proposal, and I was conscious how great a burden was being urged upon me and how great was the danger. My consent was unwilling, but consent I did, for it was necessary to protect our friends and affairs, for those who possess great wealth in Florence and have no share in the government suffer grievously."

Whatever his real feelings at the time, Lorenzo was fortunate in one important respect. Concerned by the uncertainties and discords which had marred the last five years, the leading men of the city were ready to see in Lorenzo the prospect of a second Cosimo and the restoration of a life-time of peace and prosperity. To this degree Lorenzo was at first sheltered carefully from the full weight of his responsibilities; this time truly loyal friends and advisers protected the Medici cause and his personal interests, while Lorenzo himself indulged the more frivolous and spirited promptings of an immensely rich and talented young noble.

He loved festivities and entertainments, and treated the populace to an unprecedented series of masques, pageants, processions and revels, not to curry their favour nor to distract attention from social problems and imminent disasters, but through sheer *joie de vivre* and high spirits, and because inside the city the times were genuinely peaceful and untroubled once again. Nurtured in the balanced atmosphere of his grandfather's financially secure and cultured household, he also fittingly developed into no mean poet—the best the Medici produced—and most of his poetry was written in his youth for these festive public occasions—the *Trionfi*, *Canzoni a Ballo* and the notorious carnival songs, bursting with scintillating wit, genuine poetic versatility and light-hearted indelicacy.

More serious cultural pursuits were increasingly patronized as he matured in his twenties. The greatest names in contemporary scholarship and learning were drawn to Lorenzo's Florence as to the hub of a wheel—Poggio, Politian (whom he employed as resident tutor to his sons), Pico della Mirandola. His long-standing friend and mentor, Marsilio Ficino, was energetically encouraged to establish within the walls of the Palazzo Medici that Florentine precursor of our Royal Society, devoted to the advancement of both culture and learning, the so-called Platonic Academy, after its titular god. Lorenzo's favourite book was the *Symposium*, which he religiously read every 7 November, Plato's supposed birthday; and without Lorenzo's patronage and sincere philosophical interests the Neo-Platonic *aether* would never have ignited and burned with such intensity, pervading so much late-fifteenth-century Renaissance culture and finding such nobly visible expression in masterpieces as diverse as Botticelli's *Birth of Venus* and *Primavera* and Michelangelo's *Pieta* in the Vatican. In cultural terms this was perhaps his greatest personal contribution; in other respects he merely pursued the well-trodden path of Cosimo in the free patronage of the arts, the purchase of books (on which alone he spent each year more than half the annual income of the city) and enriching the Medici collection of ancient coins and cameos for which they were particularly famed throughout Europe. The musician Squarcialupi was befriended and protected from his critics—Lorenzo was justly hailed as the greatest, most catholic connoisseur of the age. Even his critical biographer Giucciardini was forced to admit:

> "He showed for poetry, music, architecture, painting and sculpture, indeed for all the fine arts, and for the mechanical sciences too, the same favour and encouragement, so that the city overflowed with their grace and beauty, like to a fountain of the purest crystal."

Nor was it established and recognized genius that he promoted with such undeviating vigour. His guests were astonished on one occasion to see a young lad of obviously humble parentage in the

Leonardo da Vinci, superlatively great as painter and sculptor, engineer and architect, added a new dimension to the concept of European genius. This portrait of him as an old man was drawn by his own hand.

Lorenzo de' Medici, shown (*below*) as painted by Vasari (Uffizi Gallery, Florence) was another splendid luminary of the Renaissance period. Himself a poet and artist, he was one of the most generous patrons of the arts known to history; a focal point of that magnificent explosion of the human spirit that was fifteenth-century Florence.

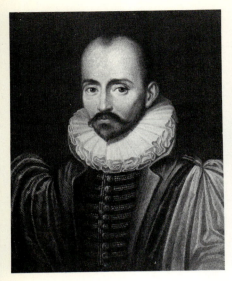

France, England, and Holland contributed these giants to the literary development of sixteenth-century Europe. Michel de Montaigne (*above*) produced essays full of the ripest wisdom and warmed with humanity. Of Shakespeare (seen *above right*, as drawn by Martin Droeshout for the First Folio) Matthew Arnold wrote, "We ask, and ask: thou smilest, and art still, out-topping knowledge". *Right:* Erasmus of Rotterdam, great humanist scholar and preacher of rational religion, writing busily in his study at Basle.

seat of honour at a banquet, on Lorenzo's right, receiving their master's undivided concentration. Lorenzo had detected what few had sensed at that time, the talent that developed into Michelangelo: to Lorenzo the Magnificent rather than his son Giovanni (as Leo X) or his brother's illegitimate child Giulio (as Clement VII) ultimately belongs the credit for that long association of the Medici with the sculpture and architecture of Michelangelo, the association which gave Europe the present monumental facade of San Lorenzo, the Laurentian Library with its superb staircase, and the New Sacristy or Medici Chapel, with its universally acclaimed statues of Night and Day, Morning and Evening, flanking the tombs and portrait statues of Lorenzo's youngest son, Giuliano, duke of Nemours, and his grandson, Lorenzo the Younger, duke of Urbino and father of Catherine de' Medici.

But if the local Florentines enjoyed the sunnier radiance of Lorenzo's youthful disposition in the early 1470's, two neighbouring cities had an early foretaste of the more ruthless side of his character. Exiled enemies of the Medici hoped to topple the fresh new heir immediately from power and stirred the citizens of Prato to revolt in 1470. At Lorenzo's insistence the revolt was suppressed with signal speed and no mercy.

A year later Volterra tried to divert into its own coffers the now booming profits of the local alum mines, which Medici capital had opened up and had the controlling interest in. Some of Lorenzo's soundest advisers counselled negotiation and compromise, but they were over-ruled by Lorenzo who summoned Federigo da Monetfeltro, the *condottiere* duke of Urbino. Volterra surrendered at the approach of his men, but Lorenzo made only a formal pretence at preventing their enforced entry and sack of the city. The severity shown on both occasions was a highly effective deterrent; for many years even greater powers trod cautiously in the Florentine presence.

Then, after almost ten unassailed years, came the domestic crisis of 1478, a turning point once again in the whole Medici fate and fortune, with Lorenzo triumphantly surviving a deeper and much more vicious plot by the Pazzi family than his grandfather's troubles with the Albizzi. With the powerful backing of Lorenzo's mortal enemy, Pope Sixtus IV, who had long been striving for the papal states' domination of the various Italian municipalities and dukedoms as against Lorenzo's championship of their separate freedoms and individualities, and with the eager assistance of the

Pope's nephew, who was to govern Florence in his uncle's name, and the anti-Medici Archbishop of Pisa, Francesco Pazzi persuaded his father and the rest of his relatives and associates to assassinate Lorenzo and his brother Giuliano and free Florence from Medici "tyranny" for ever.

The first plan was to murder the brothers during a banquet at Lorenzo's villa at Fiesole to which all had been invited, but Giuliano felt unwell and retired to bed, so the plot was postponed to the following day, Easter Sunday. From this point it assumes the dimensions of a ghastly tragi-comic charade. It was decided to strike during High Mass in the Cathedral, at its most solemn climax, the elevation of the Host. But Francesco's fellow-assassin suddenly felt reluctant to commit both murder and sacrilege at the same time and fled. Three substitutes were quickly found, two of them priests! Then it was observed that Giuliano was again absent, so Francesco went to the Palazzo Medici, found him nursing a bad knee and gallantly helped him limp from his bed to his doom. At the appointed moment one of the priests struck Giuliano from behind, followed by Francesco, who lost control of himself, wildly stabbing Giuliano again and again, and in the process knifing himself in the leg.

The attack on Lorenzo was less successful. Bleeding heavily from a gash in the neck, he managed to escape behind the bolted doors of the sacristy until his friends could muster assistance. Meanwhile the Archbishop headed the deputation which aimed to seize control of the government. The deputation unfortunately locked itself in an ante-chamber while the Archbishop nervously harangued the council; the pro-Medici *gonfaloniere* finally hung the Archbishop from the council-chamber windows, and when Francesco's father failed to rouse any support in the streets for the Pazzi the conspiracy collapsed; Francesco bled to death hanging beside the Archbishop, "a cluster of comrades swinging overhead", and the corpses of his father and two of his beheaded brothers were flung into the Arno.

The golden daydream was over, shattered by the crude realities of power politics. Lorenzo was old enough and tough-minded enough to raise and henceforth maintain his own armed bodyguard in preference to the counsel of family and business friends, and to enforce his iron will and determination through a newly formed privy council instead of the democratic and more indirect processes formerly pursued in imitation of Cosimo. There was little pretence any longer of republican government in Florence: the Medici no longer took pains to disguise the absolute and personal nature of their rule, their *palazzo* took on the open appearance of a royal court.

For fourteen years Lorenzo exercised what was nevertheless a most benevolent despotism, boldly wrestling in its closing stages with the larger economic decline of central Italy and closer at home facing the hysterical denunciations of the puritanical demagogue, Savonarola, who raged against "the tyrannical oppression of the Medici", prophesying its destruction in a second Armageddon. In 1491, contemptuously rebuffing approaches by the still tolerant Lorenzo, Savonarola predicted his death within the year. Ten months later, in the summer of 1492, Lorenzo collapsed with a stomach disorder at his favourite country villa at Careggi. His doctors fed him powdered pearls, which made things worse, and in a final attempted act of reconciliation, Savonarola was invited to administer the last rites. Adamant as ever the fanatical priest demanded that "all ill-gotten gains" be restored to the people and their liberty guaranteed thereafter. Hovering between the promise of the first and the second (or as others reported, turning his back in lofty disdain) Lorenzo died, unabsolved.

Even in his lifetime Lorenzo had been called "the pivot of Italian politics". The aftermath of his death conclusively proves what his life had all along suggested. After two years of ineffectual bungling by his weakling of an elder son came the predictable revolution of 1494. The Medici were exiled, their *palazzo* sacked and the Florentine Republic violently restored. All of which comes as no surprise.

Like Charlemagne and Winston Churchill, Lorenzo was too massively independent an individual to leave anything but a vacuum behind him: such men can have no successors. Those of his family who brought continued honour to the Medici name did so outside Florence, from early-sixteenth-century High Renaissance Papal Rome, overshadowed not only by the memory of Lorenzo the Magnificent, but by more impressive Popes like Julius II. When the Medici finally returned to rule Florence for two further centuries as Grand Dukes of Tuscany, the rich blood of Cosimo and Lorenzo had run thin and exhausted itself; these others were Pierfrancesci Medici, men of lesser magnificence, the descendants of Cosimo's brother.

Lorenzo de' Medici was many things—a traditional Medici

financier who made and spent more money than his great-grand-father and grandfather combined, a statesman and politician of greater daring, resolution, vision and ultimately more ruthless ambition, and one of the world's greatest ever patrons of art and literature. Unlike his more reserved and business-minded ancestors, he also had the humanity of soul to be an accomplished and vigorous poet in the Byronic mould, and when it came to the pursuit of women, more than enough romantic elegance of manner to over-come what some record as the swarthy coarseness of his features and nasal voice.

But Vasari's painting of him, now in the Uffizi, is surely closer to the truth, in this as in all respects of Lorenzo's character—the intensely dark eyes, knitted brow and huge, grimly jutting jaw, the mighty shoulders, powerful raking posture of the seated body, the fierce sensitivity of the iron hands, the green opulence of the one half of his cloak, the sinister black of the other, and the mysterious horror of the masks in the background: it captures what the man himself must have been—a figure of almost Satanic beauty, majesty and irresistible accomplishment.

LEONARDO DA VINCI
(1452–1519)

LEONARDO was born in Tuscany in 1452 and died at Amboise on the Loire in 1519. According to that incomparable Renaissance journalist, Giorgio Vasari, Leonardo expired in the arms of the King of France, a story which is, unfortunately, just a piece of journalistic licence. It is significant, however, that Vasari felt the need to perpetrate this charming exaggeration, for it gives us an idea of the immense prestige which surrounded Leonardo's name.

A legend in his own day, he was commonly credited with divine talents and magic powers. And yet at his death there was very little to show for his genius. He had left behind a trial of abandoned projects and a host of admiring but exasperated patrons. Of those few projects he had completed, some were already deteriorating, others had been destroyed. It was only a rumour that Leonardo possessed incredible notebooks which would reveal his genius, for he had published nothing. But the notebooks did exist, and they are the key to Leonardo's achievement. They reveal a remarkable intellect unhindered by the limitations of conventional scholarship, uninhibited by the assumptions of ideology or dogma, an intellect of such prophetic inventiveness, such persistence, that it encompassed the concepts of the aeroplane and the submarine.

To understand Leonardo's contribution to European thought, to separate the truth from the legend, it is necessary to look at him in his own time.

When Leonardo was born, Italy was the richest country in Europe, and was divided into a number of prosperous city states dominated by Milan, Venice, Florence, the Papal States and Naples. Italy's commercial prosperity was due to her geographical position on the trade routes to the Orient. The ports of Venice, Genoa and Naples thronged with merchant ships bringing silks, carpets and spices from the East to satisfy the rapidly expanding European market. Italian merchant princes had grown rich, and the rivalry between families and city states had become notorious.

It was a rivalry which was both cultural and political, in which everyone was involved from Popes to painters. Nouveaux-riche princes wooed not only the finest intellects to their courts, but hired the finest mercenaries for their private armies. And as the mercenaries followed the leader who paid the most (even changing sides in the heat of battle!), so were scholars, poets, scientists, and artists on the look out for the most generous patrons.

This, then, was the world into which Leonardo was born, the illegitimate son of Ser Piero da Vinci, a notary, and Caterina a local girl. His childhood was spent at his birthplace, Anchiano, a hamlet near the market-town of Vinci, about twenty miles west of Florence. The countryside here is lush and mountainous, crossed by narrow, winding rivers, the skyline articulated by cypresses and hilltop towns. Leonardo's ability to evoke the atmosphere of a landscape in paint astonished his contemporaries. His notebooks are crammed with minutely detailed drawings of plants and animals. This evidence of his fascination with nature surely grew out of innocent boyhood observations of his surroundings. But not content just to observe and record, Leonardo went further and asked the question "Why?" refusing to be satisfied until he had reasoned out the answer.

We know from records that by 1469 Leonardo's father had moved to Florence taking his son with him. Leonardo's illegitimacy was not a problem; it was a permissive age when society looked kindly upon such lapses. It did, however, have two important effects on Leonardo's life. It probably accounted for the fact that the boy had no formal education, and it also meant that he could not become a lawyer like his father. The fact that he was self-taught seems to have secretly embarrassed Leonardo later on, and possibly explains his reluctance to publish; it might explain the secrecy surrounding the notebooks and his habit of writing his notes in mirror-writing. Yet now it meant that the young man could approach learning with a completely fresh mind, unspoiled by a conventional education. Since Leonardo could not become a lawyer, his father was forced to apprentice him to a more humble trade. Posterity must be grateful that Ser Piero, recognizing his son's talent for drawing and modelling, decided to send him to the workshop of Verrocchio as a pupil, for there could have been no more stimulating apprenticeship for the young Leonardo.

In architecture it was fifty years since Brunelleschi had engineered the dome of the cathedral and had set down the rules for pictorial perspective. Alberti had just published his great treatise on architecture, an achievement which Leonardo intended to emulate for painting, but never did. (His celebrated *Treatise on Painting* was, in fact, compiled from his notebooks after his death.) In painting the elegant international Gothic style had been overtaken by the austerity of Masaccio, the clarity of Veneziano and the sweetness of Fra Angelico. Uccello, the fanatical exponent of pictorial perspective, was an old man. Now young painters were agog with the Flemish masters whose "oil" paintings were much admired by connoisseurs.

Oil was beginning to take over from tempera as a medium as painters experimented in order to achieve their brilliant, luminous colours and subtle details. Such experiments were later to lure Leonardo to disaster. In sculpture Ghiberti, who designed the great bronze doors of the Cathedral, was dead; and so was Donatello, whose bronze statue of the boy *David*, inspired by the sculpture of ancient Rome, had taken Florence by storm.

It was the generation of Brunelleschi, Masaccio and Donatello which had established new ideals for art, based on pride in man and built on reason. Their humanism rejected the mysticism of the medieval church and looked to the scientific, the "naturalistic", representation of nature through the study of perspective and anatomy. Ancient Rome was their inspiration, and Florence University became the centre of Renaissance humanistic studies, based on the philosophy of Plato.

Florence was at the height of her glory. The Medici family had ruled the city for forty years, providing stability in a dangerously insecure world. The court of Lorenzo the Magnificent demanded extravagant monuments, religious and secular paintings, objects to decorate its palaces and jewellery to decorate its courtiers. Verrochio epitomized the omnicompetent Renaissance master. Goldsmith first, painter last, he could turn his hand as skilfully to the making of suits of armour, church bells, jewellery, bronze and stone statues, portrait busts and mosaics as he could to the creating of altarpieces and ceiling frescos. Verrocchio not only had to design and supervise the carrying out of work in the studio, he also had to obtain and pay for materials: gold, marble, wood, lime, pigments, bronze; he had to organize carpenters to make up frames and scaffolding, prepare furnaces for casting bronze, and even provide lodgings for his pupils. But he was not just a great craftsman and administrator; he was an artist whose works express the spirit of the age. Verrocchio's statue of David was not Roman like Donatello's, it was utterly Florentine. Slim, elegant, refined, with a wry smile and long curls, it could have been modelled on the young Leonardo himself.

Verrocchio's pupils included Botticelli, Perugino and Lorenzo di Credi, and his workshop was the meeting place of the most fashionable and influential members of Florentine society. Here Leonardo first saw paintings of the Tuscan landscape, drawings of beautiful hands and of hair flowing in long, twisted tresses. Here the golden rules were precision of draughtmanship, the importance of characterization and the laws of perspective. Together Verrocchio and Leonardo studied anatomy and geometry and the laws governing the movement of water.

As an apprentice, it was Leonardo's task to complete the commissions obtained by the master. Thus Leonardo's hand is first identified in the heads of the kneeling angels in Verrocchio's *Baptism of Christ*. Already in contrast to Verrocchio's clear, bright colours there is evidence of that muted, shadowy, twilight world we see in the paintings of Leonardo's maturity. Of the other works executed as a pupil of Verrocchio, perhaps the most successful is the portrait of *Ginevra de Benci*, her pale face contrasting with the spiky juniper tree. Leonardo was enrolled in the painter's guild of St. Luke in 1472 and, although still living with Verrocchio, was already launched into Florentine society.

The legend is that Leonardo was beautiful, strong, graceful, a great horseman and musician, a brilliant talker, a talented, fashionable, popular young man, loved and admired by everyone. The truth seems to be that this was only one side of his character. There is evidence that during this period he was engaged in building up a personal library, studying avidly, indiscriminately, all the authorities he could understand. Limited by his lack of Latin and Greek he preferred to read Classical writers in translation. His unorthodox education and the gaps in his knowledge that he wished to keep hidden perhaps drove him to secrecy. A contemporary said he lived an austere and studious life.

He must have worked prodigiously, for he soon gained a reputation as a scholar; he also seems to have gained a reputation for being eccentric. His friends remarked on his extraordinary compassion. Apparently he refused to harm any living creature; he bought caged birds in order to release them, and he might even have been a vegetarian. In 1476 came the first hint of his homosexuality.

Although the case in which he was involved was dismissed, his later life seems to confirm the fact.

In 1478 Leonardo was given his first important commission, an altarpiece for a chapel in the Signoria, the Florentine council chambers. He received an initial payment, but never delivered the work. It was eventually carried out by Filippino Lippi. Then in 1481 he was commissioned to paint an *Adoration of the Magi* for the convent of San Donato a Scopeto. That was also left unfinished. So even while still young, unknown and an outsider, he had the audacity not to complete his commissions. Thus began a story of unfinished work which was to be excused by his friends as a result of his restless, creative urge, his eternal desire for perfection, his wish to experiment, and the calls of important scientific research; and blamed by his enemies on his sloth, obstinacy, incompetence and time-wasting experiments.

Meanwhile, Leonardo was restless. He felt that Florence was not offering him enough. The literary, neo-Platonist atmosphere did not suit him. Leonardo was developing into a scientist and mathematician, accepting nothing which could not be proved by experiment, and he was determined to treat painting as a science.

In 1478 a group of nobles had assassinated Lorenzo's brother in the famous Pazzi conspiracy which, although the house of Medici remained in power, was an ominous warning of further political unrest. When a chance came to go to Milan, he did not hesitate.

Leonardo carried to Milan a recommendation from Lorenzo de Medici praising his ability as a performer on the lyre and as a singer. Lorenzo even gave Leonardo a silver lyre in the form of a horse's head as a personal gift to the Duke. Leonardo's letter of introduction to Ludovico Sforza in which he offers his services and lists his skills is most revealing. There are ten items. Nine of them refer to his skills as a military engineer. He claims to be good at bridge-building, at making devices for use during seige warfare, at designing battering-rams, mines, covered chariots, guns and catapults. The tenth item refers to his abilities as an architect and as a water engineer. Almost as an afterthought, and not even itemized, he says: "I can carry out sculpture in marble, bronze or clay, and also I can do in painting whatever may be done as well as any other, be he who he may".

The letter was not exceptional, such military skills were much admired, and needed. What was exceptional were the extraordinary inventions appearing in Leonardo's notebooks, for his imagination prompted the design of machines far removed from the practicalities of modern warfare.

Leonardo's letter was sent from the address of the painter Ambrogio da Predis, and, while waiting for a reply, he agreed to help Ambrogio and his brother Evangelisto on a commission for the completion of an altarpiece for the Church of San Francesco, of which the carved wooden frame was already made. A contract was drawn up on 25 April, 1483, between the Brotherhood of the Immaculate Conception of Milan and the three friends. As usual, the contract listed every detail of the composition and decoration of the painting. The centre panel was to be a representation of the Madonna in a mountainous landscape with the infant Jesus, angels and prophets. The agreement was that the altarpiece should be completed and delivered by the December of the same year. The idea of the composition of the *Virgin of the Rocks* seems to have stemmed from an existing painting of the subject which Leonardo had done in Florence and brought with him to Milan. For two versions now exist: the Louvre version which is stylistically earlier, and the version in the National Gallery, London, which is thought to be later and probably the one commissioned in Milan. Although Leonardo completed the central panel of the Milan commission, the rest lay unfinished for many years.

Eventually Leonardo met Ludovico Sforza and was offered a permanent position as court painter and engineer. This was exactly what he needed. Now he had the freedom of a salaried job under the patronage of one of the most lavish and liberal courts in Italy. These were, indeed, happy years for Leonardo. He found at Ludovico's court much more congenial company than in Florence. There were scientists, mathematicians, doctors, engineers and painters. He founded cannon, designed costumes for pageants, organized tournaments and painted portraits of Ludovico's mistresses. His private experiments extended in all directions. He drew a plan for a model city with running water in the houses, underground drains, and split-level roads with pedestrians above and traffic below. He composed music for the lute and wrote fables and prophecies. Always in the background was Ludovico's plan to erect an equestrian monument to Francesco Sforza, the great mercenary leader and founder of the present house. But it was not until 1489 that Ludovico finally asked Leonardo to prepare a model for the monument. Leonardo's notebooks are crammed with sketches of horses in all kinds of postures. The one that seemed to please him most was rearing up on its hind legs, its front legs wildly pawing the air.

The notebooks were also full of notes for his proposed treatise on painting in which he claims that painting is superior to sculpture and poetry.

When Ludovico sent Leonardo to Pavia for two weeks to prepare plans for some restoration work, the visit trailed into months. For his passion for scientific research had been stimulated by the great Library at Pavia where he found many new friends. Now he was carried away with the laws of optics. His notes describe how light travels in straight lines, and explain the angles of reflection. Back in Milan his scientific experiments continued. He was seen bouncing balls, and throwing pebbles into water, all for science. His muddled notebooks, confused by the inclusion of domestic trivia, reveal the diversity of his inventions. He investigated the power of steam, the secrets of anatomy, the significance of fossils, and the idea of an aeroplane. "A bird", he wrote, "is a flying machine, that works according to the laws of nature and it should be possible to construct such a machine artificially." And among his notes is a drawing of a leather bat with silk tendons. Fascinated by the human body he began a book, *Della Figura Humana*. After intensive studies he deduced that the heart was a muscle and that it had four chambers, not two as had previously been thought.

Ludovico allowed Leonardo to pursue his studies, but was growing increasingly impatient for the equestrian monument. More drawings were prepared by Leonardo, but nothing satisfied him. He was still intent on the rearing posture, a design which would cause a major problem of casting in bronze. In comparison, Donatello's equestrian monument to the mercenary Gattamelata had a raised hoof carefully resting on a cannon-ball. More recently Verrocchio had overcome the problem in his monument to Colleoni and had successfully achieved a raised front hoof pawing the air, in the manner of the much admired Roman statue of Marcus Aurelius. But to have two front legs suspended in mid-air seemed an impossible task. Eventually a more conventional but gigantic statue was cast in clay; it was erected in the piazza in front of the Castle, and was viewed with amazement and admiration.

Meanwhile, Leonardo had acquired a young servant, a boy called Giacomo Salai. The notebooks for this period are filled with items bought for the child from shirts to velvet cloaks. "Thief, liar, glutton", he comments. But Salai stayed, alternately loved and despised, for the rest of Leonardo's life. His notebooks continue to carry his observations of natural phenomena and every item of his environment: animals, people, some beautiful like the recurring St Sebastians, some wild and ugly like the soldiers and beggars.

In 1495 Leonardo began a fresco of the *Last Supper* for the friars of Santa Maria delle Grazie. His conception of the scene utterly broke with convention: by the realistic expressions and gestures of the apostles (drawn from the characters in his notebooks) he reveals the significance of this profound psychological drama, seemingly cut off as if time was standing still. The event had never before been recorded in such deeply moving terms. But Leonardo's inability to be disciplined by the technique of fresco painting was to lead to tragedy. Ideally in true fresco painting the wet pigment is rapidly painted onto a section of wet plaster. As a result it dries as part of the wall, unaffected by variations in humidity, water or heat. Leonardo insisted on painting on the dry plaster, dabbling here, changing his mind there, over a period of two years. Moreover, in order to achieve the subtlety of oil paint he used an oil-bound pigment. Even as it was finished the paint had begun to flake. Now it is a wreck. At the time, however, before the weakness of the technique became apparent, the *Last Supper* was recognized as a masterpiece and carried fame for Leonardo to artists and connoisseurs across Europe.

Meanwhile, Milan's ally, Louis XII of France, who had been invited into Italy by Ludovico himself, had suddenly turned his armies on the city. Ludovico fled to the Emperor Maximilian at Innsbruck for help, while the French entered and took Milan. Ludovico returned the following year to do battle with the French. Eventually he was captured and taken prisoner to France. Leonardo had struggled to carry on during these troubled days, working at his notebooks and on his model of a flying machine, in the knowledge that in the Piazza his clay statue was being used by the French for target practice. When Louis XII at last arrived in Milan he took his captains and allies to see the *Last Supper*, and summoned Leonardo to his presence to congratulate him. Although he was at liberty to carry on his work, Leonardo found life too disturbed in the occupied city; reluctantly he packed his bags, and with the wicked but faithful Salai he left for Venice, travelling via Mantua.

In Mantua he was welcomed by the Duchess of Mantua, Isabella d' Este, who begged Leonardo to paint her portrait. The sketch was completed, but Leonardo moved on to Venice without beginning the painting. The Duchess was doomed to disappointment. For years she bullied, begged and pestered Leonardo to complete the painting, pursuing him with letters and agents as he moved from city to city, but without success.

In Venice, Verrocchio's *Colleoni* monument was already cast in bronze, the Bellinis were in their prime and Flemish paintings were all the rage. Venice offered Leonardo a new interest: geography, stimulated by the discoveries of Columbus and Vespucci. But Venice herself was threatened, by the Turks. Leonardo produced plans for the scuttling of the Turkish fleet by means of divers wearing breathing apparatus. But his plans were rejected on the grounds that they were too fantastic. Still in need of peace and patronage, Leonardo decided that Venice could offer neither, and he set off once again, this time back to Florence.

In the years since he had left, Florence had endured a serious economic recession. Lorenzo the Magnificent was dead, and his son Piero had been driven from the city when the religious fanatic Savanarola had whipped up public feeling against the Medicis. Paintings, sculpture, books and previous objects had been burned at the height of the revolt, but ironically, when public opinion changed, Savanarola himself was burned at the stake.

Leonardo brought with him an international reputation as a scholar, philosopher, artist and scientist, and he was soon commissioned to paint *St Anne and the Virgin* for the convent of the Servants of Mary, a project which never passed the cartoon stage. But Florence was still suffering from the ravages of its recent past, and Leonardo, unable to settle down, wrote to Cesare Borgia whom he had met briefly in Milan, taking up the Duke's previous offer of patronage. Cesare Borgia was at the time increasing his domains around Rome by a series of successful military campaigns. Leonardo met him in Faënza where he was appointed chief military engineer, and then accompanied him throughout the following campaigns as his armies took one town after another from Perugia to Ravenna, Urbino to Pesaro; all the time he made plans for buildings and fortifications, sketching and annotating his innumerable schemes and observations. It was during the campaign that he met Niccolo Machiavelli, who was Florence's ambassador to the Duke at the time. They were immediately on good terms, although so different in character. Machiavelli spent his life in the thick of politics, while politics was one of the few subjects which never seemed to interest Leonardo and never appears in his writings.

Leonardo returned to Florence in 1503 to find signs of a return to peace and prosperity, although the Medicis were still in exile. An arrogant young man named Michelangelo was carving a huge statue of David. The painter Perugino was delighting art lovers with his paintings of lyrical religious scenes, and Raphael was working in his studio. Leonardo, now fifty, found himself in another generation. He held his own court to which Raphael, Andrea del Sarto and Benvenuto Cellini were all welcome; Michelangelo was the notable exception. Machiavelli, also back in Florence, was Secretary to the Republic, and it was probably his influence which gained Leonardo the position of military engineer to the Republic. Machiavelli was certainly involved in Leonardo's plans to divert the Arno away from Pisa as part of the current war effort.

Leonardo was also commissioned to paint a fresco for the great hall of the Council Chambers, and he set to work to prepare the cartoon for a painting of the *Battle of Anghiari*, a famous victory of 1440 over the Milanese. Michelangelo was also invited to submit a cartoon for a similar fresco in the great hall, a decision which could hardly have pleased Leonardo. Now his notebooks began to be filled with passionate drawings of men shouting, fighting, killing and dying, of arms and armour and magnificent horses with their elaborate trappings. But once again, delay followed inevitable delay. The Council even threatened to ask for the return of all advance payments. Eventually, having designed his own scaffolding for the painting of the fresco, he set to work. Again Leonardo insisted on using oil-bound paints in his effort to achieve subtle effects. The painting was doomed from the start.

Meanwhile, the plans to divert the Arno had ended in tragedy when seasonal floods had washed away all that had been achieved. Machiavelli was blamed, and in turn blamed Leonardo. There were other troubles too. Leonardo's father, Ser Piero, had died, leaving him out of his will. Leonardo filed a lawsuit against his step-brothers which was to last for six years, during which time he was accused of being a traitor to Florence, for being irreligious, for being a sorcerer, for violating the dead and, once again, of sodomy.

In spite of all these problems Leonardo managed to produce his most famous masterpiece, the *Mona Lisa*. Madonna Lisa, or La Gioconda, was the young wife of a Florentine merchant, Francesco del Giocondo. The *Mona Lisa* reveals all Leonardo's skill at atmospheric effects. Here is the famous *sfumato*, the blurred edges of the face and landscape, which holds the secret of the flickering smile and the haunting eyes. His love of the oil technique, his understanding of its possibilities is expressed in the *Mona Lisa* beyond anything that had previously been achieved. The painting was immediately recognized as a masterpiece, and was admired and copied from the start. Leonardo for his part refused to admit that it was finished and never in fact delivered it to Francesco del Giocondo.

In 1506 he was invited by the Governor of Milan, a Frenchman called D'Amboise, to visit the city. He longed to get back to the place where he had been most happy and creative. Florence allowed him leave of three months, on pain of a heavy fine if he did not return. Milan welcomed him as court painter and scientist, and he once more found himself surrounded by his old friends and colleagues. He took with him to Milan his favourite paintings: the *Mona Lisa*, an unfinished painting of *St Anne and the Virgin* and a painting of *Leda and the Swan*. (The first two are now in the Louvre, the third is lost.) When three months had passed, D'Amboise wrote to Florence begging an extension of Leonardo's stay. But he was told that Leonardo must return to Florence to finish the *Battle of Anghiari*. The King of France then added his plea that Leonardo should be allowed to remain in Milan in time for his forthcoming visit. Diplomacy prevailed, and Leonardo was granted further leave.

He did return to Florence, briefly, to settle the lawsuit over his father's will, but returned again to Milan in 1510. The following year the French left Milan and Ludovico's heir was returned to power. In Florence the Medicis returned from exile. Giovanni de Medici was made Pope, calling himself Leo X, and Leonardo was invited to Rome by the Pope's brother, Giuliano. In Rome it was the heyday of Raphael and Michelangelo. With the *Mona Lisa* by his side, Leonardo was treated as the grand old man. Giuliano set him up in a studio and the Pope commissioned a painting, but Leonardo, as always, was carried away by his experiments. He set to work to make a pure, clear varnish, longer lasting than those in current use. The Pope was in despair. "What a man—to think of the varnish before he has painted the picture!"

Soon the French were back in Italy, this time with the young king, Francis I. The king took the opportunity of asking Leonardo if he would go to France as royal painter, offering him a pension and a home, the mansion of Le Cloux near the palace of Amboise, an offer which Leonardo could not resist. In this pleasant part of France, he passed the last years of his life, the pampered genius of Francis I's civilized court, making music, organizing pageants, arranging feasts, planning canals and filling his notebooks much as he had done in his youth at Milan. He was persuaded to sell the *Mona Lisa* to Francis I, but the king allowed him to keep it during his lifetime. He died on 2 May, 1519, leaving to his friend Francesco Melzi his drawings and his notebooks.

What was it about this extraordinary man which made him sought after and honoured by the most distinguished men in Europe, and who even now captures our imagination so many years later? There has, perhaps, always been in Europe an admiration for the unconventional genius, for the man who defies tradition. Leonardo recognized only the evidence of his own experiments, regardless of the opinions of earlier authorities. The spirit which he epitomizes, and which we recognize with such pleasure is best expressed in his own words: "Any one who in an argument appeals to authority uses not his intelligence, but his memory."

ERASMUS
(? 1466–1536)

DESIDERIUS ERASMUS is the name he is given in the histories and reference books; and a very great name it is too, denominating as it does one of the prime movers in the intellectual development of modern Europe out of the comparative obscurity of the Middle Ages. But when his mother first held him in her arms she called him Gerhard ("the beloved"), of which Erasmus is a Greek rendering and Desiderius a Latin. Surname he had none, since he was illegitimate.

Just how that came about is not at all sure. According to the story contained in the *Compendium*, a biographical compilation for which Erasmus is supposed to have been responsible, and on which the famous Victorian novel by Charles Reade, *The Cloister and the Hearth*, is based, Erasmus's father was one Gerhard or Geert, the one of a large family whom his family had planned should become a priest in the Roman Catholic church. The youth himself, however, had other ideas, and was already living, no doubt with a view to eventual matrimony, with a girl named Margaret, daughter of the village physician. His family made things so uncomfortable for him that he went off to Rome, where he supported himself by copying MSS, which indicates that he was a man of some learning. Margaret was already pregnant, and during his absence their son was born. His family thereupon wrote to him at Rome and told him that Margaret had died, and in his grief he entered the priesthood. On returning home he learnt of the cruel deception that had been practised upon him. As a priest he was not allowed to marry, and the idea of living with Margaret as his concubine (after the way of so many clerics at the time) was repugnant to both of them. In the circumstances the best he could do was to help her to support their child.

This is the story, and it has been pointed out that there is one strange omission, namely, that Erasmus had a brother Peter, three years older than he was, which would lead to the conclusion that the relationship of Gerhard and Margaret was quite a long-standing one. Because of this discrepancy some scholars have queried the authenticity of the *Compendium*; and yet, when it was composed in 1523, Erasmus had no apparent motive in concealing the facts; and in an application to the Pope for a dispensation relieving him of the disabilities attendant upon illegitimacy he had made the frank avowal that he was born of a union which, he had reason to believe, had been of a "sacrilegious character". One thing is beyond dispute, that he was born at Rotterdam, but then another doubt supervenes: was this in 1466, or 1467 or 1469? Erasmus seems to have been none too certain himself, but the consensus of present-day opinion points to 1466.

After a short time in the village school at Gouda, the boy served for about a year as a chorister in the cathedral at Utrecht, after which he and his brother went to a school at Deventer kept by the members of a pietistic order known as the Brethren of the Common Life. Here Erasmus learnt very little, except for a smattering of Greek imparted by the master, whose ability to do so must have been rare indeed in the Holland of that time. But when he was thirteen his mother, and shortly after his father, died of the plague, and the care of the two brothers devolved on three guardians, who promptly got them transferred to another school of the Brethren, at Bois-le-Duc (Hertogenbosch). Here they remained for some two years, when they petitioned their guardians to be sent to a university. This was ruled out on grounds of expense, and the boys were told that the only way in which they could obtain the education they desired was by becoming monks. At the age of sixteen, then, Erasmus agreed to enter the college of Steyn, near Gouda, but only on the understanding that he should be allowed to leave if he found the life there intolerable.

For the next six years he lived the life of a monk, although the rules were modified in his case, to the extent that he should not be required to keep the nightly vigils, since they interfered with his sleep, nor confine himself on fast days to fish, since even the smell of it made his stomach heave. Even so, his experience of monastic life left Erasmus with a deep sense of repugnance, and he might well have quitted the place but for the fact that it possessed a good library. At nineteen, in 1486, he was so far reconciled to the situation that he made his profession as a monk, and in 1492 he was ordained priest by the bishop of Utrecht, something which in later life he most bitterly regretted.

For the next few years he spent most of his time in the library studying the Christian Fathers and, perhaps even more avidly, the pagan classics of Greece and Rome. He also did a good deal of writing, tracts and essays on such subjects as the advantages and disadvantages of the monastic life, and the wickedness of war, which he later revised for publication. But he was increasingly bored and resentful, until deliverance came, quite unexpectedly, in the form of an invitation from the bishop of Cambray to serve him as his secretary. His monastic superiors raised no objections, and, feeling like a new man, he emerged into the world again.

The secretarial post proved disappointing, but the bishop gave him leave of absence and provided him with funds to enable him to attend the university of Paris and study for a doctorate in Theology. About the middle of 1495, then, he enrolled among the "poor students" at the Collège Montaigu at Paris. He was now getting on for thirty, not at all strong in constitution, rather set in his ways no doubt, and nicely fastidious in his personal habits. The life at the college shocked him. The food was poor and inadequate, and the lodging abominable. As for the instruction, it was steeped in the Scholasticism of the Middle Ages, and there was not even a suggestion of that Renaissance culture and enlightenment which was beginning to spread beyond the Alps.

The professors were on the whole a poor lot, dogmatic in their ignorance and fierce in their treatment of unruly scholars, whom they flogged until the blood came. Such foolish questions they debated too, with such furious zeal. God is omnipotent, agreed; but does that mean He can contradict Himself? Can he make the past not to have been, so that, for instance, a harlot is restored to virginity? Another was concerned with the fires of Purgatory: were they material? Such a pointless question, protested Erasmus; the only sensible thing was to live in such a way as not to get into the flames, whatever they were composed of. . . .

After a time Erasmus was allowed to live in lodgings in the city, while still attending lectures at the college. He added to his income by taking private pupils, since the allowance from the bishop of Cambray was far too small to meet the expenses of an existence which was reputed to be convivial if not actually loose. For these pupils Erasmus composed several little textbooks, including a manual on letter-writing and another that might be described as "Etiquette for Schoolboys". At Paris, too, he produced the first version of his *Colloquies*, which was originally intended as a guide to conversation. All these remained in manuscript for years, but

Erasmus's first printed work appeared at this time—a highly laudatory introduction to a history of France written by Robert Gaguin, a humanist churchman who taught Rhetoric at the Sorbonne. After several years spent in this way, one of his English pupils, Lord Mountjoy, invited him to become his guest in England, and with intense relief Erasmus left the Collège Montaigu. As he grimly recorded in the *Colloquies*: "I carried nothing away from it but a body infected with diseases, and a plentiful supply of lice."

Perhaps it was towards the close of 1497 that Erasmus paid his first visit to England, but it may have been in the summer of 1498, and some authorities even prefer 1499. Whenever it was, the visit proved to be one of the pleasantest and most rewarding periods of his life. The country was newly emerged from the Wars of the Roses, and the New Monarchy under Henry VII was showing an interest in the New Learning. Mountjoy proved himself a most gracious host, and introduced Erasmus not only to members of his family circle but to many of the most promising of the younger generation of scholars and teachers, as well as to several of the most up-and-coming in the royal service.

It must have been decidedly gratifying to discover that his reputation as a man-of-letters had gone before him, and that he was to be accepted on terms of equal friendship. His letters to friends in Paris are filled with ecstatic descriptions of men and manners. "The air is soft and delicious," we find him writing when he was not long arrived. "The men are sensible and intelligent; many of them are even learned, and not superficially either. The number of young men here who are studying ancient literature is astonishing." From London he moved on to Oxford, and his enthusiasm was unbounded. John Colet, who was about the same age as Erasmus, was lecturing on the Epistles of St. Paul; Erasmus heard him, and "I might have been listening to Plato". From Colet, who a few years later became Dean of St. Paul's in London, Erasmus absorbed a method of Scriptural interpretation altogether superior to that of the old Scholastic theologians. Even more important to his intellectual development was his contact with William Grocyn, who had studied Greek in Italy from Greek refugees and was the first to teach it at Oxford. Erasmus lived at Oxford in Grocyn's house, and he describes him in summary form as a "mine of knowledge".

So warm and flattering was the reception given him at Oxford that he deemed it necessary to explain to Colet just what kind of man he was, in case they were inclined to take a too high opinion of his merits. "You will find me", he wrote, "a man of small fortune or of none, and with no ambition in that direction. But a man who craves for friendship, with a slight knowledge of literature and a burning desire to know much more. A man who reverences goodness in others, but who has none of his own to boast about; simple, frank, open, without pretence or concealment; of moderate ability, but what he has, good of its kind; not much of a speaker. . . . in short, one from whom you must look for nothing but good will."

This may sound a trifle *too* deprecatory, and rather different is the self-portrait given in a letter addressed to his friend Faustus Anderlin in Paris (but it should be understood that Anderlin was no ascetic scholar like Colet, but a lively young man of the world). "Your friend Erasmus gets on well in England. He is a fair horseman, and can make something of a show in the hunting-field. He can make a tolerable *bow*, and can manage to smile graciously whether he means it or not. If you are wise you will make haste to cross the Channel yourself: a witty fellow like you should not be wasting his life among those French——" and here he uses a very rude word indeed.

Was Anderlin still undecided? Then here was something more, that would surely put wings to his ankles. "The English girls . . . ! Divinely pretty! soft, gentle, as charming as the Muses! They have one custom that really cannot be too greatly admired. When you go anywhere on a visit all the girls come up to kiss you. They kiss you when you go away, and they kiss you again when you return. Go where you will, it is kisses all the way. And, my dear Faustus, if you could taste those soft and fragrant lips but once, you would want nothing better than to spend the rest of your days here."

After this osculatory luxuriance, it is sadly depressing to be informed that in later years Erasmus condemned the practice of kissing as unsanitary. . . .

However much he liked England and the English, Erasmus decided at length to return to France, probably in 1499. For the first time in his life his pockets were well filled, so generously open-handed had been his English patrons. But on his arrival at Dover he ran into serious trouble. He had been warned in London that the exportation of specie, whether gold or silver, was strictly prohibited, and had thereupon changed his English gold coins into French currency in the belief that this would be exempt. The customs officers, however, insisted that the ban was on coin of every description, and Erasmus's little hoard was seized, with the result that he was almost penniless when he was allowed to resume his journey across the Channel.

Back on the Continent, he moved for years from place to place, country to country, perpetually hard up and often reduced to the most humiliating expedients to obtain the wherewithal to continue his life of study and authorship. He became a past-master in the fine art of writing begging-letters, and some of those that have come down to us can fairly be described as greasy in their flattering importunity. When one sees, for instance, the sort of thing that he addressed to Lady Anne of Veere, who often welcomed him to her chateau of Tournehem in Flanders, one wonders how even that ardent patroness of men of genius can have failed to be nauseated. At the same time it is hard to see how otherwise he could have avoided having to sell his much prized independence for some Church appointment.

In 1506 Erasmus was again in England, at first in London, where he formed a lasting friendship with Thomas More and was treated most generously by Archbishop Warham, and then at Cambridge where he furthered his studies in Greek. After only a few months, however, a favourable opportunity presented itself of satisfying his long-felt ambition of visiting Italy. Dr Boerio, physician to King Henry VII, was seeking a man of high repute and learning to accompany his two sons thither, and offered Erasmus the post. He accepted the charge with alacrity, and accompanied the two boys as far as Bologna. In September, 1506, he was in Turin, where he was awarded a doctorate in Divinity, and then he sought an introduction to Aldus Manutius, the celebrated printer of Greek and Latin texts at Venice. Erasmus spent many happy hours in the Aldine printing-shop, and Aldus Manutius came to think so highly of him that he agreed to publish a new and greatly enlarged edition of Erasmus's *Adagia*, a collection of gems of wit and wisdom culled from the authors of antiquity, which he started in his early days at Paris and of which a first edition had been published in 1500. The purpose of the "adages", so Erasmus explained, was "to persuade, adorn, and inform," and he gradually expanded his collection until from the original eight hundred items it amounted to over five thousand. Of all his writings this was one of the most popular, and deservedly so.

From Venice, Erasmus moved on to Padua and thence to Rome, where he received every mark of distinction. Scholars and prelates claimed his attention, and he was given to understand that a distinguished and profitable career in the Church lay open to him. He was sorely tempted, and he might well have lived out his days in the Holy City, with a cardinal's hat on his head or (who knows?) even the Papal tiara. But in May, 1509, there came a letter from his friend Mountjoy in England, informing him of the death of Henry VII and the accession of the brilliant young Prince Henry as Henry VIII. The new ruler was known to be very favourably disposed to the New Learning, and surely Erasmus, as one of its most distinguished embodiments, might look forward to a splendid future under his patronage. The invitation was flattering, and indeed more flattering than it actually was, since Mountjoy had hinted that it came from the young king himself. Even so, he found it hard to tear himself away from Rome, where he had made so many excellent friends, where there were magnificent libraries and collections of antiquities such as no other city in the world could equal. But at length he took the plunge, and in 1509 he again crossed the Channel to England.

In London he was the guest of Thomas More in his pleasant home at Chelsea. He and his host got on famously, and a permanent memorial of their happy intercourse is the book that Erasmus proceeded to write under the title *Encomium Moriae*, which is usually translated as "In Praise of Folly" although it might also be rendered "In Praise of More". The pun was no doubt intentional. The book had its rise in Erasmus's conversations with More, and in it Folly, *Moria*, uses the typically Erasmian language, so witty and whimsical, so ironic and melancholy, to make fun of greedy monks, strutting friars and quarrelsome theologians. Then it is the turn of princes and courtiers, but before the book closes Erasmus is harrying and exposing yet further the absurdities and worse of the monkish tribe. Here he was voicing the popular mood, and it is no wonder that *Encomium Moriae* achieved widespread fame.

For perhaps two years Erasmus kept in close touch with the English court in London, enjoying considerable patronage but denied the preferment that he had so confidently expected. In the autumn of 1511 he moved to Cambridge at the invitation of John Fisher, bishop of Rochester, and was given rooms in Queen's college, of which Fisher was president. Here he lectured on Greek, the study of which was in its infancy in Cambridge. It used to be supposed that he was appointed Lady Margaret's professor of

Divinity and was later Regius reader in Greek, but it now appears that he was given no such substantial appointments. His only certain income was the fees paid him by the students, most of whom were poor, and thus he had to continue to rely for the most part on the contributions of patrons. Of these Archbishop Warham was the most lavish, and among his gifts was a pension of twenty pounds per annum derived from the little parish of Aldington in Kent.

If the promises that had been made him (so Erasmus wrote later) had been made good, he would have been glad to spend the rest of his days in England, but in this he was disappointed. Thus it was that in the autumn of 1513 he returned to the Continent, and for the next seven years moved up and down the Rhine, between Flanders and Switzerland, and not doing at all badly, what with sundry pensions that were granted him, a shower of presents, and the proceeds from the sale of his books. For some time his head-quarters were in Louvain, but the bigotry of the Flemish clergy and the predominantly monkish atmosphere of the university at length led to his accepting the offer of John Froben, head of a publishing house at Basle, to join him in the capacity of general editor and literary adviser. The partnership thus established was of much mutual advantage, and until Froben's death in 1527 the press at Basle was recognized as the most important in Europe.

The first project on which Erasmus was employed by Froben was a carefully annotated edition of the letters and other writings of St Jerome, in which he did not hesitate to point out the extent to which contemporary Christianity had departed from what had been taught by the great Father of the Church a thousand years before. This was published by Froben in nine volumes.

Much more significant was the publication in 1516 of the first printed edition of the New Testament in Greek, something on which Erasmus had been engaged for many years. True, as a work of scholarship this left a good deal to be desired. In the first place, the manuscripts available to him at Basle were few in number and of late date; and secondly, he had been required to work against the clock, since Froben was anxious to forestall the publication of a rival version made by Cardinal Ximines that was already in print and only awaited Papal approval for its issue. But Erasmus's Greek New Testament was the first in the field, and through it educated men everywhere were enabled to get a far better understanding of the basic records of their faith than had been possible hitherto. Furthermore, Erasmus had attached to his Greek text a fresh Latin translation, from which it was made clear beyond any doubt that the Vulgate, the Latin version made by St Jerome which had been accepted for ages as the Bible of the Church, was in many passages grievously in error.

Of course, only the educated could read Erasmus's New Testament, but he was confident that very shortly it would be made available in the vernacular. Not long before the translation and publication of the Scriptures in the language of the common people would have been prohibited under pain of the stake, but now we find Erasmus writing in his preface: "I wish that even the weakest woman might read the Gospels and the Epistles of St. Paul. I should like them to be translated into all languages, so as to be understood by the Scotch and Irish, by Turks and Saracens. I long for the day when the husbandman shall sing portions of them to himself as he follows the plough, the weaver hum them to the tune of his shuttle, and the traveller use them to alleviate the weariness of his journey."

In addition to providing an improved Greek text and a more accurate Latin translation, Erasmus added much by way of elucidation in the form of *Paraphrases*, written in Latin as all his writings were, but in simple language. These were speedily translated into French, German, Bohemian, and English; it is interesting to note that one of those engaged on the English version was the Princess Mary, who was responsible for most of St. John's Gospel. In 1547, in the first year of Edward VI, the English government ordered that a copy of Erasmus's *Paraphrase of the Gospels* should be set up in some convenient place in every parish church.

Now in his fifties, Erasmus was at the peak of his influence as leader of the liberal reform movement in the Church and the most celebrated and influential man of letters in Europe. The *Adagia* still retained its popularity, and the *Praise of Folly* ran it close. A firm favourite with the serious-minded was his *Enchiridion Militis Christiani* ("The Christian Soldier's Dagger"), that originated in the request from an admirer for a book which might help to reclaim her husband from evil courses. Then there were tracts and treatises in great variety but too numerous to mention. Soon there was to appear the first edition of a book on which Erasmus had long been working—since his early days in Paris indeed—the *Colloquia*, consisting of "colloquies" or familiar conversations in which he records, with characteristic vivacity and clear-sighted observation, what he himself had seen and heard in the course of his journeyings here and there on the Continent and in England. Erasmus had the human touch. Nowhere better than in the pages of this book can we meet the people of the time—the high-born and the lowly, the wealthy and the down-at-heel, abbots and bishops, monks and parish priests, lords and commoners, soldiers of fortune, thieves and cheats, tavern keepers, and (not to forget the other sex, which Erasmus never did) ladies of the utmost respectability and flighty girls with no morals to speak of. No wonder that the *Colloquies* became the most famous of all his works, and was generally regarded as his masterpiece. To this day it has remained the most widely read and appreciated of all that he wrote.

No man of letters in Europe's long history had ever reached such a pitch of general appreciation and renown, and Erasmus should be excused if on looking out at the world from his window in Basle he found the prospect pleasing and the future bright. Not that he did not recognize the existence of many abuses, especially in the Church: he had done much to expose them, and had suggested ways in which they might be remedied. Education was the key—education, together with a proper exercise of the human reason in the interpretation of Divine truth. As we look back at the Erasmus pictured in Dürer's drawing—hooded and muffled against the cold, busily writing at a desk flanked with ponderous tomes but with a vase of flowers at his elbow—one must feel a pang of pity for a man who was born when he was, in the Europe of such Popes as the infamous Julius II and the near pagan Leo X, when he would have been so altogether at home, so deeply revered and so generally regarded in the ecumenically-minded world of Pope John XXIII.

If Erasmus ever dreamed of a serene old age, spent in the pleasantest company in which the talk was as good as the wine, his dreams were shattered by the thunderous hammering of Martin Luther, as on 31 October, 1517, he nailed his *Theses* to the door of the church at Wittenberg. After that, all was fury and discord as the Reformation pursued its tempestuous progress. Both sides in the struggle appealed to Erasmus to come off the fence and take his place in the arena. He believed that to a large extent Luther was thoroughly justified in making his "protest". The Church *was* riddled with abuses; the monks (many of them at least) *were* a disreputable lot; Tetzel selling his "indulgences" ("as soon as the coin in the coffer rings, the soul from Purgatory springs") ought to be repudiated by all decent men. On the other hand, however, not all the Popes had been bad; many of the so-called superstitious practices were harmless and had endeared themselves to generations of pious souls; and the overthrow of ecclesiastical order and good discipline, the smashing of images (the noise reached him in his study at Basle and for a time drove him into exile) and the desecration of churches were altogether too horrible.

In mind, body, and soul Erasmus was a man of the Renaissance, and the rough and rude activities of the Reformers, especially in the Low Countries and Germany, filled him with disgust, alarm and near despair, so that he mournfully concluded that the century that had opened with such promise was the very worst since Jesus Christ. And yet to the end of his days he never ceased to preach a gospel of intellectual reason and a truly Christian charity. After a month's painful illness from dysentery, he died at Basle on 12 July, 1536, and was buried in the cathedral there.

NICHOLAS COPERNICUS

(1473–1543)

> "Copernicus, a man of great learning, of much experience, and
> of wonderful diligence in observation, hath renewed the opinion
> of Aristarchus Samius, and affirmeth that the earth not only
> moveth circularly about his own centre, but also may be, yea and
> is, continually out of the precise centre of the world thirty-eight
> hundred thousand miles."

THUS WROTE Robert Recorde, an English mathematician, some
twenty years after the publication of the book which revolutionized
Man's conception of the universe, *De Revolutionibus Orbium Coelestium
Libri Sex* (*Six Books on the Revolutions of the Celestial Spheres*). Its
author was Nicholas Copernicus, canon of Frauenberg Cathedral
on the Baltic coast of Poland, which he himself described as
the "farthest corner of the earth", but from this far corner of
Europe Copernicus upset the firmly held beliefs of over a
thousand years and established the modern basis of astronomical
science.

He was born in 1473 at Torun (Thorn), the "Queen of the
Vistula", a trading city midway between Danzig and Warsaw.
Nicholas's father Mikalaj Kopernik came from Cracow, the ancient
capital of Poland, and probably engaged in the copper trade; he
married into a prosperous bourgeois family, and became a substantial citizen. Thus the earliest years of Nicholas Copernicus (he
later Latinized his name, as did many humanist scholars) were
spent in reasonable comfort, for even after his father's death, when
Nicholas was only ten, the family was well supported by a maternal
uncle, Lucas Watzelrode (1447–1512), an able cleric who became
Bishop of Varmia and was adviser to the Polish crown. In 1497 he
obtained a canonry at Frauenberg (Fromborg) through his uncle's
influence, and this appointment ensured Copernicus's material
security, since the Chapter of Frauenberg was wealthy, controlling
one-third of the province of Varmia, but his position also carried
heavy responsibilities in administration.

From 1512 to his death in 1543, Copernicus was in residence at

Frauenberg as the statutes demanded, unless the business of the Chapter called him away. In many respects he led the life of a land-lord, supervising the church estates; he examined farming accounts, inspected the properties of the Cathedral, admitted peasant farmers to their new holdings and sat in manorial courts. Occasionally there was drama in this work: from 1516–21 Copernicus administered the districts of Allenstein and Mehlsack, successfully defending Allenstein castle when it was besieged by the Teutonic Knights in 1521. He led an active life until the year of his death, when he was seventy, but it consisted largely of the humdrum routine of official business: he never achieved higher office than the position which his uncle had given him at the age of twenty-four. However, it was largely this condition of stability and certainty in his personal life which enabled him to make his great contribution to the intellectual and scientific life of Europe.

The foundation of Copernicus's work was laid by his lengthy education, through which he received the best of the European intellectual tradition of his day. He attended the local University of Cracow while still in his teens (1491–94), and later spoke highly of the mathematical and astronomical training he had received there. His uncle and patron, Bishop Watzelrode, next sent him to Bologna, one of the oldest and most distinguished universities of Europe. For four years (1496–1500) Copernicus studied canon law and was imbued with the spirit of humanism, the study of classical literature and thought which was to influence his own work con-siderably: he would naturally have mastered Latin at an early age, since it was the international language of scholarship and the Church, and at Bologna he began the study of Greek, which would enable him to read Plato, Aristotle and Ptolemy at first hand.

In 1500 Copernicus visited Rome for the celebrations of the Year of Jubilee, and according to Rheticus, he gave lectures on mathematical topics to an interested circle of learned men. How-ever he had not yet fulfilled any of the duties of his canonry, and so in 1501 he returned home to Frauenberg. The Chapter agreed to extend his leave for study, provided that he also studied medicine in order to act as a physician, and Copernicus returned to Italy to complete his education. In 1503 he obtained his doctorate of canon law at Ferrara, and continued to study medicine at Padua: when he returned home for good in 1506 he joined his uncle's household as the bishop's physician, and in effect became his secretary and personal assistant. When Bishop Watzelrode died in 1512 Copernicus left the episcopal household, and at the age of forty for the first time took up his duties as canon of Frauenberg.

During his lifetime Copernicus was the classic example of a humanist scholar: trained in several disciplines, he was "familiar with six languages, and proved himself capable in mathematics, physics, medicine, law, geography, philosophy, history, biography, philology, finance, engineering, epistolography, painting and estate management" as one admirer later asserted. He wrote an essay on money and currency reform in which he pointed out the evil effects of debasing the coinage, since bad money will drive out the good. He used his medical knowledge in the service of his uncle and the cathedral chapter, and it was said that he helped the poor without charging any fee. His legal training was undoubtedly useful in the administration of the Chapter estates, and Copernicus's breadth of learning must have impressed the people of his Baltic province, but outside this area he was little known to his contemporaries, except for a select group of astronomical mathematicians.

It is not known what first attracted Copernicus as a young man to his study of the celestial world. Indeed, there is much about his character and motivation which can never be fully explained, but a good deal is known about the intellectual background by which he was influenced in his formative years. The universities of late medieval Europe were dominated by the work of ancient philosophers, scientists and men-of-letters to a remarkable degree, and such was the respect given to the wisdom of the classics that direct observation and experiment took second place to a minute consideration of the texts of ancient authors. For example, Copernicus would have studied medicine by reading the works of Galen, Hippocrates and Aristotle: there was a practical demonstration of human anatomy once a year only at Padua, and the dissection was carried out by surgeons since such an activity was judged unworthy of a gentleman physician. The basic syllabus at any university for the first degree (in the School of Arts) reflected this preoccupation with classical learning; the intending Master of Arts would study grammar, rhetoric and logic, and then progress to arithmetic, geometry, music and astronomy, all of which depended heavily on the works of Aristotle and other classical authors. The great wave of humanist enthusiasm for classical literature and Renaissance admiration of classical art stimulated rather than displaced this firm belief in ancient authorities, although inconsistencies and contradictions now became apparent.

The great authority in astronomy, one of the basic fields of study, was Ptolemy of Alexandria, a Greek of the second century A.D.: his manual of astronomy, usually known by its Arabic name of the *Almagest*, was widely used for a thousand years, not only by Christians but by Jews and Moslems as well. Writers of the ancient world were interested in astronomy for a variety of reasons: for many peoples like the Babylonians and the Egyptians, the heavenly bodies had a mystical or religious connotation, and Greek mythology was woven round the constellations of the stars. But the study of astronomy also had a practical advantage, for the passage of the sun gave man some notion of time, the direction of the stars enabled sailors to navigate when they had lost sight of familiar landmarks, and celestial observations enabled travellers to locate their positions on the globe. Since astronomy had such wide applications it became an important topic of study in medieval universities, and during the lifetime of Copernicus it continued to attract considerable public interest.

In spite of their Christian faith, many men still firmly believed that the constellations and the planets influenced the lives of individual men, and in the sixteenth century many astronomers earned their living by casting horoscopes for wealthy patrons. It was said of Pope Paul III, to whom Copernicus dedicated his book *On the Revolutions*, that he "would call no important meeting of the Consistory and take no trip, without choosing his days and observing the constellations. An alliance with the King of France met with the objection that the Royal and Papal nativities did not conform". The Hapsburg Emperor Rudolph II was obsessed with astrology and the quest for the philosopher's stone, though to his credit he patronized Tycho Brahe and Kepler: the great general Wallenstein refused to march if the stars were unfavourable. If the leaders of society were so credulous, it is not surprising that popular belief attached the greatest importance to the predictions of wise men from the stars.

The more scientific application of astronomy was also rapidly developing during Copernicus's career. Voyages of discovery around the coasts of Africa to Asia created a demand for accurate maps and measuring equipment, which stimulated the development of the scientific instrument trade and a European interest in geography and geophysics. The discovery of the New World, a whole continent unknown to the wisest of the ancients, prompted men to reconsider some of their assumptions, especially when they seemed to conflict with the observable truth, but only in astronomy had enough observations been accumulated to enable new hypotheses to be put forward and tested on the basis of recognized mathematical methods.

Copernicus first studied astronomy at Cracow, where the principal teacher of mathematics was Albert Brudzewski, and then at Bologna, where Maria da Novara taught. According to Rheticus, Copernicus was "not so much the pupil as the assistant and witness of observations of the learned Dominicus Maria". He had already acquired considerable theoretical knowledge of astronomy by a close study of Ptolemy's *Almagest*, which had just appeared (1496) in the first printed edition as the *Epitome of Ptolemaic Astronomy*, edited by Peurbach and completed by Regiomontanus. These celebrated fifteenth-century mathematicians and astronomers had done much to rationalize the Ptolemaic system without needing to upset the basic structure.

Ptolemy's view of the universe, which was still therefore accepted in 1500, may be summarized as follows: at the centre of the universe is the spherical earth, fixed and unmoving, around which revolve the spheres of the Moon, Mercury, Venus, the Sun, Mars, Jupiter and Saturn, and beyond the last planet the sphere of the fixed stars. Ptolemy had refined the views of earlier Greek astronomers, particularly Aristotle, in order to take into account all known celestial phenomena, especially the movement of the planets, which he attempted to explain by a series of complex geometrical formulae. Ptolemy's elegant mathematical proofs ensured the supremacy of his system at the expense of earlier theories, but these were not completely lost, for Ptolemy himself relied heavily on the work of his predecessors. He included in the *Almagest* a catalogue of over one thousand stars, with a note of their positions, and Copernicus used this table in his own work.

Before Ptolemy's theories could be of much practical use to a later generation, either for the purposes of astrology or of scientific study, accurate tables had to be drawn up of the movement of the celestial bodies, especially of the planets. The tables most widely in use in 1500 were the *Alfonsine Tables* based on the meridian of Toledo and drawn up in Spain under Arabic influence in the late thirteenth century. However, these tables were by no means accurate in their predictions, and Tycho Brahe found that by the

Not since Charlemagne had there been a European sovereign who ruled over so vast a collection of territories as Charles V. All Western Europe came under his sway, and his captains added to his domain in the Indies, East and West.

In this luxuriantly splendid painting by Vasari, now at Florence, of Charles being crowned by Pope Clement VII, he is shown holding a massive orb, symbolical of the world-wide extent of his dominions.

Even in these post-Einstein days we may still detect truth in Pope's famous couplet, "Nature and Nature's laws lay hid in night: God said, 'Let Newton be!' and all was light." This portrait of England's greatest mathematician and natural philosopher (*left*), by J. Vanderbank, is in the National Portrait Gallery in London.

Newton lived in a century when scientific ideas were "in the air", as it were. The century preceding was essentially a theologizing one, and there was no more influential theologian than John Calvin, who not only formulated a vast system of dogmatic belief but devised a method of church organization which remains to this day one of the most popular expressions of the Protestant witness. The painting by Labouchere (*below*) shows Calvin in argumentative mood at the Council of Geneva in 1549.

mid-sixteenth century they were a whole month out. Copernicus had also been struck by their lack of accuracy, for he wrote:

> "I was led to think of a method of computing the motions of the spheres by nothing but the knowledge that Mathematicians (i.e. astronomers) are inconsistent in these investigations . . . I therefore took pains to re-read the works of all the philosophers on whom I could lay my hands to find out whether any of them had ever supposed that the motions of the spheres were other than those demanded by the mathematical schools."

Copernicus thus tackled the problem of how to find a more convincing explanation of the movements of the spheres in a thoroughly conservative fashion, by going back beyond Ptolemy to the theories which he had discarded. On the other hand, he tested the validity of any plausible system by painstaking practical observation, making full use of the observations of others, including Ptolemy and the Greek astronomers: in fact, his acceptance of Ptolemy's data resulted in the perpetuation of many inaccuracies, although Copernicus's new conception of the movement of the spheres enabled Erasmus Reinhold to compute his *Prussian Tables* (1551) to a greater degree of accuracy than the Ptolemaic *Alfonsine Tables*.

Copernicus took an active interest in the practical work of contemporaries, and for thirty years he checked his theories against his own observations. However, he was most important as a mathematical rather than an observing astronomer, which is not surprising when one considers the simplicity of the scientific equipment he was using. The telescope was not developed until more than fifty years after his death, and so all observations were limited to the powers of human sight. Apart from devices for measuring the passage of time, including a complicated sundial, Copernicus used the triquetrum, a simple wooden device which he made himself for measuring the altitudes of the sun, moon, planets and fixed stars, and for measuring their distances from the point of the vernal equinox. He must have used the astrolabe, the quadrant and other instruments in common use at the time, but he had no special advantage over contemporary observers: Rheticus commented that "he disliked bothering with the determination of minute distances, as sought by others who with painstaking exactitude believe they have found the place of the stars to two, three or four minutes, while actually erring by entire degrees".

E

However, Copernicus did point out to Rheticus the errors of Ptolemy's star catalogue where they were obvious, and urged him to recalculate their positions—a task completed by Tycho Brahe.

Copernicus's great achievement was not therefore so much the result of new discoveries in the heavens as a reinterpretation of existing data to fit the known celestial phenomena more exactly. There were a number of natural occurrences to be explained within the framework of a simple system: the seasons of the earth, the circling round the Pole of all the heavenly bodies, the movement of the sun against the background of the fixed stars, and the motion of the planets. The explanation which Copernicus gave of these complex movements was simple in conception but revolutionary in consequence. Instead of regarding the earth as the fixed centre of the universe, he placed the sun at the centre instead:

"In the middle of all sits the Sun enthroned. In this most beautiful temple could we place this luminary in any better position from which he can illuminate the whole at once? He is rightly called the Lamp, the Mind, the Ruler of the Universe; Hermes Trismegistus names him the visible God, Sophocles's Electra calls him the All-seeing. So the Sun sits as upon a royal throne ruling his children the planets which circle round him."

There is almost a mystical element in Copernicus's conception of a heliocentric universe; moreover Man has been displaced from the place of honour in creation. No doubt human vanity helps to explain why Aristotle and Ptolemy had placed the earth at the centre of the cosmos, and had been followed by astronomers for nearly two thousand years. It required tremendous freedom of mind to challenge the assumptions of his predecessors, but Copernicus took strength from the fact that a heliocentric system had been suggested by some Greek astronomers, notably Aristarchus of Samos in the third century B.C.: although Copernicus does not mention him by name, he was well aware of his theory.

The second assumption of the Copernican system was that the earth itself was in motion, following an orbit around the sun and accompanied by the dependent moon. In fact Copernicus ascribed two motions to the earth: its circular annual orbit round the sun accounted for the sun's apparent yearly motion through the skies and the movement of the planets, and when the inclination of the earth's axis was taken into account, it explained the seasons as well. The daily turning of the earth about its own axis explained why the whole of the heavens appeared to rotate: in his system Copernicus retained the outer sphere of the fixed stars, but they were now at rest, since their apparent motion was really that of the earth.

The greatest problem facing Copernicus's new system was the apparent movement of the planets. These sometimes remained stationary in the heavens (the stations) and then moved backwards and forwards (retrogression and procession) across the sky. According to Ptolemy, the planets were in orbit around the earth, and their movement must conform to a logical pattern based on circular motion, since this was the most natural course to take. In order to accommodate the known behaviour of the planets, Ptolemy introduced a complicated series of epicycles (a circle whose centre moves through another circle), deferents, equants, eccentrics and other geometrical formulae into the orbit of the planets: the resulting system was so complicated that Alfonso X of Castile was led to remark: "If He had consulted me beforehand I would surely have given the Creator a better plan". Copernicus showed mathematically that if the earth itself was in orbit round the sun, the motion of the planets seen from earth was apparent rather than real: since, for example, Jupiter takes nearly twelve years to complete its orbit while the earth takes only one year, the distant planets will usually appear to be moving more slowly across the sky, even backwards against the stars. Copernicus was not able to dispense with the epicycles and eccentrics completely, for he assumed like Ptolemy that planetary orbits must be circular: it was not until the following century that Kepler showed that they are in fact elliptical.

The beauty of Copernicus's system was its simplicity, which seemed to confirm the belief that the laws of the universe were all derived from a single cause:

> "I think it is easier to believe this (the heliocentric theory) than to confuse the issue by assuming a vast number of spheres, which those who keep Earth at the centre must do. We thus rather follow Nature, who producing nothing vain or superfluous, often prefers to endow one cause with many effects."

On the other hand, it was open to a number of objections, and a century of debate ensued after Copernicus's death before his system was generally accepted. The most far-reaching criticism of any new scientific theory in the sixteenth century was likely to come from the Church: Copernicus in fact dedicated his revolutionary work to Pope Paul III, commenting that:

"If perchance there should be foolish speakers who, together with those ignorant of all mathematics, will take it upon themselves to decide concerning these things, and because of some place in the Scriptures wickedly distorted to their purpose, should dare to assail this my work, they are of no importance to me to such an extent do I despise their judgment as rash."

In practice, the Protestants with their devotion to the Bible were amongst Copernicus's earliest critics: Luther referred to him as:

"The new astronomer who wants to prove that the Earth goes round, and not the heavens, the Sun and the Moon; just as if someone sitting in a moving waggon or ship were to suppose that he was at rest, and that the Earth and trees were moving past him. But that is the way nowadays; whoever wants to be clever must needs produce something of his own, which is bound to be the best since he has produced it! The fool will turn the whole science of astronomy upside down. But, as Holy Writ declares, it was the Sun and not the Earth which Joshua commanded to stand still."

When Copernicus's disciple Rheticus tried to find a publisher for *On the Revolutions* in the Lutheran city of Wittenberg in 1542 he met opposition, and so the book was published at Nuremberg in the following year. It contained a preface written by a Lutheran pastor, Andreas Osiander, to whom Rheticus had entrusted the publication, in which Osiander maintained that the Copernican system was only a convenient scientific hypothesis, and did not necessarily represent the physical arrangement of the universe. This preface was completely unauthorized, for all the indications are that Copernicus did intend his system to be taken as physically as well as mathematically correct, but this argument may have helped to protect the Copernican system from initial attack. But once the ideas of the Copernican Revolution had achieved European fame, the radical challenge to the established authorities of science fell under suspicion, for might not the authority of the Church which still approved of Aristotle also be undermined by free thinkers? From the middle of the sixteenth century, the zealous but limiting spirit of the Counter-Reformation resulted in an increasing disapproval of the work of the Copernicans by the Catholic Church, until Bruno died at the stake in 1600 and Galileo was imprisoned by the Inquisition. But the posthumous reputation of Copernicus himself was not materially affected, and only a few sentences of his works were expunged.

Copernicus's system was also open to serious scientific objections, and these considerations may well have delayed the publication of his book *On the Revolutions*. If the earth really moved round the sun, there ought to be changes in the apparent positions of the fixed stars from different positions in the Earth's orbit, but none of the stars exhibited this phenomenon of parallax, even to careful observers like Tycho Brahe. Copernicus rightly assumed that this was because the distance of the stars from the earth was so great that the changing position of the earth made little difference to their appearance, but contemporaries found this notion of an enormous universe difficult to accept. It was not until 1838 that stellar parallax was first observed with a telescope and confirmed Copernicus's theory.

A practical objection to the theory that the earth was in motion round the sun was the common-sense one, that it appeared to be completely motionless. Copernicus argued that this motion could not be appreciated by an observer on earth because it was motion relative to the other spheres of the universe:

> "It is but as the saying of Aeneas in Virgil—'We sail forth from the harbour, and lands and cities retire'. As the ship floats along in the calm, all external things seem to have the motion that is really that of the ship, while those within the ship feel that they and all its contents are at rest."

Copernicus could not give a fully satisfactory explanation of the mechanical forces at work in the moving world: when a weight was dropped, why did it fall vertically to the earth, instead of being left behind in its flight by the rotation of the earth? Ptolemy and the Greeks had taught that all objects naturally seek their place of rest at the centre of the universe, which was the centre of the earth, and Copernicus's theory seemed to make mechanics unnecessarily complicated: it was not until the time of Galileo and Newton that a solution was offered compatible with the Copernican model. An even more baffling question was to determine what kept the planets on their courses, since the forces of a gravitational field were unknown. Both Ptolemy and Copernicus assumed that the orbits of the planets followed a regular course which could be mathematically determined, but their conception of the physical arrangement of the celestial bodies was largely derived from Aristotle, who believed that each planet was attached to a rotating, transparent, crystalline sphere. The accurate determination of the path of a comet by Tycho Brahe in 1577 shattered the validity of the celestial spheres and two thousand years of astronomical theory.

In view of the powerful objections to his system and his own innate caution, it is understandable that Copernicus should have delayed publishing his views for many years, until they had been subjected to as many proofs as possible, both by Copernicus's own observations and those of others. But it was impossible to prove or disprove some aspects of his theory by observation and Copernicus was afraid to submit his work to the ridicule of the uninformed. He considered circulating his theories amongst mathematicians who would understand the problems involved and he did prepare a *Little Commentary* (*Commentariolus*) in manuscript form, but this was not printed during his lifetime. This *Little Commentary* sketches seven assumptions which are the basis of the full Copernican system, but scholars disagree about the date of its composition, which may have been as early as 1512.

Copernicus's reputation was considerable in the limited circle of mathematical astronomers, who urged him to publish his work in full, but it was a young man forty years junior to Copernicus who finally brought his theories into print. Georg Joachim Rheticus (1514–76) was a professor of astronomy at Wittenberg University, and in 1539 he travelled to Frauenberg to discover more about Copernicus's teaching for himself. With the master's consent, Rheticus published a *First Narration* (*Narratio Prima*) in 1540 summarizing Copernicus's work, though without mentioning his name. The favourable reception given to this work persuaded Copernicus to entrust a longer publication to Rheticus, although it was finally Osiander who saw *On the Revolutions of the Celestial Spheres* through the printing-press in 1543. Tradition has it that Copernicus received a copy of his great work on his death-bed: he certainly died soon afterwards, on 24 May, and was buried in the Cathedral, next to Bishop Watzelrode. Without the intervention of Rheticus, the results of his life's work might have been lost, and he would have remained the learned but obscure canon of Frauenberg.

Others quickly developed the system which Copernicus had introduced. The Great Danish observer Tycho Brahe (1546–1601) rejected the Copernican view of the arrangement of the heavens, maintaining that the sun and all other celestial bodies circled round the unmoving Earth, while at the same time the planets were also in orbit round the sun; but by his painstaking observations set new standards of accuracy which enabled Johann Kepler (1571–1630) to determine mathematically the true path of the planets in an elliptical orbit round the sun, and so to vindicate Copernicus. By the time of Galileo's great discoveries in the early seventeenth century, Man's conception of the universe had undergone a profound change: the fundamental significance of this intellectual revolution was not fully explained until the time of Newton. The rise of the inductive method of scientific enquiry is an outstanding achievement of the European mind, and while it is true that any major development in science must depend on the contributions of a series of investigators, the importance of the pioneer must not be overlooked; hence the Copernican Revolution in astronomy is justly named.

CHARLES V
(1500–1558)

CHARLES V has been described as "the last medieval Emperor", for in his lifetime he witnessed a major transformation of European government and society while he himself remained faithful to the traditions of an earlier age. But he was not a passive observer of these developments: by virtue of his unique position, Charles exercised a personal influence on events rivalled by few men in European history.

At the age of nineteen, he was King of Castile, Leon, Aragon, and the Two Sicilies, of Jerusalem, Sardinia, Corsica, the Canary Isles and the Indies, inheriting these titles from his maternal grandparents the Catholic Kings, Isabella of Castile and Ferdinand of Aragon (d. 1516). Through his paternal grandparents, Mary of Burgundy and Maximilian of Austria, he became Duke of Burgundy, Brabant, Lorraine, of Styria, Carinthia, Carniola, Count of Hapsburg, Flanders and Tyrol. He was the fortunate heir to a series of dynastic marriages amongst the ruling families of Europe, although his ancestors can hardly have anticipated such an outcome from their matrimonial intrigues. Already possessing enormous power through these hereditary lands, Charles had little difficulty in obtaining his own election as Holy Roman Emperor in succession to his grandfather Maximilian in 1519, defeating the ambitious Renaissance princes Francis I of France and Henry VIII of England. Thus Charles added at an early age the prestige but also the heavy responsibilities of the Imperial title to the government of a diverse and ultimately incompatible collection of territories, which dominated Europe in the early sixteenth century.

Charles's immediate family background was not very promising: his mother, the Spanish princess Juana, was chiefly distinguished by her melancholia, which prompted her to convey her husband's coffin with her for nine months after his death, and made her unfit to govern Castile, although she lived in seclusion at Tordesillas until 1555. She had married an Austrian Archduke, Philip the Fair, and their elder son Charles was born on 24 February, 1500, in the Prinzenhof at Ghent, the chief town of Flanders. The death of his father in 1506 and the resulting insanity of his mother confirmed Charles's ultimate right of succession to the throne of Spain, but he was brought up in Flanders under the care of his aunt the Archduchess Margaret of Austria until his sixteenth year. His education in the traditions of the Burgundian court, under his tutor Adrian of Utrecht and his governor Guillaume de Croy, lord of Chièvres, exercised a profound influence on his character and political outlook in later years.

Adrian of Utrecht was a conscientious churchman who established his reputation as a theologian and was ultimately rewarded by his election as Pope Adrian VI (1522–23) through his former pupil's influence. He developed in Charles a genuine devotion to the Roman Catholic church and a personal piety which later distinguished the Emperor from the cynicism of many contemporary rulers. This sincerity of faith was the hallmark of a spiritual Renaissance which the church in the Low Countries had experienced at the turn of the sixteenth century under the influence of the Brethren of the Common Life and their famous pupil Desiderius Erasmus (1469–1536), whose learning and fervour for the regeneration of the Church inspired great enthusiasm for moderate reform in the 1520's. Although this movement was soon swamped by the extreme demands of the Protestants, Charles did not forget the great moral responsibilities entrusted to a king, as set out for his instruction by Erasmus in his *Institution of a Christian Prince*, for the fulfilment of the Christian humanist plan for the moderate reform of the Church remained a major objective of his policy in adult life.

Chièvres was largely responsible for the political education of the young prince in the traditions of the Burgundian dynasty, of which Charles was the last representative. The court of Philip the Good and Charles the Bold had been celebrated throughout Europe as the centre of chivalry and knightly virtue, exemplified by the Order of the Golden Fleece, whose members were the greatest nobles in the land. The unreal world of the knight errant was out of place in sixteenth-century Europe, as the fate of the Imperial Knights in Germany showed, but Charles retained the best of the chivalric tradition in his character. He was a man of honour, whose mind could not comprehend the duplicity of a ruler like Francis I who broke most solemnly-given oaths; he was a man of action, fond of riding and the chase, who led his own troops into battle; he protected his subordinates and rewarded those who served him well.

Equally significant for Charles was the cosmopolitan nature of the Burgundian court: in an age of growing national rivalry, Charles maintained the tradition of a court open to men of all races, where advancement depended on loyal service alone. In adult life Charles displayed little national prejudice, but perhaps a sense of humour when he allegedly remarked: "I speak Flemish to my friends, French to the ladies, German to my horse and Spanish to God".

His election to the Imperial title was also a major formative influence in Charles V's career. The Empire was called *Roman* in emulation of the glories of the ancient world capital, and this implied that the Emperor was the chief secular authority of the whole civilized world. Most sixteenth-century rulers strongly resisted any suggestion that the Emperor's authority could be exercised directly over them, but a more shadowy claim to the moral leadership of Christendom was generally conceded. One practical result of his Imperial obligations can be seen in Charles's determination to protect Europe from the invasions of the Ottoman Turks by uniting the forces of the Christian West under his leadership, though in practice the burden largely fell on Charles alone.

The Emperor had always stood in a special relationship with the Pope ever since the Holy Roman Empire had been revived by Pope Leo III in A.D. 800: medieval writers depicted them wielding the secular and spiritual swords of Christendom respectively. The Emperor had traditionally been the secular defender of the Papacy, although the relationship had often been stormy, but Charles V took this responsibility seriously: it was one of the great ironies of history that it was his undisciplined army which sacked the Eternal City in 1527. The Imperial coronation was a symbol of the Emperor's exalted status, and Charles was crowned by Clement VII in Bologna Cathedral in February 1530, significantly the last Emperor to seek such recognition. No doubt Charles's personal inclinations made him a staunch and unwavering Catholic, but in a sense his position linked him inextricably with the Catholic Church and the Papacy.

Beyond his steadfast loyalty to the institutions and traditions which he had inherited, there were other facets of Charles's character as a young man which contemporaries noted. In appearance he was slight of build, with a pale complexion and the pronounced Hapsburg jaw, but he conducted himself with dignity and grace. He was a good horseman, and enjoyed hunting and jousting more than study in his youth: his interest in history was natural for a Burgundian prince, but in theology and mathematics his progress was not rapid. His knowledge of European languages was the product of experience rather than linguistic ability, and his ignorance of Spanish at the beginning of his reign was a considerable handicap. He was fond of good food, and enjoyed the companionship of a lively Court, including the ladies, but early in his career Charles developed a reserve in his bearing which sometimes made him appear haughty but generally commanded respect. The ability to withdraw from the pressures of public life and consider his affairs dispassionately was vital for the achievement of Charles's political ambitions.

At the outset of his career, Charles fully realized that his wide possessions, his *monarchia* as they were collectively termed, offered tremendous potential for the unity of Europe and for Charles's personal status, if only they could be welded together as an effective political unit. "Sire, God hath set you on the path towards a world monarchy", Charles was told by his grand chancellor Mercurino di Gattinara, who after the death of Chièvres in 1521 became Charles's chief minister and the leading advocate of Imperial unity until his own death in 1530.

Gattinara, a Piedmontese lawyer in origin, was an ardent Christian humanist who shared Erasmus's vision of a universal empire which would bring peace to the warring factions of Europe. This imperial dream strongly appealed to Charles and to the administrators trained in Roman law, with its emphasis on the authority of the law-giving sovereign, who had followed him from Burgundy and the Franche-Comté and now provided the imperial secretariat: it also attracted clerics, merchants and noblemen who saw great opportunities for advancement in the service of so powerful a monarch. However, the political obstacles which confronted Charles and Gattinara rendered their idealism ineffectual: proposals were made for a common currency and free trade within the empire, but in 1530 customs barriers still stood between Aragon and Castile, and after Gattinara's death imperial offices such as those of the treasurer-general and the grand chancellor were abolished, the secretariat being divided into a southern department under Francisco de los Cobos, and a northern department under Nicholas Perrenot.

It was chiefly the particularism of his various territories which prevented the unification of Charles's empire: in the Netherlands alone there were no fewer than seventeen provinces, each jealously preserving their local rights and customs. The only factor which linked this heterogeneous collection of states together was their common allegiance to Charles as ruler. Since experience had shown the purely personal nature of Charles's empire, he determined to preserve it and to maintain his hegemony in Europe by the same principle of dynastic alliances which his ancestors had so effectively followed. There was scarcely a ruling family in Europe to whom Charles was not directly related as a result of this policy: Charles's wife Isabella was Infanta of Portugal; his aunt Catherine of Aragon was the first wife of Henry VIII of England; of his sisters, Eleanor married Francis I of France, Isabella married Christian II of Denmark, Mary married Louis II of Hungary and Catherine married John III of Portugal. Charles regularly appointed members of his family to act as regents during his frequent travels: Margaret of Austria and later Mary of Hungary were Regents of the Netherlands; Charles's brother Ferdinand, who had been brought up in Spain, assumed control of the German government and the hereditary Hapsburg lands in 1522, while Charles's son Philip conscientiously obeyed his father's instructions in Spain and the Netherlands.

After 1530 it is clear that Charles's chief objective with regard to his dominions was to safeguard the ultimate succession rights of his family by strengthening the power of the House of Hapsburg in Europe. However, Charles's reign was beset with problems which threatened the very existence of his empire, and monopolized his attention for thirty years: chief amongst them were the rivalry of France, the intrigues of the nobility in Germany, the Lutheran Reformation and the Turkish invasions. The formidable combination of these difficulties put Charles's wider schemes into abeyance and finally brought about his abdication from the cares of state.

The prospect of a "universal empire" in Europe may have appealed to Erasmian reformers and Burgundian diplomats, but to successive rulers of France the reality of Hapsburg encirclement seemed to threaten the very independence of their country. Charles's chief opponent was Francis I, King of France from 1515 to 1547, an able politician who revived Valois claims to the Duchy of Milan and the Kingdom of Naples, and by his major victory at Marignano (1515) gained control over the former.

Charles's accession clearly threatened French imperialist designs in Italy, but this was not the only reason for the conflict which ensued: frontier disputes over the control of Rousillon, Cerdagne and Navarre in the Pyrenees, which Ferdinand of Aragon had annexed, and over the County of Burgundy and Lorraine, which the French had occupied within living memory, created a permanent cause of war. There was also a strong element of personal rivalry and injured pride in the conflict, for Francis could never forget his defeat in the Imperial election and his own imprisonment by Charles after Pavia, while to the Emperor, Francis was a perfidious individual who broke his most solemn oath and so far belied his title of "Most Christian King" as to make a military alliance with the Turks. Finally, Francis's fear of Hapsburg encirclement was a very real one, even if it were unfounded: on every frontier of France lay territory belonging to Charles V, from Spain to the Low Countries, and the requirements of national security demanded that the struggle should be continued by Francis's successor Henry II, even after the original protagonists were dead.

Francis first tried to stir up discord within Charles's Spanish possessions by encouraging the revolt of the *comuneros*, but Imperial forces retaliated by driving the French commander Lautrec out of Milan, while Charles launched an invasion of France herself (1522). Alarmed at the Emperor's successes, and motivated by their national longing to free Italy from foreign domination, compounded with shrewd self-interest, Florence, Venice and the Papacy encouraged the French to reoccupy Milan, but in February, 1525, Charles V's army decisively defeated Francis at Pavia and captured him. Another anti-Hapsburg coalition, the League of Cognac, was shattered when the Imperial troops mutinied for lack of pay and sacked Rome (1527), and after the failure of his attempts on Naples, Francis made peace by the Treaty of Cambrai (1529). He reaffirmed the renunciation of French claims in Italy and the Low Countries which he had first made in the Treaty of Madrid (1526), but Charles agreed in return not to press for Burgundy.

A new and dangerous factor in international politics was the defensive alliance with the Turks which Francis concluded in 1536. In 1543 the Turkish fleet wintered in Toulon harbour and attacked the coast of Italy, carrying Christian subjects off into slavery. Charles once again invaded France, but he did not have the resources nor the inclination to push the war to a military solution. His Lutheran subjects in Germany were becoming an even greater threat to his empire, for they formed a state within a state, making a military alliance with France in 1552. In the renewed struggle, Italy was no longer the major theatre of war: the focus had shifted northwards to the border between France and the Empire, a change which proved highly significant for later European conflicts. In many respects the Hapsburg-Valois rivalry was a singularly wasteful and purposeless conflict, but underlying the struggle was the issue of the hegemony of Europe and the future of Charles V's empire: the war was only concluded by the treaty of Cateau-Cambrésis (1559), after Charles had permanently divided his territories between his brother and his son.

Although French intrigue was a constant threat to the security of his empire, it was in Germany that Charles suffered the most serious setback to his imperial ambitions. In an age when feelings of national identity were rapidly developing, and monarchs in Western Europe were centralizing government and strengthening royal authority, Charles saw the necessity of making his Imperial title politically effective and creating greater unity within the Holy Roman Empire if it was to survive. The machinery of central government was weak, however, so Charles was obliged to rely on the co-operation of the great and lesser princes, the imperial knights and the imperial cities who effectively controlled their localities. The German princes had always strongly resisted any attempt to increase the authority of the Emperor, and Charles's schemes of reform were sabotaged by princely opposition: a Council of Regency was established in 1521 but soon lapsed, and from 1531 Charles was obliged to delegate the everyday responsibilities of government in Germany to his brother Ferdinand. While the Emperor was distracted by his commitments elsewhere, the princes consolidated their position, both legally and socially, until they had gained virtual independence from Imperial authority.

The social unrest of the 1520's in Germany strengthened the power of the great princes at the expense of both the knights and peasants. Led by the militant Franz von Sickingen and the poet Ulrich von Hutten, the revolt of the Imperial Knights in 1523 was a final protest against the encroaching power of the princes and the central government. Then in 1525 the peasants of Swabia broke out in revolt, driven by declining social and economic status and urged on by apocalyptic preachers, but they were brutally crushed at Frankenhausen by the Protestant Philip of Hesse and the Catholic

Duke George of Saxony. Even the religious divisions which further weakened Germany could be turned to princely advantage, for the demand for religious freedom might provide a cover for political and economic self-interest: Luther deliberately appealed to the princes for mutual support in his *Address to the Christian Nobility of the German Nation*.

Charles could not afford to alienate the great princes while the Empire was threatened by the French in Italy and the Turks in Hungary. In return for continued military and financial assistance, he was prepared to temporize over fundamental issues like a religious or constitutional settlement, and his prolonged absence from Germany (1532–41) created a power vacuum which the princes willingly filled. In the 1540's Charles again took the initiative, but his crushing defeat of the Protestant princes at Mühlberg (1547) alarmed all the princes of the Empire: fearing the imposition of Imperial absolutism, many allied with Henry II of France, with such effect that by 1553 Charles was forced to flee across the mountains in winter to his Austrian possessions. The Peace of Augsburg (1555) was an unequivocal admission of failure, for the power of the princes to determine the religion of their territories was a major concession on the part of the Emperor. Although in theory Charles passed on full authority over the Holy Roman Empire with the Imperial title to his brother Ferdinand in 1556, in practice he was the last Emperor who had a real opportunity to create a strong centralized state in Germany, for later Emperors concentrated increasingly on building up the hereditary Hapsburg lands in Austria, until their title became a mere formality.

The existing difficulties of containing the political ambitions of the German princes were intensified by the development of the Protestant Reformation at the beginning of Charles's reign. In 1520 Martin Luther declared, "God has given us a young and noble ruler to reign over us and has thereby awakened our hearts once more to hope", but his hope that Charles would support the Protestant cause was dashed at the Council of Worms (1521). Having heard Luther's refusal to retract any of his opinions, the twenty-one year old Emperor reminded the assembled German princes:

"Ye know that I am born of the most Christian Emperors of the noble German Nation, of the Catholic Kings of Spain, the Arch-dukes of Austria, the Dukes of Burgundy, who were all to the death true sons of the Roman Church, defenders of the Catholic Faith, of the sacred customs, decrees and uses of its worship, who have bequeathed all this to me as my heritage . . . from now on I regard him [Luther] as a notorious heretic, and hope that you all, as good Christians, will not be wanting in your duty".

However, not all the princes followed Charles's advice to shun Luther as a heretic; the Elector John of Saxony, the Landgrave Philip of Hesse, the Duke of Brunswick and the prince of Anhalt protected the expanding evangelical faith in the League of Torgau (1525) while Charles was preoccupied with the French in Italy. Another Imperial Council or Diet at Speyer (1526) deferred the question of reform until a General Council of the Church should be called: meanwhile each prince "is to live, govern and bear himself as he hopes and trusts to answer to God and his Imperial Majesty". Charles was in a stronger position by 1529 and at the Second Diet of Speyer cancelled all concessions to the Lutherans by "his imperial and absolute authority", but this evoked the celebrated *Protestation* which gave the Protestants their name and symbolized the permanent nature of the division within the Church. After the failure of attempts at doctrinal reconciliation at Augsburg (1530) the Protestant princes and cities formed the Schmalkaldic League for mutual defence if any should be attacked "on account of the Word of God".

Ironically enough, Charles sympathized with the demand for reform, provided that the Church maintained her unity. He hoped that a General Council of the Church would promote reform, reconcile the factions and decide doctrinal issues, but successive Popes regarded any scheme resulting in the diminution of their own authority with suspicion: Charles was faced with prevarication and deviousness by the very pontiffs whose position he sought to uphold. In 1532 in face of the Turkish threat Charles effectively granted toleration to the Protestants by the Truce of Nuremberg until a General Council was called, but the first session of the Council of Trent, convened by Paul III in 1545, came too late to heal the schism in the Church, although it did much to revitalize the Catholic faith.

While the Papacy hesitated, the Lutheran princes continued to secularize church lands and extended their faith into the Rhineland. By 1544 Charles was prepared to sacrifice all his other commitments to deal with the Schmalkaldic League, which had developed into an independent power in European politics. He defeated

Philip of Hesse and John Frederick of Saxony at Mühlberg (1547) and tried to enforce acceptance of the Augsberg Interim (1548) which made slight concessions to the Lutherans. But Protestantism was too firmly established to yield to intermittent force, and in 1555 Charles reluctantly recognized the right of each prince to determine the religion of his state (*cuius regio eius religio*) by the Peace of Augsburg. Further secularization of church property was forbidden, but no account was taken of the growing Calvinist movement, which made future difficulties inevitable. Charles's failure to maintain the religious unity of the Empire was perhaps the most deeply felt disappointment of his career.

The ultimate threat to Charles's empire came from the Turkish advance against western Europe in the sixteenth century. The Ottoman Turks already controlled the southern Balkans, and were inspired by the fierce missionary zeal of Islam to expand their empire further by military conquest. The whole state system was geared to war by formidable warrior sultans like Selim the Terrible (1512–20), whose conquest of Mesopotamia, Syria, Egypt and Arabia was a prelude to an assault on Europe, led by Suleiman the Magnificent (1520–66), who captured Belgrade in his first campaign (1521) and threatened to occupy all the central European plain. Charles thus became Emperor at the moment when Europe faced the most serious challenge to its security for many centuries. He was keenly aware of his responsibility to defend Christendom from the infidel Turk, but the powers of Europe were divided and self-interested in attitude.

In 1526 the Turks advanced against the Kingdom of Hungary; at the battle of Mohács its young King, Louis II, and many of the Hungarian nobility were killed, and Budapest the capital fell, creating an immediate threat to the Hapsburg Austrian lands. Preoccupied by the challenge to his authority in Italy, Charles entrusted the defence of the Empire to his brother Ferdinand, but he aggravated the situation by laying claim to the vacant throne of Hungary, although the nobles preferred John Zapolyai, voivode of Transylvania, as their ruler. Zapolyai appealed to Suleiman for support, so in 1529 the Turkish army invaded the Balkans for a third time and laid siege to Vienna, the Austrian capital, for eighteen days. This campaign in fact marked the limit of Turkish success on land in Europe in the sixteenth century, for the great distances which the Sultan's army had to march shortened the campaigning seasons and exposed their lines of communication, but Charles was shaken by their power: in 1531 he wrote to his wife:

> "The Turkish menace has increased so much that I have even considered coming to an agreement with the Lutherans in order to prevent worse disaster."

However, it was the Mediterranean rather than the Balkans which proved to be the weak point of Christian Europe in resisting the Turkish advance in the 1530's, largely as a result of the intervention of the Barbary pirates of North Africa as allies of the Sultan. In 1529 their renowned leader Khaireddin Barbarossa seized Algiers, which he turned into a formidable base for attacking Western shipping. Charles handed over Malta and Tripoli to the Knights of St. John, who had been dislodged from Rhodes in 1522, but Barbarossa retaliated by occupying Tunis, controlling the Straits of Sicily. In the true tradition of the Crusaders, Charles himself led an expedition which successfully recaptured Tunis in 1535, but only three years later Turkish naval domination of the Mediterranean was confirmed by Barbarossa's victory at Prevasa over the Genoese admiral Andrea Doria and the allied Christian fleet: it was left to Charles's sons Philip II of Spain and Don John of Austria to redress the balance of power by the defence of Malta in 1565 and the victory of Lepanto in 1571.

Charles's last years were overshadowed by the magnitude of the problems which had confronted him all his life: in Germany his imperial policy had met with total defeat, Henry II of France continued the unremitting struggle against Hapsburg domination until Charles himself was dead, while at sea Dragut emerged as a worthy successor to Barbarossa and seized Tripoli in 1551. Even the Netherlands, loyal for so long to their Burgundian overlords, but now burdened with heavy taxation and frequent war with France, showed the first signs of that discontent which finally erupted in full-scale revolt under Charles's successor. But Charles's successes should not be underestimated: the Turks had been checked on land, Imperial authority in Italy had been consolidated, Spain had been raised to the dominant position in European affairs which she was to maintain for a century, enriched by the wealth of the New World. It was fitting that Charles should choose to retire to Spain, the most loyal of all his possessions, after his formal abdication of responsibility in favour of his brother Ferdinand in Germany and his son Philip in the Netherlands and Spain in 1555. At Yuste in

Estremadura a royal residence was constructed adjoining the Hieronymite monastery, and this inscription may still be seen there:

"To this holy house Charles the Fifth withdrew to end his life that he had wholly devoted to the defence of the Faith and the maintenance of justice, the most Christian Emperor, invincible, King of Spain. He died on 21 September 1558."

Charles V must be esteemed as a man of principle, who adhered faithfully to his beliefs even when it might have been politically advantageous to abandon them. Although excessive zeal could be held responsible for some of the darker events of history, Charles's idealism is representative of the best European tradition, in which the exercise of political power is seen as the means to a higher purpose and not as an end in itself. Many of Charles's contemporaries, and later European rulers, have preferred the precepts of Machiavelli, that the authority of the state should be untrammelled by any moral considerations, but Charles believed that his authority conferred responsibilities as well as privileges, and sought to respect the rights of his subjects and to further their interests.

Above all else, in an age when national prejudice and racial intolerance were dividing Europe into the armed camps of nation-states, Charles's career transcended these barriers of race and land, and although his schemes for drawing the regions of his Empire into a closer union were not fulfilled, he bequeathed the vision of a united Europe to future generations.

JOHN CALVIN

(1509–1564)

FEW movements have affected European society as profoundly as the Protestant Reformation of the sixteenth century, and in its development John Calvin stands out as undisputed leader after the pioneering work of Martin Luther.

John Calvin was born at Noyon in the French province of Picardy on 10 July, 1509. His father was a successful church lawyer, whose influence with the Chapter of Noyon Cathedral enabled him to obtain a benefice to pay for his son's education, and at the age of fourteen Calvin was sent to begin his studies at the University of Paris. At the Collège de la Marche he was taught Latin by Mathurin Cordier, a humanist scholar and educational reformer, and learned to express his thoughts in the elegant yet forceful style which greatly impressed his contemporaries. At the Collège de Montaigu he studied philosophy and theology, and took his M.A. degree in 1528; the University of Paris was renowned throughout Europe for its faculty of theology (the Sorbonne), although it was rather obscurantist by this time; but Calvin was a willing student, and laid the foundations of his formidable knowledge of Christian theology, and learned the art of rational debate.

His father now decided that the study of law would be more profitable than further preparation for the priesthood, and in 1528 Calvin moved to the University of Orleans, the best centre for legal studies in France, where he studied under Pierre de l'Etoile. But Orleans was also a leading centre of humanism, the study of classical literature and thought which was sweeping sixteenth-century Europe, and Calvin developed a keen interest in linguistic and classical scholarship. He took his doctor's degree in law at Orleans, having completed his legal education at Bourges, but the death of his father in May, 1531, left him free to follow his own inclinations, and he returned to Paris to immerse himself in literary studies. In 1532 he published his first book, an edition of Seneca's *De Clementia*, and he might have become a distinguished classical scholar but for an unexpected development—his sudden experience of a spiritual conversion some time in 1533.

Remarkably little is known of the circumstances surrounding this crucial event. In the Preface to his edition of the Psalms, Calvin later wrote: "By a sudden conversion, God subdued and reduced to docility my soul, which was more hardened against such things than one would expect of my youthful years." It is most likely that this experience was the outcome of Calvin's study of the Bible and early Christian writers, but it was much more than a change in intellectual outlook, for the retiring scholar was transformed into a fearless propagandist for the Reformed faith.

The extent of Calvin's spiritual transformation could be seen when he supported his friend Nicholas Cop, Rector of the University of Paris, who delivered a highly controversial official address on All Saints Day, 1533, in which he defended not only humanist but also Lutheran ideas. In the ensuing outcry Calvin hastily left Paris, seeking refuge from the authorities at Basle in Switzerland, and here he published the first edition of his famous *Institutes of the Christian Religion* in 1536. He intended to settle permanently in Strasbourg, where a colony of French Protestant emigrés was already established, but on his way he passed through the Swiss city of Geneva: he planned to stay for a single night, but he was destined to undertake his life's work there.

Geneva was undergoing a political and religious revolution when Calvin arrived. With the aid of the Protestant city of Berne, the citizens had expelled the representative of the local prince, the Duke of Savoy, and the Catholic bishop, and inspired by an ardent French reformer, William Farel, had abolished the Catholic mass (1535). But although Farel was an eloquent preacher he was a poor organizer, and the situation at Geneva was confused. Calvin was extremely reluctant to accept Farel's invitation to stay, but Farel's insistence won the day: "You make an excuse of your studies", he told Calvin, "but if you refuse to give yourself with us to this work of the Lord, God will curse you, for you are seeking yourself rather than Christ." Calvin accepted a position as reader in Holy Scripture, and in 1537 he submitted articles to the City Council for the reorganization of the Church on distinctively Protestant lines. However a number of Genevan citizens opposed this plan which would impose effective church discipline over the laity, and when Calvin and Farel refused to accept the liturgy of Berne in their churches in 1538 they were dismissed.

Calvin made for his original destination, Strasbourg: a free city within the Holy Roman Empire, it had accepted the reforms of Martin Bucer, and during his short stay in the city (1538–41) Calvin learned a great deal. He was influenced directly in his ideas more by Bucer than by any other reformer: the doctrine of predestination centred on the saving grace of Christ, the four-fold ministry of the Church and the use of congregational psalm-singing were all part of Bucer's scheme at Strasbourg before Calvin developed and refined them. But Calvin was never purely derivative in his thinking, and while he was minister of the French congregation at Strasbourg he wrote some of his most important works, including his own translation of the *Institutes* into French (1541). Like Luther, Calvin appreciated the need to appeal to his fellow-countrymen in the vernacular, and his masterly style remained a major influence on French prose for a century.

In the summer of 1540 Calvin was asked to return to Geneva by the city council, and although reluctant—"I would submit to death a thousand times rather than to that Cross on which I had daily to suffer a thousand deaths"—he returned to the turbulent city which was to be his second home until his death. This time his scheme of church government, the *Ordonnances Ecclésiastiques*, was accepted in modified form by the city council (1541), and the Ordinances later served as a model wherever Calvinism was established. Calvin's legal training and administrative ability were clearly revealed in his plans for rescuing the Ministry of the Church from the depressed state into which it had fallen: the authority and very purpose of the priesthood had been challenged by anti-clerical extremists, and part of Calvin's great achievement was to revitalize the concept of the Christian ministry by returning to the model of the early Christian church. He envisaged a four-fold scriptural ministry, the orders being the pastors, teachers, deacons and elders.

The "Venerable Company of Pastors" were the ordained ministers of the Church, whose function was to preach the word of God, and to administer the sacraments. Calvin placed great emphasis on regular preaching from Biblical texts, and the pastors met every week to study the Scriptures together; in each parish church three sermons were given during the week, and three on Sundays. Young people were catechized by the pastor, and were not admitted to communion before they had been properly instructed and had professed their faith. Calvin wanted a monthly celebration of the eucharist, but he had to concede that it would be held only quarterly: thus the preaching of the Word replaced the mass as the central act of worship in the Calvinist system.

The services in Geneva were based on Calvin's own revision of the liturgy of Strasbourg, published in his *Forme des prières et chants ecclésiastiques*, in which any practices remotely tainted with Popery were omitted. However, Calvin was willing to accept ceremonial in the church rather more than his ardent followers: he wanted to retain the laying-on of hands at ordination, and he encouraged the congregational singing of metrical versions of the Psalms, although he would not allow any instrumental accompaniment.

The teachers (or doctors) and the deacons were chosen by the pastors, but they were not ordained. As befitted a man of international repute for his learning, Calvin attached great importance to the education of the young, and the order of teachers was responsible for instructing them "in sound doctrine in order that the purity of the Gospel may not be corrupted by ignorance of false opinions". Calvin attracted many great scholars to Geneva, and regularly gave lectures himself to large audiences on Biblical and theological subjects, but his educational policy did not mature until the Geneva Academy was established in 1559 under the Rectorship of Theodore Beza. The Academy was based on Sturm's famous Academy at Strasbourg, where Calvin had lectured during his exile, and it included a secondary school and a university establishment, which quickly won an international reputation: by the time of Calvin's death in 1564 the Academy contained 1,200 pupils, many of whom were destined to spread Calvin's teaching throughout Europe.

The deacons fulfilled the social and charitable responsibilities of the Christian community, and levied a rate on householders to maintain a high standard of welfare, caring for the sick, elderly, orphans and the infirm. Begging was strictly prohibited, however, since it encouraged the poor to rely on charity rather than their own work.

The twelve elders formed the most distinctive order of Calvin's scheme. They were all laymen, appointed by the city council after consultation with the pastors, and their function was to exercise moral oversight over the whole city of Geneva, serving with the Venerable Company of Pastors in the Consistory. This was an independent Church court, which met every week under the presidency of one of the four syndics, or city magistrates, to investigate any breach of the strict code of morality which Calvin struggled to impose. The court exhorted wrongdoers to repentance, and Calvin fearlessly condemned the vices of the great: he demanded the imprisonment of all the guests at a wedding-feast who had dared to dance, even though they included one of the syndics! Lewd songs were banned, and superstitions corrected: one woman tried to cure her husband by hanging round his neck a walnut containing a spider, another knelt at her husband's grave and said "*Requiescat in Pace*" and others copied her.

Most offenders who were summoned before the Consistory admitted their guilt and promised repentance: in fact the court could not impose sentence of imprisonment or excommunicate without the consent of the magistrates, but the civil authorities were often prepared to impose severe penalties: adulterers were liable to suffer the death penalty if detected, and a young man was beheaded for striking his parents. On the other hand, many cases were incredibly trivial: after a long argument, the wearing of slashed breeches by the city militia was solemnly forbidden.

In some respects Calvin personally wished to see the moral code enforced even more rigorously than the citizens of Geneva would permit: he wanted harlots to be more severely punished, and campaigned to have the public baths closed as they were a place of assignation. Calvin's master-stroke was to persuade the city council in 1546 to close all the taverns and replace them with evangelical cafés, where bawdy entertainment and light conversation were banned, a Bible had to be available for consultation and no meal could be served until grace had been said. This interesting experiment met with little success, and popular pressure resulted in the reopening of the taverns.

Because of the wide-ranging activities of the Consistory, Calvin's Geneva has seemed to many observers to be the classic example of a theocratic state, in which the secular authority was subordinate to the Church. In fact, Calvin intended that his Reformed Church should have an organization quite distinct from the secular state; this view was in complete contrast with the Zwinglian system of the "godly magistrate" where the secular authorities also exercised spiritual responsibilities, a practice commonly adopted in Swiss Protestant towns like Berne, Lucerne and Zurich. In Geneva the city council carefully preserved their constitutional position against clerical domination by adding this note to the *Ordonnances Ecclésiastiques*:

"These arrangements do not mean that the pastors have any civil jurisdiction, nor that the authority of the Consistory interferes in any way with the authority of the magistrates and the secular courts."

The civil authorities maintained their right to reject any candidate for the ministry whom they considered unsuitable, they took the final decision in theological disputes, and they alone chose the elders, though in deference to Calvin's wishes this was done with the pastors present during the last few years of his life. The crucial issue was the right of the Consistory to excommunicate offenders: this was a serious matter, because it meant social and economic ruin for the offender's family as well as spiritual damnation, and not until 1555 did the civil powers fully concede this power to the church court.

Although there can be no doubt that in the last decade of his life (1555–64) Calvin was the most distinguished and influential inhabitant of Geneva, he encountered considerable hostility and opposition during most of his stay, and the popular image of the Protestant patriarch ruling his chosen city with an iron rod is largely the product of imagination. In fact, Calvin's own situation was rather curious: he did not even become a citizen of Geneva until 1559, and he never held any civic office; he was no more than the leading pastor of the community. There was a substantial body of critics of Calvin's policies amongst the oligarchy of merchants and patrician families who ruled Geneva, and these so-called "Libertines" created a formidable opposition during Calvin's first stay (1536–38). After his triumphant return in 1541, criticism of Calvin's methods was muted, but by 1546 the Libertines became vocal again, and persisted in their opposition until Calvin's final triumph in 1555 when the leaders went into exile. Public opinion in Geneva had swung in favour of Calvin, partly as the result of the inflow of Protestant refugees from France, Germany, the Low Countries and the British Isles, many of whom became citizens during this period.

Calvin's force of character was such that nobody could remain indifferent towards him for long: men were either his disciples or his enemies. We know a good deal about his temperament and his prejudices from his contemporaries, although Calvin was personally reticent, seeing himself as the agent of Almighty God, whose duty it was to subjugate his personality to his divine mission. In his manner of life he was austere, living quietly in a house on the Rue des Chanoines which the city council allotted him on his return in 1541: he maintained a simple household on the stipend given to the ministers of Geneva, with some further income from his teaching. In 1540 he had married a widow, Idelette de Bure, and they lived happily together until his wife's death in 1549, but he did not marry again. He was not the kind of man to attract close personal friends, and it could be said of the citizens of Geneva, as Calvin said of those of Berne: "They have always feared me more than they loved me." His relations with the Genevans were rarely smooth: he called them a "perverse and ill-natured people", and at heart he was always a Frenchman.

For all the determination with which he pursued his religious objectives, Calvin was never an extroverted character, and shrank inwardly from the violent encounters with which his career as a reformer was marked: it was the supreme irony of his career that so often he was obliged to enter the arena of public controversy. In public affairs some of the less attractive aspects of his character were revealed: he could be harsh and dogmatic, and condemned the harmless pleasures of others, like dancing, through personal prejudice. Perhaps his greatest moral fault was the vindictiveness with which he sometimes pursued his opponents: when Pierre Ameaux called the reformer a wicked man, a preacher of false doctrine and an ambitious intriguer it was not sufficient that he later retracted these statements and apologized—at Calvin's insistence, he was obliged to tour the city, clad in a penitential shirt and carrying a torch to implore the forgiveness of God for criticizing His ministers.

Like many great men who are utterly convinced of the justice of their cause, Calvin readily equated his own inclinations with the will of the Divine, which naturally infuriated his opponents. But Calvin at least avoided the temptations towards self-aggrandizement which such a belief often brings, and the problems of his age demanded a reformer with a strong and determined will.

Calvin's determination to preserve the truth at any price was clearly shown in the prosecution of Servetus for heresy. Michael Servetus (?1511–1553) was a Spanish physician whose intellectual ability had enabled him to make a number of significant medical discoveries, but in the realm of theology his speculations proved highly dangerous, for he denied the validity of the central Christian doctrine in his book *On the Errors of the Trinity* (1531). He managed to avoid persecution by adopting a pseudonym, and continued on his dangerous course by attacking Calvin's *Institutes* and amplifying his heretical views in *The Restitution of Christianity*, published at Vienne in 1553. On being detected he escaped and turned up at Geneva, where he was promptly recognized and arrested: he was charged with subverting religion and society by teaching false doctrine, and the pastors of Geneva took a leading part in the prosecution. As the trial was progressing, the opinions of the Reformed Churches of Switzerland were sought, and they unanimously declared that Servetus's doctrines were heretical and dangerous. He was condemned to death by the court, and burned at the stake outside Geneva in October, 1553. Although no doubt his cruel death fitted the intolerant spirit of the age, it also casts a shadow over Calvin's Geneva.

The last years of his life brought Calvin recognition and recompense for his years of dedication to the Protestant cause. In his fiftieth year the Geneva Academy, which was to send missionaries throughout Europe in his name, was formally inaugurated in his presence, while later the same year the city magistrates demonstrated their complete reconciliation with the fiery reformer by offering him the freedom of the city on Christmas Day. He remained intellectually vigorous and alert until the year of his death in 1564, writing polemical pamphlets on the eucharist and advising on the structure of the Huguenot church in France. Ill-health frequently troubled him in these latter years, however; never strong in body, he had suffered frequent bouts of fever and asthma, to which were now added stone and the gout.

The overwhelming difficulties presented by the French Wars of Religion which began in 1562, and the revival of the Roman Catholic Church by the Council of Trent, which ended in 1563, renewed his fears for the future of international Protestantism when he would no longer be its leader. In February, 1564, he preached his last sermon, and took farewell of his associates in the ministry in April. He died at his home on 27 May, 1564, in the arms of Theodore Beza, and was buried the next day without pomp "in the common cemetery called *Plain Palais*": at his own request his grave was unmarked, and its site cannot be positively identified today.

The personal failings which Calvin sometimes revealed during his lifetime should not however conceal the greatness of his achievement, which has far outlived the man. His European reputation rests firmly on the foundation of his thought, and Calvin himself

was undoubtedly most happy in his work as a scholar: his exact
and penetrating mind marked him out as one of the foremost
intellectuals of his day. Although he had been trained in several
disciplines while young, particularly in classical literature and
law, theology was his exclusive interest after his conversion, and
all his earlier experience was brought to bear on this study. The
Institutes of the Christian Religion provide a systematic exposition of
Protestant theology for which Calvin was justly celebrated in his
own lifetime: first published in Latin in 1536, the *Institutes* were
translated into French (1541) and expanded three-fold by the
definitive edition of eighty chapters in 1559, but the fundamental
ideas were present in the earliest version, written when Calvin was
only in his twenties.

In many respects Calvin's theology differed little from Luther,
and he was strongly influenced by Bucer and Melanchthon, but
whereas Luther's writings were penetrating but diffuse, Calvin's
work was systematic and precise, and it provided European
Protestants with a complete vindication of their beliefs. The key to
Calvin's thought was his study of the Bible, and his humanist
education in Latin, Greek and Hebrew enabled him to become the
greatest Biblical and patristic scholar in Europe for a generation.
He published commentaries on all the books of the New Testament except Revelation, and on many books of the Old Testament,
including his great *Commentary on the Psalms*. He was no funda-
mentalist, and appreciated the need for textual criticism, although
Castellio was expelled from Geneva because he described the Song
of Solomon as a love-song. Calvin helped to establish a new tradition
by regarding the Old Testament as having equal validity with the
New Testament as a revelation of God working through history and
his chosen people, a highly significant concept for the Calvinist.

Calvin's theology is resolutely theocentric, and he places great
emphasis on the sovereignty of God—"set in a profound and
impenetrable mystery, the Divine Will dominates all persons and
things". This was the God of the Old Testament, an awe-inspiring
judge who demands the highest standards from erring humanity,
to whom later Calvinists frequently appealed; but recent theological
research has shown that Calvin himself also stressed the redemptive
work of Christ, and that divine mercy as well as heavenly retribution is central to his theology.

However, Calvin's name is particularly associated with the
doctrine of predestination. The idea that God has predestined some

men to eternal salvation (the elect) while others are doomed to damnation (the reprobate) was certainly not new, but Calvin revitalized this doctrine, linking it with God's special providence towards mankind. He wrote:

"We assert that by an eternal and immutable counsel God hath once for all determined both whom He would admit to salvation and whom He would admit to destruction. We confirm that this counsel, as concerns the elect, is founded on His gratuitous merit totally irrespective of human merit."

Calvin was more concerned with the nature of God than theories about predestination, and although he did develop his ideas in later editions of the Institutes, it was later theologians who expanded and refined predestination until it seemed to be the centre of the Calvinist creed. In times of persecution, the certainty of God's special favour gave Calvinists a boundless confidence and great moral fervour, and in the second half of the sixteenth century it was the Calvinists who led the attack on behalf of international Protestantism.

Calvin had always intended that his ideas should be put into practice beyond the walls of Geneva, and during his lifetime many Protestant refugees who came to the city were trained as missionaries to continue the work of reform. The first country to be strongly affected was France, where Admiral Coligny estimated that there were 2,150 Huguenot (French Protestant) congregations as early as 1561. Nearly all traces of earlier Lutheran-inspired reform had been crushed in France by the persecution of Francis I which had driven Calvin into exile, and Catholicism remained strong in many areas. Calvinism was however readily accepted by many of the lesser aristocracy, the merchants and provincial town-dwellers, and in some regions like Navarre and Languedoc by the nobles and the peasantry: sometimes religious grievances provided an excuse for regional separatism and aristocratic ambition to flourish. Huguenot congregations met secretly in private houses and outside towns: after 1559 a series of weak rulers made persecution less effective, and a complex national network of Calvinist churches was quickly evolved, the first National Synod being held in Paris in 1559. Between 1559–61 at least 120 ministers were sent into France from Geneva, and a strong Catholic reaction against this Huguenot expansion resulted in the so-called French Wars of Religion, which ended when Henry IV, himself a former Huguenot, granted French Protestants liberty of worship in the Edict of Nantes.

Calvinism also had a considerable influence in the British Isles. During the persecutions of Mary Tudor and Mary of Guise, many English and Scottish Protestants took refuge in Geneva, which John Knox described as "the most perfect school of Christ that ever was in earth since the days of the apostles". When these reformers returned, Queen Elizabeth of England strove to moderate their influence on the national church settlement which she had undertaken, but the Puritan faction who were mostly Calvinist-inspired remained vociferous and influential for most of her reign. During the seventeenth century English Puritans emigrated to the New World to practise their religious beliefs in freedom, and perhaps in New England Calvin's own principles were most faithfully observed after the reformer's death; thus Calvin's ideas have influenced the development not only of Europe, but of the New World as well. In Scotland the Lords of the Congregation and John Knox were irresistible, and the Presbyterian Kirk modelled on Calvinist lines remains the established church of Scotland to this day.

Elsewhere in Europe Calvinism also struck roots in the sixteenth and seventeenth centuries. In the Dutch Republic it helped to strengthen the resistance of the seven provinces against Catholic Spain, and in the Rhineland it began to advance at the expense of Lutheranism: even in Poland and Eastern Europe Calvinism had appeared by 1600. The rapid spread of Calvinism to many parts of Europe and its subsequent influence have prompted a number of questions amongst historians: did Calvinism encourage political revolution and the development of more equal forms of government, and did it stimulate the growth of western capitalism?

Calvin himself was certainly no political revolutionary: he dedicated the *Institutes* to King Francis I of France, and he strongly supported the city authorities of Geneva in their civil capacity. However, Calvinism has been linked in the European political tradition both with egalitarianism and revolution, and while the system of Church government which Calvin adopted in Geneva depended little on popular democracy, nevertheless there was an inherent tendency for power to move upwards from the people rather than downwards from a bishop or prince. In terms of a political revolution, Calvin was very cautious indeed, and shared the fear of social chaos which beset his contemporaries. However, medieval theologians had maintained that rebellion against an unjust ruler could in some circumstances be justified, and Calvin also admitted that while no individual subject had the moral right to rebel, certain "intermediate authorities" might lead the people against an unjust ruler who forced his subjects to act against their consciences. These "intermediate authorities" might include the Estates or Parlements of France, or even the great nobles: in 1561 Calvin wrote to Coligny that resistance to the King of France would be legitimate if it were approved by the Princes of the Blood. Calvin's successors were less cautious in their attitude, and by the end of the century some like Buchanan in Scotland were justifying tyrannicide.

Many historians have attributed considerable importance to Calvin's pronouncements on economic matters in their interpretation of the growth of the European economy in the sixteenth and seventeenth centuries. The Marxist historian would maintain that Protestant ethics produced conditions suitable for the growth of a capitalist system, and this theory is supported by the fact that Protestantism, and especially Calvinism, often appealed to merchants and tradesmen of Western Europe. However, the validity of this simple correlation between the bourgeoisie and Calvinism has been challenged with success in recent years, and a closer examination of Calvin's writings may also bring into question their revolutionary impact on the ethics of capitalism.

Medieval moralists had condemned the taking of interest on capital as usury, and Luther repeated the view that since money was unproductive, it should not multiply itself without work. In reply to questions about usury, Calvin made a distinction in the case of a productive loan, which was made to increase a borrower's capital, and so stimulate production, but he wisely refused to specify a permissible fixed rate of interest. However, Calvin regarded all human wealth as a God-given gift, to be used for the good of the community: instead of encouraging private enterprise and individualism in economic activity, Calvin was simply restating a traditional Christian view.

It is an indication of Calvin's immense influence on European society both as a thinker and a leader of men that such historical theories have been developed. The church which he organized revitalized the Protestant movement and took Europe by storm during his lifetime: his ideas have continued to provide a rich element in the cultural heritage of the West to the present day.

MICHEL DE MONTAIGNE

(1533–1592)

"This book was written in good faith, Reader. It warns you, from the outset, that in it I have set myself no goal but a domestic and private one. I have had no thought of serving you or my own glory. I want to be seen here in my simple natural ordinary fashion, without straining or artifice; for it is myself I portray. Thus, reader, I am myself the subject of my book; you would be unreasonable to spend your leisure on so frivolous and vain a subject. So Farewell."

THIS was Montaigne's preface to his *Essays*, about two-thirds of which appeared in 1580, the last part some years later. The world did not accept this advice; and in fact there are very few books which, century after century, have been more often read, not merely by *literati* and thinkers, but by ordinary people, young or old, who reflect at times on themselves, on other people, and on the problems of life. Montaigne was the most truthful of writers and what interests him, in himself and in other matters, is *the facts*, not emotions which confuse facts, nor the rationalizations which falsify them, nor religious and philosophical theories which are concerned with explaining them. Because he is, above all, a truthful observer he is, when writing about himself, contradictory. "Do I contradict myself? said Walt Whitman. Very well, I contradict myself."

Montaigne, long before Proust, with whom he has many similarities, perceived that the human being is not one, but many people; that he is, in Montaigne's phrase, *ondoyant et divers*—that life brings out constantly changing aspects of the same man. Then, though he is the subject of his book, he was so little egocentric that the *Essays* are a prolonged monologue about every aspect of life from sex to politics. European literature abounds in confessions and private revelations. Many writers, under cover of writing about nature or a political situation, or a foreign country are really only writing about themselves, their consciences, scruples, or emotions. Montaigne is the plumb opposite. His observations of himself are a pretext for writing about life in general. So, in a sense, Montaigne's preface to his *Essays* is deceptive. There is the world in his book. All the same, its originality and uniqueness—only Pepys wrote about himself so frankly and with as complete an absence of self-justification—is that it is a self-portrait, without pretensions or explanations.

Michel de Montaigne was born in 1533, in the chateau of Montaigne, some thirty miles east of Bordeaux, in the Perigord. His great-grandfather, one of a family of prosperous Bordeaux merchants, had bought the chateau and lands and, with them, a title of nobility. His father Pierre Eyquem de Montaigne served the King of France, as befitted a noble, and was a lawyer belonging to the Parliament of Bordeaux, as was his son. An enlightened, and eccentric man was Pierre Eyquem, whom Montaigne describes as "the best father that ever was". Full of the Renaissance passion for the New Learning—which was largely the rediscovery of classical literature—his house was open to scholars and theologians; the only fault Montaigne ever found with his father was that he valued learned men above their deserts and himself too low.

Pierre Eyquem was determined that his eldest son should grow up with a well-balanced nature. Until the age of six he was to be awakened from sleep by music; and until that age, no-one, not even his nurse or his mother, was allowed to speak anything but Latin to him. This was not altogether unpractical because Latin was very largely the language of the law, and this early knowledge served Michel well when he went to the College de Guyenne in Bordeaux, then one of the best schools in Europe. Montaigne's father also gave him as god-parents two peasants from the village near the chateau, with whose families Michel mixed, so that he would be familiar with men of every kind.

Both father and son lived at a period of strife between Catholics and Protestants. Tolerance was so strongly believed in by Pierre Eyquem that, though a devout Catholic himself, he allowed two of his five children to become Protestants. With all his generosity and benevolence, Pierre Eyquem increased the family fortune, a thing that his son did not do, remaining content that he had not allowed it to decrease. Montaigne did not like household cares. He also dropped the patronym Eyquem. It is curious that throughout his *Essays*, there is no mention whatever of his mother, Antoinette de Louppes, who was of Spanish-Jewish descent. It is possible to see a certain snobbery in these two facts. On the other hand, the absence of reference to his mother may have been due to politeness, for she outlived him.

Montaigne so cherished his father that he usually dressed like him in black and white. He notes of himself "a vain and stupid pride", and he liked aristocratic carelessness in his dress, such as a cloak worn like a scarf, the hood over one shoulder. He was short and thickset, as was his father, with a build well suited to horseback and a face not fat but full. He describes himself as having "clear soft eyes, a nose of moderate form, suitably small ears and mouth, a smooth thick chestnut-beard, fresh colour and a pleasant facial expression". But, he adds, all these do not make a small man handsome. His father excelled at all sports and exercises; not so Montaigne. Nor was he any good at playing musical instruments, or at dancing, or at managing dogs, falcons or horses. His father enjoyed exceptionally good-health and died fairly suddenly of a kidney stone at the age of sixty-six. Montaigne described his own health as vigorous, blithe and ebullient, which kindled in his mind "some of the lustiest, even the most extravagant, enthusiasms".

He was always distracted by his thoughts and in church, even with a good preacher, "where I have seen even ladies keep their eyes steady, I have never succeeded in keeping some parts of me from always wandering; even though I may be seated there, I am hardly settled there". The same illness that struck his father, struck Montaigne at the age of forty-five, though in a less severe form. It was in large part to help cure his bladder that Montaigne— who liked travelling in any case—undertook his long journey to Italy, whose baths and spas were famous, at the age of forty-seven. The result of this was his surprisingly little known Travel Diary that contains the most vivid descriptions of contemporary life.

On his father's death, Montaigne served as a judge belonging to the Bordeaux Parlement, a legal body of great importance. He visited Paris and the royal court frequently and became the friend both of Charles IX and Henry III and, particularly, of Henry of Navarre, who had become King of France, though not master of Paris, before Montaigne died in 1591. In the almost continuous disturbances of the time, Montaigne belonged to the King's party which was trying to keep the peace between the Protestants and the extreme Catholics known as the League, headed by the Duke of Guise.

During this period of his life Montaigne, already appreciated as a wise and prudent councillor and, in public affairs, a man of discretion, had a great number of love affairs of which he writes with considerable frankness. He considered sex as a normal part of life and in no sense anything to be ashamed of. Most men, he noted, are not ashamed of undertaking treacherous policies, of lending themselves to murder and assassination—he was horror-struck by the massacre of St Bartholomew—or of being avaricious, or of legally robbing the poor or their relations; but they feel themselves to be good honest men because they do not go to the brothel or do not indulge in extra-marital relationships. Montaigne found sexual desire natural and never fought against it. Writing about his old age, in an essay called "On some verses of Virgil", which is devoted to the subject of love, he says regretfully: "I have no other passion to keep me in breath. What avarice, ambition, quarrels, lawsuits do for others who, like me, have no assigned occupation, love would do more agreeably. It would restore to me vigilance, sobriety, grace, care for any person . . . it would take me back to some wise studies . . . would divert me from a thousand troublesome bad thoughts." But he adds: "We demand more when we bring less . . . knowing ourselves in what we are, we have become less bold and more distrustful; nothing can assure us of being loved, knowing our condition and theirs . . . I am ashamed to find myself amid this green and ardent youth."

Montaigne's great friend at this time, M. Etienne de la Boétie, who was of a more serious nature and happily married, used to warn his friend against his amorous tendencies, though not censoriously. Their friendship, based on a common love of the classics and a common attitude to the troubled and violent times, was one of the great events of Montaigne's life. Twenty years or so after de la Boétie's early death, whilst Montaigne was in Italy, he still recalls his friend with anguish. When la Boétie died, Montaigne redoubled his amorous ardours, seeking to drown his sense of loss. After two years, he married a girl of a noble family of Bordeaux, Françoise de la Chassaigne. Of this marriage he writes: "Of my own choice, I would have avoided marrying Wisdom herself, if she had wanted me. But say what we will, the custom and practice of ordinary life bears us along. Most of my actions are conducted by example, not by choice."

The essay "On the Verses of Virgil" (none of the titles of Montaigne's essays give the reader much idea of what the subject is about) is one of the essays which in the pious sixteenth century led Montaigne, though much read and secretly admired, to be considered a licentious writer, essentially unsound. This essay certainly contains, in its long rambling structure with the frequent examples from Latin and Greek literature, more true observations about man and woman and the nature of love than any other work that the writer has knowledge of. It is in no way pathological—Montaigne was essentially the natural man. It is not a treatise on how to make love—that was not Montaigne's line either. It is far more down to earth, concerned more with animal passion than Stendhal's admirable *De l'Amour*. One wonders whether some of Montaigne's admirers in the Victorian age skipped through this chapter or deliberately ignored it. Montaigne states that his approach to women was "impertinently genital", but also that that he loved, admired and sought to guide most of his mistresses. Women, he points out, have by their constitution a greater sexual capacity and aptitude for love and sex than men. Men condemn them for their desires and their infidelities; yet society, from their childhood, brings them up as objects of desire. "They can allege, as we can, the inclination to variety and novelty common to us both, and allege, secondly, as we cannot, that they buy a cat in a bag." Montaigne suggests that Plato was right in advocating that men and women should be invited without discrimination into all studies, functions, warlike and peaceful occupations. "I say", he writes—at the end of the "Verses of Virgil"—"that males and females are cast in the same mould, and, except for education and custom, the difference is not great. . . . It is much easier to accuse one sex than to excuse the other. It is the old saying—the pot calls the kettle black".

Montaigne's attitude to marriage is all the more astonishing in view of his liberal one to women in general. In a good marriage, Montaigne held, love is dangerous and what he calls "the wantonness of ordinary sexual love"—of which he clearly did not disapprove—is an offence against the dignity of marriage. He advises married people to make love infrequently and to take their time when they do. He married when he was thirty-six and she a beautiful and, by all accounts, lusty girl of twenty. La Rochefoucauld said "there are no delicious marriages", and this was what Françoise must have thought. His wife bore him six children only one of whom, a girl Léonor, lived beyond three months. In addition Montaigne, who was in many ways so reasonable and tolerant, hated the idea of managing a household, was always at loggerheads over domestic details with his wife and his mother, who lived with them. One of the reasons why travel was a delight was that it removed him from domestic duties. The *Essays* were written not in his chateau, but in a bare room in a tower attached to the main building, where he sometimes slept and even heard mass; so the picture of a peaceful sage, working in his "panelled library", drawn by Andrew Lang, is nonsense. In spite of all this it is evident that Montaigne's marriage, from guarded references to his wife in the *Essays*, worked fairly well, and man and wife maintained affection and respect for each other.

After his retirement from the Bordeaux Parlement in 1571 he continued to be active at times among the moderate Catholic or King's party in his region, and was fetched back from his travels in Italy in 1581 to become Mayor of Bordeaux. But Montaigne never put more than one foot in politics, and his experiences as courtier and diplomat are not much reflected in the *Essays* which, after all, are not memoirs. He was reluctant to undertake being Mayor of Bordeaux, the second city of France and one which was constantly threatened by Protestants and by the League. The office of Mayor of a great city with a charter was something quite different from what it is in modern times. Montaigne was the direct representative of the King.

His first two years of office were comparatively uneventful, and he was elected Mayor for the second term. The King's heir, the Duke of Anjou, had died and Henry of Navarre was now the heir to the throne. Navarre was also, with the bulk of the Pro-testant army and his principal supporters such as the Prince de Condé, much in the neighbourhood: indeed, he slept for two nights at Montaigne's chateau. His accession was at once resisted by the Catholic League, who also menaced the royal power in Bordeaux. However, Montaigne kept both the Protestants and Catholics at bay. On his retirement, he did not attend the meeting of the *jurats* of Bordeaux who were formally to elect his successor. The plague raged in the city and Montaigne felt it would have been mock heroics to go into the city at that time.

In holding public office Montaigne believed in avoiding extreme involvement, stating that it was the enemy of efficiency. "People adore everything that is on their side; as for me, I do not even excuse many of the things I see on mine." Reflecting on being Mayor of Bordeaux, he wrote: "I have been able to take part in public office without departing one nail's breadth from myself . . . we should play our parts bravely, but as the part of a borrowed character ... I see some who are prelates to their very liver and intestines and drag their position even into their privy ... The Mayor and Montaigne have always been two, with a very clear separation." Although Montaigne, as one of his best biographers, Mr Donald M. Frame, has pointed out, was not the most dedicated of public servants, he had shown himself vigilant, conscientious and effective.

Montaigne refused to see absolute right or virtue in anything, and certainly not in the struggles of individuals to attain power and wealth. He was not a religious man either, though he remained an adherent of the Catholic Church. He thought it was foolish to try to settle questions of belief, and wiser to live according to those of his forefathers. He served the King and his government diligently, but without servility and with the mental reserve of a man who is not hoodwinked. Christians, he considered, harmed themselves by trying to support their beliefs by reason, since religion is conceived by faith and by the inspiration of divine grace. He did not believe that man was as superior to animals as he thought himself because of human reason and imagination. He had a great passion for animals, and at his chateau was surrounded by dogs, cats, birds and other wild creatures. He considered animals as a whole more beautiful than human beings, and more intelligent than most people believed. "When I play with my cat, who knows if I am as much of a pastime to her as she to me?"

In several of his *Essays* he inveighs against the outstanding event of his period, the conquest of the New World by the Spaniards. He denounced the cruelty of the conquerors and deplored the destruction of a civilization in many ways superior to ours. He had the opportunity of examining a group of American Indians— known as "cannibals"—who had been brought to France and found them, even though they did not wear breeches, kinder and more natural than civilized Europeans. Although he did not believe—as Rousseau did in the eighteenth century—in the Noble Savage, he thought that the conquered and enslaved peoples of the New World had lived better without magistrates and laws than European nations, who are overrun with them. He saw in animals and savages more courage, charity and magnanimity than among civilized men.

Montaigne's motto was *Que Sais-je*—What do I know? The dominant characteristic of the Essays is the exposure of the folly of thinking we understand things we don't, of building intellectual systems and trying to impose them on ourselves and others. He refuses to have an aim, much less a system and, if people learn from him, he wants them to do so naturally and pleasurably—as, in fact, he writes his essays. He valued truth in human relation above all things: "We are men and hold to each other by our words." If there was any wisdom, it came from observation of oneself and other people, and from books as well. Man should reflect more on what he really valued, and Montaigne thought that a large part of man's unhappiness was that he feared to shut himself up alone in a room.

His aim was truthfully to describe all that went on, however foolish and sometimes wise, in the mind of Montaigne. In all his last and greatest essays, and particularly the two "On Vanity" and "On Experience", he points out that all other parts of nature except man appear to study themselves first and, according to their needs, limit their desires and labour. He makes the Delphic oracle say of Man: "There is not a single thing as empty and needy as you who embrace in your mind the universe; you are the investigator without knowledge, the magistrate without jurisdiction and, all in all, the fool of the farce." At the end of "On Experience", he says that man is continually trying to go outside of himself because he does not know what it is like inside. "Yet there is no use mounting on stilts, for, on stilts, we must still rely on our own legs. And on the loftiest throne in the world, we are still sitting only on our bottom." If Montaigne has a creed it is expressed in the words: "It is an absolute perfection and virtually divine to know how to enjoy our being rightly."

It is hard to think of any book that has had a more continuous and pervasive influence on European thinking than the *Essays*. From the start Montaigne's attitude to human experience appealed to the English, and later to the Anglo-Saxon world as a whole. Shakespeare, Bacon, Ben Jonson and Marlowe were all admirers, and it was said that the *Essays* was the bed-side book of Elizabethan gentlemen. In his own country, during the great age of French literature in the seventeenth century, he was attacked as an immoral and licentious writer by Pascal and others, but it was clear, from the frequency and virulence of some criticisms, that he had been much read and pondered on. The French eighteenth century considered the *Essays* as rather inelegant and gross, and he was somewhat patronizingly praised by Voltaire. But many French writers and thinkers in that century, including Diderot and

Montesquieu, admired him, the latter comparing him to Plato and saying, "In most great authors, I see a man writing; in Montaigne, a man thinking". Rousseau borrowed greatly from the *Essays* in his impassioned attack on civilization in the name of Nature.

At the time of the French Revolution, it was considered that the bones of this great revolutionary, Michel de Montaigne—his book was then on the Index—should not be dishonoured by remaining in the church in Bordeaux where they had been laid after his death. His body was disinterred, but, strangely enough, it proved to have been the wrong body. In the nineteenth century his admirers were legion—both Classics and Romantics. Flaubert, who constantly read the *Essays*, said he thought of Montaigne as his foster-father. In America, Emerson praised him, though deploring what he called "his savage indecency". Hazlitt said that such was Montaigne's range of investigation into the human condition that he had left little for his successors to achieve. In the twentieth century he has more admirers than ever, and his works have been translated and commented on by scholars in Poland, the Soviet Union, Turkey and Japan. A French writer, Jean-Jacques Revel, wrote recently that in Montaigne we learn that it is not a fault to be sleepy, to desire, to day-dream, to be lazy, to waste time, to fear death and illness. Not only is it not a fault, but these weaknesses are intimately connected with strengths and, as Freud has shown, it is an error to repudiate a part of ourselves.

Montaigne was one of the most intelligent men who have ever lived, and one of the most sceptical. Yet the positive message of the *Essays* is a moral one. The responsibility for evil, we learn from the *Essays*, begins not with wayward thoughts or inconsistency of mind, but with personal or political acts which adversely affect other people. In this, far from making a public morality impossible, he makes it possible. The revolutionaries of 1789 were probably mistaken in thinking that Montaigne would have been one of them. He would have taken neither side, nor would he have welcomed Napoleon Bonaparte as a restorer of order. He was not a politician, and he was not a progressive looking forward to a bright future. Why is it that he is to be numbered among great Europeans? Europeans have not shown themselves more humanitarian or, generally, wiser in their conduct than men of other continents; nor, as the rat race of the affluent society of today shows, more inclined to value the quality of life before material progress. Nonetheless, among the virtues of European civilization is that some of the best Europeans have realized that the world is one, that it is Man who matters, not nations, societies or ideologies.

Montaigne said that had it not been for Paris he would as soon be born a Pole as a Frenchman; and he wrote "Nature put us into the world free and unfettered, yet we imprison ourselves in certain narrow districts". In Montaigne, who never preached, the message of human brotherhood was implicit, and because men read his book for pleasure it has been more powerful than a bomb and has subtly helped to destroy bigotry and the foundations for believing that one man is superior to another because of his skin, or his skill. Montaigne's scepticism and tolerance were never made into a political credo, but this has made them the more effective and enduring an influence. Others have probed, maybe, deeper into the human condition; but no-one has looked at it with such attractive good humour and devastating detachment, and pointed out that the enemy is not the confused and passionate nature of man, but self-delusion, deceit and lies.

CERVANTES
(1547–1616)

MIGUEL DE CERVANTES SAAVEDRA, to earn world-wide and immortal fame, near the end of a long and singularly unsuccessful life, as the author of *Don Quixote*, was born in 1547: the exact date is not known (it was about 29 September). His baptism took place on 9 October in the Spanish university town of Alcalá, which was also the birthplace of Catherine of Aragon.

He was the third child of Dr Rodrigo de Cervantes, licensed for simple surgery as "a physician without Latin", and therefore in a humble position of his profession, although the doctor's father had been a lawyer of some standing. The family was descended from a line of Castilian nobility which took its surname of Cervantes from the castle of San Servando, or Cervantes, near Toledo; but the branch had declined into the lower middle class of shabby-genteel poor, and poverty was to dog Dr Rodrigo's children for the rest of their lives.

Nevertheless, although the family moved about from Alcalá to Seville and finally to Madrid, as the doctor sought better fields for his limited abilities, Cervantes seems to have obtained an education of sorts, although he is not registered in the rolls of any University. In Seville, between 1563–66, he attended the best schools and made friends who would eventually hold high offices. He was nineteen when he arrived, in 1566, in Madrid, a city which had been created capital of Spain two years earlier. Here he attended the leading academy, the Estudio. In 1568 the humanist professor Juan López de Hoyos, who had recently been appointed principal of the Estudio, was asked by the city authorities to compile a volume to commemorate the death and funeral rites of the tragic heir-apparent to the throne, Don Carlos. Contributions by his own pupils were included, and outstanding amongst them were those by Miguel—"our dear and beloved disciple", as Hoyos termed him.

When Queen Isabella died, early in 1569, Miguel was selected to write the Estudio's own formal elegy, and won high praise for his verses. Thus at the age of twenty-one Cervantes made his first appearance as a writer, and was fired with a literary urge which never left him. But social and financial circumstances were not favourable to his becoming a professional author, and Cervantes did not improve his prospects by directing his ambition towards poetry and the stage, for neither of which he was to prove to have special gifts.

He was attracted to the theatre in his youth by seeing the principal actor of the time, Lope de Rueda. But de Rueda belonged to a strolling-player type of troupe which played not in theatres (there were none then in Spain) but in public squares, performing pastorals and interludes of dubious quality. The great Spanish age of the theatre had not begun, and Cervantes's style was outmoded almost before the ink was dry on the comedies he cared so deeply about (he published them in 1615, after the success of *Don Quixote*, but sold only a few, with small success, to theatre managements in early life). The great dramatist Lope de Vega, fifteen years Cervantes's junior, was to sweep de Rueda's pastorals and interludes and whole theatre style into oblivion, and Cervantes was by then too old a dog to learn new theatre tricks.

The thought of trying to earn a living as a writer may have occurred to Cervantes in youth, but fortune disposed otherwise, In December, 1569, he was in Rome, acting as chamberlain in the household of the young prelate-diplomat Giulio de Aquaviva, soon to be made a Cardinal and recently on a mission to Madrid. It has been conjectured that he obtained this rather surprising post through the influence of Hoyos, although a document of September, 1569, ordering the arrest of a "Myguel de Zerbantes", in hiding after wounding an adversary in the Court precincts, has been taken by some to refer to Cervantes and explain his flight abroad. To draw a sword anywhere near royalty was an offence throughout Europe, bringing severe penalty.

After a year of service with Aquaviva Cervantes apparently felt the call to arms and adventure, and left his post to enlist in Diego de Urbina's company of infantry, in Rome. Whatever the cause, it was not antipathy to Aquaviva, a cultivated man to whom Cervantes later paid tribute in the Preface to his pastoral novel, *La Galatea*. It is probable the young Cervantes was fired, like many, by the need to protect Christendom from a new threat from the Turks, whose Sultan Selem II had taken Cyprus from the Venetians (Shakespeare was to touch on this aspect of history in

Othello). A new twenty-three year old leader, Don John of Austria—
the natural son of the Emperor Charles V and half-brother of
Philip II—had also shown the personal magnetism that pulled
many young men to his service. When, as Generalissimo of the
Holy League, Don John fought and won the decisive sea battle of
Lepanto, Cervantes took part in the battle on the galley *Marquesa*
with such initial gallantry (he was suffering from fever and had
been ordered below deck) that he was given the command of twelve
men. He received three serious gunshot wounds, one crippling
permanently his left hand, and was under the surgeon for three
months. Notwithstanding his injury, he was then drafted to
Naples as a soldier of the first class with extra pay, Don John having
personally recommended him for a commission.

He spent four further years as an active soldier. His younger
brother Rodrigo had joined him in the army and fought with him
at Corfu and Navarino; but in Naples Cervantes combined
garrison duty with a study of the language, so that he was able to
read Petrarch, Boccaccio, Tasso and Ariosto in the original. All
these things were to prove grist to the mill of the writer, as was the
next, disastrous, period of his unusually adventurous life.

In 1575 he was granted leave, after the fall of Tunis, to return to
Spain and apply for a captain's commission. Carrying letters of
recommendation from Don John and the Viceroy, he boarded the
galley *Sol* with his brother on 20 September. The *Sol* became
separated from the flotilla bound for Spain and six days later was
captured by three Turkish galleys. The Spanish prisoners were
taken to Algiers, with the prospect of a hard fate. Slavery and
ransoming were features of Algerian life and the Turkish ruler or
"Dey", Hassan Aga, was not noted for lack of cruelty. It would
appear, however, that Cervantes attracted him, both by his
courage and charm. Across the years the indomitable captive
engineered at least three doomed escape bids with fellow prisoners
(once getting as far as the coast where a ship was waiting by
arrangement). In each case, under threat of torture, he refused to
implicate the others but took full responsibility for the planning;
yet he virtually escaped punishment. Much of this history was to
appear in the Captive's Tale in *Don Quixote*, but Cervantes's
unselfish heroism was freely vouched for by other prisoners who
shared his captivity.

After five years he and his brother were ransomed through the
agency of two Trinitarian friars. Cervantes's family, with much

sacrifice, had been able to raise only 200 of the 500 escudos demanded for his ransom, and as Hassan Aga, who was due to leave Algiers at the termination of his office, refused this, Cervantes actually found himself among the slaves on his ship, about to set sail for Constantinople. Just in time, Spanish merchants in the town made up the full sum of his ransom and at last, in 1580, Cervantes sailed for Spain, reaching Madrid *via* Valencia on 24 October.

Cervantes was now aged thirty-three. The young Don John of Austria had died, aged only thirty-one, in 1578, so that his letter recommending Cervantes's qualities of leadership had become useless. In any case, as in times before and since, the war hero had ceased to be of interest in civilian life. From now on Cervantes lived from hand to mouth, although in May, 1581, he earned a welcome 100 ducados carrying despatches from Tamar, Portugal (where King Philip II currently was) to Omar.

We do not hear of him again until 1584, when following a brief affair with a minor Madrid actress, Ana de Rojas—which produced an illegitimate daughter, Isabel, to whom Cervantes remained devoted and who eventually lived with him and his sisters—he courted the nineteen-year-old Catalina de Palacios Salazar y Vosmediano, of Esquivias. She seems to have been very much his opposite in character—as down-to-earth and home-loving as he was idealistic and restless; but she loved him, and she was rich, so he married her, in December, 1584. The union was not a successful one. Resentful of his wife's attempts to tie him down to her estate, Cervantes absented himself more and more frequently, until at length he was away altogether.

In January, 1584, Cervantes's first substantial work, a pastoral novel in prose and verse called *La Galatea*, was submitted to the censorship. It was published in his birth town, Alcalá, in 1585 and earned a modest *succès d'estime*, though little money, for Cervantes was glad to accept a modest sum for the work. Like so much of the literary work of the time (including that being produced in Elizabethan England) it was much influenced by Virgil. Its plot was also full of the currently popular duels, kidnappings, voyages and assassinations, and perhaps for this reason the work sold through three editions. Nevertheless it had a slightly tongue-in-the-cheek quality, perhaps heralding Cervantes's satiric bent which came to full flower in *Don Quixote*. In fact he was to achieve, in *Don Quixote*, the humour of self-quotation, in the episode where the parish priest and barber go through Don Quixote's library during his illness, and find a copy of "the *Galatea* of Miguel de Cervantes".

"That Cervantes has been a great friend of mine for many years," says the priest, "and I know him to be more versed in misfortune than verse. His book has some good inventions, but it sets out to do something and achieves nothing. We must wait for the second part he promises us . . ."

The second part of *La Galatea* was never written, but in March, 1585, the stage-struck Cervantes achieved a dearer object when he sold two plays. They have not survived, and the other comedies written over the years by the ever-hopeful author only went to fill a precious trunk, from which he would never be parted. He was compelled to scrape a living by less stimulating means. In 1587 he became a Treasury official at Seville, requisitioning wheat, barley and oil for the fleet that was to carry out the projected Spanish invasion of England. After the defeat of the Armada in 1588 he was employed in other forms of Treasury work, which at length included tax collecting. The pay was poor and over the years Cervantes was several times in trouble with the authorities over the accuracy of his accounts. In 1597 a banker to whom he had entrusted public money, to be paid into the Treasury in Madrid, went bankrupt and his bill was dishonoured. Although this was not Cervantes's fault it was his responsibility, and as he was unable to make up the full sum from the bankrupt's estate he was imprisoned for about twelve weeks. It was not the only time—his character seems to have been Micawber-like—but in spite of his early release it lost him his government employment.

From now on he led a bohemian life, particularly in Seville, where he mixed as an amiable outsider among the drifting and criminal fraternity of the city. Upon this he drew much for his subsequent works, in particular for the story of *Rinconete y Cortadillo* in the twelve *Novelas Ejemplares* published later. These "cautionary tales" used not only the characters of the Spanish underworld but its "double-talk" or jargon, which Cervantes came to know well. Its obvious English parallel is Gay's *Beggar's Opera*. He lived with two widowed sisters, a niece and his own illegitimate daughter Isabel for much of this time and later.

In 1591 he published a short drama in verse, called *La Casa de Los Celos* (*The House of Jealousy*); in 1595 he won three silver spoons

in a verse competition held by the Dominicans of Saragossa; and
in 1596 he published a satirical sonnet against the Duke of Medina
Sidonia, very much the butt of Spanish wit ever since his disastrous
command of the Armada. This time the unhappy Duke, immediately after the sacking of Cadiz by the Earl of Essex, made a belated
entry into the city, "scaring the populace at least" as Cervantes
sardonically put it. The elaborate ceremonies on the death of
Philip II in 1598 brought another lightly satirical sonnet by
Cervantes: irony of a political kind was apparently countenanced
in Spain, for in another piece Cervantes, on the subject of the
State's well-known empty coffers, remarked drily that his late
Majesty doubtless invested all his treasure in Heaven.

Cervantes was now over fifty, ceaselessly writing, almost always
unpublished, and one would have thought just one more tattered
remnant of a failed author, sinking into obscurity and death. When
he began *El Ingenioso Hidalgo Don Quixote de la Mancha* is uncertain.
It could not have been much later than 1600, and it has often been
said that he began it during his time in prison. In 1603 and 1604
he was living in Valladolid, hanging about the fringes of the
Court of Philip III and putting the finishing touches to Part I of
this great picaresque novel. By August, 1604, the coming work
was already talked about, for Lope de Vega was writing in a
letter of 4 August: "As for poets ... this is a good season for
them ... None is so bad as Cervantes, and nobody is sufficiently
foolish to praise Don Quixote." The publisher, de Robles, had in
fact applied for a licence (*privilegio*) for the book which was granted
in September. The first part was published in Madrid early in
January, 1605.

Cervantes, as usual, sold the work for only a small sum and
reaped no reward but fame; but that at least, despite Lope de
Vega's prophecy, was instantaneous. The literary failure—
"elderly, shabby, obscure, disreputable"—had become a lion.
Later, in Madrid (where the Court, on public supplication, returned in 1606, with the Cervantes ménage in tow), Cervantes was
even elected to the Academia Selvaje.

Lope de Vega was president of this literary society, and he and
Cervantes at last met at one of its evening functions. De Vega by
now had expressed more admiration for Cervantes, who had
at least one advantage over him as a writer, being a much-travelled
man with a knowledge of foreign countries and customs, whereas
de Vega never left the shores of Spain.

Yet its capturing of the essential quality of Spanish life (much as Chaucer's pilgrims, travelling down the dusty roads of England, caught the essence and variety of English character and life in the fourteenth century) was to be one of the most highly-praised elements in *Don Quixote*. By chance, Cervantes had hit upon a theme which was to sweep and enchant the world: a theme of failure sustained by natural nobility, something which began as a satire of the more absurd chivalric romances and developed, as D. B. Wyndham Lewis has written, "into an epitome of the human comedy". It was also a study, long before our time (which has also been obsessed by the theme) of the nature of truth: that razor-edge between reality and fantasy on which Don Quixote moves, a crackpot whose sense of justice sends him tilting at windmills and slaying wineskins under the impression that they are giants. It is one of Cervantes's remarkable feats that Alonso Quixado (or Quesada—the author is engagingly not sure which), surnamed "the Good", although he plunges into absurdity—a scarecrow who sees himself as knight errant—never loses the affection of his readers.

The device of using his shrewd peasant servant as his foil ends in a curious psychological development that binds the episodic adventures together. For Sancho Panza's matter-of-fact scepticism, as the tale proceeds, undergoes a curious process of fluctuation, so that at the end of Part I we find him telling his wife Teresa, in all seriousness, about the governorship promised him by his master. The two characters so deliberately contrasted, react on each other; each episode becomes later a source of memory and conversation, so that in Part II, delayed for ten years, the novel grows in stature until the point where farce becomes tragi-comedy. "The man who ruins himself and others by his romantic and generous illusions and by his over-confidence in the goodness of human nature," as Gerald Brenan has commented in his *Literature of the Spanish People*, returns in the end to "the empty state of sanity". When Don Quixote's lunacy leaves him he has nothing to sustain him but death. Salvador de Madariaga, in *Don Quixote: an Introductory Essay in Psychology* (1934), saw it as the tragedy of "the believing man, passing from the wealth of total conviction to the bankruptcy of utter scepticism". With this some more orthodox Catholic commentators have naturally disagreed.

The theme of Cervantes, Wyndham Lewis has pointed out, is that life is treacherous, hard, cruel and unpredictable. But despair is a sin, and, though Lewis does not add this, there are escape routes through the imagination. For Cervantes the route was the novel; for Don Quixote the transformation of the world about him into the chivalric fantasies of the lunatic. But both were battered by experience, and became a part of the picaresque scene of Spanish vagabond life, and the novel's richness of social fabric came from this. In the end, Cervantes's disastrously unsuccessful and bohemian existence provided the material for a masterpiece that immortalized him.

It would not have done this had his mind not been of a type which not only assimilates but psychologically and philosophically transforms with an innate wisdom. His reading in Italy, his unending process of self-education, contributed to a genius that grew out of a vast capacity to absorb the sights and sounds of humanity and supplement observation with detached but humorous comment. Cervantes's social comment is not political; it is simply drawn out of the hardships and low company into which life had thrust him, and which failed to quench his indestructible optimism of the knight he invented. It is not for nothing that Cervantes wrote, with a flash of intuition into the nature of his genius, "Don Quixote was made for me, and I for him. His to act and mine to record. We two alone are one. . . ."

Nevertheless, Cervantes did not get down at once to the task of recording that second set of adventures for which the world was clamouring. The dramatic sense of *Don Quixote*—its sense of comedy climax which, like the tumultuous end of Act II of Wagner's *The Mastersingers*, is based on chaotic explosions of quarrelling, screaming and fighting humanity—only confirmed Cervantes in his rooted conviction that he was a born dramatist and poet. Perhaps, too, the concentration on the novel had temporarily sapped him and he genuinely needed a rest from it. His output was diverse. In *La Española Inglesa* (1605), there were unexpected and even charming glimpses of England's Queen Elizabeth I (in May that year the Earl of Nottingham was in Valladolid to ratify a peace treaty), and a satire in verse, *Viaje del Parnaso*, based on an Italian original, contained an engaging comment on the poet's poverty, well known to Cervantes:

Timbreo: Wrap your cloak round you.
Poet: Sir, you cannot have noticed I have no cloak.

Shakespeare's Don Armado, the "fantastical Spaniard", in *Love's*

Labour's Lost (written a few years before *Don Quixote*, although commentators have occasionally erroneously suggested that the character must have been influenced by Cervantes), admitted his poverty with shamefaced dignity with the words "The naked truth of it is, I have no shirt". There is no evidence that the plays of Cervantes's greatest contemporary were known in Spain, but one inevitably wonders if the Italian source was common.

The *Novelas Ejemplares*, published in 1612, were dedicated to Cervantes's first real patron, Conde de Lemos, and have often been admired: there were six editions before Cervantes's death, and Goethe commended them warmly to Schiller. But the treasured trunkful of rejected plays, published at last in November, 1615, brought Cervantes little praise at the time or later, although a few of the comedies have had isolated admirers and Schlegel, among others, highly praised *La Numancia*, an heroic drama in classic style on Scipio Africanus. The satiric sketches known as the *Entremeses* have, however, earned the epithet "brilliant" from some critics. One of them, *The Show of Marvels*, is about charlatans exploiting the credulity of country people, and contains a nice fancy involving the presentation of "multicoloured descendants of the original rats of Noah's Ark". Ben Jonson's Volpone, masquerading as the quack fair doctor, would have fitted without difficulty into this scene.

At last, in December, 1615, Robles was able to publish the long-awaited Part II of *Don Quixote*. The first part had been widely pirated and plagiarized in the ten years since its appearance, but Cervantes's pen was given a final push by the publication in July, 1614, of a false "Second Part of the Ingenious Gentleman Don Quixote de la Mancha", written by one Avellaneda (probably a pseudonym) and prefaced with an insulting reference to Cervantes. Its reign was short-lived, for Cervantes's own Second Part was immediately hailed as an improvement even on the first, and it consolidated its author's world reputation. In the book's final total of nearly seven hundred characters, it has been remarked that not a single one is wholly bad-natured, not even the professional bandit Ginés de Pasamonte, with his buoyant literary pretensions (de Pasamonte is one of only two non-fiction characters in the work). It is a reflection of Cervantes's own tolerant charm that this is so.

Much ink has been spilled on the question as to whether Cervantes's territory as a Treasury official covered La Mancha. He certainly showed intimate knowledge of the whole arid area, and at Argamasilla (Don Quixote's village) it is still maintained that Cervantes served there one of his brief terms of imprisonment. The thought adds piquancy to his famous opening line: "In a certain village of La Mancha, the name of which I have no desire to recall. . . ."

Cervantes spent the last seven years of his life in Madrid. His brother Rodrigo had been killed in action many years before, and his sister Magdalena also died: otherwise his life did not greatly change, although his circumstances (in spite of absence of income) eased a little at the end, due, it would seem from one of his letters, to the generosity of his patron Lemos. He knew he was dying for some time, but worked until four days before his death. This was on 23 April, 1616—the same date as the death of Shakespeare, his younger contemporary, allowing for a ten days' difference in the Spanish and British calendars (England had failed to adopt the Gregorian reformed calendar along with the rest of Europe). His burial place is unknown. He left behind *Pérsiles y Sigismunda*, a huge, rambling romance and fantasy, which went through six editions up to 1630 and thereafter disappeared from print like most of his work apart from *Don Quixote*.

Even in his lifetime Cervantes's fame had spread abroad. Francisco Torres, Spain's censor of printed books under the Cardinal Archbishop of Toledo, called in February, 1615, on the French Special Envoy in Madrid and mentioned the licensing of *Don Quixote*:

"They questioned me eagerly on his age, profession and situation. I was obliged to inform them that he was old, a soldier, a gentleman and poor . . .

'What! A man like this? Has Spain not enriched him? Is he not on the Civil List?' was the horrified reaction.

Following this up, another gentleman remarked with some acuteness: 'If he is forced to write by necessity, pray Heaven he never finds himself well off! His staying poor enriches the entire world'."

The enrichment is through a world literature and art which have continued to draw inspiration from Cervantes's immortal knight. Perhaps the most famous example among novels is *The Pickwick Papers*: the master-servant relationship and growing bond between Don Quixote and Sancho Panza was Dickens's acknowledged model in the creation of Mr Pickwick and Sam Weller. George

Eliot's adaptation of country proverbs has been described as almost as skilful as Cervantes's use of the rich fund of Spanish proverbial wisdom in the dialogue of Sancho Panza. Fielding's *Jonathan Wild* is a rogues' gallery with a similar sense of irony, and Smollett and Scott also consciously adapted Cervantes's style. Scott also derived the Whitefriars scenes of *The Fortunes of Nigel* directly from *Rinconete y Cortadillo*.

Even earlier, the Jacobean dramatists Fletcher, Massinger and others had plundered the *Novelas Ejemplares* for the stage: England was the first country to publish a translation of *Don Quixote*, and its influence was lasting. Byron declared Cervantes and Le Sage his favourite writers, and in *Don Juan* called *Don Quixote* a "real Epic". On the charge of scoffing "at human power and virtue and all that" his response was:

> I say no more than has been said in Dante's
> Verse, and by Solomon and by Cervantes.

Coleridge thought *Don Quixote* should be read through not once or twice, but regularly. Macaulay proclaimed it the finest novel in the world.

In France, it was the favourite book of Henri IV (Henry of Navarre), who read Part I in the original in 1608 (Spanish was a regular language at the French Court), and thereafter addressed the young Charlotte de Montmorency, in his love letters, as "Dulcinée", after the highly idealized "Lady Dulcinea" of Don Quixote's imagination. In Germany, in the eighteenth-century romantic revival, Christoph Martin Wieland (1733–1813), whose *Oberon* influenced Byron, wrote a satirical novel modelled on Cervantes (*Don Sylvio von Rosalva*, 1764); and an Essay on Cervantes (comparing Nietzche with Don Quixote) was among the works of Thomas Mann.

In art Don Quixote has remained a perennial theme, from Goya to Daumier and Doré. Films (Chaliapin played the Don in one of them with George Robey as Sancho Panza), operas, ballets and musical plays have constantly used the story, and in 1956 Ingmar Bergman, in one of his greatest films, *The Seventh Seal*, created a knight and his squire returning from the Crusades, in a more serious Quixote-Panza image. It has been said that no hero of romance, not even Hamlet, has been more microscopically examined. In the critical works of the most famous world commentators the Don and his author have sometimes become inextricably confused, and the book is reinterpreted, as *Hamlet* is reinterpreted, in the light of each new era and generation.

It has been translated into more than fifty languages and into English alone some eight or nine times, and is certain to be many more times, as each new age finds some reflection of itself in a work which originated nearly four hundred years ago. The first English translation was by Shelton within three years of the publication of Part I (i.e. 1608), and in almost as short a time Don Quixote and Sancha Panza were figuring in a fiesta in far-off Peru. Few books have spanned the world so instantaneously, with so much effect on the author's fame, and so little on his pocket.

WILLIAM SHAKESPEARE
(1564–1616)

WILLIAM SHAKESPEARE, by world-wide consent the greatest of all dramatic poets, was born at Stratford-on-Avon in Warwickshire, England, towards the end of April, 1564. As he was baptized on the 26th of April, and died on the 23rd of the same month in 1616, it has become customary to regard 23rd April, which is also St George's Day, as his birthday: in any case the association of the Spring and the countryside seems appropriate for a poet whose initial inspiration was lyrical, and whose work to the end of his life was to reflect the lasting impressions of a childhood never far from English rural surroundings. The teeming plant life of the Stratford meadows invaded his verse irrespective of geography, and can be traced right through his plays from the "Wood near Athens" of *A Midsummer Night's Dream* to the mythical island of *The Tempest*: it was a groundwork of the poet on which the later sophistications of London life close to the Court, and the darker impress of tragedy, were built, enlarging without destroying the base. In this he could be said to be a harbinger of the great line of English lyric poets, such as Keats, Shelley and Wordsworth, a breed practically non-existent in the seventeenth and early eighteenth-century, whose versifiers regarded Nature with a cold eye.

He was, as well, a unique creator of psychology, tragedy and comedy in the theatre. Until Marlowe's day the height of English drama had been such crude comedies as *Gammer Gurton's Needle*, and the primitive tragedies and histories Shakespeare himself was to revivify.

The immense scope of Shakespeare's genius, which seems in his plays to encompass, at various periods, all aspects of the human psyche and a whole range of the history of men and nations, is as in so many cases of supreme talent inexplicable in terms of heredity or background. He was of humble stock, the son of John Shakespeare, a respected glove-maker and dealer in corn and timber who could not write his name but progressed from Alderman to be High Bailiff of Stratford in 1568. His mother, Mary Arden, inherited a small estate from her father, a well-to-do farmer. William, the third son, appears to have attended the local grammar school, where he acquired a basis, but certainly not an erudite knowledge, of Latin and Greek, to which some French and Italian were added. This later gave rise to Ben Jonson's celebrated gibe at Shakespeare's "small Latin and less Greek", but in fact the lack of too rigid a classical education allowed Shakespeare's genius to flow unrestricted by the erudition that militated, in the end, against Jonson's wider penetration as a dramatist. Shakespeare's scholarship was of the kind that "soaks up knowledge like a sponge", transforming its essence into a microcosm of humanity, politics and the arts.

Although surprisingly little is known of his personal life, certain key movements can be traced. From 1578 his father's financial affairs caused concern and the boy was taken from school, to be apprenticed, it is most widely conjectured, to a butcher or an attorney. The latter would certainly explain the many legal references in his plays, and it has some support in allusions of Shakespeare's contemporary, the playwright Nashe. His first encounter with the "theatre" can only be guessed at. In 1575 Queen Elizabeth I's favourite, Robert Dudley, Earl of Leicester, promoted lavish masques to entertain Elizabeth at nearby Kenilworth, and the eleven-year-old Shakespeare may well have attended with other local children, and experienced for the first time the magnetism of theatrical entertainment. Oberon's reference to the "mermaid on a dolphin's back" in *A Midsummer Night's Dream* is said to apply to the Queen and these Kenilworth revels.

On 28 November, 1582, a bond previous to marriage was made between Shakespeare and Anne Hathaway, daughter of a substantial yeoman of Shottery, and eight years Shakespeare's senior.[1] The marriage followed later. As their daughter Susanna was baptized on 26 May, 1583, it may have been in the nature of a shotgun wedding, but there is no indication that the youthful bridegroom, then only eighteen, seriously regretted the alliance or tried to evade responsibilities. Twins, Hamnet (who died young) and Judith, were born in 1585, and although very soon Shakespeare left Stratford and was next heard of among the actors in London, he returned periodically to his family and home town and eventually retired and died there.

[1]Though even her identity is open to doubt; one Anne or Agnes Whateley has been favoured by some scholars as the true wife of the poet.

Shakespeare's first biographer, Nicholas Rowe, writing over a century later, referred to deer-stealing in the park of Sir Thomas Lucy as a contributory cause of his leaving, but there is no record of the source of this story. It has also been suggested that he joined Lord Leicester's players during their known visit to Stratford in 1587. Whatever happened, the opportunities which opened up after he left Stratford were rich for the development and practice of Shakespeare's genius. He was soon a valued young actor in the Lord Chamberlain's company, which was much favoured by royalty from 1594 onwards, and simultaneously he was proving of immense service on the literary side.

It was an age in which the theatre had suddenly become brilliantly articulate: playwrights like John Lyly, with his courtly comedies, Robert Greene, and above all the mercurial and enigmatic sceptic, Christopher Marlowe, of the "mighty line", had established a repertoire of actable plays and Shakespeare learnt from all of them, particularly Marlowe. It was Greene's reference in 1592, the year of his death, to the "upstart crow, beautiful with our feathers, that with his *Tygers heart wrapt in a player's hide* supposes he is as well able to bumbast out a blanke verse as the best of you", that first pinpointed Shakespeare's active literary work in the theatre, as a toucher-up of earlier plays. The italicized words are a parody of the line "Oh, tiger's heart wrapt in a woman's hide" from the third part of *King Henry VI*, an old play on which Shakespeare had already worked some of his magic.

The three parts of *Henry VI* (of which the first seems to bear little evidence of his hand) were probably the first of the many earlier plays on which Shakespeare, in the manner of the time, was put to work; and already Parts II and III show the unmistakable hallmark of his genius for character and the dramatic vitalizing of history. Marlowe with his *Tamburlaine the Great* and *Edward II* had already set the model, and Shakespeare's *Richard II*, the tragedy of the anti-heroic king, was soon to show much influence of Marlowe's Edward. It was a time highly sensitive to the historic past, growing partly out of a consciousness of the Elizabethans' own recent defeat of the Spanish Armada and the greatness of the reign of a Queen already over thirty years on the throne, and not yet quite listing into the decline of old age.

History was a constant subject in the theatre, and with its corollary themes of pride flawed by ambition it was to remain a dramatic fascination for Shakespeare, moving from the scintillating, almost tongue-in-the-cheek sardonic villainies of *Richard III*, through the artistic sensibilities and tragically misplaced belief in the divinity of kings of *Richard II*, to the over-reaching, murderous clutch at a throne of *Macbeth*: the study of a trusted officer who, once tempted into crime, finds that blood can only beget blood.

Beginning as a revivifier of other men's plays, Shakespeare was to turn to the histories of Plutarch (recently translated by North) and Holinshed with a dramatic instinct heightened by practice, enriching and moulding character, analyzing the responsibilities of power, and in the end shaping tragedy into new reflections of the human condition. His King Lear, beginning in overweening senile pride, is not crushed by the elements but transformed by suffering, coming out of the storm broken physically but, even through the aura of madness, with a new appreciation of social injustice, of the "poor, naked wretches" who passed unnoticed before his eyes as a King. In the Roman plays Caesar becomes the Nemesis of his assassins, the clash of temperament being between the assassins themselves, Brutus and Cassius, as well as the new "rulers of the world", Mark Antony and Octavius. Antony, the great man slave to his passions, and defeated by them, is the subject of a further, mature study in *Antony and Cleopatra*.

None of this was a steady, inexorable development, for Shakespeare was not only artist but artisan, working usually to a time limit and with a definite theatrical company in mind. His close relationship to the stage and its immediate demands was the ruling factor in his work and can never be overlooked. The fluid technique of his plays, comparable in many ways to film techniques today, derived from the shape of the Elizabethan theatre, jutting into the audience and encouraging movement from scene to scene without changing scenery. Modern theatres throughout the world are returning today to this style and form. Although his work as a dramatist came to overshadow his work as an actor, he was still acting as late as 1603 and probably for some years afterwards. In this year, as in 1598, he was playing at least two long parts in plays by Ben Jonson, and as Ivor Brown has written: "He was memorizing, rehearsing and performing at a time when he was most busily and triumphantly engaged as a dramatist."[1] He seems to have been a respected if not major actor, admired as Ghost in his *Hamlet* and a number of other parts, both in his own and other plays. The work gave him a "feel" for the stage that reinforced his

[1]Shakespeare and the Actors (Bodley Head, 1970).

remarkable facility as poet and play constructor. His fellow actors, Heminge and Condell, who edited the First Folio edition of his plays in 1623, after his death, referred to the fact that they "scarce received from him a blot in his papers".

Shakespeare worked within the theatre itself, in a company close to the Court. This too inevitably had reflections on the nature of his work, especially as courtiers were among the regular playgoers. The points of contemporary historic reference in his plays are numerous, for the Elizabethan was a compact society, and even without a Press to inform it was intensely aware of Court events. The plays were subject to censorship, although only once did a play of Shakespeare's—*Richard II* in a revival in February, 1601— come into official disfavour. This revival was engineered by adherents of the Earl of Essex, then in fatal insurrection against the Queen, and it was rightly considered by authority to be a dangerous and deliberate emphasis of the precedent of a monarch's deposition. The play was suppressed, although Shakespeare himself was not personally named in connection with the incident. His early patron, the young Earl of Southampton, was, however, involved with Essex's rebellion and only with luck escaped with his life. Shakespeare certainly showed himself conscious of Essex, and Ulysses's urging of Achilles, sulking in his tent, to return to activity, in *Troilus and Cressida*, has always been taken to be metaphorical advice to the young, hotheaded Essex, who at the time had similarly withdrawn from Court life.

It was as a lyric, not a dramatic, poet, that Shakespeare first gained distinction, and the connection with the Earl of Southampton (sometimes, although his rivals are numerous, taken to be the mysterious patron to whom the Sonnets were dedicated in admiring terms) was longstanding. His first published work, in 1593, was the narrative poem *Venus and Adonis*, described by Shakespeare as "the first heir of my invention". It was followed by *The Rape of Lucrece* in 1594, and both works were frequently reprinted. The full genius of his lyric verse crystallized in the Sonnets, whose theatrical counterpart was the early tragedy of *Romeo and Juliet*, already showing the elements of earthier character, in the figures of Mercutio and the Nurse, which were to grow in later years into the gargantuan wit of a Falstaff. Shakespeare caught the intensities of young love in a fashion which has captured every new generation down to our own time, but in other respects, he showed himself still a dramatic apprentice, not yet fully capable of fusing character and verse. The poetic response flows even from such unlikely characters as the fussy, quick-tempered and convival old Capulet, whose lines at Juliet's death

> Death lies on her like an untimely frost
> Upon the sweetest flower of all the field

are as purely lyrical as the phrasing of a Sonnet—the form given to the first meeting of Romeo and Juliet. Later, Shakespeare was to develop enormously the structure of his verse, using freer and more varied forms including light endings and the carrying over of the sense into a second line. His range of emotional emphasis and imagery was also to grow.

The style of verse of the Sonnets and *Romeo*, typical of the young romantic Shakespeare, is found too in *Love's Labour's Lost*, a comedy which some scholars believe to be his first work for the theatre. The chronology of Shakespeare's plays is disputable and can never be finally resolved, although of the general dates of certain clusters of plays, all bearing hallmarks of their period in the dramatist's development, there is little doubt. *Love's Labour's Lost* heads a list of early comedies including *The Two Gentlemen of Verona*, *The Comedy of Errors* and *The Taming of the Shrew*. Of these *Love's Labour's Lost*, unlike the other three plays, derived from no one else's plot but was entirely original in conception. Some of the characters bear almost contemporary historic French names (Longueville and Navarre, for instance) and there is a touch of the *commedia dell arte*; but its sense of style and elegance is highly developed, and its wit in repartee, in particular between the lovers Berowne and Rosaline, anticipates Benedict and Beatrice in *Much Ado About Nothing*. There is also a certain amount of dated scholastic parody, but it has been described, for a first or early play, as a "miracle".

The Comedy of Errors, performed at Gray's Inn in 1594, derives from Plautus, and Latin influences, such as Plautus and Seneca, were strong in the Elizabethan theatre, although Shakespeare, unlike Jonson, broke away from the more academic bonds of the Senecan influence. *A Midsummer Night's Dream* (First Quarto—i.e. published version—1600) was a culmination of the first group of comedies, again original in plot and imaginatively combining native folklore with classical legend, and rustic comedy with a fairy enchantment.

A second group of comedies, probably beginning with *The*

Merchant of Venice (First Quarto also 1600), develops Shakespeare's mastery of theatrical incident and climax, here allowing, perhaps involuntarily, a natural compassion to add power and humanity to the nominal villain, Shylock (who probably derived from Marlowe's Jew of Malta) and yet retaining the earlier sense of fantasy in the romantic scenes at Belmont. *Much Ado About Nothing*, dated about 1599, greatly strengthened the characterization of the two lovers in the ageless sex war, even although its Renaissance sub-plot is a weak feature in the comedy's structure, and alienates us today like some of the Jew-baiting young Christians in *The Merchant*.

As You Like It (1599–60) is as transparently English in its pastoral scene as *A Midsummer Night's Dream*, in spite of its French Forest of Arden and banished Duke. Touchstone, the clown, Jacques, the melancholy professional cynic, and Rosalind, the most radiant to date of Shakespeare's women in love, show a new ease of character invention which became even further matured in *Twelfth Night*, with Viola adding a new and sadder depth to Rosalind's "many fathoms deep" in love, and the contrasting characters of Sir Toby Belch, Malvolio and Aguecheek balancing, with comic sureness, ebullience, self-conceit and the endearing quality of witless innocence. The play was described by John Masefield as "the greatest English comedy".

The histories continued to mature, with the strange, rambling, sometimes compelling tragedy of *King John*—"a solemn reflection on civil commotion, of whose dangers Shakespeare was acutely aware", in the words of Professor B. Ifor Evans—followed by the masterly Parts I and II of *Henry IV*, which expand on the theme of usurpation set in motion by *Richard II*. "Shakespeare with his singing robes on" was Coleridge's phrase for *Richard II*, and its delineation of the King was a first exercise in the poetic tragedy of character that led to Hamlet (Brutus in *Julius Caesar* was another step). Both parts have been continuing challenges to the great actor, although for long Richard was underrated while Hamlet has never for one moment released his hold upon the playgoer's imagination in any part of the world. It is not easy to define its fascination: yet its introspective analysis of thought and action seems to reflect the dilemma of every generation. Modern scholarship (in particular that of Professor Dover Wilson) has successfully linked the character's instability of mood and inertia with the fashionable Elizabethan concept of melancholia propounded by Robert Burton, but the play and the part go much beyond this and notoriously can be absorbed into the personality of differing actors and the philosophy and spirit of changing times. A melodrama of revenge and kingship has been transformed by the dramatist into a tragedy for Everyman: even modern dress productions have revealed new facets without seriously distorting its effect of universality. It was the foundation from which Shakespeare moved on to the study of jealousy and apparently motiveless evil in *Othello*, the convulsive battle of conscience in *Macbeth*, and the cataclysmic power of *King Lear*.

Two other groups of plays suggest that Shakespeare's personal development was by no means as straightforward as these greater tragedies imply. From 1601 to 1604 there appeared the bitter comedies of *All's Well That Ends Well*, *Troilus and Cressida* (called "a tragedy" in the Folio, 1623) and *Measure for Measure*. All deal with faithlessness in varying degrees, and contain elements of both comedy and tragedy, and all have yielded more psychological interest in the twentieth century than was usual in the past. The study of Angelo in *Measure for Measure* is particularly subtle by modern standards: actors now recognize the conflict of conscience behind the puritanical façade. *Troilus and Cressida*, as has been indicated, has Elizabethan parallels in politics that are by no means inapplicable today. The plays have been termed "dark comedies".

Into their orbit come also the tragedies *Timon of Athens* and *Coriolanus*; the first, perhaps only partly by Shakespeare, a bitter and savage indictment of ingratitude, the second a study in patrician pride (c.1606) that never quite takes off the ground after the passion of *Antony and Cleopatra*, yet uses a corrosive imagery consistent with these later plays of Shakespeare. Politically, it stresses the necessity of many co-ordinating parts to the proper functioning of the body politic.

Then again, near the end, Shakespeare turns to romanticism, but a romanticism now darkened by experience and the bitter dregs, as it were, of the *All's Well that Ends Well* period. *Cymbeline*, loosely based on early Roman/British history, is the lightest, an uneven play with a Renaissance-style villain (Iachimo), a jealous husband with faint echoes of Othello (Posthumus) and a wronged heroine of great charm, Imogen. Some of its poetry, including the dirge "Fear no more the heat of the sun", has a beauty which, like the character of the heroine, transforms the story. Imogen is the last of a long line of Shakespearean heroines *en travestie* (i.e. who dress as youths to further the plot), a device born in part of the convention of employing boy actors for the women's parts in Shakespeare's own time. *Pericles*, again only partly by Shakespeare, the narrative links of Old Gower being obviously untouched by his pen, has fairytale elements and one of Shakespeare's later charmingly guileless and unstained young heroines, Marina: her reconciliation with her father, after the black comedy of the brothel, is a tender echo of that of Lear and Cordelia.

The Winter's Tale contrasts the pastoral Perdita with the savage jealousies of Leontes, her father; it is an almost Freudian psychological picture, healed in the end by the grace of a second generation grown up in rustic innocence. *The Tempest*, a once underrated play (it is still believed by many to be Shakespeare's last) is also far more than an exercise in masque and magic: in Prospero's revenge is a despair of humanity, with the semi-human Caliban the pre-Darwinian image of the natural savage. Yet once again there is a feminine counteraction to despair, the daughter Miranda, and Prospero proceeds in the end from disillusion to forgiveness, drowning his book as perhaps Shakespeare meant to finish with the magic of the theatre.

Certainly, soon afterwards, he retired to Stratford where his roots lay, and to the young growing daughter Susannah whose image seems to have been reflected in his last heroines. He died at New Place, the house he had bought many years before, after a short illness on 23 April, 1616. Legend, probably of seventeenth-century origin, attributes his death to a chill caught while drinking with London cronies outside the Falcon Inn at Bidford-on-Avon. Shakespeare's younger daughter, Judith, had married the previous month. All that remains of New Place is its garden, foundations, and well. It was destroyed by a mean and vindictive seventeenth-century clergyman.

Little is known of Shakespeare's personal life in London. We know that in 1604 he lodged in Silver Street, Cripplegate, at the home of Christopher Mountjoy, a maker of jewelled tiaras (some, perhaps, for the theatre). Records of Ben Jonson and others depict him as mild and likeable: Mercutio's description, obviously mocking, of the peaceable Benvolio in *Romeo and Juliet*, as having a head "as full of quarrels as an egg is full of meat", is sometimes assumed to be an "in-joke" of Shakespeare's at his own expense, as his head appears to have been egg-shaped and he is said to have played the part of Benvolio in the original production. It is probable he had little time for adventure or even lively tavern interludes: the study of acting parts, the writing and re-writing of nearly forty plays, the supervision of the boy actors who must always be borne in mind when assessing the emotional limitations of his female parts, and whose training must have needed care—these must have constituted a full and exhausting life quite apart from his business interests in the theatre. For Shakespeare early acquired enough money from his acting (which would have been poorly paid) and writing to take shares in the theatre for which he worked. He sold these shares in the Globe Theatre some time between 1611 and 1613, the year the theatre was burnt down. The fire was caused by an exploding cannon in *Henry VIII*, the late historical play (in which Fletcher as well as Shakespeare is believed to have had a hand), which, like the last tragi-comedies, was designed to fit the new fashion for pageantry and the masque that came in with the Jacobean era.

As a man of the theatre Shakespeare adapted his talents without question to the demands of the times, and also to the company of actors for which he was writing: many of his greatest roles might have been different but for the talents of the admired actor, Richard Burbage, for which they were originally shaped. Yet his genius transcended what to many might seem limitations, just as great composers transcend the structural limitations of the symphonic and sonata form.

Shakespeare's genius, as both poet and dramatist, was so unique that his world influences have been critical rather than dramatic. His shadow in England obliterated a deadening succession of imitators in blank verse, only the Jacobean John Webster (writing far darker and more violent tragedies of Borgian influences) and the Stuart John Dryden attaining any real distinction in the form (although Otway's *Venice Preserv'd*, in 1682, showed some of the elements of Shakespeare's republican tragedies and was dramatic enough to attract notable leading actors, for a number of years, for its two principal parts). Not, however, till Congreve and Sheridan developed the comedy of manners, in totally different style, did the English theatre recover any originality. In Victorian times other poets, including Tennyson, tried the theatre again but without success, until Bernard Shaw, in the footsteps of Ibsen, developed a new strain of social comedy and coruscating wit and the British theatre acquired its second great genius, Irish-born and entirely original.

In France Shakespeare, defeating the translators, has had little influence: he was considered uncouth by a nation whose whole dramatic outlook derived from the Greeks, as developed nationally through the rigid Alexandrines and classic "proportions" of Racine (only *Macbeth* of Shakespeare's tragedies shows some hints of ancient Greek tragedy in style). "Shakespeare is a savage," wrote Voltaire, "with sparks of genius which shine in a dreadful darkness of night." Molière's legacy of satiric comedy was also very different from Shakespeare's, and in fact more akin to the satires of Ben Jonson. In Germany Schiller and Goethe were certainly aware of Shakespeare, and the greatest German actors have always played Shakespearean parts; but Shakespeare's deepest influence, perhaps, on German dramatic thought has been through the immense volume of Shakespearean criticism and philosophy, written by Heine, Nietzsche and others, and paralleling that of Hazlitt, Coleridge, Lamb, Bradley, and so many others in England.

From Italy Shakespeare himself took many basic stories, showing in his adaptations the characteristic Elizabethan awareness of Machiavellian politics and Renaissance character. The evidence of Shakespeare's experience of the sea, and his frequent references to Italy, suggest strongly that he visited that country, and set his scenes there whenever possible; but Italy did not reciprocate, through her dramatists. Nevertheless, in some form Shakespeare, partly through the actors who cannot resist his parts and, partly through the poets who study him in translation, has penetrated the world consciousness, and modern developments in production have continued to be an international stimulus. Gordon Craig's designs for a production of *Hamlet* in Moscow in 1911 were of notable influence in the European theatre, and Stanislavsky wrote a book about his Moscow Art Theatre production of *Othello*. Today Peter Brook, working a great deal in Europe, is among the producers spreading Shakespearean influences in revolutionary ways. And recently there has been a new production of *Richard III* at the *Comédie Française*, which was well received by French audiences.

The artistic influence of Shakespeare on the world cinema has also been striking. Sir Laurence Olivier (Britain), Innokenti Smoktunovsky (Soviet Russia) and Maximilian Schell (Germany) have all played film Hamlets in recent years, the first two being particularly notable productions visually and imaginatively, with a world-wide distribution, and Olivier's productions of *Henry V* and *Richard III* also set a famous standard. Since the formation of the

National Theatre in London, Olivier's Othello, one of his greatest performances, has been transferred to film, although in this case as a more literal transference of the stage production to the screen. Sir John Gielgud, once the most famous of modern stage Hamlets and Richard IIs, has also put on film record his masterly Cassius in *Julius Caesar*. Peter Brook's film of *King Lear*, with Paul Scofield, has been another attempt to capture a great stage performance for world viewing. Scofield's Lear was, in fact, also seen on many European stages, in eight different countries, and also in New York. This international exchange of Shakespearean productions and performances seems likely to continue extending the culture of many nations.

Perhaps the best summing-up of Shakespeare is still that of his contemporary and rival Ben Jonson: "He was not for an age, but for all time."

JOHN LOCKE
(1632–1704)

JOHN LOCKE is widely regarded as the greatest, and certainly the most influential philosopher of English birth. And yet there are critics who say that Locke was not a philosopher at all. Such critics are usually those who think that only metaphysicians are philosophers; and Locke was assuredly no Leibniz or Spinoza, he offered no all-embracing system to explain the nature of the universe. On the contrary, he tried to show that the human understanding is so limited that comprehensive knowledge of the universe is beyond men's powers to reach. Locke did not give the answers; his achievement lay in setting out the problems, in suggesting, as no one had ever done before, how the pursuit of knowledge should be conducted.

Two powerful streams in seventeenth-century thought, the semi-sceptical rationalistic theorizing of Descartes and the *ad hoc* scientific experimenting of Bacon and Boyle and the Royal Society, came together in Locke. Their union was not perfect, because the streams were so different, but his mind was the meeting place, a point which marked a new beginning, not only in philosophy, but in the way in which men thought about the world. Locke, one might almost say, had the first modern mind. Descartes, though more original than Locke, remained in many ways a medieval thinker, his philosophy was still subject to theology. Locke made the break; he separated philosophy from theology and set the proper study of philosophers within the boundaries of man's experience: "Our portion lies only here in this little spot of earth, where we and all our concernments are shut up."

Yet Locke was not a sceptic, and in his capacity as theologian he had thoughts of his own about God to expound. He quarrelled with prelates and the orthodox, he maintained that a Christian need believe no more than the single proposition "that Christ is the Messiah", but to that bare minimum of doctrine he held with the deepest assurance. The New Testament was the basis, was indeed the sum of Locke's moral teaching, and his whole temperament was, like Newton's, a religious one.

Locke was a man of middle-class birth. His father was a West of England lawyer, and a Puritan. The Civil War between Charles I and the Puritan Parliament broke out when Locke was ten, and his father was mounted as a captain of Parliamentary Horse by Alexander Popham, a wealthy magistrate turned colonel. Apart from demolishing some "Popish" images in Wells Cathedral, the two officers saw little action, but a grateful Alexander Popham became the patron of his captain's eldest son; and when, a few years later, Westminster School was taken over by Parliament, the colonel found a place for his protégé in what was then the best school in England.

At Westminster the boy came under the influence of Richard Busby, the Royalist Master of the school, and when Locke left in 1652 to become an undergraduate of Christ Church, Oxford, he was well prepared to react against the rule of the Puritan Saints which then prevailed in the universities. By the time of the Stuart Restoration, Locke had become sick and tired of political fanaticism of any kind.

He stayed at Oxford as a college tutor, and took up the study of medicine which was the nearest thing to science he could find there.

In the summer of 1666, Locke met and made friends with Anthony Ashley Cooper, then Lord Ashley, later first Earl of Shaftesbury. "Shaftesbury" for simplicity's sake I shall call him here. He was not yet the leader of a party, but he was already the outstanding politician of progressive liberalism, the most forceful champion of religious toleration. Shaftesbury opposed the Corporation Bill, the Bill of Uniformity, the Five Mile Bill, and every other measure designed to curb the freedom of Nonconformists. He had thus been a spokesman for liberty before he met Locke and undoubtedly influenced Locke politically.

A year later, at the age of thirty-four, Locke went to live at Shaftesbury's house in London. It was under Shaftesbury's patronage that Locke discovered his own true gifts. First he became a philosopher. At Oxford he had been as bored and dissatisfied as Hobbes had been with the medieval Aristotelian philosophy which was taught there. Reading Descartes first opened Locke's eyes to the "new philosophy", and discussions with Shaftesbury and other London friends led him to write, in his fourth year under Shaftesbury's roof, the earliest drafts of his masterpiece, the *Human*

Understanding. He also became an economist, educationist and medical reformer.

Shaftesbury, little, ugly, and vain, has a bad name in the history books. But he was no fool. He was interested, with Locke, in philosophy and in science, and he did much to defend and enlarge the liberties of Englishmen. Admittedly his concern for religious toleration was not prompted by Christian forbearance and compassion. He advocated religious freedom because he believed that religious persecution divided a nation which would be stronger, and richer if it were united. Shaftesbury was self-consciously the imperialist and the capitalist. He saw more clearly than most of his contemporaries that colonial expansion and international trade might bring at the same time great fortunes to men like himself and great power to the country as a whole.

When Shaftesbury pleaded for religious toleration he wished to have it primarily on behalf of Protestant dissenters. Charles II, who favoured religious toleration primarily for the sake of Catholic recusants, was for some time in agreement with him against the intolerant Anglican majority. This was the position in the earliest years of Locke's connection with Shaftesbury. Shaftesbury was then anti-Dutch. He had studied Holland closely, and his kind of liberal imperialism was largely based on the Dutch model. He saw Holland as England's greatest rival in trade and therefore her greatest potential enemy. Later Shaftesbury came to regard France, not Holland, in this light, and he altered his policy accordingly. As Charles II was pro-French this change put Shaftesbury into opposition, but it also gave him a principle besides trade and toleration on which to take his public stand. That principle was the Protestant religion. France was Catholic, and everything Catholic served the interests of France; France was England's natural enemy, therefore everything Catholic was inimical to England's interests. The case was easily argued, though indeed it hardly needed to be argued. The very name of "popery" was enough to agitate the public.

Shaftesbury, however, liked to argue; he liked to be able to express his ideas in theoretical terms; and as his physician was also a philosopher, he invited Locke to reflect on the general principles involved in these matters of political expediency. Was it illogical to stand both for religious toleration and for the suppression of Catholics? Locke came to the conclusion that it was not. Catholics were not just religious dissenters, they were a body of men who acknowledged allegiance to a foreign potentate, the Pope, and who were therefore allied through Rome with the Pope's true friends, the French. No country, Locke believed, could tolerate within it people who were potentially disloyal. It was not a question of religious liberty, but of the security of the realm, and the defence of the realm was the first duty of any government.

Locke stayed with Shaftesbury on and off until Shaftesbury's death in 1682. In those fifteen years Shaftesbury's Protestant zeal carried him to the point of organizing a rebellion. Charles II refused to deny his Catholic brother, James, his legitimate right to succeed him to the throne. Shaftesbury persuaded Parliament to pass a measure designed to make James's succession illegal. When Charles thwarted this manoeuvre, Shaftesbury replied by calling on his friends to rise and exclude James in favour of a Protestant successor by force of arms. The Protestant successor he unwisely named was Charles's bastard, Monmouth. But Shaftesbury's supporters hesitated, and he himself withdrew to Holland, there, soon afterwards, to die.

These were the events which stand behind Locke's *Two Treatises of Civil Government*. The book was not published until eight years after Shaftesbury's death, by which time Englishmen had come round to Shaftesbury's way of thinking to the extent of expelling James II by force of arms and enthroning his Protestant nephew, William. Locke in the preface of the published version of his book said he hoped it would "help to justify the title of King William to rule us". But Locke had conceived the book and written most of it, when Charles II was still alive, and when the question of whether a nation had the right to rebel against its ruler was not a backward-looking moral problem but a forward-looking moral challenge.

Throughout the years when Shaftesbury's house was his London home, Locke retained his Studentship of Christ Church, though he seldom spent as much as a full term in Oxford. His comings and goings were the subject of speculation. In 1675 he was thought to be after a place as a medical don, but he went to France for three and a half years instead. In 1682, after Shaftesbury's disappearance, Locke seemed once more about to settle down in Oxford, and would probably have done so had not the alleged conspiracy of Shaftesbury's Whig successors to kidnap Charles II and his brother at Rye House precipitated such a feverish witch-hunt that Locke felt it would be unsafe to remain in England. He fled, as Shaftesbury had done, to Amsterdam.

In 1684 Locke was expelled in absence from his Studentship of Christ Church by the King's express command. The following summer, after James's succession to the throne, came Monmouth's abortive rebellion in the West of England, and Locke was named by the English government as one of Monmouth's agents in Holland. Locke went into hiding as "Dr van der Linden", but a few months later his name was removed from the list of wanted men, and he emerged from hiding, though he did not return to England.

Locke's friends in Holland included some of William's English courtiers, but Locke himself was seldom at The Hague. When William and his supporters sailed in 1688 to invade the English coast, Locke complained of ill-health and stayed in Rotterdam. His Swiss friend Jean le Clerc called him *"plutôt timide que courageux"*, but the remark was hardly just, for Locke, at the age of fifty-six could reasonably feel that he had had his share of danger. He returned to London quietly in 1689 in the company of Princess Mary.

Jean le Clerc's words have been seized upon by Locke's biographers because they can be used to support the theory that Locke had never anything to do with such hazardous activities as revolutionary plots. Their story is that Locke was Shaftesbury's friend and aide while Shaftesbury's actions were constitutional, but not at other times. While Shaftesbury was preparing a rebellion, Locke, we are invited to believe, was a remote and harmless Oxford don. Other dons were not of this opinion, and at least one in Christ Church believed that Locke had a hand in the Rye House plot, that he was working with Monmouth in Holland, and that he was the author of seditious tracts which had been smuggled into England from Amsterdam. This may have been partly true. Shaftesbury, according to his grandson, had employed Locke "for his secretest negotiations", and Locke was certainly in close touch with some of the conspirators in Holland but it is difficult to believe that he wrote any of the smuggled pamphlets.

In Holland between 1683 and 1689, as in France between 1675 and 1679, Locke travelled about the country making notes of what he saw, but because he had no eye for beauty and no sense of history his notes make dismal reading. He would go to great trouble to visit some great cathedral or chateau, and then spend much of his time there working out the exact dimensions. He detested ceremonies and show, which he thought irrational and wasteful, and was clearly pleased to find that one of the best

Dutch universities had the most nondescript architecture. It proved "that knowledge depends not on the stateliness of buildings, etc."

"Knowledge" is the word which matters here. For Locke's philistinism was in no sense an aberration. Locke wanted to get away from the imagination, from the vague glamour of medieval things, from unthinking adherence to tradition, from enthusiasm, mysticism, and *gloire*; away from all private, visionary insights and down to the publicly verifiable, measurable, plain, demonstrable facts; and this desire was central to his whole mission as a philosopher and reformer. His antipathy to imaginative artists was coupled with contempt for ivory-tower scholars who "converse with but one sort of men and read but one sort of books", and thus:

> "canton out to themselves a little goshen in the intellectual world where the light shines, and, as they conclude, day blesses them; but the rest of that vast *expansum* they give up to night and to darkness; and so avoid coming near it. They have a pretty traffic with known correspondents in some little creek; within that they confine themselves and are dexterous managers enough of the wares and products of that corner, but will not venture out into the great ocean of knowledge . . ."

Venturing out into the great ocean of knowledge made Locke a polymath, but he was in no sense a smatterer. Admittedly his expertness was not equally marked in all the subjects he chose to study. Compared to Boyle and Newton, who were his friends, Locke was an amateurish scientist; his knowledge of the Scriptures was questionable; and although he was an original as well as an influential economist, he could not appreciate the subtlety of other theorists in that field. What was important in Locke's case, how-however, was not his versatility itself, but that each department of knowledge was related in his mind to all the others.

During his exile in Holland he wrote, from drafts he had made in 1671, his *Essay concerning Human Understanding*, his first *Letter for Toleration*, and his *Thoughts on Education* (or, more accurately, the letters which were afterwards published under this title), and he may have done some work on his *Civil Government*. The *Letter for Toleration* was published in Locke's original Latin at Gouda in 1689, and an English translation made by the Socinian William Popple—made, Locke afterwards said, "without my privity"—was published in London a few months later. The *Human Understanding* and the *Civil Government* were also brought out by different

London booksellers in the winter of 1689–90. Only the *Human Understanding* bore Locke's name, but its success was so great that it made its author famous throughout Europe even in his lifetime.

Locke was a liberal: but he was certainly not a democrat. He was untouched by that belief in equality which Rousseau was to make the dominant sentiment of the Left. In one of his books on monetary theory, Locke pointed out that "the labourers' share" of the national wealth "being seldom more than a bare subsistence, never allows that body of men time or opportunity to raise their thoughts above that", or even to assert their interests against the rich unless "some common and great distress, uniting them in some universal ferment, makes them forget respect . . ." Locke did not mean with these words to suggest that labourers ought to have more than a bare subsistence, but rather that governments should ward off any "common and great distress" which might make labourers forget the respect they owed their superiors.

Precisely because they had not more than a bare subsistence, working men were excluded from the full responsibilities and privileges of political society. For, as Locke said more than once, "the great and chief end . . . of men's uniting into commonwealths and putting themselves under governments is the preservation of their property". And although Locke said he used the word "property" to mean "that property which men have in their persons as well as their goods", he often also used the word in its more limited and familiar sense. The labourer's only "goods" was his capacity to work, and the sale of that to an employer left him with nothing. If the labourer had therefore little material interest in the commonwealth, neither had he much rationality to contribute to it. "The greatest part of mankind have not the leisure for learning and logic."

Locke's writings on the rationality of men are decidedly ambiguous if not contradictory. I think it is not unfair to say that he believed in the rationality of all men when it suited him and not otherwise. When he was writing as a champion of the right of rebellion, as a revolutionary pamphleteer, Locke emphasized the rationality of men as he emphasized their natural rights. In this context he had perforce to minimize the disadvantages of natural anarchy and in doing so he came very near to a "Garden of Eden" picture of pre-political human history. Locke consulted the reports of travellers who had visited remote parts of the globe, to see what life was like among the pre-political savages, and the reports which came from

North America and the Pacific islands tended to confirm his theory that life in a condition of natural anarchy was in many ways an agreeable one—agreeable because men were naturally rational and naturally quite good. To this extent Locke *did* have something in common with Rousseau: they were both believers in man's original innocence.

But Locke was not carried as Rousseau was from the idea of natural goodness to a preference for democratic republican government. From the thought that all men were innocent in a state of nature Locke never for one moment passed to the thought that all men in a political society were equally rational. The moment Locke stopped thinking about Natural Laws and thought about practical politics, he stopped thinking about men's equality and their common rationality. Men were so obviously *not* equal. Some were much more intelligent than others, and some were much better than others. The idea of *social* equality at no time entered Locke's head.

When William Penn told him about the social services he wished to introduce in Pennsylvania, Locke protested that such innovations would be inimical to the liberty of subjects. To sacrifice liberty for the sake of philanthropy seemed to Locke mistaken; the object might be good but the price was too high. If anyone had suggested sacrificing liberty for the sake of equality, Locke would have thought the sacrifice disastrous and the object foolish.

In the preface to the English edition of the first *Letter for Toleration* is a sentence which reads: "Absolute liberty, just and true liberty, equal and impartial liberty is the thing we stand in need of." Many people have supposed these words to be Locke's, and Lord King used them as an epigraph for his biography of the philosopher, but in fact the words were written by William Popple, the translator of the *Letter*.

Locke did *not* believe in absolute liberty, any more than he believed in absolute knowledge. Locke wanted as much liberty as possible and he wanted as much knowledge as possible; and he thought the way to achieve as much as possible of each was to face the fact that both were limited and then to find out what the limitations were. The limits of knowledge, he thought, were set by the limits of men's cognitive apparatus; the senses gave men data (or "ideas") of the universe, but men had no means of comparing the data with the universe itself. Once men recognized that certain information could be had only in one or two fields, they could go on to acquire a great deal of probable information in other fields. Hence the seeming paradox of Locke's attempt in his *Human Understanding* to show how much knowledge men can have by explaining how little knowledge they can have. He used the same method to show how much freedom they can have by explaining how little they can have.

The impact of Locke's thought was probably more extensive than that of any other philosopher of modern times. In the narrow realm of pure philosophy he was perhaps less influential than either Descartes or Hegel, but he had a far greater influence than either of those theorists on the day-to-day thinking and way of life of ordinary people. In politics, Locke's doctrine of the rights of man—and more precisely the rights to life, liberty and property—became the central axioms of reformers and revolutionaries everywhere. His doctrine of religious toleration gradually permeated the minds of Christians of all denominations. His ideal of the life of practical business became a model for the rising middle-class culture. His belief in the harmony of private gain and public good made him a powerful champion of industrial and scientific progress. Romantic poets disliked Locke's prosaic utilitarian view of life, as much as he himself detested the mysticism of poets; but the poets were surely right to see in Locke a great intellectual force in modern life, a thinker who had diverted men's minds away from the unseen world of the spirit and imagination towards the visible world of working and trading and legislating and investigating nature.

If there is such a thing as a liberal ethos, Locke was its first and most powerful exponent. But he was much more than that. His books, which were published in French and Latin in his lifetime, were read eagerly throughout the civilized world; his style was very English, but his mind—which was partly shaped by years of travel in France and Holland and the reading of books in various languages—was entirely cosmopolitan. Locke was a European, a creature of Europe, and in turn, one of the creators of Europe as a cultural reality and not just a geographical expression.

LOUIS XIV
(1638–1715)

LOUIS XIV, the son of Louis XIII and Anne of Austria, was born in September, 1638, and was called Louis the God-given because it seemed miraculous that a child could be born to these parents after twenty-three years of marriage. He succeeded to the throne in 1643, when he was still an infant and his first experiences were of civil wars. These were brought about by a variety of causes, in which economic and political grievances went hand in hand with the ambitions of certain nobles, the intrigues of foreign powers, and mob violence.

The King was frequently exiled and it was not until 1652 that he was able to return to Paris and Cardinal Mazarin, his mother's closest friend and adviser, was able to resume his effective government. In March, 1661, the Cardinal died and to the general surprise of the Court, Louis announced that he intended to be his own chief minister. Thus began one of the longest and most remarkable reigns of any French king; one too which was of great importance in the history of Europe.

France was already the outstanding kingdom of the continent. Since Charles V had abandoned his enormous Empire in 1556 in order to lead a life of contemplation, the Hapsburg inheritance had been divided into two. From this time onwards the Hapsburg Emperors in Vienna who ruled over Austria, Bohemia and Hungary, found themselves faced with Lutherans and Calvinists. The Hapsburgs of Madrid found themselves in unsuccessful wars, notably with England and the Low Countries. France, under Richelieu and under Mazarin had profited from this, and within the time of Louis XIV's minority rule had expanded into Alsace and Lorraine, as well as southwards to Roussillon and northwards to Artois.

The most important act of Louis XIV's life after his accession to the throne was his marriage, and this was given a typically European meaning. He was obliged, and he accepted, to renounce Marie Mancini whom he appears to have loved; and he married the Infanta of Spain, Maria Theresa. Thus Louis who was, through his mother, a direct descendant of Charles V, married another descendant of the Emperor. In the marriage treaty it was stated that Maria Theresa renounced her claim to the Spanish throne, on receipt of a dowry to be paid by her father. The fact that this dowry was never paid added a further element to both France's real and potential supremacy in Europe. Louis had the most powerful army and the most effective diplomatic service; he had many allies; his neighbours appeared weak and divided. There was no reason why he should not shape the continent according to his desires. On the other hand the Vienna Hapsburgs had never accepted that the terms of the Treaty of Westphalia, in 1648, extending French power in the east, were permanent, and they perpetually sought to have them changed. In a sense therefore, Louis was on the defensive.

The first opportunity for Louis to take decisive action occurred in 1665 when the King of Spain died. Louis had prepared for this by allying himself with several other powers, so that Spain was isolated. Louis then launched a series of attacks against Spanish possessions in the name of the French Queen's rights. He concentrated on the Spanish Netherlands, and when the Spanish government made peace at Aix-la-Chapelle in 1668, France acquired a number of important towns, such as Lille, Oudenarde, Douai and Tournai. This improved the French strategical position and left Louis favourably placed. But Louis had accepted to make peace, against the advice of his military advisers, who thought that France stood to gain much more. In the first place he had come to an agreement with the Emperor, whereby the two of them were to divide the Spanish empire between them, should the new king, the invalid Charles II, die soon and die without children. In the second place, Holland, England and Sweden had formed a Triple Alliance, and Louis was aware that this was being directed against him. Naturally Holland had no reason to wish for the strong power of France to be consolidated on her frontier. The British ambassador at The Hague, Sir William Temple, was very influential and he was conscious of the fact that "a great comet", as he called Louis, had arisen and was demanding admiration from the rest of the world.

It seems that Louis quite early determined that he would break the power of the United Provinces. He saw them as an obstacle to his expansion. He objected to their religion and to their republicanism. Preoccupied as he was with sharing out the Spanish inheritance, he was particularly anxious about the Netherlands. He succeeded in allying himself with Sweden and with England, as well as with a number of German princes; in 1671 he sent his armies into Lorraine as part of a strategical preparation. In May, 1672, he ordered a large force to attack the Low Countries. This gained many initial successes, but as time went by it seemed that Louis had underestimated his enemy. William of Orange emerged through a welter of intrigue and confusion as the leader and king of the Dutch; the Dutch navy scored a number of successes; gradually European opinion hardened against Louis, as his operations alarmed, offended or shocked other rulers. The Emperor, the King of Spain, the German princes, even under the pressure of public opinion, the King of England, turned against him and abandoned their agreements. Instead of easy victories against an isolated enemy Louis was obliged to contemplate a long series of campaigns involving most of the states of Western Europe.

In 1678 and in 1679 he accepted to make a series of peace treaties (signed at Nimwegen) with the Dutch and with the other powers. By these treaties the French gave up Maastricht, which they had captured; they evacuated some of the towns in the Low Countries which they had gained by the earlier war; but they took Franche Comté in eastern France, together with a line of strong places running from Dunkirk to the river Meuse. In this way, although there was an element of compromise, Louis continued to strengthen his frontiers. Since his army had never been beaten, he continued too to enjoy the reputation of the foremost military power in western Europe.

It was clear that the magnificence of Louis in Europe could not be maintained without a firm basis in France itself. Ever since the king's decision to rule he had emphasized the importance and grandeur of his own person. From the late 1660's this was to be expressed in the importance of the Palace of Versailles. The Court, the Council of Ministers, the representatives of foreign governments, all that was fine and important in the kingdom was to be concentrated in this great building, which was rebuilt and surrounded by gardens. It was the centre of government in the most obvious sense of the word. Louis XIV, as king, lived in the full glare of publicity, never for one moment ceasing to play the rôle of the monarch, whether demonstrating his splendour in hunting or festivity or his power in administration and diplomacy. The aristocracy were expected to be on parade in order to assist in this ornamental demonstration of the king's supremacy. What was important was that the king should be seen to be the sole master of the kingdom, the man upon whom everything depended.

In reality it was difficult for the king to supervise personally the business of the state which was for ever growing in quantity and complication. Although he worked long hours, particularly after he had abandoned the frivolities of his youth, nevertheless he was very dependent upon assistance. There were the men of the upper levels of government, such as Colbert, who had served Cardinal Mazarin and who was a remarkable administrator for some twenty-two years. There were the aristocratic friends and associates, whom he felt able to trust, and who were sometimes made governors of distant provinces. There were the *intendants*, officials who were responsible for the administration, especially in fiscal matters, of the provinces, and who often made practical compromises between the principles of central government and the pressures of local interests. There was the bureaucracy, many of whom had purchased their positions. There were local courts, local parliaments, a whole set of customs and traditions, which the monarchy could not ignore. Above all there was the fact that Louis XIV always wanted money. This constant need could not be satisfied by too frequent a resort to force, which tended to disrupt society. There had to be negotiating and bargaining. In consequence the practical power of the king had very real limitations.

But in Europe these limitations were hardly recognized. The palace and the court of Versailles seemed to epitomize all that was meant by kingship. Other monarchs, such as the Emperor of Austria, built palaces which were imitations of Versailles. Even where some German princeling could only build a miniature Versailles, he was accepting this as the model of what government should be. Although Colbert was anxious for there to be economies in governmental expenditure, he nevertheless believed that the prestige and reputation of a government was bound up with its buildings as much as with its military victories. Louis himself was never tired of personally supervising the decoration of his buildings, much of which was devoted to his personal glorification. But Versailles was not only a temple elevated to the cult of royalty. It was also a monument to a form of government which had become the symbol of a form of civilization. The reputation of Versailles included that of the theatre, music, literature and thought as well as architecture and painting. It almost seemed that European civilization had become French civilization.

The prestige of the court was fundamental to the government of Louis XIV. This was all the more striking since the court of the Valois during the sixteenth century had been perpetually on the move and had had no possibility of establishing any careful etiquette. Under Louis XIV the order of the court was the idolization of the king. The whole life of many important noble families was devoted to the ceremonies and celebrations of the court, and many a noble ambition consisted of seeking for some mark of royal esteem. Even such a critical mind as Madame de Sévigné would savour the pleasure and the triumph of a few words from the king, and the greatest of dukes and marquises would make a point of never missing *le lever du roi*, the "getting-up" ceremonial. And this was in spite of the admitted inconvenience of life at court, particularly at Versailles, which from 1682 onwards was the permanent residence of the court. With its 8,000 valets, Versailles was totally inadequate to house the noble courtiers. The rooms were small, the sanitation was deplorable, the whole palace thronged with thieves, adventurers, prostitutes and other undesirables. Attendance at court was always expensive and could be ruinous; it was often very boring. But people wanted to be there. As one aristocrat said to the king, away from Versailles one was not only unhappy, one was also ridiculous.

The atmosphere of the court changed in the course of the reign. At first, when the king was often at Fontainebleau or Saint Germain, there were magnificent fêtes, ballets, operas, plays. The king would be with his mistresses, most famous of whom were Louise de la Vallière and the Marquise de Montespan, the latter bearing him four children. But by the late 1670's, Louis had formed his attachment to Madame de Maintenon, the governess of his children. After their marriage court life became severer, strict, religious and dull, without ever losing any of its complicated ceremonial.

It is often said that it was thanks to Louis XIV that this was such a magnificent period in French literature, art and architecture. It has been suggested that this was the great period of French classicism, and that in order to achieve such a moment in a national culture, it was necessary for there to be some organization to give the tone, to devise and impose the rules, to provide the patronage, and that this organization could only have come from the king and the court. In many ways this is true. The government gave pensions to the writers and artists of whom it approved; the *Acádémie*

Française attempted to control the French language; other Academies organized painters, sculptors, architects and decorators; the king created the *Comédie Française* in 1680 so as to give official approval to certain plays; the musician Lulli prospered thanks to the royal patronage, as *Tartuffe* could only be played thanks to royal protection.

But in spite of this one cannot assimilate the reign entirely with this cultural splendour. Much had been accomplished before. Malherbe had laid down the rules of classicism, Pascal and Descartes were dead, Corneille had written all his great plays, Molière had had his first successes, all before the king had started to rule personally. Many of the great names had disappeared before the end of the century and well before the end of the reign; Molière in 1673, La Fontaine in 1695, Madame de Sévigné in 1696, Racine in 1699. Nor were the great names always appreciated: Molière was always at odds with the authorities, Racine was regarded by many as being inferior to several authors whose names are now forgotten. Most important is to remember that just as behind the harmonious façade of Versailles were to be found many examples of the baroque, so can one find a great variety in the cultural life of the time. The strict Catholicism of the court could not stamp out the heresy of Jansenism, the classicism of Corneille could not conceal his romanticism, the writers and thinkers of the end of the reign, such as Fontenelle and Perrault attacked the classicism of Boileau. It was this variety which gave vitality to French civilization.

From 1680 onwards Louis determined to extend his power by legal means, although this was always backed up by the use of force. He took up claims on behalf of the French crown which had lain dormant but which were permissible by the terms of the Treaty of Westphalia. Special tribunals were established in Flanders, Alsace and Franche-Comté in response to requests which had usually been inspired by the French government. The result was a series of French annexations. Eventually only Strasbourg remained independent, and in 1681 the French army occupied this town which had been virtually independent, like a Swiss canton. Louis himself entered Strasbourg with great pomp, and it was clear that he attached great importance to the fact that the French frontier had been established on the Rhine. But there was no reason to believe that French ambitions were ending there. Louis himself said that he regarded Alsace as a passage through which he could invade Germany. On the same day that Strasbourg was occupied French troops seized a base in northern Italy near to Turin. It was widely reported that Louis sought to have himself made Emperor.

French policy was successful because of French military strength, because of skilful diplomacy which separated his potential enemies, and because he profited from the Turko-Hungarian attacks on the Hapsburgs and the siege of Vienna in 1683. Had Vienna been captured then Louis would have appeared as the master of Europe, the protector of Germany and of Christianity, in spite of the encouragement he had given to the Hungarians and the friendship which he had professed for the Sultan. Even though Vienna did not fall the Emperor was forced to abandon his ambitions in the west, and in 1684 he signed with Louis and with the Spanish government the Truce of Ratisbon which recognized most of the French annexations, including those of Strasbourg and Luxembourg. It was generally agreed that the reign of Louis had reached a new *apogée*, although it was necessary to turn the truce into a regular treaty for the advantages to be made certain.

It is no accident that during these years the names of Constantine and of Charlemagne were frequently recalled in France. It was widely recognized, by some with fear and resentment, that the King of France intended to make himself a king of Europe. One element only was lacking, particularly since the Turks had failed in their attack on Vienna. This element was that of religion. Louis saw no reason why France should not stand forth as the champion of Catholicism, and take over the rôle once played by Philip II of Spain. It is true that this coincided with his own marriage (the Queen having died in 1683) with the austere Madame de Maintenon and an affirmation of his own piousness. But it seems that Louis began his persecution of the French Protestants, the Huguenots, as a political rather than a personal act. The annexation of Strasbourg was depicted as an important stage in the destruction of Lutheranism. The Emperor was criticized for not protecting the German Catholics adequately. The new king of England, the Catholic James II, was offered troops to help him convert his subjects. The Pope himself incurred the displeasure of the French king, for being inadequate in his defence of religion. The Barbary pirates of North Africa were attacked in a new French crusade.

These actions were greeted with a variety of emotions in Europe. There was cynicism when it was known that the military successes of Europe were to be seen as victories for Jesus Christ. There was revulsion at the news of persecutions. There was disturbance when many French Protestants fled to England, Holland and parts of Germany, and helped to create hostility against France and facilitated the task of William of Orange, the ruler of the Low Countries, in organizing coalitions against France.

All this was taking place at a time when Louis, like other European rulers, was contemplating what was still thought to be the imminent death of the King of Spain, and the inheritance of his considerable dominions. Louis showed that on certain matters of international dispute he was prepared to be amenable, but when anything arose concerning the future of Spain and the Spanish possessions, then he was prepared to be difficult. At the suggestion, for example, that the Elector of Bavaria should become Governor of the Spanish Netherlands, Louis massed his troops on the Pyrenees and made some threatening statements.

However it must be remembered that whilst Louis was usually aggressive in his conduct of affairs, and invariably gave the impression that it was French policy to take the initiative and to determine the outcome, there always remained an element which was defensive. Hapsburg power was considerable and the possibility of some Hapsburg ruler controlling Spain, the Empire and the Spanish Netherlands was the nightmare of many French diplomats. This fear of encirclement seemed to take on a concrete form when in 1686, Spain, Bavaria, the Elector Palatine and Sweden came together in the so-called League of Augsburg. This claimed to be a purely defensive agreement among rulers who had interests in the Low Countries and in Germany, and who were anxious that existing treaties should be adhered to and that the King of France would cease his aggression. Louis, however, saw no reason why William and the Emperor Leopold should not use this League for their own purposes. This was all the more likely since the Emperor was winning his battles in the east (Belgrade was to be captured in 1688) and was appearing more and more as the defender of Christendom against the Turk and the Champion of Catholicism against the Lutheran Hungarians. There was reason to believe that Leopold's allies extended beyond the states who had united at Augsburg, and that they represented a formidable combination.

With the conviction that war was bound to come, Louis was determined to seize the initiative. He profited from a complicated affair over the electorate of Cologne in which he claimed he had been badly treated, and in September, 1688, he unleashed his troops. The Papal possession of Avignon was seized since Louis objected to the continual resistance of the Pope to his schemes; French troops invaded the Palatinate and began to devastate it. In this way the French would either be secured for a long time from any attack from this area, or they would become the undisputed masters of the Rhine. The English Revolution of 1688, in which William of Orange replaced James II and thereby greatly increased his power, probably meant that the major French preoccupation was to leave only light forces in the east so as to concentrate on attacking Flanders, and the destruction of the crops and the towns of the Palatinate meant that no army could be maintained there. But the action of the French armies caused great indignation, and in Germany it was said that the real descendants of Charlemagne were to be found east of the Rhine.

A number of German princes who had been admirers and even imitators of Louis XIV formed a coalition against him and reoccupied the Palatinate in spite of the devastation. The French were also attacked in Flanders. In view of these circumstances and because the French King, having to fight on various fronts at once, was essentially weak, Louis pursued a largely defensive policy. Certain of his projected offensives did not materialize. For example, James II, who was supported by some French troops, failed in his invasion of Ireland, and the idea of invading England had to be dropped when a combined Anglo-Dutch fleet defeated the French admiral Tourville at La Hogue. But under the command of Luxembourg the French army continued to win important battles. In 1693 he gained a decisive victory against the Dutch at Neerwinden.

By the end of 1693 Louis began to think seriously of making peace. 1694 showed a stalemate, with little military activity on either side. It was clear that France's enemies had considerable resources which they were slowly developing, whilst in France itself there were many reports of how the country was suffering from over-taxation and from war-weariness. There were famines and there was disorder, one witness describing France as "a huge hospital".

But the diplomatic negotiations were slow and complicated. Louis still believed that he could impose his will to the extent of reversing the English revolution and reinstating James II as king of England, and this created an impasse between him and William III which seemed unbreakable. It was on another front that the situation began to move. The Duke of Savoy was induced to abandon his German allies in return for the restitution of Nice (which had been conquered by the French). Once the coalition had been broken, then the differences between William and Leopold became more open and negotiations started up in earnest. Louis now showed himself to be very conciliatory. The reason for this was that he had had news that the ill and childless King of Spain, Charles the Sufferer, was certainly dying. Having failed to terrorize Europe, he now believed that he would have to have the co-operation of the other European powers if he were to hope for the Spanish succession. He therefore gave back the territories which he had annexed by quasi-legal means since the 1680's, with the exception of Strasbourg. He returned Lorraine to its ruler. He recognized William III as King of England and he allowed the Dutch to garrison certain towns in the Spanish Netherlands. In 1698 the Treaty of Ryswick was signed by France, England, Holland, Spain, and after a short delay, by the Hapsburg Emperor. In France this treaty was received with consternation. But Louis had his eyes fixed on the greater prize of the Spanish succession.

The principal claimants to the Spanish throne were Louis himself, or his children or grandchildren (by direct descent and by his first marriage), Leopold and his descendants (also by direct descent and by a first marriage) and Leopold's grandson, the infant Elector of Bavaria. At first it was thought that some compromise could be reached whereby the Spanish inheritance could be partitioned. But Louis was in a delicate position. William would never accept that the French should occupy the Spanish Netherlands, and Leopold would never accept that the French would inherit the Spanish possessions in Italy. In 1699 the Elector of Bavaria died and Louis and Leopold confronted one another. Then it was that the invalid King of Spain determined that the greatness of Spain could only be preserved by unity; and rejecting any idea of partition, his will declared that Philip of Anjou, grandson of Louis, should succeed to all his dominions, whilst renouncing any expectations of the French throne. Charles died in November, 1700, and after some hesitation Louis accepted the will, feeling that he had no real alternative.

It seemed that war was inevitable, certainly against Leopold who immediately began his preparations. Assuming that the other powers would join him Louis took various initiatives. He declared that Philip could succeed to the French throne, and he interfered openly in matters of state in Spain. He attacked the Dutch garrison troops. He recognized the new Stuart pretender as King of England. It appeared that the Pyrenees had ceased to exist and that the power of the French King might be overwhelming.

The long war which followed was notable for many things. The victory of Marlborough at Blenheim in 1704 was the first serious defeat that the French army had suffered under the rule of Louis XIV. To underline the fact that Louis was not invincible Marlborough was to win other victories. These military defeats were made all the worse by the terrible conditions within France, where bankruptcy seemed to threaten along with many murmurings of distress and discontent. As absolute ruler the king was held responsible and he was openly criticized. In 1711 and 1712 there occurred several unexpected deaths of those who were in the line of succession and it was as if fate itself had joined the coalition against the French King. But the French armies were resilient and in spite of all their set-backs succeeded in gaining certain victories.

It was these victories which facilitated the final making of peace. War-weariness was not confined to France. A new government in England refused to serve Dutch interests, whilst the deaths of Leopold (in 1705) and his successor Francis (in 1711) facilitated Hapsburg acceptance of peace terms. By the Treaty of Utrecht, in 1713, Louis gave up the Spanish Netherlands, which were to become Austrian, as were the Italian territories belonging to Spain. But his grandson remained in possession of Spain and the Spanish overseas empire, whilst abandoning his claim to the French throne. Anne was recognized as the Queen in England, and the Elector of Brandenburg as King of Prussia. This was very far from being a great expansion of French power and territory, and although he had avoided a Hapsburg inheritance in Spain, this might have contributed to the sadness of Louis's final days until he died in September, 1715.

These French wars of conquest were to stand as a warning to other powers. In one way, they helped to emphasize the differences between states. England was more committed to the continent than before and was emerging as a great power. The Hapsburgs had expanded into the Netherlands and Italy and had finally defeated the Turks. It was not yet clear that this was going to deprive them of their role in Europe, and people were only conscious of the extension of the ensemble of territories under their rule. With the decline of Swedish control on the mainland of Europe, it was also clear that Prussia was going to play an important part in the future, whilst the same could be said of Savoy in Italy. But whilst Louis can be held responsible, to some extent, for this increasing divisiveness in Europe, the concept of the balance of power, based upon some sort of a consensus amongst the European states was also strengthened. The influence of the French language, of French culture and thought was also much more considerable than it had been. Perhaps it was in these years that the idea grew that France thought the thoughts that the world had need of.

ISAAC NEWTON

(1642–1727)

LEAVING aside, for the moment, the famous incident of the falling apple, Newton's life's work is perhaps most elegantly summarized in the Latin inscription on the monument above his tomb in Westminster Abbey, which, translated, reads:

> "Here lies Sir Isaac Newton, Knight, who, by a vigour of mind almost supernatural, first demonstrated the motions and figures of the planets, the paths of the comets and the tides of the ocean. He diligently investigated the different refrangibilities of the rays of light and the properties of the colours to which they give rise. An assiduous, sagacious and faithful interpreter of nature, antiquity and the Holy Scriptures, he asserted in his philosophy the majesty of God, and he exhibited in his conduct the simplicity of the Gospel. Let mortals rejoice that there has existed such and so great an ornament of the human race. Born 25th December 1642, died 20th March, 1727."

There is no significance in the fact that Newton was born on Christmas Day, but he was certainly born in troubled times. He was six years old when Charles I was beheaded and Cromwell seized power for eleven years. He was a contemporary of Samuel Pepys, to name but one of the many famous people who emerged during the post-Reformation and Renaissance era. He had reached his mid-twenties at the time of the Great Plague and the Great Fire of London. He lived through the Restoration of Charles II and the subsequent reigns of James II, William of Orange, Queen Anne and the first of the Hanoverian Georges. Indeed, he died in the same year as George I.

The year 1642 marked both the birth of Isaac Newton and the death of Galileo, the famous astronomer and philosopher. Newton's birthplace was the manor house of Woolsthorpe-by-Colsterworth, about six miles from Grantham, in the valley of Witham in Lincolnshire. The parish register still contains the record: *Isaac sonne of Isaac and Hanna Newton Baptized Jan, 1, 1642/3.*

The manor house still exists; a plaque over the front door

commemorates Newton's birth, and not far away is the orchard in which an apple falling from a tree triggered off a line of thought that led to Newton's discovery of the law of gravitation. An off-shoot of that original apple tree is said to be there to this day.

Newton did not start life with the best of advantages, even though his father, a farmer, was "lord of the manor". For one thing, his father died three months before his son was born; for another, he was born prematurely and was so frail and weak that he was not expected to survive. Finally, his mother remarried within two years and moved to another village to live with her new husband, the Reverend Barnabas Smith, leaving baby Isaac in the care of his grandmother. Genius, however, is often stimulated by early adversity.

While Cromwell's Ironsides and King Charles's Royalists were fighting the civil war, Newton was being taught the "three Rs" at a local school within walking distance, where he stayed until the age of twelve. The next four years were spent at Kings School in Grantham where, incidentally, he carved his initials and name in the woodwork ledges. They can still be seen in the old school building where he was educated.

His training at that point was dramatically interrupted by the death, in 1656, of his step-father. He was withdrawn from school and brought back home to learn to be a farmer and manage the estate. The point here is that Newton was not particularly bright at school, nor was he interested in games; perhaps his only prowess at that time was an inventive facility for handicraft and experimentation. The true Newton had not yet emerged. Like Einstein, centuries later, he was a slow developer.

The enforced return to farm life proved to be a disastrous failure—young Isaac was simply not interested in farm work. During his years at school he had been an avid reader of books, and had revealed a mechanical turn of mind, making various gadgets and using his pocket money to buy materials and tools. He built a practical model windmill for grinding grain, which worked well, and then modified it to be driven by a mouse, which also worked well, except that the mouse ate the grain. He also made paper kites with illuminated lanterns attached to their tails, which at night caused some alarm to local inhabitants.

One of the more interesting devices was a water-clock made of wood. It stood about four feet high, and had a dial face on which the hours were indicated by a floating piece of wood which moved upwards as the reservoir was gradually filled by water dripping from a container. Some years later at a meeting of the Royal Society he perceptively pointed out the faults of this primitive method of timekeeping, namely, gradual furring-up of the tiny water-drip aperture due to impurities in the water. In the same way hour-glasses using sand were also inaccurate after a period because "the sand will wear the hole thro' which is transmitted bigger."

One can detect the emerging pattern of logical thought, and the balancing of practical advantages against disadvantages, an attitude of mind which was to develop more rapidly in succeeding years and become a characteristic of the adult man. But back to Grantham school again, and then to university. He was admitted to Trinity College, Cambridge, on 5 June, 1661.

By this time Newton's character was beginning to crystallize. He was single-minded and capable of exercising self-discipline. He belonged to nobody (apart from an abiding affection for his mother), and could be suspicious and bad-tempered even with his best friends. He seemed to gravitate towards controversies, and often said or did things that pained his admirers. He loved solitude, and, like Einstein, was very much of a "lone wolf". Part of this may have been due to an inherent artistic temperament, for he possessed a notable talent for drawing—whether birds, animals, ships or men. Throughout his life he kept detailed notebooks, but some inner sensitivity compelled him to destroy all those of a personal nature, and it is mainly in surviving letters that a reasonably true picture of the man himself emerges.

On the whole, he tended to be a friendless person—that is to say, he had colleagues rather than friends. His open hostility to critics was probably indicative of an innate sensitivity. To most people outside his family; he was somewhat remote; he was cool and even offhand to his friends, who generally took care not to offend him, for he could be very vindictive.

He tended to be careless and slovenly in dress and habits, and in his eating habits he was totally erratic. It was not unusual for him to be two hours late for dinner, and his breakfast was invariably cold by the time he reached it. He was not, however, the typical "absent-minded scientist"; if his thoughts often seemed far away, it was because of concentration and not distraction.

Newton had no desire to travel and lived almost as a recluse at Cambridge, though later in his life he moved to London as he assumed a more public life, in Parliament and at the Mint. In general, however, he rarely travelled, other than to visit his family at Woolsthorpe.

Although when he first went to Cambridge he was engaged to be married, he never did so, and his life became more and more scholastic and, indeed, monastic, for theology was another of his great interests. He remained at Cambridge for nearly forty years—the first seven years as a student until he gained his M.A. degree, and the rest of the time as Fellow of Trinity College and Lucasian Professor of Mathematics.

His early years at Cambridge were presumably not particularly happy since, not being a public-school entrant, he had joined as a subsizar (a kind of fag) paying for his tuition and board by carrying out menial tasks, running errands, helping in the kitchen, waiting on his tutor, and so on. He studied classics, logic and some elementary mathematics. Yet it was during these undergraduate years that he discovered the binomial theorem—an important algebraic formula for expanding any power of $(1 + x)$.

The mathematical tuition may have been elementary, but Newton's approach to it certainly was not, for very quickly he devised original forms of analytical geometry and trigonometry. At the same time he was interested in the mathematics of optics, and in the practical aspects of grinding and polishing lenses. He became thoroughly versed in Latin which at that time was virtually an international language for the publication of all important scientific and theological tracts. He was proficient in Greek and knew some Hebrew, but was hardly aware that the French and German languages existed. That was the overall pattern of classical education in those days.

Newton's creative invention was at its peak during the two or three years of the Black Death and the Great Fire of London. When the plague started the university closed, so he returned to Woolsthorpe for nearly two years. During that period, continuing his personal studies, he made three major discoveries in science; the mathematical method of "fluxions" (i.e. calculus), the composition of light, and the law of universal gravitation. Oddly enough, Newton was always reluctant to disclose his findings, probably because of his extreme sensitivity to criticism. Although he wrote five important papers while at Woolsthorpe, some of his results were deliberately withheld and not made public until the end of the century.

Leaving calculus and gravitation aside Newton developed a

high proficiency in grinding optical lenses, based on studies of the Copernican theory and work by Kepler and Descartes. In doing so, however, he came upon the irritating phenomenon of chromatic aberration in which a lens separates out the colours of white light in a spectrum-like fashion. The reason for this was not known at that time. To overcome this problem, in his characteristically practical fashion, Newton experimented with concave mirrors instead of curved lenses, where the phenomenon of chromatic aberration does not occur, and thus laid the foundation for today's giant optical telescopes which use concave mirrors several hundred feet in diameter.

Then, during the same short period, came the theory of gravitation—and here the famous apple enters into the picture. Newton's biographer, Conduitt, recorded that "in the year 1665, when he retired to his own estate on account of the plague, he first thought of his system of gravity, which he hit upon by observing an apple fall from a tree". An historical moment indeed.

Newton's own observations on the phenomenon of the falling apple were not made until he was eighty-four years old, when he said to a biographer: "Why should the apple always descend perpendicularly to the ground? Why should it not go sideways or upwards, but constantly to the earth's centre? Assuredly, the earth draws it. There must be a drawing power in matter . . . it must be in proportion to its quantity. Therefore the apple draws the earth, as well as the earth draws the apple. There is a power that we here call gravity which extends itself through the universe."

When Newton returned to Cambridge in 1667 he was elected a Minor Fellow, but became a Major Fellow in 1668 and achieved his M.A. degree in the same year. In less than eight years he had risen from the humble rank of subsizar to the high status of Fellow of Trinity College. One year later he became the Lucasian Professor of Mathematics, one of the highest honours in the scientific world. His income was now adequate and he had freedom to pursue his own scholarly studies and research.

The period from 1668 to 1678 has been called the "optical decade" of Newton's academic career (characteristically, his lectures were never published until 1704). His first practical major achievement, having rejected the principle of the refracting telescope because of chromatic diffraction, was the construction of a small reflecting telescope embodying a concave metallic mirror instead of a normal objective lens. This instrument was about six inches long with an aperture of just over one inch, and it gave a magnification of 40 diameters. Newton considered that it gave a more distinct image than a conventional four-foot telescope: "I have seen with it Jupiter distinctly round and his satellites, and Venus horned . . . I do not doubt but in time that a six-foot tube may be made after this method, which will perform as much as any 60 or 100-foot tube made after the common way."

Although the first telescope was lost, Newton made a second and better one which he demonstrated to the Royal Society. It was inspected personally by King Charles II. It exists today, and is one of the most valued possessions of the Society. It was as a result of this invention that Newton was elected a Fellow of the Royal Society in January, 1672.

Newton's next important work concerned the nature of light and colour, using prisms to study refraction and the spectral composition of white light. He was able to formulate three laws on the nature and constitution of light, and anticipated modern ideas by accepting that light could be regarded as either a particle or waveform since under different conditions it would behave as either. The first edition of his work *Opticks* was published in English in 1703— and promptly attracted criticism of his scientific methods because they appeared to contradict established hypotheses.

Criticism made Newton angry and defensive, particularly when some of the criticism was abusive. His response was to withdraw more and more into his cloistered academic world and show increasing reluctance to make his work public. Some biographers say it was vanity; others modesty. It was probably a combination of both, accentuated by an inherent sensitivity.

One of his opponents was Robert Hooke, seven years older than Newton, who had also carried out work on the composition of light and had produced a hypothesis, whereas Newton's theory was based on practical experiment and measurement. Newton would not accept purely hypothetical reasoning and the formulation of laws which could not be substantiated by experiment.

Hooke's career had paralleled that of Newton's. He had been puny at birth and not expected to survive. He was educated at Westminster School which had a high reputation for scientific education, after which he went to Oxford University, itself a responsible body in the development of the Royal Society. He also possessed a mechanical bent, inventing an air pump for Boyle in his work on gas pressure, coiled springs for clocks, and a man-powered flying machine (which did not work). He became curator and "official experimenter" of the Royal Society until his death, in which position he was well placed to attack Newton's work. Indeed, at one point he charged Newton of plagiarism of his own studies on light and lenses. Certainly the ideas of Hooke and Newton about light were never far apart; also Newton was an avid reader and often "borrowed" from various relevant material without always acknowledging the source.

Hooke went further. In his Royal Society function of evaluating the new work of others he advised Newton "as a novice" to continue the practical development of the telescope, but to leave the question of light to those who had developed a satisfactory hypothesis—and, in any case, he claimed, most of the discoveries had already been made by himself. Newton was not the man to ignore such a challenge. In reply he published a scathing counter-attack in which he not only defended his own work, but criticized Hooke's hypothesis in very great detail. And so the battle began—although it was a pattern to be repeated over and over again with other critics of Newton's work if they chose to enter the lists.

Perhaps the most famous dispute in which Newton was involved was that with Gottfried Wilhelm Leibnitz, the German philosopher and mathematician four years younger than Newton, who was elected a Fellow of the Royal Society in 1673 for the invention of a new complex calculating machine. The focus of the dispute was, who had invented the differential and integral calculus? Leibnitz made the claim in 1673, but Newton had written his original paper on "fluxions" (which embraced both differential and integral calculus) in 1665, although it was not actually published until 1674—one year after Leibnitz's claim. This was the kind of situation likely to arise because of Newton's dilatoriness in the publication of his work.

Until the learned societies were formed and chartered in the mid-seventeenth century there was no public way of disseminating the results of research other than by correspondence, and the habit died hard. The fight for recognition in respect of calculus continued for nearly forty years, when finally the Royal Society appointed a committee to investigate the matter. The committee's findings were in favour of Newton. Leibnitz refused to accept the decision as final, especially as Halley, the astronomer, an important member of the Royal Society committee, was a known supporter of Newton. The row continued unhappily until the death of Leibnitz in 1716.

(For the mathematical reader, Newton used a dot placed over the algebraic letter concerned to represent the "fluxion". It was Leibnitz who introduced the symbols dx and dy for the differentials of x and y, and this is the system of notation that has survived today—so perhaps Leibnitz is not entirely without immortality in this matter, even though Newton is officially credited with the invention of calculus. In any event, Leibnitz's reputation rests securely on his great achievements as a metaphysical philosopher.)

The French mathematician, Professor J. Hadamard commented: "Leibnitz had only become acquainted with Newton's discovery, at any rate directly, some years later. Let us simply notice that Newton's creation was one thing, Leibnitz's another, and that in his epic discoveries the former was not inspired by the latter."

The trouble was that in the emerging scientific climate of the day there existed much sensitivity about the possible plagiarism of inventions and discoveries, and this was one of the reasons why many scientists and mathematicians declined to publish their results, or, if they did, omitted proofs and even used special codes to conceal their reasoning. It was always possible that a number of people in different countries might, unknown to each other, be working simultaneously on identical problems, so that the question of claiming priorities became important.

Newton's theory of gravitation was also a source of argument and controversy. He postulated the "mutual attraction" of matter and light, which nearly three centuries later became one of the basic tenets of Einstein's gravitational theory and was duly verified by precise observation of the positions of stars visible near to the sun's "blacked-out" disc during a total eclipse. Newton also accepted the apparent ambivalence of light in its behaviour as both a particle and a vibration—again, one of the paradoxical fundamentals of modern physics.

It was Clerk Maxwell who much later, in 1873, was to predict that an electromagnetic oscillation would be propagated through space at the velocity of light, thereby implying that light itself was in the form of an electromagnetic wave. Thus, the existence of "ether", the all-pervading medium in which light travelled, began to die a slow death, though even today the true nature of light remains much of a mystery, despite the brilliant work of scientists such as Lorentz and Einstein.

The situation has been summed up thus:

> Nature and nature's laws
> Lay hid in night.
> God said, *Let Newton be!*
> And all was light.
>
> *Alexander Pope*

To which came the riposte:

> It did not last:
> The devil howling, *Ho!*
> *Let Einstein be!*
> Restored the status quo.
>
> *Colling Squires*

Newton's work on light was eventually published, much delayed, in 1704. The following extract from the preface to the book (written when Newton was over sixty) is indicative of his reluctance to publish a work that might result in dispute and controversy.

"To avoid being engaged in disputes about these matters, I have hitherto delayed the printing, and should still have delayed it had not the importunity of friends prevailed upon me. If any other papers writ on this subject are got out of my hands they are imperfect, and were perhaps written before I had tried all the experiments here set down, and fully satisfied myself about the refraction and composition of colours."

And the first sentence of the first of the three books which make up *Opticks* is typical of Newton's philosophy: "My design in this book is not to explain the properties of light by hypothesis, but to propose and prove them by reason and experiment." Hence Newton's oft-quoted statement—*hypotheses non fingo* (I do not frame hypotheses). Many of the experiments involved the commonplace phenomena of the colours on soap bubbles and the coloured patterns produced by a thin film of oil on water or pieces of flat glass in close contact which today are known as Newton's rings, and are due to the interference of reflecting light waves at different frequencies.

Newton's original tiny reflecting telescope was the forerunner of today's giants throughout the world, the largest of which is the 200-inch on Mount Palomar in the U.S.A. In the Royal Greenwich Observatory at Herstmonceux, Sussex, is a 98-inch reflecting instrument named the Isaac Newton Telescope, the mirror of which was made in America and presented to the observatory by the University of Michigan and the Tracy McGregor Fund.

Perhaps Newton's most important work lay in his laws of motion and gravitation, and were developed from earlier work by the great astronomers Kepler, Tycho Brahé and Galileo, all of whom encountered hostility because of their radical and even "heretical" views. The fundamentals of Kepler's work on elliptical planetary orbits and the mathematics involved appeared in a book published in 1619 and dedicated to James I. Newton went further and produced a generalized system of celestial and terrestrial mechanics, taking into account the effect of gravitation.

His early work on gravitation started around 1666, but it was not until a generation later, in 1687, that his ideas were published in his famous work, *Philosophiae Naturalia Principia Mathematica*, which is usually known as the *Principia*. What he proved was that any two bodies mutually attract each other in direct proportion to the product of their masses and in inverse proportion to the square of their distance apart. The *Principia* also states Newton's three laws of motion, which are still valid today. They, are briefly: (1) absence of force implies uniform motion in a straight line; (2) rate of change of motion is determined by force; and (3) for every force there is an equal and opposite reaction. The latter principle is the foundation of space flight, for rockets are propelled by such a reaction and not because they "push against the air".

Because of the bitter dispute between Hooke and Newton, the *Principia* might never have been published at all. The Royal Society was also short of funds. In the event, Halley acted as patron and undertook to pay the printing costs, and many of the plates and engravings were donated by others (including Samuel Pepys, who paid for about 80 of them). The first edition of the *Principia* contained 500 small quarto pages and sold at nine shillings per copy. The second edition did not appear until 1713; it was priced at 21 shillings (or 15 shillings unbound). A third edition appeared in 1726.

Newton's motivation was always the pursuit of simplicity in seeking an explanation of phenomena, and the *Principia* clearly states his "Rules of Reasoning in Philosophy", thus:

(1) We are to admit to no more causes of natural things than such as are both true and sufficient to explain their appearances.

(2) Therefore, to the same natural effects we must, as far as possible, assign the same causes.

(3) The qualities of bodies, which admit neither intensification

nor remission of degrees, and which are found to belong to all bodies within the reach of our experiments, are to be esteemed the universal properties of all bodies whatsoever.

(4) In experimental philosophy we are to look upon propositions inferred by general induction from the phenomena as accurately or very nearly true, notwithstanding any contrary hypothesis that may be imagined, till such time as other phenomena occur, by which they either be made more accurate, or liable to exceptions.

That was Newton the scientist, but it is often overlooked that he was also intensely interested in theology, and in the later decades of his life he wrote extensively on that subject—indeed, it has been estimated that he wrote more than one and a quarter million words on theological subjects, equivalent to seventeen books. Philosopher John Locke wrote: "Mr. Newton is a very valuable man, not only for his wonderful skill in mathematics, but in divinity too, and his great knowledge of the Scriptures, wherein I know few his equals." But Newton's theological writings were not published for more than two hundred years, presumably because of the turbulent religious atmosphere of his age. In one of his books he refers to the fact that in Queen Mary's reign 284 Protestants (800 according to another report) were burnt at the stake, quite apart from those imprisoned and deported.

It was as recently as 1934 that the first detailed research into Newton's theological writings was carried out by Professor L. T. More of the University of Cincinnati. After the Second World War a large collection of Newton's original theological manuscripts was donated to King's College, Cambridge, by Lord Keynes.

Newton's public life began when he was elected to represent the University in the Convention Parliament. He left Cambridge to take up residence in London, and there is little doubt that he left reluctantly. His room at Cambridge was virtually a laboratory which, according to a contemporary, "was well furnished with chymical materials as bodyes, receivers, heads, crucibles, etc., which was made very little use of, the crucibles excepted, in which he fused his metals. He would sometimes look into an old mouldy book which lay in his laboratory, I think it was titled *Agricola de Metallis*, the transmuting of metals being his chief design".

Was Newton genuinely interested in alchemy? He was certainly interested in chemistry, and for a man who travelled little had a surprising knowledge of mineral deposits and refining operations in Europe. But it seems more likely that his experiments in "alchemy" were in the pursuit of knowledge rather than the transmutation of base metals into gold.

All that was to be replaced by a different kind of life in London. The Convention Parliament lasted only two years before its dissolution. Then in 1693, Newton's mother died, which upset him greatly. For months he slept little, and went through a long period of ill health. But by the end of the year he had recovered sufficiently to be able to take up a new appointment with The Mint, of which he was to become Warden, at a salary of £400.

The Mint in those days was housed between the inner and outer walls of the Tower of London, and was patrolled by sentries. A new mechanical process had been introduced which could strike a coin every two seconds to replace the old manual punch-and-hammer method. A process of "recoining" was under way, for the old silver coins not only lost physical value by normal wear and tear, but were only too frequently filed or clipped by those who could sell the accumulated silver clippings. All the old handstruck silver coins were being withdrawn. It is worth noting that at that time Sir Christopher Wren recommended a system of decimal currency but some three hundred years were to pass before it finally achieved reality. The Bank of England was established in 1694 to handle the increasing National Debt and also to provide a borrowing facility for the Government to finance its Continental wars.

While at the Mint, Newton continued his work and research into mathematics and theoretical physics. When the existing Master of The Mint, Thomas Neale, died in 1699, Newton took over full responsibility; he was then fifty-seven years old. Two years later he again stood successfully for Parliament, but this lasted only one year until Parliament was dissolved. His political life was short-lived. Nevertheless, in the 1705 election he was again a candidate, but was defeated.

Newton's period at the Mint created in him an interest in the design of medals and medallions, and he carried out a survey for the Treasury of international coinage. One of the medallions he designed was for the Royal Mathematical School within Christ's Hospital, showing three boys in the traditional "bluecoat" dress. Indeed, Newton was one of the original Governors of Christ's Hospital, along with Samuel Pepys, Locke, Wren and others. Christ's Hospital today remains one of Britain's oldest public schools, the main boy's school being located at Horsham in Sussex, and the girl's school at Hertford in Middlesex.

In the closing years of his life he was elected President of the Royal Society, the chair which had held so many great men before and so truly joining the ranks of the illustrious. And two years later, in April, 1703, he was knighted by Queen Anne. It is recorded that on this occasion the University of Cambridge was so short of funds that it had to borrow £500 in order to entertain the royal visitor in the manner to which she was accustomed.

In his later years, Newton lived in Jermyn Street in London, moved to Chelsea, then Westminster, and finally Kensington. It is said that he often amused himself by blowing soap bubbles from a clay pipe—but probably for reflective or even nostalgic reasons, still studying the changing colour patterns of light diffraction.

From 1722 onwards his health deteriorated rapidly; he suffered from a stone in the bladder, followed by gout and then serious lung trouble. He died on 20 March, 1727, at the age of eighty-four a grand old man of science who had, by his own genius, laid the foundations on which in the centuries to come other men of genius, particularly in Europe, were destined to build towards today's advanced technologies, resulting in such extremes as the H-bomb and human footprints in the dust of the dead moon. Without Newton there could never have been an Einstein, though whether the world would have been happier or sorrier is a question for historians and philosophers to answer retrospectively.

Perhaps the point is that Newton, although virtually a recluse, doing little but thinking a lot, made an impact on science and society which spread throughout Europe and then throughout the world. Even now, after three centuries, his reasoning is still valid, though it may have been modified and extended here and there.

The mortal proof of his importance to mankind is that after his death he lay in state in recognition of his greatness, and was duly buried in Westminster Abbey in London.

Of Newton's own notebooks, seven still exist today. One is in a New York library, and the other six are at Cambridge University, where he spent so much of his creative life. In the ante-chapel of Trinity College, Cambridge, is a memorial statue of Sir Isaac Newton bearing the brief but dignified inscription:

NEWTON

Who surpassed all men of genius

PETER THE GREAT

(1672–1725)

PETER the Great was neither the first nor the last Russian ruler to try to transform his country into a European power, but his attempt was certainly the most dramatic. Historians are less certain how successful he was. Lord Acton's verdict was characteristically uncompromising: "In a single reign, by the action of one man, Russia passed from lethargy and obscurity to a dominant position among the nations." More recently Richard Charques has written: "A semi-Asiatic and medieval land before he set to work upon it, Russia remained largely semi-Asiatic and medieval after he had done." Yet there is no doubt that Peter's efforts were heroic—even in failure.

Contemporary travellers regarded Russia as an oriental state—certainly more Byzantine than European—and were forthright in condemning the barbarism of its inhabitants. Olearius of Holstein wrote in 1643 that "if a man considers the natures and manners of life of the Muscovites, he will be forced to avow that there cannot be anything more barbarous than that people".

The circumstances of Peter's rise to power were barbarous enough. His father, Alexis, who ruled as Tsar from 1645 to 1676, had married twice. Peter, the first child of his second wife, Natalia Naryshkin, was born in the Kremlin on 30 May, 1672. When Alexis died four years later, it was Theodore, the eldest son of the first marriage, who succeeded him. But when he in turn died in 1682, Peter was illegally proclaimed Tsar in preference to Theodore's younger brother, Ivan. Ivan's relatives staged a counter-coup with the aid of the *Streltsi*, the imperial palace guard, who butchered most of the Naryshkin faction in the corridors of the Kremlin before the terrified eyes of Peter and his mother. Peter, still only ten, was theoretically to rule jointly with Ivan under the regency of Ivan's sister, Sophia; but he and his mother were in fact exiled to their country estates. In 1689 rumours of a fresh coup drove Peter to seek sanctuary in a monastery in the forest. This time the coup failed. It was now Sophia's turn to be confined to a convent, and Peter's mother became effective regent. Ivan continued to fulfil the ceremonial functions of a ruler, in partnership with Peter, until his death in 1696.

Engelbert Kämpfer, a German traveller in the temporary employment of the Swedish envoy, described the impression that the two boy-tsars made on him when he was presented to them in 1683. Whereas Ivan, with the imperial crown well down over his eyes, sat like a lifeless statue on his silver throne and stared at the floor, Peter, a lively, handsome eleven-year-old wearing a replica crown and sitting on an identical throne, looked eagerly and confidently about him and found it difficult to keep still.

Peter's restlessness and untiring energy were to become as proverbial as his ruthlessness. He walked so quickly and with so long a stride that his companions had to run to keep up with him. He found it difficult to sit through banquets without jumping up to stretch his legs. He had a great interest in practical techniques and insisted on trying to master every new technique himself. He even practised dentistry—and not simply for sadistic reasons. He was forever making things, from chairs to snuff-boxes, and his enthusiasm for ship-building is well-known.

This zest for manual work, combined with the notorious boorishness of his behaviour, made it difficult for the ruling classes of western Europe to take him seriously when he arrived in their midst on his diplomatic tour in 1697. The eight volumes of Louis XIV's dispatches for that year contain only one incidental reference to Peter's European visit, while the commemorative plaque in the royal park at Brussels (which marks the spot where he stopped to be sick after a heavy drinking bout) describes him simply as the Duke of Muscovy. The European courts did not greatly relish the drunkenness of the Tsar and his retinue, his liking for practical jokes and fireworks, or his ill-sustained attempt to travel incognito under the name of Peter Mikhailov. What were they to think of a ruler who scorned protocol and worked for four months in the ship-yards of Holland, wearing the garb of a Dutch sailor?

Peter's interest in ships was genuine enough. The ostensible reason for the Grand Embassy—the first foreign tour by a Russian ruler since the eleventh century—was to try to build up a European coalition to fight the Turks. But he also needed a navy. The leading members of the embassy were given secret instructions to look for capable naval captains and lieutenants "who had reached their present rank through merit and not through influence", and to recruit "as many trained men as possible". While he was working in the shipyards of Amsterdam and Deptford, learning new construction techniques, another mission of nineteen noblemen had been sent to Venice with a letter of introduction informing the Doge that the Tsar wished them to "learn the new methods of warfare as practised in Europe". William III of England delighted Peter by making him a present of the new yacht, the *Royal Transport*. Indeed, the British government carried courtesy to the point of sending Vice-Admiral Mitchell with a squadron of two warships, two yachts and a sloop to bring the Tsar from Holland to England. Meanwhile Admiral Benbow was turned out of Sayes Court, John Evelyn's country house which had recently been leased to him, in order to allow Peter to live conveniently close to the Royal Docks. Evelyn had complained that the Admiral was not a "polite tenant", but he was soon to regret displacing him in favour of the Russians. He recorded in his diary for 9 June, 1698: "I went to Deptford to view how miserably the Tzar of Muscovy had left my house after three months making it his court."

From the Tsar's point of view, the Grand Embassy had been a great success—even though he had to cut it short in order to hurry home to deal with another revolt of the *Streltsi*. He had recruited nearly 1,000 experts for service in Russia and shipped 260 cases of naval stores and munitions back to Moscow. The experts, chiefly in naval and military engineering and in mining, included Captain John Perry, an hydraulic engineer who was to be responsible for constructing a dam linking the Don to the Volga, and Henry Farquharson, who later established a school of mathematics and navigation in Moscow. Peter had also obtained £12,000 in advance payments of customs dues as a result of granting a monopoly to a group of English merchants to import tobacco into Russia. Lefort, the leading member of the embassy, described it as "a fine stroke of business". As he sailed out of Margate in the *Royal Transport* on 25 April, 1698, Peter could congratulate himself on having achieved much in England—even if he had failed to create his hoped-for coalition against the Turks.

The Turks were not Russia's only enemy. A century earlier, in the so-called Time of Troubles (1585–1613) the Swedes and Poles had over-run the Muscovite lands almost completely. The seventeenth century had seen a gradual and painful recovery of those lost territories so that by 1682 the western frontiers of Russia ran from just above Pskov in the north, through Smolensk and Kiev, to the shores of the Caspian in the south. But the Russians were still denied access both to the Black Sea and the Baltic.

In 1695 Peter had attacked the Turks in order to force a way through to the Black Sea. His first attempt to seize Azov, the Turkish fort at the mouth of the Don, had failed dismally through lack of naval support. But with the help of a hastily assembled flotilla of galleys, he succeeded in taking the fortress in the summer of 1696. The capture of Azov was not enough, however, since the outlet from the Sea of Azov into the Black Sea itself was controlled by another fortress—Kertch. The failure of Peter's plans for a new anti-Turkish coalition forced him to conclude peace in 1700. (The Austrians, Venetians and Poles had made peace with the Turks by the Treaty of Karlowitz in the previous year.) This upset Peter's Black Sea strategy, for the peace left him with Azov, but without Kertch. Indeed, when a second Turkish war broke out in 1710 he would be forced to give up Azov, too. Meanwhile he turned his attention from the Black Sea to the Baltic.

In 1700 he invaded Ingria and laid siege to the Baltic town of Narva with a force of some 40,000 men. But the eighteen-year-old King of Sweden, Charles XII, with an army of only 10,000, came to the relief of Narva and completely routed the Russians. The extent of Peter's humiliation may be gauged from the fact that the Swedes killed nearly a quarter of the Russian army and captured eighteen generals, 145 cannon and 151 colours, for the loss of about 700 officers and men. Luckily for Peter, the Swedish king chose not to follow up this decisive victory. Instead Charles turned against Augustus of Saxony, whose recent election to the Polish throne he was determined to dispute. However, in undertaking not merely the seizure of some suitable slices of Polish territory, but the actual dethronement of Augustus, Charles was setting himself a colossal task. His Swedish biographer, F. G. Bengtsson, put it even more strongly: "There is no doubt that his decision to depose Augustus is the great lunacy of Charles XII's life, corresponding to Napoleon's Spanish hallucination." Not until the spring of 1708 did Charles invade Russia.

For Peter, this respite was all-important. During much of the seventeenth century the Tsar's armies had been made up mainly of feudal levies. By the time of Peter's accession, however, a system of conscription was already well under way: about half the Russian army of nearly 200,000 in 1682 was made up of peasant conscripts, mostly under foreign officers. It was still not a very effective fighting force, as events at Narva had shown. Peter's answer was to put conscription on to a more systematic basis and to extend conscription to other classes of society: sons of nobles and courtiers, sons of tradesmen, even sons of the clergy were now to be recruited.

Each year from 1705 to 1709 there was a general levy of about 30,000 recruits—at first bachelors aged 15 to 20, later of married men of 20 to 30. New recruits (one man for every twenty tax-paying homesteads) were billeted in the nearest town in companies of 500 to 1,000. They were trained by retired officers, and, when trained, were sent to fill vacancies in existing regiments, or to form new ones. The purpose of these training-centres or "muster-points" was succinctly expressed by Peter: "When fresh drafts are asked for, let there always be some available to fill the gaps." If a recruit died while at the training-centre, or deserted, the district that had sent him must immediately send a replacement "in order that the complement be maintained and everybody always be ready to serve his sovereign".

No doubt there was some discrepancy between theory and practice. In 1718 there were reckoned to be as many as 20,000 deserters; and, in spite of the introduction of western-style uniforms and the creation of a commissariat, the army lost more men from starvation and exposure than in battle. That was probably true of most eighteenth-century armies. Charles XII's main invading force when he entered Lithuania early in 1708 numbered 35,000. After a wet summer and a freakish winter, his army had shrunk to 22,000 when he at last confronted 45,000 Russians at Poltava in June, 1709. Even so, the odds would scarcely have alarmed Charles, since at Narva his victorious army had been outnumbered by four to one. But this time Peter's troops stood firm and the Swedes were routed. More than 9,000 of Charles XII's troops were killed or captured and a further 13,000 surrendered. Charles struggled southwards with a few hundred survivors to seek asylum with the Sultan.

The significance of the Russian victory at Poltava has often been stressed by historians. It can scarcely have been overlooked by contemporaries. Peter's defeat by the Turks on the banks of the Pruth in 1711, and the consequent abandonment of his hopes of a port on the Black Sea, could not alter the fact that Russia would now control the Baltic. By Charles XII's death in 1718 Peter's armies had occupied Livonia and part of eastern Finland, and the Treaty of Nystadt (1721), which formally ended the Great Northern

War, confirmed the Russian conquests. Peter's control of the Baltic shore gave him "a window to the west", a port that did not, like Archangel, become ice-bound in winter. By the end of his reign in 1725, Peter had created a fleet of 48 ships of the line, 800 galleys and smaller vessels, and 28,000 sailors. Whatever else, Peter is the unchallenged founder of the Russian navy.

Of even greater symbolic, if not strategic significance was the building of St Petersburg, capital of Russia until 1919. He started work on it as early as 1703, characteristically cutting the first sod with his own hands. It was built on the marshes of the River Neva— a Finnish word meaning "mud". The unhealthiness of the marshes contributed to the death of no less than 200,000 conscripted labourers during the construction. But if many peasants died there, the nobility were compelled to live there; and even if the walls of their palaces were soon to show alarming cracks, the fact that they were ever built bears witness to the force of the Tsar's will. By the time of his death, St Petersburg was not only a capital but an international port. The number of foreign vessels using the harbour increased from 16 in 1714 to more than 200 in 1724.

Less spectacular, but no less significant, was Peter's reform of the machinery of government. At the centre stood the traditional *Boyar Duma*, the Tsar's council. This had originally been the preserve of members of the oldest noble families of Moscow, but their influence was steadily diluted as nobles from more remote provinces were summoned to attend. In 1613 the *Duma* had numbered only 30; by 1682 there were more than 150. As its membership increased, the importance of the *Duma* declined. Although it met every morning to consider policy, government decisions were more often taken by committees of the *Duma* or by the Tsar's more informal group of favourites and confidants. In 1711, on the eve of his departure for the Turkish wars, Peter transferred its functions to a new body: "Having to absent ourselves frequently during the wars, we appoint the Senate as ruler." The Senate, though it remained an informal body subject to the Tsar's pleasure, was intended to supervise the new provincial administration, set up in 1708, under which Russia was divided into ten *gubernia* administered by a governor with the help of a council elected by the nobles. These new provincial units were preserved by Catherine the Great, though she greatly increased their number.

Regional reorganization could scarcely be expected to work so

long as the central administration was in a state of confusion.
The old central state departments or *prikazi* had multiplied during
the seventeenth century until there were as many as fifty, with
frequently overlapping jurisdictions and often with geographical
rather than functional responsibilities. Tsar Alexis, Peter's father,
had tried to improve matters by creating a special office to co-
ordinate them "to the end that the Tsar's thoughts and acts be all
fulfilled according to his wish". It was not a success. In 1718 Peter
replaced the *prikazi* by nine (later 12) administrative "colleges" on
the Swedish pattern. Each was to be responsible for a separate
branch of government, with authority over the whole country, and
each had a board of twelve members: a president, vice-president,
four councillors, four assessors and two secretaries, of whom one
councillor or assessor and one secretary were to be foreign.

The administrative reforms were intended to increase revenue.
Modern methods of warfare cost more money. The largest part of
the state revenues in the seventeenth century had come from
indirect taxes such as customs duties and the granting of trade
monopolies. The need for increased direct taxation was well
recognized, however, even before Peter's accession, and in 1679 the
old system of permitting each *prikaz* to levy and collect its own taxes
for its own needs had been replaced by a unified household tax. But
the inadequacies of the fiscal arrangements were shown by the
need for the Tsars to resort to emergency measures such as forced
loans.

Here, as in so much else, Peter's policy was a mixture of old and
new. He granted state monopolies not only in tobacco, but in salt,
cod liver oil and oak coffins. He sought also to give state encouragement to trade and industry. In 1696 the first ironworks had been
established near Moscow; by 1725 there were 86 ironworks, 15
cloth mills and six cotton mills. Foreign trade increased, and by
Peter's death the value of Russia's exports was probably as much as
double that of her imports. But the chief new source of revenue was
the substitution of the poll tax for the insufficiently productive
household tax. The new tax, announced in 1718 but not collected
until 1724, was levied on all male "souls" and imposed a much
heavier burden on the already over-taxed peasant. After one year of
operation the poll tax was 843,000 roubles in arrears. But Peter
had balanced his budget: state revenues rose from an annual
average of over three million roubles for the years 1705 to 1707 to
nearly nine million for 1724.

Financial considerations were the chief motives behind Peter's attack on the Church. After the defeat at Narva, he confiscated the bells of some 300 churches to be turned into cannon, seized the monastic estates which then employed some 900,000 serfs, and limited the jurisdiction of Church courts. While the clergy as a whole were critical of Peter, the Church itself was divided over the liturgical innovations of the Patriarch Nikon, which had provoked the schismatic group known as "Old Believers". This made it easier for Peter, on Patriarch Adrian's death in 1700, to leave the patriarchate vacant until 1721 when he finally abolished it, creating in its place a Holy Synod to manage Church affairs under the supervision of a lay official, the high procurator.

The clergy had objected to Peter's westernizing policy, which seemed to involve, not merely greater military and administrative efficiency, but a complete re-orientation of social customs. The calendar was reformed in 1700; the alphabet was simplified; nobles were encouraged to wear western clothes and were taxed if they continued to wear beards. In 1716 forty civil servants were sent to Berlin to learn German, while in 1717 appeared *The Honourable Youth's Mirror*, a manual on the manners of western society. It was an attempt to Europeanize the Russian nobility. The young nobleman was urged not to spit in the drawing-room and taught how to behave himself at table. He was advised to learn foreign languages—if only to prevent his servants from eavesdropping on his conversation—and, besides mastering the arts of horsemanship, dancing and duelling, to "show evidence of learning to the extent that he is acquainted with most popular books".

How successful was Peter in civilizing Russia's ruling class? There is some evidence that the nobles acquired the more expensive European tastes—not least the taste for good cooking. In this respect "westernization" of the nobility meant their increasing alienation from their own peasantry. The second half of the eighteenth century in Russia has been aptly described as "the golden age of the nobility and the zenith of serfdom". Under Peter, however, the nobles were made more aware of their duties than of their privileges. He compelled them to enlist in either the army or the administrative service for life. The new system of a conscript army had removed the need for the feudal obligation of the nobles to raise troops when summoned; it was replaced by the obligation to serve as an officer in a permanent army. Equally, the reforms in government called for a new class of bureaucrats, and in the circumstances of eighteenth-century Russia, only the aristocracy could staff a bureaucracy.

The way had been prepared for Peter by the ending of the traditional rules of precedence by which a man was not supposed to accept a government post less exalted than that held by any of his predecessors. Tsar Theodore changed all this shortly before his death in 1682 by the simple device of having the precedence registers burned. Similarly the distinction between hereditary estates and estates held in return for service to the state had been breaking down before Peter's accession. His decree of 1714 required all estates to be left in their entirety to a single son or relative. This measure was doubtless intended to make it more difficult for noblemen to escape the obligation of state service by retiring to a country estate, however small. In the autumn of 1714 Peter ordered all noblemen between the ages of 10 and 30 to appear during the course of that winter and register themselves at the Senate. In order to discourage evasion, anyone who denounced an absentee would receive all his wealth and estates—even if the informer was a serf. In 1722 the penalties for evasion were stiffened still further: from now on defaulters would be declared outlaws. Yet even such draconian measures did not altogether prevent noblemen from avoiding the new responsibilities that Peter was anxious to impose on them.

The system of state service was formalized in 1722 by the famous Table of Ranks with its fourteen grades of service divided into parallel ladders, civil and military, ranging from registry clerk to chancellor and from ensign to field marshal. The top eight grades carried with them hereditary nobility with its associated privileges of the right to own land and serfs, and exemption from direct taxation. Nobility of birth would no longer qualify anyone for high office: service alone could do that. And those who earned their places in the first eight ranks "whatever their birth, become the equals of the best and most ancient families, and enjoy the same dignity and advantages". Not surprisingly, the number of nobles increased until by the 1760s foreign observers put the number of nobles and their families at half a million out of a population of 28 million.

Peter may not have civilized his nobles, nor entirely succeeded in disciplining them; but he controlled them more effectively than later eighteenth-century Russian rulers managed to do. Of Peter's six immediate successors, three were women and one was a child. The Empress Elizabeth and Catherine the Great were indeed formidable women, but the nobility steadily re-asserted their privileges, and in Catherine's case it was the nobles who frustrated any ambitions she may have had of introducing reforms befitting a true "Enlightened Despot".

Peter, though called "the Great", could hardly have been an "Enlightened Despot" in the strict sense, even if he had wanted to. For one thing, he died (1725) before the writers of the French Enlightenment had begun to command a European public. For another, the motive behind almost all Peter's reforms was frankly military: he regarded his people as cannon fodder. The new machinery of government he introduced never had a chance to work properly. A further administrative unit, the regimental district, was simply superimposed on the newly established pattern of local administration, and collection of the poll tax was entrusted to the military—for whose upkeep the tax was of course intended. Similarly the new criminal code imposed on the whole population in 1716 was borrowed in its entirety from the new military code of 1715, and included various forms of the death penalty (from burning alive to impalement) for over one hundred offences.

What about educational reform—the litmus-test of an eighteenth-century ruler's "enlightenment"? In 1689 Russia's sole educational institutions comprised the theological Kiev Academy, the Moscow Academy for Slavonic, Greek and Latin, and a few scattered church schools. Apart from encouraging young Russians to acquire an education abroad, and inviting foreign experts to come to Russia, Peter created a Naval Academy, an engineering school and an artillery school. In 1714 he attempted by a series of decrees to set up a network of "cipher" or mathematical schools throughout the provinces. Children of noblemen, civil servants, secretaries and under-secretaries had to learn arithmetic and elementary geometry, and, in the words of the decree, "are forbidden to marry until they have done so". Schools were to be built in all provinces, near churches and large monasteries; teachers were to come from the Moscow mathematical colleges founded in 1703. Attendance at these schools was compulsory for all children between 10 and 15. A decree of 1723 forbade pupils to remain at school beyond the age of 15 "even if the pupils so desire, in order to prevent them from using their studies as an excuse for avoiding reviews and their military service". In the event the real problem was how to persuade the children to come to these cipher schools rather than how to get them to leave.

Peter's other principal educational foundation—the Academy of Sciences—was scarcely more successful. The Academy, which opened in St Petersburg shortly after his death, had a university and gymnasium or high school attached to it. The university began bleakly enough: most of the professors and students came from Germany, and the professors were sometimes obliged to attend one another's lectures because of the shortage of students. The gymnasium got off to a better start with 126 pupils on the roll in its first year, but by 1728 the total number had dwindled to 13.

It is easy to poke fun at the superficial nature of Peter's "westernizing" policy. But geographically speaking at least, Russia moved west during Peter's reign. His Swedish conquests and the new port of St Petersburg had brought Russia firmly into the commercial orbit of Europe. Not for the first time, new ideas and new fashions followed the trade routes. And in the long run not even the traditions of the Orthodox Church or the self-interest of the Russian nobles would be able to resist the slow percolation of European influences. Communist Russia has good cause to be proud of St Petersburg—even though it has chosen to call it Leningrad.

VOLTAIRE
(1694–1778)

THE Works of Voltaire! There they stand, row upon row of them on the library shelves. Even the first collected edition, made before the eighteenth century was out, could not be contained in fewer than seventy volumes, and before long the "hundred volumes of Voltaire" had become an acceptable figure of speech. Today, what with the retrieval of numbers of fugitive pieces that were published anonymously but have since been identified, and the ever-swelling stream of his correspondence—twenty thousand letters to date—the number is considerably greater. No European writer, it is safe to assert, ever wrote so much or was rewarded so handsomely or enjoyed such unbounded popularity. And yet this is not the most extraordinary thing about him. It is not so much what he wrote but what he *was* that has most powerfully and permanently influenced the developing intelligence of Europe.

Voltaire was not his name to begin with. Born in Paris on 21 November, 1694, he was baptized, the day following, Francois Marie Arouet. Why the hurry? Because it was feared that such a puny little morsel could not live for more than a few hours. Yet he *did* live, and somehow managed to hold on to life (notwithstanding innumerable illnesses, real or imagined) until he had attained to his eighty-fourth year. And even then it was not so much of old age that he died as of over excitement.

Although his paternity has been questioned, the consensus of opinion remains that he was the son of Francois Arouet, a notary (lawyer) with an excellent practice in Paris. His mother was likewise middle-class, but rather more so, since she had some pretensions to superior gentility. He had an elder brother, with whom in later life he had little to do, and a sister, of whom he was fond. His mother died when he was seven. Three years later, in 1704, he was entered at the Jesuit College of Louis le Grand, where he received a sound classical education. Even as a schoolboy he gave evidence of a marked gift for clever versifying, which was not at all to the taste of his father, who had it in mind to make a lawyer of him. A counterbalancing influence was exercised, however, by the boy's godfather, the Abbé de Chateauneuf, who, notwithstanding his clerical style, was very much a man of the world and introduced him into the witty, gay, and often licentious life of the capital.

From the time he left school in 1711 he mixed more and more in this rather questionable company, and so much neglected his legal studies that his father packed him off into the country, and then agreed to his joining the train of the new French ambassador to The Hague, presumably in the hope that on his return he would settle down. Hardly had young Arouet arrived in Holland than he got himself entangled in an emotional attachment with a young lady who was not only penniless but a Protestant. Nor did the young lady's mother regard a young fellow of nineteen, of no family to speak of and without definite profession or prospects, at all a suitable match. She complained to the ambassador, with the result that the youth was sent back to Paris in disgrace.

Very much against his inclination he submitted to being articled to a notary, but whenever possible he escaped into the brilliant society of young wits and easy-going ladies who were prepared to overlook his comparatively modest origins in recognition of his personal charm, literary ability, and social accomplishments. Very early he was producing dramatic poetry of a high order, but it was his extraordinary gift for persiflage that won him most acclaim. It also got him into serious trouble. A specially scurrilous libel on the Regent, the Duke of Orleans, was traced home to him, and, despite his perfervid denials, he was given a spell of imprisonment in the Bastille.

This lasted for nearly a year, and it was not at all rigorous or even uncomfortable. Arouet spent most of the time composing a long epic poem on Henry IV, the renowned founder of the reigning dynasty, and putting the finishing touches to his first play, the tragedy *Oedipe*. But the experience had one vastly important consequence. Soon after his release in April, 1718, Francois Arouet disappeared from the scene. Henceforth he was to be known as Arouet de Voltaire, or more simply, VOLTAIRE. The origin of the famous name has been much disputed, but the generally accepted conclusion is that it is an anagram of "Arouet the younger" in French.

Once adopted and announced to the world, the new name was soon on everyone's lips, as its bearer pursued his chosen career of poet and dramatist, made all the easier when on the death of his father he came into the possession of a considerable property. His *Oedipe* and other plays were well received, and his *Henriade*, when published in 1723, won him the title of the French Virgil. He stood well with the Court and had aspirations to becoming a Minister, in which case the name of Voltaire might have been worth a footnote in the political histories. But he happened to fall out with a worthless young sprig of the aristocracy, one Chevalier de Rohan, who had him beaten up in the street by a bunch of his servitors. Bursting with rage, Voltaire challenged him to a duel, which was contemptuously ignored; and when it was reported that Voltaire was still threatening vengeance, the Rohan family influence got him imprisoned in the Bastille for a second time. This was in April, 1726, and then after a fortnight Voltaire was given his liberty on condition that he should leave the country for a while, and he chose England.

The English visit lasted about three years, just when George I's reign was ending and George II's beginning. At first things were difficult, since although his pocket-book was bulging with introductions, he had brought very little cash with him. But after the first distressful few days he was given a most generous reception. He met all the literary men of note, and was made much of in Princess Caroline's drawing-rooms. He was a regular attendant at the theatre. He set himself to learn English, and was soon able to read it with ease and also to write it, with some agreeable idiosyncrasies of spelling. He studied the best books on philosophy, religion, politics, and science, Newtonian physics in particular. He tried hard to appreciate Shakespeare, and if he continued to think *Hamlet* a "vulgar and barbarous play" he more than any other man was responsible for introducing Shakespeare to a European public as a poet of the "greatest imaginable power and grandeur".

For the English political system he had hardly anything but praise, and he noted with wondering admiration the way in which the social classes seemed to mix and merge. He admired, too, the easy-going ways of the established church, and the way in which numerous sects were able to flourish under the safe toleration of English law. In particular was he impressed by the Quaker scheme of things, with its insistence on brotherly love and utter abhorrence of murderous war. Of course, he saw many things that were not there, and missed seeing a good many things that were. If he had crossed the threshold of an English gaol he might not have thought so highly of the English penal arrangements, nor might he have

drawn so rosy a picture of the lot of the English labourer as compared with the French peasant's if he had investigated the workings
of the English poor law. All in all, however, his acutely observant
brain did not play him false, and when at length, in 1729, he was
enabled to return to France he was a very different man from when
he first crossed the Channel—far better informed, far more comprehensive in his understanding, much more sympathetic to social
aspirations and reforming ideas.

For some years, however, his career followed much the same
lines as before. Still above all else he was the literary idol, the
darling of French intelligence, busying himself with the production of plays and poems, essays and histories that were generally
very well received and added to the lustre of his name. But then in
1734, whether with rash carelessness or premeditated design, he
arranged for the publication of his *Lettres Philosophiques sur les
Anglais* (of which an English edition had appeared the year
previous). The little book, witty and characteristically graceful,
purported to be a critique of the people amongst whom he had
spent the years of his exile, but those in authority who explored its
pages must soon have reached the conclusion that it was much
more a eulogy of English ways and institutions, with the pretty
obvious implication that these were on the whole very much better
than the French ones.

The *Lettres Philosophiques* was ordered to be burnt by the public
executioner because of the grave danger it was alleged to present to
"religion and public order", a warrant was issued for Voltaire's
arrest, and his lodgings were ransacked for treasonable material.
But he had received advance warning of what was afoot, and was
safely away, first to the camp at Philippsburg, near Karlsruhe,
where his friend the Duc de Richelieu held a command, and then
to the chateau of Cirey, on the borders of Lorraine and Champagne,
where he was to remain for years as the honoured guest of its
owners, the Marquise du Châtelet and her accommodating spouse
the Marquis.

Thus opened what was to prove one of the most memorable
chapters in Voltaire's life. In this year of 1734 Madame du
Châtelet was twenty-eight and nine years married to a man who
came of an even more aristocratic family than her own. She had
borne him several children, but for some years now the couple
had agreed to go their separate ways while maintaining all the
customary *convenances*. She took lovers in steady succession, the

most recent being the Duc de Richelieu, Voltaire's friend. She was handsome rather than beautiful, and much more *intellectuel* than *chic*. She could not be bothered to spend hours every day with her dressmaker or coiffeur, when she could never find time enough for her studies, her reading of abstruse works on mathematics, science, and philosophy, and her work at her desk translating Newton's *Principia* into French. A veritable blue stocking, and yet at the same time a woman of great charm, Voltaire was gratified with the reversion of her person, and not only assumed responsibility for a large proportion of the household expenses but paid for the construction of a new wing and the repair of what was a somewhat dilapidated place.

At Cirey Voltaire was perpetually occupied, writing in particular his *La Pucelle*, a burlesque on Joan of Arc, and the *Siècle de Louis XIV*, the most deservedly celebrated of his historical works. In 1744 his contribution to the festivities accompanying the marriage of the Dauphin were recognized by his appointment as Historiographer-Royal, which carried with it a substantial salary, and a couple of years later he was elected to the *Académie Française*. On the whole, things were going very pleasantly with him, and so they might have continued indefinitely if Madame du Châtelet, after thirteen years of closest companionship with Voltaire, had not sensed some falling off in his attentions and adopted a more ardent lover in the person of the Marquis de Saint-Lambert, who was twenty years her junior. Voltaire accepted the changed situation with philosophical resignation—at least this is what has been generally supposed. But he deserves no congratulation on this score since letters that have been unearthed and published by Dr Theodore Besterman (editor of the great 107-volume edition of Voltaire's correspondence) have made it clear that for some little time Voltaire had been having a passionate affaire with his niece Madame Denis (the elder of the two daughters left by his long-deceased sister) who, upon becoming widowed, had been invited to join the household at Cirey. The situation was an intriguing one and (apart from the incest) not without its farcical element. But farce turned into tragedy when Madame du Châtelet, at the age of forty-three and a grandmother several times over, was made pregnant by Saint-Lambert and on 10 September, 1749 died suddenly in childbirth, to the consternation and grief of all around her.

Deprived thus tragically of the woman who had been for so long the central figure in his life, Voltaire was in a most unsettled state until in 1750 he was invited by King Frederick of Prussia, in the most flattering terms, to visit him at Berlin. Such an invitation had been sent him several times before, but Madame du Châtelet had always dissuaded him from acceptance. Now her good counsel was no longer available, and in June, 1750 Voltaire (unaccompanied, it may be noted, by Madame Denis) set out on the long and tiresome journey across the continent. He arrived at Berlin in July, and his reception at the Prussian court was princely. Honours and hard cash were lavished upon him, and nothing was left undone that might contribute to his comfort and convenience. Voltaire could not fail to be intensely gratified, and at first his letters home were filled with encomiums of Frederick, a philosopher-king if ever there was one; in page after page he expatiated on the pleasures of living in daily intimacy with one who was not only a martial hero but a true lover of literature and the arts. Really it was quite remarkable how well his Majesty performed on the flute; he wrote verses too, and they were not at all bad . . .

But after only a few weeks a different note is sounded. Voltaire's nerves, it is clear, were getting somewhat frayed, what with the constant tumult of fêtes and military parades, the drum-bashing and trumpet-blowing, the ritual gluttony of banquets and receptions. Writing to Madame Denis he informed her that he had asked to be allowed to withdraw from the king's dinners since there were so many princes and generals at table, and he now supped with his Majesty in a much smaller and more select company, where everything was more natural, gayer, and shorter.

Very soon, however, there were more troubles, and much more serious ones. Voltaire was always inclined to behave like a spoilt and mischievous child, and he was never more childish than now. He quarrelled with almost everyone and made friends with hardly anybody. He resented, with the utmost unreason, the favours that the king extended to other visitors to his court, who included some of the most distinguished men of letters, philosophers, scientists, and mathematicians in Europe. He insulted them to their faces, and intrigued against them behind their backs. When Frederick teased him, as was his barrack-room habit, Voltaire either sulked or indulged in impertinent responses. As a rule Frederick laughed the matter off, since he was still congratulating himself on having enticed so great a European into his net, but when Voltaire was detected in a discreditable, not to say illegal, speculation in foreign exchange, his wrath boiled over. "You have behaved outrageously," he wrote to Voltaire; "I kept peace in my house until your arrival, and I warn you, that if you want to indulge your passion for scheming and plotting, you have come to the wrong place." Voltaire was all contriteness, and the uneasy love-hate relationship between the two continued for a while longer.

The end of March, 1753, saw Voltaire on the way home, however, and the king's farewell had been curt to say the least. After a leisurely progress across Germany, Voltaire arrived at Frankfort on 25 May. Here fresh trouble awaited him. Although Frankfort was nominally a free city of the Empire, it was very much under the Prussian king's control, and orders arrived from Berlin that Voltaire was to be detained until he returned, among other things that he was alleged to have taken away with him without permission, a copy of Frederick's poems. Voltaire protested that he had not them with him: he had sent them to Leipzig, or it may have been Hamburg. But Frederick, knowing full well the sort of use that Voltaire might make of his effusions, was adamant, and after six weeks' unseemly wrangling the poems were produced and handed over to the Prussian representative. Then in company with Madame Denis, who had joined him from Strasbourg and had shared in the humiliations of his detention, Voltaire proceeded on his journey.

Very probably he would have liked to return to Paris or its neighbourhood, but it was made clear that he would not be officially acceptable. So the next couple of years were passed in wandering uncertainly along the border country of Alsace and Lorraine, until in 1755 he found a resting-place in the vicinity of Geneva. Here just outside the city gates he bought a chateau so commodious and pleasantly situated that he named it *Les Delices* (now the seat of the Voltaire Museum and Institute). He also acquired a winter residence at Lausanne. But before long he was made aware that life in the little and strongly Protestant republic had its drawbacks. One of his early improvements at *Les Delices* had been the building of a theatre, where he proceeded to put on his own plays, directed and stage-managed by himself. The authorities at Geneva now informed him, politely enough, that stage performances were not allowed within the republic. No actual injunction was delivered against him, but Voltaire had seen the red light, and in 1758 he bought yet a third property, the lordship and estate of Ferney, just over the border in French territory. Henceforth this was his principal dwelling, with Mme

Denis as his housekeeper, and it was as the "Patriarch of Ferney" that he gained in course of time his unique place in the popular imagination. Indeed, he has a patriarchal appearance, as he sits, immobilized in Lambert's bronze, at the entrance to the modern township of Ferney-Voltaire.

Voltaire was now in his middle sixties, but looking considerably older than his years; still full of energy, however, and overflowing with ideas for the improvement of his estate and the welfare of humanity at large. Both aims received his immediate attention.

So far as Ferney was concerned, when he bought it the place was a wretched hamlet inhabited by some hundred and fifty serfs whose condition was one of squalor, ignorance, and general misery. Like one of those good English landlords he had so much admired years before, he embarked on comprehensive, and expensive, schemes for reform. He rebuilt cottages and built new ones to accommodate the numbers of newcomers. He laid out fields and plantations, lined the main road to Geneva with trees, some of which still remain. He started a village school; he even built a church, and the present-day traveller may look up at the inscription above the door: DEO EREXIT VOLTAIRE. Then like the excellent man of business that he was, he established industries at which his people might earn a decent livelihood. Among these watch-making and the manufacture of silk stockings had pride of place; he advertised his wares in his vast correspondence, and the visitors who swarmed to enjoy his hospitality found that they were expected to buy a watch or a clock or a pair or two of silk stockings made in the Ferney workshops.

For all the years he lived there Ferney was a "must" on the itinerary of the European traveller. Sometimes the old man was heard to grumble that he was expected to act the "Innkeeper to Europe", but no one took his complaining seriously. Many of the visitors were from England, which is fortunate, since it is from the accounts of such men as John Wilkes, Adam Smith, Boswell, Gibbon, and Dr Burney that we are enabled to visualize the patriarch in his domestic surroundings. So many were the callers that it may be wondered that he ever managed to get any work done. But four hours' sleep were enough for this shrivelled ancient who after a life-time of authorship had so much still to say and was determined to say it. In fact, Voltaire was never so busy as in the last two decades of his long life.

When he removed from Geneva to Ferney he took with him the

manuscript of *Candide*, the most brilliant specimen of that form of literature, the *conte philosophique* (a tale or short story conveying a serious moral in the most agreeable way) of which it may be claimed that he was the inventor. This was published in 1759 and soon became, what it has ever since remained, the outstanding best-seller of Voltaire's immense output. On the face of it, it is a delightful adventure story, full of incident, amusing, satirical, and spicy in its sexual passages, and yet it was written when Voltaire was emerging from the shock given by the Lisbon earthquake of 1755 to his hitherto reasonably optimistic philosophy, followed by the case of the English admiral Byng who, to quote *Candide's* most famous line, was shot *"pour encourager les autres"*. As for the "moral" of the little book, it is to point out the absurdity of the egregious Dr Pangloss's contention that this is the "best of all possible worlds" and secondly, that it is incumbent on mankind to do their best to change it for the better—or, to use the words that Voltaire puts into Candide's mouth, "let us cultivate our garden".

With Voltaire this involved "crushing the Infamous". What did he mean by "the Infamous"? Not Christianity, not Catholicism even, but religious bigotry, intolerance and persecution, ferocious penal laws, flagrant social iniquities, unjust privileges, belief in witchcraft and other superstitions, and the cruelty, folly and futility of wars. *"Ecrasez l'Infâme!"* ("Crush the Infamous!"), the phrase he often used in place of his signature on his letters, became the battle-cry of the tremendous campaign that, until the end of his days, he planned and organized and directed from his base at Ferney.

His only weapon was a pen—but what a pen! For the first time in history a great writer appealed over the heads of the authorities in State and Church to something that he was largely responsbile for creating—public opinion. Naturally enough, he thought in terms of books and pamphlets, and for years these poured from his study at Ferney in unceasing flood. Most important was his *Dictionnaire Philosophique* (1764), which is not a dictionary nor is it primarily concerned with what we generally mean by philosophy; it is a fascinating compendium of articles on a great variety of subjects, but mainly theological and educational, intended to appeal to and inform the great mass of ordinary people. Innumerable reforms are outlined in its lively pages, and in its successive editions it was the textbook of the liberal-minded reformers who launched the French Revolution.

Voltaire was now in the full flood of his propagandist activity. His writings circulated everywhere, and, hot from the printing-press, were read in the original French or when translated into every tongue that mattered. But this was not all. Mighty as was Voltaire's pen, his example was mightier yet, since it could be understood by multitudes who never read a book (and couldn't perhaps if they tried). These began to hear his name and carry it on their lips, as Voltaire, in defiance of aching bones and quivering nerves, took his place as prosecuting counsel at the bar of the world's opinion.

The first and most famous of the many "cases" he took up was the judicial murder of Jean Calas, a humble tradesman of Toulouse, who was broken on the wheel for having killed (so it was alleged) a son whom he suspected was about to abandon Protestantism for Catholicism. When the case was reported to Voltaire he was soon convinced that a horrible miscarriage of justice had occurred. At once he went into action: letters to influential people, abusive articles in the newspapers, appeals to justice, pamphlets made out of Madame Calas's pathetic communications. The sentence on Calas was revoked, but the poor fellow was dead. Somewhat similar was the case of the Sirvens, who were convicted in their absence of the murder of their daughter, a weak-witted girl who had been a nun. Years afterwards Madame Suard, a young Frenchwoman, was visiting at Ferney and remarked on a picture over Voltaire's bed showing Calas, "this victim of Fanaticism", taking leave of his family before going to execution. "Ah, Madame," commented the old patriarch, "for eleven years I was continually occupied with that unhappy family and that of the Sirvens; and in all that time I reproached myself, as if for a crime, if I even caught myself smiling."

One other case must be mentioned, that of the young La Barre, who in 1765 was charged with having mutilated a crucifix on the bridge at Abbeville. At his trial it was proved that he had been reading, among other books, Voltaire's *Philosophical Dictionary*. He was found guilty, and beheaded. "The atrocity of this event fills me with rage and horror," raged Voltaire; "I repent indeed of having ruined myself in building houses and doing good on the borders of a land where, in cold blood and before dinner, people commit abominations which would revolt a parcel of drunken savages." It was rumoured that a *lettre de cachet* had been issued with Voltaire's name on it; if they did such horrible things to a poor, inoffensive young devil like La Barre, what might they not do to *him*? To his eternal honour the old man refused to be intimidated; but the iron entered into his soul, and years later he wrote: "This innocent blood cries out, and I cry out too, and I shall go on crying out till I die."

Early in 1778 Voltaire returned to the Paris that he had not seen for nearly thirty years. He came home like a conquering hero. Immense crowds pushed and shoved to greet him, and among the hundreds of callers at his lodgings in the Rue de Beaune were Benjamin Franklin and the British ambassador. Many of those who roared their welcome can have read not a word he wrote, but they knew him as a man: "'Twas he who avenged Calas!..." When his last play, *Irène*, was put on at the *Comédie Française* his bust was crowned amid delirious enthusiasm with the victor's laurel wreath. The excitement proved too much for the old man, and on 30 May he died. Thirteen years later his body was reinterred in the Panthéon among the Revolution's most honoured sons, and the catafalque bore the words:

"Poet, philosopher, historian, he gave wings to the human mind; he prepared us to be free."

JEAN-JACQUES ROUSSEAU
(1712–1778)

JEAN-JACQUES ROUSSEAU took good care to see that posterity should know what sort of a man he was. In his *Confessions*, one of the lengthiest expressions of the autobiographical urge, he set out to "show a man in all the truth of nature", and on page after page he reveals a whole heap of things such as most men would prefer to keep to themselves. As a work of literature the book is superb; and notwithstanding the numerous lapses from strict historical accuracy that the critics have pounced upon, it remains the fount and foundation of everything most worth knowing about this most extraordinary of romantics, this most vitally effective of the parents of revolutionary ideas.

Born at Geneva on 28 June, 1712, he came of a French family that had been settled in Paris until the Reformation when, having become Protestants, they found it best to migrate to the "city of refuge" that Geneva had become. In the "Protestant Rome" they proved themselves good citizens in an unpretentious way, earning their livelihood by honest industry and regular in their religious duties. Jean-Jacques's father, Isaac Rousseau, was a watchmaker by trade; his mother, Suzanne Bernard, was a pastor's daughter, and as such rather better educated than her husband. There was an elder son of the marriage, but he very early left home and disappeared without trace, so that Jean-Jacques was to all intents and purposes an only child. Unfortunately his mother died in giving him birth. As he was to write in due course, "I cost my mother her life, and my birth was the first of my misfortunes."

Thus tragically deprived of a mother's love, the child might not have long survived if one of his father's sisters had not taken charge of the little household. She must have been an excellent woman. To the end of his days Jean-Jacques remembered her as always kind and cheerful, recalled her old-fashioned ways of dressing and coiffure, and her pleasant rendering of the simple airs of the country people—to her he attributed the taste, or rather passion, for music which developed in him in later life. Isaac Rousseau seems by comparison to have been a rather unstable character, but if he liked a convivial glass he was also very fond of reading, and he encouraged it in his boy. Father and son took it in turns to read aloud to one another, first the romances that had belonged to the mother and then the more serious books that had stood on her father's shelves. Plutarch's *Lives* was Jean-Jacques's favourite, and as the frail little fellow read the tales of the ancient heroes and patriots his voice rose high and shrill and his tears of excitement watered the page.

When the boy was about ten years old, these happy days came to a sudden end. His father got involved in a quarrel with an influential fellow citizen, and, rather than admit he was in the wrong, preferred to go into voluntary exile. So the home was broken up, and Jean-Jacques was sent to school at Bossey, a neighbouring village, where the pastor, one M. Lambercier, taught "along with Latin, all that sorry stuff which goes under the name of education".

For two years he remained under M. Lambercier's roof, with another boy of the same age, one of his Bernard cousins, as his bosom friend. He made good progress with his studies, and learnt some things not found in the books. Two experiences stand out in the narration. The first has raised a good many eyebrows, but in these psycho-analyzed days it may not appear so shocking. The minister had a sister, who shared in the conduct of the school. She was close on forty (not thirty as Rousseau states in the *Confessions*) but obviously possessed of some charm still; and Jean-Jacques, at the age of eleven or twelve, found that being whipped by Mlle Lambercier was not without pleasing accompaniments. He felt a growing affection for her, and committed further misdemeanours in the hope of another whipping. But the good woman was not as primly ignorant as might have been expected, and she calmly announced that she was going to do no more whipping since it tired her too much . . .

The second experience was also connected with Mlle Lambercier, though less immediately. One day Jean-Jacques was learning his lessons in the room next to the kitchen where some of her hair-combs had been left to dry after washing. When these were taken off the stove it was found that the teeth of one of them had been broken, and the boy was blamed. He strenuously denied the accusation, but he was disbelieved and thrashed all the harder for persisting in his denials. The memory of this first injustice was still fresh in his mind when, nearly forty years afterwards, he wrote that "when I read of the cruelties of some ferocious tyrant, or the atrocities of some villain of a priest, I would fain start on the instant to poniard such wretches, though I were to perish a hundred times for the deed".

At the age of twelve his schooldays came to an end and he returned to Geneva to live in his uncle's house. To begin with he was found a place in the office of the town clerk, but after a few weeks' trial was dismissed as hopelessly inadequate. Next he was apprenticed to an engraver, a rough, ill-natured fellow who treated him with extreme harshness, and the drudgery and blows might have ruined his spirit if he had not had the good chance to discover a tiny lending-library and was thus able to indulge his passion for reading. He also made friends with a number of youths of his own age and standing, and sometimes joined them in boisterous excursions beyond the city walls. Once they had to spend the night in the open since they got back when the gates had been shut, and Jean-Jacques was savagely beaten and warned that much worse things would befall him if he offended in the same way again. There *was* another occasion, and rather than face his master's anger Jean-Jacques turned his back on Geneva and embarked on a series of wanderings that he was to describe with such inimitable grace and charm in the opening books of his *Confessions*.

This was when he was about sixteen, and although he was not yet anything like skilled enough to earn a living at his craft he was not in the least despondent. On the contrary, he was filled with the most absurdly optimistic hopes of exciting adventures and dazzling achievements. For some days he roamed among the villages of the Genevan countryside, and then crossed the border into Savoy, then part of the dominions of the king of Sardinia and as solidly Catholic as Geneva was Calvinist. For generations the priests of Savoy and the Genevan ministers had been ardent rivals in proselytizing activity, and when the youth reached the village of Confignon he was warmly received by the parish priest. So excellent was the dinner provided, and so persuasive the Frangi wine, that he fell in readily enough with his host's suggestion that he might do very well for himself by changing his faith. The morning after he may well have had second thoughts, but it was now too late (or so he supposed) since he had been given a letter of introduction to a Catholic lady at Annecy who was known to be most helpful in the conversion business.

At Annecy, on the morning of Palm Sunday in 1728, Jean-Jacques saw this lady for the first time, as she was on her way to church, and was instantly captivated. Louise Eleonore de Warens her name was, and she was then twenty-nine, in the efflorescence of buxom beauty. She was born at Vevey, in the Swiss canton of Vaud, the daughter of a prosperous country gentleman, and at the age of fourteen had been married to a Monsieur (later Baron) de Warens. In 1726, however, the marriage had broken up, with no recriminations on either side, and the husband was no longer in the picture. Madame de Warens had then crossed into Savoy, where she sought the protection of the king and was converted to Roman Catholicism. Henceforth she was to live on a pension from the royal purse, in return for which she was employed on diplomatic missions that demanded a certain feminine finesse and in keeping a kind of hospice or reception-centre for converts to Catholicism; it seems to be now pretty well established that she was something of a political spy.

Jean-Jacques's first encounter with this prepossessing lady was but a brief one. She took pity on him, provided him with funds and letters of introduction, and dispatched him to Turin, the capital of the Sardinian kingdom, where there was a Catholic recruiting-centre. Arrived there, the youth was still full of the most delightful hopes, but the reality turned out to be something very different. When he presented himself at the address given him, he found the place a monastery that was also a prison. He had to mix with scoundrels who, professing to be Jews or Moors, made a living by wandering through Italy and Spain and getting themselves "converted" to Catholicism. There were women, too, and young girls, of the most abandoned description, who followed the same career. One of the Moors, attracted by his air of boyish innocence, made loathsome pederastic approaches which he barely managed to repel. Some slight "instruction" was given him, and then, after just nine days in the monastery, filled with shame and hopeless remorse and not seeing any way of escape, he abjured his "sectarian errors" and was received into the bosom of Holy Church. At the ceremony a collection was made among the congregation for his benefit; twenty francs it came to, and with this in his pocket he was shown the door, although not so speedily as the reader of the *Confessions* is given to understand.

For some time he wandered about Turin. His money was soon spent, and he was reduced to desperate straits. But kind-hearted people took pity on him, especially among the poor, and at last he obtained a post as lackey in the house of one Madame de Vercellis. After three months this lady died, and on her effects being gone through it was found that nothing more important than a small piece of ribbon was missing. Jean-Jacques had taken it—he thought it so pretty—but when it was found in his possession he brazenly declared that it had been given to him by a fellow servant, a young girl of unblemished character named Marion. When charged with the petty theft the girl gave Jean-Jacques a reproachful look that he never forgot, but he persisted in his story and, since there was no time to investigate the matter more fully, the master of the house dismissed them both, with the remark that the guilty one's conscience would avenge the innocent. "Not a day passes", is Jean-Jacques's comment, made years afterwards, "on which the prediction has not been fulfilled."

Before long the youth found other employments, generally of a somewhat menial character, and he may have spent as much as three years in Turin. But ever and again the vision of his patroness at Annecy made a tantalizing return, and so in the early summer of 1731 (this date seems more likely than the 1729 preferred by earlier writers, but the chronology is most confused) he presented himself again at Madame de Warens's door. She received him most kindly, provided him accommodation in her household, arranged for his further education, and introduced him into society. She also encouraged him to persevere in his musical studies.

After about a year of this most pleasant existence she ordered him to accompany one of her pensioners, a musician named Le Maitre, on his way to Lyons. The pair reached Lyons, and two days after their arrival Le Maitre was taken in an epileptic fit and fell down foaming in the street. Whereupon Jean-Jacques was so scared that he left the poor fellow lying where he was and took to his heels. This was the third of the "disgraceful confessions" that Rousseau felt obliged to make (the others being his juvenile passion for Mlle Lambercier and the affair of the ribbon); if he had many more as bad to relate, he wrote, he would abandon the book that he had begun.

On his way back from the ill-starred visit to Lyons, he learnt to his consternation that Madame de Warens had left Annecy, and it was not until near the close of 1732 that he joined her at Chambéry, where she had now made her home. As before, she received him with smiles and caresses, and the strangely intimate relationship thus begun continued in a slowly ripening development for some eight or nine years. More than once she obtained for him quite well-paid and promising appointments; he was willing to try them, but always he threw them up after a while, and returned most gladly to the extraordinary woman whom he has immortalized in page after page of limpid prose. She was flighty, and as careless in money matters as of decorum. Her pension was generally mort-gaged before she received it, what with her lavish hospitality and innumerable charities. Jean-Jacques knew very little of business, but he strove to act honourably as her manager. She called him her "little one" and he called her his "Mamma", and Rousseau would probably have been quite satisfied with the relationship that these terms imply. But when he had grown to manhood and showed signs of an active interest in young women, *Maman* told him, by look and gesture more expressive than words, that (the place having become vacant through the death of its previous occupant) he might have his devotion and services rewarded by becoming her lover.

If his story is to be believed, he was not as excited at the prospect as might have been expected, and when he held her in his arms (the first woman he had ever actually possessed) he had a feeling that he was committing incest . . . But she, for her part, had no qualms or compunction. She remained cool if not frigid. Although she con-sidered herself to be a devout Catholic, she had no scruples over indulging in something that to her seemed neither important nor particularly enjoyable, but nevertheless appeared to be the most effective means of attaching a man to her person and her interests. As Rousseau somewhat bitterly remarked, she "could have slept with twenty men every day and thought nothing of it". What really interested her were her social gatherings, her amateurish experiments in chemistry, and (above all perhaps) the devising and working out of the schemes and contrivances with which she earned her pension.

At Chambéry Rousseau spent his time in reading, writing music and giving music lessons to the young ladies of the town, and in doing his rather inadequate best to keep his mistress from going bankrupt. But his health began to give cause for anxiety, and largely on account of this Madame de Warens took a country house, Les Charmettes, just outside Chambéry, for the summer months. Here Jean-Jacques led an idyllic existence: "I was happy . . . I did the things I wanted to do, and was the man I wanted to be." But the idyll came to an end, as idylls always do. For the benefit of his health he went on a trip to Montpellier, and on the way met a charming lady named Madame de Larnage with whom he shared a love-making that must have made the embraces of Madame de Warens seem positively chaste. The latter, however, would seem to have become aware of a certain deficiency in Rousseau's make-up, for when he returned home he found to his intense chagrin that another young fellow had been introduced into the household and was apparently doing all that was required of him to Madame's complete satisfaction. For a time Jean-Jacques endeavoured to adapt himself to the very changed situation, but in 1741 he finally broke away from Madame de Warens and made his way to Paris.

This brings us to the end of the sixth book of the *Confessions*, which is not quite half way, with another six books to come. But the separation from Madame de Warens constitutes a great divide in Rousseau's life. As he himself explains it, up to then it had been "quiet and idle," but the story of his second thirty years would be, alas, very different, composed as it must be of "misfortunes, mistakes, treasons and perfidies and heart-rending recollections".

At Paris the little money that he had brought with him was soon spent, and a system of musical notation he had invented and hoped would make his fortune was rejected by the Academy of Sciences as being neither useful nor original. But he managed to keep himself afloat by copying music and giving music lessons, until one of the influential friends (there always seemed to be plenty of such about, however shockingly he treated them) obtained for him the post of secretary to the French ambassador in Venice. There he was able to enjoy the most agreeable feminine society, and although the salary attached to his appointment was not much he might have obtained some advancement if, after eighteen months, he had not taken umbrage at the way he was treated by his master. So he handed in his resignation and went back to Paris, there to engage again in music copying, supplemented by some article writing for Diderot's *Encyclopédie*.

Not long after his return to Paris he decided that it was incumbent upon him to take a permanent mistress, who would provide him with the home comforts that he had enjoyed under Madame de Warens's roof. The girl he settled upon was a poor drudge at the hotel or boarding-house where he had his quarters. Thérèse le Vasseur her name was, and she was then twenty-two or

Louis XIV, as painted from the life by Hyacinthe Rigaud in 1701 (the picture is now in the Louvre at Paris), is indeed the *Grand Monarque*, the *Roi Soleil*, who in one of the longest reigns in history dominated Europe with his statecraft and military might. The picture (*below*) by the nineteenth-century painter J. L. Gerome represents a king who has not yet become imprisoned by his ideas of grandeur. To the obvious amazement of his courtiers the young Louis is engaged in affable conversation with one of those men of genius who reflected such real glory on his reign—the playwright who is so generally known by his stage name of Molière.

In Europe's literary firmament no star burns brighter than Voltaire's. In his own day (as often since) he was denounced as a mocker of sacred things, of long-cherished beliefs and institutions; but in the longer view of history he stands out as the unrelenting foe of superstition and tyranny, of ignorance and fanaticism, of social injustices and individual wrongs. Here we see him as J. A. Houdon saw him, the shrivelled ancient who had become the "Patriarch of Ferney"; and (*below*) in a contemporary engraving we see him again, but now in the tremendous climax of his career when, having returned to Paris after years of absence, he went to the *Comédie Française* to see his last tragedy performed. And there, in a scene of delirious enthusiasm, he was crowned by the beautiful young Marquise de Villette with the laurel wreath of the victor.

twenty-three. She was no beauty and was almost completely illiterate; furthermore, she had a horrid old hag of a mother, whom she supported out of her meagre earnings, and a whole troop of most mercenary brothers and sisters. In her manners and ways of behaviour she revealed her working-class origins; but then, Rousseau's were much the same. She was affectionate, modest and kind, a splendid cook and first-rate housekeeper, and, although amongst his more deplorable "confessions" is the claim that he never had any real love for her as an individual, she answered to the full his sensual needs. She bore him five children, each of whom he promptly popped into the reception-bag outside the foundling hospital. Of course, he has his excuses ready. Thus, he was not in a position to maintain a family, and surely it were better that they should be handed over to the care of the State, when they would be brought up to become honest workers or peasants instead of adventurers and fortune-hunters? He did not see himself as an unnatural parent, but rather as a good citizen of Plato's Republic. (All the same, in after years he felt some compunction, and had inquiries instituted as to their fate. But no trace of them was ever found.)

Nothing, surely, can excuse Rousseau's conduct in this particular; it stands for all time as the blackest page in his confessions. Even in his lowest straits he was never anywhere near starving. He was never without wealthy friends who would have been glad to open their purses to him (as they very often did), and time after time they obtained for him employments in the secretarial line which he always threw up for the most insufficient reasons. What is more, before long he was earning a quite substantial income by the exercise of his genius, first as a composer of light operas and then as the author of literary works of immense charm and popular appeal.

This was something he had never thought of, and he might never have embarked upon the seas of authorship if he had not come by chance on an announcement of a prize being offered by the Academy of Dijon for the best essay on the effects of the progress of civilization on morals. Rousseau seized on the subject, developed with rare ingenuity the paradoxical idea of the superiority of the savage state, and won the prize. When his essay was published in 1750 he found himself famous, and his position as a man of letters was consolidated with a second essay on the "Origin of Inequality." So celebrated had he become that in 1754 he ventured to make a visit to Geneva, which he had quitted years before as a friendless vagabond. The city authorities made much of him and he aspired to citizenship. This was something that no Catholic might aspire to, but the obstacle was removed by Rousseau's abjuration of his juvenile abjuration. As a Protestant he was soon enabled to boast of the proud title of "Citizen of Geneva".

This visit to Geneva was made memorable also by his first encounter with Madame de Warens since his departure from Chambéry thirteen years before. He found his *Maman* sadly changed, and all for the worse. He offered her some financial help and even (if his story is to be trusted) invited her to make her home with Thérèse and himself. But she declined the invitation and he never saw her again. She died eight years later, in 1762, in obscure poverty.

Rousseau returned to Paris, where rich and powerful friends were more than willing to give him every succour. But city life oppressed him, and in the spring of 1756 he accepted the offer of a cottage near Montmorency made by Madame d'Epinay. "The Hermitage" it was called, and here he produced the first of the three great works of literature for which his name will ever be remembered.

La Nouvelle Heloise was about the first and must still be ranked among the greatest of romantic novels, so that Rousseau may be regarded as the originator of this most popular form of reading-matter. It is composed of letters passing between three young people—two girls, Julie and her bosom friend Claire, and a young man named Le Preux, who is Julie's tutor. She is well born and well off, while he is of humble origins and penniless—just the sort of young fellow, indeed, as Jean-Jacques had been, and occupying the same sort of place he had so often imagined for himself. The location of the romance is Vevey, on the Lake of Geneva, which had been Madame de Warens's birthplace.

Notwithstanding their so different social circumstances Julie and Le Preux fall in love, and (a highly original touch this, since in those days young ladies waited until they were safely married before they took a lover) consummate their passion. Whereupon Mlle. Julie suddenly reveals something in the nature of a moral conscience (or awareness of the value of social convention). In a gush of tears and embraces she sends Le Preux about his business, while she, in a mood of sacrificial ardour, marries her father's choice of suitor, and in no time at all becomes an altogether admirable wife and mother. If the plot were all, *The New Heloise* would have been damned long since as unbearably preposterous, but as in almost everything that Rousseau wrote there are many saving graces. There is, first, the deep feeling for Nature, in all its changeful loveliness; but even more, generations of readers have responded to the extraordinarily perceptive revelations of a man and a woman in the delirium of love. As Madame de Staël was to put it a generation later, Rousseau was the first to dream that "the burning agitations of the human heart" might be expressed in literature. And he made the dream come true.

With the publication of *The New Heloise* in 1760 Rousseau reached the peak of popularity, but his literary triumphs were overshadowed by personal mishaps. After rather more than a year at the Hermitage he quarrelled bitterly with Madame d'Epinay, and, even worse, with her sister-in-law Madame d'Houdetot, for whom he had developed a richly emotional attachment—"the first and only love in my life" is how he describes her in the *Confessions*—which was responsible for much of the sensitively sensuous feeling and some of the incidents that set the pages of *The New Heloise* aglow. Quitting his rural retreat in a fit of morbid self-pity, he was provided with a cottage on the estate of the Duc de Luxembourg, another of his rich and influential protectors. Here he produced the second of his masterpieces, *Le Contrat Social*.

In the whole vast collections of political polemic there is surely nothing more audacious than his opening statement: "Man is born free; and everywhere he is in chains!" To explain this terrible contradiction he goes back to the beginnings of human society, and imagines our savage ancestors concluding something in the nature of a "social contract", whereby each member joins with every other member in pooling their persons and whole power, "under the supreme direction of the general will". Rousseau knew very little of history, and of course this conception of his is completely illusory. But it contained the germ of something that was to ripen into a terrible harvest—the idea of Popular Sovereignty. This it was that made so strong an appeal to the discontented masses, and still more to the discontentedly restless and groping, comparatively enlightened few. From the pages of *Le Contrat Social* were deduced those principles of *Liberté*, *Egalité*, *Fraternité*, that, combined, became the tremendous watchword of the French Revolution.

The *Social Contract* was published in 1762, in Amsterdam, to escape the attentions of the French censors; and two months later appeared, likewise in Amsterdam, the third of Rousseau's great trilogy. This is *Émile, or Education*, and it takes the form of a philosophical romance in which the three characters are a boy and a girl, Emile and Sophy, and Jean-Jacques himself. Most of the book is taken up with Emile's educational process, and (although there must seem to be something indecently incongruous in a man setting up as the instructor of youth's instructors who had consigned his own offspring to the foundling-hospital) there is much in Rousseau's apostrophizing commentary that is altogether admirable. Sophy is not introduced until the fifth book, and, notwithstanding her creator's insistence that she is "as truly woman as Emile is a man", she must strike many readers as a blushing little piece of feminine complaisance. No higher tribute to the book's essential worth may be found than the fact that Pestalozzi, one of the world's most successful educationists, borrowed heavily from its pages, and in Germany such men as Goethe and Schiller and Jean-Paul Richter were fired with thoughts they first came across in *Emile*.

Nor should we omit to mention that inserted in this book is the "Confession of a Savoyard Priest", an intensely interesting piece of spiritual biography in which Rousseau combines the characters of two Catholic priests who, in his days of juvenile vagabondage, furnished him with religious instruction (albeit highly unorthodox) and moral guidance when he was most desperately in need of both.

For twelve years Rousseau's reputation as a thinker and man of letters had been steadily growing and it was now higher than ever. But fortune is fickle, and hardly had *Emile* been published when he found himself in serious trouble with the authorities. The book was condemned by the Paris *Parlement*, and an order was issued for its author's arrest. Rousseau had been warned in time, however, and had already taken flight. For some years he was a wanderer from place to place, country to country, pursued by fears that were not all imaginary. Early in 1766 he went to England, where his admirers, the philosopher-historian David Hume in particular, did everything possible for his comfort. But he was not the sort of man to accept favours with a good grace, and his morbid sensitivity, intensified by a most painful urinary condition, put him beyond the help of friends and would-be benefactors.

In May, 1767, he went back to France and eventually to Paris, where he maintained himself and Thérèse (with whom by this time he had gone through some form of marriage) by music copying.

So the years passed, and Jean-Jacques sank deeper and deeper into an abyss of misery and half-lunatic imaginings. In 1778 a rich financier offered him the use of a cottage on his estate at Ermenonville, and there on 2 July of that year he died, physically a wreck and mentally so disturbed that there were grave suspicions of suicide.

ADAM SMITH

(1723–1790)

IF EVER a man may be said to have founded a science, then Adam Smith was the founder of the science of economics, or political economy as it was called in his day and up to much later. This he did through the writing and publication of one single book, known throughout the world as *The Wealth of Nations*.

He was a Scotsman, or Scotchman as he would have preferred to spell it. He was born at Kirkcaldy, a small seaport on the east coast of Scotland, in Fifeshire on the opposite side of the Firth of Forth from Edinburgh, on 5 June, 1723. His father, also Adam Smith, was a writer to the signet (i.e. a lawyer approximating to the English solicitor), who held a number of appointments under government including that of collector of customs at Kirkcaldy; his mother, born Margaret Douglas, was the daughter of a small laird or landed proprietor in the neighbourhood. Adam Smith senior died a few months before his son was born, and the child was brought up by his mother in comfortable circumstances enough.

When he was nine or ten he was sent to the Kirkcaldy Burgh School, which was reputed to be one of the best secondary schools in Scotland. From thence he proceeded at the age of fourteen to the College or University of Glasgow, where he was taught Latin and Greek, natural and moral philosophy, mathematics, and logic. The place had a high reputation for scholarship, and some of the professors were first rate. Adam Smith was attracted in particular to Professor Hutcheson, who held the chair of moral philosophy and delivered courses of lectures in which he was inclined to take an unusually favourable view of the human situation. Nearly half a century later, when Smith was elected Lord Rector of Glasgow University, he paid tribute to his old teacher as "the never-to-be forgotten Hutcheson", and careful readers of Hutcheson's lectures have detected passages which were reflected in *The Wealth of Nations*. As a glance at the dictionaries of quotations will confirm, it was Francis Hutcheson who said "that action is best, which procures the greatest happiness for the greatest numbers"—a dictum that was absolutely fundamental in Adam Smith's very practical philosophy.

Smith was at Glasgow for a little short of three years, until in the spring of 1740 he was awarded an exhibition to Balliol College, Oxford. On a June morning he set out on horseback for Oxford and rode the whole way there. He was seventeen, and everything he saw impressed him as new and strange. Hardly had he crossed the border than he noticed how much better the English fields looked than those he had left behind him in Scotland, and indeed at that time most of the Scottish lowlands was uncultivated waste. Even the Scottish cattle seemed to be lean and poor compared with the fat oxen of the English farms.

After several weeks on the road, Smith reached Oxford, and matriculated at Balliol in the middle of July. Here he felt himself to be a stranger in a strange land, and to make matters worse, he was a Scotchman arrived at a time when Scotchmen were particularly unpopular with the English students. He was six years at Oxford: he never went home once in the whole time he was there, for the very good reason that he could not afford to. His exhibition was worth only £40 a year, and out of that he had to pay £30 a year for his board and lodging and £5 for tuition, which left him precious little for all his other expenses.

Compared with Glasgow, Oxford made but a poor showing. "It will be his own fault if any one should endanger his health at Oxford by excessive study", he wrote in one of the very few letters that have survived from this early period of his life, "our only business here being to go to prayers twice a day and to lectures twice a week". In the *Wealth of Nations* he bluntly declares that: "In the university of Oxford the greater part of the public professors have, for these many years, given up even the pretence of teaching." He ascribes this deplorable state of affairs to the system of paying the professors a fixed salary, irrespective of whether they carried out their duties or no: how very much better was the Scottish practice of making the teachers dependent in part at least on their students' fees.

All the same, his time was not wasted. Balliol possessed a very fine library, and here Smith laboured at the congenial task of teaching himself. At Glasgow he had been a good Latinist and an indifferent Grecian, but now he developed into a ripe scholar in both of the ancient tongues and literatures. Better still, perhaps, for the promotion of what was to be his life work, he read widely and deeply in the Italian poets and the French classics.

In August, 1746, he returned to Scotland, and for the next two years lived with his mother at Kirkcaldy, doing nothing in particular and with no settled career in prospect. Then by a fortunate chance some friends in Edinburgh invited him to give a course of public lectures on English Literature. Nothing of the kind had been attempted before, and the course was so successful that Smith was invited to repeat the performance in each of the two following winters.

But the lectures had a much more important consequence. Smith had displayed such capabilities as a public lecturer that in 1751 he was appointed professor of logic in the university of Glasgow. Then in the year following he was enabled to exchange this chair for that of moral philosophy, which suited him much better, since the subject could be made to cover pretty well what he chose. So began a period of thirteen years of active academic work at Glasgow which in after years he looked back upon as "by far the most useful and therefore by far the happiest and most honourable period" of his life.

As a professor, Smith's emoluments seem never to have risen much above £170 per annum, but he was provided with a house in the precincts rent free. The first of the day's classes was held at 7.30 a.m., and it must have been a good lecturer who could hold the attention of a crowd of young fellows just out of bed. Yet Adam Smith managed it. He had a sense of humour, and made them laugh with his quaint expressions and homely illustrations. He was very down-to-earth, and although his subjects would seem to have been abstruse enough—natural theology, ethics, and the place of justice in political relationships—he gave them a twist of practical application that was warmly appreciated. There is good reason to believe that it was in the murky light of a winter morning in a crowded classroom at Glasgow that Adam Smith first elaborated the doctrine of free trade that was ultimately to enlighten the world.

Glasgow in the middle of the eighteenth century was little more than a provincial town, with a population of round about twenty-five thousand, and a general aspect not undeserving of Defoe's description of it a generation earlier, as "one of the cleanliest, most beautiful, and best-built cities in Great Britain". But dramatic changes were only just round the corner, if they had not already begun. The union of the two kingdoms in 1707 had thrown open the trade with the British colonies in the West Indies and North America, and the "tobacco lords" in their scarlet cloaks and cocked hats were becoming a familiar sight on the quays. Factories and workshops of one kind and another were demonstrating their noisy presence, the first of the city's banks was open for business, and the Clyde was being deepened so as to take ships of considerable tonnage. There was work for everybody who was prepared to use his hands or his brain.

No one was better aware of the fact than Adam Smith. He had come to Glasgow not only to teach but to learn, and he made a habit of buttonholing anybody and everybody who might seem to have something interesting and valuable to relate. There was nothing of the superior academic about him. He visited the naileries, the potteries, the tanneries—where on one famous occasion he fell into one of the pits when he was showing a friend round. He made friends with the merchants of the place, and in particular with Andrew Cochrane, whom years afterwards Smollett was to describe in his novel *Humphry Clinker* as "one of the first sages of the Scottish kingdom". It was Cochrane who founded the "Political Economy Club"—the first of its kind to be established anywhere—and Smith was one of its members.

What he learnt, Smith was not slow to put into practice. Walter Bagehot, brilliant Victorian man-of-letters, no doubt thought he was being very clever when in his essay on Adam Smith he wrote that "the founder of the science of business was one of the most unbusinesslike of mankind", but in fact he was talking rubbish. The records of Glasgow College provide abundant evidence that Smith was generally the man chosen to carry out any important piece of business, and he served for years as the College Treasurer and business manager.

There is something more than coincidence in the fact that it was while Adam Smith was a member of the faculty that Glasgow university furthered a number of highly important or scientific enterprises. One of the first was a chemical laboratory in which the brilliant young professor of chemistry, Joseph Black, might pursue his researches. Another was a printing establishment in which the Foulis brothers produced magnificent editions of the classics. And a third, and most important, was the welcome accorded to James Watt, when he had been forbidden by the Corporation of Hammermen to establish himself in Glasgow as a maker of mathematical instruments, on the simple ground that he had not served his apprenticeship to the craft. Fortunately Watt had done some skilled work for the university some years earlier, and now when he applied for help they promptly placed at his disposal a workshop, wherein he proceeded to make those experiments on the force of steam that led to his revolutionary development of the steam engine. Adam Smith often dropped in on Watt for an exchange of talk, and the incident provided him with much of the ammunition he later employed against the obnoxious privileges of craft corporations and the vicious operation of the laws regarding apprenticeship.

In the midst of all this varied activity Dr Smith (as we may now call him, since he had been made LL.D. by the University) found time to write *The Theory of Moral Sentiments*, a typical piece of eighteenth-century philosophizing in which the greatest emphasis is laid on sympathy as the origin and justification of our ideas of right conduct. The book was published in 1759 and won for its author a reputation extending far beyond Scotland, even to learned circles on the continent. But it had also a profound effect on Smith's personal fortunes. The book happened to be read, and deeply admired, by Charles Townshend, one of the most promising of the younger politicians of the day. Now Townshend had married the widow of the eldest son of the Duke of Buccleuch and thus became the guardian of her two sons by her first marriage. Francis, the elder son, was now the duke, and was about to leave Eton and be sent on the customary "Grand Tour" of the continent. The boy would require a tutor to accompany him—and what better person could there be than the distinguished author of the book just mentioned? So the offer was made, and the terms were so advantageous—a salary of £300 a year, with all travelling expenses paid, and a pension of £300 a year thereafter for the rest of his life—that Smith felt it impossible to decline. Towards the end of 1763 he resigned his professorship at Glasgow, and made ready to accompany his young charge; and it is altogether characteristic that he insisted, much against their will, in returning to each of his pupils that part of their fees which they had paid in advance and which he considered he had not fairly earned.

Early in 1764 Adam Smith and the young duke set off for the continent together. Some people thought they made a very ill-matched pair, but in fact they got on very well together. After ten days in Paris, spent very largely under the wing of the Scottish philosopher-historian David Hume, who was secretary at the

British Embassy, they moved on to Toulouse, capital of the province of Languedoc, with its own *parlement*, university, archbishop, and social advantages that made it a favourite winter resort. Here they stayed for eighteen months, and at first Smith found them rather boring, since the inadequacy of his French prevented his mixing with society. "The life which I led at Glasgow was a pleasurable dissipated life in comparison of that which I lead here at present", we find him complaining in a letter to Hume; but he added, "I have begun to write a book in order to pass away the time". This book became *The Wealth of Nations*, so that in the circumstances we have no reason to regret that the time hung heavy on his hands.

By way of diversion the pair made a trip to the great port and industrial centre of Bordeaux, where Smith formed a most favourable opinion of the French habit of drinking wine as compared with the mad indulgence in gin that went so far to demoralize the English populace. What an excellent thing it would be, he surmised, if French light wines could be imported freely into England, instead of being loaded with crippling duties which were responsible for the dangerous activities of smugglers (for whom, it may be noted, Smith had some very understanding things to say in his book).

Sometimes surprise has been expressed that Adam Smith seems to have taken a much more favourable view of the state of France and her people than Voltaire and other observers did. But it should be remembered that when he went to France the Revolution was a quarter of a century in the future; and besides, he spent most of his time in Languedoc, which was then the best governed, with a large measure of local autonomy, and most prosperous of all the French provinces. Even so, his picture of the France he saw is not all that favourable. Notwithstanding its greater size and population, France (he wrote) "is perhaps in the present times not so rich a country as England," and although a much richer country than Scotland was not going ahead so fast. The profits of trade in France were greater, it was true, but the wages of labour were generally lower. The great roads were kept in excellent order, but most of the others were neglected. The French taxation system was in every way far inferior to the British. The country was divided into a number of regions, each of which had its own fiscal system, so that a multitude of revenue officers were employed in hampering the internal trade of the country. The main burden of taxation was borne by the common people, and Smith was in no doubt but that their condition was worse in many respects than that of the British.

Thus he noticed such a thing as that in England leather shoes were a necessary of life, so that the poorest "creditable person of either sex" would be ashamed to appear in public without them, whereas in France they were not so regarded, "the lowest rank of both sexes appearing there publicly, without any discredit, sometimes in wooden shoes and sometimes barefooted".

Quitting Toulouse at length, Smith and his young companion paid a visit to the little republic of Geneva, where the former made many friends among the leading citizens and the distinguished foreigners who generally abounded there. Among these was Voltaire, and Smith lost no time in paying his respects to "the Patriarch" who had recently added to his tremendous fame by championing the unhappy Jean Calas, who a few years earlier had been judicially slaughtered by verdict of the Toulouse *parlement*. Smith seems to have visited Voltaire at his chateau of Ferney five or six times, and to the end of his life he never spoke of the great Frenchman save in terms of the deepest respect and admiration.

When 1765 had only a few days to run, Smith and the young duke were back in Paris, and they remained there for the next ten months. If Smith had been bored at Toulouse, he had nothing to complain of now; in fact, these months were probably the most interesting period in his life. Hume was just about to leave France for home, having been granted a very comfortable pension, but he was able to introduce his friend to the people most worth knowing in the capital. So Adam Smith went into society as never before, or after. He joined clubs, he attended the theatre regularly, he was welcomed into the literary ladies' salons, and he became very much at home with Baron d'Holbach and D'Alembert and the other chiefs of the great publishing enterprise of the *Encyclopédie* (which he seems to have read from the publication of the first of its thirty-five folio volumes in 1751), up-and-coming statesmen such as Turgot and Necker, and a great number of men of business, merchants and manufacturers, writers and artists, bishops and generals and so on. If there was one of these new acquaintances who especially aroused his interest and esteem it was Dr Francois Quesnay, one of the king's physicians, with a suite of rooms in the royal palace at Versailles, and who (as we may read in *The Wealth of Nations*) was the master of "a pretty considerable sect, distinguished in the French republic of letters by the name of the Economists".

This "sect" or school of economic theorists constituted the

main opposition to the "Mercantile system" which had been practically dominant in France since the days of Louis XIV a century earlier. According to the Mercantilists, a rich country was one abounding in money, and the government accordingly did all in their power to encourage exports and reduce imports, when the gap would be necessarily filled by hard cash. As a corollary, they strongly favoured the manufacturing interest at the expense of the agricultural, since it was they who produced the surplus of goods for export.

The *Economistes*, or Physiocrats as they were alternatively styled, held an exactly contrary view, in that they regarded "the labour which is employed upon land as the only productive labour". Adam Smith was of the opinion that this notion was perhaps "too narrow and confined", and yet he agreed with them "in representing the wealth of nations as consisting, not in the unconsumable riches of money, but in the consumable goods annually produced by the labour of the society". He might spare a smile for the unbounded admiration of the sect for their master, "a man of the greatest modesty and simplicity", but all the same, Quesnay's system was, perhaps, "the nearest approximation to the truth that has yet been published upon the subject of political economy". Whether (as has been sometimes supposed) he learnt much from Quesnay may be doubted; more likely, in his frequent discussions with the doctor and his followers he was confirmed in beliefs that he had first worked out for himself when he was a professor at Glasgow.

Adam Smith and his companion returned to England in October, 1766, their stay at Paris having been cut short by the sudden illness of the young duke, in course of which he was nursed by Smith with the most solicitous assiduity and tended by Dr Quesnay in his professional capacity. Both travellers had every reason to be satisfied with their experiences. The Duke of Buccleuch had established a friendship with his tutor that was terminated only with Smith's death; and Smith, for his part, had seen something of the great world, met a host of most interesting people, and accumulated a detailed knowledge of France and the Mercantilist system that was of inestimable advantage to him when he applied himself to the composition of his great book.

For some months after his return to England Smith remained in London, enjoying the intellectual life of the capital and spending many profitable hours in the reading-room of the British Museum.

Then in the spring of 1767 he went back to Kirkcaldy and made his home with his now aged mother, with his cousin, Miss Jean Douglas, to undertake the housekeeping. The book that had been forming in his mind for so many years now began to take shape and form. Starting early in the morning, he dictated to the young man who acted as his secretary. Most of the book was on paper by 1772, but there remained a good deal of revision to be done, mostly, it would seem, in London. Then on 9 March, 1776, any one with 36s. to spare might purchase the two big quarto volumes of *An Inquiry into the Nature and Causes of the Wealth of Nations*, stated on the title-page to be by "Adam Smith, LL.D., F.R.S., formerly Professor of Moral Philosophy at the University of Glasgow".

Although the book does not seem to have had much notice taken of it in the reviews, the first edition, probably of a thousand copies, was sold out in six months, and four more editions appeared in Smith's life-time. Nearly everybody whose opinion was worth anything spoke most highly of it: thus Hume wrote to his old friend that "it has depth, and solidity, and acuteness, and is so much illustrated by curious facts that it must at last take the public attention", and Gibbon hailed it as an "excellent work . . . an extensive science in a single book, and the most profound ideas expressed in the most perspicuous language".

The Wealth of Nations is a very long book, so long that summaries of it have sometimes required a volume to themselves. Beyond any doubt it is the greatest exposition of economic principles that has ever appeared, but what gives it a uniquely individual character is that Adam Smith treated his subject as a branch of the study of Mankind. He was a philosopher, in the eighteenth-century meaning of the term, and he illustrated his general theme of the supreme value and necessity of Economic Liberty with material drawn from history, philosophy, law, politics, sociology, religion, ethics, and literature in general. He never made the mistake (made by so many of his successors) of forgetting that economics is about *people*, and not figures in a table or lines on a graph. He was a man of the broadest human sympathies. He had many hard things to say about landlords, manufacturers and merchants, shopkeepers and the employing classes in general, but for the great mass of the population, mostly poor, he had a warm and understanding consideration. To quote one of the book's great key passages: "No society can surely be flourishing and happy, of which the far greater part of the members are poor and miserable. It is but equity, besides, that they who feed, clothe, and lodge the whole body of the people, should have such a share of the produce of their own labour as to be themselves tolerably well fed, clothed, and lodged."

Because Adam Smith laid such emphasis on the "human touch", his pages are dotted with interesting little details of things he had observed, or made a note of in his reading; such things, for instance, that there was "a village in Scotland where it is not uncommon for a workman to carry nails instead of money to the baker's shop or the ale house", "the first person that wore stockings in England is said to have been Queen Elizabeth", "there is no city in Europe in which house rent is dearer than in London, and yet I know no capital in which a furnished apartment can be hired so cheap", and "the common people of Scotland, who are fed with oatmeal, are in general neither so strong nor so handsome as the same rank of people in England who are fed with wheaten bread". There are numerous indications of his interest in and knowledge of the life of the common people, e.g. "soap is a real necessary of life", "coals are a less delightful fuel than wood", "that beautiful and happy invention" of glass windows, and "one half of the children born die before the age of manhood".

There are statements drawn from business life, as "Money makes money. When you have got a little, it is often easy to get more. The great difficulty is to get that little". Bold expressions of belief in the virtues of private enterprise and the capitalist system: "The natural effort of every individual to better his condition." The "sacred rights of private property". "There is no art which one government sooner learns of another, than that of drawing money from the pockets of the people." "It must be in the interest of the great body of the people to buy whatever they want of those who sell it cheapest." It was Adam Smith, it seems, who first referred to the English as "a nation of shopkeepers".

Added to the breadth of his understanding was his sagacious farseeingness. Writing when the "troubles" across the Atlantic had not yet broken into the War of American Independence, he speculated about a "Utopia" in which there would be an imperial Parliament, with American M.P.s at Westminster, and an imperial system of taxation, with possibly as a later development the transfer of the imperial capital from the banks of the Thames to somewhere in North America. And sundry references to the drawbacks and disabilities imposed on commerce by national boundaries leave us in no doubt that if he were alive today there would be no more convinced and eloquent champion of the European Community.

Very soon after the publication of *The Wealth of Nations* quotations from it were illuminating the speeches from both sides of the House of Commons. Most notable of the early converts to the great principle of free trade that it advocated was William Pitt, who as Chancellor of the Exchequer and then as Prime Minister attempted to give its arguments practical implementation. On the continent translations of the book soon appeared, in German, French, Italian, Spanish, and Danish, and began to exercise a fertilizing influence. The France that emerged from the Napoleonic wars had been swept clean of internal trade barriers, and something of the same kind was accomplished in Germany with the creation of the customs union known as the *Zollverein*. With the abolition of the Corn Laws in 1846 Britain became virtually a free trade country. Up to the time of the First World War Adam Smith's ideas may be said to have been predominant, and after the outbursts of economic nationalism in the "between the Wars" period they are once again receiving the attention of those responsible for the world economy.

To return to Adam Smith: until 1778 he lived in London, but in that year he was appointed (through the good offices of his former pupil, the Duke of Buccleuch) one of the commissioners of customs in Scotland and took up his residence at Edinburgh. The salary was £500 per annum, which was sufficient to enable him to take a house in a good residential district, keep a very hospitable table, practise much quiet charity, and indulge in his only extravagance, the formation of an excellent library. His mother and cousin joined him there, but Mrs Smith died in 1784, when in her ninetieth year, and the death of Miss Jean four years later left him a lonely and rapidly ageing man.

In 1787 he was elected Lord Rector of Glasgow University, and he acknowledged the honour in a letter couched in the most grateful terms. One thing that worried him greatly as his end approached was the feeling that he "had done so little", and he forthwith gave orders that a number of bundles of unfinished manuscripts should be burnt. He died on 17 July, 1790, and his body was laid to rest in the churchyard of the Canongate.

JOHANN WOLFGANG VON GOETHE
(1749–1832)

WHAT Dante is to Italy, what Shakespeare is to England, what
Voltaire is to France, that is what Goethe is to Germany. He was
born at the west German city of Frankfort-on-Main on 28 August,
1749, and was named Johann Wolfgang after his maternal grandfather. Nothing in his ancestry goes far to explain his extraordinary
genius. His great-grandfather was a farrier in Thuringia. His
grandfather gave up shoeing horses to become a ladies' tailor, and
eventually settled in Frankfort, where he did well, first in tailoring
and then as an innkeeper and wine-merchant. His second son
Johann Caspar (the elder son was an imbecile and was kept
hidden away in an attic) was given a good education, studied law,
made the Italian tour, and then returned to Frankfort to collect
coins and pictures. He would have liked to play some part in
municipal affairs, but the city fathers could not forget that this
well-to-do dilettante was the grandson of a tailor's apprentice,
and he was obliged to content himself with buying the title of
imperial councillor.

At the age of thirty-eight he married a girl of seventeen, one
Elizabeth Textor, daughter of a highly respected lawyer who rose
to become the chief magistrate of the city. Johann Wolfgang was
their first child. A year later was born a girl who was given the name
of Cornelia; she was Goethe's dearest companion in childhood and
early youth, and an intimate relationship continued until her
death in 1777 at the age of twenty-seven. Four other children died
very young.

Goethe's father seems to have played but a small part in his
development, but his debt to his mother must have been far greater
than he was prepared to acknowledge. She was only eighteen when
he was born: "I and my Wolfgang have always held fast to each
other," she said, "because we were young together." She was
cheerful, good-natured, and transparently sincere, with a great gift
for friendship. Her schooling must have been of the slightest, yet
she read Luther's Bible and Voltaire and fashion papers. She never

learnt to spell, and her punctuation was her own. In speech she was frank and salty, as when she referred in perfect naturalness to her son's mistress as his "bedfellow" and to her husband's collection of sculptures, as "those bare-bottoms". She dressed in complete disregard for fashion and suitability, and her ways were decidedly eccentric, so much so that the son in whom she took the greatest pride and interest was careful to avoid the embarrassments of her presence. She lived at Frankfort until her death in 1808, at the age of seventy-seven, and her last concern was that those attending her funeral should be given a good dinner. Goethe had not seen her for eleven years.

Of his boyhood there is little to recall or that has been recorded. His education was almost entirely at the hands of his parents and tutors, but he picked up much miscellaneous information in the streets and houses of the old city, where he mixed easily and often with people of all classes and occupations. This was the time of the Seven Years War, in which Frankfort as an Imperial city welcomed French troops as allies against Frederick of Prussia. The boy met a number of French officers, some of them men of culture, and he was a frequent visitor at the theatre in which French plays were performed. When he was about fourteen he had his first delightful experience of falling in love. His sweetheart is supposed to have been the daughter of a tavern-keeper at Offenbach, somewhat older probably than he and sturdily sensible, so that when she said "no kissing!" she meant it. "She treated me like a child", he grumbled, but he remembered her well enough to immortalize her under the name of Gretchen.

In the autumn of 1765 when he had just completed his sixteenth year Goethe was sent to Leipzig to study law at the university, since this was the career that his father had decided upon for him. At Leipzig he did indeed study many things, but law was nowhere near the top of the list. *Belles lettres* was his first preference, and for some time he was regular in attendance at the lectures of the professors of literature. Then he came under the influence of Oeser, director of the Academy of Arts, who gave him drawing lessons. His real university education, however, was derived from intercourse with the friends who dined with him at the professors' tables or in the local inns and boarding houses. He tried his hand at writing, and penned some pretty little pieces of a romantically erotic character, which were well received by his friends.

Being young and handsome and with money in his purse, he was never at a loss for a sweetheart, and his letters home to his sister are full of mentions of Annette or Auguste or Lisette or Löttchen or (most often perhaps) Käthchen (Kitty) Schönkopf, daughter of a wineseller who welcomed paying-guests to his luncheon table. With most of the girls the parting was little more than a saucy tilt of his student's cap, but Käthchen at nineteen was a woman with, as he put it in the poem commemorating the occasion, "only one fault —she loves me". Leaving her, then, meant a stormy wrenching of the emotions, but it had to be done. For already he was beginning to experience that nightmare that was to torment his sleep for years, of a woman "beckoning at the door, kisses in passing, and then, suddenly, she has put me in a sack!"

Towards the end of his third year at Leipzig, Goethe was taken seriously ill with a form of hysteria, brought on probably by too many late nights and drinking too much beer and strong coffee, although some biographers have attributed it to a venereal infection. His recovery was slow, and all the slower because of a tumour that developed in his neck. By August, 1768, he was sufficiently recovered to leave Leipzig, and for the next eighteen months he was at Frankfort, doing nothing in particular but extending his acquaintance among the townspeople. One of the most rewarding of his fresh contacts was with Fräulein von Klettenberg, who presided over a coterie of mystical pietists and dabblers in alchemy and provided him with material which he was to use to advantage in *Faust*. But his father was still insistent that he should embark on a legal career, and in the spring of 1770 Goethe proceeded to Strasbourg, to spend a few terms at the celebrated university.

Strasbourg had been French since 1681 but it still retained the characteristics of a German imperial city. Goethe was soon thoroughly at home there. He put his name down for courses of law lectures, and booked a seat at a table d'hôte kept by two maiden ladies in the Kramergasse, where the guests, about ten in number, were in the main medical students. With several he was soon on terms of friendship. One was J. H. Jung, who as "Jung Stilling" was to win fame as an operator for cataract and as author of pietistic romances in which much traditional lore of the common German people was embodied. More important, however, to Goethe's developing intelligence was Johann Gottfried Herder, who not only impressed him with the importance of folk songs and stories but introduced him to Shakespeare. But to begin with, Goethe was chiefly engaged in preparing a series of theses which he hoped would be found good enough to win him a doctorate in Law. Whether he actually got anything more than the licentiate is a matter in dispute, but there is no doubt that from his Strasbourg days he assumed the title of *Doctor* Goethe.

The question is of small importance compared with some other things that Strasbourg did for him. The Herder-Shakespeare connection has been just mentioned. A second was his awakening to the merits of Gothic architecture as a result of a prolonged study of the glorious pile of the cathedral, and this at a time when "Gothic" was generally synonymous with barbaric. And the third? Well, here *she* comes—a trim little maiden of nineteen, with blue eyes often wrinkled up with laughter, rosy cheeks, deliciously turned up nose, and pig-tails of fair hair falling almost to her waist; while as for her dress, it is the national costume of Alsatia—tight bodice, short white full skirt (short enough to disclose the neatest of ankles), black taffeta apron, and a straw hat which, when Goethe sees her first, is negligently hanging over her arm. This is Fräulein—no, Demoiselle—Frederike Brion, the second of the three daughters of the Lutheran pastor of the little village of Sesenheim, a day's ride out from Strasbourg.

Goethe owed his introduction to one of his fellow-boarders. Recently at Herder's prompting he had been reading Goldsmith's *Vicar of Wakefield*, and at once he was recognizing in Pastor Brion just such a man as Mr Primrose, and in his two elder girls who else but Olivia and Sophia? Frederike was Sophia, and from their very first meeting she and Goethe were most powerfully attracted. Successive visits contributed to form a passionate attachment. Hand in hand or arm in arm they strolled along the fieldpaths and over the daisied meadows, joined in boating expeditions on the river, and shared in many a jolly picnic. They danced together in the close-clasping dances of the country. She played on the harpsichord and sang the simple songs that he composed specially for her. In the family circle he was the young girl's accepted suitor, but there was no formal engagement. Weeks slipped into months and still the idyll continued. But the end came at last: Goethe mounted his horse and rode away.

Eight years later Goethe, when on his second visit to Switzerland, broke his journey to call once again at the Sesenheim parsonage. Great was his relief to discover that Frederike seemed to bear him no ill will and made him feel quite at his ease. Again he rode away, and for forty years seemed to have put her quite out of his mind. But one day when he was dictating his autobiography her entrancing shape swept into his vision, and (after a pause of silent melancholy) he proceeded to give to the world a matchless picture of a German maiden in all her freshness and unpretentious charm. Frederike might have read it, since she lived until 1813, but she is unlikely to have ever done so. If she had ever heard of the "Sesenheim idyll" she kept well away from the exploiters of the Goethe legend. She never married, and her life seems on the whole to have been a rather unhappy one.

Back once more in Frankfort, Goethe wanted nothing so much as to be allowed to follow his literary bent. Hitherto his output had mainly consisted of romantic poems and sentimental songs, but now, in his newborn enthusiasm for Shakespeare, he had in mind the writing of a drama of splendid theme and majestic construction; and one, moreover, that should be essentially *German*: he had no time now for the "three unities" and other stilted contrivances of the classical theatre. A dry-as-dust biography of Götz von Berlichingen, known as Götz of the Iron Hand, provided him with a suitable subject. Götz was a robber baron, or, looked at from a different standpoint, a bold, courageous survivor of the feudal age who managed to survive and flourish in sixteenth-century Germany. The play was sketched out in a few weeks, and Goethe read it to his sister, who made all the encouraging noises. But before he could polish it for publication he had one more clash with his father, who insisted that he should qualify as a jurist by enrolling among the young attorneys at the Imperial Supreme Court at Wetzlar. Goethe was still so completely dependent on his father that he could do nothing else but comply. He went to Wetzlar, and for some weeks gave some half-hearted attention to law suits that his father put in his way. After that, however, he seldom put in an appearance in the court's dusty corridors and chambers, and when that summer of 1772 came to an end he had decided that, whatever his father might say, never again would he wear a lawyer's wig.

That summer was not without its compensations, however. As usual he had made many new friends, of both sexes. Amongst the young men was J. G. C. Kestner, who held a secretarial post at the Hanoverian Legation, and amongst the young women, above all nineteen-year-old Lotte Buff, who was Kestner's betrothed. Lotte seems indeed to have been what Goethe calls her, a "desirable creature". She was the eldest daughter (in a family of twelve children) of the bailiff in charge of the Wetzlar properties of that feudal relic, the Order of Teutonic Knights; her mother was dead, and she performed wonders in keeping the home together. Goethe was always very fond of children, and he found the company under the Buffs' roof altogether delightful. For Lotte, indeed, his admiration soon expanded into love. What an excellent little mother she made! And how pretty she looked as, in her curly coiffure, tight-laced bodice and dress of many flouncings, she sat at the parlour table cutting bread and butter! Goethe felt so *comfortable* with her, and the fact that she was engaged to his friend enabled him to take little liberties that otherwise might have put thoughts of another kind in the dear girl's head. Even as things were, Goethe began to feel that he was on the slippery slope to matrimony, especially when Kestner hinted that he loved Lotte so well that he would be ready to give her up if he found that she loved Goethe more . . . Goethe saw the red light of danger, or, to change the metaphor, the terrible "sack" of his nightmares. Without bidding a formal adieu, he rode away.

Lotte shed a few tears, but she was not disconsolate. A year or so later she married Kestner, and she may well have concluded that she had done better for herself than would have been the case if she had married that brilliant but not very reliable young Goethe. If fecundity is a sign of happiness in marriage then she should have been happy, since she bore Kestner a dozen children. All the same, she was never to escape entirely from Goethe's clasp, as we shall see in due course.

On the whole, then, that summer at Wetzlar was something that furnished Goethe with richly rewarding experience and the pleasantest of recollections. The contrast with his renewed life at Frankfort was harsh, and his father's grumblings must have been hard to bear. But soon the situation was changed beyond measure. That play he had carried about with him and revised so long and lovingly was at length ready for publication, and in the summer of 1773 *Götz von Berlichingen* burst upon an astounded world. The clattering panoply of medieval knighthood, recreated by Goethe's genius, opened the first chapter in modern German literature and gave a vigorous thrust to the *Sturm und Drang* ("Storm and Stress") movement.

Although the name comes from one of the tragedies of Maximilian Klinger, it was Goethe who was hailed throughout the length and breadth of Germany as the movement's principal spokesman. Greatly celebrated as he became, he was still not satisfied. He had no ambition to go down in history as one, even the leader, of a movement: he was an individualist, and so his pen resumed its experimental wanderings.

After quitting Wetzlar he had kept in touch with Lotte and Kestner, and one day he received tidings of a tragic happening that moved him deeply. A young attaché of the name of Jerusalem, whom he had known slightly in Leipzig and had met again at the luncheon table in Wetzlar, had borrowed Kestner's pistols and shot himself. Apparently an unhappy love affair was the reason, coupled with social slightings and professional failure. Goethe could not get the incident out of his head, and before long we find him making it the central theme of a work which, though announced as fiction, was largely composed out of facts conveyed to Goethe in letters from Kestner. This is understandable and indeed allowable; but Goethe with a shocking insensitivity introduced into his story a Lotte who was so like the Lotte of real life that the identification was soon made. Kestner, too, discovered that he had been subjected to similar treatment. Very naturally, the pair were deeply pained and indignant, and it says much for their forgiving spirit that in the end they did not allow the affair to affect their friendly intercourse with Goethe.

Die Leiden des Jungen Werthers—in English, *The Sorrows of Werther*, was published in the autumn of 1774, and was an immediate bestseller, as it fully deserved to be. On the face of it, it is but the tale of an ill-starred love—but what pathos there is in the telling, what consummate simplicity in its use of words, what deep understanding of the moody melancholy that afflicted so many youthful spirits of the time, a weariness with life and a longing for the unending sleep of death. If the book's sentimentality seems forced, it was real enough to send the tears streaming down the cheeks of men and maidens alike. Young fellows imagined themselves as Werther, dressed themselves in the Wertherian costume of blue tail coat, yellow waistcoat, and black leather breeches, and (some of them) followed the procedure of the suicide to the last detail, the finalizing bullet. Preachers railed against the book in the pulpit, critics filled columns in the newspapers and periodicals. Not only the educated but the common people lapped it up, in cheap pirated editions that were hawked through the streets. Its fame even penetrated to China, where Lotte and Werther were modelled in porcelain.

Werther gave Goethe an European reputation. Now at last he could look his father in the face and insist on following his own chosen path. And that path led him, not for the present to fresh literary triumphs (the plays and poems that followed *Götz* and *Werther* were not in the same class of excellence), but through the gates of an insignificant little town in one of the most minor of the host of German principalities. That town was Weimar, capital of the duchy of Saxe-Weimar, in Thuringia. Goethe had first met its duke, Karl August, at Frankfort some years earlier. The acquaintance had been improved by fresh meetings, and now an invitation had come for him to pay the duke a visit. The invitation came at a most opportune moment, just when Goethe was recovering from another love affair, in which he had so far forgotten himself as to enter into a formal engagement. Glad indeed was he to make good his escape, and so, on 7 November, 1775 we see him entering the town where he expected to stay for a few weeks only but which in the event was to become his home for the rest of his long life.

Weimar in those days showed not the slightest signs of becoming the "German Athens". It was a poor little place of about six thousand inhabitants, mainly peasants but with a thin sprinkling of tradesmen and artisans, and a still thinner layer of upper-class courtiers. Its duke, Karl August, had just come of age at eighteen (Goethe was twenty-six), and his "palace" was no better than the house of a substantial Frankfort burgher. There was nothing of the intellectual about him. He loved hunting, cross-country riding, and indiscriminate wenching among the peasant girls of his domain. But he had a shrewd understanding and knew a good man when he saw one: how else could he have seen in the young literary lion the makings of a lifelong friend, a most trustworthy counsellor, and an administrator of statesmanlike ability?

The first few weeks in Weimar were an extravaganza of boisterous amusement. Goethe joined the duke and his party in helter-skelter gallops across country, boar-hunts, sleigh-rides, rough practical joking, and the rough and tumble of rural debauchery. But when the excess of youthful energy had been worked off he took a cold, hard look at his situation and prospects. The duke was more than kind: he provided him with a comfortable dwelling and offered him a salary which, though small, would be sufficient in a place where living was so cheap. He might have gone back to Frankfort, or pushed his fortune in some livelier and grander centre. But winter passed and the spring came and, since he got on so well with the duke and his family and the work he was invited to do proved so congenial, he decided to stay. But there was another perhaps even more compelling reason that kept him in Weimar, and, need it be said? this had a woman's shape. Not a young girl this time, not an unsophisticated innocent of virginal integrity and with lips hardly kissed, but a mature woman of thirty-three, eleven years married and with three children living of the seven she had borne her husband. This was the Frau Charlotte von Stein, wife of the duke's master of the Horse, a very accommodating gentleman who seldom found it necessary to put in an appearance at his own home. She was not beautiful, but she was elegant in dress and person, thoroughly well bred, and of exquisite manners. For ten years she and Goethe were on intimate terms, but whether the intimacy reached the ultimate is a matter that continues to exercise the curiosity of biographers. Seventeen hundred letters written her by Goethe have been preserved, but she was careful to get back all that she wrote to him and committed them to the flames.

Those ten years covered the period when Goethe was primarily concerned with running the affairs of the little state. After only a few months at Weimar he was given a seat on the ducal council, and in 1782 a patent of nobility entitled him to place the much-prized *von* before his name. His first ministerial appointment was as director of Roads and Services, but his responsibilities were soon extended to cover practically all the affairs of the several territories (containing perhaps a hundred thousand souls) that comprised the state of Saxe-Weimar. Under his influence and guidance Duke Karl August became a worthy exponent of that "enlightened despotism" that Goethe conceived the best form of government for the times.

But with middle age the spirit of restlessness again took charge of his mind and actions. Without so much as a "by your leave" he suddenly slipped away from Weimar and made for Italy, where from the autumn of 1786 until the summer of 1788 he passed his time in fascinating explorations of classical ruins, vain efforts to prove himself a painter, and earthy love affairs with women of low degree. When at length he made his reappearance at Weimar he was a changed man, physically as well as mentally. He was relieved of the routine of daily business, and devoted himself to botanical and other scientific studies, in particular the search for the "primal plant" and investigation of the nature of light.

At the same time his personal life took a dramatic turn. The Frau von Stein no longer pleased him. He sought a simpler, more sensuous companion, and he erelong found her in a plump little piece of unaffected femininity who one day approached him when he was walking in the park and in proper bashfulness sought his good offices on behalf of her young brother who was out of employment. Christiane Vulpius was her name; she was twenty-three, obviously marriageable but still unwed, and she earned her livelihood as a workgirl in the artificial-flower factory that was Weimar's principal industrial establishment. Goethe fell for her at once; he took her into his home as his mistress, and as such she answered his every need. She bore him several children, of whom only the first-born, his son August, survived infancy, but it was not until 1806 that he saw fit to reward her near twenty years of devotion by making her his wife in regular form. The nightmarish menace of the "sack" was thus exorcized at last.

The advent of the French Revolution did not surprise Goethe: he had felt its preliminary rumblings for some little time. Nor did it disturb him much. He had no revolutionary enthusiasms, no sympathy whatever with the masses, however oppressed they might be made out to be. Nor had he any feelings for German patriotism; German culture he could understand, to contribute to German intelligence was his life's work—but "Germany" was for him nothing more than a vague geographical expression. All the same, when Saxe-Weimar joined in the alliance against the French revolution he felt it his duty to accompany his duke in the campaign, travelling in his own carriage with a man-servant. He found it all very interesting, and at the "battle" of Valmy in 1792 he deliberately ventured near the front in order that he might note his own reactions to being under fire.

As soon as might be, he was back in Weimar, busying himself as before with his ordered course of ministerial duties, direction of the theatre, writing and scientific studies, and the war did not catch up with him again until 1806 when French troops occupied Weimar and he was threatened by marauders in his own house. Christiane sprang to his protection, and it was shortly afterwards that he married her. In 1808 he was among those summoned to attend Napoleon at the Congress of Erfurt. The Man of War was pleased to patronize him. "*Voilà un homme!*" he exclaimed, as he saw him approach. How old was he, he enquired? Sixty? You are well preserved. That *Werther* now; he had read it seven times (so he claimed), but he couldn't help feeling that the story was rather muddled. . . . The Man of Letters bowed in appreciation, and was extremely proud of the *Légion d'Honneur* with which he was invested. The War of Liberation left him cold: Napoleon was a "demonic force", and it really was not the slightest use attempting his overthrow. . . .

The ten years about the turn of the century were chiefly remarkable for his intimate literary partnership with Schiller, so close and so mutually responsive that henceforth the names of the two great writers were indissolubly linked. It was largely owing to Schiller's encouragement that Goethe produced his *Wilhelm Meister*, a novel of crowded incident which he had begun even before his Italian journey. But his outstanding contribution to the literature of the new century was *Faust*.

Since the days of his youth he had been fascinated by the figure of the medieval necromancer who entered into a compact with the Devil to sell his immortal soul for gold, women, honour, and, above all perhaps, knowledge. There really was a Doctor Faustus: he lived in Germany in the early years of the sixteenth century, and his story was related in a succession of books—vulgar, obscenely sexual, and horrific for the most part—and presented to the populace in stage plays and puppet-shows. Goethe was acquainted with these things, and his interest was stimulated by the goings-on among the chemical flasks and mysterious salts of Fräulein von Klettenberg's laboratory. These provided the material for the confrontation of the Magician with Mephistopheles, but for the core of eventual drama—the love-tragedy of Faust and Margaret-Gretchen—Goethe was almost certainly indebted to a case that occurred at Frankfort in 1772, soon after his return from Strasbourg, of a girl named Susanna Margaretha who was found guilty of infanticide and doomed to the horrible death by beheading laid down by law. To these essential ingredients he added much later the "boisterous crew" of naked young witches storming through the air on Walpurgis Night to their orgiastic revels on the Brocken.

Much of the First Part was in manuscript when Goethe went to Italy, and from time to time he added fresh lines and scenes. What he called a "fragment" was published in 1797, and then in 1808 the whole of the First Part was included in the collected edition of his works issued by Cotta at Tübingen. The second (so very different) part was many more years in the writing, so that it was an old man of eighty who put the finishing touches to what a young man in his twenties had begun.

Faust stands at the summit of Goethe's literary achievement: it puts him among the Immortals, not of Germany only, not of Europe only, but of the world. And yet there was something more to come.

Goethe's declining years were one long golden sunset. When death had swept the board almost clean of his old-time friends and associates he found refreshment in the company of men and women belonging to the younger generations. New ideas too ("If one isn't to stagnate, one must be constantly changing, regenerating oneself, growing young again") spurred his pen to produce more lovely poems, more delightful recollections, more scientific excursions, more letters; and that his conversation had lost none of its ripe wisdom and pregnant thought is clear from what his secretary, J. P. Eckermann, so faithfully recorded. His wife was dead and his son, but he was well looked after by his daughter-in-law Ottilie. Life still seemed good to him and he was in no hurry to die, even though he was sure beyond the least doubt of some continued existence beyond the grave.

When the end approached, those standing by were appalled by the intensity of his death struggles, as he sat in the armchair beside his bed. "More light!" he murmured, probably in reference to a closed shutter. And then, "Look at the lovely woman's head—its black tresses—magnificent colouring—against the dark background!" At noon on 22 March, 1832, the age-worn fingers that had been as though writing on the coverlet, slowly uncurled and lay quiet. Goethe had finished his last, and greatest work.

NAPOLEON BONAPARTE
(1769–1821)

THE STORY of Napoleon Bonaparte is one of the great adventure stories of modern European history. He came from a little known island, Corsica, best known for its addiction to brutal civil wars, wars in which Bonapartes had long been conspicuous, and whose own sovereignty had just casually changed hands from Genoa to France; he had no connections in France; he was short and swarthy and, except for the deepset eyes, unprepossessing in appearance, looking and acting like a rough foreigner in a still aristocratic France; at his artillery school at Brienne—where he went on a scholarship—he was lonely, inward-looking, and dedicated—not to France, but to the struggle for freedom in Corsica, to Robespierre's politics, and always to his own career. He was, first and last a Corsican adventurer, a *condottiere*.

He tried to seize Ajaccio in 1792 and in 1793, without success. It was only after the expulsion of his family from Corsica in 1793 that he identified himself with his new cause, Revolutionary France. But he remained to the end what he had called himself on the eighteenth Brumaire of the Year VIII (9 November, 1799), "the god of fortune and of war". Indeed on that day, in particular, his fortune held, for that was one of the rare occasions when for a few hours he lost his courage. It was the firmness of his brother Lucien and the promptness of the grenadiers in clearing out the Five Hundred, that made Napoleon First Consul. But he seemed in 1799 after ten years of unparalleled turmoil to be clean, fresh and unsullied. After that, until Moscow, both fortune and war—and France—were his to command.

Napoleon's career would have been impossible but for the Revolution, which offered a career to a talent like his, and equally impossible without the chaos that followed it, which gave that talent its stage. By 1795 France was in a state of civil war, divided between royalists dominating the south and west and practising a Counter-Terror of their own, constitutionalists—the Clichiens notably Carnot—hoping for a "mixed order", and the "perpetuals"

—mainly Girondins and notably Barras and Rewbell—who wanted to carry on the Revolution and the war against the old order, against royalism, the clergy and the emigrés. France was threatened by foreign enemies, by the hunger riots of 1795, by a rising of the *sans-culottes*—of which the only result was the abortive Babeuf conspiracy (May, 1796)—and by the royalist conspiracy of the Abbé Brottier (January, 1797). There was rampant inflation, administrative chaos and business corruption. Boissy d'Anglas talked of a country ruled by property-owners; what this meant in practice was the rule of speculators and war-contractors, in which Robespierre's civic puritanism disappeared in a wave of sexual indulgence and licence, and Republican virtue was lost in a tide of venality. The situation called for leadership, and the leadership came from this Corsican outsider, trained as an artilleryman caught up in Revolutionary ideas but in no man's party except his own, and who had made his mark not as a politician but as a brilliant, ruthless and clinically cold soldier.

It was his direction of the artillery that led to the recapture of Toulon from the British (18 December, 1793), which made him a brigadier, aged twenty-four. Less than two years later (5 October, 1795), he suppressed the insurrection of Vendemiaire with a "whiff of grapeshot"; he became Commander of the Army of the Interior at twenty-six, a major-general, and the husband of Josephine de Beauharnais—Barras's former mistress. Within a year, he became commander of the Army of Italy because the Directory had no funds to pay its quarter-of-a-million men on active service, and could only tempt them with foreign booty.

Napoleon, himself an adventurer now twenty-seven, led an army of hungry adventurers with a war chest of only 2,000 louis in coin; he told his troops they were on a plundering expedition. He won 26 battles in less than 12 months, and his booty included 750,000 francs and the portrait gallery of the Duke of Modena, 21 million francs from the Kingdom of Naples, and 20 million and the promise of more, plus 500 manuscripts and 100 pictures, from the Holy See. His armies dominated northern Italy and he was now a public hero, a man with a future.

At the age of twenty-nine (1799) he was given command of the "Army of England", but the Directory decided to strike at Britain through Egypt. Napoleon, aware now that complete power in France was possible but that "the pear is not ripe", and fascinated by the East—he had once thought of service with the Sultan—

was away for sixteen months, in the course of which he took Malta and routed the Mameluke forces at the Battle of the Pyramids. But he had his fleet destroyed by Nelson at Aboukir Bay, and he was checked at Acre; the army he abandoned had later to capitulate, and to evacuate Egypt—but his own reputation stayed unsullied.

He returned in September, 1799, to help Sieyès, who, like a Madison, sought a Washington and found a Caesar. Sieyès thought of Joubert as his ally but Joubert was killed at Novi. Moreau and Bernadotte refused to help him. Thus Bonaparte was not—no more than was Franco—a first choice. But once invited, he, like Franco, took over totally. But history will see Franco as an infinitely more skilful, if less significant, figure. After Brumaire (1799, aged thirty) he was First Consul. Only he could appoint and dismiss officials and promulgate laws. In 1802 he became First Consul for life, with the right to nominate his successor. In 1804 he crowned himself Emperor, taking the crown from the Pope's hands. He himself then crowned Josephine. He was thirty-four.

The roots of the success lay on the battlefield. Napoleon had a remarkable eye for the broad perspective of a campaign, and equally remarkable tactical insight on the day; he could see the weak spot of an enemy, as at Waterloo—and he was usually opposing uneasy coalitions; he was a master of timing, as Austerlitz showed; even when exhausted, he had striking powers of recuperation, as witness the manoeuvres against Blücher and Schwarzenberg in 1814; and because they lived off the country his troops could move with speed. He was a great planner of a campaign but he never in fact relied on plans when it came to action. The art of war, he said, was "all in the execution". And he was able to establish a *rapport* with his men of a rare kind. "It is by speaking to the soul that men are electrified." He had exceptional physical strength—in 1808 he rode from Valladolid to Paris in 6 days, and in the 4 days of the Waterloo campaign he was on horseback for 37 hours and had less than 20 hours sleep. But he was not—until the legend grew—by any means universally popular with his men; he was prodigal and profligate with their lives, as witness Borodino; it was his Imperial Guard, who were largely ceremonial troops, who cried *Vive l'Empereur*; by the end there were mass desertions, though there was by that time also, inevitably, a wild fascination about his appearance among his troops, for this clearly was a man cast, for good or ill, in an heroic mould, and with a magical flair, it seemed, for military success.

Perhaps indeed his major legacy was as a military tactician. Wars after his day were fought according to his rule-book: the selection of the enemy's vulnerable point and the massing of force against it; heavy preliminary bombardment; the use of an advanced guard to engage the enemy while the main force manoeuvred for an advantage; the importance of a powerful reserve and its use at the strategic moment.

But Bonaparte's success was more than military. He was not only a successful soldier, but a natural authoritarian. He worked with the concentration, and the command of detail, of a Louis XIV; like the young Louis also he chose well, and his success and efficiency bred loyalty. This was a truly Enlightened Despot, and superbly served—by Talleyrand as Foreign Minister (1799–1807), by Berthier, War Minister (1800–1807), by Fouché, Police and Interior (1799–1802, 1804–10) of whom Talleyrand said that he was a man who minded his own business, and other people's; by a parade of brilliant marshals, Massena, Soult, Ney, Davout, Murat, Augereau, Bernadotte. Some of these were noble indeed and paid the supreme price—for Ney, the "Bravest of the Brave" who joined him after Elba was executed by the Bourbons; and Berthier, living in Bavaria, was pulled in both directions in 1815 and committed suicide. Napoleon had no such emotions, nor such loyalties. But he could choose well, and not just marshals. Men like Berthollet, Chaptal and Laplace were as important and as devoted as his military lieutenants.

His revolutionary ardour soon cooled, and efficiency and merit became the watchwords. "The more I read Voltaire", he said, "the better I like him. . . . Up to the age of sixteen I would have fought for Rousseau against all the friends of Voltaire. Today it is the opposite. Since I have seen the East, Rousseau is repugnant to me. The wild man without morals is a dog". He was ready to pay verbal tributes to representative government and to elections; the life consulate of 1802 and the Imperial title of 1804 were consecrated by plebiscites; and the gains of the Revolution were never put at risk; but all Napoleon's natural instincts were for order and obedience.

This was patently true in politics. After 1799 the First Consul was in fact a supremo. The Senators were nominated for life by the Consuls, and they themselves selected both the Tribunate, which discussed legislation, and a Legislative Assembly which voted without discussion; in 1802, however, the Tribunate was purged

No great writer has given to the world a more intimately revealing account of his own life than Jean-Jacques Rousseau (whose fine bust by Houdon is pictured on the right). Not surprisingly, his *Confessions* has caught the fascinated attention of generations of readers, and if his reputation has suffered then it is very largely his own doing. But he wrote much more. His *La Nouvelle Heloise* is one of the earliest of novels of romantic sentiment. His *Emile* shows him (the man who deposited his own children in the bag at the foundling-hospital) as a most enlightened educationist. His *Contrat Social* reveals him as an out-and-out democrat, the parent of a host of the most revolutionary ideas. Small wonder that when the day of Revolution dawned, perfervid partisans hailed Jean-Jacques as their forerunner, and there appeared such pictures as the artistic medley on the right, in which Rousseau's portrait appears above a variety of patriotic symbols and emblems, arranged in a landscape in which move peasant and soldier and the Julie and Claire of his romantic masterpiece.

As the eighteenth century was nearing its
close, there stepped on to the European
stage the demonic figure of Napoleon
Bonaparte. Just a daring young soldier to
begin with, he soon revealed qualities of
greatness as a military commander and the
manipulator of political arrangements.
For years he was the apparently invincible
master of Europe, the arbiter of its
destinies. This is the Emperor Napoleon
who is portrayed here by Antoine Vernet,
the French painter whose vast battle-pieces
of Marengo and Austerlitz won him the
Emperor's favour. At length the man who
had toppled so many of the ancient
dynasties resolved on the creation of a
dynasty of his own, and, having put away
his wife, married in 1810 the young
Archduchess Marie-Louise, daughter of
the Austrian emperor—the occasion
pictured here by Rouget in all its showy
magnificence.

and in 1807 dissolved. After 1804 the Emperor himself nominated the Senators. There was universal suffrage, but it was for the selection of a list of 10 per cent of the electorate, regarded as suitable for local office. Local government in any event was controlled by a prefect, chosen by Paris, and wielding autocratic powers, in fact a Napoleon in miniature, heir to the Intendant of Louis XIV. Mayors of major cities were named by the Emperor. Local councils, though elected, were elected from among the principal taxpayers and sat for 15 or 20 years, so that local notables re-emerged to positions of power. Judicial posts—made elective by the Revolution—became life appointments; and special courts became frequent features.

Gradually the trappings and ritual of authority were introduced also; the Legion of Honour, modelled on the Order of St Louis, in 1802; at his coronation in 1804, princely titles for the Bonapartes, with Kingdoms to follow for all the brothers except Lucien; in 1808, an Imperial nobility with hereditary titles and hereditary estates also—31 Dukes, 388 counts, 1,090 barons, 1,500 knights; 16 generals became marshals of France, and Murat, the ally of Vendemiaire, became grand admiral; and in 1810, came marriage to the most august dynasty in Europe and an eighteen year-old bride for himself, whom he found eminently satisfactory. In 1811 with the birth of the King of Rome his own dynasty seemed assured. It all seemed a reversion to the France of the Bourbons, and many old *aristos*, with or without a title but holding on firmly to land, crept back into local society. But it was done with total candour and obvious calculation, indeed with near-contempt. And what was given could always be taken away. The basis of the Napoleonic system was not honour but fear. If he was the child of the Revolution, he was also its destroyer.

But in the legal codes the emphasis also was authoritarian. The codified laws were, it is true, for the most part based on Revolutionary legislation, and they enshrined the basic principles of the Revolution—equality before the law and the equal distribution of property, freedom to work and worship, and the secular character of the state. The objective, and it was novel not only in France but in Europe, was a law that was uniform and rational. But Napoleon put his own stamp on the codes. The authority of the father in the family was made clear—he could imprison his children, withhold consent to their marriage and control his wife's property. Family cohesion was seen as basic to cohesion in the state. If the principle of divorce was admitted, it was not to be allowed after ten years of marriage, and only once. In criminal trials, there was no *habeas corpus*, juries were nominated by prefects and the preliminary investigations were secret—none of them giving any assurances for the accused. The law was seen as the buttress of the state, not as a protection against the abuse of arbitrary power. But the objective was rationalism and universality, and the Code has remained the basis of French civil law.

Moreover the Press was tightly controlled. The number of licensed printers was limited, and Fouché and his police kept a careful eye on all that was written and as far as possible on all that was said. In 1810 the single newspaper in each department was under the prefect's control; by 1811 Paris had no newspaper at all.

Education too bore the marks of the despot. A new style of grammar school appeared, the *lycée*, in which military training was as important as the classics—it was to be one of Napoleon's great contributions to France. In 1808 the Imperial University was established, a degree from which was a prerequisite for teaching. The *Écoles* set up by the Convention, notably the *École Polytechnique*, to train engineers, and the *École Normale Superieure*, to train teachers, were encouraged and supported. But they too gradually reflected the authoritarianism of the regime—by 1810 the *École Polytechnique* was no more than a training school for the army. And primary education was sadly neglected. French education, even after a century of shocks and revolution, still bears the notably centralized and "hot-house" character that Napoleon gave it.

The government was almost as much involved in economic affairs. Laws were issued to regulate the supply of food, for the registration of workers with the police, and to establish the metric system. The policy was protectionist, and if the primary intention of the Continental System was the destruction of Britain it was, in embryo, a European-scale *zollverein*. There was a concerted attempt to promote industry, with government subventions for agriculture, notably for sugarbeet. And there was, despite the blockade and the wars, a flourishing silk, wool, and cotton trade, which enriched the bourgeoisie. The pattern, again, was that of Louis XIV, and even of Colbert, with the sharp difference that the French peasant now had a stake in the soil, and in the state; he was the real beneficiary of the Revolution. He has ever since called himself as a result a radical and a revolutionary, but he has been utterly conservative in his instincts, for he has a lot to lose.

In one area, however, secular authority met a countervailing force: Caesar faced the challenge of the viceregent of God. For, despite the age of reason and the worship of the Supreme Being, France was still in essence a Catholic country; Chateaubriand, an early admirer of Napoleon—though his admiration turned to hatred after the murder of the duc d'Enghien in 1804—had considerable impact with his *Génie de Christianisme* in 1802. The Revolution had frightened and alienated many Catholics, and Napoleon, first and last a realist, even a cynic, wanted to end the tension. He saw religion as a necessity not for the sake of the Church but for the stability and contentment of the State; it was a useful buttress to patriotism. "In religion", he said, "I do not see the mystery of the Incarnation but the mystery of the social order." "If I were governing the Jews, I would restore the Temple of Solomon."

In 1802 a Concordat was signed with the Pope. Bishops were required to resign their sees, and the bishoprics were reduced to 50 in number, with 10 archbishoprics; they were nominated by Napoleon and consecrated by the Pope. In exchange for a fixed salary, the clergy took an oath of obedience to the state. But the Church lands confiscated by the Revolution stayed firmly in the hands of the bourgeoisie and the peasants who had acquired them. Roman Catholicism was recognized as the "religion of the great majority" of Frenchmen, but equal rights were granted to other faiths—a basic principle of the secular state which was unknown anywhere before the Revolution. In other words, the spirit, like the mind, was disciplined in his service, and the Church, like the schools, became a Department of State. The *Journal des Curés*, the only clerical newspaper to appear after 1806, carried his imprimatur, sermons were strictly censored, and there were to be no papal bulls, papal legates or investigations from Rome. But if it was to gain little for Pius VII, at least most of the religious orders returned, as did the Sabbath, and the Gregorian calendar.

Yet when the quarrel with Rome came it was not over these issues. The strongly Gallican spirit in France long pre-dated Napoleon; his attempts to exploit it for his own purposes had the effect of driving his clerical opponents into ultramontanism, that is they recognized the Pope as the supreme head of the Church. Pius VII disliked the extension of the Code Napoleon to Italy, since it authorized divorce; Napoleon despoiled Rome of the Legations of Bologna and Ferrara, which he added to the Kingdom

of Italy, and he handed over Ponte Corvo and Benevento to
Bernadotte and Talleyrand respectively. Pius objected to Joseph
Bonaparte's accession to the throne of Naples, and in 1806 he
refused to expel the enemies of France from the papal states. In
May, 1809, Rome was annexed by France; in June Pius excommunicated Napoleon, and the Pope was arrested in the
following month and imprisoned in Fontainebleau.

In the end the Pope returned to Rome as a result of the allies'
triumph at Leipzig, and his steady resistance undermined all
Napoleon's efforts. Napoleon found that it was his own unbridled
ambition and not the Concordat which succeeded in alienating
many Catholics, for he tied Church and State so closely together
that their alliance has been a continuous source of tension and
danger to France. However, the Concordat survived the quarrel
and remained in force until 1905.

Napoleon produced, then, a cohesive, highly centralized, tightly
disciplined state. His reforms were in the spirit of the Revolution, a
Revolution made tidy and orderly. But it was as if he knew the
Revolutionary words but had forgotten the tune. His Empire at
once enshrined the ideas of the Revolution, and in the process
undermined them. He had been prepared to eradicate the mob
with grapeshot; for him they were *canaille*. His reforms in education
sought and trained an *elite*; in his codes and in his Concordat the
emphasis was not on liberty and equality, and certainly not on
fraternity, but on discipline and obedience—and on talent. As he
instructed his brother Jerome when he made him King of Westphalia—"talented men should have an equal right to your consideration and to office, whether or not they are of noble birth".

The reforms were largely the work of Napoleon as consul. By
1804 he was an Emperor, and he planned an all-out war with
Britain, with invasion for a time his dream. At this point French
historians fall basically into two camps. If they all agree that as
lawgiver and planner this was a great and constructive genius,
they do not agree on much thereafter. There are those—notably
Mme de Stael in his own day, Taine, Aulard, Lefebvre and Peter
Geyl—who see him after 1805 as a tyrant, driven by power and by
megalomania. And there are those—like Thiers, Sorel and Madelin
—who see him as a prisoner of the European situation; as drawn
into wars he was not keen to fight but which he found inescapable.
Certainly there is some validity in the view that he did not seek
the war with Prussia in 1806, and that in the Rhineland, Italy and

Poland he was seen as liberator rather than as conqueror. Many Rhinelanders fought in his armies. And certainly 1806 was a year of total victory. After Austerlitz Austria made peace; Russia withdrew into its own territory; and the Holy Roman Empire was declared abolished. When Prussia moved, she was defeated at Jena (October, 1806), and the Continental System—a vast blockade of Britain by Europe—was announced in a series of decrees made in Berlin. And in 1807 the Russians were overwhelmed at Friedland. In July, 1807, the two Emperors, of France and of Russia, met in high ceremony on a richly decorated raft in the River Niemen, and signed the Treaty of Tilsit.

Tilsit is the climax of the reign, and it witnessed the carving up of Europe between the two men. Poland and Prussia were treated with special harshness. A Grand Duchy of Warsaw was set up mainly built up from East Prussia; Prussia west of the Elbe became the Kingdom of Westphalia, governed by brother Jerome; and Prussia's army was to be limited in size and she was to close her ports to British trade. There was still the rationalist's dream of a united Europe, with "one set of laws, one kind of opinion, one view, one interest, the interest of mankind". But it was now translated into effect by war, military or economic. And Napoleon's methods in the end were destructive of the dream.

For the last eight years were years of total absolutism and all but total carnage. To enforce the Continental System, the extremities of Europe as well as the French heartland had to be controlled. Spain was torn by civil war, and in the struggle against Napoleon the nationalist cause there gradually became the cause of high conservatism; in the end, as he said himself, the Spanish ulcer was to destroy him, but it was also to halt all notions of progressive political change at the Pyrenees. By 1810 the uneasy alliance with the Tsar was over. The march on Moscow in 1812, on which 600,000 men set off and from which only 30,000 returned, was the beginning of the end, as decisive a turning point as Hitler's invasion in 1941. The nationalism of the peoples, that had been the secret ally of the Revolution and of the early Napoleon, was now turned against him. The arbitrary carving up of territories, the Corsican-style nepotism of the "kingdoms", the re-appearance in the satellite states not of liberators but of men of property usually from the major families of the old regime, all these were anathema to the rising spirit of national resurgence and bourgeois assertion. And at the centre of the dream was less a new vision of Europe than an enlarged France. In 1810 Holland, the papal states and the north-west coast of Germany were all annexed to France; this was not the new liberalism of '89 but old-style conquest. It appealed neither to the rulers nor their subjects, the rulers because it upset the balance of power, the people because it destroyed their own self-respect.

In the end the spirit of nationalism, itself a product of 1789, was Napoleon's own undoing. This, plus his failure by 1813 to be capable of any measure of moderation. Even after Leipzig (October, 1813), by bargaining and blandishment he could still have retained his throne, even perhaps an Imperial title. It was by that time not in him to compromise; the major cause of his final tragedy, first at Elba, and then in the 100 days to Waterloo, was thus less the Spanish war or the Moscow campaign, Wellington's armies, or nationalism, but the man's own megalomania. At the end as at the beginning the nature of the usurper and the *condottiere* was all too transparent. He had done it all. Why should it end?

What then was the Napoleonic legacy, for France and for Europe? Albert Guérard has said that he left behind no permanent conquests, except "an architectural style and a legend".

"The style, a stiff Roman pastiche, had dignity and consistency; it was to be the last definite one for over a hundred years. The legend is multiform. It is a grand epic of battle with the taut gray-coated figure, impassive, commanding, ever in the centre. Even Napoleon's worst failures—Egypt, Russia—enriched his prestige through their exotic colour or their tragic magnitude. The legend is also a perfect "success story"; the petty noble from an outlying, half-tamed province, who rises vertiginously, marries an arch-duchess, refers to Louis XVI as 'my uncle', and gives crowns to his brothers. The legend, finally, is a romantic myth of the same period, with the same appeal as Faust, Don Juan, Prometheus. Napoleon was his own poet and his own hero; he consciously cultivated his prestige; he won the most lasting of his triumphs, a place in world folklore, by the side of Alexander, Caesar, Charlemagne; by the side also of King Arthur, Siegfried and William Tell."

The legend had and has abiding meaning for France. The career of Napoleon III, and in some degree the careers of Petain and De Gaulle, were shaped by it. If for the Presidency of the United States the strongest myth of all is "from log cabin to White House", so for France the notion of a career open to talent, and a call to high patriotic adventure, are part of the national mythology. To him, as to Louis XIV before him and De Gaulle after him, France was a great nation, marked out by a special destiny. And her dictators always seek plebiscitary, if not truly democratic, approval.

In fact, however, even if the mould was that of a dictator, the Napoleonic system left other legacies. French industrial progress was twisted by the blockade into fiercely protectionist forms. Money went into land rather than industry, and the French industrial revolution was delayed for two generations. His system exacerbated the division between Church and State, and pushed French Catholicism towards ultramontanism and reaction. Ever since, in the politics of State as well as of Church, there has been a clear role in French history for the ultra, and the non-constitutionalist, and a readiness to appeal to force that is conspicuously absent from British history. The continuous wars drained the country of its resources of men and goods. Freedom of thought was stifled, not only as compared with the Revolution but even with pre-revolutionary France.

But the legacy was positive too. The legal codes were the most durable part of his achievement. They ensured that the state was secular, that private property was protected, that civil law was free from religious influence, that all men—if by no means all women—had equal rights. A uniform system of law, concrete and specific, was a great benefit to France and of even more value to Europe. For it was carried by his armies wherever they went. The assumptions of a lay state and of the equality of all citizens before the law were truly revolutionary notions in Europe. Outside France, if not in it, Napoleon was still the Revolution made personal.

In France Bonapartism became in essence an efficient form of Bourbonism ruling, for a decade at least, with popular acceptance. Outside it, it was libertarian, even revolutionary in its effects. Constitutions, judiciaries and social reforms followed in the wake of his armies, and feudalism received its death-blow; notably in northern Italy and the Netherlands, even if not always permanently. Many Germans supported him, especially in the smaller south German states like Bavaria and Wurttemberg; German princes were glad in particular to see the end of the Holy Roman Empire. And it was after the Prussian defeat and during the French occupation that Stein and Hardenberg began their reforms. The abolition of serfdom and the guilds, and local self-government, came because of the French model. There are some who would call Napoleon the creator of modern Germany. And in Russia Speransky's legal code and the Constitution of 1809 owed much to plain imitation of France. Whatever he might be at home, and however impermanent his achievement, Napoleon was seen abroad as an Enlightened Despot. The map of Europe was transformed by him, and the national spirit of Germany and Italy were his legacy.

Napoleon was cast in a heroic mould, and for a decade and a half bestrode a continent. He was passionately admired, in his own day and later, and not only by Frenchmen—by Hegel and Goethe, by Beethoven and Hazlitt, by Carlyle and Rosebery. Along with Byron, he became for nineteenth-century Europe the great embodiment of romantic individualism. Yet despite all his legacies his incandescent quality, his glamour and his glory, this was not an admirable man. Even if history is not a court of morals, Napoleon condemns himself by his own frank admissions—his comment on the 29,000 dead at Eylau was "small change!" and on Borodino, where 80,000 lay dead, was that it was the most beautiful battlefield he had ever seen. In 1813 he told Metternich that a man like him did not care for the lives of a million men. As women conspicuously were but the instruments of his lust, so, most of the time, were men but the instruments of his quest for power. He was utterly devoid of charity or of scruple, his sole emotion was the satisfying of his own vanity. It is impossible to quarrel with the verdict and the indictment of A. J. P. Taylor:

> "He was a monster. He found France great; he left her small . . . It would have been better for everyone if he had never been born; and there was nothing for it but to eliminate him."

Or as Alexis de Tocqueville put it—and he was brought up as a boy in Napoleon's France:

> "He was as great as a man can be without virtue."

GEORG WILHELM HEGEL
(1770–1831)

GERMANY was unified, so Bismarck said, by iron and blood. Successful war (against Denmark 1864, against Austria 1866 and against France 1870) made the nation. Economic historians have subsequently argued that German unity was in fact the product less of iron and blood than of iron and coal and railways, and of the skills—developed at universities and technical high schools—with which Germany exploited her industrial resources inside a free trade area or *zollverein*.

But in yet another sense it could be claimed that the idea of German national unity represented in essence the fusion of Prussian authoritarianism and the romanticism born of the French revolution. The movers and shakers of opinion in Britain in the eighteenth century were the agricultural improvers and the industrial entrepreneurs. In Germany they were the men of the study, the writers, university teachers, philosophers and musicians. And if there is one single man who developed this ideal of a single organic unity called the nation, and of the state as its essence, it is Georg Wilhelm Hegel. But he was more than a conservative and a nationalist. He so dominated the thinking of his time that the idea of a German state owes much to him.

It is possible to describe Hegel's career quite simply. He was born in 1770 at Stuttgart, the son of a revenue officer, and studied theology at Tubingen, where he became a friend of Hölderlin and Schelling. He was more interested in the classics than in theology, however, and the theological certificate he obtained in 1783 stated, ironically in the light of his later career, that he was deficient in philosophy. After a spell as a private tutor in Berne and Frankfurt, he became a *privatdozent* or lecturer at Jena in 1801. From 1802 to 1803 he was joint editor with Schelling of the *Kritisches Journal der Philosophie*, to which he contributed many articles. Hegel was appointed to a chair at Jena just before Napoleon's victory in 1806 which closed the university, and he had to spend the following decade as a newspaper editor in Bamberg and as a headmaster of a gymnasium in Nuremberg. He married Marie von Tucher, twenty-two years younger than himself, in 1811. In 1816 he became a professor at Heidelberg, and in 1818 he succeeded Fichte in the chair of philosophy in Berlin, where he remained until his death in the cholera epidemic of 1831.

Partly by his own writing and close relations with the Prussian government, partly by the range of his scholarship, and above all through his influence and that of his followers on generations of German students of philosophy and history he dominated German thought throughout the nineteenth, and in some measure into the twentieth century. He had much influence on Idealist philosophers like Bradley and Bosanquet in Britain. He was a great philosopher of history, and one who—like Marx—also changed its content and its direction.

> "... A historian recently raised the question whether the struggle of the Russians and the invading Germans in 1943 was not, at bottom, a conflict between the Left and the Right wings of Hegel's school. That may seem to be an exaggerated statement of the problem but it contains a nucleus of truth."[1]

It is possible to describe Hegel's career even more simply by his major books. He described them himself as an attempt "to teach philosophy to speak in German". Hegel's first major published work, *Die Phänomenologie des Geistes* (*The Phenomenology of the Mind*) appeared in 1807. In his second work, *Wissenschaft der Logik* (*The Science of Logic*) (3 vols., 1812, 1814, 1816) he developed his system fully for the first time and, in particular, his famous view of the dialectical process. Every truth, he held, is a synthesis of two contradictory elements; the formula of thesis, antithesis and synthesis was clearly spelt out. The book made his reputation and brought him the offer of three chairs. In 1817 he produced his *Encyklopadie der philosophischen Wissenschaften* (*Encyclopedia of the Philosophical Sciences*). His views on political philosophy were expressed in his *Philosophie des Rechts* (*Philosophy of Rights*) in 1821. His lectures on art and aesthetics and the philosophy of history were published after his death, as were his proposals for the German Constitution, from the collated lecture notes of his students. His collected works extend to 19 volumes.

But no philosopher, least of all so academic a figure as Hegel—

[1] Ernst Cassirer, *The Myth of the State*, New Haven, Yale University Press 1946, p. 249.

who never intervened directly in politics—can be understood merely as a writer and teacher. Indeed as teacher and personality Hegel was dull and unimpressive. The reason for his importance lies in part in his doctrines, but even more in the coincidence of the man and his times. For Hegel's career spanned the end of the *ancien régime* and the years of Revolution. In the year of his birth, Marie Antoinette of Austria married the Dauphin of France, James Cook was sailing round the world and discovering Australia, and British troops fired on a mob in Boston, causing five Americans to die—for a "country" none of them knew. In the year of his death, Napoleon had been dead ten years, the U.S. was now an independent republic reaching the western ocean, and Karl Marx was thirteen. Hegel's death took place a few months after the revolutions of 1830, and thus his life spanned the years of hope passing through dictatorship to the emergence of nationalism. And he died four years before the first German railway was opened in 1835.

His thinking reflected the anxieties and turmoil of a preindustrial age in which rationalism first bred revolution, and then nationalism, counter-revolution and conservatism. It can be summarized by saying that for him reason as explanation and analysis gradually came to mean not rationalism but history. World history he saw as "reason on the move". And history revealed itself through the dialectic deployed in time, the "truth" of each moment and event appearing a half-truth to its successor, negating its antecedent and absorbing it. Each stage is an advance on the last, a step forward.

The dominant influences on the young and theologically-minded student were the French Enlightenment, the Revolution and Napoleon. Hegel began by believing, with the *philosophes*, in the ruthless application of reason to all the affairs of men. "What is real", he said, "is rational". Like Kant he saw the facts of history as in themselves devoid of meaning; the only way to grasp and understand the past was, he believed, by the application of reason, for order rests not in the chaotic world around us but in the mind of man. And what he particularly admired in France was that the ideas of the *philosophes* were put into action—they now appeared to be the cause and the instrument of political change. It was possible for philosophers to be in a measure kings. Bliss was it indeed, in the dawn of 1789, to be alive.

Moreover, by contrast with France, Germany, in Hegel's youth, was a backward and divided land. Reason was sadly needed there.

It was a congeries of some 300 small independent states and cities, free towns and bishoprics, with none of the political unity of Britain or France. Though in form part of the Holy Roman Empire—which Voltaire described as neither Holy, Roman, nor an Empire—it was in practice a collection of untidy petty principalities; and what pleased the prince, whether his choice of religion or the size of his army, had the force of law. His religion was accepted by his subjects; they had freedom only by his consent—indeed freedom was not thought of as freedom "from" or "against" the ruler, but as service to and for him.

Whereas in Britain or France and the U.S. reason had been the radical instrument used against the state, reason in Germany had been an instrument of the state and of the prince's will. Even the Enlightenment was part of a system of despotism, a tool of the state; science, agricultural improvements, religious freedom were—as to Frederick II—all instruments for strengthening the state. And this diversity and division were sharpened by the different laws and customs, by the absence of a key intellectual or cultural centre in this divided Germany, and by the rigid class structure and pettinesses of provincial life. In his essay on the Constitution of Germany, written in 1802, Hegel concluded that Germany was "no longer a state". There was a memory of past greatness only. Culturally, Germany was certainly a nation, but its quest for political freedom had proved anarchic and self-defeating.

There was thus from Hegel and from Germany a welcome for the French Enlightenment—witness the Storm and Stress period in German literature, the dreams of Schiller, the poetry of Lessing and the music of Mozart. There was an even warmer welcome for the Revolution itself, from the poets Wieland and Herder, from Kant and Fichte, from Schlozer the teacher of constitutional law and Johann von Muller the historian of Switzerland's struggles for freedom—who declared the fall of the Bastille to be the happiest event since the birth of Christ. Kant's ideal was the *Rechtsstaat*, the state based on the rule of law. Fichte's first writing was an anonymous tract written in 1793, *A demand for freedom of thought presented to the Princes of Europe who have hitherto suppressed it.*

But once the movement unleashed violence, there was a sharp revulsion, and admiration cooled. It was the Napoleonic *blitzkrieg* far more than Parisian ideals that transformed and convulsed Germany. Hegel welcomed Napoleon's victory over Prussia at Jena. Napoleon indeed he saw as a "world soul". But these were years of tumult and chaos. The Empire disappeared, and many petty princes, abbeys and cloisters and free towns went with it. A Rhenish Confederation was set up, essentially a French satellite. Napoleon decreed his Continental System from the Prussian capital Berlin. After 1807 Prussia itself became a secondary and frontier state in eastern Europe. Germany was reduced to a smaller number of dynastic states but they were all under French tutelage.

German nationalism was born partly in admiration of Napoleon, partly in revulsion from him. In part it was also the product of the reforms of Stein, Hardenberg and the Minister of Education Wilhelm von Humboldt. The University of Berlin was founded in 1809. So were a host of secret societies. For in Germany from the first the spirit of reform—the plans for improved administration, for financial reform, for municipal self-government and a free peasantry—marched uneasily with anti-liberal, anti-revolutionary and anti-Semitic opinions and with the exaltation of the fatherland. Stein wanted to revive the Empire. Hardenberg urged the King of Prussia in 1807 to do "from above what the French had done from below" and in the spirit of the *volk*. The finest product of the blend was the new model army of Scharnhorst and Gneisenau; just as Prussia had first grown as a military state, the Mark of Brandenburg, so now she became a nation in arms. Napoleon could be beaten only by his own methods. He himself saw the significance of it too late, only in fact when he was on St Helena; he said then that his greatest mistake had been not to wipe out Prussia completely. The idea of the German nation was born when an army was established that was a professional corps led by officers now openly recruited on merit, and backed by a national volunteer militia. It came from the border state, Prussia. "In the north breaks the dawn of freedom", sang Korner. Now nationalism was as strong as rationalism and Revolution.

The idea of a greater Germany came less from the administrators than from the writers and agitators. It came from Niebuhr the historian and Böckh the philologist in the University of Berlin, from the poets Heinrich von Kleist and Clemens Brentano, and from philosopher Johann Gottlieb Fichte's *Addresses to the German Nation* in 1807–8. In these the man who in his youth had wanted to become a French citizen now called for an awareness of German greatness. The unity of mankind could only be reached by way of service to the fatherland. It was voiced by Ernst Moritz Arndt and by Friedrich Ludwig Jahn (1778–1852) who wanted to revive the national spirit through gymnastic exercises in order to develop the physical and moral powers of German youth, and who also fostered pride in German language and its sense of its own distinct past. The brothers Grimm, in their research in language and folk-lore, tapped a folk memory and stirred the imagination; Germans through all their divisions and wars had always at least retained their identity through their language. Running through all of these pan-Germans like Novalis and Herder, Moser and Fichte, was pride in a sense of community that owed nothing to France or to a Latin world of rationalism and liberalism. There was much here that Hegel would share.

The first and strongest note in Hegel's philosophy, however, is that of change, of challenge and response, of progress as a central fact in history, and as the product of the constant clash of opposites. Hegel began, then, like Goethe, as a man of the Enlightenment. It was the spread of knowledge that gave meaning to history. But in contrast with the *philosophes* he never divided men into good and bad; early on, he accepted that even those who opposed progress conditioned its course and direction, by the very fact of opposition. To him the essence of history is the dialectic of struggle and conflict. The fact of change was basic. In contrast with many of his pre-decessors he did not see mind or nature as static.

The historical consciousness was strong in him. As with Herod-otus, whom he greatly admired, his philosophy is a philosophy of challenge and change, and the method—the dialectic—owes much to Heraclitus. Moreover, he was influenced as much by German mysticism as by French rationalism. This, and the Romanticism of his youth, reinforced his strong sense of change and mutability. It gave him also a strong sense of the imperfections, and the concreteness, of the human situation.

But what the Revolution also did for him was to make him aware that the world could be changed, and by philosophers. Philosophers and poets became increasingly concerned with politics. Hegel himself abandoned the study of theology for philosophy because he said theology could save souls but not the body politic. Philosophy's task was to demonstrate the unity and rational order behind the material world, but it was also to be, to him as to Bacon, a guide to statesmen.

But, secondly, change and turmoil were not always welcome. Hegel felt acutely the sufferings of his country under the impact of the Revolution. In *The German Constitution* written when he was thirty-two, but not published, he bewailed German feebleness. He saw the essence of her weakness in the absence of statehood; it was this, he believed, that gave France and Britain their unity and hence their power and wealth. Moreover, by 1802 the excesses of the Revolution were all too clear. Order, he believed, is essential to society. "A settled government is necessary for freedom." What he most admired and envied in the Napoleonic Empire was its strong central government, its sense of order and Codes of Law. The alarms at German weakness in 1802–6 were redoubled after 1815. If part of him rejoiced in the fact that there had been an impressive struggle fought by Germans in their War of Liberation, and that some of the South German states had now constitutions, he was worried by the unrest in Universities. Such was his prestige that he was called on by the Prussian Minister of Education, Von Allenstein, to lecture to students and Army officers, to act as guide and counsellor, a philosopher made king indeed. Against this unrest he wrote his *Philosophy of Rights* in 1821, and here the essential political conservatism of the man is most clearly expressed. He became an admirer and defender of the state and the idealization of the state is the third, and most characteristic, feature of Hegel's philosophy.

By 1821 the state is now seen by Hegel as sacrosanct, the product of the centuries, of history and of reason. It is "the divine Idea as it exists on earth". Since it had emerged, it was an expression of the idea of reason in history; the "is" was for Hegel also an "ought". His state was less an actual state than the state as ideal, and an actual state only in so far as it contained the ideal elements. Its best form is hereditary monarchy, since a guaranteed succession represents unity and guarantees continuity. There is a place for a representative legislature, but the will of the people is quixotic, impulsive and unreliable. "To know what we want, and still more to know what reason wants, and what is good for the state, is the fruit of deep knowledge and insight, and is therefore not the property of the people." Government calls for special skills and for a special class of administrators. For the sovereignty of numbers, the Rights of Man and other such abstractions and universals he had the same scorn as had Burke. He held, in any event, that the whole was greater than the parts, the individual not only less important than the state but inconceivable, empty and isolated without it. Only in the state does he find himself and express himself. In this sense the state is not only the instrument of order but the guarantee of the liberty of all.

This is a basic part of the Hegelian doctrine. *Freiheit* is not liberty, not freedom from restrictions, but freedom to fulfil oneself in society, to become part of a larger whole, and in doing so to escape from the limitations of self. There is here something of St Augustine, and something of Plato, and much that is later found in T. H. Green. But the whole which offers an individual escape and salvation is for Hegel not God but the state. He was scornful of the adage "Know thyself". "Man knows himself only in so far as he knows the world. He becomes aware of himself only in it and it in him". To Hegel, as to Aristotle, man realizes himself in the state.

Believing as he did in struggle and conflict as part of a natural order, it followed that Hegel could not accept a higher law than the state. No state could be bound by any laws that in any way diminished its own will and freedom to act. Differences between states must be settled by war; and war is a fact of life, not a matter for moral judgment. He saw in Machiavelli and Richelieu the two heroic figures in modern politics. This was not a glorification of war but a plain recognition of the facts of life and history.

All of this suggests the steady remorseless evolution of an arch-conservative and an authoritarian. But much as Hegel admired the German state and saw in it the actualization of an Idea, his awareness of the constancy of change and of the dialectic operating in history meant also an awareness that there was no final form. At the end of the historical process when the state has fully realized itself, a global state of universal reason would be attained. The origins of Marx's vision is here. Hegel chose as his motto for the Lectures on the Philosophy of History the phrase of Wilhelm von Humboldt, "World history is incomprehensible without world government".

So Hegel is no mere glorifier of German statism, nor of might makes right. He knew that his own view was but partial; when he concluded his Lectures on the Philosophy of History, he wrote: "To this point, consciousness has come." He saw America not Germany as "the land of the future". And if from one angle his disciple is Marx, from another it is Whitman, least authoritarian and most democratic of voices:

> "In the future of these States must arise poets immenser far . . .
> poets not only possessed of the religious fire and abandon of Isaiah,
> luxurious in the epic talent of Homer, or for proud characters in
> Shakespeare, but consistent with the Hegelian formulas."[1]

[1] Whitman, *Democratic Vistas*, The Little Library of Liberal Arts, p. 63.

Hegel's conservatism was in any event counter-balanced by his belief in freedom and in progress, by the remorseless working of the dialectic through History. For him History had gradually replaced Reason, or in a measure become its voice. He began by claiming that Reason "is regnant in history". But by 1821 he sees God and Reason as one and the same; he had subtly altered the meaning of Reason. It no longer connoted, as it did to the *philosophes*, the intellect or the critical analysis of existing institutions. Gradually it becomes to Hegel the idea of God—and gradually this idea is spelt with a capital "I". It represents perfection, the fusing of will and power. Alongside this Absolute Idea, which exists only in the mind, is the material universe, imperfect and finite. Between the two is the spirit, the creative urge which makes it possible for man to realize his potential. History, he says, "is the development of Spirit in Time, just as Nature is the development of the Idea in Space". The spirit, Hegel contends, enters a certain people for a time and then leaves them. When the spirit is most intense, the individual is fused with the state and absorbed in it. It is this spirit—at once mind or reason or God and also Energy or Will—that is the creative force through history.

Much of this sounds, and is, like the language and approach of the *philosophes*. Robespierre also saw progress as the march of reason. But to Hegel, Reason and God are one—he never quite escaped the grip in the formative years of his youth of the mystic Christian tradition going back to Meister Eckhart of the thirteenth century. Whereas to Diderot and the Encyclopedists the advance of reason and enlightenment was episodic, a series of inexplicable and little-related events, Hegel sees progress as a universal force. But it is the work of men, who must will it and struggle for it. Reason means effort and will and conflict, not just the revelation of great truths. And it is in the struggle that man perfects himself. He is part of history by willing himself to be so. Here Hegel is the forerunner of Marx.

Hegel takes over in fact the old Christian dualism of mind and matter, or God and Nature, the two antitheses. Man stands between the two, having in him aspects of both, and having an untapped potential both for good and evil. Man is the agent of the Idea, and predestined only for struggle and tension. No single individual can fulfil these potentials. Only the state can. And only in proportion as the institutions are rational and orderly is the Idea realized in history.

By the time he was teaching in Berlin, Hegel had reached the view that the World spirit worked through history and that it would lead to the emergence of an ideal Prussia, an ideal state where in the end law and freedom would co-exist. Cynics have said that for him the kingdom of Prussia and the kingdom of Heaven became one and the same. But most political philosophers who look to history as mentor are in fact prophets in disguise. Hegel's own years were years of war, chaos and national striving. It was natural that, disillusioned in the end by the Revolution and scornful of the restlessness of Young Germans like Gotzow and Heine, he should voice conservative views. His Idealism was bred by disillusion. The future for Germany could not fail to be better than the past. The state, which it had lacked, would be its instrument of transformation, its magic and its myth.

In the last decade of his life he wielded immense influence. He helped to make Berlin a rival to Vienna as an intellectual centre. His colleagues were equally influential as scholars—and as myth-makers. Friedrich Karl von Savigny, the friend of the Grimms, taught law, and was for a time a Prussian minister; he preached the importance of German rather than French law and founded a new system of jurisprudence to match the new doctrine of the folk-nation. And the young Leopold von Ranke, who began that careful collection of historical sources that is the real beginning of scholarly history, infused with this an acceptance of the Hegelian view that the power struggle is the most important theme in history.

Hegel began as a Romantic and ended up as a conservative. It is by no means an unfamiliar course, as man's experience widens. But unlike Savigny, and despite his own influence and renown, he was an Ivory Tower philosopher. He was first and last a metaphysician and a system builder, interested not in men but in Mankind. Like Kant he dealt in generalizations; and some of his concepts are elusive, and they are not always clearly presented. Yet he was through it all a rationalist, not a dreamer; a conservative, but not a Hitlerian. Although abandoning theology for philosophy, he never entirely outgrew his early mysticism or his interest in Christianity. One of his first pieces of writing was a life of Jesus, and what interested him in Jesus was what it was that made him the hope of mankind; he found him a noble spirit appealing to the divine in all men. He also expresses the view, to which he holds consistently, that life is more important and of a higher order than any or all of the incidents in it. Only the whole, what he later called the Absolute, is rational and true. "Religion", he said, "anticipates philosophy; philosophy is nothing but conscious religion". The two great forces in Western civilization were the free intelligence of Greece and the moral insights afforded by Christianity. For him history is the progressive incarnation of the Absolute Spirit. If this Truth is reached by the processes of dialectic —thesis, antithesis and synthesis—when it is reached it is non-self-contradictory. The whole truth rests in both yes and no, in a thing and its opposite, and in the end in the Absolute, which absorbs and transcends both.

The two striking features of Hegel's writing are thus his method— the dialectic—and the result, the nation state as idea and ideal. To him they were inseparable. But in the end they became distinct. His notion of progress as dialectic was used by Marx to become the economic interpretation of history and as the intellectual instrument of socialism; in the end therefore it became internationalized and assumed the withering away of the state. Nationalism for its part gradually lost its radicalism and became conservative in essence. In his method and in the content of his writing Hegel can be seen as the author of the two dominant political philosophies of the twentieth century.

Hegel, and still more the school of his disciples, are responsible for developing that worship of the idea of the state to which late nineteenth-century and early twentieth-century Germany and Europe fell victim. His lectures, though delivered without style or oratory, were treated in contemporary Europe as the work of a sage. As the proponent of Will and Power, his name was invoked by Bismarck and William II. His notion that progress is the consequence of a dialectical process of thesis and antithesis working out through history has been one of the great seminal ideas in European philosophy and sociology; it was taken over in different form by Marx. Consequently, Hegel is at once the founding father of European conservatism and the unwilling grandfather of European Communism.

LUDWIG VAN BEETHOVEN

(1770–1827)

> "Liberty and progress are the goals of art just as of life in general," declared Ludwig van Beethoven in a letter; and, on another occasion, "Words are bound in chains, but happily sounds are still free."

THE MUSIC of Beethoven's so-called "second period", from 1800–15, has been widely held to symbolize the spirit of the new age of European freedom in which he was living. The Bastille had been stormed in 1789, when he was nineteen, and the years following had seen the ending of much aristocratic and clerical domination throughout Europe, the institution of government by parliament in most countries, and a significant acceptance of concepts of individual liberty. That this new-found freedom would in due course become submerged under new regimes of autocracy is another matter: when Beethoven was composing the most outward-looking of his works, liberty was Europe's *leitmotif*.

Beethoven did not deliberately set out to express democracy in musical terms. He happened to be a fervent believer in the brotherhood of man; a pugnacious individualist in personality, who said what he felt like saying without cant or fear; and a musical innovator at the very moment when music was due for its own revolution. The conjunction of all these made him the perfect example of the man born exactly for his time, whose art and personal nature would mirror, and come to symbolize, the prevalent mood of the majority of his fellow men. His music has perhaps inspired as much thought about freedom as any words have done. Again and again, its passages strike exactly those vibrations in the individual listener of whatever nationality which conjure up the realization of what liberty, equality and fraternity are really about. Yet he himself, hearing someone remark "Vox populi, vox dei", growled "I don't believe it," and it is a mistake to read too much symbolism, conscious or unconscious, into his work. It has no need of it. Simply as music it represents one of the supreme achievements of mankind, and a short list of the greatest, most universally acknowledged individuals who ever lived would inevitably include the name of Ludwig van Beethoven.

He was born in Bonn, in Germany, on 16 December, 1770, in a house which is preserved today as a museum to his memory. The birth date is conjectural: he was baptized on the 17th, and it was the custom in his time for this to be done the day after birth. The name *van* Beethoven, instead of the German *von*, indicates his family's origins in the Low Countries. His musician grandfather, Louis, had moved from his native Antwerp at the age of eighteen to Bonn, then the seat of the Electoral Archbishop of Cologne, at whose court he had at length become Kapellmeister. His son Johann, Ludwig's father, became a tenor in the Electoral Chapel.

In addition to music, a great deal of alcohol flowed in the Beethoven blood. In order to supplement his income, Louis had established a wine-trading connection between Germany and the Netherlands, and his wife Josepha had become enthusiastically addicted to his wares. Her taste for tippling was inherited by Johann, and, together with a chronically bad temper, no doubt attributable to a never-ending sequence of hangovers, made him an often disagreeable person about the home and an ineffectual father to Ludwig and his two brothers, Kaspar Anton Karl, born 1774, and Nikolaus Johann, born 1776. Their father was not all bad, though, and there was light as well as gloom in Johann van Beethoven's household, with his wife, Maria Magdalena, proving as loving a mother as anyone could have wished. Undoubtedly, though, the erratic life of an alcoholic's family resulted in some of the less admirable of Ludwig van Beethoven's personal traits—his uncouthness, unkemptness and untidiness—which were to offend many people who would cross his path and may to a large extent have deterred any woman from marrying him and bringing him the domesticity and sexual stability he often craved.

Though in later life Johann van Beethoven's drinking got the better of him and resulted in the loss of his job and his expulsion from Bonn, he was shrewd enough in the 1770s to be able to discern exceptional musical talents in Ludwig, and to give him his grounding of tuition. There was a good deal of self-interest in this, though. The example of Mozart as a child prodigy was very much in Johann's mind, and he determined that his son should achieve similar precocity and reap its rewards. The boy never did fulfil these hopes to the extent Mozart had done; but he absorbed enough from his father and others to be able to appear in public as a pianist at the age of eight (his father advertised him as being six). Fortunately for Ludwig, the newly-appointed Court-organist at Bonn in 1779 was Christian Gottlob Neefe, a fine performer, composer and writer of musical criticism. Ludwig was in due course enrolled as his pupil and from then on began to develop and civilize his talents much more broadly and quickly. Neefe set exceptional store by the works of the Bach family, at that time not yet properly appreciated, and especially the keyboard works of Johann Sebastian Bach's second surviving son, Karl Philipp Emanuel, whose influence carried music out of the baroque era of mathematical counterpoint into the classical and romantic styles based on harmony: Beethoven would later declare, "K. P. E. Bach is the father of us all."

It was Neefe, too, who taught him to extemporize. When, at the age of seventeen, he visited Vienna and was given an interview by Mozart, his playing made little impression at first. Then Mozart gave him a theme and asked him to improvize. The brilliance and originality with which he did so moved Mozart to prophesy to some others who were present that the young man would make a great name for himself. At this time it seemed that such fame, if indeed it did come, would be for his solo playing. Although he could play other instruments, it was at the piano keyboard that Beethoven showed himself at his idiosyncratic best. His technique, like his personality, was violent, impatient. He punished the keyboard, made excessive use of the loud pedal, sacrificed clarity of individual notes for startling rapidity. He threw himself about on the piano stool, crouched low over delicate passages, grimaced—all in complete contrast to the old-fashioned style, precise and prim, for which Mozart himself had been so much admired.

Beethoven might have learnt much from Mozart, all the same, had he been able to remain in Vienna; but in that same year his mother and small sister died. Heavy-hearted, he returned to Bonn, to recognize his feckless father's incapability to rule the family and order its routine. Ludwig took over, and settled down to five years in the Elector's service, receiving half his father's salary from which to educate his brothers. His father was ordered to leave Bonn in 1789 and died three years later.

The five years were by no means wasted. As a member of the Court orchestra—a good one—Beethoven made many friends amongst musicians and wealthy and influential patrons of the arts. He was also able to meet Josef Haydn, whom the orchestra entertained on his way to England in 1790. When next they met, two years later, Beethoven had two quite substantial compositions to show him: cantatas he had written on the death of the Emperor Joseph II and the coronation of his successor, Leopold II. That same year, 1792, Beethoven obtained leave to go to Vienna, where he moved into cheap lodgings and enrolled himself as Haydn's pupil.

"With hard work you shall receive Mozart's spirit from Haydn's hands", Beethoven's aristocratic friend Count von Waldstein had written to him in a note of farewell as he left Bonn. Mozart had died the previous year. Beethoven did receive something of Mozart and Haydn—his early compositions are much in their style—but this was more attributable to his own study of their works than to Haydn's teaching. The master-pupil relationship did not work well. Haydn was kind, considerate and helpful in many ways, but he seems to have glanced only vaguely over Beethoven's exercises, instead of subjecting them to the relentless criticism that the young man expected of the old master; and when Haydn did criticize Beethoven, on musical or other grounds, his pupil, being what he was, resented it and made his resentment plain. All the same, he was avid to learn, and went to several other teachers in Vienna.

His stipend from Bonn was cut off abruptly in 1794, when the Electorate of Cologne ceased to exist, in the wake of the French Revolution. It did not dismay Beethoven. Even if his income was slenderer than ever, he was a free man, in nobody's service, and his emancipation, which had been brought about by political and social revolution, was a revolution all of its own. Even Mozart and Haydn had been to a large extent the hirelings of aristocrats, having to show due deference for the far-from-generous patronage on which their lives depended. Beethoven, too, relied for much of his livelihood on the favour of the many rich Viennese who gave private musical entertainments in their homes and vied with one another to show off the latest celebrity: although he claimed that Haydn had taught him nothing, he had him to thank for many valuable introductions. But his relationships with those who "employed" him were always on his own terms. He bowed the knee to no one, saying exactly what he felt, rebuffing in forthright manner any attempt to patronize him in the belittling sense of the word, and demanding the respect due to the great artist he knew himself to be. The cultivated aristocrats recognized the justice of his claim and gave him that respect. He might offend them by his untidy appearance at some glittering occasion; by his keeping them waiting for him to turn up at all, and not apologizing when he did arrive; by the arrogance with which he rejected opinions contrary to his own: but they treated him as a friend and as an eccentric giant.

Physically, Ludwig van Beethoven was anything but a giant. He stood only five feet four inches high. His head was small, but made leonine by the thick black hair which streamed behind him. His nose was stubby, his complexion coarse, dark and pock-marked. His eyes were piercing and his scowl daunting. He was untidy, clumsy, and quick to take offence and fly into violent rages. Some people found him detestable; others were prepared to overlook his faults for his artistic gifts; but those who took most trouble to study him found much virtue in him, much fellow-kindness, and a disarming readiness to apologize when he had calmed down and seen how wrong he had been or how badly he had behaved.

Many women, especially, found him a fascinating specimen of manhood and he had numerous love affairs. He proposed marriage in 1795 to Magdalena Willman, whom he had known in Bonn and who had found fame in Vienna as a singer. She turned him down, but he seems not to have regretted it much. Much speculation has been devoted to the identity of a woman to whom he wrote several letters from which it is clear that she and Beethoven were more than just good friends: she has come to be known as *Die Unsterbliche Geliebte* (The Immortal Beloved), and has been generally acknowledged to have been Josephine von Brunswick, a married woman who is believed to have had an illegitimate daughter by him in 1813. But although he was a fascinating object for romantic fancy, and high-born ladies wrote him adoring letters and poems and perhaps expressed their feelings for him in even more interesting ways, any woman who married Ludwig van Beethoven would have had a hard life before her, and no doubt they sensed as much.

Some biographers, though, have resisted the idea that he had sexual relations at all, insisting that he was spiritually above such things and would sever friendships with men or women whom he found to be morally tainted. Some have said that he reserved himself entirely for his art, and had no passion to spare for other purposes. But there may have been another reason for his never having married. More than once during the years of increasing isolation by deafness and growing unhappiness, he lamented that he would never be able to share other men's domestic bliss by having a wife and family. We may never know the truth that will settle the endless arguments, the "proofs" and denials. There is a lot of evidence to the effect that Beethoven had syphilis, either hereditary or contracted in his youth, knew it to be incurable, and dared not marry because of it. It would account for much more in his life: perhaps even for the devastating deafness itself. It would account for the almost hysterical vendetta against his brother Johann's immoral wife and the depth of disillusionment he suffered over his attempts to bring up his nephew Karl in the rectitudinous way he wished. It could account for so much in his music that sounds like anguished cries of defiance in the face of Fate, or sad surrender and acceptance, such as in the last quartets. But this is adding conjecture to a subject about which more conjecture than fact has been forthcoming. The evidence of Beethoven's doctors and other contemporaries is confusing, the opinions of early and modern commentators conflicting. Beethoven may have had syphilis; it may have been the cause of this and that; or he may not have had it at all. At any rate, for whatever cause, he never married, and he did become tragically deaf.

The deafness was already making itself apparent by the turn of the century. He hurried to doctors. When the orthodox ones seemed to be achieving no results, he resorted to quacks. He raged against the Almighty for treating him, of all people, in this way:

"Your Beethoven is most unhappy, in discord with nature and the Creator. More than once I have cursed the latter for exposing his creatures to the slightest accident, so that often the loveliest blossoms are broken or destroyed."

By 1801, when he was still only just turned thirty, he knew that his hearing was leaving him altogether. When people spoke he could hear the murmur of their tones, but not the words themselves; yet if someone shouted to try to make him hear he flew into a fury. He could not hear music except from the closest quarters, and even this ability would leave him before long. His career as a solo pianist was virtually at an end, though he continued to play in chamber works until 1814 and to direct performances of his pieces from the piano, as was then still the custom.

As he entered the solitude of deafness, Beethoven also entered his period of greatest creativity as a composer. His life's work is generally recognized as falling into three distinct phases: the first, up to 1800, when he was finding his feet, concentrating upon his reputation as a keyboard virtuoso and experimenting with composition, echoing Mozart and Haydn to a large extent but already showing abundant evidence of an emerging style of his own; the second, to 1815, when he achieved the height of his contemporary popularity and composed the works which are best known to the modern audience—most of the symphonies, the violin concerto, several piano concerti, many of the sonatas and songs, and his only opera, *Fidelio*; and the third, darker phase of twelve years until the end of his life, during which the works least comprehended in his own century—the last five quartets, the ninth symphony ("The Choral"), and the mass *Missa Solemnis*—were composed against a background of increasing depression, illness, disenchantment and self-neglect.

If the third period of Beethoven's work was inevitably the most introspective, reflecting his own disillusionments and mental torments, the second was the one which mirrored most the European mind at that time. It was an heroic age, and heroic is the word for much that Beethoven wrote in it. Napoleon, born only the year before Beethoven, was in the ascendant during the first decade of the nineteenth century, watched by many progressive Germans as the ideal of the kind of man they needed to lead them out of their centuries of corrupt medievalism. Beethoven's rise as the composer who would, above all others, make music speak messages, and messages of freedom, rose in parallel to Buonaparte: the "Eroica" symphony, the opera *Fidelio*, with its expression of the individual's fight against tyranny and imprisonment, the overtures *Egmont*, arising from the story of the struggle for independence by the sixteenth-century Dutch, and *Coriolanus*, inspired by the rise to power of one of the greatest of Rome's generals—all spoke to the German people as music had never spoken to anyone before, and were soon speaking to other nations in a language which needed no translation.

But it is not only the message inherent in some of his pieces that has made Beethoven, of all composers, the most widely performed in the world. He wrote so much else that is magnificent in quite different ways and often on quite miniature scale. It is as though he were able to interpret virtually the full range of human emotion in terms of most "listenable" music. He influenced a whole line of composers after him, from Schubert, Schumann and Brahms, to

Schoenberg and Bartok, contributed to the development and growth of the symphony orchestra, and established the piano as the pre-eminent solo instrument. When one stops to think that this was done by a tormented, ill-disciplined man who for some two decades of his life was stone deaf and suffering from other ailments, real and imagined, and from the depression which they and disputes with his family and quarrels with colleagues and friends brought in their train, his achievement is staggering. He wrote some 250 substantial works, all of which remain in constant performance today.

There is a well known story that after he had conducted the first performance of his Choral Symphony on 7 May, 1824, and that massive blend of instruments and voices in the setting of Schiller's *Ode to Joy* which forms the final movement had come to its end, Beethoven went on beating time, too deaf to realize that the music had ceased and that the audience was applauding wildly. He had to be turned round by one of the soloists to *see* the applause. Some people say this was the summit-point of his career, and that the ninth symphony is the noblest of all symphonic achievements. Others say that the five last quartets, much of whose music is totally different from anything Beethoven had ever written, mark the highest point he attained. They were written against all odds in the last two years of his life. His brother Karl had died in 1815 leaving a widow whom Ludwig had strenuously tried to prevent his marrying in the first place—he called her the "Queen of the Night", and so she proved to be—and a son, Karl. Thinking, as always, that he knew best, Beethoven defied his dead brother's wish that the boy should remain with his mother, and that she and Beethoven should patch up their antagonism. He fought a series of lawsuits to get control of the younger Karl, succeeded in 1820, having spent what money he had in the process, and then found the boy an ungrateful disappointment. From Karl's point of view, life with his eccentric guardian must have been almost intolerable: the boy ran away, was brought back by the police, was put into an institution, was fought over through the courts again and yet again, pulled to and fro between his mother and uncle, and at length attempted suicide. Beethoven loved him deeply but was quite incapable of bringing up a youth. This failure of the only approach to a family life of his own that he had ever achieved weighed dreadfully on him. In his youth he had said "I will take Fate by the throat". Now, he accepted all that Fate had done to him, yet still refused to bow the knee, and blended acceptance and strength into those last quartets.

After a series of operations for dropsy, Ludwig van Beethoven developed pneumonia and died in his untidy room in Vienna on 26 March, 1827, during a violent thunderstorm which he could not have heard, even had he been conscious. Ironically, the world at large had not known that he was dying. He had been ill so often that no one thought to find out, and deathbed comforts and companionship which would have been readily forthcoming were never offered. But eight composers carried his coffin at a grand public funeral, watched by some 20,000 Viennese, in whose city he had spent his mature years and done his greatest work.

All they needed to carve on his tombstone was the single word BEETHOVEN. His music and his influence are his memorial; and it is a singularly appropriate tribute to both that the Council of Europe, the cultural, social and economic brotherhood of free nations founded in 1949, should have chosen his setting of the *Ode to Joy* from the Choral Symphony for its official anthem.

GIUSEPPE GARIBALDI
(1807–1882)

"I say with pride that I dare take rank with the most staunch of Italian patriots, and in writing this my conscience tells me that I am not making a vain boast. My life, all spent for Italy, is my witness; to unsheath a sword for her is the paradise of my belief: my wife, my children, the desire for rest, nothing has ever been able to restrain me from fighting for the holy cause."

Giuseppe Garibaldi, writing these words in 1857, was making no vain boast, bombastic as his statement may appear. For the most part of his fifty years he had been dedicated to the unification of a kingdom without a king, war-torn and disorganized as was no other European country. The plight of Italy inspired men of blazing courage and genius to come to her aid; among them, Garibaldi's name is pre-eminent.

As so often, Fate suited the man to the times. He was born in 1807 in Nice, once a city of Sardinia, but conquered by Napoleonic forces in 1792 and retained by France until 1814. Swarming across Europe like resistless locusts, Napoleon's armies had disseminated Revolutionary principles wherever they trod. The "little kings" of Italy began to stir uneasily on their thrones, the thrones of those provinces they had hitherto held securely. The House of Hapsburg's tentacles had extended from Austria to control Milan, Tuscany and Naples, while Spain's Bourbons held Parma and Sicily and shared the rule of Naples. Over central Italy the Pope was supreme, while Venice and Genoa were ill-governed republics.

In 1804 Napoleon proclaimed the French Empire, and shortly afterwards, in May 1805, crowned himself King of Italy in Milan Cathedral with the iron crown used by the ancient Lombard kings. "God gave it to me," he declared in the old ceremonial words, "let him beware who touches it."

Five months later at Trafalgar British sea-power under Nelson struck a blow at the man who thought himself unconquerable.

His policy of nepotism failed, for the Bonapartes and other kindred installed by him as rulers lacked his own strength. His *Code Napoléon* was unpopular, particularly in Rome, where the Vatican had been obliged to cede so much of its previous authority. Elsewhere, the Napoleonic laurels were beginning to wither. The terrible Russian campaign of 1812 included a strong Italian force led by Napoleon's stepson, Eugene Beauharnais; of the 27,000 who marched with him to Moscow, only three hundred or so came home to Italy. The rest lay, unburied skeletons, among Russian snows.

In 1814 the Treaty of Paris ended Napoleon's rule in Italy, which now reverted to conditions more or less the same as before his entry. The Treaty of Vienna, signed in 1815, implemented them. But the complacency of the restored Hapsburgs and Bourbons was ill-founded. Napoleon had brought with him ideas and methods of administration which attracted people who had before his time lived in semi-medieval conditions. The influence of British occupation in Sicily had had similar effects. Italy, so long stifled by one or another oppressive rule, was beginning to breathe again. Faction sprang up between dismissed soldiers and papal agents anxious to regain power. And over a wide terrain there began an ever-increasing number of lodges of the Carbonari (charcoal-burners), an underground league of revolutionaries who might be land-owners, peasants, members of the nobility, all united by a longing for Italian freedom from foreign rule.

Agitations, revolt and bloodshed followed the foundation of the Carbonari. Its ideals spread to France by 1820, and in England young Lord Byron, a lover of Italy, supported it warmly. In 1831 it was replaced by a movement calling itself "Young Italy", headed by the patriot Giuseppe Mazzini. With his attempted siege of Genoa the name of Garibaldi entered history. Garibaldi's father, a sailor, had sent his son to sea at an early age. Now he was twenty-six, stalwart, intrepid, a natural leader, and already a master in the merchant service. On a voyage through the Black Sea he had met one Cuneo, a fervent member of Young Italy, and had become infected with his enthusiasm. Soon he was in Marseilles, talking with Mazzini himself, afire with plans for involvement. He intended to join the Piedmontese navy and spread revolt among its personnel. Already, as a Young Italian, he had taken the name of Joseph Borel; now he boarded the frigate *Eurydice* under the flamboyant nom-de-guerre of Cleombroto.

Word reached the Admiral, and "Cleombroto" was hastily

transferred to the admiral's flagship. Good sense conquered any desire for martyrdom. He escaped, fled to the mountains, and disguised as a peasant reached Marseilles. There he read that a court-martial had passed sentence of death upon Giuseppe Maria Garibaldi, for treasonable conspiracy. Only by voluntary exile could he remain free to serve his country's cause; he sailed for Buenos Aires, and in 1836 received letters of marque from the state of Rio Grande de Sul.

The man who had distinguished himself at sea now proved himself on land as a guerilla fighter. A career of operatic romance opened before him. Captured and set free, he eloped with and married the creole Anita Riviera de Silva, a girl of Madonnaesque beauty, with whom he led for ten years a life of complete happiness. Anita was not only wife but companion and helpmeet in her husband's dangerous wanderings, during which she bore him two sons, Menotti and Ricciotti, and a daughter, Teresa.

To the energetic and versatile Garibaldi nothing came amiss if it would enable him to stay free and active in the movement which was now spreading beyond its place of origin. Not only a Young France but a Young Europe now existed, and even, under the leadership of the Tory Benjamin Disraeli, a Young England. It was, admittedly a movement more romantically nostalgic than fiery, and in years to come Disraeli was to censure Garibaldi's methods as "piratical"; but it was at least a genteel cousin to the Italian ideal. Mazzini had fled to England, where his literary and political activities earned him fame and influence, and his personal charm popularity with the English intelligentsia, including the Carlyles and John Stuart Mill.

Garibaldi, meanwhile, had kept himself and his family by working as a cattle-drover, a ship-broker, and a teacher of mathematics, before the war between Montevideo and Buenos Aires brought him again to sea command. In 1846 he formed the Italian Legion, and with its strength won the battles of Cerro and Sant' Antonio which decided the freedom of Uruguay. At last, perhaps, he could return to Italy. He offered his services to Pope Pius IX (Pio Nono), known for liberal sympathies, but the papal reply was evasive. The Pope's invocation "*Dio Benedici l'Italia!*" and election-policy promises of enmity to the hated Austria had made Italy ring with cries of "Viva Pio Nono!" and "Viva l'Italia!" but while he campaigned against the tyranny of Austria and of the despotic old Bourbon King of Naples Pio Nono did not lose sight of the importance of retaining his own power. Garibaldi might well prove a dangerous henchman.

But in England Mazzini kept watch on Garibaldi's growth into the stature of a hero, and made sure that Italy knew of his great deeds by reporting them for the *Apostolato Popolare* and in the English press. In 1847 he and his ever-growing band of English supporters founded the International League. Mazzini's first project for the League was the re-making of half the map of Europe, but he was tactfully persuaded to modify this to something more realistic. The first address, given by the League's secretary, W. J. Linton, stated clearly and reasonably the aims of this, the first true bond between England and Italy.

> "The insularity of England, her concentration on the affairs of her own country, is admittedly an anomaly, and deprecated because it encourages absolutism to interfere with national rights in a way it would not dare to do were England to object; but England has not hitherto cared even to understand the workings of absolutism in Europe."

1848 would go down to history as the Year of Revolutions. In January revolts broke out in Palermo and Naples. Piedmont demanded a constitution; influenced by Camillo Cavour and his powerful paper *Il Risorgimento* demonstrations took place on such a scale that a charter was granted which laid the foundations of the future United Italy. In Paris the Bourbon Louis Philippe was deposed and Louis Napoleon Bonaparte, later Napoleon III, elected Prince President. Berlin, Vienna, Prague and Budapest were in revolt; and Garibaldi returned to Italy to put his sword at the service of the King of Sardinia, Charles Albert, who had declared war upon Austria. Not surprisingly, the meeting was cool: it had been Charles Albert who had signed Garibaldi's death-warrant in 1834. "I saw him," wrote Garibaldi,

> "saw the man who had executed Italy's noblest sons, who had condemned me and so many others to death, and I understood the coldness of his reception, and yet I would have served Italy under a king, as under a republic . . . to free her from the accursed foreigner."

Again, somewhat frostily, Garibaldi was told to "go and ply his trade of corsair in the Adriatic". The Minister of War in Turin, who issued this instruction, was offended that Garibaldi had gone

Across a tempest-torn landscape strides the stocky little figure of Ludwig van Beethoven. Because of his deafness he hears nothing of the wild discordances of nature—but what tremendous music sobs and surges through his brain! (From the painting by Bac.)

Goethe's house in Weimar has been for generations one of the principal literary shrines of Europe. His private apartments have been preserved very much as when he lived there—in particular his workroom-study, with its bookshelves and filing-cabinets in which he kept his natural history and geological specimens—the room in which he wrestled like Faust with the problem of good and evil.
J. J. Schmeller's picture (*left*) was painted in 1831, the year before Goethe's death.

G W f Hegel

In this drawing done in 1828 the German philosopher G. W. F. Hegel is shown seated at his desk in the lecture-room at the university of Berlin, expounding to a class of young men what is generally considered to be the most profound (and mystifying) of philosophical systems.

No lesser claim can be advanced on behalf of Adam Smith than that he was the founder of the science of Economics. Here we see him as he was sketched by the Edinburgh artist John Kay, walking between two friends.

over his head by seeking a personal interview with the king. He was only slightly mollified by the appeal of a friend, the dying patriot Anzani: "Garibaldi has received such gifts from Heaven that it is our duty to follow him. He is predestined, and I am convinced of his great mission."

In July, 1848, Garibaldi was in Milan, where he had been grudgingly put in charge of the volunteers. Under his banner inscribed "God and the People" his corps of young men fought gallantly against superior Austrian forces under the seasoned warrior Radetzky. An armistice was signed, and Garibaldi, disappointed and lowered with fever, returned home to Nice, where he had left Anita and the children.

The climate of revolution had spread to England, where the Chartist movement was at its peak; a peak from which it was to descend with some ignominy. But in the Spring of 1849 the revivified Garibaldi was back in command of a small but intrepid band of men who under his unerring leadership entered a war-torn Rome on which French, Austrian, Spanish and Neapolitan troops were converging. His campaigns of that summer amount to a saga. Knowing his own powers, and confident of them, he wished to be "unlimited Dictator or a simple soldier". Mazzini, who with him defended the threatened Roman Republic, was for holding out to the bitter end against the long and terrible siege, while Garibaldi wished to end the useless butchery of the brave young men, his red-shirted legionaries, who were fighting a losing battle.

At the end of June the gallant defence was over; Rome fell to the French. Garibaldi, who had led his troops, sword in hand, was exhausted; the campaign of blood, sweat and tears was over. But his courage and daring were unsapped. Calling the survivors together, he offered them "hunger, thirst, forced marches and constant combats" if they would stay with him. As ever, they rallied loyally round that now tattered banner. And as they set off on that perilous journey, there rode at Garibaldi's side his dauntless wife. In spite of his protests, she had joined him in Rome, leaving their children in Nice, and had been in the thick of the bombardment. Even now she would not leave him, though she was pregnant and worn down with privations. She cut off her long, beautiful black hair so that it should not hinder her on the dreadful journey that lay before them.

Pursued by the four enemy armies they travelled on through

central Italy. Tuscan soldiers, discouraged, dropped out. Death thinned the ranks, deserters stole away in the night. When they reached the little Republic of San Marino Garibaldi realized that to remain there would be to expose the city to Austrian reprisals. At last he ordered his men to lay down their arms and disband. All but two hundred obeyed, and they, taking up his cry that "Venice is still left to die for!" marched on towards the Adriatic. At Cesenatico, after an incredibly tortuous journey through mountainous country, they reached the ocean. Garibaldi chartered thirteen fishing-boats and they set sail confidently for Venice; only to be betrayed by a shaft of moonlight that showed them to the Austrian blockade.

The tiny fleet was decimated. Eight boats were captured, but Garibaldi, by the strange fortune which had so often befriended him, escaped to Mesola. There, at last, Anita collapsed. Garibaldi and his one-armed friend Leggiero, themselves exhausted, somehow carried her to a farm and brought a doctor to her. It was too late. She sipped the cup of water held to her lips, and died in her husband's arms.

For ten years, known as the *decenio della resista* (decade of resistance), Garibaldi remained in the wings of a drama in which he could take no active part. After an interlude in America, where he worked for a time as a candle-maker, and later as captain of a Pacific merchantman, he returned to Italy and bought the island of Caprera, which he made his new home. Mazzini, again in England, was, as he himself said, "a voice crying *Action!*" while in Italy the increasingly forceful Cavour worked for the banishment of the Austrian yoke from Italian necks and the establishment of Piedmont as a North Italian kingdom under the young Victor Emmanuel, who had become king of Sardinia on the abdication of his father Charles Albert. With Cavour as his Prime Minister, Victor Emmanuel, "the honest king", was able to bring about social and military reforms; and on the outbreak of the Crimean War in 1854 sent an army of 10,000 men to fight with France and England against Russia, a gesture which greatly heightened his popularity in both European countries. Through the wiles of Cavour, Napoleon III of France was persuaded to join Victor Emmanuel in an alliance against Austria. But the slippery Emperor feared the threat to France of a powerful, united Italy; he made peace with Austria.

Cavour had resigned in disgust. Austria still held Venetia;

Italy was as far from unification as she ever had been, her people as restless. The Società Nazionale was born. An alarmed Austria, in April 1859, declared war; France followed suit. Garibaldi, again exulting in command, led the Alpine infantry to victory and liberated Alpine territory to the borders of the Tyrol. He had become a hero once more, almost overnight. Newspapers announcing his exploits were avidly read in the streets, his photograph was displayed in every size, from buttonhole-medal to bill-poster, his enlisting volunteers flaunting their scarlet shirts and kepis. It was clear that the way lay open for Italy to become one nation, under Victor Emmanuel. Garibaldi issued his famous proclamation to his fellow-countrymen.

"The day in which Victor Emmanuel should again summon my warriors for the redemption of the Fatherland I shall be found armed, side by side with my brave companions. The miserable feline policy which retards the majestic march of Italian affairs ought to make us rally, more than ever, round the brave and loyal soldier of Italian Independence, who is incapable of receding from his sublime and generous purpose, and to prepare money and arms to withstand whomsoever shall attempt to throw us back again into our ancient miseries."

Wherever his followers met his Hymn was sung.

Al l'armi! Al l'armi! Si scopron le tombe, si levano i morti,
I martiri nostri son tutti risorti!
Le spade nel pugno, gli allori alle chiome,
La fiamma ed nomme d'Italia sul cor!

(To arms! To arms! The graves are uncovered,
                the dead come from far,
The ghosts of our martyrs are rising to war.
With swords in their hands and with laurels of fame,
Their dead hearts are glowing with Italy's name.)

Complex political moves and counter-moves held the final victory in abeyance. But when the invasion of recalcitrant Sicily became necessary, and Garibaldi knew that the sympathy of powerful Britain was with him, taking the concrete form of two loaned ships, *Intrepid* and *Argus*, he landed in Marsala on 11 May, 1860, and on the next day was proclaimed dictator. A series of victories culminated in the triumph of Garibaldi at the siege of Messina and the battle of Reggio, on 21 August. On the evening of

6 September he and his officers entered Salerno in open carriages, his troops two days' march behind. Naples was his to take, unless King Francis II chose to fight. Salerno went wild with joy, almost destroying the conquerors with their demonstrations of affection. Bonfires on every hilltop celebrated the arrival of the new Dictator; while at the Palazzo Real of Naples the last Bourbon king and queen prepared to leave their kingdom, never to return. In the course of a few weeks Garibaldi and his volunteers, the glorious Thousand, some of them boys no older than twelve, had overcome more than 24,000 regular soldiers. "The age of miracles is not dead!" was the cry of Europe.

On the morning of 26 October Garibaldi went out to meet his King. Stationing himself beside a rustic tollgate inn, he watched the handsomely caparisoned royal regiments march by, he himself clad in a rough poncho, a scarf tied round his head, his red shirt as shabby as those of his officers. Suddenly the shout went up: "*Il Re! Il Re!*" The little gathering by the inn mounted their horses and moved forward to greet the approaching cortege. Victor Emmanuel, dashing and resplendent on his fine Arab steed, stretched out his hand to the man who had made his entry into Naples possible. They spoke together like two chance-met acquaintances.

"*Come state, caro Garibaldi?*"

"*Bene, Maesta. E Lei?*"

"*Benone.*"

("How are you, my dear Garibaldi?")

"Fine, thank you, Your Majesty—and you?"

"Splendid.")

They rode together side by side, chatting, for a time; then the King moved on towards Teano. It was noticed that Garibaldi's expressive face wore a look of gentle melancholy. He was quiet that evening. Next morning he told the gallant Englishwoman, Jessie Mario, who had been the Florence Nightingale of his campaigns, "Jessie, they've sent us to the rear". In that short ride Victor Emmanuel had told him that his services were no longer required.

It was not the end of his military career. Active in politics during the following year, 1861, he was once more in the field in August, 1862, marching hopefully on French-occupied Rome. But on the plains of Aspromonte he encountered the troops of the King, who fired on his own men. He ordered them not to return the fire; but already a bullet had penetrated his ankle, causing an angry wound which was long in healing. *Punch*, that sharp eye of England, had seen with its usual clarity the true situation between King and Liberator when, on the occasion of Victor Emmanuel's entry into Naples, a caricaturist had shown Garibaldi, a peasant-like figure, kneeling with dignified humility to fit a boot inscribed ITALY on the arrogantly outstretched leg of Victor Emmanuel, rakishly crowned, tomcat-moustaschioed, dapper in uniform and cloak. England loved Garibaldi, claimed him as her own hero.

In 1864 he received full testimony of her adoration, when he visited her shores. Half a million Londoners struggled round the carriage that bore him to Stafford House, by St James's Palace, and when he stepped out of it the vehicle which had been clutched by so many hands fell, literally, to pieces.

His visit was significant. Freedom and democracy were spreading over Europe. Since the death of Chartism the Trades Union movement had begun to take shape; the much-disputed Reform Bill would be carried by Disraeli within three years of Garibaldi's arrival in London. To the man in the street Garibaldi represented liberation from upper-class domination, while to England's nobility and intelligentsia his heroic qualities were almost beyond praise, and his personality immensely likeable. Gladstone epitomized the impression he made.

> "We who then saw Garibaldi for the first time can many of us never forget the marvellous effect produced on our minds by the simple nobility of his demeanour, by his manners and his acts . . . Beside his splendid integrity, and his wide and universal sympathies, besides that seductive simplicity of manner which never departed from him, and that inborn and native grace which seemed to attend all his actions, I would almost select from every other quality this, which was in apparent contrast but real harmony in Garibaldi—the union of the most profound and tender humanity with his fiery valour."

Elizabeth Barrett Browning had already celebrated his deeds and bitterly attacked Victor Emmanuel for his treatment of the hero: she, dwelling in Italy herself, was still a poet of England. The Poet Laureate, Tennyson, invited Garibaldi to plant a tree in his garden in the Isle of Wight, and listened with rapt attention to Garibaldi's recitation of an Italian patriotic poem, of which he understood not one word. At a grand reception at Stafford House, where the guests understandably consisted mainly of Liberals, the Dowager Duchess of Sutherland paid Garibaldi the unheard-of compliment of inviting him into her sumptuously-appointed private boudoir, and, even more startling, permitted him to smoke there. Mazzini, living humbly in one room in Fulham, shared modestly in his triumphs, and would-be revolutionary leaders from all over Europe, and from Russia, began to converge on London.

The Government was embarrassed. The celebration of such a major world event as the unification of Italy was certainly an occasion for rejoicing, but it was far from Gladstone's wish that political agitators anxious to follow in Garibaldi's footsteps should make England their headquarters. Politely, but pointedly, Garibaldi was told that a return home would probably benefit his health. He was hurt; not that his public triumphs were to be curtailed, but that he was personally not wanted. A pension for himself and his family was offered; he curtly refused it. A provincial tour which had been arranged for him was cancelled, by his own desire, and he wrote to its organizers a simple, direct letter.

"Dear Friends,—Accept my heartfelt thanks for your sympathy and your affection. I shall be happy to meet you under more favourable circumstances, and when I can enjoy at ease the hospitality of your country. For the moment I am obliged to leave England. Once more accept my ever-abiding gratitude."

On the eve of his departure he was visited by the Prince of Wales, very much against Queen Victoria's wishes. She grudgingly admitted the hero's honesty, disinterestedness and bravery, but regarded him as a dangerous revolutionary who had had an inflammatory effect on the Liberal Party. The Prince of Wales, courageously flouting maternal disapproval, paid a private visit to Stafford House, talked with Garibaldi, and even more courageously wrote his mother an account of the meeting, at which he had been "much pleased" with Garibaldi's dignified, noble appearance, quiet manner of speech, and lack of self-aggrandizement. The royal visit, however private it had been intended to be, was soon public knowledge and increased the Prince's popularity.

Garibaldi left England with a sad heart. There had been a sour taste about his last days there. It would probably not have amused him greatly to know that England's lasting memorials to him would be a biscuit of currants encased in pastry (known to schoolboys as Squashed Flies) and an innumerable quantity of pottery figures from the Staffordshire kilns. The most famous shows him bare-headed, simply clad in shirt and trousers, his hand poised near the pommel of his sword, a pillar supporting him with a clock inset.

The eighteen years remaining to him saw him still constantly in action. In 1866 he led Italian volunteers against the armies of Prussia, and when ordered to retire from the projected siege of Trent, obeyed against his will. His attempt to liberate Rome in 1867 led to defeat and imprisonment. When the Franco-Prussian War broke out three years later, he fought for France in the battles of Chatillon, Autun and Dijon, successfully in each case. The Peace of Frankfurt, which followed, established The German Empire. In 1874 he was elected deputy for the now liberated Rome; for in the same war Victor Emmanuel's Bersaglieri had finally taken the city after its French garrison had been withdrawn to fight elsewhere. The dream of the Liberationists was at last realized.

But Garibaldi was old and rheumatic. His last years were spent peacefully in his white house at Caprera. On a summer evening, as he lay dying, two little moorland birds sat chirping for food on the window-sill of his bedroom. His nurses would have driven them away; but Garibaldi smiled and issued his last order—that the small creatures should come and go at their pleasure, then and after his death.

Of the four great figures responsible for the Italian *Risorgimento* and the eventual unity of Italy, Garibaldi alone has captured and endured in popular imagination. Mazzini has been called its "purest hero", he who worked with such devoted diligence for his country and was so poorly rewarded, dying after long exile, a stranger in his own land. The brilliant brain and extraordinary administrative ability of Cavour provided the nerve-centre of the Liberation movement, particularly in its later stages. Victor Emmanuel proved a capable constitutional monarch and a useful foreign ambassador, but was hardly of a stature worthy of the immense monument raised to him in Rome. Each of these men played an important part in the movement which symbolized and solidified the spirit of nationalism begun by the French Revolution and the rebellion of the American states; liberalism, the realization of a national identity and the discovery that union and strength are synonymous, were all ideals that would spread throughout Europe in the nineteenth century and into Asia in the twentieth. And the great figure of Garibaldi, man of the people, soldier of dauntless courage, honest and simple, the "happy warrior" beloved of poets and people, was the instrument, the stalwart body, rather than the brain, of the conflict by which Italy and eventually all Europe found freedom.

CHARLES DARWIN
(1809–1882)

WHEN Charles Darwin died they buried him, not in the village churchyard he would have preferred, just across the road from his home, but in Westminster Abbey. A roll-call of the assembled company would have borne witness to a world-wide expression of honour and esteem. But if we may imagine his spirit to have been hovering over the scene as they lowered his coffin into the history-saturated ground we may equally well catch his murmured expostulation. All this public display, the eloquent tributes and deep organ notes, the flowers and the shuffling crowds . . . when he was such a simple fellow really, old and tired now, who (as he had written a few years before) regretted that he had not been able to do more direct good to his fellow creatures, but, all the same, believed that he had done rightly "in steadily following and devoting my life to Science".

Charles Darwin was born in his father's big, plain, and comfortable house rising above the Severn at Shrewsbury, on 12 February, 1809. His ancestors were Lincolnshire yeomen, until there emerged in the family tree one of those men who are the delight of those ever on the search for the why and wherefore of genius. In the middle of the eighteenth century Erasmus Darwin adopted medicine as his profession and practised first at Lichfield and eventually at Derby, where he became celebrated as a man of radical and freethinking opinions, an ardent cultivator of botanical science, and the author of poems (such as the *Loves of the Plants*) in which, so it has been claimed, may be found some inklings of the principle of Evolution.

Charles Darwin's father, Robert Darwin, was Erasmus Darwin's son. He, too, was a doctor, and a highly successful one, possessed of a bedside manner which the ladies of Shrewsbury found wonderfully soothing. Even if he had had to rely on his practice alone he would have become wealthy, but he had the good sense, and good fortune, to marry Miss Susannah Wedgwood, the eldest daughter of the great potter, who contributed to her husband's bank account a very substantial dowry. Mrs Darwin died when Charles was only eight, so that he had few recollections of her, but Dr Robert survived until 1848, when he left the exceedingly handsome fortune of round about £280,000.

The mixture of Darwin and Wedgwood genes provided Charles Darwin with a wonderfully rich inheritance of brain if not of much muscle, but it should be recognized that it was the reeking kilns of the Wedgwood works at Etruria, near Burslem, that eventually made it possible for Charles Darwin to lead a life of unharassed ease, free to do his life's work just how and when and where he wanted.

In 1817, the year in which his mother died, Charles was entered at a day school in the town, preparatory to going the next year to Shrewsbury School, one of the most famous of English public schools. He was there for seven years, until he was sixteen, but (as he wrote in his *Autobiography*) "as a means of education to me the school was simply a blank". The curriculum was almost entirely made up of Latin and Greek, and Darwin was never any good at learning languages, living or dead. Then the headmaster, Dr Butler, although regarded as one of the country's leading educationists, was entirely unsympathetic; when he learnt that Charles had been amusing himself with his elder brother in messing about with chemicals in a tool-house in their garden, he publicly rebuked him for wasting his time in such an ungentlemanly fashion.

Since he was doing no good at Shrewsbury School, his father took him away earlier than usual and sent him to Edinburgh University, where his brother was completing his medical studies. There was some idea of Charles becoming a doctor like his father and grandfather, but the subject of human anatomy was taught in so uninteresting a fashion that it completely disgusted him, and the two occasions on which he was required to assist at an operation were so horrifying, what with the blood and the screaming patients being held down in those pre-chloroform days, that he decided that he had had more than enough of surgery. The only good thing that came out of his Edinburgh period was an interest in natural history, for which his membership of several students' societies was mainly responsible.

But if life at the university was dull and apparently meaningless, the vacations were filled with the most pleasurable exertion. In the days of his youth there was no hint of the ill-health that was to make so much of his later life miserable. He delighted in field sports. He loved angling, horse-riding, and shooting, particularly the last, so that he became a very good shot. He might well have developed into a country squire, one of the fishin' and huntin' set, with no interests beyond his rod and gun and bottle. This seemed all the more likely when, his father having come to the conclusion that he would never make a doctor but might perhaps make the grade as a clergyman, sent him to Christ's College, Cambridge, with that end in view. Here his black marks multiplied. Although he had scruples about expressing belief in all the dogmas of the Church of England, he quite liked the idea of becoming a country clergyman; but now his passion for shooting and hunting and riding across country got him into a sporting set where, as he put it years afterwards, "we sometimes drank too much, with jolly singing and playing cards afterwards". When the inevitable morning-after dawned, he may well have remembered something that his father had flung at him, years earlier when he was still at school: "You care for nothing but shooting, dogs, and rat-catching, and you will be a disgrace to yourself and to your family!"

Who knows, something like this may well have happened to him, but for the fact that in these Cambridge years he was developing an ever greater involvement in natural history. Collecting insects, beetles in particular, became a passion with him, and "no poet ever felt more delighted in seeing his first poem published" than he did in seeing in a volume of *Illustrations of British Insects* the magic words, "captured by C. Darwin Esq". It was at Cambridge, too, that he formed a friendship which was to influence his whole career. This was with Professor Henslow, who lectured on botany, but was also thoroughly well informed on chemistry, entomology, and geology. From their early acquaintance Henslow recognized some extraordinary quality in Darwin's mental processes; he encouraged him in every way, made him welcome to his classes and his home, and chose him as his almost daily companion in long walks over the countryside. Not that Henslow was alone in his appreciation. Several other of the dons allowed Darwin an unusual measure of association, notably Professor Sedgwick, whom Darwin accompanied on an excursion among the rocks of North Wales in the summer of 1831. Darwin thoroughly enjoyed the trip, but he took good care to be back home in time to join his Uncle Josiah Wedgwood's shooting party, for at that time, so he very candidly admitted in his *Autobiography*, he would have thought himself "mad to give up the first days of partridge shooting for geology or any other science".

But already he had in his pocket a letter that was to prove of the most momentous importance. It was from Professor Henslow, who wrote that he had been asked to recommend a naturalist to accompany Captain Robert Fitzroy, R.N., on an expedition that was being sent out to survey the coasts of the most southern parts of South America. Henslow had at once thought of Darwin, and was sure he was just the right man for the job: was he willing to go? Darwin would have accepted on the spot, but his father made some difficulties that were not easily overcome, such as that a journey round the world could hardly be regarded as a suitable preparation for a man destined for the Church, and the fact that it had been offered to several other better qualified young men, who had turned it down, suggested that there was a catch in the offer somewhere. At length Dr Darwin agreed that Charles might go if he could find a man of undoubted common sense to recommend it, thinking, no doubt, that this would be the end of the matter. But Charles appealed to his Uncle Josiah, who gave him his strong backing.

Forthwith Darwin hurried off to London to meet Captain Fitzroy, and everything was soon fixed up. Not until much later did he learn that Fitzroy, who was something of a phrenologist, had thought of rejecting the young fellow, since he suspected from the shape of Darwin's nose that he would not possess sufficient energy and determination for the voyage!

Darwin joined his ship—H.M.S. *Beagle*, 242 tons, rigged as a barque and classified as a ten-gun brig—in October, 1831, but south-western gales delayed her sailing, and it was not until two days after Christmas that she was able to leave Devonport, and set a south-westerly course across the Atlantic.

Years afterwards Darwin was to deliver his considered judgment, that "the voyage of the *Beagle* has been by far the most important event in my life". To begin with, he was horribly seasick, and he often had to "take the horizontal", as he called it. The quarters allotted to him were abominably cramped, and he soon discovered that Captain Fitzroy (who though only four years his senior, was already a seasoned navigator) was possessed of a vile temper. Fortunately Darwin never once lost his own, and the two men got on well together for most of the time. The crew found Darwin's dredging for natural-history specimens highly amusing, but they were soon referring to him as "the Flycatcher", while in the officers' mess they spoke of him, behind his back, as "dear old philosopher".

Somehow or other he managed to clear a space on the chart-table and, day by day, wrote up the journal which he later expanded into a volume.

Their first land-fall was the island of St Jago in the Azores, and Darwin was very glad to get ashore and stretch his legs. A month later they arrived off the Brazilian coast, and Darwin went ashore and paid his first visit to a tropical forest. When that evening by the light of a swinging lantern he wrote his account of the day's happenings he said that "delight" was too weak a term to express his feelings: "to a person fond of natural history, such a day as this brings with it a deeper pleasure than he can ever hope to experience again." And yet this was but the beginning of a succession of wonderful days, of breath-taking prospects, of fantastic explorations of flora and fauna, of human contacts that left behind them unforgettable memories, fierce and terrible some of them, sad and degraded others, and yet others tender and graciously moving. Looking back, he recalled such things as the glories of the tropical vegetation, the sublimity of the great deserts of Patagonia, and the forest-clad mountains of Tierra del Fuego. Writing of the last-named, he remarked that "the sight of a naked savage in his native land is an event which can never be forgotten."

The voyage had been originally planned to take a year or two, but there was no definite time-table and the term was extended again and again. From South America the *Beagle* sailed into the Pacific and visited Tahiti and New Zealand and Tasmania, and then to the Keeling Islands in the Indian Ocean (where Darwin made a pioneering investigation of coral reefs). So they sailed on, round the Cape into the Atlantic again—when, to the pretty general disgust, Fitzroy decided that they must pay a second visit to South America to check on some discrepancies discovered in their previous reckonings of longitude. But at long last the *Beagle* cast anchor at Falmouth. The date was 2 October, 1836, not much short of five years since they had set out.

When Darwin had sailed on the *Beagle* in 1831 he was twenty-two, as unsettled in his opinions as in his ways, and with no clear idea of what he wanted to do in life. When he returned to England in 1836 he was twenty-seven and looking and seeming older, far better informed, much more serious-minded, and with a brain cleared of a good deal of intellectual rubbish. The changes were speedily noted when he first made his reappearance at home. "Why, the shape of his head is quite altered," remarked his father. The question of his becoming a clergyman was never even raised. Darwin himself was quite sure what he wanted to do. Ever since he had been at Tierra del Fuego his mind had been made up. Briefly stated, it was "adding a little to Natural Science".

For a couple of years he was engaged in clearing the ground. He was perpetually busy, although his health had begun to show signs of strain, which eventually made him an invalid. After a round of family visits and to friends at Cambridge and London, he took lodgings in London, where he busied himself in preparing for the press the record of his travels, which was published in 1839 under the title, *Journal of Researches into the Natural History and Geology of the Countries visited during the Voyage of H.M.S. Beagle round the World*. The book was as well received as it deserved to be, and has remained the most generally popular, as it is certainly the most readable, of his many writings.

That same year he was married, and he was as fortunate in his choice of wife as he had been in that of career. His bride was his first cousin, Miss Emma Wedgwood, the youngest child of his Uncle Jos; she was thirty, nearly a year older than he was, and she outlived him by many years, not dying until 1896, when she was eighty-eight. They had known one another from childhood. All that we are told about her suggests that she was one of the nicest of nice women. She was well-educated, she could play the piano and loved reading, she was good-looking and had all the housewifely virtues, such as knowing how to keep the fire burning brightly in the grate and how to arrange the cushions on the sofa to which her husband was increasingly condemned. She was mature, with a mind (as well as plenty of money) of her own, and her children (she bore ten, but several died young) thought her wonderful. And her husband's opinion? Nearly forty years after their marriage he put it down on paper for the benefit of his children: "She has been my greatest blessing . . . I do not believe she has ever missed an opportunity of doing a kind action to any one near her . . . she has been my wise adviser and cheerful comforter throughout life, which without her would have been for a very long period a miserable one from ill health. She has earned the love and admiration of every soul near her."

Married on 29 January, 1839, they seem to have had no honeymoon but gone straight to the house they had taken in Upper Gower Street. Describing her first week's experiences as a married woman, she wrote to her mother that they had had their first dinner-party, had bought a piano at Broadwood's, and the cook didn't know how to boil the potatoes properly. Next week she wrote to her sister that she had sacked the cook. . . .

For between three and four years they lived in London, but going into society did not agree with Darwin, and interrupted his work. So they started looking for a house in the country, and found one in the little village of Downe, in Kent, some sixteen miles from London. Down House (without the final e) was squarely built and unpretendingly plain, with plenty of accommodation (but no modern conveniences: water had to be drawn from a well, and the "sanitation" was earth closets), and the garden and grounds extended to eighteen acres. This meant servants, and the Darwins had plenty: a manservant for Darwin, a cook, four housemaids, two menservants or footmen in livery and an uncertain number of gardeners, coachmen, and stablehands.

Altogether it must have been an expensive place to keep up, but money was something the Darwins were never short of. When they were married, Darwin's father made him an allowance of about £500 a year, to which Emma's father added another £400 a year. What this would represent in present day terms is impossible to determine with any accuracy, but no doubt about it, it would be a very substantial sum. In course of time he received large legacies, and, although not at first, he even managed to make money from his writings; from first to last his books brought him just over £10,000. But there was something else, which may be gathered from the reply he made to his cousin, Francis Galton, who, when in search of data for his study of English men of science, invited Darwin to mention any "special talents" that he might possess. Darwin's reply is astonishing. "None—except for business as evinced by keeping accounts, replies to correspondence, and investing money very well."

"*Investing money very well.*" Here, surely, he was being even more modest than usual with him. From the first days at Downe, he saved money and started investing it in Government stocks and land mortgages but above all, it seems, in railway shares. Every day after lunch he would retire to his sofa in the drawing-room, smoke a cigarette, and listen to his wife or one of his daughters reading aloud from a work of history, travels, or a novel (he liked a good novel, provided it did not end unhappily, "against which a law ought to be passed.") Then he would take up his *Times*, which, so his son tells us, was the only non-scientific matter that he read to himself. Could there be a more vividly revealing picture of an "eminent Victorian" taking his ease in his home circle? There he lies, the world-famous scientist, with his feet up, studying the City Page and then proceeding to speculate, very profitably, in railway shares!

Darwin's estate at his death has been estimated at £282,000—a large sum in his days and one which today might bring him into the millionaire class. Yet, like many another wealthy Victorian, he was inclined to be "near". It is with mixed feelings that one is allowed to handle the couple of dozen account-books, in which Darwin, day by day over all the years between his marriage until his death, recorded every penny that he received and every penny that he spent or saved. One cannot help feeling sorry for Mrs Darwin, who was required to keep a strict record of every article of domestic expenditure, of such things as cab fares and theatre tickets, gifts and charitable contributions, and what happened to her dress allowance (which, incidentally, was remarkably small for a well-to-do Victorian lady). This insistence on the meticulous recording of the trivial may be seen as a reflection of Darwin's life-long passion for collecting; but, all the same—poor Emma!

In justice to Darwin, however, it should be recognized that great wealth did not enervate or corrupt him. When other men in his position might have been inclined to take things easy, he drove himself to the limit in pursuing the satisfaction of a noble ideal, a disinterested search for truth about the processes of Nature. This is speaking generally; and to particularize, for the greater part of his working life he was primarily and absorbingly concerned with one problem in particular—that "mystery of mysteries, the origin of species".

The problem had first begun to worry him when he was on board the *Beagle*. At Cambridge he had never thought to question the orthodox teaching, that all the infinite species of flora and fauna had come into being by individual acts of special creation; but not long before he sailed from England he had bought a copy of Professor C. Lyell's *Principles of Geology*, and he took it with him on the voyage. Lyell, writing as a geologist, challenged the view that in the history of the world there had been a succession of stupendous catastrophes or cataclysms, in which animal and plant life had been wiped out and so enabled a fresh start to be made; on the contrary, he maintained, in the geological structure of the world there might be seen the evidences of an unbroken, regular development from the primeval chaos to the conditions of the present. When Darwin went ashore at St Jago and at Bahia, in South America, he found plenty to support Lyell's argument, and he asked himself whether living creatures might not be the products of an orderly, gradual development, equally with the dead rocks? On every hand, he discerned "organisms of every kind beautifully adapted to their habits of life"—but *how* had they become so adapted? The question haunted him, and for the next quarter of a century he was preoccupied with finding an answer.

The first thing to do was to collect as many facts as he could about the variation of plants and animals, both in a state of nature, i.e. wild, and domesticated. "My first note-book", he tells us, "was opened in July, 1837." He read widely, corresponded with animal breeders and horticulturists, and exchanged views with Lyell and many another scientific authority. In June, 1842, "I first allowed myself the satisfaction of writing a very brief abstract of my theory in pencil," This was enlarged in 1844, but Darwin kept the manuscript in his desk, only taking it out now and again to make additions or some revision. In 1856 Lyell urged him to "write out his views pretty fully", but still he dithered. After all, there was no hurry, was there?

We can understand his consternation when on 18 June, 1858 he received a letter from an English naturalist named Alfred Russel Wallace, who was then collecting natural history specimens in the East Indies, which made it perfectly clear that *he* had arrived at a theory of "Natural Selection" that was in all essentials the same as the one which Darwin had spent so many years in getting down on paper! "Your words have come true with a vengeance", he wrote forthwith to Lyell, "that I should be forestalled. I never saw a more striking coincidence; if Wallace had had my MS sketch written out in 1842 he could not have made a better short abstract!" His first reaction was to scrap his own work and let Wallace have all the credit; but his friends at length persuaded him to agree with the suggestion—one in which Wallace had at once concurred —that the two of them should prepare a joint paper to be presented to a meeting of the Linnean Society in London. This was done, the paper was read on 1 July, 1858—and, after all, none of those who heard it seemed very much impressed.

Darwin now went ahead with his own book, and after a year's hard work it was sent to the printers. In November, 1859, it was published by John Murray, its full title being, *The Origin of Species, by means of Natural Selection, or the Preservation of Favoured Races in the Struggle for Life*. It was a large book, running to about 600 pages, and its price was 15s.—no inconsiderable figure in those days. Notwithstanding, the first edition of 1,250 copies was sold out on the day of publication, and a second edition of 3,000 copies was soon exhausted. By 1876 some 16,000 copies had been sold.

The Origin of Species was, as Darwin himself claimed, the chief work of his life. Its importance derives from its double aspect. In the first place, it is an exposition of the evolutionary principle. In the second, it gives an account of Darwin's own theory—Natural Selection—of the way in which plants and animals have evolved through the ages. The two things are quite distinct, although they have been often confused. When Darwin wrote, nothing was known of genes, and he is unlikely to have even heard the name of Mendel. Since his time, the science of Heredity has come into existence, and it is now held that there are other ways than Natural Selection in which variations can have occurred. But it was as the Apostle of Evolution that Darwin caught and held public attention. Others, including his grandfather Erasmus Darwin, had made groping approaches to the problem, but it was he who, as it were, put Evolution "on the map".

Within a short time of his book's appearance, Darwin (one of the most retiring of men) was the centre of a violent intellectual storm. Although he had refrained from definitely including Man in his evolutionary scheme, he was loudly denounced as "the man who says we are descended from monkeys". For some years he was exposed to the most virulent misrepresentation, abuse, and denunciation. But he had many influential supporters in scientific circles, notably Professor Thomas Huxley, who thoroughly well earned the designation of "Darwin's bull-dog".

While the uproar was continuing, Darwin held quietly and steadily on his way. A small book on *The Fertilization of Orchids* was published in 1862, and this was followed by one on *Climbing Plants* and another on *The Variation of Plants and Animals under Domestication* (1867). Then in 1871 was published *The Descent of Man*, a work hardly less important than the *Origin* and far exceeding it in human interest. By this time the "high antiquity of Man" had become pretty generally accepted by educated opinion, thanks to works published by Lyell, Huxley, Lubbock, and others; but even so, there were plenty of angry voices raised against Darwin's demonstration that Man, like every other form of life, is "the modified descendant of some pre-existing form". However, the reviewer who wrote that the *Desecnt* was raising "on every side a storm of mingled wrath, wonder and admiration", was pretty near the mark. But the row was nothing like so violent as the *Origin* had aroused, which in itself was a tribute to Darwin's success as a propagandist of the evolutionary idea.

Now in his last decade, Darwin's output was unabated. As a scientific expositor he appealed to the general reader with such books as *The Expression of the Emotions in Man and the Animals, Insectivorous Plants, Climbing Plants,* and *The Formation of Vegetable Mould through the Action of Worms,* the last published a few months before his death; his writing was marked by a not ungraceful simplicity, but without the least indication of a vulgar popularization.

For the last twenty years of his life he was in the front rank of scientists at home and abroad. His books were translated into French, German, Italian, and other European languages, and foreign academies and scientific societies hastened to do him honour. As early as 1867 he received from Germany the distinguished decoration, the Order *Pour le Mérite*, which, it may be noted, anticipated by ten years the award by Cambridge University of an honorary degree of LL.D.

Towards the end of 1881 Darwin showed signs of increasing fatigue and weariness, and in the following spring he had severe heart attacks. On 7 March he took his last "constitutional" along his beloved "sandwalk" in the grounds of Down House, and on 19 April, 1882 he died.

WILLIAM EWART GLADSTONE
(1809–1898)

EDMUND BURKE once wrote that while men love to hear of their power, they have an extreme disrelish to be told of their duty. So long as W. E. Gladstone was one of Britain's leading political personalities they were never kept in ignorance of their duty or, at least, of their duty as Gladstone conceived it.

Not that Gladstone was unaware of his own power. He failed in some of his purposes, but he enjoyed many stirring triumphs and left behind him a reputation which has meant as much to posterity as it did to his own generation. His admirers were usually extravagant in their praises. What could be more eloquent, for example, than the tribute of his close friend, Lord Acton, the great nineteenth-century historian of liberalism?

> "Looking abroad beyond the walls of Westminster, for objects worthy of comparison, they will say that other men, such as Hamilton and Cavour, accomplished work as great; that Turgot and Roon were unsurpassed in administrative craft; that Clay and Thiers were as dexterous in parliamentary management; that Berryer and Webster resembled him in gifts of speech, Guizot and Radowitiz in fullness of thought; but that in the three elements of greatness combined, the man, the power and the result—character, genius and success—none reached his level."

The list is appropriately international, as Gladstone would have wished it to be, and in the twentieth century Gladstone is far better known than most of the other names in it.

Much, though not all, of Gladstone's political strength derived from the fervour with which he held moral conceptions of the duties both of individuals and of nations. Indeed, in an age when political parties were being fashioned afresh he was exceptional as a party leader in becoming a politician in spite of himself. When in 1878 he published seven volumes of articles which he had written during the previous thirty-six years, three and a half were devoted entirely to religion. His diaries, now in the course of being published for the first time, reveal the depth of his religious conviction. Thus, for example, he wrote in 1840 that "a political position is mainly valuable as instrumental for the good of the Church; and under this rule every question becomes one of detail only". In public he made it abundantly clear throughout his long political life that he put principles first and political calculations second. The remarkable fact was that from the public platform he could effectively communicate his moral ideas and passions to others even in the roughest of political meetings. One of the common labels attached to him while he was alive was "the People's William".

Yet Gladstone reached the pinnacles of popular success only after a fierce personal struggle and a never easy shift from old-fashioned toryism to liberalism. His father, John Gladstone, was a rich merchant who made his fortune by trading skilfully in the difficult conditions of the revolutionary and Napoleonic Wars. He was one of Britain's biggest slave-owners, and he was highly suspicious of his son's politics even before he became a Liberal. This was an awkward inheritance. Not surprisingly, what the son called "detail only" could be sufficiently intricate to force him as a Liberal in the making into ambiguous positions. Nor was his moral stance congenial to all his fellow countrymen. He was Prime Minister four times, and throughout each period in office the force of his own convictions led him into complications with his own supporters as well as into bitter confrontations with his opponents. He never had the whole of Britain behind him. In another Acton letter—this time of 1881, when Gladstone was Prime Minister for the second time, with a sizeable majority in the House of Commons but with a very precarious control over his own cabinet—the historian wrote:

"To many people the idea is repugnant that there is a moral question at the bottom of politics. They think that it is only by a great effort and the employment of every resource that property and religion can be maintained. If you embarrass their defence with unnecessary rules and scruples, you risk defeat, and set up a rather arbitrary and unsanctioned standard above the interest of their class or of their church. Such men are not at ease with the prime minister, especially if he is against them, and even when they are on his side. I am thinking of Argyll in Lytton's first debate; of Kimberley always; of soldiers and diplomatists generally."

Acton did not include the name of Disraeli, who deeply distrusted

Gladstone, or of Joseph Chamberlain, a radical member of Gladstone's own government, who represented a totally different approach to politics and was to move from radicalism to support of the Conservatives. Yet his comprehensive reference to "soldiers and diplomatists generally" covered a substantial group of people who mattered.

Gladstone's moralism is an even more important and crucial factor in his life than his strong European sense, though the two were entangled together. When he rounded off his Oxford education with a continental tour in 1832, the year of the Great Reform Act, the main question in his mind was whether he had "betrayed the cause of God to my worldly ambitions". His first interest in Europe was twofold—concern for its classical origins and preoccupation with its religious traditions and its spiritual future. In Italy he displayed no sympathies with Italian liberalism or, indeed, with Italian nationalism. "It seems almost inexplicable," he observed, that Italy as it then was "should ever have nurtured such hardy nations as the generality of its ancient inhabitants are stated to have been."

Later in 1832 Gladstone was elected member of parliament for the pocket borough of Newark, and nine years afterwards he entered the government of Sir Robert Peel as Vice-President of the Board of Trade, a post for which (despite his father's business) he felt he had no prior training or preparation. Two years later he joined Peel's cabinet. (The statues of the two men in Westminster Abbey were to be so near to each other that they almost touched). He resigned from Peel's cabinet not on the issue of free trade, which was to split the cabinet irrevocably in 1846, but on whether or not Peel was right to give state support to the training of Catholic priests in Ireland. On free trade itself, which his father found difficult to accept, he was a staunch Peelite, and he remained a Peelite after Peel's death during the complex political manoeuvres of the 1850's.

On more than one occasion he might have rejoined the main group of Conservatives, led by Lord Derby, who abandoned protection, the cause of the break with Peel, in 1852. Instead, he became Chancellor of the Exchequer in Aberdeen's coalition government of 1852 and in Palmerston's government of 1859. There was an element of irony in this last and decisive choice since he had been the most fierce of Palmerston's Peelite critics during the late 1850s. Europe played an important part in helping him to make up his mind, particularly the place of Italy in Europe, and once he had made it up there was to be no road back to the Conservatism of his youth.

Much has been written about Gladstone and Italy. Whatever he had thought on his first visit, a further visit in 1850 had drawn him for the first time into public discussion of European politics. Shocked by a trial of Neapolitan liberals and by their subsequent imprisonment, he appealed beyond the diplomatists to the growing reading public, and in *Two Letters to Lord Aberdeen* (who was not very happy about receiving them) urged that it was the sacred duty of Christians everywhere to protest against "the negation of God erected into a system of government". "The present practices of the Government of Naples," he thundered, "are an outrage upon religion, upon civilization, upon humanity and upon decency." He was at pains to insist in private that he was not supporting Italian nationalism—or liberalism—but his writings encouraged many people to believe that he was. And by 1859, when he made his crucial choice, he really was, though he retained a number of what to him seemed adequate qualifications. "We doubt whether anywhere in Christendom," he wrote in the *Quarterly Review* in 1859, "there be an instance corresponding with the Austrian power in Italy . . . where a people glaringly inferior in refinement rule, and that by the medium of arbitrary will, without the check of free institutions, over a race much more advanced."

At the moment of choice, the Conservatives seemed to Gladstone to be irredeemably pro-Austrian, and much as he disliked Palmerston's foreign policies during the 1850s he was in near agreement with him and Lord John Russell on all questions relating to Italy. "Lord Aberdeen," he said of his old colleague in the Peelite group, "can look at nothing except through Austrian spectacles. At this juncture he holds me to be the most extravagant and abandoned of English politicians." The Prince Consort, whose approach to European politics was very different, described Gladstone succinctly as "violently pro-Italian".

In November, 1860, Gladstone wrote to the Italian exile Panizzi that Italy had been to him "for the last eighteen months a principal cause, not only of joy and satisfaction, but even of the desire for political existence". And he stood by this judgement retrospectively, noting in 1865, the year of Palmerston's death, that it was "the overwhelming interest and weight of the Italian question, and of our foreign policy in connection with it, joined to my entire distrust of the former [Conservative] government in relation to it, that led me to decide without a moment's hesitation".

Whether or not there was any hesitation, there was certainly a change of view. He had once told Panizzi in a well-known passage that if there were two things on earth which John Bull hated they were an abstract proposition and the Pope, and that any idea of creating a new Italy on the basis of abstract propositions was likely to command little support. Now he challenged his own earlier verdict:

> "We distrust the abstract doctrine of nationality, not so much for fear it should be applied in a manner unfavourable to our own interests as because it appears to us incapable of general use by way of rule for political demarcations, and assumes therefore in our eyes the character of a symbol of disorganization . . . It has become plain that the passion for nationality in Italian (*sic*) is inseparable from the desire for freedom."

As events in Italy moved fast, Gladstone urged, however, that France and Britain should keep close together. He was corresponding at this time with Richard Cobden who was negotiating a commercial treaty with France which was to influence the first of Gladstone's new sequence of budgets. "If we engage in this matter [the Italian question] with France," he wrote in 1860, "it will be because we think that united with France we are strong enough to cause justice to be done." At this point "power" entered Gladstone's calculations. He had objected to Palmerston blatantly displaying British strength to the world from the time of the Don Pacifico debate in 1850 onwards. But he was prepared to use power "upon great occasions" to secure great objectives. "To repair a political wrong, or undo a political crime if it has long subsisted, is in many cases almost beyond the power of man." In the case of Poland it was: in the case of Italy in 1859 and in 1860 it was not.

The currents of Franco-Italian relationships were more strange, at times more muddy, than Gladstone realized, but he convinced himself first that Italian unification would "help to keep France in order" and second that through the commercial treaty which Cobden secured with Napoleon III's France it would be possible "to knit together in amity those two great nations whose conflicts have often shaken the world". The events of the next ten years, however, were calculated to foster more fears than hopes.

In September, 1870, Napoleon III was defeated by the Germans at Sedan and eighteen days later Italian troops entered Rome, where the Pope's position had been protected by the French. Gladstone had wished the Pope to renounce his temporal power on condition that his "sovereignty" was underwritten by a European guarantee. Now the King of Italy formally incorporated Rome and the Roman provinces into Italy. At the same time the Pope, to Gladstone's anger, was magnifying his spiritual power: in July, 1870, the Vatican Council had decreed the dogma of papal infallibility in matters of faith and morals by 533 votes to 2. Gladstone was Prime Minister in 1870, and it cannot be said that the foreign policy he pursued in this troubled year or between then and his fall from power in 1874 did much to convince either his fellow-countrymen or most foreigners who were concerned with Britain's role in Europe.

In 1869 he reiterated his belief that Britain should seek "to develop and mature the action of a common, or public, or European opinion . . . but should beware of seeming to lay down the law of that opinion by her own authority". He looked to the idea of a concert of Europe, since international opinion and international law could not be "sustained by physical force alone, still less by the physical force of a single power". Such an approach to international relations was beyond the comprehension of Napoleon III, and even more seriously it was academic nonsense to Bismarck, the man of action in 1870. When during the Franco-German War Gladstone tried to mobilize the support of the neutral powers to protest against the German annexation of Alsace-Lorraine, he may well have had moral principles to back him, but he could gain no support even from his foreign secretary, Lord Granville, who warned the Prime Minister not to run the risk of alienating the new Germany from the moment of its birth. Later in the year when Russia, encouraged by Bismarck, denounced the clauses in the Treaty of Paris of 1856 which had closed the Black Sea to Russian warships, Britain could do nothing (despite strong anti-Russian public opinion). Moreover when for once a European "concert" really came into existence and an international conference was called in London, it legalized Russia's unilateral action. A declaration that treaties could not be abrogated without the consent of all the signatories was the kind of sop that made a mockery of moral principles.

Few would have predicted in 1874, when Gladstone lost the

general election to Disraeli, that he would return to politics triumphant in 1880 on issues concerned mainly with foreign affairs. Indeed, he wrote to his wife in 1874 that "the welfare of mankind does not now depend on the State or on the world of politics; the real battle is being fought in the world of thought". A year later he resigned the leadership of his party and concentrated on the intellectual and moral implications of the Vatican decrees and on the problem of Homer which had long fascinated him. It must be emphasized that his concern for these two subjects was a more active element in his "European sense", as it has been called, than the pressures of day-to-day diplomacy or the movements of troops. Unlike most Englishmen of his time, he saw the struggles within the Catholic Church in their European and not in their insular framework and in long-term not, short-term perspective. Other Englishmen were as devoted as he was to the study of the ancient world, but few conceived of Homer as the key figure in the origins of Europe. Gladstone turned to the Homeric poems not in the spirit of a specialist scholar, but in a mood of meditation. Far back in time, "Homer" was where European civilization had begun, and by "civilization" Gladstone meant, as he once wrote, "a thing distinct from religion, but destined to combine and coalesce with it. The power derived from this source was to stand in subordinate conjunction with the Gospel, and to contribute its own share towards the training of mankind".

Given such feelings, it is not surprising that Gladstone was unimpressed by the attitude of many of his fellow-countrymen towards Europe. They put their own country first and did not understand the whole. They seemed to him to be "arrogant", to wish to talk about other people's faults all the time instead of noting or confessing their own. Few British Prime Ministers would have said as he did that "the English are a very strange people. They have very great qualities; but they also have great faults." Gladstone was never tempted by the idea of overseas adventure either in Europe or in the Empire, and he was cautious even in his attitudes towards national defence. One of his best replies to a question was his simplest. "Are you at all afraid of war," he was asked late in life, "especially with Germany?" "Not in the least," was his first reply. The questioner went on, "Are you not afraid of our small army being attacked by their huge army?" This time Gladstone replied with a question: "How are they to cross the Channel without ships? They would get very wet."

It is easy to understand how such feelings were to make it possible for Gladstone, unlike most Englishmen, to see the Irish question both in moral and in European terms and, in consequence, to arouse a majority of his fellow-countrymen against him. This was to be the main theme of the 1880s. Yet when he returned to politics from the world of thought in 1876 it was the fortunes not of the Irish but of the Balkan Christians which aroused him. His views on foreign policy and on Britain's role in Europe were diametrically opposed at this time to those of Disraeli, the Prime Minister, and the drama of their relationships raised popular feeling to fever pitch. The gap in thought and feeling was immense. Gladstone heralded Disraeli's acquisition of Cyprus at the Congress of Berlin in 1878, for example, as "an act of duplicity not surpassed and rarely equalled in the history of nations". His further description of the act as "insane" stung Disraeli into dismissing him as "a sophisticated rhetorician inebriated with the exuberance of his own verbosity".

The rhetoric may have divided liberals and conservatives, but Gladstone emphasized that the Eastern question was one in which "all Englishmen have a common interest". He touched a moral chord in thousands of people, some of whom, indeed, saw the moral implications of the Bulgarian atrocities before he did. A conservative wrote to him that in face of Turkish atrocities "the enthusiasm and indignation of the English nation is unbounded and unparalleled", and begged him "to save a suffering and outraged people, and render an inestimable service to religion and humanity".

There had never been such public excitement on issues connected with foreign affairs even though such issues had often stirred public opinion during the previous twenty-five years, and in less than six weeks nearly five hundred popular demonstrations were held throughout Britain. Some of Gladstone's strongest supporters were nonconformists, a sector of society with no comparable European counterpart. Their zeal showed that Gladstone depended for the political success he acquired not only upon his own abilities, but upon a particular configuration of society during a particular phase of national history when immediate interests could be sacrificed to great causes. The German theologian Dollinger wrote that what was happening in Britain in 1876 and 1877 would be almost inconceivable in any other country, and certainly in this context also the English were "a very strange people".

Not all Gladstone's eager supporters during the Near Eastern crisis followed him during the 1880s when he was converted to the cause of home rule for Ireland, a cause which split the Liberal party in 1886 just as dramatically as the cause of free trade had split Peel's Conservative party forty years before. In face of the troubles of the 1880s Gladstone came to the conclusion that the only way to secure justice for Ireland was to grant home rule, and in 1886 he addressed an Irish delegation at his home in Hawarden in these terms:

"I feel that the man who has exposed the conduct of foreign Governments ought, on principles of justice, to pursue the same course with regard to his own country; and I could not consent to keep back or describe in qualified terms, misdeeds for which England is responsible ... Attacks made upon the Turkish Government, attacks upon the Napolitan Government, made by me, certainly received a very cordial and hearty welcome in England, because it was thought that they were justly made."

Gladstone was pulling together the threads of his own life. Yet his belief in "the wise and generous justice of the nation" was ill grounded and the opportunity of securing home rule at the most favourable moment in the nineteenth century was lost. He was ostracized in many quarters, lampooned in others. *The Times* drew a very unfavourable parallel between him and Bismarck, "a statesman who is no novice or visionary—who is unsurpassed by any of his contemporaries in practical wisdom and resources". Bismarck had just expelled 37,000 Poles, not because they were seditious agitators but because the Polish population in East Germany was increasing faster than the German. *The Times* hailed this "solution" which eschewed "laborious efforts to follow every winding and evolution of national sentiment". The "vigorous application of stringent measures" was what was most needed. "We in this country have been far too much blinded by specious nonsense about justice and its infallible efficacy as a breeder of affection. It is time to recognize the truth written large in history, in contemporary events and in human nature, that there are antipathies which have to be accepted as ultimate facts, and which neither justice nor generosity can soften."

This epitaph on Gladstonian liberalism sharpens the contrast between Gladstonian approaches to foreign policy and *realpolitik*. Yet it is important to bear in mind that during the early 1880s Gladstone's foreign policy had led him not only into such terrifying disasters as Gordon's death at Khartoum, but into serious mis-understanding of the motives and tactics of Europe's leading politicians. He was out of touch with many realities which could not be corroded by rhetoric, unaware of many social and political forces which were to change Europe more than it had changed in his own lifetime. He was right to hate "the fiend of Jingoism" in Britain itself, wrong to put his trust in a "concert of Europe" dominated by the foreign policy-makers of his time. He had said in 1880 that "the ideal of my life" in foreign policy was a European concert working "for purposes of justice, peace and liberty, with efficiency and success". But the actual European concert, when it was brought intermittently into existence, did not work for these purposes. Bismarck, who could use concert as well as war as an instrument of policy, could treat Britain's Prime Minister as "Professor Gladstone", a professor in shining armour.

Gladstone's last years were years when Britain itself was moving further and further away from the ideal of his life. He foresaw some of the horrors of the twentieth century, and remained convinced himself of the need to maintain the moral values for which he had always stood. When there were Armenian atrocities in 1894 Gladstone once again in great public speeches during the following two years tried to rouse the crowds, arguing this time that the Turkish Empire deserved to be rubbed off the map. He was rebuked by a Liberal Prime Minister, Rosebery, who told him that by coming forward to advocate a policy which the government could not support he had "innocently and unconsciously" dealt official policy (which was to maintain "concerted action of the Powers") a *coup de grâce*.

The words "innocently and unconsciously" linger in the mind in relation to many of Gladstone's specific policies. Yet his vision of Europe as a family of nations, of which Britain was a necessary part, was a warm and enlarging one, and one which could attract to the last. As he passed through the streets of Liverpool on his way to give his final speech on the Armenian massacres there was a sense in which, as one of his biographers, appositely quoting Homer, puts it "he beheld again the wonder of the common man gazing upon him as a god".

OTTO VON BISMARCK
(1815–1898)

BISMARCK, like many other great men, has gone down to history as somebody he was not; as austere, ruthless and unscrupulous, the Iron Chancellor. By the use of the army in three short wars, and by a carefully thought out policy for unification, he made the German nation into an empire. He was a gruff, hard-headed Junker from the Pomeranian plain. He dominated the new state for twenty years. And then he was thrown overboard ungraciously by William II.

The facts tell another story. He was, as Mr A. J. P. Taylor has described him, "a clever sophisticated son of a clever sophisticated mother masquerading all his life as his heavy earthen father". He was half country squire and half urban and revolutionary intellectual, at once both neurotic and decisive; he was capable of great piety, but could equally be swept by waves of rage and resentment (he once said "I have spent a whole night hating"). He loved Byron, Chopin and Walter Scott, and the arch-cynic could be the great Romantic, writing lyrical letters to his wife and addicted—like Churchill—to easy tears. Sometimes in his clashes with the Emperor after 1871, one would be found in one room weeping, and the other next door, also weeping. He could be domineering, but at the same time charming and supple—he has been described as a Byronic hero whose model was Frederick the Great.

He has sometimes been presented as a pre-Hitler figure, a Nazi before his time, but if there is a comparison to be made it is probably with Richelieu, whom in character and capacity for work he most closely resembles. He had, like him, a sharp awareness of the possible; and could trim and tack, and take time, and opportunity, by the forelock. And he had in him the essentials of a statesman, a capacity for identifying himself with events and mastering them, even if they took him down strange and contradictory paths. "I do not recognize the term 'right' and 'wrong' in foreign policy; I recognize only the term 'convenience'." He became a legend in his own day, and cultivated the plant warmly. He said that the man who had not drunk 5,000 bottles of champagne and smoked 5,000 cigars could not properly be said to have lived. Certainly he did his best: he smoked 14 cigars a day; and when he left the Chancellorship in 1890 he took 300 crates of paper and 13,000 bottles with him. He went most unwillingly. The last act of his public career was to throw out of the house the miserable parson who preached on the text—"Love your enemies".

He is, then, a figure of astonishing paradox: a gentle husband and devoted father but, to the world outside, a fire-breathing autocrat; a gargantuan eater and drinker, but also a hypochondriac; a wily diplomat, but a vigorous and outspoken hater of Poles, Jews and Frenchmen. He was inconsistent, vindictive, and mendacious. But, however unlovable to those outside the Junkers' world, to some of whom he seemed a monster, intellectually and physically Bismarck was a giant. Most Germans and almost all Prussians see in *der alte Herr* a twin-figure to Churchill: an extension and a prototype of the nation's personality.

When Bismarck was born, 1 April, 1815, three months before Waterloo, Germany was—despite Napoleon's reduction of the number of German states—still a congeries of principalities and duchies. In 1789 there had been 300 of them. After Waterloo there were still 38. Of these the Hapsburg Empire was the largest, and included Austria, Bohemia and part of Hungary; it dominated the Germanic Confederation set up in 1815. If Germany had a capital city it was Vienna, and it had been so for over five hundred years. By contrast Prussia was small and seen as a northern and barbarian outpost, which after all had been its original purpose. The electorate of Brandenburg and the little Baltic duchy of East Prussia had come under the rule of one family, the Hohenzollerns, in 1525; and by 1740 Frederick the Great, King of Prussia and Elector of Brandenburg, was in a position to challenge the power of the Hapsburgs in Germany. He made his kingdom in his own lifetime almost as important as the Empire itself. But the need for co-operation between Prussia and Austria during the Napoleonic wars made it seem that Prussia was once more in a secondary position, and after 1815 Austria resumed her dominant place among the German states. Prussia by the settlement at Vienna had been cut down the middle, and her Rhineland provinces were separated from the main kingdom of Brandenburg—Prussia—by the sovereign states of Hanover, Hesse and Nassau. The smaller German states that surrounded Prussia like Saxony and Thuringia were under Austrian influence. And Prussian expansion, which over the previous two centuries had been based on a policy of a strong army and state conquest, would now have to take a different shape. In 1834 she formed the *Zollverein*, a custom union that grew in importance as industry developed. Her logical role was to put herself at the head of the emerging German nationalist movement; but Frederick William III (1797–1840) and Frederick William IV (1840–1861) were not ambitious men, and seemed prepared to accept the hegemony of Austria. And when the opportunity came, in 1848, the King proved timid.

The 1848 revolution—the revolution of the intellectuals—left unchanged the balance of power in Germany and inside Prussia. The revolution was crushed, and crushed by Austria, with Russian assistance. If it did leave Prussia with a constitution, it greatly favoured the propertied classes. When the imperial crown of the proposed German empire was offered to Frederick William IV by the delegates of the people meeting in St Pauls Church in Frankfurt, he rejected it because it had not been offered to him by the German princes. Yet he did not entirely abandon the idea of a united Germany under his own leadership. For a time he favoured the nationalist schemes of Josef Maria von Radowitz and the idea of a federal union of princes, which would include in it the strictly German areas (*Kleindeutschkonzept*), as against the inclusion of states like Austria with their great numbers of non-Germans (*Grossdeutschkonzept*). Naturally this scheme was opposed by Austria and by the Prussian Junkers. As solid conservatives the Junkers disliked the sacrifice of Prussian rights that would follow from the formation of the union, the dominance of Catholic German states in it, and the liberal and national ideas that were coming out of Frankfurt. Frederick William for his part was ready to accept Junker resistance in order to justify his abandoning the scheme. By 1850 it had collapsed, and the Germanic confederation continued essentially under Austrian control.

It was the crisis of 1848 that first brought Bismarck on to the public stage.

Otto von Bismarck was born at Schönhausen on the river Elbe. The Bismarcks were an old Brandenburg family, indeed as old as the Hohenzollerns—Bismarck once said, "Not only older than the Hohenzollerns but in no way inferior to them". His father was a not very efficient farmer, and lived like most Junkers on his estates. His mother was city-bred and highly intelligent, and descended

A great new chapter in Italian history opened in May, 1860, when Giuseppe Garibaldi and his "thousand heroes", as they were later celebrated, landed in Sicily, within three months liberated it from the Bourbon tyranny, and a few weeks later crossed the straits and entered Naples in triumph. In the hour of victory (26 October, 1860) the red-shirted Garibaldi met King Victor Emmanuel, and handed over to him his command. But in 1862 he embarked on a rash expedition for the capture of Rome, was wounded and taken prisoner. This photograph (*right*) shows the great Liberator in hospital.

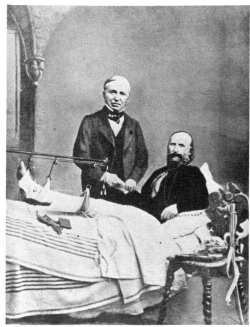

It was as naturalist to HMS *Beagle* in her voyage round the world in 1831–36 that Charles Darwin acquired that extensive knowledge of fauna, flora, and geology that stood him in such good stead when, on his return, he set about the formulation and establishment of the evolutionary theory that was given expression in his *Origin of Species*. *Above:* the *Beagle* overshadowed by the great mass of Mt. Sarmiento, in the southernmost parts of Chile; this engraving dates from 1838. *Right:* photograph of Darwin taken in 1860, the year following the publication of his great book. *Above right:* a contemporary caricature, exemplifying the popular (but quite false) belief that Darwin's theory propounded the intimate cousinship of Man and Monkey.

from the Mencken family, which had provided Brandenburg with some distinguished civil servants. She had great ambitions for her sons, particularly for Otto the youngest, and especially wanted him to become a high government official.

He was educated in Pomerania on another family estate, and attended school in Berlin with the thought of becoming a farmer like his father. He went to the University of Gottingen in Hanover, studying Law, but his attendance was erratic and he was not interested in his studies. He disturbed the public peace by many a night's roistering and spent some time in the University gaol. He fought no fewer than twenty-five fencing bouts with sabres in not untypical German student fashion. In 1836 he took up his first post as a Prussian civil servant at Aachen but did not enjoy it. From 1839–1849 he managed one of the family estates at Kniephof. In 1847 he married Johanna von Putkammer, a plain and very pious girl to whom he was devoted, as he was to his able but disagreeable son, Herbert, whom he hoped would be ultimately his successor in politics. At the time of the 1848 revolution he was therefore a restless farmer with a strongly conservative background.

In 1847 Bismarck was elected from the province of Saxony to the united Prussian Diet, which was summoned by Frederick William IV to discuss the drafting of the constitution. When he learned of the outbreak of the revolution he was on his estates in Pomerania, and was outraged at what he thought the threat to the Prussian system. He thought of mobilizing the countryside and marching on Berlin to free the King; he proudly hoisted the Prussian colours of black and white on the church tower near his estates. The King, while flattered by his emotions, treated his enthusiasm coolly and his approaches were ignored in Berlin. But he had made plain his devotion to traditional monarchy and his contempt for liberalism. The system that he thought the ideal was a monarchy built on and supported by a landed aristocracy. In practice this meant a policy of total defence of the *status quo* and of the rights of the nobility.

These sentiments and his right-wing enthusiasms attracted the attention of the King, who invited him to the general surprise to become the Prussian ambassador in the Germanic Confederation at Frankfort. He thought him one of the few Prussians who was able to work with Austrians and who actually liked Austria; certainly his conservatism would be acceptable. If this had been the case it rapidly ceased to be true after Bismarck's arrival in Frankfort.

The reasons were partly personal—he disliked the attitude of superiority of the Austrian Chairman of the Council of Ambassadors, Count Thun. He was himself seen as arrogant and crude—"He dressed like a gentleman but acted like a boor". But what became clear was that his own objective was German national unity under Prussian leadership.

He had opposed the nationalism of 1848 because it was then identical, it seemed, with liberalism and revolution. To the national cause in the shape of German unity under Prussian leadership he now became devoted, and these years were decisive in giving to Bismarck his basic political purpose. He became not only a critic of Austria but a sympathizer with Russia, and his consistent efforts to keep Prussia neutral during the Crimean War, as later during the Polish revolt of 1863, won him great support in St Petersburg. He was never to change in his view that there must be a genuine accord with Russia in order to guarantee the security of Germany's eastern frontier. But he was determined to try to divert Austrian interests and aspiration away from Germany and towards Roumania and the Balkans, thus imperilling her relations with both Russia and Italy. These eight years from 1851 to 1859 were decisive in his training as a diplomat. In 1859 the King asked him to become the Prussian ambassador in Russia. In 1862 he moved in a similar capacity to Paris. He did not stay there long. Disraeli met him in Paris and was impressed. "Take care of that man", he said. "He means what he says".

What proved decisive, however, for Bismarck's career was his relationship with the King's brother William, who in 1857 became the Prince Regent on the illness and subsequent insanity of Frederick William IV; William became King in his own right on his brother's death in 1861. He was able and industrious, and a good judge of men. In background he was a soldier and an absolutist—on becoming King he declared that he ruled "by the favour of God and of no one else." It was assumed that his wife Augusta and his son, the Crown Prince Frederick (later Emperor Frederick III), who was married to Queen Victoria's daughter, would be liberal influences upon him, but if so their persuasions were ineffective. The beginning of the reign was marked by a sharp constitutional struggle. This was still a period in Britain as well as Germany, when the army was seen as the monarch's to control, and William I placed great faith in a strong military machine. He wanted an increase in the budget for the army, in order to restore the three-year enlistment period, to strengthen the regular army at the expense of the militia, and to expand military equipment. The Prussian legislature wanted a tightly controlled budget and a small army. In the course of this struggle the King even contemplated abdication. In this situation the Minister of War, Albrecht von Roon, persuaded the new ruler to summon Bismarck to guide him, and in 1862 this die-hard Junker from his Pomeranian estates, whose experience had been exclusively in diplomacy, was appointed Prime Minister and Foreign Minister of Prussia.

His solution for the conflict was simple: he dissolved one assembly after another, he muzzled the members and he dismissed all officials who sided with the Assembly. Germany should look, he said, not to liberalism, to speeches and majority votes, but to its own power, to blood and iron. For four years from 1862–1866 he ruled without legislative consent, ran the State and paid an army, which was twice successful in war, without sanction of the Chamber or the people. He realized the strength of feeling against him and carried a pistol in his pocket out of fear of assassination, but his victory against Denmark in 1864 and the lightning war (*Blitzkreig*) against Austria in 1866 gave him immense public and royal standing. In 1866 the Assembly passed an indemnity bill legalizing all his acts during its absence. His success abroad brought him acclaim at home. Moreover, a majority of the liberals split off from the Prussian Progressive Party to found the National Liberals which was to rule Prussia for the next thirteen years. This proved to be the party foundation on which Bismarck's power rested for a decade or more.

But Bismarck's authority was not just the result of his dictatorial methods. It was bound up with the three wars of 1864, with Denmark; 1866, with Austria, and 1870, with France. Success in each of these made his state, and, for his lifetime himself, the dominant forces in Europe.

The war with Denmark arose because of the complications of the status of the two border duchies of Schleswig and Holstein. Lord Palmerston's comment on that status is famous: "Only three men have ever understood it. One was Prince Albert, who is dead. The second was a German professor who became mad. I am the third and I have forgotten all about it." After the Treaty of Vienna in 1815, the two duchies of Schleswig and Holstein, both of which had large German populations, had been united with Denmark in a personal union. Holstein was a part of the German Confederation, and the King of Denmark, as Duke of Holstein, was a member of the Confederation and was represented in the Diet at Frankfurt. During the Revolution of 1848 the Germans in Schleswig and Holstein rebelled against the "Danish foreigners", but their insurrection collapsed when Prussian support was withdrawn.

From the beginning of his ministry Bismarck intended to annex the provinces to Prussia. "I have not the smallest doubt," he said, "that the Danish business can be settled in a way desirable for us only by war." All that was necessary was a favourable opportunity. It came in November, 1863, when the Danish Rigsraad passed a new constitution which Bismarck interpreted as incorporating Schleswig into Denmark and as a violation of the promise that the Danish king had given to Austria and Prussia in the Protocol of London in 1852. The death of Frederick VII brought the matter to a head.

Bismarck concluded an alliance with Austria, probably reasoning that he could eventually pick a quarrel with her over the spoils. On 1 February, 1864, Prussian and Austrian armies crossed the frontiers of Schleswig. The Danes elected to fight, hoping desperately that England would come to their aid. Bismarck selected his moment shrewdly, for the British asked only that the integrity of the Danish monarchy not be violated. By 18 April, the whole of Schleswig was in the hands of the invaders. Abandoned by the Great Powers, Denmark was forced to sue for peace. By the Peace of Vienna, August, 1864, Denmark had to give up the Duchies to Austria and Prussia. By the Convention of Gastein, 14 August, 1865, the Austro-Prussian condominium of the Duchies was ended by dividing them. Austria was given control over Holstein and Prussia over Schleswig.

The legacy of one two-month war was another: the war with Austria over the spoils. It lasted seven weeks. With speedy communications and superb military organization, and with an alliance with Italy that kept her neutral and held out the hope of gaining Venetia from Austria, the Prussians led by their King in person defeated Austria at Sadowa. It was a quick war; it brought Bismarck immense popularity; it was followed by a peace treaty of remarkable and shrewd generosity. The Treaty of Prague (1866) required Austria to recognize the end of the German Confederation, the incorporation of Schleswig-Holstein with Prussia, and the annexation of Venetia by Italy. Austria was to pay a small indemnity of twenty million talers, but she lost no territory.

In 1867 Bismarck consolidated Prussia's position in the north by creating the North German Confederation, a union of twenty-two states and the principalities of North and Central Germany. It was a union of Prussia with all the German states north of the Main—all that is except Bavaria, Württemberg and Baden. A Reichstag was called on the basis of the universal suffrage law of 1849. But real power lay with the *Bundesrat*, which consisted of appointees of the member states. The constitution of the confederation, written largely by Bismarck, was similar to the one adopted by the German Reich in 1871. It made the *Bundeskanzler* the responsible minister of the confederation and the political and administrative head of the government, which was precisely Bismarck's aim. All military forces were pooled and foreign policy was determined by the Federal Government which was dominated by Prussia.

The third and decisive stage came in 1870. Napoleon III was naturally alarmed at the speed and character of German unification. If the three south German states were to join the North German Federation, "French guns", he said, "would go off by themselves". For his purpose Bismarck was very willing that they should. He proposed that a member of the branch of the Hohenzollern family, Prince Leopold von Hohenzollern-Sigmarin, should be a candidate for the vacant throne of Spain, knowing him to be unacceptable to Napoleon III. The French reacted with the anger that he expected to the thought of being encircled by a Hohenzollern empire. Nevertheless, they did not want war. Benedetti, the French Minister, called on King William at Ems, and while indicating his peaceful intentions was rash enough to ask the German government to abandon all claims to the Spanish throne. When Bismarck was sent by the King a telegram describing these discussions he released to the press a version of it which sounded disturbingly like a French ultimatum. Each side treated it as such and France declared war at once.

In less than two months the French army suffered a series of defeats along its eastern frontier, and was forced to surrender on the 1 September at Sedan where Napoleon III was himself captured. Marshall Bazaine surrendered another French army of close on 200,000 men at Metz in October. From September to January 1871 Paris was besieged and bombed by Prussian guns and fell mainly because of hunger on the 28 January 1871. The Peace terms were harsh: she was to surrender to Germany the province of

Alsace and most of Lorraine including Metz; she was to pay an indemnity of five billion francs and a German army of occupation would remain until the indemnity was paid; Napoleon III went into exile and the Third Republic was proclaimed; and most bitter irony of all, the new German empire with William of Prussia as Emperor was proclaimed in the Hall of Mirrors at Versailles. Bismarck himself became a prince.

He was undoubtedly the architect of the new empire and of French defeat. Except where France was concerned he acted, and was to continue to act, with remarkable restraint. His three wars had been carried through at bewildering speed and with immense sureness of touch. His greatest skill of all indeed lay in his foreign policy after 1871. He sought to keep France isolated by setting up the *Dreikaiserbund* which began as a tacit royal alliance against potential revolutions between Germany, Austria-Hungary and Russia in 1872; but by 1881 it had blossomed into a formal and secret pact, in which each party guaranteed its neutrality if one of the three were to be at war with a fourth power (meaning France). It was renewed in 1884 and when in 1887, tensions in the Balkans between Austria-Hungary prevented its renewal, Germany then made a separate Reassurance Treaty with Austria. In this Treaty each ally promised its neutrality unless Germany attacked France or Russia attacked Austria-Hungary. A similar secret Treaty between Germany, Austria-Hungary, and Italy in 1882— renewed every five years up to 1915—guaranteed support for each ally if any were attacked by France. Again, Bismarck presided over the Congress of Berlin in 1878 to prevent the *status quo* in the Balkans being violently upset by Russian successes in her war with Turkey. After 1871 peace and diplomacy, not war, were the essential bulwarks of the new empire he had created. He could speak softly on occasion. It was a foreign policy of restraint and success.

Bismarck was equally successful in creating a constitutional system of autocracy and efficiency. The new empire was a federal union of twenty-five states with a central government in Berlin. The Emperor was Commander-in-Chief of the army and navy and had, with the consent of the *Bundesrat*, the right of declaring war and making peace. The twenty-five states had 58 representatives in the *Bundesrat* and of these Prussia had 17. It was this body which passed legislation and governed the empire. The Reichstag, which was elected by universal manhood suffrage, could not initiate legislation nor dismiss the Chancellor, and was little more than a debating society. The Chancellor, Prince Bismarck, was appointed by the Emperor and responsible only to him. He was supported by an efficient civil service and by, for the most part, a loyal and patriotic public opinion. Bismarck was not only federal Chancellor, Chairman of the *Bundesrat* and head of the Prussian delegation in it, but he was also Prime Minister of Prussia. For the next nineteen years he was in fact the government of Germany.

He left an immense impact in domestic policy. At a time when sweeping social and industrial changes were taking place, he held Germany on a conservative course for two decades. To maintain German military supremacy all citizens were required to be conscripted for military training. He unified the railways, introduced a national coinage and organized an imperial bank. Although at first an advocate of free trade in 1879, he moved over to a policy of protection for home industries. These policies made Germany immensely prosperous. She had a commanding central position in Europe; her access to the Baltic facilitated commerce with Russia and Scandinavia, the Rhine gave her an entry into the Low Countries. The Danube commanded the trade of Eastern Europe. The acquisition of Alsace-Lorraine brought the resources of iron ore to the coal of the Ruhr Valley, and the Ruhr became the centre of European heavy industry.

There was a rapid shift of population to towns and cities—in 1850 less than 3 per cent of the German population lived in cities of more than 100,000, by 1910 it was 30 per cent; Berlin in 1820 had 200,000 inhabitants and by 1920 almost two and a half million—by that time the fifth largest city in the world. Between 1860 and 1910 German railway tracks were increased six-fold, and in the same period her coal production increased from 30 million metric tons to almost 200 million. Great iron and steel empires were created by the Krupp and Thyssen families; and two great shipping companies, the Hamburg-America line and the North German Lloyd line of Bremen, became among the most powerful merchant fleets in the world. Only Russia had a larger population. But whereas that population consisted mostly of uneducated serfs the Germans were well educated. Not only had Goëthe, Heine and Schiller large audiences for their writings, German technical education and scientific skills were outstanding, and her chemical and electrical industries virtually dominated the world. And her dyes and dynamoes were in great demand. To all of this, and because of it, the Germans added immense self-confidence and pride in their new-found national unity.

But Bismarck struck some false notes. The empire he built had enemies. The first of them in his view was the Pope, who, in 1864, in the Syllabus of Modern Errors had condemned secular education and civil marriage and who had in 1870 proclaimed papal infallibility on matters of faith and morals. Until 1870 German history had been notable for its tolerance, especially its tolerance towards Catholics. But in 1871 Bismarck launched what his liberal allies called the *Kulturkampf*, the fight for civilization. He expelled the Jesuits in 1872 and by the May laws from 1872 and 1878 gave the State control over marriage and education, confiscated Church property and tightly controlled the Catholic press. Archbishops, bishops and priests were persecuted, imprisoned or expelled. One result was the rapid development of the Catholic Centre Party as a force in German politics. But this struggle was less between Catholic and Protestant as between those who did and those who did not put the interests of the State above those of religion.

In 1878, however, the accession of the moderate Pope Leo XIII in succession to Pius IX brought a change of policy. The primary reason was that Bismarck came to be more alarmed by the rapid rise of socialism than he was by any threats there might be from Rome. By 1887 most of the anti-Catholic laws were repealed, but a campaign was under way against socialists. In 1878 the Chancellor enacted a series of Exceptional Laws which denied freedom of the press to "socialist machinations dangerous to the common weal". But it was by no means a policy of hostility alone. Bismarck passed a striking number of measures that were indeed the first of their kind in Europe: Sickness Insurance (1883), Accident Insurance (1884) and Old-Age Insurance (1889). These were seen by many inside and outside Germany as models, and were especially seen as such in Britain by David Lloyd George, who enacted similar measures two or more decades later. Despite these measures the socialist cause flourished in Germany. In 1890, the year of the Grand Old Man's retirement, the Exceptional Laws of 1878 were allowed to lapse.

In March, 1888, the Emperor died. Bismarck announced the event in the *Reichstag* with tears running down his cheeks. He himself, now 73, expected dismissal at the hands of the new liberal Emperor Frederick III, but Frederick III, aged 56, was already suffering from that cancer in the throat from which he died 99 days later; and German liberal hopes died with him. His son William II was 29. He was intelligent and sincerely patriotic, but he was also impulsive, erratic and bombastic. A clash between the old man and the new was inevitable, but was more than a clash of personalities. Bismarck wanted to continue the policy of friendship with Russia, whereas the Emperor foresaw an eventual war between the two and preferred war sooner rather than later. Bismarck wanted to continue his campaign for the passing of anti-socialist measures, and was not averse to the stirring up of labour unrest so that he could use troops to crush the red international. The new Emperor saw himself as a "Workers' Emperor" and a "King of the Poor", and did not want to begin his reign with a blood-bath. Moreover, Bismarck had by this time hopes of a Bismarck dynasty in the person of his son, Herbert, who as State Secretary seemed to be in line to be his successor. In 1890 the Prince Chancellor was forced to resign and, as the famous Punch cartoon of the day indicated, the German Ship of State "dropped the pilot".

Bismarck had in 1871 along with the title Prince been given two large estates, Varzin in Pomerania (now in East Germany), and Friedrichsruh near Hamburg where his family still lives. He had used these estates as strategic retreats, places to sulk and brood and plot, and sometimes he would stay in one of them for months at a time. On his resignation in 1890 he became Duke of Lauenburg. He was reconciled to the Emperor in 1894 and died in 1898. His son Herbert retired on his father's resignation, and himself died in 1904.

Frederick William IV had said of Bismarck in 1848 that he "smells of blood and will be useful later". He had been useful indeed. He had not only created the German Empire, he had thereafter limited his aims, averted hostile coalitions and never taken on more than one enemy at a time. He was neither a militarist nor an imperialist but a supreme example of a nationalist, who knew at each shift in the international scene exactly what he wanted and when to call a halt. What was supreme about him was neither his ruthlessness nor his lack of scruple, though he had both of these qualities in abundance, but his moderation in success. Moreover, he had created an empire, and in the process had separated nationalism from liberalism. Like Napoleon III he sensed that nationalism and liberalism were not natural allies, and the state he created was a synthesis of German nationalist pride, Prussian militarism and the federalism of the Hohenzollerns. He made of this blend a state that prospered even as socialism grew. As Bertrand

Russell noted of him: "It was only through Bismarck that German patriotism became respectable and conservative, with the result that many men who had been liberal because they were patriots became conservatives for the same reason." To use a Disraelian phrase, he had caught the Liberals bathing and run away with their nationalist clothes, or, as he himself put it to Napoleon, "Only the Kings make revolution in Prussia". Moreover, this nationalist emotion did move the German people and it overcame their particularist loyalties.

His success came at a time of immense industrial expansion, and that expansion reinforced his political achievements. But he did not create the *Zollverein*, and the industrial development of Germany owed little to him directly; as A. J. P. Taylor has noted, he never saw a coal mine in his life, he was never in the Ruhr and he did not visit the Rhineland between 1871 and 1892. A German Empire in an industrial sense might well have emerged whatever he did or did not do. Even in his change of course from free trade to state control and social legislation in 1879, he followed a European movement away from liberalism. His social reforms, which now seem so original and creative, did not seem important to him—he forgot even to mention them in his memoirs.

But he left a legacy behind in which his prudence and skill were forgotten and the image of him has dominated his own and later generations—the image of blood and iron and of the man of deeds. It is not quite true since he was neither a Jingoist nor a totalitarian. But he had no richly developed conscience, and the success of the blend of militarism and autocracy certainly contributed to Germany's twentieth-century wars and to the Nazi movement. He was venerated by Hitler, who saw in Bismarck and Frederick the Great his greatest predecessors. Bismarck not only created the German Empire, of which the Austrian Hitler saw himself as head, but did so by military *blitzkrieg* and political opportunism; his methods, even more than his goals, were revered by many Germans and by some outside the Reich. If his own interest in or understanding of economic forces was never very sophisticated, economic and technical power were seen to be at best as important as military.

Europe admired Bismarck's success and skill, if never fully aware of his restraint; his great service to Europe as distinct from Germany was his twenty-year effort after 1870 in preserving the Balance of Power, preventing any major clash in the West and ensuring an alliance to protect Germany against the inevitable cry of revenge from France. But he was a nationalist first, and a European only in order to buttress the security of his construct, the German Empire. Ironically, Europe was most in debt to him for his social insurance and welfare measures, which were the first of their kind, which did much permanently to weaken the Socialist movement in Germany, and which, first in Britain and then gradually elsewhere in Europe, were widely imitated.

KARL MARX
(1818–1883)

NOTHING written on Marx can either be composed or read with detachment. This is so not merely because of the passion that Marxism, Marxists and neo-Marxists have excited since his day or because of the wide range of his writing and its effect on great events, but because with him the purpose of political philosophy changes totally. None of his immediate predecessors—the Idealists, Fichte and Hegel, from whom he drew some of his basic principles, the Positivist Comte, with his laws of society, or his contemporary the liberal John Stuart Mill—regarded themselves as social revolutionaries or as departing from the basic cultural tradition in which their ideas had been formed. But with Marx, philosophical positions are taken up of a totally new and radical kind.

His goal was not just to understand the world but to transform it. Marx considered the socialist thinking that preceded his own—especially that of Proudhon and Blanqui whom he sharply critized in *The Communist Manifesto*—as Utopian, whereas he claimed, or Engels claimed for him, that his own was Scientific. Socialism with him became a body of doctrine resting firmly on an economic base. His ideas were rooted equally firmly in a special interpretation of Hegelian philosophy. Seeing all history, however, as a struggle not of ideas or notions but of classes, he held that reconciliation could come only from the abolition of classes, and this gave him an agenda for political action as well as an economic and philosophical system.

The revolution of the proletariat and the classless society that would follow were, he believed, the inevitable consequence of the contradictions inherent in a capitalistic economy. They are, he held, not only likely to occur but are certain to do so. He not only recognized class-hatred as a central fact in history, he saw it as a conscious instrument of revolution. Only through revolution could progress take place. "Force", he wrote in *Das Kapital*, "is the midwife of every old society pregnant with a new one." In other words, his philosophy is a mixture of eighteenth-century French rationalism, of German Idealism and of British and French Utopian Socialism. Yet his theories in the end owe little to all of these sources—except radically to transform them; for his theory of the State is in the end a theory of force and his interest is in action. As the eleventh thesis on Feuerbach asserts, hitherto philosophers have thought about the world, now it is time to change it.

It is of course possible to point to the many contradictions in his philosophy. It is equally easy to attribute his interpretations and his opinions to a brusque temperament, to ill-health, to a sense of unfulfilled ambition, to a long and hard life in London, and to his almost total personal failure to win friends and friendship. Carl Schurz summed it up when he said: "I have never seen a man whose bearing was so provoking and intolerable. To no opinion which differed from his own did he accord the honour of even condescending consideration; every argument that he did not like he answered either with biting scorn at the unfathomable ignorance that prompted it, or opprobrious aspersions upon the motives of him who had advanced it. I remember most distinctly the cutting disdain with which he pronounced the word bourgeois; and as a bourgeois— that is, as a detestable example of the deepest mental and moral degeneracy—he denounced everyone who dared to oppose his opinions. . . ." But none of these things really matter. For many people in many countries came to accept his views, and to act politically on that acceptance. He was more than a thinker, he was a prophet. He was, if not the greatest, certainly one of the most influential political thinkers of the nineteenth century or indeed of all time.

His intellectual development is usually divided into three periods: a philosophical phase from 1840–1845 when he finished his studies at German universities; a socio-political phase from 1845–1850 when he lived and wrote in France and Belgium; and an economic phase from 1850 until his death, when he developed his system of economic theory in London after the failure of the revolutions of 1848, and when it seemed that the chance of radical working class action had become remote. But this is much too simplified and shortened an interpretation of his career.

Karl Marx was born in 1818 in Trier, in the Rhineland, the son of a Jewish middle-class lawyer, Hirschel Marx. The date, the family and the region are all significant. The continent was just beginning to recover from the dislocations of the Napoleonic wars and to suffer the anguish of the Metternich reaction. The 1820s and

1830s were years of intellectual ferment especially in the Rhineland. Marx as a young man was both impressed and depressed by the inhumanity of the industrial system as it was developing around him and in Britain and France. He was conscious of living in an area that was undergoing rapid development and, while he wanted to see modernization take place, he was coming to condemn those aspects of modernization that threatened the sense of identity of his own community. In a similar way Dostoevsky in Russia was horrified by the threats to Russian values that were coming from industrialization and urbanization. Marx's views on this subject make his writing very relevant to students of development in the twentieth century.

The boy was born, however, into a world of solid comfort. His father was a cultured man and the family was accustomed to a background of books and discussion. Rhinelanders saw themselves as culturally superior to the Prussians; to them Prussia was a land of backward Junkers, the Siberia of Germany. This sense of superiority made Rhinelanders very sensitive about Prussia's political control after 1815, especially when the Napoleonic reforms were reversed by Prussian officials. Marx's father found it more and more difficult to practice his Jewish faith, and was converted to Christianity when his son was six. Thus the young man was conscious of being in part German, in part a Rhinelander, and in part a Jew.

Almost as a matter of course he looked towards a university career and studied primarily in jurisprudence and history at Bonn, Berlin and Jena. He mixed with the Hegelians but they were by that time really Hegelian revisionists, and they were trying to liberate the Hegelian logic from its subservience to philosophical and political conservatism. He took over Hegel's view of the dialectic, and saw progress as a result of a clash of thesis and antithesis, a conflict of opposites. But while busy with his thesis for a doctorate at Jena there came the Prussian conservative reaction of 1841, of which he became a savage critic. In the same year his father died and he needed money. In any event he was never—unlike Hegel—an Ivory Tower philosopher; he always sought to combine the theory of politics with organization and action; he was always a man of two worlds, the study and the forum. By nature combative, he turned towards politics and journalism and abandoned his dream of becoming a university teacher. Perhaps the words he wrote in the preface to his dissertation, a preface he did not show to the university authorities, were to be his real creed: "In a single word, I hate all the gods."

He was, until the paper was banned, on the staff of the *Rheinische Zeitung* which he made a powerful radical journal in Cologne, and in 1843 he moved to Paris, accompanied by his bride, Jenny von Westphalen. Until her death forty years later, and despite all the trials and turmoils of his public life, it was a marriage of utter happiness. There were to be four daughters and two sons, but both sons and one daughter died in infancy.

Paris was at this time a hot-bed of socialist activity and discussion. He met Proudhon, the philosophical anarchist ("What is Property? It is theft"), and attacked him savagely in *The Poverty of Philosophy*; he met Heine, Blanqui and in particular Friedrich Engels, who became his life-long friend and later his financial patron. Expelled from Paris in 1845, he moved with other exiled German socialists to Brussels, where he wrote in collaboration with Engels *The Communist Manifesto*, published in 1848. Expelled from Brussels in 1848, he spent a month in Paris. When he returned to Germany in that year, the year of revolution, it was as a fully-fledged and convinced socialist. He found employment as editor of a radical paper, the *Neue Rheinische Zeitung*, but in 1849 had to escape again, this time with a threat of high treason hanging over him. And so, aged thirty-one, he moved to London, and it was in and around 28 Dean Street, Soho, Haverstock Hill and the British Museum that he spent the rest of his life.

For the first few years his circumstances were darkened by poverty and ill health—his young son died of malnutrition and when his daughter Francesca died, there was no money for the funeral—and he survived only by work as a journalist and with an allowance from Engels. He became the organizer and propagandist of the International Communist League. By 1855, however, his circumstances were improving, and he was endlessly engaged with pamphlets, addresses and newspaper articles. In 1864 he helped to found the First International Working Men's Association, whose programme he helped to draft, and which he led through a series of faction-ridden squabbles, especially with Proudhon, until its dissolution twelve years later.

He helped Liebknecht and his associates in Germany to found the Social Democratic Party in 1869. But by that time his reading in the British Museum was beginning to bear fruit, and the first volume of *Das Kapital* was published in 1867. His last eight years,

1875–83, however were embittered and sad. The task of finishing *Das Kapital* proved too great; the next two volumes were prepared by Engels from notes Marx left uncompleted at his death. His wife died. His health declined. He was now committed to a form of intellectual guerrilla warfare with continental socialist like Lassalle, and charges about stealing ideas and bookish indebtedness were freely and waspishly exchanged. He became at the end irritable and testy. The small group who attended his funeral at Highgate cemetery, now a place of pilgrimage, heard an oration by Engels in which Marx was hailed as the "provider of the key to social change"; in terms of social development he had laid bare "the circulation system" of human society.

Marx was a child of German Idealism but he became highly critical of it. In 1846, along with Engels, he published an attack on it under the title *The German Ideology*. "In direct contrast to German philosophy", he said, "which descends from heaven to earth, here we ascend from earth to heaven. That is to say, we do not set out from what men say, imagine, conceive, nor from what man has narrated, thought of, imagined, conceived, in order to arrive at man in the flesh. We set out from real active men and, on the basis of their real life process, we demonstrate the development of the ideological reflexes and echoes of this life process." He moved away, in other words, as Feuerbach had done before him, from Hegel's emphasis on spirit to matter. "Life is not determined by consciousness but consciousness by life." Schiller had said that hunger and love make the world go round, and Marx in a sense agreed. To use his own phrase about Feuerbach, he turned Hegelianism on its head. "While the French and the English at least hold by the political illusion which is morally close to reality, the Germans move in the realm of the pure spirit and make religious illusion the driving force of history". He could not accept Hegel's Idealist interpretation of history, which ascribed to ideas and ideals a controlling power over historical change. Nor could he accept Hegel's view of the Prussian state as the realization of the idea of humanity. In his essay, "Towards the critique of Hegel's philosophy of Right", printed in 1844, Marx merged his study of German philosophical humanism with an interest in British and French economic realism.

Marx was writing at a time when the Industrial Revolution was rapidly developing man's wealth and at the same time condemning large numbers of workers to soul-destroying life in a grim environment. He believed that the explanation for the eruption of European revolutionary ideas lay in the harsh economic realities of the world of the new industrial regions of Europe. In his view the decisive feature of the new society was that the worker by signing a wage contract surrendered all share in his product. The product of his labour became a commodity which he had to buy in the market place. Moreover, the work in which he was engaged was not necessarily one he himself chose; he was the victim of his inheritance and his location. The increasing division of labour reduced the worker's share and sense of partnership in his work, and removed from his labour its genuine creativity. He was the prisoner of a form of industrial slavery.

Moreover, the value of the goods he produced far exceeded what he got as wages—the difference being known as "surplus value". While this provided the profits for the capitalist and funds for the business, and by doing so financed technical advance and expansion, it also led to more intense competition and the elimination of less efficient firms. Employers and their work people were in these circumstances often thrown out of work and into the ranks of the proletariat; and in this way the worker not only lost his fair share as a producer but had his own purchasing power restricted and his own dignity threatened. As competition increased so did the division of labour, and the means of production accumulated in fewer and fewer hands. Not only did the modes of production and distribution foster competition and social bitterness, they produced an intricate and vulnerable society, in which most workers and some employers felt themselves at once alienated and victimized. And it was, he believed, these modes of production, by giving rise to specific forms of private property and social classification, that determined the structure of each epoch in history.

One way of putting this is to say that Marx transferred Hegel's principle of dialectic from the world of ideas to the actual living situation, and that he did so by incorporating with it the labour theory of value. It is certainly true that the dominant motives in life were, he believed, materialist, and that the actions of men were governed by the struggle to control the means of production— land, labour and machinery. He saw the clash not as a clash of ideas, but of classes, between those who own the machinery of production and those who do not; and history became for him the record of this struggle—in his famous phrase, "The history of all hitherto-existing society is the history of class struggle". "The final causes of all social changes and political revolutions are to be sought", he said, "not in men's brains, not in men's better insight into eternal truth and justice, but in changes in the modes of production and exchange." If it was to end in a synthesis, as he believed it would, that synthesis would take the form of a communist society in which private property would in the end be abolished. He saw this as a historical process, so that just as the capitalist class had ousted the landowning and feudal classes, so the working class would, by revolution, replace the capitalist. They would do so by the dictatorship of the proletariat, by which he meant a dictatorship over the prolerariat by their chosen leaders. In other words, he not only transformed Hegelianism, but produced a totally new body of philosophic and economic thought which was in its implications truly revolutionary. Economics he saw as a science of history as well as a method of analysis.

In seeking to understand Marx one must distinguish clearly between terms like Society, Government and the State. By Society Marx meant all who live and work together to satisfy human needs, and by Government, he meant the administrative machine by means of which these needs would be satisfied and furthered. But where the State was concerned he was original and penetrating, even if its characteristics have changed since he wrote. In his eyes the State was "the organized public power of coercion to enforce the decisions of that group or class which controls the government". Its special characteristic was that it controlled and operated an armed organization standing over and above the rest of the population. As his friend and collaborator Engels said, the State presupposes a public power of coercion "separated from the aggregate body of its members". And in their eyes this power was the power of one class to oppress another. To them there was no "ought" in politics, no ethical obligation; there was only a "must" backed in the last analysis by force.

But Marx was a pamphleteer, a publicist and a propagandist for action, as well as a philosopher. In *The Communist Manifesto* he advocated a series of specific reforms, some of them now either enshrined in law in many countries, all of them accepted as the goal for socialist and communist republics. They can be summarized quite baldly:

1. The expropriation of landed property, and the use of rent from land to cover state expenditure.

2. A high and progressively graded income-tax.
3. The abolition of the right of inheritance.
4. The confiscation of the property of all emigrants and rebels.
5. The centralization of credit in the hands of the state, by the establishment of a state bank with state capital and an exclusive monopoly.
6. The centralization of transport in the hands of the state.
7. An increase in the state ownership of factories and instruments of production, and the redistribution and amelioration of agricultural land on a general plan.
8. Universal obligation to work and the creation of labour armies especially for agriculture.
9. The unification of agricultural with industrial labour, and the gradual abolition of the differences between town and country.
10. The public education of all children. Abolition of factory labour for children in its present form. Unification of education with economic production.

What is clear now in the late twentieth century is that, however original Marx's views were, he is open to major criticism on a number of basic points. First, if it is possible to read history in terms of thesis and antithesis, why will this dialectical process halt with the coming of Communism? And in any case does the thesis hold throughout history that society is stratified into two classes, and that the oppressed class can perceive its interests and has the necessary wisdom to promote them? There is no record of a class struggle marking the collapse of a primitive communism and the arrival of slavery. Throughout the history of Greece and Rome there are many stories of group clashes, but there is no evidence that the downfall of Rome was the result of the struggle between two classes, one basically pro-slave and the other basically pro-feudalism; nor is there any evidence that feudalism was necessarily a higher order of civilization than the society of ancient Greece or Rome. As late as 1848 Marx expected a bourgeois revolution in Germany, which in the *Communist Manifesto* he likened to the revolution of the seventeenth century in England and of the eighteenth century in France. No such bourgeois revolution ever came in Germany. Nor was the October Revolution of 1917 in Russia a contest between a feudal class and a new bourgeoisie. As history, the doctrine of the class struggle is impossible to sustain.

Again, the striking feature of the late nineteenth century in the advanced countries, and of the twentieth century throughout much of the world, is precisely that the working class has acquired greater and greater privileges and much economic and political power. The State far from being the instrument of capitalism has moved in with laws to provide social and health insurance, to recognize trade unions in law, and indeed to foster factory and industrial development on a considerable and on a very healthy scale. The same Blue Books and Public Health Reports on which Marx drew to compile, in *Capital*, his vivid picture of the contrast between rich and poor in capitalist England led governments to act.

Societies have been transformed not by cataclysm but by law, and peacefully. Moreover, the whole development of the managerial revolution has separated the ownership of industry from its technical management, so that neither the story of recent past nor any agenda for present action can be based on a picture of the wicked capitalist risking his own resources and exploiting everyone else's; and there has been a vast development of workers' participation at all levels of industrial society. The petty bourgeoisie has not identified its interest with the working class. Marx did not indeed foresee the extent to which the salariat would grow, nor expect it to be so hostile to the proletariat. His view of the class struggle proved to be altogether too simple. His famous paragraph in *Capital* now reads as dated and extravagant.

> "While there is thus a progressive diminution in the number of capitalist magnates (who usurp and monopolize all the advantages of this transformative process), there occurs a corresponding increase in the mass of poverty, oppression, enslavement, degeneration, and exploitation; but at the same time there is a steady intensification of the wrath of the working class—a class which grows ever more numerous, and is disciplined, unified and organized by the very mechanism of the capitalist method of production. Capitalist monopoly becomes a fetter upon the method of production which has flourished with it and under it. The centralization of the means of production and the socialization of labour reach a point where they prove incompatible with their capitalist husk. This bursts asunder. The knell of capitalist private property sounds. The expropriators are expropriated."

Proletarians, Marx said, had nothing to lose but their chains. In fact they had much more to lose than their chains, and they did not really want to unite.

Again, Marx's indifference to ethical questions, to the fundamental question of what is the public good, is a sharply limiting factor in his work. In all his writing, production is seen as the major and indeed sometimes the sole criterion. There is no acknowledgement that non-economic factors do play a formative part in life. Nor is there any emphasis on the interaction of intellectual and spiritual factors with those that are purely economic. There are political, social, racial and religious barriers among work-people, as among employers, which have not always been overcome by economic factors, and have sometimes, as in 1914, prevented consistent unity of action by the working class. A major phenomenon in recent history has been the bid for power by an army or a totalitarian party concerned less with social justice than with power-mania. Fascism revealed the elements that were missed in an interpretation that was based purely on economic man. In other words, there are many omissions from Marx's contribution.

Nevertheless, it is impossible to underestimate the profound contribution he made to sociological thinking and to the study of politics and history. If he was less gifted as a prophet than many Marxists have imagined, the concepts of historical materialism, surplus value and the nature of the dialectic process have been of immense value to philosophers and sociologists. His idea of the power of the proletariat makes him far more significant a figure than either Gladstone or Bismarck. His faith in class-hatred as a factor in history allied to a doctrinaire temperament made him the great advocate of revolution. Foreseeing the age of the masses, he is scornful of classical liberty as a chimera. He described the age of *laissez-faire* capitalism as the age of "liberty, equality, property and Jeremy Bentham". For the whole generation brought up in the late nineteenth and to many others in the twentieth century, Marx was the great visionary figure and it is impossible to assess the role played by Lenin or Jaurès or a host of socialists and communists in France, Italy and Germany without a study of Marx. He said of himself that he was not a Marxist, but Marxism has dominated and conditioned the political thinking of twentieth-century Europe.

The motive power of his thought and action was less scientific than he claimed; his view of history was too simple; and his impact came less from his scholarship than from his fierce moral indignation and his awareness, and his reader's awareness, of the persistent inhumanity of man to man throughout history. But he reminds us that the central problem in politics is not the seizure of power, where he proved a poor guide, but the purposes to which it is put to use. He imposed himself on his contemporaries, says E. H. Carr, and he has imposed himself on history, with all the sheer force of a unique and dominant idea.

This eccentric philosopher, loved and lovable in his stormy and difficult domestic setting, outwardly crusty and ill-tempered, was one of the great Europeans of the nineteenth century. His economic interpretation of history and his philosophy of dialectical materialism were to become the dominant methods of approach to history, philosophy, economics and social studies; Marx's view of development and progress in history as being the result of thesis—antithesis—synthesis has become the accepted basis of much European thinking, even by those who deny both his materialism and the primacy he gives to economic forces. Moreover, this philosopher of the study was a failed 48-er, and his own motivation was never just understanding for its own sake but action. *The Communist Manifesto* was one of Europe's first blueprints for an international-style revolution. Marx's activities in organizing the International Working Men's Association in 1864 and his stormy involvement in it kept the idea of revolutionary Socialist activity alive; and both the Communist International of 1919 and contemporary international terrorist movements derive logically from his propaganda and his activities.

HENRIK IBSEN
(1828–1906)

HENRIK IBSEN, poet and virtual creator of a new kind of social drama, was born in the small town of Skien in southern Norway on 20 March, 1828. His genesis is the more remarkable in that Norway, at the time under Swedish domination after centuries under the Danes, had almost no literature of its own, although the eighteenth-century Norwegian-born dramatist Ludwig Holberg had reached celebrity in Denmark, writing for Danish readers.

The written Norwegian language, *riksmaal*, was practically indistinguishable from Danish, but there was a movement to use the natural rhythms and idiom of peasant dialects which was to attract Ibsen himself for a time later. The theatre in the capital, Christiania (now Oslo), was wholly in the hands of Danish writers and Danish players, and long before his name reached Europe Ibsen was to become part of an attempted theatre revolution to create a national Norwegian drama. In this the rediscovery of indigenous ballads and folk-tales was to play a part, and affect Ibsen's earliest work as a poet and writer of verse plays. Beginning as a slowly progressing revolutionary in a new-born national theatre, in which he took more practical part as a producer than as a writer, he was to develop only late in life, by constant experiment, into the progenitor of a form of psychological drama, questioning social and moral values, which was to revolutionize the theatre throughout the world.

As with so many writers of genius, his parentage and background provide few genetic clues to his gifts and their direction. His mother before her marriage was said to have been fascinated by travelling players (the nearest thing to a theatre the district could provide), and even after marriage she retained the habit of playing with dolls, possibly using them like theatre puppets. (Solness's unhappy wife, years later in Ibsen's *The Master Builder*, was to mourn to the point of mental imbalance the loss of her dolls in a fire). Ibsen's father, Knud, was a merchant of merchant-mariner stock, in a good way of business until a financial collapse and bankruptcy in 1836 reduced the family to poverty and a deprived existence in rural districts.

Henrik was the second son (the first had died) and persistent local rumour later suggested that he was really the illegitimate child of his mother's previous fiancé, Tormod Knudsen, who came frequently to Skien on business; but although Henrik in youth, his tongue loosened by drink, is said to have admitted that he believed this, there is actually no evidence of it. In later life Ibsen bore a striking likeness to his presumed father, Knud Ibsen. The fact remains, as Ibsen's biographer Michael Meyer has written, that "bankruptcy and illegitimacy recur spectre-like throughout his work", and these early home troubles may have had more influence than actual education (which in Skien was limited) on the boy.

Ibsen left school in 1843, before he was fifteen, and went to work as apprentice to an apothecary at Grimstad, a much smaller town and a centre for the building of sailing ships. *Pillars of Society* was to draw much on Grimstad for its atmosphere. He lived on the cramped premises and at the age of eighteen became the father of an illegitimate son by a servant girl, ten years his senior. For the next fourteen years his meagre resources were to be stretched to their limit to support this child, living with its mother in the country.

When the chemist's shop changed hands in 1847 Ibsen's position changed also for the better. He had always been a keen reader. One of his earliest influences had been a history of London, left at his family's home by a visiting sailor: it is the work over which the young Hedwig, in *The Wild Duck*, pores so avidly. Now, he read books by Dickens, Scott, Holberg and (his favourite) Voltaire, and at last made intellectual friends, all young and with radical views. These were fomented by the widespread European revolutions and abdications of 1848. "All this", wrote Ibsen later, "had a powerful and maturing effect on my development." He was nineteen, now taking private lessons from a tutor, for whom he wrote in 1848 a composition, *On the Importance of Self-Knowledge*, which was to become a major theme in all his later works.

"While a great age thundered outside I found myself in a state of war with the little community within which, by the circumstances of my work, I sat imprisoned," he wrote. The state of war with society, and the sense of imprisonment in a stifling small provincial community, were to persist when he became a dramatist, but his first play, the blank-verse tragedy *Cataline*, was written at this time under the influence of Sallust's *Cataline* and Cicero's speeches. Ibsen, however, here as in later plays, diverged from history in order to penetrate character, and the play already showed the self-questioning theme in its depiction of Cataline, who in his opening lines acknowledges a voice within his soul urging him on to "a better, nobler life than this", and in the last Act queries:

> "Is life then not an unabating struggle
> between the hostile forces in the soul?"

This psychological conflict, as well as the tragic character of the reformer doomed to failure by his own mistakes, were to run like a thread through Ibsen's plays, personified by Cataline, Brand and Julian and Apostate, Gregers Werle and John Gabriel Borkman. Technically he was to change his methods spectacularly, from historical verse plays to modern social drama; but his psychological impetus, although it was to develop immense subtleties, grew from seeds sown in his youth. *Cataline* was published privately by his admiring friend Schulerud in 1850, though later the two young men had to use the unsold copies for wrapping paper. It was the first Norwegian play to be published for seven years, and the only one to reflect the spirit of world rebellion.

Ibsen wrote, a quarter of a century later, in a preface to a revised edition: "I found that it contained a good deal that I was able to acknowledge." It has customarily been written off by Ibsen scholars as unactable, but in fact it was performed in London, with Donald Wolfit as Cataline, in 1936, and the critic Audrey Williamson in her book *Theatre of Two Decades* wrote of it: "This Roman historical drama has, in theme, some similarities to Shakespeare's *Julius Caesar*: it is a study of revolution and the clash of democratic and tyrannous principles, but lacks the dramatic cohesion and subtlety of character which keep Shakespeare's play alive in the theatre."

In 1850 Ibsen left Grimstad for Christiania, with some idea of studying medicine. This intention was short-lived. He was already deeply immersed in poetry and philosophy, with a revolutionary bias, and took an enthusiastic part in student activities. He came under the influence of the workers' movement founded by Marcus Thrane, who had visited Paris and the London of the Chartist Manifesto. His horizons were spreading towards Europe and in September, 1850, his second play, *The Warrior's Barrow*, achieved production at the Christiania Theatre. Laura Svendsen, the actress who as Laura Gundersen was to create the parts of Ellida in *The Lady from the Sea* and Gunhild Borkman in *John Gabriel Borkman*, played Blanka. The play, about a pagan Viking, was moderately praised but unimportant; but it gave Ibsen prestige and free seats at the theatre, which enabled him to practise as dramatic critic, as well as political commentator, in the student paper, *The Man*. Although entirely unmusical throughout his life, he also covered opera, and remarkably anticipated both Wagner and his own disciple, Bernard Shaw, by calling for a new form of music drama with greater harmony between music and text. This was in a review of Bellini's opera, *Norma*, which inspired Ibsen to write a political parody of the story.

The Man, with the whole workers' movement, was suppressed, when Thrane and Ibsen's friend Abilgaard were imprisoned in July, 1851. But that same year Ibsen was offered the post of resident dramatist at the new Norwegian Theatre in Bergen, which had been founded two years before by the famous international Norwegian-born violinist, Ole Bull. Ibsen moved to Bergen in November, 1851, and stayed at the theatre until 1857. In the next few years he wrote a number of plays, including *St John's Night*, *Lady Inger of Østrat* (his first play in prose) and *The Feast at Solhaug*, which were produced for a few performances only. Lady Inger was a character of many doubts and conflicts, at once courageous and cowardly, and psychologically an obvious forerunner of Mrs Alving, Ellida, Rebecca West and Hedda Gabler. The play dealt with an early Norwegian rising against Danish rule, and although a failure was a step forward for Ibsen as a dramatist.

Ibsen's major work at the theatre was as producer, and it was mainly in this connection in 1852 that he was given a grant to travel with two of the company's actors to Copenhagen, Dresden, Hamburg and Berlin, to study theatre conditions. He took a particular interest in scenic design, for he was himself a good artist, and in Dresden, as later in Italy, he found much inspiration from paintings and sculpture.

In Copenhagen he saw his first four Shakespearean plays—*Hamlet*, *King Lear*, *Romeo and Juliet* and *As You Like It*—as well as Mozart's *Don Juan*, and admired the famous tragedian Michael Wiehe, whose acting must have underlined the defects of that of the young, inexperienced Norwegian players at his theatre in Bergen, where the stage conditions were primitive, no classics were performed, and the repertoire of plays had to be chosen, for financial reasons, mainly to suit the indifferent popular taste of the time. Although Gogol, Turgenev and Ostrovsky were already writing plays of some social realism they were totally unknown to Ibsen

(*The Government Inspector*, 1836, and *A Month in the Country*, 1850, did not reach Norway until 1890). Nevertheless his European trip widened Ibsen's horizons, and he brought back valuable books of costume and design.

He stayed at Bergen six years, until in 1857 he was released to take up the position of director at the recently opened Norwegian Theatre in Christiania, which had followed Ole Bull's lead in attempting to attract national actors and writers. It was a theatre in a working-class district, attracting a very different audience from the major Christiania theatre, which employed only Danish actors and played to socially affluent audiences. Again, its patrons were not educated to accept anything but the lowest popular fare and Ibsen found his appointment even less culturally rewarding than that at Bergen. But it enabled him to marry, in 1858, Susannah Thoresen, whose step-mother, Magdalene Thoresen, had herself written plays.

Magdalene later described Ibsen as "a silent, withdrawn person whom no one got closer to than he, Ibsen, wished". It seems to have been generally true (and accounts for a certain detachment—which some actors find chilling—in the character-dissection in his plays). Nevertheless, his marriage to Susannah was to prove a successful partnership for many years. They had one son. Susannah was a strong-minded woman with a great understanding of Ibsen's work, and must have been the source of much encouragement in the face of the frustrations under which he was having to work at this time.

Despite his frustrations as a producer, Ibsen's talent expanded as a dramatist. In 1858 *The Vikings at Helgeland* was produced at his theatre with (as in the case of so many later Ibsen plays) explosive controversial effect. It had been turned down by the larger Christiania theatre, and over-taxed the resources of the Norwegian one. As Hans Heiberg has written in *Ibsen: A Portrait of the Artist*, "it presages the claws of the lion". Eighteen years later, in 1876, it was to be the first Ibsen play staged outside Scandinavia, when performed at the Hoftheater in Munich where he was then living. In London, Gordon Craig designed a famous production for his mother, the actress Ellen Terry, and the play was also performed during the nineteen-twenties at the Old Vic, which in 1923 had staged the first English production of *Peer Gynt*.

In Norway *The Vikings* was Ibsen's first substantial success. By 1900 it had received more performances in Christiania than any of

Ibsen's more mature works. Bjørnstjerne Bjørnson, a younger rising dramatist with whom Ibsen throughout his life was to be involved in a love-hate relationship, described it as "the best play that has yet been written in Norway". But controversy raged at its nationalistic language and tone, and it was three years before the major Christiania theatre condescended to stage it, with Laura Svendsen in the part of Hjørdis. It was then an immediate success.

Ibsen's next play, *Love's Comedy*, was published in 1862. Although this work, on the theme of the dilemma of commitment, was not performed until eleven years later, its satiric scorn for society and its institutions, and theme of a young man and woman who rebel against marriage, stimulated the usual antagonism and discussion. Ibsen maintained strongly that marriage should be based more on spiritual ties than passion, if it was to be successful, and probably only its rigid verse-system precludes this play of very modern ideas from revival today.

During these years with the Norwegian Theatre it was as a poet that Ibsen was still most admired. His poem *On the Heights* anticipated the loneliness and call of the mountains which were soon to become themes of his first great play, *Brand*. Michael Meyer has termed this poem "perhaps the finest of his non-dramatic works". In 1862 Ibsen also wrote *Terje Vigen*, a long narrative poem of the Napoleonic Wars, which as late as 1916—ten years after Ibsen's death—was made into a silent film by Victor Sjöström, the famous Swedish director who made his last appearance as an actor in 1957, in the leading part in Ingmar Bergman's film masterpiece, *Wild Strawberries*.

In 1862 the Norwegian Theatre became insolvent. The following year Ibsen was given a part-time position at the Christiania Theatre, at last committed to a more Norwegian policy, and there, in 1864, he was able to produce his own prose play *The Pretenders*, set in Norway in the early thirteenth century. It was the first of the epic quartet which was to be completed by *Brand*, *Peer Gynt*, and the long-delayed *Emperor and Galilean*, the 10-Act play about the Emperor Julian's fatal attempt to combine the best in Christianity and paganism, which Ibsen was to take nearly a decade to write. *The Pretenders* was a palpable success, but too far removed from the style of work to which the theatre's administrators and their patrons were accustomed to be given an important place in the repertoire.

Disillusioned, refused an official pension such as had been granted to Bjørnson, and dismayed by his countrymen's failure to support the Danes, who had been invaded by German armies, Ibsen took his wife and son out of Norway altogether, to live in Rome. On the journey across the Alps he was struck, as he wrote, by the "bright light" of the south, which "suddenly revealed itself to me, gleaming like white marble. It was to affect all my later work."

It is probable that Garibaldi, whose autobiography Ibsen borrowed from the Scandinavian Club library in Rome, influenced his next great work, the verse-drama *Brand*. "I offer neither pay, nor quarters, nor provisions. I offer hunger, thirst, forced marches, battle and death", Garibaldi had written; and the essence of Brand's tragedy is in the lines:

> "require All or Nothing.
> No half-measures. There is no forgiveness
> For failure."

This titanic play in rhymed four-beat verse, like its successor *Peer Gynt*, was not written for stage performance, and both dramas for this reason gave Ibsen a free-ranging technique with infinite opportunities for experiment. Nevertheless, the more sophisticated techniques of staging available to the modern theatre have shown both plays to be brilliantly actable, although it was 1959 before *Brand*, in an heroic performance by the actor Patrick McGoohan and the '59 Theatre Company, was actually staged in London. Its emotional power and imaginative scope proved, in the event, overwhelming, and threw a new light on Ibsen as a creator of poetic tragedy, far removed from the sociological dramas on which his European name mainly rested. The influence of Michelangelo, "Ibsen's master" as he has been called, also cannot be overlooked in the creation of Ibsen's colossal and anguished anti-heroes. *Brand* was recognized officially by the grant of a State pension to Ibsen, thereby relieving him of the threat of poverty.

Peer Gynt, the epic verse drama which followed, was, as often with Ibsen, an antithesis of the previous play's characterization. If in Brand the ego was sublimated with disastrous consequences to himself and all around him, in the rapscallion Peer we see the ultimate emptiness—like the onion, in his most famous soliloquy, which peels away to reveal nothing—of the totally selfish man for whom individualism is the only concept. There was admittedly something of Ibsen in both characters; even his socialism had a curious ambivalence at times.

Peer Gynt is satiric and comic where *Brand* was tragic. It drew on folklore and transformed it for political parody, some of it lost on us today, although the theme of the individual living in a fantasy world, unable in the end to perceive the dividing line with reality, remains remarkably contemporary. The play is a sprawling masterpiece, half-fantasy, half-morality. The Boyg, identified with the Sphinx, is a riddle of life which cannot be answered, and in the lunatic asylum scene we see individualism literally run mad: "Here a man is himself, and can utterly sever Everything else from himself for ever." The symbolism is exhaustive, and Audrey Williamson, in *Old Vic Drama*, has commented on the play's "finely correlated technical machinery in which even the smallest episodes are designed to heighten the theme, and to provide a suggestive link with later character developments and events". This was written of the revealing (and probably only) stage production of *Peer Gynt* in its entirety, given by the Old Vic Company at Sadler's Wells in London in 1936, which followed a shortened version by the same company in the autumn of the previous year. This revival (with a dinner interval) was a spectacular public success and the highlight of the Old Vic's distinguished record of *Peer Gynt* productions. The play was not produced at all on the stage until nine years after it was first published in 1867. It was *Brand* which established Ibsen in Scandinavia as a pioneer of revolt against dead tradition, having the same explosive effect there, as Meyer has pointed out, as *Pillars of Society* on German audiences and *A Doll's House* on the whole western world.

The technical mastery of *Peer Gynt*, revealed in the full version, was to be repeated and heightened in all Ibsen's later realistic dramas, which became the foundation of dramatic technique in the modern theatre. In 1868 Ibsen moved with his family to Dresden and *The League of Youth* was published, and produced at the Christiania Theatre, in 1869. Its social satire once again sparked off controversy, but the same year Ibsen revisited Stockholm for a conference and was selected by King Carl XV as one of the two delegates from Norway and Sweden to attend the official opening of the Suez Canal. Ibsen, whose passion for medals of recognition was to be much remarked upon (perhaps the natural result of his prolonged fight for acceptance against attack, and continuing financial hardship), celebrated this event with a fine poem on the desert around the Nile. His major volume of *Poems* was published in 1871.

At last, in 1873, emerged the mighty *Emperor and Galilean*, which did not receive its first stage production until 1896, by the Civic Theatre in Leipzig. "What I desired to depict were human beings, and therefore I would not let them talk in 'the language of the gods'," Ibsen wrote to his young English disciple, Edmund Gosse, of the illusion of reality which he had tried to create in this vast play, which freed an ancient Grecian theme from classical conventions of manner and language. In this sense, although it is historical and contains some over-flown passages, the play formed a bridge to the modern dramas he was about to write.

In 1874 Ibsen revisited Christiania, but remained unreconciled to the political attitudes of his fellow-countrymen, which provoked in him much cynicism. He believed that politicians, once they achieved power, compromised on their ideals: a view in which he would not be unsupported today. He thereafter lived alternately in Munich and Rome. In 1872 his total earnings had still only reached £56, in spite of his growing fame. He was dependent on his meagre state grant, but fortunately both he and his wife Susannah were frugal in their household requirements. It was just as well, for this situation was long to continue, partly owing to the fact that Norway and Denmark had failed to enter into European copyright agreements.

Pillars of Society, in 1877, was the first of his great line of modern social dramas. Its theme was the sending to sea of rotten ships for commercial reasons, a theme inspired partly by Ibsen's knowledge of the sea town of Grimstad, and partly by a world controversy on the subject which in England, following Samuel Plimsoll's famous attack in the House of Commons in 1868, resulted finally in the Merchant Shipping Act of 1876. The play's questioning of the morality based on money was to spill over into world drama and politics for many decades.

It was an implied theme also of his next play, *A Doll's House*, 1879; the first blast of the trumpet for Women's Liberation which was to deafen the eardrums of the world. "There are two kinds of moral laws, two kinds of conscience, one for men and one, quite different, for women", wrote Ibsen in *Notes for a Modern Tragedy* (1878). Although *A Doll's House* is very much an expression of Ibsen's view of the struggle of individual versus society, and might have employed a man as protagonist for the purpose, women's emancipation was a subject in which he had long been interested, having early met Camilla Collett, the Norwegian feminist pioneer, who had gone so far as to complain of Solveig's passivity in *Peer Gynt*.

To say that the world was shaken by his message is an understatement of fact, although the outrage was soon to be dwarfed by the almost literally speechless horror which greeted the publication of *Ghosts*, 1881, about the unmentionable subject of venereal disease; a play refused production in Norway and for long more or less swept under the world's carpet as a subject quite unmentionable in society. Nora's bid for independence in *A Doll's House* had its sympathizers (although the leading German actress of the part insisted on introducing a "happy ending", with Nora brought to her wifely senses by her husband's indication of the deserted children in the nursery); elsewhere the door she slammed on her husband's home reverberated not only on the world's stages but in political and feminist groups not unready for the challenge. The play owed something in plot to Ibsen's friendship with Mrs Laura Kieler, who in desperate circumstances had forged a cheque and been repudiated by her husband as a criminal.

A Doll's House was immediately produced in Copenhagen and Norway, and in the same year as the Norwegian production (1880) William Archer's translation of *Pillars of Society* reached the English theatre for a single performance at the Gaiety Theatre, the first English production of any Ibsen play, heavily abridged, adapted and even retitled. Later *Ghosts* was to be particularly savaged by English critics, but the dogged persistence of Ibsen's admirers, headed by Edmund Gosse, the first English critic to recognize his qualities, William Archer, his first English translator, and Bernard Shaw, won him an honoured place eventually on the English stage.

Between 1881 and 1890 Ibsen produced a line of masterpieces: *Ghosts*, 1881, *An Enemy of the People*, 1882, *The Wild Duck*, 1884, *Rosmersholm*, 1886, *The Lady from the Sea*, 1888, and *Hedda Gabler*, 1890; yet his total income for the period was under £6,500. His fame, however, grew, not least from the controversy surrounding *Ghosts*, which, despite its most immediately apparent subject, is also very much a reflection of Ibsen's view of the fatal effects of a woman's compromise in not having the courage of her convictions, and leaving her husband. Mrs Alving was the answer to the critics of Nora. *Ghosts* was also a play about "the joy of life", stifled by what Henry James, writing on *Hedda Gabler* in *The Scenic Art*,

When this photograph of Bismarck and his young wife was taken, he was the rising bureaucrat, the minister of ultra-royalist leanings—but not yet the "man of blood and iron". That came later, when he engineered the defeat of Austria and the humiliation of France at Sedan. As such we see him in the photograph below—the virtual creator of the German Empire which endured until the close of the First World War in 1918.

W. E. Gladstone's intellectual powers were matched by a splendid physique: the photograph (*left*), showing him engaged in wood-chopping at Hawarden was taken in 1877, when he was not far short of seventy. *Above:* the "Grand Old Man" of his last premiership.

Karl Marx was only twenty-four when he became editor of the *Rheinische Zeitung*. Because of his virulent attacks on the established order, the newspaper was soon closed down: the cartoon (*above left*), dating from 1843, shows him as Prometheus chained to his broken printing-press, while the Prussian eagle preys on his liver. *Above right:* Marx as the world-famed founder of international socialism.

described as "the pervasive air of small interests and standards, the sign of limited local life". It was to be a constant Ibsen theme, frustrating Hedda Gabler and Mrs Alving alike.

Ghosts, rejected viciously by the old and middle-aged, found its champions in the young. Students read it, openly and defiantly or surreptitiously, all over the world, and young German actors and actresses used it for audition purposes long before it was allowed to be performed on the public stage. Its superb construction and psychology have kept *Ghosts* alive in spite of medical repudiation of the cause and effects of Oswald's disease; for as Bernard Shaw wrote: "The universality of Ibsen makes his plays come home to all nations."

It is one of the oddest facts of dramatic history that *Ghosts* achieved its first production in America—at Chicago in 1882. This was a presentation in the original language, for Scandinavian immigrants, which later toured Minneapolis and cities of the mid-West. It was over a year before any European production followed.

An Enemy of the People landed Ibsen in trouble with liberals, owing to Dr Stockmann's rejection of majority opinion in favour of an educated minority. But Ibsen elsewhere explained the line "The minority is always right" in another way: "I mean the minority which forges ahead in territory which the majority has not yet reached". As he well knew, Ibsen was, in this advanced position, echoing the political reformers. It had been a theme of John Stuart Mill (whose work he admired) in *On Liberty* ("The initiation of all wise or noble things comes and must come from individuals; generally at first from some one individual"); and Ibsen's disciple Bernard Shaw was to propagate the idea, with similar attacks and misunderstanding. It is notable how Dr Stockmann's "the strongest man in the world is he who stands alone" anticipates Shaw's Caesar and also his Saint Joan, who makes not dissimilar remarks. It is incidentally interesting that Ibsen, according to William Archer, had "the most vivid sympathy" for Charles Bradlaugh, the radical English politician; and that Dr Stockmann was the favourite part of Stanislavsky, who played the role with the Moscow Arts Theatre in Petrograd at the time of the 1905 rebellion and massacre, to terrific audience response.

An Enemy of the People, with its theme of a spa town's officials savagely resisting the doctor's revelation of contaminated baths, was Ibsen's last wholly "realist" play. *The Wild Duck* with its symbolistic attic, a world of human fantasy and escape from reality, set the key for the "white horses" and millrace of the couple's suicide in *Rosmersholm*, the towers of *The Master Builder*, Solness's frantic climb in search of lost youth, the Rat Wife in *Little Eyolf*, and the misty and enigmatic background of Ellida's Stranger in *The Lady from the Sea*.

Although Ibsen complained, doubtless with truth, of critics "eager to find a double meaning, a hidden symbol, in every word or action"—that constant complaint of imaginative and elliptical writers—the symbolism remains. It is a return in a new prose form to the poetry of his youth; partly inspired by his own sense of age, of youth (as Solness felt) thundering at the door, and partly also by the decline of his marriage and his successive platonic infatuations in old age with the young girls Emilie Bardach and Hildur Andersen (the pianist granddaughter of his one-time Bergen landlady), both of whom may have contributed to the character of Hilda Wangel in *The Master Builder*.

On another level, *The Wild Duck* was a further change of direction for Ibsen: the reverse side of idealism, demonstrated through the crank, Gregers Werle, who must blurt out the truth and destroy human happiness in the process. "Nothing Ibsen has written makes us respect him more", wrote the English critic Desmond MacCarthy, reviewing a performance of the play in 1905. "He had always declared that, 'What is wanted is a revolution in the spirit of man'; in this play he faces the reformer's worst trial, the conviction of the fundamental weakness of human nature."

John Gabriel Borkman (1896) and *When We Dead Awaken* (1899) finish Ibsen's work. They are studies respectively of a potential if criminal greatness (the financial wizard) eclipsed by prison, and of the artist's egoistic creative urge and its shattering effect on other human beings and the nature of love. In the end Rubek (Ibsen, the artist) ascends the mountain with the woman his art sacrificed, and perishes like Brand. Ibsen had returned to his old theme, solitariness and the call of the mountains.

What still distinguishes all these plays is Ibsen's continued mastery of dramatic technique and increasing subtleties of characterization; he explores the whole spectrum of the human psyche and remains the unique master of feminine psychology, one of the few dramatists whose parts are worthy of great actresses. From Nora and Mrs Alving to Hedda Gabler, the coward living vicariously through the profligate she drives to suicide, Ibsen's range of feminine character is remarkable and extraordinarily subtle. Perhaps the best writing on his last phase is Shaw's in *The Quintessence of Ibsenism* (extended in 1913 to include the last four plays):

> "Ibsen now lays down the complete task of warning the world against its idols and anti-idols, and passes into the shadow of death, or rather into the splendour of his sunset glory; for his magic is extraordinary potent in these four plays, and his purpose more powerful. And yet the shadow of death is here; for all four, except *Little Eyolf*, are tragedies of the dead, deserted and mocked by the young who are still full of life."

What is certainly true is that Shaw was the greatest dramatist to work under Ibsen's influence, and also, with Gosse and Archer, the major force in spreading appreciation of Ibsen in England. *An Enemy of the People* has been described as the most Shavian of Ibsen's plays; but without Ibsen not only Shaw's sociological comedies, such as *Mrs Warren's Profession* (full of echoes of *Ghosts*), but many of his later more imaginative works would, if written at all, have taken perhaps a different colour. Shaw described *Heartbreak House* as Chekhovian, but Captain Shotover, with his platonic attachment to the young girl Ellie, has more than an echo of the Ibsen titans and eccentrics.

Ibsen died on 23 May, 1906, having done no work for several years owing to a stroke. His last words, characteristically enough, are said to have been "To the contrary"; but he was given a State funeral. He had returned to Christiania in 1891, affluent at last and honoured in the theatres of the world. The effect of his work has been continuous. Dramatists notably influenced by him, apart from Shaw, included John Galsworthy in England, Brieux in France and Ugo Betti (in particular in *The Burnt Flower Bed*) in Italy. Ibsen's works have been little translated into cinema: an early attempt was by the famous actress Alla Nazimova as Nora in a silent film of *A Doll's House*. Television and radio have proved more successful media for bringing his work to the mass audience.

It is in the theatre that he continues to command the highest regard; and it is only in recent years that techniques and influences which first emerged from his works have begun to be supplanted by others (although some of these revert to a style not dissimilar to that of *Peer Gynt*), and symbolism has taken a new form through Ionesco, Samuel Beckett and Harold Pinter.

LEO TOLSTOY
(1828–1910)

Count Leo Nikolaevich Tolstoy, author of two of the greatest novels ever written and later the exponent of a revolutionary, wholly Christian way of life, was born on 28 August, 1828, at his ancestral estate of Yasnaya Polyana ("Bright Glade") some 130 miles south of Moscow.

His mother died when he was two years old and his father seven years later, when the family was living in Moscow for the sake of the children's education. The family life both in town and country (the Tolstoys owned several farms and estates) was nevertheless extremely happy; the children were looked after by an adored Aunt Tatiana, and Leo was completely devoted to his three elder brothers and sister, as they to him. The position of the estate servants and labourers as serfs did not early trouble him. He took their slavery and punishment as a matter of course, as children brought up in positions of wealth, in a long-established social system, almost invariably do.

On the death of his father Leo, as the youngest son—under the Russian system—inherited Yasnaya Polyana, and although part of the house had later to be sold to pay his youthful gambling debts (and was removed elsewhere by the new owner), Tolstoy lived largely in what remained of the mansion and estate for over eighty years.

As they grew older the Tolstoy boys all proved to have questioning and enquiring minds. In particular, Nicholas, the eldest, deeply influenced Leo, who was greatly affected by his brother's death from consumption in 1860. "The humility which Leo Tolstoy extols in theory", wrote Garshin, according to Leo Tolstoy's son, "was applied by his brother directly to life." Nicholas's death came long before the crisis which led to Tolstoy's own total change of life, but his character and memory lived on in his mind, subtly reinforcing his own conclusions. Another brother, Sergei, became the inspiration of Volodia in Tolstoy's autobiographical trilogy *Childhood*, *Boyhood* and *Youth*, and his sister Maria, who had an illegitimate daughter by a Swedish lover and later became a nun, was the prototype of Luba in *Boyhood*.

At sixteen years of age, Tolstoy followed his brothers into the University of Kazan, but he failed his examinations partly owing to a passion for social life and a good deal of dissipation. Like Young Marlow in Goldsmith's *She Stoops to Conquer*, an intense shyness with aristocratic women turned him towards the company of women of a lower class. Highly sexed throughout his life, he was in his later development to become a moralist acutely aware of the conflict between the physical and the spiritual in man's nature, culminating in the ferocious rejection of lust and the sexual side of marriage in *The Kreutzer Sonata*, a product of his old age. In the interim both Pierre in *War and Peace* and Levin in *Anna Karenina* were reflections of Tolstoy's own struggle with his own nature, and to some extent philosophical and sociological reflections also. But in spite of womanizing and heavy gambling, and of an absorption with fashion and party life, the young Tolstoy characteristically retained the capacity for equal mental activity.

Already he was speculating on the great enigmas of life: its meaning and the reason for suffering. He was also an avid reader from childhood, not only of novels by Turgenev, Dickens and later George Eliot, but of the works of Jean-Jacques Rousseau, which had an inevitable effect on his political and educational thinking. The affinity with Rousseau was so strong that Tolstoy once remarked of Rousseau's works that he felt as if he had written them himself. It was at this time that he began to keep a diary, a habit he continued to the end of his life, thus providing much illumination for posterity on his thought-processes and complex psychological battles.

In 1847, when he was only nineteen, he had a spell in hospital with venereal disease, a condition which caused him considerable mental anguish. He left the university and returned to his estates, already concerning himself with the welfare of his serfs. A year later he returned to Moscow and the following year to St Petersburg, where his gambling debts reached a climax, although he briefly studied law at the university. His social life continued until 1851, when his brother Nicholas, now an artillery officer, returned to the Caucasus, taking Leo with him as a cadet. This Caucasian expedition was profoundly to influence Tolstoy's writing. He was to remain there for three years, becoming an expert horseman with a penchant for dangerous adventure, narrowly escaping capture by the Tartars and absorbing the spirit of the scenery and people.

He continued both heavy reading and debauchery, and in 1852 published his first story, *Childhood*, semi-autobiographical in a few respects (like much of his later work) and owing something to the influence of the childhood sequences of Dickens's *David Copperfield*, a work he specially loved and admired. It was published in a journal, *The Contemporary*, and Tolstoy described it to the editor as the first part of a novel, *Four Periods of Growth*. Although *Boyhood* and *Youth* followed, the novel as such was never written; but already Tolstoy's work, it has often been pointed out, combined the individualizing detail of a Dickens or a Gogol with the psychological analysis of a Stendhal. Stendhal was also to be the inspiration of Tolstoy's methods of describing war in *War and Peace*. "I am greatly indebted to him. He taught me to understand war," Tolstoy wrote. "Re-read the description of the Battle of Waterloo in *La Chartreuse de Parme*. Whoever before so described war? Described it, that is, as it is in reality?"

The Cossacks, although not published until 1863, the year after his marriage, was also born directly out of Tolstoy's experiences in the Caucasus; so was one of his last stories, *Hadji Murad*, based on the history of the Russian penetration of the area. In *The Cossacks* the whole life of the Caucasus is seen through the eyes of Olenin, a young traveller from Moscow with romantic preconceived notions of the area who fails in the end to become absorbed into the community. "The form of *The Cossacks*," writes John Bayley in *Tolstoy and the Novel*, "gave Tolstoy a great deal of trouble. He worked on it intermittently for ten years, between 1852 and 1862, interrupted by his service in the Crimea and visits to Europe."

Tolstoy was stationed at Sevastopol in 1854 after the allied landing in the Crimea and was present at the siege, noting with the clinical eye of the author the incidents of war and the amputations of the wounded, which Florence Nightingale, England's "lady with the lamp", was to make a matter of history. Some of this, with Stendhal influence, was to penetrate *War and Peace*, but the immediate results were two works, *Sevastopol in December* and *Sevastopol in May*, both published, with *Memoirs of a Billiard Marker* and *The Woodfelling*, in 1855 (a *Sevastopol in August* followed the next year). *Sevastopol in May* was the more artistic of the two works: it is, writes R. F. Christian in *Tolstoy: A Critical Introduction*, "the first of Tolstoy's works to strike an uncompromisingly hostile attitude to conventional thinking about war, and, within the limits of censorship, to expose and denounce militarism." Its opening picture of "the angel of death hovering unceasingly" over the trenches will strike a chord in the minds of those who remember another war in another century, and "the angels of Mons". Its literary sense of ironic contrast is already striking:

> "Hundreds of newly bloodstained bodies of people who, two hours before, had been full of various lofty or trivial hopes and desires lay with stiff limbs in the dewy vale of flowers which separated the bastions from the trenches and on the smooth floor of the mortuary chapel in Sevastopol; hundreds of people with curses and prayers on their parched lips crawled, writhed and groaned, some between the corpses in the vale of flowers, others on stretchers, on beds, or on the bloodstained floor of the ambulance station; and still, as on previous days, the dawn broke over Sapun Hill, the twinkling stars grew pale, the white mists spread from the dark roaring sea, the rosy dawn lit up the east, the long purple clouds spread across the pale blue horizon; and still, as on previous days, the sun rose in power and glory, promising joy, love and happiness to all the awakening world."

In *The Woodfelling*, too, Tolstoy dealt with militarism and military types, categorizing them, with further subdivisions, into three groups: the submissive, the domineering, and the reckless (both the amusingly and the viciously reckless).

The next year Tolstoy left the army. He published several more minor works and resumed an active social life including membership of the literary circle, the "Contemporary", of which Turgenev was the leading spirit. In the summer at Yasnaya Polyana he conceived an abortive project to free his serfs, but the next year, 1857, he spent largely abroad in France, Switzerland and Germany. In Paris he witnessed an execution by guillotine which made him a lifelong fervent opponent of capital punishment.

Although he continued to publish stories, Tolstoy largely retreated from literature in the next few years, devoting his time to farming and hunting and founding both the Moscow Musical Society and a school for peasant children on his estate. Here he found great happiness as a teacher of original style, having total success in interesting the children, and it was in connection with this project that in 1860 he travelled to Germany again to study educational theory and met Froebel. In 1861 he was also in Italy, and in Brussels, where he met Proudhon. In addition he visited London, where he was bored by a three-hour oration by Palmerston in the House of Commons and moved to tears by a public reading given by Charles Dickens. His admiration for Dickens was expressed not only in his work: his son Sergei, in his book written in old age, *Tolstoy Remembered*, recalls the family pet and favourite setter named Dora, after David Copperfield's young wife.

Tolstoy continued teaching, and also publishing an educational magazine, until 1862, when he married Sonya Behrs, an eighteen-year-old girl from a good social background in Moscow. Tolstoy was full of theories about marriage and hoped to educate a young wife to suit his tastes; but the marriage was to cause him both family happiness and disaster. He perhaps did not help matters, at the outset, by insisting that his youthful bride should read his diary, a confessional of all his earlier dissipations which were not psychologically soothing to a woman who was, in the words of her eldest son, jealous by nature.

Both husband and wife now kept a diary, showed the entries to each other, and increasingly lacerated each other as the years passed. "The resultant frictions grew more severe with time," wrote Sergei Tolstoy, although in fact Tolstoy's faithfulness to his wife, once married, seems to have been complete. But Sonya missed the bright life of the town; she was isolated on the vast, unapproachable estate and increasingly burdened with a succession of pregnancies, and in the end the burdens defeated her sense of proportion, exploding in neurosis and self-dramatization.

Yet at first there was a certain mutual devotion and happiness: the family circle made its own entertainments and Tolstoy was a loving and entertaining father, reading the children novels by Jules Verne and Dumas. The two daughters, in particular, grew particularly close to him and more antagonistic towards their mother than the boys. They were deeply imbued with their father's ideas. And in the first years of marriage it was Sonya who sustained Tolstoy in his writing, copying out *War and Peace* more than once by hand in the days before the invention of the typewriter.

Tolstoy started work on *War and Peace* in 1863, the year after his marriage. He had begun by planning a novel about the Decembrists, the young intellectual officers who had brought back from a Russian campaign in Europe new ideals of political and social enlightenment, and planned a *coup d'état*. Most of them were executed, or exiled to Siberia, under Nicholas II. Pierre, a key character in *War and Peace*, was to be one of them; but Tolstoy found his historical interests going back in time and in the end he did not, as at one time planned, even depict Pierre as a Decembrist in old age. He had found the whole vast canvas of 1805–1812, with its conflict of the great Russian general Kutuzov and Napoleon, sufficient unto itself. He would not even term his monumental work a novel: "It is not a novel, even less is it a poem, and still less a historical chronicle. *War and Peace* is what the author wished and was able to express in the form in which it is expressed." It is worth noting by foreign readers that the Russian title is *Voina i Mir*, and *mir* in Russian means not only peace but both universe and community. Its full implications therefore are virtually untranslateable.

This great merging of history and fiction may not fit into Tolstoy's own not entirely lucid definition of a novel; but then neither does *Don Quixote* and many other panoramic works, including those by Gogol and Dostoievsky, as Tolstoy noted. The history was transformed into psychological studies of people in the upheavals of war: even in the case of Kutuzov, that formidable one-eyed colossus of strategy and personal fascination, Tolstoy suppressed certain facets—the known womanizing for, instance, and aggression—for a greater purpose. It is the story of Kutuzov and Napoleon and their opposed concepts of war; but it is also the story of two families intertwined by that war and their own passionate involvements and relationships, weaving a human pattern among the triumphs and disasters of history.

The great battles are meticulously reconstructed from research, but never pedantically. Natasha with her girl's indecision of attachment, all sincere and absorbing at the time; Prince Andrey with his Tolstoyan prevision of death; Nicholas Rostov finding the way to courage in battle; Pierre who gains Natasha in the end, his character a complex centrepiece, a Tolstoyan commentary, to the whole work—these show the wonderful psychological subtlety and sense of character development Tolstoy had attained from his experience and intuition, in addition to creating innumerable other characters who act both in their own human right and as a philosophical spring.

Tolstoy uses coincidence without self-consciousness to interweave his characters and intensify his plot-line; he absorbed the influence here of Sir Walter Scott, another of his favourite novelists. Another influence was the philosopher Schopenhauer, both in the awareness of death and sense of fatalism in the story. The individual will is always in Tolstoy hedged by accident of circumstance. It was Isaiah Berlin who pointed out, also, that Tolstoy's conception of history resembled in many ways that of Marx, of whom he had never heard at the time he wrote *War and Peace*; and that this applied to his sense of personal history as well as the history of nations.

Tolstoy's first draft of *War and Peace*, called *1805*, appeared in 1865: succeeding volumes appeared until the fifth and sixth (the final) in 1869. The following year Tolstoy began studying drama and the Greek language, becoming able, it is said, to master Herodotus in the original in a remarkably short time. It was during this year that he began to think about *Anna Karenina*, his first "real novel" as he termed it, but it was long before he actually started on the project.

War and Peace had brought fame, but in 1871 Tolstoy had an illness and went for convalescence to his farm in Bashkiria, where his son Sergei remembered with nostalgia his recovery, his activities on the farm, and arrangement of Bashkiri horse races in their traditional form. Tolstoy also planned a stud and bought some fine stallions, not for the last time in his life; his love and understanding of horses was a feature of his work. The death of Vronsky's mare Frou-Frou in the steeplechase was to be one of the most significant scenes in *Anna Karenina*, a symbolic anticipation of the rider, Vronsky's, later responsibility also for the death of Anna. And in 1885 (although it had been written earlier) Tolstoy published an imaginative story, *Strider*, on the life and death of a horse, some of it narrated by the horse itself and poignant in effect. "The consequences of being different (a piebald and a gelding)" writes R. F. Christian, "the themes of alienation, injustice and the inconstancy of love inevitably arouse pity; while the vision of human beings and their system of private property, incomprehensible from a horse's point of view, provides the sort of opportunity for trenchant and well-aimed satire which some earlier writers found in the juxtaposition of European and oriental civilizations based on widely different conventions". It was, in fact, not a realistic study of animal psychology, but a reflection on human society written with compassion on the plight of the animal.

After his return from Bashkiria, Tolstoy still showed no sign of resuming work on a novel. The vast enterprise of *War and Peace*, which had included research at Borodino on the actual battlefield, had perhaps drained him creatively. In 1872 he published primers for children called the *A.B.C. Books*, in connection with the school at Yasnaya Polyana: working with characteristic thoroughness and originality at the arithmetic and astronomy sections (for which he sat up all night examining the stars).

These school books were a great success and went on selling for many years. His educational experiments also included entrusting the teaching of village children to his own young children: this also, according to his eldest son, was a surprising success. He did work intermittently on an abortive novel on Peter the Great, but in 1873 returned to his estate in Bashkiria, raising a fund during the famine in the province. However, at last the same year he returned to his three-year old, half-forgotten idea for *Anna Karenina*, in addition to planning new primers, and he wrote to his friend Strakhov in May, 1873, "This novel, the first I have attempted, I'm taking very seriously." The first instalment was published in 1875 and the final one in 1877. The following year *Anna Karenina* appeared in book form.

Anna Karenina, no less than *War and Peace*, has caught the imagination of the world. Its canvas is domestic and social, more concentrated than in *War and Peace*. Its study of a woman caught in the toils of an uncontrollable passion, isolated from the society whose rules she has defied, and finally driven to her death by the discovery that life does not stand still and the *liaison* is disintegrating under pressure, is penetrating psychologically and notable, at that time, for its honesty. The book is a reflection on society, but far more on human relationships: the cheerful, likeable rake Oblonsky, Anna's brother, and his long-suffering wife Dolly, and the happier alliance, after storms *en route*, of Levin and Kitty, are set as contrasts to the rash and illicit union of Anna and Vronsky.

The contrasts are all psychological, and bring their own problems and their own solutions or disasters. Anna's inability to love her illegitimate daughter by Vronsky as she loves her son, whom she has lost, by Karenin, is one of the book's revelations of the unexpected quirks of human nature; and Karenin himself is an ambivalent figure, tied to convention yet capable of fleeting pity for Anna, and sympathy in himself. Levin takes the king-pin position of Pierre in *War and Peace*, a complex figure whose spiritual questioning and agricultural experiments parallel, to some extent, Tolstoy's own. As Merezhkovsky wrote in *Tolstoy as Man and Artist*; "And so by the motions of muscles or nerves we enter shortly and directly into the internal world of his characters, begin to live with them, and in them."

Yet for all the emphasis on character reaction to circumstances, *Anna Karenina* also follows Tolstoy's basic sense of fatalism. Anna's suicide is the natural, inexorable consequence of her first, fatal decision to live with Vronsky whose, comparatively shallow and physical-based character finds it impossible, in the end, to satisfy Anna's craving. He has other interests, she none. But it is part of the imaginative subtlety of Tolstoy's drawing of character that he does not, like many novelists, depict them only responding to the major theme of plot and circumstance; they have a natural human resilience that simultaneously copes with tragedy and the mundane details of life and observation. Even Anna, at the station preparing for suicide, is momentarily seized with the idea that life is still perhaps worth living, and at her death Tolstoy comments: "The candle . . . flared up with a brighter light than before, lit up for her all that had been dark, flickered, began to go dim, and went out for ever." It was Shakespeare's "lightening before death", long understood by genius.

The suicide, the fatalistic view of Anna's life, was built into the novel from the start. Tolstoy had been profoundly influenced by the similar suicide, under a train, of the mistress of a neighbouring landowner at Yasnaya Polyana. He had seen the young woman's body, with her dark hair, and been haunted by it. It was, in every sense, the starting point of his novel.

It was after *Anna Karenina*, in the 1880's, that Tolstoy's rift with his wife became painful and irreconcilable. It was the result of new, deep thinking on his part and a concentration of his writing time on the Gospels and problems of theology. Dogma and much of the Bible he came to reject as completely as Thomas Paine had rejected them, in *The Age of Reason*, almost a hundred years before, although in spite of his attachment to the even earlier teachings of Rousseau, which influenced the whole eighteenth-century age of the enlightenment, it is doubtful if he had ever read Paine.

His theological writings led inevitably to a severance from the orthodox Christian church (which ultimately excommunicated him) and the embracing of social equality not in theory, but as far as possible in practice. "His whole order of life changed abruptly", wrote his son. "He rose early, tidied his room himself, pumped water from the well and rolled it home in a barrel, chopped wood, made boots. He stopped drinking wine, became a vegetarian, and tried to give up smoking, although it was only in 1888 that he actually succeeding in doing so."

This spartan personal life, and seeking for humility, were accompanied by a wish to reject all royalties on his work and give the money to social causes: a plan that so bitterly provoked the antagonism of his wife that he was forced to abandon it. As a slave to his conscience he made over the estate and the book money to her and his children, living on at his home as a tenant in increasing friction, and tormented by a sense of the difference between his actual situation, still living in surroundings of comparative luxury, and his ideals. He was a man, as his son wrote, who lost his happiness through compassion for the world's miseries. Yet politically he did not satisfy the growing Russian liberal movement either; for his doctrine was total passivity in the face of provocation, a line of non-resistance which was later deeply to influence Gandhi in India. (A comparative interest in religions, including those of the orient, was part of Tolstoy's study in later life.) He warned, nevertheless, that revolution was inevitable, and came in the last year of his life to the view that "No one is guilty in this world": the real culprits were the conditions under which human life was lived, and the environment.

His wife in particular resented the change in his writing and its concentration on theology and social ills, although in 1886 Tolstoy wrote the most admired of his plays, *The Power of Darkness*, a tragic view of peasant life, and in 1890 the savage indictment of sex and marriage, *The Kreutzer Sonata*. His works were now widely censored, but they were published in translation and his house became a constant place of pilgrimage for Russian and international admirers, all of whom he received patiently.

In 1898 his *What Is Art?* showed his now almost complete rejection of normal literary values, dismissing his own works as well as those of Shakespeare and many others, and making his criterion for excellence a work of art's ability to appeal to the majority, educated or uneducated. "Great works of art are only great because they are accessible and comprehensible to everyone". It was a criterion instantly rejected by Bernard Shaw, in a lively review in the *Daily Chronicle* of 1898; but the essay was not unwise in some of its wider points of reference, as Shaw realized, in spite of "the inevitable obsolescence of an old man's taste in art". It was Tolstoy's social premises that interested him. "In vain do we spend hours in a highly superior manner in proving that Tolstoy's notions are unpractical, visionary: in short, cranky; we cannot get the sting and startle out of his flat challenge as to how much we have done and where we have landed ourselves by the opposite policy. No doubt the challenge does not make all of us uneasy. But may not that be because he sees the world from behind the scenes of politics and society, whilst most of us are sitting to be gulled in the pit? For, alas! nothing is plainer to the dupe of all the illusions of civilization than the folly of the seer who penetrates them." What Shaw probably did not know was that *What Is Art?* was written partly to obtain money to help a persecuted religious sect, the Dukhobors, to emigrate to Canada.

In 1899, at last, Tolstoy published another full-length novel, *Resurrection*, far more a social document and criticism than his previous ones and therefore less highly rated, but the result of immense research into the penal code, official inertia, details of prison life and prostitution in prisons. He had visited a friend of his son Sergei in prison in Moscow, a young man condemned to Siberia for revolutionary activities. This was the initial spark that ignited the work.

The story of *Resurrection* is one of expiation. Nekhlyodov (a character first encountered in Tolstoy's *Boyhood* and *Youth*, but greatly developed) finds himself on a jury trying a prostitute, Maslova, for murder, and recognizes in her the young servant girl he had seduced on his rich relative's estate, long ago. Feeling growing responsibility for her plight, he follows her to Siberia and wishes to marry her; but for his sake she ultimately rejects him for a platonic marriage as social helpmeet to a Christ-like eccentric. The whole book is a rejection of sex in totality; but it is also an uncompromising rejection of what Pierre, in *War and Peace*, had already referred to (in strangely modern anti-Establishment terms) as "the system", a whole social order of incompetently and inhumanly administered "justice" and punishment, that, its opponents claim, degrades those who administer it as much as the criminal. It was not a new outlook for Tolstoy: "The state is a conspiracy for the purpose not only of exploiting the citizens but of demoralizing them as well," he had written in a letter in 1857.

Maslova, in comparison with Natasha and Anna Karenina, remains an enigmatic figure, a stranger to Nekhlyodov to the end of the book, when he gazes into her "unfathomable squinting eyes", the eyes of a woman who has endured every form of degradation yet finally, by some mysterious process, has attained a resurrection and a purity of the spirit he cannot understand.

Tolstoy said that the only two works of his last period that he valued were *Hadji Murad* and *The Live Corpse*, the story of a man who pretends suicide to release his wife, but finds in the end ironically that only real suicide is the solution. Nevertheless common consent places *War and Peace* and *Anna Karenina* at the head of his many and varied works, and it is an irony that so much concerned marriage. "He presents the *marriageness* of marriage," writes John Bayley, "more directly and exhaustively than any other writer. In *Family Happiness* he envisages it; in *War and Peace* and *Anna* he describes it; in *The Kreutzer Sonata* he denounces it."

In 1910, when he was eighty-two years old, his own marriage, with his wife's increasing neurotic outbursts and suicide attempts, became finally unbearable. "It is as if I was the only sane man in a madhouse, run by madmen; my family does not understand the torment that I live in", he had written in his diary. He left home, took a train journey to an undecided destination, and died from a chill in the station-master's house at Astapovo. Most of his sons and daughters, who largely sympathized with him, found out where he was dying and were with him at the end; but his wife, on doctor's orders, was admitted only after he became unconscious. Thousands flocked to his funeral, and the world showed itself for once fully conscious of the passing of a great genius, and in his way a great and good, although deeply tormented, man.

His influence lingers on most of all through his novels, *War and Peace*, *Anna Karenina* and *Resurrection*, which are still widely read and have been several times filmed: the Greta Garbo impersonation of Anna Karenina becoming as classically famous, in its own special brand of suffering and personal magnetism, as the original. Hemingway, notably among modern writers, was influenced by *War and Peace* and *The Cossacks*, and Thomas Hardy's annotated copy of *War and Peace* shows how strong was its influence on his Napoleonic epic poem, *The Dynasts*. In Tolstoy's own time, Chekhov's story *My Life* was inspired by Tolstoy's sensitivity to the gap between man's ideas and the world as it is.

Although his political attitude was non-violent, he remains a figure of special honour in the Soviet Union, for he was one of the first to preach the need for social and judiciary reform, in so many directions, to a world public.

SIGMUND FREUD

(1856–1939)

ONE would like to offer another definition of existence, not the Cartesian "I think, therefore I am" nor, as has been suggested, "I suffer, therefore I am", but: "I seek, therefore I am." Human beings are insatiably curious and in all of us, buried beneath the habits of routine, suppressed by the increasing difficulty of finding it, is a thirst for adventure and discovery.

In former times the outer world was the oyster, luring to exploration, but now, except for the ocean depths, we know it and have tamed most of it. It shrinks—breakfast in London, lunch in New York, dinner in Tokyo—and with energies pent up, proliferating races rage against one another for dominance of territories long since inhabited and familiar. Is there no alternative to destroying ourselves through frustration and, as we cannot all take a weekend in space, is there no territory left to explore? Yes, indeed there is: ourselves. Here is a *terra incognita* of vast, possibly limitless proportions and as man once, of necessity, explored his physical environment to subdue it to his will it may well be that we must now explore those inner regions lying beneath the conscious mind, with the same object and for the same ultimate purposes: survival and the continuance of evolution.

Sigmund Freud was a pioneer in this daring adventure, and in case we should doubt whether this seemingly calm and inscrutable professor could really be compared to a Columbus or a Stanley let us hear what he said about himself. "I am not really a man of science, not an observer, not an experimenter, and not a thinker. By temperament I am nothing but a *conquistador*—an adventurer— with the curiosity, the boldness and the tenacity that belong to that type of being." Aged thirty, he wrote to his fiancée: "My ambition will be satisfied in learning to understand something about the world", and he confessed: "I am violent and passionate with all sorts of devils pent up that cannot emerge." Josef Breuer, a Viennese physician who led him onto the path to psychoanalysis, called him "an infinitely bold and fearless person", and on this Freud commented: "I have often felt as if I could joyfully cast away my life in a great cause." The cause became the exploration of the human psyche, the jungle in the mind. The tool, or machete, became psychoanalysis, free association coupled with the interpretation of dreams; the territory discovered was the dynamic unconscious with infantile sexuality; the new map became Freudian theory; and the minds investigated were those of mentally sick people, whom today few of us, even in self-protection, would be inclined to distinguish fundamentally from the so-called normal.

Freud's investigations were heroic enough, as we are all reluctant to face the truth about ourselves, but the climate of Vienna, where his great discoveries were made, was peculiarly difficult for the development of his work. The *conquistador* needed all his courage. Firstly, he was a Jew, eldest son of the second wife of an obscure cloth-merchant from Freiberg in Moravia, the family having settled in Vienna when the young Sigmund was four. In a city where social acceptance was a matter of genealogy and anti-Semitism was rife, the Freuds counted for less than nothing. No Jew could become a professor, for instance, unless he had powerful backing from influential Gentiles. Thus from the start the social environment was indifferent if not hostile.

As for a sexual explanation of the aetiology of mental illness, there were two enormous obstacles to its acceptance. One was the current medical attitude to such illness. In the 1890's, when Freud first voiced his opinions, psychology was a static, purely descriptive science dealing with conscious mental processes and the understanding of "madness" had not gone much beyond Shakespeare's famous definition, the theological concept of diabolic possession or conjectured physical causes. Some superficial electric stimulation of the skin, warm baths, rest, a few words of advice, and most doctors were glad to be relieved of such patients, whom they suspected anyway of suffering from inoperable brain tumours. But far more dangerous was the hornet's nest of sex. In a schizoid society where the right hand refused to know what the left hand was doing, the suggestion that sexual disturbance had a direct connection with mental sickness was abhorrent; even worse was the assertion that this was not adult sex (whatever that might be), but a sordid amalgam with residues from something called "infantile sexuality", things to do with sucking and excreting, with auto-eroticism and wanting to rape mother and murder papa. Here the unforgiveable crime was being committed. Not only adults but innocent little children, who flocked starry-eyed to Jesus in coloured engravings, were being attacked by the Jew Freud daring to call them "polymorphously perverse". Ostracism, violence, hatred was the response of human beings who refused to accept their humanity, and across the years comes to us the voice of the Hamburg professor who as late as 1910 crashed his fist on the table at a congress of German psychiatrists and roared: "This is not a topic for discussion at a scientific meeting; it is a matter for the police!"

But in 1885 these convulsions were yet to come. In that year Freud went to Paris to study under the greatest neurologist in Europe, Professor Charcot, who ran the Salpetrière Hospital where he was experimenting with hypnosis in connection with hysteria. Freud had started a medical career in 1873, studying at the University of Vienna and himself specializing in neurology, later gaining some experience of psychiatric cases after he had qualified as a doctor. At that time, hysteria with its baffling physical symptoms and character disorder was usually swept under the carpet by the medical profession as an insoluble phenomenon. The underlying cause was assumed to be a structural fault in the nervous system, but none could be found. What then was wrong with such patients?

At the Salpetrière Freud watched as Charcot hypnotized non-hysterical patients, producing in them by suggestion the exact symptoms of hysteria. Charcot ascribed the fact that they could be hypnotized at all to neurological degeneration, but as hypnosis was obviously a psychological process Freud asked himself whether there might not be a psychological cause for the symptoms of genuine hysteria. Returning to Vienna, he found that his friend and medical colleague, Josef Breuer, was actually relieving these symptoms by hypnosis, combining suggestion with the "cathartic" method, invented by a patient of his, Fräulein Anna O., now famous in psychoanalytical literature, who insisted in talking out her troubles in what she called the "talking cure" or "chimney sweeping". By this method she managed to revive traumatic experiences with the emotions attached to them.

Freud himself now took up hypnosis with hospital and private patients, bit by bit using less suggestion and more of the talking-out process, until in 1893 he and Breuer published a joint work entitled *Studies in Hysteria*, which established that the disease can be produced by psychological conditions in which highly charged emotional material shut off from the conscious mind has become inaccessible to a direct effort of memory. This discovery had led to a new concept of repression: an automatic, compulsive locking away of emotions whose release, the patient obscurely felt, would swamp and imperil the personality. They were locked in the unconscious mind, now seen by Freud and Breuer not as a kind of waste-paper basket for inert and de-energized memories, as hitherto assumed, but as essentially dynamic with drives so powerful that their repression could produce crippling physical symptoms.

But what were these drives? From a study of the copious clinical material collected by both men Freud saw that they were nearly always sexual in nature, urges laden with fear or guilt that had been repressed in childhood or infancy. There was no doubt about this, nor of the tremendous resistance opposing their acceptance into the adult conscious mind. Indeed, Breuer himself, who had helped to uncover the facts was the first to deny their implications and only a year after publication of the *Studies* he dropped out of further collaboration. Later, when Freud was stressing yet more strongly the significance of sexuality in the development of neuroses, he came to realize that Breuer had merely been the first in time to "show the reaction of distaste and repudiation which was to become so familiar to me . . . my inevitable fate".

From now on, almost until his death which occurred from cancer in London in 1939, after the Nazis had reluctantly given him an exit visa when they occupied Austria, Freud treated patients at his home, often more than ten a day in sessions lasting twenty minutes to start with, later expanding to fifty minutes, one person coming as often as five times a week over a period of months. He abandoned hypnosis (he was not a good hypnotist in any case) and adopted the method of free association still used today. In this, the patient lay on a couch and was encouraged to say anything that came to his mind of a personal and emotional nature, however irrelevant, obscene or nonsensical it might seem, on the principle that, as iron filings are drawn towards a magnet, so the associations would slowly reveal the buried material that was causing the sickness.

The method worked despite the strong resistances encountered and to his astonishment Freud found that in many cases the underlying trauma (from the Greek word meaning a wound) was a sexual experience in early life involving one or both parents. It seemed that Vienna was full of unscrupulous adults who had erotic relations with their children. Could this possibly be true? The experiences were certainly recounted in every vivid detail, with all the accompanying emotions of desire, fear or guilt. They sounded true, but, to Freud's even greater amazement, careful investigation revealed that in most cases they almost certainly were not and in some, owing to absence of parents, could not possibly have been.

The result, as he wrote to a friend, was at first "helpless bewilderment . . . reality was lost". But then a sense of victory supervened rather than defeat. What mattered, he now saw, was not the factual truth of these sexual "experiences", but their psychic reality, their importance for the individual and their power to affect his life. From this realization, reinforced from many directions, grew two concepts which revolutionized psychology, that of *psychic determinism* of the most literal kind, the assertion that nothing in the whole of mental life is fortuitous, even to the odd lapse of memory or slip of the tongue, but that everything is caused and can be explained in terms of *goal-directed drives*. Increasingly Freud came to see that his first great discovery, the dynamic unconscious, was responsible for the production of neurotic illness and through its emotional drives and conflicts operated in all men to a degree that shook reason on her throne and made it almost true to say that we are "lived" by unconscious forces.

Viewing mental life in this way, Freud at an early date began to see a new significance in dreams, those strange fragmented dramas that had always haunted the human race but that no one before had tried to explain psychologically. Freud saw them within the framework of determinism as "the royal road to the unconscious".[1] They were not fortuitous as we may suppose, or irrelevant to our lives. Every dream ever dreamt was "the distorted substitute of unconscious dream-thoughts"[2] and offered a key to the hidden processes, what was really going on in the depths. In his book, *The Interpretation of Dreams* (1899), which has been called "one of the great classics of human thought",[3] Freud expounded the method of interpretation, distinguishing between their manifest and latent content. The manifest content is what is remembered on waking, usually incoherent and disjointed. The latent content— what the unconscious is really saying, in Freud's view always related to a wish—is discovered by free association with the disconnected objects or events of the dream.

Sometimes the apparent wish of the dream is the reverse of the

[1] All quotations so far from "The Life and Work of Sigmund Freud", Ernest Jones, Pelican Books, 1964.
[2], [3] "What Freud Really Said", David Stafford-Clark, Macdonald, 1965.

true wish. For instance, a patient dreamt that she wanted to give a supper party, but had nothing in the house but a little smoked salmon. It was Sunday; the shops were shut, and when she tried to ring a caterer at his home, the phone was out of order. So she had to abandon the party. "How do you fit that in with your theory?" she asked Freud. But the true position came to light in the course of questioning. The day before the dream she had visited a female friend of whom she was jealous because she thought her husband admired her. Fortunately the friend was thin and the husband liked plump women. But the friend said she wanted to put on weight, and then to the dreamer: "When are you going to ask us over again? You always have such good food." In this light the dream meant something quite different. The dreamer did not want to give a party so that the other woman could become fat and even more appealing to the husband.

Here we come upon Freudian *theories*, expressed in terms of his basic concepts, which is more controversial ground. No one today would deny that mental events are in some sense caused, nor the existence of purposeful drives towards goals of some kind, nor that of the dynamic unconscious. But the theories are in varying degrees subject to criticism, though in all of them there are recognized areas of truth. The first coming to our notice here is that of personality structure, of which Freud's final views were published in the 1920s, in *The Ego and the Id*. We can illustrate the theory from the dream. The manifest content implied a wish to give a party, whereas the latent content contained the opposite wish. Why was it wrapped up and distorted? Because, said Freud, of "ego defences", the Ego being defined as the conscious self in direct touch with external reality and the defences, in this case, springing from the dreamer's refusal to admit the full extent of her jealousy. Why not? Because of her Super-Ego, which in Freudian terminology is both more and less than what we usually call conscience and derives from the incorporation into the personality of parental standards of good and bad, right and wrong, starting at about the age of three. Freud believed only in derived, not innate morality. But what of the lady's sexual jealousy? Where did that come from? Here we encounter the most controversial element of the theory.

To Freud, people are the product of their history, of all the forces, internal and external, which have operated on them since birth and his theory sought to define the subsequent stages of development. The new-born child he saw as a seething mass of instinctual drives, as yet uncontrolled by a discriminating Ego. The infant is entirely spontaneous, possessed by its impulses to which, because of their impersonal nature, he gave the Latin name, the Id, meaning the It. The energy investing these impulses he called Libido, sexual energy which, in the case of the infant, seeks sensual satisfaction from bodily functions. (Later, Freud maintained that all human activity, whether overtly sexual or not, sprang from Libido or its frustration.) In the first, called the oral phase of development, the infant finds satisfaction in sucking, and the object of attention is the breast. After about six months, the oral merges into the next, the anal phase, when pleasure is obtained from defecation and also, according to Freud, from retention of faeces, seen as an early and negative assertion of individuality in the face of parental wishes. All this is called pregenital sexuality which again merges after three years into the early genital or phallic phase, when interest becomes centred on the penis and sexual attraction is shortly aroused towards the mother, with fears of paternal punishment in the form of castration.[1] This is the well-known Oedipus situation (named after the King in Sophocles's play who married his mother and murdered his father) which, owing to the conflicts and sense of guilt aroused, strongly reinforces the developing Super-Ego and results in a succeeding latency phase, when sexuality is largely dormant, lasting up to puberty. The Oedipus complex is not finally resolved until the maturing adult finds a partner outside the family.

Thus in Freud's view the child is very much father to the man, and few indeed are the adults who have escaped unscathed from over-strict parental attitudes, their condemnation of an interest in bodily functions natural to a child and overt demonstrations of their own repressed guilt. Moreover, Freud did not believe that any of these early phases are ever completely surmounted; residues remain which we carry with us, often in thinly disguised, partially sublimated forms into adult life. Examples are not far to seek, and Freud saw adult life and indeed civilization as an uneasy compromise between the biological drives seeking satisfaction and their expression in a form acceptable to society and one's associates.

[1]Noting their own less impressive equipment, little girls were said to experience "penis envy" and then, accepting their lot, to become attached to their fathers. As the fault lies with nature and not themselves, they are, according to Freudians, incapable of developing a strong Super-Ego—whence exists, no doubt, the fascination of Eve.

In his picture, the Ego is in a highly vulnerable position, being assailed from two directions: from the unconscious where primitive impulses have been repressed but still exist, and from the Super-Ego, which is only partly a conscious phenomenon containing, sometimes in a highly active and aggressive amalgam, the moral standards imbibed from parents and the conventions and taboos of society. Civilization itself is unstable, brought about at the price of suffering and self-denial.

Freud's view of human nature does not give much ground for optimism, for, curiously enough, in his later work he did not see sexual satisfaction as the most difficult problem (*The Future of an Illusion, Civilization and its Discontents*, 1927–1931). Most men and women, he thought, could obtain a partner and achieve equilibrium in the sexual sphere without much interference from society. But Libido needed other outlets. Man, he believed, was essentially self-seeking, and in pursuit of wider pleasures would willingly dominate or murder his neighbour, who to him was either a tool to be exploited or an obstacle to be destroyed. Aggression was a drive as inherent as sexuality. Hate was fundamental; love, cooperation, tenderness were secondary phenomena, sublimations of sex. All that prevented men in a given society from killing one another was self-interest, the fear of retribution. It was this that impelled them to call a truce with their neighbours, so that they could survive to pursue their narcissistic goals by other means. But the abandonment of overt aggression remained a heavy burden and the Super-Ego, individual and collective, was the sole means of preventing, in the long run, the disintegration of society.

This dark picture was drawn from theory, of which one element was the universality of the Oedipus Complex. On this pin-point Freud constructed speculations concerning the origins of religion which he declared to be fundamentally an illusion, "the obsessional neurosis of mankind". It arose from the situation in primitive tribes where the father of the horde possessed all the women and was killed by the other males so that they could enjoy them. The dead leader, both revered and hated by the survivors, who felt deep guilt at the murder, then became symbolized by the totem, a familiar animal believed to incorporate the qualities of the leader now raised to the status of a god. Throughout the year the animal was sacred and might not be hunted. except on one day when it was killed and eaten by the tribesmen who thus took into themselves the qualities it symbolized. Part of the rule of the totem was also the institution of a taboo against marrying within the family, whereby the tribesmen expiated their original incestuous wishes. Religion in Freud's view thus became a largely ineffectual attempt on the part of humanity to resolve a collective Oedipus Complex, ineffectual because the ambivalent feelings towards the father-god remained.

All this, the discovery of the dynamic unconscious, the new psychoanalytical method together with the interpretation of dreams, the vast clinical material produced, the concepts, the theories (including that of the neuroses which has been excluded for lack of space) and, less importantly, the speculations about human nature, society and religion, comprises Freud's legacy to the world. What is its significance for us today?

First we must deal with a difficulty, the one-sidedness of Freud's doctrines, and doctrines they were, raised by him to the status of a quasi-religious dogma. It is entirely reasonable to accept the importance of infantile sexuality in general terms and its power to disrupt human life if not successfully absorbed is beyond doubt, but it is meaningless to maintain, as he did, that the unconscious contains nothing positive but sexual drives or that every achievement of man, from a Mozart symphony to the building of a motorway, is the outcome of sublimated sexuality. Yet to Freud this not only was, but had to be so, and the reason was his own neurosis, never resolved, which centred on highly ambivalent feelings towards his father, making it impossible for him to accept a Creator with paternal qualities or explore the realm of spiritual experience. The tragedy of this situation for Freud has been movingly described by C. G. Jung in his book *Memories, Dreams, Reflections* (1963) and the danger today in the sphere of psychiatric treatment is that people may be discouraged from seeking a spiritual basis for their lives.

But with this important qualification, the Freudian legacy has been of tremendous value in helping us to know and understand ourselves better, not only revolutionizing our attitude to the mentally sick but presenting human nature in a new perspective, its influence spreading to every corner of life in the West, especially in Europe and the United States, to child care, education, criminology, the social sciences, politics, industry, the arts, to the roots of civilization itself. After the first glimpse that Freud gave us into the vast complexities of the human mind, depth and group psychology continue to open up new spheres of investigation and offer new insights. We know now something of the polarity in the psyche, the eternal interchange between the conscious and the unconscious mind, and beyond this we see a deeper significance, for thanks to Freud our attitude to their relative importance has been profoundly changed.

Modern man is sick from neglect of his unconscious, and science with its toys and its distractions is making him worse. In the first half of this century we have been uprooted from our past. All that connects us with our ancestry, with the slowly evolving life of the millenia, including nature, the soil of our existence, is being torn up and replaced by a utilitarian superstructure which does not speak to us except in the language of chilling alienation. Man's work, for the most part of insufferable tedium, is geared to the demands of an economy given the status of a jealous god, to be served and satisfied or else he will die. Mechanical movement and the manipulation of things fill his existence, and with this goes a severance from his personal roots, those deep sources which provide him with a feeling of true identity and life. Empty, restless, dissatisfied, he pins his hopes on a future of material opulence where, as in a cocoon, he can manipulate more gadgets and admire their own smooth functioning, if not his own. Industrial civilization is organized to support this existence, dominated by a moloch of man's own creation which now has him enslaved. Can we wonder that violence frequently erupts, born of the tension between falsity and new life struggling to be born?

Life must come from within, from the unconscious. Its discovery involves a readiness, a desire to know more and understand more. Here Freud, the bold pioneer, stands at the gateway, bidding us explore. But we have to go further than he did, strengthen collectively and individually the links with our past, our primitive ancestry and the spiritual life of the universe. The urge to this development does not spring from calm and rational decision, but is imposed on us by the impulses of the unconscious, and like physical exploration it is a messy and unpredictable business.

Today it is already taking place and we have the spectacle of scientists, on the one hand, achieving wonders by rational analysis of life's framework, while other people with growing enthusiasm explore its non-rational content. Young people's emphatic rejection of bourgeois standards, the fervour of religious revival, a new interest in archaeology and man's animal origins, even the frenzies of pop-addicts and the passion for drug-taking (highly dangerous and unnecessary though this method is)—these are only a few illustrations of the inward-turning which man is driven by the unconscious to perform to find more of himself and reverse the process of impoverishment. Man's destiny, wrote Jung, "is to create more and more consciousness. As far as we can discern, the sole purpose of human existence is to kindle a light in the darkness of mere being"[1], while Teilhard de Chardin, that great scientist and mystic, noting the "threadbare millenium" which materialists offer us, declared: "It is right that our hearts should fail us at the thought of so 'bourgeois' a paradise. We need to remind ourselves yet again that it is not well-being but a hunger for more-being which, of psychological necessity, can alone preserve the thinking earth from the *taedium vitae*"[2]. Elsewhere, he too wrote of this search in terms of human destiny. In three successive steps in four centuries, by the discoveries of Galileo, Darwin and Freud, man had "seemed definitely to redissolve in the common ground of things", astronomically when the earth was engulfed in the anonymity of the cosmos, biologically when man "vanished in the crowd of his fellow-species, psychologically, last of all, when an abyss of unconsciousness opened in the centre of his *I*"[3].

But Teilhard did not see this "return to the crucible" as a regressive step, but foretold that man would re-emerge "more than ever at the head of nature . . . with the possibility and power of forming in the heart of space and time a single point of universalization" for the very stuff of earthly existence. Jung joined with him in speaking of *"reculer pour mieux sauter"*, while Freud glimpsed this result when he wrote that "our civilization imposes an almost intolerable pressure on us and calls for a corrective"[4], and proudly and rightly claimed that he had troubled the sleep of the world. So, if we wish to sum up our debt to him, it is that he showed us the need to find more life. It is up to us now to grasp the opportunity, for whatever the urge of the unconscious may be to seek the light of day, it is we who hold the key and can lock or open the door.

[1] *Memories, Dreams, Reflections.* Collins and Routledge and Kegan Paul, 1963.
[2] Pierre Teilhard de Chardin. *The Future of Man*, Collins, 1964.
[3] *The Appearance of Man*, Collins, 1965.
[4] David Stafford-Clark. *What Freud Really Said.*

DAVID LLOYD GEORGE
(1863–1945)

WHO THAT heard him in his prime can ever forget the stocky little fellow in a grey suit, with untidy hair, bushy moustache, a pair of twinkling eyes and a monitory forefinger; and above all, that extraordinary voice of his, now low-pitched, soothing, soft and caressing, like the murmuring of young lovers, and then rising with an impetuous surge until it came crashing about one's ears like one of those sudden tempests that torture the mountains of the land he loved so well?

For forty years and more that voice of David Lloyd George dominated the platforms from one end of the country to the other. In peace and in war he "rode the whirlwind and directed the storm", and at the end of his long day, as Winston Churchill said in his magnificent memorial tribute in the House of Commons, "the pillars of his life's toil" stood "upstanding, massive, and indestructible".

David Lloyd George was a Welshman, descended from a long line of Welsh peasant-farmers, and of nothing was he prouder than the Celtic blood that ran in his veins. When as sometimes happened in the early stages of his tempestuous career his racial origins were made into a bitter jibe, he answered the taunt with the unanswerable claim that the Celts, oppressed and trampled upon as they had been so often in the course of history, yet maintained an irrepressible love of freedom.

Born on 17 January, 1863, his birthplace was not, as one might expect, a cottage on a lonely hillside in the heart of Wales, but a dreary-looking little brick house in a suburb of Manchester, where his father, William George, who as a young man had quitted the family farm in Pembrokeshire to become a school-teacher, was headmaster of a National school. His mother, too, was Welsh through and through; she was Elizabeth Lloyd, daughter of the village shoemaker at Llanystumdwy, on the outskirts of Criccieth, in the northern parts of Wales. David was their second child, the first being a girl; a second boy was born posthumously, for William

George, who a few months after David's birth had suffered a breakdown in health and gone back to a farm in Pembrokeshire, died suddenly of pneumonia in 1864, when only in his middle forties. Mrs George was thus left a widow at thirty-six, with two little children to support and another on the way, and she would have been hard put to it if she had not been able to call on her brother for help. Without a moment's hesitation Richard Lloyd answered the appeal, and took his sister and her children back with him to Llanystumdwy, where he was carrying on the business of shoemaker that had been their father's.

At Llanystumdwy, in the modest dwelling next door to his uncle's workshop, David Lloyd George spent the days of his infancy and youth. Richard Lloyd was a sterling character, who remained a bachelor very probably for the excellent reason that with his assumed responsibilities he could not afford to get married. He was self-educated, but a great lover of books and reading, and he instilled the same interest into his young nephew. When he was between three and four, little David was sent to the village school, and he remained there until he was just on fourteen. The school was a "church" school, maintained by the Anglican Church in Wales, while the Lloyds were Nonconformists, regular attendants at a tiny Baptist chapel where Uncle Richard sometimes preached (as David himself was to do as a teen-ager). Very early, then, the boy became aware of the existence of not one Wales but two; the one English in tradition, religious observance, and political interest, and the other deeply Welsh, speaking the Welsh tongue, listening to Welsh preachers, and stoutly Liberal or Radical in their politics. As soon as he appreciated the differences between them, David Lloyd George had not the least difficulty in deciding where he stood. Wales was the first altar at which he worshipped, and so it remained for the rest of his life.

At school the boy had shown much promise, and his juvenile passion for learning had been fostered in every way by his uncle and his mother. When the question of a career came to be discussed there was some talk of his becoming a preacher, but in the little denomination to which the Lloyds belonged the ministers received no salary. However, there was another career in which a "gift of the gab," to put it vulgarly, was of decided value. Earnestly the mother and her brother deliberated, whether the boy might not become a lawyer? At first they were astounded at their own presumption, but in the end they resolved to make the necessary sacrifices, and by dint of much tuition from his uncle by candle-light after the day's work was done, David sat for the first examination of the Law Society. He was successful, and when he was just turned fifteen he was articled to a firm of solicitors in Portmadoc.

Towards the end of 1881 he went to London to take an examination, and he seized the occasion to visit the gallery in the House of Commons. The words he used to describe the experience have a peculiar significance. "I will not say but that I eyed the Assembly in a spirit similar to that in which William the Conqueror eyed England on his visit to Edward the Confessor. O Vanity!" Two years later he was in London for his final examinations (which he passed with honours), and this time he attended a debate in the House of Commons when Gladstone spoke.

By this time the shoemaking business had been given up, and his mother and uncle were living in Criccieth, where Mrs George let rooms to summer visitors. Now the front door of the small house bore a brass plate on which was inscribed *D. Lloyd George, Solicitor*, and from the back parlour he embarked on a lawyer's practice which was never in need of clients. He had a name to make, and in the courts and in private practice he was swift to make it. All those who felt themselves to be suffering from the petty tyrannies of landlord and parson flocked to his door. The magistrates on the local bench came to dread his appearance in cases brought before them. He was so sure of himself (usually with good reason); he was so forthright; he was occasionally so rude (as he intended to be). As a public speaker, too, he was in great demand, and he was always sure of a large and appreciative audience at Liberal party meetings and chapel congregations, at temperance gatherings and anti-tithe agitations. Life was still a struggle, but the prospect was so promising that in January, 1888, he was enabled to marry Margaret Owen, daughter of a substantial farmer in the neighbourhood—a young woman of serene and steadfast temperament, large-hearted and thoroughly capable in all domestic matters, who encouraged and furthered his career in every way.

That career was about to take a dramatic new direction. It was only to be expected that the Liberals in the constituency should have their eye on him as a man who might challenge successfully the Conservative (Tory) domination in the political field. Lloyd George welcomed their approaches, and in 1889 he managed to obtain election as an alderman on the newly established county council: he remained an alderman for the rest of his life. Shortly afterwards he was adopted as prospective parliamentary candidate for the Caernarvon Burghs in the Liberal interest, and within a few months the Conservative M.P. died suddenly and there was a by-election. Lloyd George went into battle on an advanced Liberal or Radical programme, which included Home Rule for Ireland—and for Wales too; disestablishment of the Anglican Church in Wales; taxation of land values; and a "free breakfast table", by which was meant no taxes on imported food. It was an audacious programme, but then he was an audacious young fellow with a very sensitive finger on the public pulse. He thought he knew what the people wanted, and the result proved that he was right. When the votes were counted on 11 April, 1890, it was found that he had triumphed. True, his majority was only eighteen, but it was enough, and in the event he was to remain M.P. for Caernarvon Burghs for fifty-five years without a break.

Six days later the young man of twenty-seven, black-haired and blue-eyed, slightly built and engagingly mannered, and gifted with a Celtic eloquence that could charm as it could infuriate, took his seat in the Chamber which he was to dominate for so many years. A month later he made his maiden speech, and it was a marked success. Feeling quite sure that henceforth London was to provide him with his field of action, Lloyd George with his wife and growing young family moved to a house on Wandsworth Common. In due course he established a branch of his legal business in London, while his uncle kept an eye on affairs at Criccieth. For M.Ps were not paid in those days, and in his earlier years in London, at least, Lloyd George was pretty generally hard up.

Essential though it was to keep his practice going, his main interests lay at Westminster. For fifteen years he was a Liberal back-bencher since these were the years of the long Conservative rule under the premiership of Lord Salisbury and (from 1902) his nephew A. J. Balfour. Lloyd George was sometimes in opposition, too, to his own party, when they seemed to be insufficiently interested in Welsh affairs or indifferent to the workings of the "Nonconformist conscience". As a debater he proved himself a hard-hitter, afraid of nobody, not even of the "Grand Old Man" (Gladstone) himself. When the Boer War broke out in 1899 he took up an attitude of extreme hostility to what he regarded as British imperialism run riot, and for a year or two he was perhaps the best-hated man in England. But the Caernarvon electors remained firm in their support, and he justified their confidence.

When in the opening years of the new century (and reign), Joseph Chamberlain embarked on his raging, tearing campaign in favour of Tariff Reform, Lloyd George denounced him as a food-taxer from platforms made available to him in all parts of the country. At length the Balfour government resigned, and the Liberals under Sir Henry Campbell-Bannerman returned to office after more than a decade in the political wilderness. The general election fought in the opening weeks of 1906 gave them a landslide victory, and by common consent a large part of the credit for the tremendous triumph was attributable to the fierce crusading zeal that Lloyd George had displayed.

When Campbell-Bannerman formed his ministry, he included Lloyd George as President of the Board of Trade, and an excellent appointment it proved. He showed an unexpected mastery of the intricate details of business matters, and among the measures for which he was responsible was the Merchant Shipping Act of 1906 which came to be known as the "Seamen's Charter". So well did Lloyd George do that when Campbell-Bannerman retired through illness in the spring of 1908 and H. H. Asquith became Prime Minister in his stead, Lloyd George succeeded Asquith as Chancellor of the Exchequer, the position in the administration that ranked second to the premiership.

This was the position that was most suited to his talents, the one that provided him with the opportunity of launching the vastly far-reaching "Liberal experiment" in social reform. Poverty, hardship, unemployment, poor housing, widespread squalor and malnutrition, lack of educational opportunity—these were the ills that made the lives of millions such as a truly civilized community should be ashamed to tolerate, and Lloyd George was resolved to reduce their incidence even though they could not be abolished altogether. If we look for a date which may be regarded as the birthday of the "Welfare State" then we might well choose 29 April, 1909, for this was the day on which he "opened" his first Budget, what came to be known as the "People's Budget". Just before he sat down after speaking for four hours, he declared, "This is a War Budget. It is for raising money to wage implacable war against poverty and squalidness. I cannot help believing that before this generation has passed away, we shall have advanced a great step towards that good time when poverty, and the degradation and wretchedness that always follows in its camp, will be as remote to the people of this country as the wolves which once infested its forests."

The Budget, with its proposals for land taxes and the rest, was fiercely resisted, and the House of Lords took the unprecedented step of rejecting it; it was not finally passed until another general election had confirmed the Liberals in office (though with a greatly reduced majority). Lloyd George then prepared a comprehensive scheme for National Insurance, which provided for the compulsory insurance of the great majority of workers against sickness and incapacity by the joint contributions of themselves, their employers, and the State. The contributions were 4d, 3d, and 2d per week respectively, and Lloyd George claimed that this meant that the worker was going to receive "ninepence for fourpence"; but not everybody agreed with his arithmetic. The scheme was most violently assailed, and the Northcliffe newspapers in particular worked up a massive agitation against mistresses being compelled to lick stamps to put on their domestics' insurance-cards. But when the day came the tongues did their duty, and for the first time in British history millions of sick and suffering humanity were assured of some protection against the bludgeonings of an unkind fate.

There was a phrase that Lloyd George used in one of his speeches dating from this time, something about his having joined the Red Cross and being in the Ambulance Corps, that caught the popular imagination; so much so that "Lloyd George's ambulance-wagon" became a synonym for all that aimed at social reform and human redemption. Lloyd George himself asked for nothing better than that he should be allowed to drive his "wagon" uninterruptedly and with no speed restrictions. But the intensification of the arms race with Germany left little money over for any further expansion of the social services.

Lloyd George deeply deplored the changing state of affairs. He tried to convince himself, and convince others, that the international situation was nothing like so menacing as was being made out. As late as the first week in 1914 he was protesting in a newspaper interview against what he called "the overwhelming extravagance of our expenditure on armaments", and right up to the summer of that fateful year he discounted the ever-growing talk of the inevitability of war. Not then, or ever, was he a pacifist, but he hated war from the depths of his being, and was resolved to do everything in his power to avert it. This remained his attitude until the Austrian archduke was assassinated at Serajevo at the end of June. Even then, indeed, he was not as a man absolutely without hope. War was coming—but perhaps the intervention of the great

As the years pass, Tolstoy's superlative greatness as a novelist is increasingly recognized throughout the world. Vast numbers of readers, who know his works only through translation, would admit to the belief that his *War and Peace* is the greatest novel ever written. But Tolstoy would never have been satisfied with literary acclaim. He was above all else a reformer, one who sought to win men's hearts and minds to the acceptance of a way of life based on the Sermon of the Mount. *Above:* Tolstoy—the bearded figure on the extreme left—as one of the family circle in the garden at Yasnaya Polyana. This photograph and the portrait (left) were both taken in 1906.

For the greater part of his life
V. I. Ulyanov, who assumed the name of
Lenin, was engaged in an "underground"
agitation against the Tsarist regime of his
native Russia. For three years he was in
exile in Siberia, and then from 1900 was
generally in one or other of the countries of
Western Europe, until in 1917 he returned
to Russia and, within a few months,
succeeded in establishing a "dictatorship
of the proletariat" with himself at the
head. The photo above shows him
haranguing the crowd in Petrograd,
shortly before his successful coup; on the
right of his stand is his great lieutenant,
Leo Trotsky (in military uniform). *Right:*
as he was when head of the Soviet state.

powers might succeed in confining it to the Balkans. . . . So more weeks passed, and the war clouds gathered blacker and blacker. Then on 3 August the German armies invaded Belgium, and at once his mind was made up. A little country, not much bigger than his native Wales, savagely attacked without cause, her territory violated, her towns sacked, her people massacred. . . . When some of his Cabinet colleagues were still questioning their consciences, his conscience was clear. With no more hesitation, he supported the ultimatum to Germany, and when it expired he was at the Treasury effecting the smooth transition of Britain from a peace to a war economy.

For the present he remained Chancellor of the Exchequer, and his conduct of the nation's finances was masterly. Once again he took the campaigning trail, and no voice was more eagerly listened to than his, as it called for boundless effort and sacrifice. There was much talk of "Business as usual", but he had no illusions himself as to the probable length and intensity of the struggle ahead. Some of his colleagues in the Government were highly indignant when he ventured to criticize the way the war was being run, and pooh-poohed his suggestions that since the combatants had fought themselves to a deadlock on the Western front an attempt should be made to turn the enemy's flank by an attack through Turkey and the Balkans.

In the spring of 1915 rumours began to reach London of a shell shortage in France, and the *Daily Mail* took the matter up. The disclosures were nothing new to Lloyd George. Realizing how badly things were going, he had developed an information service of his own, and artillery-officers on leave from the Front had given him information that the War Office generals had not bothered to seek, or if they had, they kept to themselves. Even before the "shell scandal" hit the headlines in the newspapers, he had urged upon Asquith the appointment of a Munitions of War Committee with Lloyd George as chairman. This was no longer sufficient: nothing less than a change in Government would do. So in April, 1915, the first Coalition ministry was formed, with Asquith as Prime Minister still, but with Lloyd George holding the key-appointment of Minister of Munitions.

Great things were expected of him, by King George, by the Government and by the people. If he had failed, the war might have been lost, or dragged on to end in an inconclusive peace born of weariness and disillusion. But Lloyd George was determined not

o

417

to fail. The Ministry of Munitions was an entirely new one. There were no precedents to work by (perhaps he rather liked that). He had no staff, his office was a single room, provided with a table and a couple of chairs—but no carpet. But in a matter of days, hours even, what a change! Never had such a tornado of human energy sent the papers flying in the offices of Whitehall.

Within a few weeks the foundations were laid of what in a few months had become the largest industrial establishment that the world had ever seen. One of the new Minister's first reforms was to throw open to general competition the contracts for munitions supply that the War Office had reserved to a small number of privileged firms. Another was the introduction into the Ministry of men who had won high positions for themselves in private industry, and real "hustlers" some of them proved to be. A third was the personal appeal he delivered to the men in the workshops and the mines to forgo for the duration of the War those restrictive practices that mean so much to the trade unionist. And yet another, and perhaps the most important of all, was the enlistment, on a scale never approached or even dreamed of before, of the woman-hood of the nation. Hundreds of thousands of women and girls showed what they could do as munition-workers, and their achievement was immense. None other of the combatant nations came near to equalling, let alone surpassing, this tremendous effort.

One thing more should be mentioned. Although he was now devoted to the production of weapons of destruction, Lloyd George had not abandoned his interest in social reform. As soon as he had got the new arms factories operating, he turned his attention to the conditions under which those employed in them were required to work. In September, 1915, he appointed the Health of Munition Workers Committee, charging them to consider and advise on questions of industrial fatigue, hours of labour, night work, and all other matters affecting the health and efficiency of the men, women, and young people employed in the factories and workshops under the Ministry's control. This was something that was altogether after his own heart, and he had good reason to be pleased with the result. As he remarked, "it is a strange irony, but no small com-pensation, that the making of weapons of destruction should afford the occasion to humanize industry. Yet such has been the case."

For thirteen months Lloyd George was Minister of Munitions, until in the summer of 1916 he was called upon to succeed as War Secretary Lord Kitchener, who had been drowned when the ship in which he was proceeding to Russia on a Government mission was sunk off the Orkneys. He was not at all keen to make the move, but he felt it his duty to accept. And in any case, his work was done. Where before his advent there had been the most shocking and dangerous shortages, there was now an almost superabundance of all the munitions of war.

At the War Office he found things far from satisfactory. He had done so much to provide the generals with all the weapons and ammunition that they could possibly require, but were they capable of using them to the best advantage? A few days before he took over his new post the battle of the Somme began, and he was appalled by the slaughter of the nation's young manhood in an offensive that never had much chance of success. But the generals were not alone to blame. There was something radically wrong in the supreme direction of the war. What he had begun to suspect long before was now abundantly plain, that, whatever his virtues as a peacetime Prime Minister, Asquith was quite unfitted to lead the country through what had become the greatest and most terrible of wars. He was well aware that many others, in the high places of government and among the newspaper proprietors, shared this view, and before long he felt himself in a position to act. At first he had no desire or intention of supplanting Asquith in the premiership; he would have been content with the setting up of a War Committee with supreme co-ordinating and directing powers, of which he should be the chairman. Asquith seemed to concur, but then drew back. Lloyd George was so convinced of the necessity for the changes he advocated that he at once handed in his resignation.

This was on 5 December, 1916, and there followed a couple of days of intense activity behind the scenes, while the great general public, who had come to recognize in Lloyd George the one political figure who had it within him to fight and keep on fighting, were left in a condition of bewilderment and deep concern. The newspapers continued to carry the most startling headlines: Asquith resigns, Bonar Law (the Conservative leader) asked to form a Government, the King (George V) calls a conference of political leaders, Lloyd George goes to the Palace. . . . Then on 7 December it was announced that Mr Lloyd George had "kissed hands" as Prime Minister of a great new Coalition Administration pledged to carry on the war until complete victory had been won.

When the new Prime Minister arrived back at his office in

Whitehall, he told his secretary, Miss Frances Stevenson, what had occurred. Then she heard him mutter, half to himself, "I wonder if I can do it?" But his native ebullience swiftly asserted itself, and he flung himself into the tremendous tasks that lay ahead. This must be said, however, that he never underrated them. His first speech in the House of Commons as Prime Minister, on 19 December, was introduced with the admission that, "I appear before the House today with the most terrible responsibility that can fall on the shoulders of any living man".

How he acquitted himself, and how the people answered his repeated calls for toil and hardship and terrible sacrifice, go to the composition of one of the most impressive and most memorable chapters in British history. In the military sphere, Passchendaele was a ghastly repetition of the horrors of the Somme the year before; Lloyd George would have sacked Haig, whose concept of generalship hardly rose above that of a mutual blood-letting, but the commander-in-chief had too many powerful friends in the Government and Court, and his own position at Westminster was none too secure. Russia collapsed, and the French army was weakened by mutinies. In the spring of 1918 the Germans made a last great desperate thrust for victory, and it was only then that Lloyd George was able to induce the Allies to appoint a Supreme Commander such as he had long been urging.

These things were terrible enough, but even more terrible was the grim battle being fought on the high seas, where the German U-boats were sinking at sight British and Allied merchantmen bringing food and other supplies to a beleaguered isle. In the spring of 1917 the sinkings were averaging a million tons a month, and there was a very real possibility of Britain being starved into surrender. It was entirely owing to Lloyd George's insistence that the Convoy system should be given a fair trial, that the frightful ravages of the U-boats were halted and the situation brought under control.

At length, as suddenly and unexpectedly as it had begun, the war came to an end. On the afternoon of 11 November, 1918, Lloyd George rose from his seat in the House of Commons to announce that at eleven o'clock that morning "the cruellest and most terrible war that has ever scourged mankind" had been brought to an end.

In retrospect, this moment may be seen as the climax of Lloyd George's career. No Prime Minister had ever enjoyed such immense popularity as was his; on every hand he was acclaimed as "the man who won the War," and there was not too much exaggeration in the ascription. His first concern was to "Make Britain a fit country for heroes to live in!" to quote his most-quoted slogan. Already, indeed, the Coalition government had passed Acts remodelling the national system of education and giving the parliamentary franchise to large numbers of women, and it was on a comprehensive programme of social reform that Lloyd George now led the Coalition forces to overwhelming triumph in the general election at the close of the year.

But for the next year or two, Lloyd George was obliged to spend most of his time away from Westminster. Beyond the Channel a continent was in the throes of dissolution, the political arrangements had broken down, millions were starving and ripe for revolution. Somehow or other, but most urgently, a new order had to be brought into being, and in the accouchement Lloyd George played a most important part; indeed, it is not too much to say that his position approached that of Prime Minister of Europe. No British statesman had ever exercised such influence in the comity of nations; as against the unrelenting ferocity of Clemenceau and the starry-eyed idealism of President Woodrow Wilson he exhibited an often startling genius for practical compromise. At Versailles he stole the show, and the eventual peace settlement owed a very great deal to his lifelong championship of small nations rightly struggling to be free.

But while he was so heavily engaged on the Continent, his position at home was being steadily undermined. Since the general election of 1918 the Coalition had been dominated by the Conservative wing, and although most of the most prominent leaders of the party remained loyal to Lloyd George, many of the backbenchers were suspicious of his Liberal instincts. When in December, 1921, he reached an agreement with the Irish rebels for the establishment of the Free State, there was deep resentment on the Conservative benches, and an occasion for bringing him down was eagerly awaited. This came in the autumn of the year following, when it seemed clear that Lloyd George was willing to go to war again in order to rescue the Greeks from destruction by a renascent Turkey. At a meeting of Conservative M.Ps at the Carlton Club on 22 October it was resolved that the party should fight the next election on their own, and Lloyd George at once accepted this as the end of the coalition. That same day he went to Buckingham Palace and tendered his resignation to the King.

In his diary that night King George wrote: "I am sorry he is going, but some day he will be Prime Minister again." Lloyd George doubtless thought so too; after all, he was not yet sixty, his prestige throughout the world was immense, his experience unrivalled, his ability and energy unimpaired. But for "some day" history was to write "never". In the first place, he was without a firm party base: the Conservatives had repudiated him, the Liberals were in disarray, and Labour deeply suspicious. Secondly, and more important even, was his own incalculable disposition; he had proved "too clever by half", he was the "Welsh wizard", and while there was ungrudging admiration for his superlative gifts and magnificent achievements, there was the most widespread distrust.

So it happened that for the more than twenty years that were left to him he was an increasingly lonely figure. During the 'twenties he instituted valuable enquiries into the state of Britain's towns, countryside, and industry, and in the 'thirties he advocated comprehensive measures to combat unemployment. As a political force, however, he was spent.

All the same, he had plenty to keep him busy, what with lecture tours in America, writing his *War Memoirs*, and running his model farm at Churt, in Surrey. In 1940 Mr Churchill invited him to join his Government, but nothing came of it. In 1941 Mrs Lloyd George died at their home at Criccieth, and in 1943 Lloyd George married Miss Frances Stevenson, who had become his personal secretary in 1915 and ever since had shared his life. He remained M.P. for Caernarvon until in 1945 he was created Earl Lloyd-George of Dwyfor. On 26 March, 1945, he died, in the village where he had spent his youth. Four days later he was buried beside the little river Dwyfor, and a big stone on which he had often sat as a small boy marks the place.

LENIN

(1870–1924)

VLADIMIR ILYITCH ULYANOV, who took the name of Lenin, was the architect of the Russian Revolution, the creator both of the modern Russian state and of the world Communist organization, and a major contributor to and exponent of Communist philosophy. It is no accident that that philosophy is now generally described as Marxism-Leninism.

Lenin was born at Simbirsk on the middle Volga—now called Ulyanovsk in his honour—on 22 April, 1870, the son of a college teacher. Long before he read Marx, he was driven to revolution by two events: his expulsion in 1887 from Kazan University for taking part in a revolutionary meeting, and the execution in 1891 of his eldest brother for taking part in a plot against the life of Tsar Alexander III. On returning to Kazan University he undertook a thorough study of Marxism and of Plekhanov, the leading Russian Marxist writer, and thereafter sought strenuously to root his revolutionary activities in a firm theoretical foundation. He believed that if the revolution was to come, it needed to be based on a definite doctrine. Theory was a guide to tactics and to action.

Lenin practised law in Samara in 1892, but in 1894 moved to St Petersburg. By the age of twenty-five he was among the leaders of potential revolution in Russia as pamphleteer, agitator and activist. In 1895 he organized the illegal "union for the liberation of the working party", took the alias of Lenin, and was arrested and spent three years in Siberia. Here in 1898 he married Nadezhda Krupskaya. On release he moved to Switzerland and founded the paper *Iskra* (*The Spark*) as a journal of revolution, designed for circulation inside the closed world of Tsardom. Its objective was to form a centralized "underground revolutionary party of Social Democrats which at the head of the proletariat should open the struggle against Tsarism". From the beginning Lenin denied that a spontaneous revolt of an oppressed working class or that isolated and sporadic acts of violence would be sufficient to generate and sustain a revolution. Something more than poverty and anger were called for. An organization of professional revolutionists was needed, precise in doctrine, dedicated and ruthless in purpose, but sharply political and therefore pliable in tactics. As he wrote in *What's to be done?* in 1902,

> "I assert: (1) that no revolutionary movement can endure without a stable organization of leaders that maintains continuity; (2) that the wider the masses spontaneously drawn into the struggle forming the basis of the movement and participating in it, the more urgent the need of such an organization, and the more solid this organization must be (for it is much easier for demagogues to sidetrack the more backward sections of the masses); (3) that such an organization must consist chiefly of people professionally engaged in revolutionary activity; (4) that in an autocratic state, the more we *confine* the membership of such an organization to people who are professionally engaged in revolutionary activity and who have been professionally trained in the art of combating the political police, the more difficult will it be to wipe out such an organization, and (5) the *greater* will be the number of people of the working class and of the other classes of society who will be able to join the movement and perform active work in it . . ."

His task was thus always twofold, that of teacher and pamphleteer on the one hand, and organizer and shaper of political discontent on the other. If theory was as important as action, organization counted for more than oratory. "Go out and organize" is a recurring theme in the Communist story. Lenin was greatly assisted by his wife, as skilled an organizer as he was. And for ten years, from 1907 to 1917, it was a task done by them in exile, from Paris and Vienna, London and Zurich and Geneva. It was to be a long slow road to the Finland Station.

The uncompromising character of Lenin's views led to a split in the movement then called Social Democratic. The break came at the London conference of 1903, a conference largely financed by a benevolent British soap manufacturer, Fels, who was persuaded to support these Russian exiles by the pleadings of a young Glasgow University lecturer in economics, H. N. Brailsford. It was at this conference that the split took place between the Mensheviks (Minority), with whom Leo Bronstein (*alias* Trotsky) was then associated, and whose policy was that of the progressive advancement of the workers' cause in alliance with the liberal bourgeoisie, and the Bolsheviks (Majority), led by Lenin and Plekhanov, who advocated a radical revolutionary plan based on a close alliance between the industrial proletariat and the peasantry. The need was for rigid discipline, secrecy, and leadership; the leadership, he held, must provide the "revolutionary consciousness" for its followers. Lenin's majority was a narrow one, but he exploited it skilfully. From now on "Social Democrat" and "Reformist" were terms of abuse applied by the Communists, as the Bolsheviks now called themselves, to their opponents. This savage scorn for liberals and moderate socialists has also been, ever since, a feature of Communist history.

But to the dedicated Marxist, Russia posed serious problems. The Revolution would come first, Marx had said, in the industrialized countries, where an urban proletariat driven to desperation would be its instrument. In Russia this class was small in numbers, and ill-educated; the country was overwhelmingly agricultural and peasant. Although the peasants had been emancipated in form in 1861, they were heavily in debt, they were politically powerless, and they were superstitious. The Tsarist secret police, as Lenin knew all too well, were powerful. The Tsarist system was tyrannical but inefficient—and dangerously explosive; it produced more anarchists and revolutionaries than the rest of Europe put together, many of whom—like Lenin before them—were either in exile or in Siberian camps.

After the defeat of Russia by Japan in 1905, there had come the first revolution, in which the Black Sea fleet mutinied and a general strike was called. Lenin returned in November, 1905, and for three months tried to organize resistance in St Petersburg, but he was forced to move abroad again in 1906. The revolution was savagely suppressed, but, after it, from 1907 to 1914 a number of Parliaments (Dumas), with merely consultative powers, were called. They had hardly any influence on the Tsar or any popular appeal.

It was on this unlikely and unMarxist soil that Lenin had to work, and for almost twelve years entirely from without. He did it by holding regular European Congresses, by propaganda and pamphleteering, and by organizing for the day of revolution. His party, while keeping its secret and illegal machinery in being, sought, by permeation of the factories and trade unions, to bring a wider circle of workmen under its influence. His plan was to achieve revolution in three stages; first, by the temporary overthrow of authority and the attainment of political freedom by the people by creating or profiting from a situation of anarchy; secondly, by the creation of new revolutionary forces consisting of soviets (councils) of workers', soldiers' and peasants' deputies, who should be ready to seize power and begin the organization of the socialist state; and then, thirdly, by the forcible and permanent "liquidation" of the employers and propertied classes. The state, in the Marxist sense of the power available to a master class, would not just "wither away" but would be ruthlessly destroyed. In the meantime, parliamentary methods were to be exploited to the utmost. Those were, in fact, the tactics actually followed by the Bolsheviks in the Russian Revolution of 1917. They remain the classical model for Communists to follow in other countries, when circumstances permit.

While waiting for his opportunity, Lenin was himself studying and developing the Marxist canon of revolutionary philosophy. His *Philosophical Note Books* show a patient reading and criticism of many philosophers, especially Hegel. In 1908 he published his *Materialism and Empirio-Criticism*, which constituted an attack on a number of "would-be Marxists", including his later ally Lunacharsky. His major intellectual contribution, however, lay in three post-Marxian developments and these have led to his name being linked permanently with Marx as a major Communist writer and thinker. First, he applied Marxism to the world outside Europe, and especially to the new phenomenon of imperialism. Drawing in part on the writings of J. A. Hobson (*Imperialism* 1902), Lenin applied the Marxist analysis to the new forms of international capitalism which had developed since the conclusion of the work of Marx. With the concentration of capital, huge trusts and combines superseded the small producers of the earlier stages of capitalism. These large capital interests became inextricably interwoven with the State, and Lenin argued that they drove governments to imperialistic policies to capture foreign markets and sources of raw materials. Capitalism was not merely a national phenomenon, but a cause of imperialism and war. Yet imperialism is the very last stage of capitalism. It harbours all the inner contradictions of capitalism in an increased degree; they explode in ever greater crises and wars until a world-wide proletarian revolution overthrows capitalism and replaces it with socialism. Moreover, out of colonial profits the big monopolies can pay higher wages to their skilled workers, and thus a labour aristocracy arises which dominates the socialist parties and leads them on the way of "reformism". The poorer classes of workers, however, continue to adhere to revolutionary socialism. This is, he held, the underlying cause of the rift between the moderate and radical factions in the socialist movement. These were the years of sharp exchanges between Lenin as revolutionary socialist and Edward Bernstein, the German socialist, who tried to develop a Marxism that was evolutionary not revolutionary.

Secondly, Lenin built upon and extended the Marxist doctrine of the State in his *State and Revolution*, written just before the revolution of 1917 and published in 1918. In this work he developed Marx's idea of the dictatorship of the proletariat, which for Lenin became a dictatorship over the proletariat by a disciplined party group. He made a sharper distinction between Socialism and Communism than Marx had done, and began to speak of "Socialism in a single country", which Marx would probably not have endorsed and which Stalin was to make his own. The major purpose of the book, however, was to "legitimize" the events of 1917, to make the Bolshevik programme of the violent overthrow of the mildly liberal regime of left-wing liberals, led by the young lawyer Kerensky, appear to follow logically from Marxist writings. Lenin saw the state as an organ of class domination, "an organ of oppression of one class by another", and to him the logic was clear:

> "If the state is the product of the irreconcilable character of class antagonisms, if it is a force standing *above* society and 'increasingly separating itself from it', then it is clear that the liberation of the oppressed class is impossible not only without a violent revolution, *but also without the destruction* of the apparatus of state power, which was created by the ruling class and in which this 'separation' is embodied . . ."

There was, however, a third strand in his thinking, just as relevant as *State and Revolution*. He saw the First World War from the safe vantage point of Switzerland, and he saw it as an "Imperialists' War". For the purpose, he developed yet another tactic, that of "revolutionary defeatism".

> "The struggle against the Government that conducts the imperialist war", he wrote, "must not halt in any country before the possibility of that country's defeat in consequence of revolutionary propaganda. The defeat of the Governmental army weakens the Government, aids the liberation of the nationalities oppressed by it and makes civil war against the ruling class easier."

This policy of "transforming the imperialist war into a civil war" was adopted, at Lenin's instance, by the left wing of the Conference of European Socialists, held at Stockholm in 1915; and when the Russian Revolution finally occurred two years later, many European socialists believed that the seizure of power by the Bolsheviks in Russia was the beginning of the end of the existing order the world over. The prospects of the revolutionary "new order" were bound up in their minds, as in the minds of many of their successors, with the success of the Russian experiment. Moscow in this view was to become the Mecca of revolutionary socialism. It was to have a mystical attraction for those whose discontent with the existing order of things prepared them to accept the most radical changes. It gave them a disposition to praise and justify, on their face value, all the economic and social achievements of the new Russian regime, even before they could occur, and to ridicule any who, however conscientiously, should throw doubts upon the authenticity of any of these achievements.

Lenin's policy of revolutionary defeatism, however, in practice played straight into the hands of the German General Staff. And, in order to break down Russian resistance, the German military authorities, in April, 1917, arranged for Lenin and other Bolsheviks, like Zinoviev, Radek and Lunacharsky, to be transported in a sealed railway carriage from Switzerland, across Central Europe, which they controlled, and smuggled into Russia.

The first revolution had already occurred, and a provisional government, mostly of Social Democrats, had been formed, first under Prince Lvov, then under Kerensky. Lenin was afraid that the Russians would be satisfied with this form of moderate democracy, and he campaigned bitterly against the Kerensky group. In his hands PRAVDA, a small daily paper, now the official organ of the Communist International, became a powerful means of organizing the demand for total revolution.

A "soviet" of workers' representatives had been set up in Petrograd in March and this was his power base. But in July he had to flee to Finland, and Trotsky who had now joined him was arrested after the first *coup* failed—at first it seemed like 1905 all over. Nor did his theories help him. The party was still divided between Mensheviks and Bolsheviks. Marxism had always rested on the assumption that revolution would come first to an industrialized society that had a militant sense of class awareness and class bitterness, and a sharp sense of working-class solidarity. The Revolution to Marx was to be the work of a class, and to be carried through by the dictatorship of the proletariat. To Lenin it became the work of a party who were to bring "consciousness" to the working class. Lenin moved yet a further step from "pure" Marxism and decided empirically to strike for power quickly.

Events, however, now began to play into his hands. The hopeless offensive which the Allies forced the Russian armies to undertake on the Eastern front, its disastrous collapse and the appalling hardships of the troops filled Petrograd with angry crowds and armed demonstrators. The workers and peasants desperately wanted peace, while the new government remained loyal to Russia's allies and tried to carry on the war. The peasants wanted to divide the landlords' estates among themselves immediately, while the Kerensky government preached patience to them, asking them to wait until the transference of land could be legally arranged. The workers in the towns, to the dismay of the government and even of the Mensheviks, were taking over some of the factories and trying to run them. They were doing at the beginning of the capitalist phase of Russia's history what, according to the Mensheviks, ought to be attempted only at the end of it; and yet the Mensheviks, whose influence depended on the workers trusting them, dared not resist their initiative.

Soldiers were deserting from the front, industrial production was diminishing, and the peasants were growing violent. The time was fast approaching when, according to Lenin and Trotsky, the Bolsheviks could make a successful bid for power.

Lenin devised three slogans to enable his party to get power: "Immediate Peace", "All Land to the Peasants", and "All Power to the Soviets". Both the government and Mensheviks were for continuing the war, despite Russia's most costly defeats, for they feared to leave her at the mercy of the Germans. The Bolsheviks alone promised immediate peace, and the peasants and workers, who wanted peace and land immediately, saw that they could get them only with the Bolsheviks in power.

The first revolution of March, 1917, was liberal and "parliamentary"; the second revolution in October was a revolution of surrender, a surrender of Liberals, Mensheviks and Social Democrats to Lenin. The army was demoralized; the soldiers deserted in droves, formed Soviets or councils, and went over to the workers' side. The call of "land to the peasants" was followed by still more mass desertions. By October, 1917, the Bolsheviks were in a majority in the Petrograd Soviet and on 7 November they struck.

By that time 20,000 Red Guards were outside the Winter Palace; only 800 Whites held it. Railway stations, post offices and barracks were occupied, and the Kerensky government collapsed. After a futile attempt at resistance, Kerensky went into exile. By the old Russian calendar, 7 November was 25 October, which was thirteen days behind the rest of Europe, so to them it was and still is the "October" Revolution. Lenin became head of the Soviet or Council of People's Commissars, January, 1918, and head of the Russian Communist state. It was then only a small area of the former Tsarist territory.

Lenin, always a remarkable blend of the philosopher as well as the tactician of Communism, was aware that he was seeking to organize a premature revolution. It ought not to have come in a backward state, vast, demoralized and disunited, itself the size of a continent, lacking an industrial base, and with a foreign army in control of all its strategic and valuable areas. He therefore devised yet another argument, that of world revolution. Russia might be backward, and therefore, if considered in isolation, unripe for proletarian revolution; but Russia was only one of several Great Powers brought to the edge of disaster by war. In Germany there was a large working class taught for some forty years to respect Marxism, and in the other great industrial countries the workers were also tired of war and bitterly hostile to their governments. The Bolsheviks, by seizing power in Russia, were in fact setting an example to the proletarians of the West; they would be giving the initial impulse to the world proletarian revolution for which the advanced industrial countries—and they between them dominated the world—were already ripe. They would be destroying "the chain of imperialism" at its weakest link. As soon as the working class held power in the industrial West the proletarian government of backward Russia would receive all the help needed to avert the calamities foretold by the Mensheviks,and it would be possible to revert to the pure doctrine of 1848—workers of the world, unite.

According to this doctrine, world revolution—in Germany Britain and the United States—was imminent. It followed that peace could be made with Germany, and an "Imperialist" war brought to a quick end because the workers' revolution would soon occur in Germany too. Accordingly at Brest-Litovsk in March, 1918, the new state made an abject surrender to Germany and withdrew from the war. Indeed Trotsky's debating tactics dragged out the negotiations in the hope that every day of debate was a day nearer world revolution. And with the French Army near revolt in 1919, it was not as fanciful as now it might seem. In March, 1918, Russia surrendered Poland, the Baltic provinces, Finland, the Ukraine and the Caucasus to Germany, and with them half of its industrial and agricultural wealth. This was revolutionary defeatism with a vengeance. The treaty was formally annulled by the German Armistice in the West in November.

The philosophy of the Bolsheviks and their ultimate purposes were not even guessed at by the great majority of the Russian people. Their promises had offered what the people most urgently wanted, and they had therefore found it easy to take power. The business of keeping it proved incomparably more difficult. For four years a civil war was fought. Ex-Imperial army officers organized resistance among the Cossacks, and White armies appeared led by Generals Kornilov and Denikin. General Yudenitch nearly captured Petrograd. The Allies, who wanted the war against Germany continued, gave support to the Whites. Japanese landed at Vladivostok. Admiral Kolchak dominated Siberia. The Poles fought for survival against Germans and Russians—a war that continued until 1921.

In the long war against their enemies—Whites, Poles, Balts, Japanese, British, French, Germans and Americans—the Bolsheviks could rely on the industrial workers; they held the heart of Russia, her largest towns and important centres of communication. But the attitude to them of the peasants was uncertain and suspicious. The better-to-do among them hated the Bolsheviks, resenting their forced levies and urban arrogance, but they also disliked the Whites, whom they suspected of wanting to bring the old landlords back. But the poorer peasants were easily won over to the Bolsheviks, who made them their agents in the villages, thus putting it in their power to tyrannize their more prosperous neighbours.

Yet the Bolsheviks were never strong while the civil war lasted, and when it ended they were widely hated. They survived only because their enemies were weaker even than they were, and politically were much less shrewd. Using the emergency as an excuse, the Bolsheviks had set up their party dictatorship and restored the political police. In 1921 Russia was exhausted; and the Bolsheviks, though more detested, and by many more people, than they had been in November, 1917, were firmly in the saddle. And the foreign intervention rallied the Mensheviks to a cause now seen as a struggle for national survival.

The expected world revolution, used by them to justify their bid for power, never happened. But, having got power and fought hard to keep it, they meant to use it. Their duty seemed plain to them. They had become the masters of a great country, and must make it the centre of a revolutionary Socialist movement covering the whole world. In 1919 the Third or Communist International was set up in Moscow, to aid and abet world revolution. At the same time, because their country was backward, the Bolsheviks had to endow it with industries and educate its people at an unprecedented speed. As Lenin repeatedly said, Communism meant revolution—and electrification.

The years from 1914 and especially from 1917 to 1921 were years of appalling hardship for the Russian people. Only a government of discipline and ruthlessness could have survived, and it ruled by terror and by a savage secret police. The Tsar and his family, after a year's imprisonment at Ekaterinburg in the Urals, were shot in July, 1918, by local Communists as Whites and Czechs advanced on them; their bodies were thrown down a disused mineshaft (though legend has it that Princess Anastasia survived, and a lady claiming to be her is now living quietly in Charlottesville, Virginia). Priests, officers, teachers and landowners were "liquidated". In the Constitution of 1918, adopted by the all-Russian Congress of Soviets, all bourgeois classes were disfranchised. Only the Bolshevik party was legal, and there was no freedom of opinion. Russia was governed now not by 180,000 landlords, but by 240,000 party members. Lenin's authority in party and state was unquestioned until his death.

They were grim years, and the policy Lenin followed did not help. By a decree of 7 November, 1917, all the large estates were confiscated and placed under soviets or councils of peasants. Workers' soviets also attempted to run industries, which were gradually nationalized. Private trade was suppressed, food tightly rationed, church property confiscated. By 1921 both industry and agriculture were in a state of collapse. Industrial output was as low as 17 per cent of that of 1913, and the yield of corn was less than half of the pre-war figures. Famine was widespread in 1920–21, and the typhus epidemic which swept across Europe after the war claimed thousands of victims. Finally, when the sailors at Kronstadt, the naval base near Petrograd, who had backed the coup of November, 1917, mutinied in March, 1921, and were only controlled after terrible bloodshed, Lenin decided on a temporary "retreat from Communism". Once again a tactical withdrawal was necessary. In order to increase production he initiated the New Economic Policy (N.E.P.), by which private concerns were permitted to engage in trade and manufacture, while the peasants were to pay a fixed levy of grain which would leave them with a surplus to sell. As a result, some improvement took place in economic conditions. But it took place slowly.

Lenin's opportunity came, in 1917, after a long exile and a long wait, when he was forty-seven. He sought to build the socialist state that his Marxism had taught him, but it came in an alien environment, where he had no book to guide him. He was both more humane and more a realist than many of his followers, but he found himself compelled to rely on a rigid party bureaucracy and to deny all criticism and all freedom even to those he sought to liberate. Russia in 1921, with its lack of press freedom and its secret police, was more the Old Russia than a New Paradise. The new dictatorship of the party, however benevolent in intent, was in practice the old tyranny writ large. The unity of state and party was maintained at the price of freedom. Lenin made it clear enough:

"The revolutionary dictatorship of the proletariat is rule won and maintained by the use of violence by the proletariat against the bourgeoisie, rule that is unrestricted by any laws."

(From *The Proletarian Revolution*)

The tragedy of the Revolution is that Lenin could not have done otherwise. The Revolution was made before the masses were ready for it, as he knew, and he had to keep power in order to allow socialism to develop. He died a disappointed man, worried not only at the situation of chaos in Russia but at the growth of bureaucracy, at the moral degeneration of his followers, and at the failure of Revolution abroad; only Hungary for a short time had a Communist regime. So the Communist International was hard to distinguish from the cause of Russia, and an ugly war of words and ideology began between a closed, suspicious, poor and conspiratorial Russia, on the one hand, and an equally suspicious and hostile capitalist West on the other. This was a bitter legacy.

Lenin died at Gorki, 21 January, 1924. He had been shot at in August, 1918, and wounded; a second attempt on his life was made in 1922. His wounds, the earlier periods of imprisonment, the long years of overwork all sapped his strength. His body was embalmed and is on permanent exhibition in Moscow; the old capital of St Petersburg, which Kerensky had re-named Petrograd, was now re-named Leningrad. Lenin is recognized as the architect of the Russian Communist state. His contribution was almost equally important as writer. His *Collected Works* in Russian run to 30 volumes with another 30 of miscellaneous writings (*Leninskie Sborniki*).

It is hardly possible to minimize the significance of Lenin for the understanding of contemporary European Socialism and Communism. He was the founder of the first European Communist state, and he is the prototype revolutionary leader. His concept of a small disciplined party of professional revolutionaries has been accepted and imitated as the model of contemporary revolutionary methodology. As writer, he contributed to the study—and the weakening—of European imperialism; and his last articles were a warning against bureaucracy and the accumulation of power by the Party's General Secretary, Stalin. Moreover, seeing Communist Russia as only the first of what would be a succession of revolutionary republics, he was responsible for the revival of the International Working Men's Association as a distinctively Communist force; Moscow for over thirty years was seen as a second Rome, the spiritual and organizational centre not only for European Communism but for the cause of world revolution.

E. H. Carr has written this assessment of him:

"It has become a commonplace to praise Lenin's realism, his flexibility, his practical commonsense in judging what could and what could not be done at the given moment; and all these qualities he possessed in pre-eminent degree. But perhaps the most vivid impression left by a re-reading of his major works is of the amazing intellectual power and consistency of purpose which runs through them. His tactical readiness to compromise, to tack, to retreat when it became necessary was an enormous asset to a politician. But what is infinitely more striking is that he seems to have known from the first where he was going and how he intended to get there, and that when he died in 1924 the revolution was firmly established on foundations which he had begun to dig thirty years before."

SIR WINSTON CHURCHILL
(1874–1965)

SIR WINSTON CHURCHILL bestrode his world like a colossus, and his career as author, soldier, politician, Prime Minister and war leader is the most colourful and dramatic in modern British history. He was born in 1874, elder son of that Lord Randolph Churchill who was Lord Salisbury's Chancellor of the Exchequer—and whose memory he revered and sought to capture in his biography of him—and he died in 1965, aged ninety. His service as a Minister of the Crown thus extended over thirty years and as a parliamentarian for over fifty-five. He served six sovereigns, of whom the first and the last was a Queen. He proved to be in war as masterful and successful a strategist as the elder Pitt, but he lived a much longer life through far more testing and far more violent, and violently changing, times. And the years described as "peace" were as challenging and restless as those of war.

The man's range and vigour are as striking as the record of his achievements. He could be fitted into no party harness: he began as a Conservative and was first elected as such in 1900; he became in 1904 a Liberal, and in 1924 reverted again to Conservatism. By nature a partisan, he was never a natural party politician. Despite his zeal for social reform in 1910, he was never fully a Liberal because he never shared the Liberal reluctance to solve a problem by force. But when he took his seat as Prime Minister in 1940, the loudest cheers did not come from the Tory benches.

He captured in 1940, and expressed through the war years in voice and pen, a sense of being specially destined for the role of war leader, and of being the voice and the hope of his country. As Lady Violet Bonham Carter, Asquith's daughter, said of him: "Though never (to my mind) a Tory, he saw and judged events in the historic framework of tradition." By capturing the spirit of Britain, he was able to lead his country through its most severe test in 1940–41, when it stood alone against totalitarian Europe; by surviving then he led it on to victory. Britain's debt to him is beyond calculation. He was the greatest Englishman of his age, and perhaps in all British history.

Winston Churchill was born at Blenheim Palace on 30 November, 1874; he arrived prematurely, in fact in the midst of the St Andrew's Night Ball, and was born in a closet to which his mother was carried. His mother Jennie Jerome of New York was a great beauty; his father, the third son of the 7th Duke, had just been elected to Parliament, and blazed across the political scene like a meteor until his light was dimmed after 1886—in part because Lord Salisbury accepted a resignation that was not really intended, in part because of the syphilis that killed him in 1894. His mother, a fervent socialite, was extravagant and somewhat feckless; she had many admirers and made a second marriage that was not successful. On her sixtieth birthday she said, "I'll never get used to not being the most beautiful woman in the room". Aged sixty-one, she married for a third time, and a man three years younger than her son. To her Winston was devoted, and it says much for him. Hers was, he said on her death in 1921, "a life of sunshine and storms".

His education at Harrow was unhappy—though to the school he was in his famous years to show a filial devotion. The legend has it that he was slow at school and especially weak in mathematics. But, patchy and unpalatable as was his education, one thing it did give him, and to it he was to owe his capacity to earn a living and to make a reputation: the ability to write. Churchill was to be first and last a historian, and indeed it was his own sense of history that helped him in 1940 to infuse his own dogged qualities into a whole people. And this depended on the cultivation of a distinctive style.

"We were considered such dunces (he recalls in *My Early Life*), that we could only learn English. Mr Somervell—a most delightful man, to whom my debt is great—was charged with the duty of teaching the stupidest boys the most disregarded thing—namely, to write mere English. He knew how to do it. He taught it as no one else has ever taught it. Not only did we learn English parsing thoroughly, but we also practised continually English analysis. Mr. Somervell has a system of his own. He took a fairly long sentence and broke it up into its components by means of black, red, blue and green inks. Subject, verb, object: Relative Clauses, Conditional Clauses, Conjunctive and Disjunctive Clauses! Each had its colour and its bracket. It was a kind of drill. We did it almost daily. As I remained in the Third Fourth (B) three times as long as anyone else, I had three times as much of it. I learned it thoroughly. Thus I got into my bones the essential structure of the ordinary British sentence—which is a noble thing. And when in after years my schoolfellows who had won prizes and distinction for writing such beautiful Latin poetry and pithy Greek epigrams had to come down again to common English, to earn their living or make their way, I did not feel myself at any disadvantage. Naturally I am biased in favour of boys learning English. I would make them all learn English: and then I would let the clever ones learn Latin as an honour, and Greek as a treat. But the only thing I would whip them for is not knowing English. I would whip them hard for that . . ."

It is clear that, if both a Churchill and a Jerome, Winston Churchill owed most, not to his parents, but to himself. Both his parents were throughout his boyhood remote and even callous when he made his appeals for help or affection, and some of his father's letters were utterly lacking in the human touch. In all the apparent opulence it was a lonely, neglected and unhappy boyhood. Moreover, when Lord Randolph died in 1894, his son was in fact left impecunious, and with a far from adequate preparation for life. Blessed, and in some respects cursed, by the name he bore, he had to stand on his own feet. Things were not won with any of the effortless superiority ascribed to Balliol men, but by an effort and application that did not come naturally. Both the writing and the oratory were difficult to cultivate. But he had immense zest— his boyhood is a series of mischievous escapades and he was clearly far from "biddable"—ferocious ambition, and great courage.

As he was to write nearly forty years later in his *Life of Marlborough*, "It is said that famous men are usually the product of an unhappy childhood. The stern compression of circumstances, the twinges of adversity, the spur of slights and taunts in early years, are needed to evoke that ruthless fixity of purpose and tenacious mother-wit without which great actions are seldom accomplished."

And in 1898 he wrote of the Mahdi:

"Solitary trees, if they grow at all, grow strong; and a boy de-deprived of a father's care often develops, if he escapes the perils of youth, an independence and vigour of thought which may restore in after life the heavy loss of early days."

There were traces of autobiography here.

He entered Sandhurst in 1893 on the third attempt, and here his interest was captured, not least by studying the campaigns of the American Civil War. He passed out with honours, eighth in a class of 150, and was commissioned in the 4th Hussars in 1895. There followed five years of high adventure. There was service as an observer and war correspondent with Spanish forces in the Cuban war of 1895. This was followed by service with his regiment at Bangalore in southern India, during which he read and re-read Gibbon, Lecky and Macaulay, on whose rolling periods much of his own superb style, at once rugged and rhetorical, was fashioned. This was a seminal period for him. It was in India that he came to the conclusion that "the orator wields a power more durable than that of a great king"; and it was in India that he came to believe in the Pax Britannica, "to the maintenance of which I shall devote my life."

The young Indian cavalry officer, fortified by the Sudan experience and his escape from the Boers, was indeed the father of the man. On leave from India, and by the happy fact of personal acquaintance with Sir Bindon Blood, he became war correspondent-turned-combatant on the North-West Frontier with the Malakand Field Force, whose task was to suppress the Pathans, then in rebellion. From this came his first book, *The Malakand Field Force*, which one reviewer described as "A Subaltern's Hints to Generals".

The book won its author favourable notice, sufficient to overcome the resistance of Sir Herbert Kitchener, Commander-in-Chief of the Anglo-Egyptian Army sent to liberate the Sudan from the Dervishes, who did not want the brash young man around. But thanks to his mother's pleadings, the War Office gave Churchill a commission with the 21st Lancers, and he also secured an assignment with *The Morning Post* as an accredited war correspondent in the Sudan. He rode in the famous cavalry charge which won the battle of Omdurman, the last cavalry charge in British history. Out of this experience came the two volumes of *The River War*, and an unsuccessful election campaign in 1899 at Oldham.

This success in turn led *The Morning Post* to send him to South Africa as a special correspondent in the Boer War, and at a special —and till then unheard of—salary of £250 a month. It was in South Africa that Winston Churchill made a national reputation. He was captured by the Boers in 1899 while trying under fire to repair a wrecked train—which made news; and he escaped— which made headlines. He engaged in battles up to the capture of

Pretoria. When he fought Oldham a second time in the "Khaki" election of 1900, it was as a national hero. He toured the country lecturing at a fee varying from £100 to £300 a night. A lecture tour in the United States brought him £10,000 in two months, and he was described as "the hero of five wars, the author of six books, and the future Prime Minister of Great Britain". In five years he had earned a reputation for high courage, love of adventure, unsleeping ambition and zestful success. He had polished his prose style, and with his pen begun to make a fortune. He was colourful, impish, a great Romantic adorning the epic age of Empire, a real-life Kipling hero. As the war correspondent G. W. Stevens saw him then, and with prescience:

> "His brief military career is interesting as an illustration of the versatility, the pushing energy, the precocious worldly wisdom of the man. He is ambitious, he is calculating, yet he is not cold. He has not studied to make himself a demagogue. He was a born demagogue and he happens to know it. The master strain in his character is the rhetorician."

Of these years his son Randolph wrote:

> "His school was the barrack-room; his university the battle-field. He has served in two regiments of the line, fought with the Spaniards in Cuba, and held a commission in the South African Light Horse. He knows life in four continents, and has smelt powder in three. He has seen more wars than any man of his years; written more books than any soldier living. He has been a war correspondent; he has been taken prisoner; he has escaped from prison. And he showed the same address in war as in politics. General Smuts told me that when he held up the armoured train on which Mr Churchill was captured he was struck by the energy and capacity of a fair-haired youth who led the defence. When they surrendered, this youth modestly claimed special privileges in telegraphing to his friends on the ground that he was a war correspondent. The General laughed 'You have done all the damage that's been done,' he said. 'You fight too well to be treated as a civilian.' 'And now,' added the General in telling me the story, 'I am going to the Colonial Office to see if I can get a favour out of that fair-haired youth in memory of our meeting on the veldt.' "

And, aged twenty-six, he was an M.P.; except for two years (1922–24) he would sit continuously in the House of Commons for over fifty-five years.

The young warrior moved socially in an Edwardian world that

had about it something of the raffish quality of the France of the Second Empire. Scandal seemed to lurk just below the surface of society; there was a touch of shoddiness in the glitter, and Soho was in reality, as in geography, disturbingly close to the Mall and the Court. But it was a world rich in characters and in drama. The House was the stage, but there were dinners with Buckle of *The Times*, Spender of the *Westminster Gazette*, and John Morley, who introduced Churchill to Seebohm Rowntree's study of *Poverty*— perhaps the beginning of his transition to Liberalism. The young hero was much in demand, and not long a back-bencher. Indeed, he was not long a bachelor either. In 1908, the year he became President of the Board of Trade, he married Clementine Hozier, "the sheet anchor of his career".

The future Lady Churchill was not his first love. He had been unofficially engaged to Pamela Plowden, and he had proposed to others, including Ethel Barrymore. Nor was the first meeting with Miss Hozier auspicious. As she later described it: "Winston just stared. He never uttered one word and was very gauche—he never asked me for a dance, he never asked me to have supper with him. I had of course heard a great deal about him—nothing but ill. I had been told he was stuck-up, objectionable, etcetera. And on this occasion he just stood and stared."

But when the friendship began four years later it proved a different story: by 1908 she found him "brilliant and dynamic". She had, said Violet Asquith, "a face of classical perfection—a profile like the prow of a ship", and she was, said the same committed lady, "a better natural Liberal than Winston". It was a marriage of remarkable and lasting happiness, and provided that bedrock of stability on which a political career of storms and epic greatness was based.

Churchill began as a Tory but with a reputation to defend and cherish, not his own but his father's. His father's enemies of the 1880's he wanted to do down. He referred in his maiden speech to "a certain splendid memory" that was to be preserved. He was researching his father's life, and this reinforced his loyalty. He called for retrenchment on military expenditure, as his father had done before him. He had hopes of a new "Fourth Party". The uneasy radicalism of his Edwardian years was a product of his filial loyalty and of his natural pugnacity—even if it was a radicalism that could denounce dukes during the week and spend week-ends at Blenheim.

The reasons he himself gave for his conversion to Liberalism in 1904 were not just distaste for those who had scorned his father, but hatred of Joseph Chamberlain's tariff reform campaign, which threatened to turn the Conservative Party into a fortress of high Protection, distaste for Jingoism, and a mounting passion for social reform. He was concerned over low wages and unemployment—"I see little glory in an empire which can rule the waves and is unable to flush its sewers"; and he was attracted, and did not hide the fact, by the intellectual calibre of the leading Liberals. "I belonged to a stupid party which I have left because I do not want to go on saying stupid things."

Indeed the natural rhetorician in him piled it on; witness his famous description of the Conservative Party:

"Sentiment by the bucketful, patriotism by the imperial pint, the open hand at the public exchequer, the open door at the public-house, dear food for the million, cheap labour for the millionaire."

This vehemence cost him what little popularity he still retained. From the first he had moved with remarkable confidence and individuality in the House—in 1900 he voted against most of his Party leaders within an hour of taking his seat. It was a less tidy and more robust political world than today's, and it could still be swayed by oratory and energy. From 1904 onwards a shiver of alarm and hate ran through the Tory ranks when he spoke; Balfour, his former friend and leader, left the Chamber when he rose to speak: when Churchill spoke of "a lack of deference and respect", other front bench Tories followed their leader. Churchill became the ogre of the drawing rooms, Lady Lugard spoke of "Wild Winston . . . an ignorant boy . . . the damage he may do appears to be colossal". And Lord Charles Beresford, who was a good judge of ambition, called him a "Lilliput Napoleon— a man with an unbalanced mind, an egomaniac".

He was, however, a successful apprentice. He served (1905–8) as Under Secretary for Colonies under Campbell-Bannerman, and actively supported the policy of self-government for the Transvaal and Orange River Colonies. With a chief, Lord Elgin, in the Lords, he piloted through the Commons the South African constitutional settlement. He joined the Cabinet as President of the Board of Trade (1908–10) and was for the following year Home Secretary. He was an interventionist in economic affairs, deliberately adopting Bismarck's State socialist measures as his model. He established machinery for the conciliation and arbitration of trade disputes, introduced daylight-saving, legislated to prevent sweated labour, set up employment exchanges, and introduced unemployment insurance. Much of Churchill's work at the Home Office was inevitably concerned with the maintenace of law and order during the industrial disputes of 1911 and 1912.

His energy as Home Secretary gave him a "strong" image but nothing would be more absurd than to regard the Churchill of those days as a reactionary. Representing predominantly working-class constituencies—Oldham, Manchester North-West and then Dundee—he found himself moving ever further to the Left to defeat the appeal of the Tory cry, "Tariff Reform means work for all". As Lloyd George's closest colleague, he gave strong support to the Lloyd George Budget and revelled almost indecently, for the scion of a noble house, in the clash which followed between the House of Commons and the House of Lords.

Recognizing the Government's dependence on the Irish vote in the House, Churchill supported Home Rule and, with more courage than wisdom, went to Belfast to defend the Government's proposals. But as the Irish crisis deepened, he grew increasingly aware of the genuine character of Ulster's resistance to Home Rule. He began to revive some of Lord Randolph's schemes of devolution, and there was speculation that he might resign over Ulster.

In 1911 he went to the Admiralty. However much a decade before he had wanted retrenchment, now he found the responsibility of defence sobering. The Admiralty, he said in 1911, could only be wrong once. He pressed for increased naval expenditure to the point of resignation. His critics—some of them his colleagues—said with some justice that he had given up Liberalism for the Navy. But when the war came in 1914 at least the Fleet was ready. The achievement went beyond the building of the Grand Fleet; it also meant the beginning of the Naval War Staff, the creation of the Royal Naval Air Service, the mobilization of the Fleet, its safe arrival at its war station in time for the declaration of war, the safe transportation of the British Expeditionary Force and its secure maintenance in France, the mobilization of imperial forces across wide oceans, the sweeping away of German commerce and the protection of Britain's own, and the confinement of the German High Seas Fleet within its harbours—it was a monument of achievement.

Yet in all his vigour—which showed through dramatically in 1914–15, especially in his repeated pleas for a military command—he was in these years politically accident-prone, over-combative and over-talkative; and some questioned his judgment. He strongly favoured the Dardanelles campaign, to strike at the weakest point in the German-Turkish Axis. The Conservative Opposition seized on its failure to demand his head as the price of the Coalition, and Asquith sacrificed it, and Haldane's. Yet the Gallipoli project proved his strategic genius, and would have succeeded (as we now know from enemy sources), if Admiral de Robeck had been less cautious and General Sir Charles Monro less pusillanimous. This soldier was the only man to whom Churchill in Lady Asquith's experience ever felt vindictive: "I should like him to starve without a pension in a suburban hovel facing a redbrick wall." In *The World Crisis*, he damns him in a lapidary phrase—"an officer of swift decision, he came, he saw, he capitulated."

Not content with getting Churchill out of the Admiralty the Conservatives soon expelled him from the War Council. He therefore resigned from the Cabinet and went to serve on the French front. It was the nadir of his career. For twenty years the cry "What about the Dardanelles?" would dog him. But to the culpability of the men on the spot there were others far more responsible than Churchill: not least Fisher, First Sea Lord, an erratic and megalomaniac 73-year-old, Kitchener and Asquith. Churchill alone carried the blame.

Churchill spent a year in the trenches, commanding the 6th Royal Scots Fusiliers. After a commission of inquiry into the Dardanelles had cleared him, and Lloyd George had replaced Asquith as Prime Minister, he returned to office in 1917 as Minister of Munitions, in time to help equip the American Army that arrived in Europe, and to produce the "tank". From 1918 to 1921 he was Secretary for War and Air, through the trying time of troubles in Ireland and troubles that became a revolution in Russia; and from 1921 to 1922 as Colonial Secretary he served through the equally trying days of the post-war settlement in the Near East.

When the Conservatives left the Coalition in 1922 over the Chanak crisis, Churchill went out into the wilderness with Lloyd George. In fact in 1922 an appendicitis operation prevented a full electioneering campaign and he was rejected by the electors of Dundee—a city towards which he was never to feel quite so affectionate again. "I came out of hospital", he said, "to find that I had lost my seat, my party and my appendix."

It was some time before he found a new constituency. He stood for Leicester and was beaten. He stood for Westminster and lost by forty votes. At last he found refuge in Epping and later in Woodford, where his loyal constituents were to send him to Parliament on eight successive occasions. When he got back in the House in 1924 he was a man without a party. He had fallen out with the Liberals and now termed himself a Constitutionalist.

In 1924, on his return, Baldwin invited him to serve as Chancellor of the Exchequer, much to his surprise, and to his pride, since it had been his father's post. His most famous Budget was that of 1925, which put Britain back on the Gold Standard and sent up the price of British goods abroad. He was in his element during the General Strike of 1926, and among multifarious activities he produced a Government journal, *The British Gazette*, which when the strike was in its eighth day was running to over 2 million copies. When the Government was defeated in 1929, he went out of office and stayed out for ten long years.

The 1930s were his second nadir. These were the years of a national depression that was more than an economic decline; of massive unemployment in particular regions, especially Scotland and Wales and the North-east of England; of recurrent crises in India, on which Churchill was consistently a hard-line imperialist; of Edward VIII's marriage, on which he was an incurable romantic and spoke of a "Royal party"; and of mounting crises, moving in the end to war, with Hitlerite Germany. On the danger from Germany Churchill was consistent, emphatic, and all too prescient. Through the years up to September, 1939, his was a lone voice; Baldwin and Chamberlain gave no heed to his call nor any place to him in their Administrations; he was an embarrassment in their noble but fruitless pacific efforts. When he was—to his surprise—invited to attend a lunch to meet Von Ribbentrop, "I suppose", he said, "Ministers asked me to come along to show him that if they could not bark themselves, they kept a dog who could bark and bite."

When Austria was seized, he crossed the Channel to meet France's leaders, the soldiers as well as the politicians. The two countries, he said, must join together to prepare to resist the Nazis. He proposed that a defensive alliance should be formed with the smaller states of Europe, with Yugoslavia, Roumania, Hungary,

Czechoslovakia, with Greece, with Turkey. One by one they might be swallowed up, but together they would be powerful enough to protect themselves. Nothing was done.

After Munich in 1938, he prophesied disaster.

"All," he said, "is over. Silent, mournful, abandoned, broken, Czechoslovakia recedes into the darkness.

"We are in the presence of a disaster of the first magnitude that has befallen Britain and France.

"We have passed an awful milestone in our history, when the whole equilibrium of Europe has been deranged. Terrible words have been pronounced for the time being against the Western democracies—'Thou art weighed in the balance and found wanting.'

"This is only the beginning of the reckoning. This is only the first sip, the first foretaste of the bitter cup."

A year later, 1 September, 1939, Germany invaded Poland and Britain declared war. On 3 September, 1939, Churchill went to his old place of 1911 as First Lord of the Admiralty, and a famous signal went to the fleets across the seven seas: "Winston is back." His old war map was hung on the wall. On 10 May, 1940, he succeeded Chamberlain as Prime Minister.

Churchill's story from 1940 to 1945 is identical with his country's. When between 1923 and 1929 he wrote what was in form an autobiography (in four volumes) it was not arrogant for him to call it *World Crisis*; the six volumes of *The Second World War* that he wrote after 1945 are a second autobiography that is identical with his country's history. It was a very percipient Edwardian journalist writing as early as 1908 who had detected his natural leanings, and they were made for the crisis of 1940, perhaps the most frightening in British history:

". . . his real political philosophy is the philosophy of Caesarism. If we could conceive him in a great upheaval, he would be seen emerging in the role of what Bagehot calls "a Benthamite despot", dismissing all feudal ideas and legitimist pretensions, sweeping aside all aristocracies, proclaiming the democratic doctrine of the "greatest happiness of the greatest number" and seating himself astride the storm as the people's Caesar—at once dictator and democrat."

It was one of his great skills to keep his war-time team happy and harmonious—unlike Lloyd George's. Despite early disasters and some heavy losses of able men, his Cabinet Ministers (of all parties) and his battle commanders were able and loyal, again unlike Lloyd George's. He was himself Minister of Defence, and there was no nonsense about where power lay. His training in Gibbon and Macaulay now brought rich dividends; the War speeches, delivered in an inimitable style, in which even the oddities of pronunciation became endearing, are now immortal classics. This was a man whose whole career of adventure and of temporary exile seemed to have been but a preparation for his real task. It did not seem to matter that, in 1940, he was sixty-six. He lived, it seemed, like Bismarck, on an unusual diet: cigars, brandy and crisis, and he needed them all.

To the tactical skill of an Elder Pitt he added an unusual—and far from expected—skill as a diplomat. He could be expected to get on well with President Roosevelt. Stalin was a very different matter. And yet—though he never had any of FDR's curious illusions that he knew how to handle him, by treating him as if he were another Cook County boss—and although he had to suffer the embarrassing anti-imperialist baitings of the President, he identified his country promptly with Russia when she was invaded by Germany in 1941. The Atlantic Charter was drawn up at sea, in August, 1941, as a statement of Anglo-American policy. On the entry of the United States into the war after the Japanese attack on Pearl Harbour in December, 1941, he visited the United States, addressed Congress and established a strong claim on American affection— after all, he said, if his father instead of his mother had been an American he might have got to Congress on his own. And there were the series of conferences at which the war-time and post-war strategy were hammered out: with FDR at Washington (June, 1942; May, 1943) Casablanca (January, 1943) and Quebec (August, 1943 and September, 1944); with FDR and Chiang Kai-shek at Cairo (November, 1943); with FDR and Stalin at Teheran (December, 1943) and Yalta (February, 1943); and with Truman and Stalin at Potsdam (July, 1945).

His policy, he was fond of saying, was "Victory". The basis of his statecraft was the American alliance and the freeing of, and restoration of stability to, Europe. He welcomed the Russian alliance, but had no illusions about Communism, and in 1943 wanted, as in 1915, to strike at "the soft under-belly of the Axis" and get to Berlin before the Russians. A master of words, he was even more a master realist of power politics.

The defeat at the polls in 1945 came as an unpleasant surprise.

He spent six years in Opposition, and was not always regular in attendance at the House. He was busy as a writer, his books still the main source of his income. The six volumes on *The Second World War* appeared at almost yearly intervals—a million words or more. His great themes after 1945 became the menace of Russia, first voiced at Westminster College, Fulton, Missouri, in which the phrase "The Iron Curtain" was first used; and the need, if Europe was to resist Communism, for European solidarity and union. At the height of the German threat to France in 1940 he had proposed an Anglo-French Union. Now at Strasbourg he was greeted as first citizen of Europe. His speeches, and his visits to Europe, were treated with veneration. It was unfortunate that the European expectations of British sympathy for European unification, and for prompt British adhesion to the Treaty of Rome when it was signed in 1957 that were aroused by his speeches, were disappointed after 1951.

When Churchill became Prime Minister again in 1951, he was seventy-seven and tiring. In 1953 he suffered a stroke, the scale of which was never fully revealed to the British public. He became a Knight of the Garter in 1953 at the hands of the new Queen, but stayed a House of Commons man to the end. He was succeeded as Prime Minister in 1955 by his war-time lieutenant and Foreign Secretary, Anthony Eden. He did not stand at the election of 1959, by which time he was becoming deaf.

Winston Churchill died in January, 1965, and his funeral was an immense pageant, of an age and of an Empire whose sun seemed to set with him. After a service at St Paul's, his body went by barge up the Thames to be interred in the family vault at Bladon, near Blenheim.

Winston Churchill was at times unpredictable, at times impossible, at times captivating. He was dependent in the war years and after on a few key figures: on Alanbrooke in war, for instance, the real organizer of victory, and he listened to Smuts and to John Anderson. He could be impulsive and arrogant. There was an almost-proud ignorance of science. There were vast inconsistencies. And there was a near-total ignorance of the ordinary world. He hardly saw it except as an audience, with himself commanding the stage ("You probably don't realize", Clemmie told Lord Moran, his doctor, "that he knows nothing of the life of ordinary people. He's never been in a bus, and only once on the Underground." She smiled, "That was during the General Strike when I deposited him at South Kensington. He went round and round, not knowing where to get out, and had to be rescued eventually. . . . He's an egoist, I suppose, like Napoleon.")

His story can be told as a failure up to 1940, and as an anti-climax after 1945. This may well be the final judgment of history. If so, those five years have still to be explained: why it was that a small and vulnerable island stood alone for eighteen months against the embattled might of the Europe of the dictators, and in doing so kept alive the cause of the free world; and how, in the end, survival was transformed into victory. However else it be explained, however it might be qualified by errata of judgment then or later, however much it was a people's rather than one man's achievement, however much it was given to him only—as he said—to provide the lion's roar, there can be no question that Churchill's leadership, oratory and courage were fundamental to that effort and to that survival. Stalin in 1945 said he could think of no other instance in history where the future of the world depended on the courage of one man. Churchill's own favourite words in his "History" are Resolution; and Magnanimity.

> "At Marrakesh in 1947 Lady Moran asked him 'Which year of all your life, if you could relive one twelvemonth, would you choose?' Winston: '1940, every time, every time.' "

Churchill's pride was fiercely patriotic, and fiercely imperial. He was first and last a nationalist, and only reluctantly a European. He spoke French execrably, and indeed made of it both a pleasantry and a challenge. But in 1940 he made a gallant offer of joint citizenship to France, in an effort to prevent her collapse; his voice in the war years was a call to European national revival; and from 1946 to 1950 he firmly advocated European unity. If his own bulldog qualities were in 1940 deliberately cultivated as "English", Europe then and later recognized that this very dourness was among the major reasons for Hitler's defeat. In this sense, if 1940 was for Churchill, as for his country its finest hour, the Europe of the Six in 1947 and later owed to him more than any other man its own democratic survival.

David Lloyd George was above all things a Welshman—as Winston Churchill declared in his funeral oration, "the greatest Welshman which that unconquerable race has produced since the age of the Tudors". Among his altogether exceptional qualities was a voice capable of the most extraordinary expression of passion and power, and above we see him, in his latter days, addressing a crowd in one of his campaigns for the re-creation of Britain after the First World War. *Right:* as he was in his young days, speaking in the House of Commons in 1904, when the Free Trade versus Protection controversy was at its height.

MR. D LLOYD GEORGE. M.P.

'COBDEN WAS NOT MERELY A FREE TRADER BUT OPPOSED TO WAR.'

"THE OLD BANNER STILL WAVES PROUDLY OVER A VICTORIOUS FIGHTING LINE."

MR WINSTON CHURCHILL M.P.

For nearly seventy years Winston Churchill was never for long off the front pages of the newspapers. He wrote history, and made it. Early in this century he was Lloyd George's lieutenant in a vast programme of social reforms. In the First World War he saw that the Navy was ready; and in the Second of the "wars of the terrible twentieth century"—his phrase—he was both the leader of the British people and the embodiment of their spirit. His voice inspired and his hand guided them on the road to ultimate victory.

Left: the young Churchill of 1904, debating in the House of Commons.

Below: outside No. 10 Downing Street in 1943, acknowledging the greetings of the crowd with his famous "V for Victory" sign.

ALBERT EINSTEIN
(1879–1955)

WHEN Albert Einstein as a youth was at school at Aargau Cantonal College in Switzerland, his Latin master once told him: "You will never amount to anything, Einstein." On 16 July, 1945, when Einstein was sixty-six years old, the first-ever atomic bomb was exploded at Alamogordo in the New Mexican desert, U.S.A., and a month later came Hiroshima and the end of the second world war.

Einstein did not invent the A-bomb, but he was the mathematical genius who revolutionized theoretical physics and made it possible for others to devise the basic formulae of the bomb. It wasn't his fault; indeed, with Bertrand Russell and others as allies, he expressed his horror, and campaigned with them to warn mankind of the unimaginable dangers of this terrible new power available from the nucleus of the uranium atom.

His immortality in history lies in his controversial, but finally confirmed, theory of relativity. Even today it is understood only by experts, but it is the foundation of modern physical sciences, and is as important as Newton's laws of motion and gravitation. Einstein did not demolish Newton; he merely extended and added mathematical sophistication to his basic premises.

He was born in Württemburg, Germany, on 14 March, 1879, in the small town of Ulm—the son of Hermann Einstein, a Jew. The family moved to Munich during Einstein's childhood, and then went to live in Milan. In 1895 Einstein travelled to Zurich to take an entrance examination for the Federal Institute of Technology, but failed! He was weak in botany, zoology and modern languages. Nevertheless, he obtained a place in the Aargau College in the country which he grew to love, and which he described as "an unforgettable oasis in Europe, Switzerland". At the age of sixteen he had already made up his mind that his future field of research would be theoretical physics. What is perhaps little known is that at that age he was also an accomplished violinist, playing Schumann, Bach, Handel, Mozart and Brahms. Music remained one of his great interests throughout life.

P

At college he studied for a specialist teacher's post in mathematics, and graduated in the year 1900. The subjects studied included higher mathematics, differential and integral calculus, geometry, analytical mechanics, physics, celestial mechanics, astronomy, Kantian philosophy, ballistics, geology, economics, statistical theory and Goethe's philosophy. Even so, he admitted to neglecting mathematics to spend most of his time in the physical laboratory—and in that respect he was a kin spirit to Isaac Newton, who put experimentation before hypothesis.

As a student he lived an austere life on an allowance of 100 francs a month from an aunt, though this ceased when he reached the age of twenty-one. His father died in Milan in 1902, and his mother died in Berlin in 1920. Einstein himself published his treatise on the general theory of relativity in 1916.

During his student days, Einstein was critical of his education and the examination system. His view was that one was obliged to study irrelevant material in order to pass examinations. He commented: "For the examinations one had to stuff oneself with all this rubbish whether one wanted to or not. This compulsion had such a terrifying effect on me that after my finals the consideration of any scientific problems was distasteful to me for a whole year." He took the view that this kind of coercion stifled truly scientific impulse. He wrote: "I believe it would be possible to rob even a healthy beast of prey of its voraciousness if it were possible, with the aid of a whip, to force the beast to devour continuously, even when not hungry, especially if the food handed out under such coercion were to be selected accordingly."

In this Pavlovian sentiment (Pavlov was his contemporary and thirty years his senior) Einstein expressed a fundamental facet of his character: his belief in freedom. Ironically, at that time he could not foresee that he would be forced into exile from his native Germany because of the ascendancy, albeit short-lived, of the opponents of freedom in the form of the Nazis.

In terms of character, Einstein was a man of great humility and integrity; the two go together. He never attempted to conceal his Jewish origin why should he? His ideals were "goodness, beauty and truth", and he never regarded comfort and happiness as a goal in life; they were "the ideals of swineherd". He wrote: "The commonplace goals of human endeavour—possessions, outward success and luxury—have always seemed to me despicable since early youth." He was also an international individual, regarding himself as a lone wolf, never really belonging to any country, to a circle of friends, or even to his own family. Even so, he married twice, and his first wife, Mileva Maric, whom he met at the age of seventeen, became the first woman to have explained to her the evolving Einstein theory of relativity.

Although this chapter is about the man himself rather than science, it is necessary to deal briefly with the subject of relativity—which comes in two forms: the special theory and the general theory. The special theory assumes that the velocity of light remains the same in all co-ordinate systems which are moving uniformly relative to each other. The general theory extends the principle to systems in non-uniform or accelerated motion. Relativity demolishes the notion of an all-pervading "ether" in which light travels, either in waves or particles, and states that all observers in space, whatever their motion, will measure the velocity of light at precisely the same value. Thus, if a space vehicle were travelling at approaching the speed of light and shining a searchlight in a forward direction, the beam from the searchlight would still be travelling at the speed of light and not at the combined velocity of the beam plus that of the moving point of origin.

Furthermore, to the observer the spaceship would appear to contract in the direction of motion until, at the speed of light, it would in effect vanish, at which point, its weight remaining constant, the mass becomes infinite and infinite energy would be required to produce any further acceleration. Therefore, the speed of light represents (to the observer) a limiting velocity in the universe as we know it (i.e., measurable with instruments). Also, to the observer on earth, clocks in the spaceship would appear to slow down as it approached the velocity of light, and would come to a stop at that velocity. This means that, in theory, the crew of a spaceship might go off on a one-year journey into space, involving acceleration and deceleration, and return to earth to find that many decades had gone by.

However, a paradox exists. From the point of view of the crew of the spaceship, they are stationary and it is the observer on earth who is moving at almost the velocity of light, and the earth appears to shrink and clocks slow down. The earth can be regarded as going on a one-year trip into space (relative to the spaceship) and returning in due course to find the astronauts aged by several decades. Well, you can't have it both ways, and both versions cannot be true simultaneously. Nevertheless, the mathematics involved has not yet been faulted. The paradox is "apparent" in the same way as that of the race between the tortoise and the hare; if the tortoise is given a start, then in theory the hare can't win, which is nonsense, but can be demonstrated in fairly plausible mathematics, just as one can prove that $1 = 2$.

Whatever the truth may be, Einstein's theory of relativity has been experimentally proved in practice, by refined astronomical observation and by sensitive measurements in modern nuclear particle physics. The mass of a fast-moving particle does in fact appear to increase if measured by suitable instruments, and light rays can be deflected by gravitation.

It has been very good material for the science-fiction authors, and no doubt Sir Isaac Newton would have enjoyed it immensely, and added his own contribution. The state of the relativity art will be advanced in due course, but the "due course" stage has not yet arrived.

One of Einstein's tutors, who had a lasting influence on him, was Dr Hermann Minkowski, who at the age of eighteen won the Paris prize for mathematics, and was one of the first eminent mathematicians to acknowledge the importance of the special theory of relativity. Another of Einstein's lecturers was Heinrich F. Weber in Zurich who once remarked: "You're a very clever boy, Einstein, an extremely clever boy, but you have one great fault—you will never let yourself be told anything!"

Another physics professor, Jean Pernet, once asked an assistant, "What do you make of Einstein? He always does something different from what I have ordered." To which the assistant replied, "He does indeed, Herr Professor, but his solutions are right and the methods he uses are always of great interest."

This characteristically independent attitude was in no way meant to be insubordinate or disrespectful. His enquiring mind would not accept the absolute authority of the earlier pioneers in physics and mathematics, and he considered that new pioneers would emerge to enhance and "up-date" scientific reasoning and knowledge. While it is unlikely that he thought of himself as a pioneer at that time, he certainly saw no reason why he should not challenge the existing text-book foundations of the then contemporary sciences. Even though an admirer of Newton, he was opposed to the "dogmatic obstinacy" which dominated the physical sciences of his time. It is interesting that when Professor Pernet, charging him with lacking capability in physics, asked,

"Why don't you study medicine or law instead?" Einstein replied, "Because I feel I have a talent, Herr Professor. Why shouldn't I at least try with physics?" Pernet replied, "You can do what you like, but I only wanted to warn you in your own interests."

His dislike of regimentation and the restriction of freedom extended to the German military tradition and militarism in general. He once wrote: "When a person can march with pleasure in the ranks in step to a piece of music, I already have the greatest contempt for him. He has only been given his big brain by mistake —his spinal marrow would have largely sufficed him." He was never required to do military service, mainly because of varicose veins.

Although in a sense he was an atheist and remained independent of any established church, he nevertheless recognized "an intuitive conviction of a superior intelligence which reveals itself to the world of experience", though he would not accept the idea of a personalized God. During his youth, his favourite reading was philosophy, particularly Schopenhauer, Hume, and to a lesser extent Aristotle, Plato and Kant. In literature his main diet was Tolstoy, Dostoevesky and Shakespeare; for bedside reading he apparently favoured *Don Quixote*. He read very few newspapers or magazines; indeed, he took the view that "a man who only reads the newspapers and, at most, books of contemporary authors reminds me of a very short-sighted man who is too ashamed to wear glasses. He is completely dependent upon the judgements and fashions of his age, and sees and hears nothing else." Once, commenting on a large new printing press which he had seen, he remarked: "Marvellous—the only thing missing is a machine to read all that stuff!"

A former pupil of Einstein's in Berne has described him thus: "Einstein is 5 ft 9 in, broad shoulders and a slight stoop. Unusually broad short skull. Complexion a matt light brown. A garish black moustache sprouts above his large sensual mouth. Nose rather aquiline, and soft deep dark brown eyes. The voice is compelling, vibrant like the tone of a cello. Einstein speaks very correct French with a slight foreign accent."

He was careless about his appearance and dress. It is recorded that in 1908, when his sister Maja attended one of his lectures, an organizing official said, "Is that scarecrow your brother? I'd never have believed it!" On another occasion in Basle, when checking in at a hotel to attend a science conference, the concierge was so surprised by his shabby appearance that he asked his unrecognized guest to pay his bill in advance. At the Calvin celebration in 1909 to commemorate the 350th anniversary of the founding of the University of Geneva, he joined the solemn procession of more than two hundred delegates to St Peter's Cathedral for the ceremonial service. All were wearing ceremonial robes, with the exception of Einstein, who was sporting a straw hat and an ordinary everyday suit. And at a reception for Einstein in a big hotel in Prague, he arrived with tousled white hair, wearing a dark blue cheap shirt. The porter took him for the electrician who had been called to repair a lighting fault.

Absent-minded professor? By no means. He was a single-minded and dedicated professor to whom the niceties of social convention and ceremony were, in his view, irrelevant to reality and not to be taken seriously. Thus, when lecturing in Prague for a period, and having been obliged to assume Austro-Hungarian citizenship as a semi-State official, he was required to wear a uniform consisting of a naval-style coat and trousers with broad gold bands, and a triangular hat. This was not Einstein's sartorial style at all, and it was worn by him on only one occasion—when assuming office. When he left Prague he sold it to a friend at half price.

Einstein's post-graduate career began modestly enough with an austerely paid post teaching mathematics at a technical college in Switzerland. In February, 1901, he officially became a citizen of the Swiss Republic. His next important post was at the Swiss Patents Office in Berne, where he was listed as a "technical expert" along with twelve others. His starting salary of 3,500 Swiss francs rose after four years to 4,500 francs. He left the Patents Office in 1909 at his own request, having decided to devote his life to teaching and scientific research. One may assume that his seven-year stint at the Patents Office was triggered by economic necessity, as within one year of taking the job in 1902 he married Mileva Maric, and a son, named Hans Albert Einstein, was born in 1904 (Hans, incidentally, migrated to the USA in 1937 where he became Professor of Hydraulics in the University of Berkeley, California).

While at the Patents Office, however, Einstein was beginning to establish his world reputation as a theoretical physicist of a new order of thinking. In 1905 he published five papers. The first, "A new definition of molecular dimensions", gained him a Ph.D.

degree, and a second paper explaining the origin of light from light quanta won him the 1921 Nobel Prize for Physics for the discovery of the law of the photo-electric effect.

Other papers were concerned with the movement of suspended particles in static fluids, the relationship between the inertia of a body and its energy content, and the electro-dynamics of moving bodies. The latter paper, consisting of thirty printed pages, embodied the groundwork of the special theory of relativity. The original manuscript became lost, but Einstein, decades later, copied it all out again in his own hand to raise money for the American War Loan in 1943—and it was bought by the Washington Library of Congress for six million dollars.

The true birth year of the theory of relativity was 1911, with the publication of a paper, "The influence of gravity on the distribution of light", but it had been gestating for many years before then. And there were many more problems to be solved before the general theory of gravitation was published in a paper as late as 1946.

Einstein had his own ideas on what might be called "the theory of scientific theory". He wrote: "The relativity theory is a magnificent example of the basic character of the modern development of theory. The original hypothesis becomes ever more abstract and further removed from experiment. In this way, however, one comes nearer to the most superior scientific goals with a minimum of hypotheses or axioms to embrace a maximum of experimental content through logical deduction." He also remarked: "Now I know why there are so many people who love chopping wood—in this activity one immediately sees the results."

The physicist Max Planck, who won the Nobel Prize for Physics in 1918 for his work on the laws of radiation, had a considerable influence on Einstein's rise to fame. Planck's life was unfortunately tragic. His two daughters died and two sons were killed in the First and Second World Wars. His home in Germany was destroyed by bombing in 1944 and all his remaining property, including valuable documents, was stolen. His one remaining son was arrested by the Gestapo and never seen again. Planck himself died in Gottingen in 1947. Another scientist who had a great deal of influence on Einstein was Ernest Mach, who was one of the first to question the dogmatism of mechanistic physics following work carried out by Maxwell and Hertz in the electro-magnetic theory of light propagation. Einstein viewed Mach's importance as lying in "his uncompromising scepticism and independence"—a description which equally applied to himself.

But the true point of origin of Einstein's theories is said to date back to his early youth, when he tried to analyze the situation of a man who runs after a ray of light, and a man falling in a lift—in simple terms the bases of the special and general relativity theories. He once told a friend that he "developed so slowly that I only began to wonder about space and time when I was already grown up. Consequently, I probed deeper into the problem than an ordinary child would have done."

Einstein's second son, Eduard, asked him why he was so famous, to which his father replied: "You see, when a blind beetle crawls over the surface of a globe he doesn't know that the track he has covered is curved. I was lucky enough to have spotted it." And on the same theme, Chaim Weizmann, the Zionist leader and later President of the new State of Israel, after travelling with Einstein, was asked if he understood the theory of relativity. He replied, somewhat drily, "During the journey Einstein explained his theory to me every day, and on my arrival I was fully convinced that *he* understood it."

The next step in Einstein's career took place in 1909, when he became Professor (Associate) of Physics at Zurich University. He lived with his family at an apartment in Moussonstrasse on the floor above a physicist colleague, Dr Friedrich Adler. It was Adler who later became involved in politics, edited the Social Democrat newspaper *Volksrecht*, became secretary of the Austrian Social Democrats—and then in 1916 shot Premier Graf Stürgk. At the trial Einstein volunteered to serve as a defence witness but was never called. Adler was sentenced to death, but the sentence was duly commuted to eighteen months hard labour. While in jail Adler wrote a paper on the Einstein and Lorentz theories which was published in 1920. It no doubt helped to pass away the long months of imprisonment, though apparently Einstein did not regard it very highly.

In his academic university role, Einstein never regarded himself as a very good lecturer. His attire was always faded, his trousers invariably too short, and he wore a heavy iron watch chain. He spoke extempore, using for reference only a tiny piece of paper on which were listed a few talking points. Occasionally he would falter in the middle of a lecture, unable immediately to solve a particular mathematical problem, but would carry on talking, meanwhile thinking simultaneously about the problem until he would interrupt his discourse a few minutes later to announce the solution.

If anything, he was suspicious of mathematics (an artifact of human logic) and more concerned with reality as it existed beyond the human brain. There is an anecdote that when he asked a friend the overall length of five matches placed end to end, each match being two and a half inches long, he challenged his friend's reply of "twelve and a half inches" by saying "That is what you say, but I very much doubt it. I do not believe mathematics."

This may sound contradictory in view of the nature of Einstein's work, but he regarded mathematics as a tool, and was more concerned with concepts. Mathematics was the language in which those concepts could best be expressed, although he was also very proficient in expressing those same concepts in ordinary plain language. Once, finding an error in a mathematical work by his colleague Max Planck he commented, "The result is correct, but the proof is faulty. ... The main thing is the content, not the mathematics. With mathematics one can prove anything."

And this same extraordinary man, when moving house, quite happily hitched himself to a cart and transported his own furniture and belongings to the new address.

Professor Alfred Kleiner, Director of the Zurich Physics Institute, wrote as follows: "Einstein ranks today as one of the most important theoretical physicists and his work on the relativity principle has been generally recognized. ... In his writings will be found an implacable striving for truth and an absolute objectivity. He has no personal ambition. He never enters into controversies or discussions which have nothing to do with science. ..."

In return, Einstein gave his own opinion of Professor Kleiner in a private letter to a colleague. He wrote: "Professor Kleiner, the head of our Institute, is not a very great physicist, but a magnificent fellow who pleases me enormously. Apparently scientific repute and great personalities do not always go together. To me a harmonious man is worth more than the most subtle composer of formulas and creator of regulations."

One year after joining Zurich University at a salary of 4,500 Swiss francs (plus lecture fees), which still meant austere living, Einstein accepted a post at the German University of Prague for an extra 1,000 francs. It was that year that he started to learn English. And a year later, finding living conditions in Prague somewhat inferior, he returned to Zurich. It was around this time that his marriage with Mileva began to break down.

It seems likely that while in Prague Einstein found himself an alien. Few people spoke German, and their attitude in general was hostile to the Germans. He apparently missed the meticulous cleanliness of Switzerland, although he wrote: "One should not take it too much to heart. The filthier a nation is, the tougher it is." Perhaps the truth is that within six months of Einstein's move to Prague his colleague Marcel Grossmann was already making approaches to persuade him to return to Zurich, and Einstein made it clear enough that he would be quite happy to return, though in the event he was not to stay there for long.

In the summer of 1913 Max Planck and a colleague, Walter Nernst, travelled from Berlin to Zurich to offer Einstein the new post of Director of the Kaiser Wilhelm Society's proposed Research Institute for Physics. He would also become a member of the Prussian Academy of Science (formed in 1700) at a salary of 12,000 marks. The Kaiser himself approved this proposition, and Einstein duly accepted "this high honour only with a certain amount of awe."

The assumption of his new office marked the end of his long residence in Switzerland (from 1895 to 1913) and also signalled the termination of his first marriage, although divorce was not possible until 1919, after the end of the First World War, during which period his wife, Mileva, and his two sons remained in the comparative safety of neutral Switzerland.

He settled in Berlin in April, 1914, and shortly afterwards the war broke out. His health suffered from the consequent food shortage and rationing, but he continued his work, dismayed by the international disruption of communication between scientist colleagues of different countries. His views on humanity remained unchanged. To a friend he wrote: "Often those men who in politics are the greediest for power and the most ruthless in their private lives could not kill a fly. There is an epidemic of megalomania abroad which, after it has caused endless suffering, will once more disappear so that future generations will look upon it with surprise as something monstrous and inconceivable." He was not to know that in less than a generation an even greater epidemic of megalomania was to erupt, to generate a war even more monstrous and inconceivable, and that he himself, inadvertently, was to provide at least part of the mathematical theory behind the most monstrous and inconceivable weapon of all time, the atomic bomb.

However, he did express some prophetic insight in a letter to a colleague written after the armistice: "Here strong anti-Semitism and mad-dog reaction reigns—at least among the so-called cultured." In the same year, on 29 March, Einstein's theory of gravitation was confirmed by practical experiment during a total eclipse of the sun observed in Brazil and in Portuguese Africa. The scientific expedition was led by Sir Arthur Eddington, and Einstein's desire (expressed in 1911) to be proved correct by astronomical measurement of the deflection of light by gravitational fields was finally granted. The experiment was repeated in 1952 during another total eclipse visible in Sudan, producing even more accurate results.

The years following the war were perhaps the most difficult of Einstein's life, due to the continuing devaluation of the German mark, the insidious growth of anti-Semitism, and the overall political instability. The Nazi movement was still to get under way, but the breeding ground was fertile enough. Einstein himself undertook active work for Jewry within the Zionist movement, but he was also a critic of many Jews, and wrote: "The greatest enemy of the Jewish people and Jewish dignity is fatty degeneration, in other words, the lack of principle induced by wealth and good living." If he was right, then all that was soon to change in a most ruthless fashion.

He travelled a great deal during the post-war years, lecturing mainly in Europe, but also visiting America to help raise money (and successfully) for the Jewish National Fund and the Hebrew University. England, apparently, impressed him greatly—"As long as this land still leads the world everything will go comparatively well." History holds its subtle ironies!

As early as 1921 the American Universities of Princeton and Wisconsin were bidding for Einstein's services as a lecturer, but nothing happened until 1933 when Hitler seized power in Germany, at which point Einstein and his colleague Professor Weyl accepted posts at the Institute for Advanced Studies in Princeton, USA. They had adjacent studies. Einstein never returned to Germany after 1933, though he visited Europe. Under the Nazi regime his property had been confiscated, his citizenship annulled, and there was a price of 50,000 marks on his head. So much for the Kultur of the Third Reich.

Indeed, in 1933 he wrote to a colleague: "My great fear is that this hate and power epidemic will spread throughout the world. It comes from below to the surface like a flood, until the upper regions are isolated, terrified and demoralized, and then submerged." And in the press he was reported thus: "As long as the opportunity still remains open to me, I shall only live in a land where political freedom, tolerance, and equality of all citizens reign." He became an American citizen on 1 October, 1940, though he still retained his affection for Switzerland and kept his Swiss nationality.

What of the older Einstein, the world celebrity, and his slovenly attire? Success did not change him in the least. Even at the age of seventy-five he would still prefer to walk to work, without a hat, wearing crumpled trousers, a worn pullover, a rather tattered overcoat and old sandals without socks. His sense of pomp and circumstance was either inept or tongue-in-cheek. Once (in 1925), in an attempt to show that he could dress smartly if he so chose, he joined a ceremonial procession of professors at Leyden University in the presence of Queen Wilhelmina. All wore formal black togas and black velvet hats—except Einstein, who was sporting a bright blue silk cape embroidered with gold lace and hat with two white ostrich feathers.

Max Picard, the Swiss physiognomist, described Einstein's face as resembling "a reliable old-fashioned shoemaker or watchmaker in a little city, who perhaps collects butterflies on Sundays and reads Fechner of an evening." And, "it is quite different from most physicists. It is not levelled like most scientists' faces, nor is it particularly buffoonish as it might have been. ... He is at home with himself in this face, however far he may travel." Nor did he change in his independent habits; when he had to travel to another town for hospital treatment for a heart condition he insisted on carrying his own luggage—even though he spent three months in bed afterwards.

His life and career during the war and post-war years are well enough documented. From 1933 to 1945 he was Professor of Theoretical Physics at Princeton University for Advanced Studies. He did not have to give lectures and was able to concentrate on his theoretical work in physics and mathematics.

In 1939, one month before the outbreak of the Second World War, he wrote a letter to President Roosevelt containing the following ominous prediction: "In the course of the last four months it has been made probable ... that it may become possible to set up a nuclear chain reaction in a large mass of uranium by which vast amounts of power and large quantities of new radium-like elements would be generated. Now it appears almost certain that this could be achieved in the immediate future.

"This new phenomenon would also lead to the construction of bombs, and it is conceivable—though much less certain—that extremely powerful bombs of a new type may thus be constructed. A single bomb of this type, carried by boat and exploded in a port, might well destroy the whole port together with some of the surrounding territory. However, such bombs might well prove to be too heavy for transportation by air."

On 6 August, 1945, shortly after 8 a.m., an American Super-fortress B25 heavy bomber flying at an altitude of 30,000 feet over Hiroshima resolved the latter doubt. The world has never been the same since. But perhaps it could have been worse, for in 1939 Germany stopped all external sales of uranium from the Czecho-slovakian uranium mines which had just been taken over, and early in the war German physicists were exempted from military service to develop an atomic bomb project. In the end it was pigeon-holed, partly because of uranium shortage, but mainly because it was decided to channel the heavy capital investment required into the more attractive missile and rocket programme which carried higher priority. The Nazi administration made the wrong decision —which was just as well for the rest of the world.

Roosevelt did not hesitate in taking action on receipt of Einstein's letter. Within two months, two billion dollars had been allocated to development work on an atomic bomb and work started at once. The project reached completion six years later on a crash priority basis.

In a press statement issued in July, 1955, Einstein and ten other eminent scientists from all over the world said: "In view of the fact that in any future world war nuclear weapons will certainly be employed, and that such weapons threaten the continued existence of mankind, we urge the governments of the world to realize, and to acknowledge publicly, that their purposes cannot be furthered by a world war, and we urge them, consequently, to find peaceful means for the settlement of all matters of dispute between them." Well, we all know what has happened since then.

Albert Einstein, as a European, was truly a citizen of the world. In 1952, on the death of Chaim Weizmann, Israel's President, he was asked if he would accept the honour of becoming head of the new Jewish State, but declined in his usual modest fashion, saying "I have neither the natural capacity nor the experience in the correct handling of men and the practice of official functions." Also, "I would be unable to fulfil this high task because my advanced age has considerably reduced my strength."

Indeed, Einstein's health and resilience were failing. The man who was described in a New York newspaper as "looking rather like Father Christmas, with his long white hair creeping out from below a woollen balaclava" was obliged to give up smoking and become a vegetarian. He underwent an operation for an enlarged aorta, and gradually it became apparent that Einstein's life was running out. But he still continued quietly with his academic work in pursuit of his general field theory which would encompass and reconcile all the physical sciences in one simple equation. It was a holy grail that he was destined never to attain.

A few days before his death, on learning that he was to be invited to record a broadcast for transmission in Israel to more than 60 million people on the occasion of the State's seventh birthday, he said wrily: "So I still have a chance of becoming world famous."

He died from internal haemorrhage on 18 April, 1955, after refusing an emergency operation. Typically, he had donated his body to a medical school, but, in fact, he was cremated at a small private funeral attended by just a few of his closest friends. The world had lost Albert Einstein for ever; but he had given it more than the theory of relativity—he had given it through his own humanity and humility a philosophy of peace, equality and brotherhood which, unfortunately, seems increasingly out of place in today's world of accelerating violence and declining moral standards.

PICASSO
(1881–   )

GATHERING together on his canvas all the aspirations of the human race along with his own enormous verve and love of life is a small man who lives and works in a French village.

Picasso was born at Malaga in 1881. He showed an early talent for drawing (his father was an art master and recognized his gift) and studied art in Barcelona and Madrid where he soaked up the lessons to be learned from the paintings in the Prado. Through these, he acquired a thorough knowledge of the painting of the past, a knowledge which he broadened by a study of the creative processes behind great works of art. In 1900, Picasso made his first visit to Paris—Paris, the Mecca of artists of all nationalities, and this trip had a decisive influence on the evolution of his art.

On his return to Spain, Picasso's pictures were full of reminiscences of Montmartre—street and café scenes, prostitutes, dancers of the Moulin de la Galette, music-hall artistes, but somehow he imbued these subjects with a Spanish flavour which enlarged their scope and gave them more vigour and pungency. A year later Picasso returned to Paris with seventy-five works which were exhibited at the Vollard Galleries in the rue Lafitte. The dealer Vollard made his gallery a rendezvous for the artists whose works he dealt in, as Théo van Gogh had made the Goupil Gallery a rendezvous some ten years earlier. Among the subjects of the paintings exhibited were Spanish scenes, bullfights and horse races, some nudes and a number of striking flower pieces. This exhibition attracted a lot of attention for Picasso, but he did not rest on his laurels and made no concessions to public taste.

Picasso was twenty years old in 1901 and his pictures of 1901–3 are alive with the fire of his own youth. To have contact with them is to have an interest roused and a sympathy stirred by a young man eager to make us share his passions and discoveries. Picasso was already a master who was creating his own pictorial language for each work; and certain motifs—the harlequin and circus figures, the mother and child, the bull fight, which recur again and again later—are already appearing. Gauguin's influence can be seen in the simplified drawing of the charming *Child Holding a Dove 1901* where the attitude is one which occurs very frequently in Gauguin's paintings. Picasso has always shown great affection for children of all ages and this picture is an example. His treatment of a subject in which the pitfalls of sentimentality are so obvious is saved by the boldness of the brushwork and the heavy outlines, characteristics which also evoke the vigour of Van Gogh.

In the poignantly expressive pastel of 1903, *The Sick Child*, a faint pink glow like a promise of health tinges the livid, bluish flesh. Technically speaking the influence of Lautrec is seen at this time. Like him, Picasso chose the subject matter of his pictures from the life around him, but though influences of this kind are apparent in these early paintings, they are permeated and transformed by the tremendous originality and drive of this new personality.

During his early development, Picasso used less colour and put more emphasis on light and shade. This exclusion of colour gave a sculptural effect to the magnificent series of portraits and still lifes that Picasso painted in the early 1900's. *The Blue Room* is one of the first in which Picasso's natural predilection for blue led him, over a period of some years, to choose this colour for the leading role in his palette. "The colour of all colours, the bluest of all blues" is how he refers to it. The years 1901–4 are known accordingly as his Blue Period although the term is too categoric as vermilion and dark colours appear too.

When he returned to Barcelona in 1903, after another prolonged visit to Paris, Picasso painted a series of emotive figures culminating in two profoundly moving pictures— *The Old Guitarist* and *La Vie*. In this break-away from appearance, forms tended to be elongated, El Greco style, limbs are separated from bodies and weave an arabesque over the picture surface and full rounded curves give way to angular outlines. These two pictures illustrate the extreme development of this new procedure.

Picasso returned to Paris for good in 1904, although he was to continue to make many short visits to his native land. In his *Self Portrait* of 1906 and in the *Two Nudes* of the same year, he was making attempts to escape from his youthful and quasi-sentimental mannerism. He was feeling his way towards a more deliberate and powerful approach and found it in one of his most important paintings which was begun in the spring of 1907. *Les Demoiselles d'Avignon* was in a completely new style, which was begun in the vein of Picasso's harlequin series but ended as a semi-abstract composition. Compared with the numerous Baigneuses of Cézanne, the derivation of the group is obvious. However, there is the essential difference that Cézanne's pyramidal structure is replaced by vertical parallels, but the pose of some of the figures is identical. It has been claimed by art historians that this picture shows the first evidence of Picasso's admiration for African sculpture, but Picasso himself has denied this. It is true, however, that in the early phases of his development Picasso was something of a roving eclectic. Influences from many sources appear in his work— Romanesque art of his native Catalonia, Gothic art in general, sixteenth-century Spanish painting, particularly the work of El Greco; and of his contemporaries he was most impressed by the work of artists like Arp and Miró, but his starting point was in Cézanne. All influences were comparatively sporadic other than the influence of Cézanne, which was permanent. Questions of derivation and resemblance are interesting but not in themselves important. It is the new style that emerges from their complete fusion that was to be decisive for the whole future of western art.

In Paris, with his energy, clearsightedness and mental and moral force, Picasso soon became a leading figure in a brilliant group of friends which included Braque, Derain, Gris and Léger. Each in his own way was to evolve what is now called analytical cubism, and the story of the new art which arose begins a decisive chapter in the history of art. In 1907, the first exhibition of cubist art was held. Cubism was an inquiry into the very nature of the objective world and its relationship to the individual. It began as a logical application of Cézanne's method, which called for the ordering, arranging and imposing of strict architectural procedure in pictorial design, but it carried this much further to mean the analysis of forms and their inter-relation. This meant in practice combining several views of the object, all more or less superimposed, which expressed the *idea* of the object rather than one *view* of it. In spite of its revolutionary trends, Cubism retained an attachment to classical tradition. It was an art-form kept within the limits and limitations of painting, but was no longer required to copy nature or even to interpret it.

In his development of Cubism, Picasso brought to it not only his amazing energy, but also an open-mindedness which enabled him to break with his own past. His practical good sense led him to tackle each of the problems one by one, as it arose, before integrating his discoveries into an organic whole; and with Braque, Léger

and Gris he concentrated on the exciting disintegration and rein-
tegration of natural forms. The rigours of the new discipline of
Cubism, were to limit the range of colour until subtle passages
from ochre to brown or grey were all that relieved it from monochrome. Colour had been set aside as a problem which should not
be allowed to interfere with the realization of form. To quote
Braque: "Colour acts simultaneously with form but has nothing to
do with it."

Cubism was a passion with Picasso for about five years, but he
did not consciously create a system. The term suggests an intellectual or methodical approach to painting, but Picasso has always
emphasized the intuitive and emotional side of his work. While his
painting was governed by the austere disciplines of Cubism, he
subjected his forms to the fierce distortions of his passions. These
distortions were the outcome of his approach, and not out of a
frivolous desire to shock people. Picasso believes "Nature and art
are two different things. Through art we express our conception
of what nature is not". Cubism used as subject matter the most
common objects of everyday use—pipe, newspaper, bottle, glass or
the human form; and at the height of the experiments Picasso and
Braque started to add lettering to their pictures. Picasso saw the
possibilities of this innovation and proceeded to use the original
textures that up to now only paint had produced. He stuck pieces
of newspaper, wallpaper, oil cloth fabric, bits of wood and other
tangible objects onto the canvas, linking these elements with areas
of paint or outlines of charcoal. This technique was given a new
name, collage, and it led naturally to a form of art where sculpture
and painting were combined. Cubism liberated a creative energy
that was to transform the art of the whole world. Its simplification
of form at the expense of representation was the fundamental step
taken simultaneously by artists in countries as distant from each
other as France, Russia, Italy and America.

Elements that appeared in embryo in the paintings of 1910–12
were to become dominant in the paintings of 1913–14. Parts of
musical instruments, fragments of typography and textures of
wood were used to construct several three-dimensional still-lifes.
Picasso's early cubist work has a clear contour, a carefully planned
space arrangement, and plastic modelling painted in cool, greenish-
grey tones which are almost monochrome. However, in a series of
charcoal line drawings Picasso used patches cut out from the
coloured patterns of nineteenth-century wallpapers and pieces of

newspaper, and with these additions came the first reintroduction of colour. Colour had been kept in reserve but now it was to return, not to describe the lighting or the relief of an object but as a delight in the sensation of colour itself. For Picasso, colour returned to his canvas with the excitement of the bullfight, a spectacle of agility and rich colour.

The upheaval caused by the First World War made a break in Picasso's creative effort. Cocteau has told us how he persuaded Picasso to go to Rome in 1917 to make the curtain and design the costumes for Satie's ballet, *Parade*, produced by Diaghileff. Picasso stepped into his new role as theatrical designer with delight and assurance. Bakst, who had been the most popular stage designer for the ballet, praised Picasso and in an introductory note for *Parade* showed how the collaboration of Picasso with Massine had led to a new choreography and a new form of truth. While in Rome with the Russian ballet Picasso was impressed by antique Roman art, and in the years immediately after gigantic nudes appear with placid expressions. They have the simplification of late classical sculpture and Picasso's paintings become magnificently plastic and monumental.

Another interest of Picasso's was sculpture itself, which began to show around 1930 with metal constructions in wrought iron and wire. These developed towards heads, cast in bronze, which had a fragmented effect produced by angular distortions of the modelled surface. Picasso had for many years enormously admired the violence, expressiveness and primitive strength of African sculpture. Its use of geometric shapes and patterns produce an abstract delight in form, and the rich variety in which these shapes are arranged and the vitality that radiates from them brought a new breath of inspiration to Picasso.

1937 was the year of the International Exhibition in Paris and Picasso was asked to provide a work for the Spanish Pavilion. Of mural proportions, the work he offered had as its theme the bombing and destruction of the Spanish town of Guernica by the German air force. Using the favourite device of ambiguity as a means of approaching truth, Picasso filled his canvas with symbolic images which savagely probe a brutal act. The elements which express a specific feeling for violence and of tension had for a long time been appearing in Picasso's work—for example in the orgiastic *Dancers*, the heat of the bull fight, the anguish of the crucifixion, and now *Guernica*—they were all painted with the same passion and conviction. Avoiding the aesthetic distraction of colour, Picasso restricted himself to black, white and greys and it is this simplicity that makes *Guernica* a picture which can be easily understood. As earlier with Picasso he uses the simplest and most traditional forms as a frame for the most revolutionary inventions. The picture of *Guernica* is more than a document of the Spanish Civil War. It is a great work of art and a crystallization of feelings about the horrors of all war, expressing a universal tragedy and the moral issues facing the whole of civilization. Over thirty years later, it has lost none of its monumental significance and its power will grow. No single modern work has had such an impact and there is not one that better illustrates the power which can be created by forcefully moving images on a canvas.

That Picasso is a socially conscious artist is without doubt, and he insists that the artist should not seek refuge in an ivory tower. He wrote in 1945 that: "Painting is not done to decorate apartments. It is an instrument of war for attack and defence against the enemy." The enemy to Picasso is one who exploits his fellow human beings from motives of self interest and profit. Picasso has always had an awareness of the problems of his age, and in presenting such a clear visual image as *Guernica* he has expressed all human suffering for all time.

The years of the Second World War were spent first in Royan, about seventy-five miles north of Bordeaux, and then, after the fall of France, in Paris. Throughout the occupation, Picasso was forbidden to show his work in public (a possible acknowledgement of the powerful influence his work could have) but the policy of the Germans was conciliatory. However, all attempts to win Picasso in any way met with complete failure. Although he had been strongly associated with many movements in the development of art, he was wary of joining any particular group; but in 1944 Picasso felt the need to actually join the Communist Party. In a statement he says: "My adhesion to the Communist Party is the logical outcome of my whole life. For I am glad to say that I have never considered painting simply as pleasure-giving art, a distraction; I have wanted, by drawing and by colour since those were my weapons, to penetrate always further forward into the consciousness of the world and of men, so that this understanding may liberate us further one day. . . . These years of terrible oppression have proved to me that I should struggle not only for my art, but with my whole being." Throughout all its vicissitudes, Picasso has remained a member of the Party because he believes that in this way he keeps a link with the common people. His faith in them is part of his fundamental humanism. Also his membership underlines his lasting disapproval of the Franco régime in Spain.

Although there have been times in his life when he could not find in himself his habitual urge to paint, Picasso never stops drawing. He has an extraordinary ability as a superlative draughtsman, and has gained a great deal of inspiration from the neoclassic grace of Ingres. Drawing is a medium which Picasso uses continuously with an increasing flow of invention. His clear, incisive outlines and his richly expressive subjects are executed with forcible directness and rigid economy of means. Drawings, engravings and lithographs all demand quality in the firmness of their line and are some of Picasso's favourite means of expression.

Picasso's versatility is almost reminiscent of that which we come to expect of the Renaissance man, and it is peculiarly unusual and impressive to-day. His work has included paintings, lithographs, drawings, engravings, ceramics, sculpture, theatre designs, poetry, posters and lino cuts and, at the end of the war, he added play writing to this long list of talents. The play was called *Desire Caught by the Tail* and it was given a public reading in Paris. Those taking part included Sartre, Dora Marr and Simone de Beauvoir, with Camus acting as compère, rapping the floor with a big walking-stick to indicate a change of scene and describing the setting and introducing the characters, who had names such as Big Foot, Fat Misery, Round End, Thin Misery and The Tart. The packed audience sat and stood in reverent attention and those in the cast thoroughly enjoyed the whole venture. Simone de Beauvoir visited Picasso in his home at this time and describes his method of work (painting not literary). "He developed a theme from one painting to the next. He would concentrate on one subject at a time—the sanctuary at Nôtre Dame, a candlestick, a bunch of cherries—and as one followed the sequence of his various interpretations it was easy enough to grasp his creative quirks and caprices where he had forged ahead and where he had temporarily halted."

In 1945, Picasso left Paris and returned to his beloved Mediteranean. Everything there was crowded and disorganized, and he found it hard to work from the hotel bedroom in Golfe Juan where he was living. At this point the Director of the Antibes museum came to the rescue. He offered Picasso the keys of the museum and invited him to use it as a studio. Happy to be in the sun of the south and inspired by his surroundings, Picasso painted innumerable fauns, goats, bulls, owls, centaurs, flautists, dancers and lovers, notably the famous *Ulysses and the Sirens*. Always alive to new outlets for his enormous vitality Picasso was attracted by the possibilities offered by the potteries of nearby Vallauris. Vallauris was a very ordinary little Provençal town with a number of potteries. Running the Madoura Pottery was Georges Ramié and his wife, and one day Picasso joined them in their work. A year later he returned to find that the clay he had modelled had been fired and kept, and his delight grew into a passion which has remained. He moved to Vallauris and began to design a variety of ceramics. The pots, jugs and plates which had been the subject matter of so much of his still life painting were now actually made by him, so combining the arts of paintings and sculpture.

Through his work at Vallauris, Picasso brought prosperity to the village and relaxation and great enjoyment to himself. His friend and biographer Roland Penrose used to watch him at work and describes it. "To see his hands as he moulded the clay, small and feminine yet strong gave a pleasure akin to watching a ballet, so complete was the co-ordination in their unhesitating movements. It seemed impossible for the clay not to obey; in such hands its future form was certain to become impregnated with their life." Also in Vallauris Picasso decorated panels for the barrel vault of the nave of its little chapel. He renamed the chapel the "Temple of Peace" dedicating it to the furthering of peace and the avoidance of war. Also at this time, Picasso designed a poster for a congress in Paris of a white pigeon which was to become familiar all over the world as a symbol of peace.

In 1957, Picasso embarked on a major project. Showing his lifelong admiration for his compatriot Velasquez, he made a series of 44 variations on Velasquez's painting of *Las Meninas*. It is an exploration into questions of spatial relationships as well as a demonstration of how fascinated Picasso was with the original. In the same year Picasso made a gigantic mural for the UNESCO building in Paris.

Picasso's private life, which has been made public by the writings of Françoise Gilot and also by his own paintings, shows a *joie de vivre* which is as appealing in the man as it is in his art. He has never in any way, emotionally, politically or artistically set himself apart from the maelstrom of life. As a result his means of expression is full of life and concern, and its impact is immediate and important.

The achievements of this great artist are immense in their variety and innovating power. Picasso's art has developed simultaneously on several planes and he often moves with fearless daring and courage into realms far beyond the scope of any ordinary artist. He did not try to imitate form but to create it. As opposed to the Impressionist preoccupation with the rendering of ever-changing and superficial appearances, he tried to make images which by the clarity of their structure could convey an idea of life and reality. His mind is always open to new ideas and he never confines himself for long to a single theme. This restlessness has led him to a constant discovery of new and intense means of expression and a deeper understanding of the world we live in.

In considering the act of perception Picasso has always been amazed at the discrepancy between seeing an object and knowing it. When he paints, he takes possession of the object or being so that he becomes its creator. Everything drawn and painted by Picasso is arresting and all his works grip the spectator by the force of the personality that produces them. Representing the superficial appearance of an object is to him absurdly inadequate. Seeing is not enough; there are other faculties such as feelings which must be brought into play if perception is to lead to understanding. It is largely due to Picasso that the conception of art as a powerful emotional medium rather than a search for the perfection of ideal forms of beauty has now become accepted. Picasso's art is not abstract as even the most violent distortions have their origin in reality; but the liberties that he has taken with the human form have made it necessary for him to invent a new anatomy of his own. By the use of his own language of colour, form, image and symbol, he has provoked emotion, enlarged sensibility and gives enormous visual pleasure.

Picasso is the most influential artist of the first half of the twentieth century, with Mondrian, Pollock and Moore being among his most important followers. His contribution to the development of modern art cannot be given to any particular phase of it. Movements were founded on his discoveries and inventions, but throughout the changing twists and turns of his styles he himself always remains apart. "When you come right down to it", he says, "all you have is yourself. Your life is a sun with a thousand rays in your belly. The rest is nothing."

Although Picasso has lived as an expatriate for more than fifty years, he is still essentially Spanish. He is Spanish in his eternal unsatisfied striving, Spanish in his humour, Spanish in his exhibitionism. In Paris as a young man he attended balls dressed as a matador; marrying again at the age of eighty, he dressed up as a high priest. Until the Second World War, Picasso made frequent visits to Spain while living in France. It was his country and it had nurtured his talent, calmed his spirits and renewed his creative impulses. He has never asked for French nationality, and has not travelled outside Europe and very little within. He has never been to Africa whose spontaneous art has influenced him so much, nor to America where his own influence has been so deeply felt. Picasso has always been firmly based in one part of Europe, in domestic life, in political thought and in social contacts, but no limitation can possibly be put on his creative force or the enormous admiration which people feel for his work all over the world.

The overwhelming success of his one-man exhibitions held in recent years shows how widespread is the admiration for his work. His greatness transcends the political frontiers between Russia and America, and Spain is anxious to reclaim its own. Picasso has been connected with many "isms" in his life, but perhaps one of the few he would agree to be fully associated with is Europeanism. While being against the present Spanish régime, he would encourage any movement which brings more people together as a group. While remaining severely individual, it was as part of a group that Picasso first made his great innovations in Cubism. Without losing any of his personal identity, he needed the group to stimulate his inspiration, evaluate his work and encourage his new ventures. The group can accept or reject, and in so doing is an invaluable stimulus towards greater achievements.

Europe to Picasso means in one sense, the small village of Mougins in Provence where he now lives, with its vineyards, olive groves and fields of flowers set among the pinewoods of the low coastal hills. Picasso to Europe means a Spaniard in origins, a Frenchman by work, a European in political thought, and a man of the world in his compassion and concern for humanity and in the enjoyment he has created by his art.

Three Men and an Idea

ARISTIDE BRIAND
(1862–1932)

JEAN MONNET
(1888–   )

ROBERT SCHUMAN
(1886–1963)

ARISTIDE BRIAND was born in Nantes, Brittany, in 1862. Before the 1914 war his activity as a politician was primarily that of a left-wing journalist and deputy, whose main concern was with domestic matters. He was particularly important in bringing about a practical and moderate solution to the Church and State issue, having first entered the government as Minister for Public Instruction in 1906. He became Prime Minister for the first time in 1913, an office which he was to hold eleven times in all.

It was during the First World War, when he was both Prime Minister and Minister for Foreign Affairs, between 1915 and 1917, that he became particularly concerned with European affairs, with the organization of Europe after the war and with the possible creation of a League of Nations. From 1921 to 1922, for a period of some twelve months, he was Prime Minister and Minister for Foreign Affairs, and was directly concerned with the details of the execution of the Treaty of Versailles and the establishment of a system of co-operation amongst various European States. It was during this ministry, when negotiating with the British Prime Minister, Lloyd George, at Cannes, that the President of the Republic (Millerand) became suspicious of Briand's policy, and believing that he was sacrificing French interests to Anglo-French co-operation, he summoned him back to Paris. Briand then resigned. It was from this time that Briand became identified with a particular approach to European problems and was to become famous as The Pilgrim of Peace, "*le pélerin de la paix*", the man whom many were to consider as their chief hope for a world which would not see any repetition of the 1914 war.

By the early 1920's the situation had clarified for the French. There were always those who realized that France was in a permanent position of industrial and demographic inferiority with regard to Germany. France had only won the First World War at tremendous cost, and because her allies included, at some time, the most important powers in the world, Britain, Russia and the United States of America. Therefore France could only have security in the future if Germany was rendered permanently weak. Since the Treaty of Versailles had failed to divide Germany into a number of different states, it was important to see to it that such terms that did exist and that did give some satisfaction to France should be rigorously upheld. In particular Germany had to pay reparations to France, both in money and in goods, and certain areas of Germany were to be occupied by the French army for specified periods of time. The policy of insisting on these terms, in the most legalistic manner, became associated with the name of Poincaré, who had been President of the Republic during the war period and who succeeded Briand as Prime Minister in 1922. It was Briand who became associated with the counter-policy.

At first, Briand's policy had various strands. He believed that if French governments followed progressive, radical policies at home, then the reputation of France would prosper in Europe. At the same time he was a subtle, clever and accommodating politician who never found it too difficult to organize, or to fit in to, different ministerial combinations. In much the same way he was able to discuss matters of policy with other foreign statesmen, always with the aim of reaching agreement. He was informal, direct, perceptive. He won the confidence of foreigners, and he was usually able to justify his actions to Frenchmen by virtue of his magnificent oratorical gifts. And in his discussions and speeches he stressed three points: the importance of the League of Nations; the need to bring about stability by a series of pacts which would guarantee frontiers in different parts of Europe; and the need for a direct *rapprochement* between France and Germany.

The first was shown when Briand became the representative of France at the League of Nations after the elections of 1924. The second was shown in Briand's great achievement, the agreements of Locarno in 1925, whereby England, France, Belgium and Germany agreed to respect the frontiers of western Europe and agreed on the procedures which they would adopt should these frontiers be violated. Briand expected that "this bundle of treaties", as Locarno was called, would be completed by a similar arrangement in eastern Europe. This did not take place, but France maintained a particular interest in eastern Europe by signing agreements with Poland, Czechoslovakia and Yugoslavia. The third was evident in Briand's presentation of Germany as a member of the League of Nations, which he believed was a definitive step towards peace and away from war; and in his secret interview with the German leader Stresemann at Thoiry, a French village near to Geneva in 1926. Briand's daring idea was to deal with the whole of the problem of Franco-German relations, and to bring France and Germany closer together by an economic agreement which would help France out of certain immediate difficulties. Nothing came of this interview, but it was an interesting example of Briand's attempt to solve the German problem by means of an agreement between France and Germany.

Between 1925 and 1932, when he died, Briand gained a complete ascendancy over French foreign policy. Whether he was Prime Minister, or whether he was serving in a government presided over by one of his former opponents, such as Poincaré, his control over the conduct of foreign affairs was virtually complete. His predominant thought was that French interests were best served by the international approach to questions and were badly served by a narrow, exclusive nationalism. "What a waste of energy it was", he once said, "that Joan of Arc should have expelled the English. Had they stayed in France, in a few generations we would have assimilated them. What a magnificent race we would then have created." For Briand, the worst periods of French history, in 1815 and in 1870, occurred when France was isolated. The finest periods in French history took place when France was the symbol of liberty and justice and was surrounded by friends and allies.

From this manner of thinking to the idea of creating some sort of European spirit, was a relatively short step. It was in 1926, on the occasion of Germany's admission to the League of Nations, that Briand declared that once Europe returned to a situation of economic and moral harmony, once European peoples realized that they possessed security, then there would develop the sentiment of being European. No other statesman at the time was able to strike the imagination of his audiences so forcibly as he held up the prospect of universal peace, as he created a mystique of the League of Nations, and presented a vision of the peoples of Europe animated by the same feelings.

In April, 1927, Briand took the initiative of proposing to the government of the United States that France and the United States of America should make a public declaration in which the two of them would outlaw war. The American Secretary of State, in return, suggested that all the countries of the world should sign a pact in which they publicly renounced the use of war. Thus it was that in August, 1928, a vast concourse of statesmen, representing many countries, gathered in Paris in order to sign what was to be called the Kellogg Pact. Briand was under no illusions as to the practical value of this ceremony. Nevertheless it was the first European Conference since Versailles which was attended by the official representative of the American Government, and it was the first time since the war that the German Foreign Minister had come to Paris. This, and the fact that the initiative had been partly French and that Paris was the centre, justified the Pact in the eyes of Briand. He believed that it was necessary to formulate ideas which were large and generous, and that the technical arrangements would follow.

It was deliberately therefore that in September, 1929, speaking to the League of Nations, Briand suggested that where peoples were grouped together geographically, as was the case with the peoples of Europe, then some sort of federal link should be created amongst them. He was careful to point out that he did not believe that this link should only be concerned with economic matters, although he recognized that these would be the most easily established. He insisted that some sort of political union should be erected. In August, 1930, after many consultations, Briand circulated a memorandum to the twenty-seven governments of Europe in which he suggested the creation of a representative European body, which would be called a European conference, an executive body, which would be called the permanent European committee, and a secretariat. The whole of this organization would be placed under the aegis of the League of Nations and none of it would in any way diminish the individual sovereignty of the member states. In September, 1930, the League set up a committee with the task of creating European unity, and Briand was made Chairman until his death.

Briand was not the only statesman to be interested in the idea of creating a European federation. It is possible too that in this, as in other aspects of his foreign policy, his private thoughts were not so bold as his public utterances. As in domestic politics, so in foreign affairs, he knew the value of the imaginative phrase and the sweeping gesture, whilst maintaining a carefully practical point of view with regard to details. It is also true that nothing was accomplished as a result of Briand's initiative. Nevertheless Briand stood for an ideal which was never forgotten in France, at least. He genuinely believed in peace and he resolutely believed in the need to create European co-operation and international reconciliation. He dramatized his own role and identified himself completely with the cause of peace. For many Frenchmen and for many Europeans there was something unforgettable about the spectacle of the old, exhausted orator who promised that as long as there was breath in his body there would be no war.

Aristide Briand died on 7 March, 1932.

JEAN MONNET
JEAN MONNET was born in Cognac, a small town in the Charente district of France, on 9 November, 1888. The region was famous for its brandy, and Jean Monnet's father was the creator of a successful firm. It was as a salesman for this family firm that Monnet, instead of going to university, went to North America. It was probably through this that he early acquired an international outlook which was rare amongst Frenchman. He also became acquainted with American business methods.

Returning to France at the outbreak of the First World War, he demonstrated ideas and techniques which were to be typical of him all his life. He learned that although France and England were allies, they were in fact competing with each other in order to acquire raw materials and other supplies. He succeeded in getting an introduction to the then French Prime Minister, René Viviani, and he persuaded him that he should be given the special mission of establishing a joint Anglo-French machinery for the organization of their purchases and supplies. For the next few months Monnet was engaged in constant negotiation over technical details before he succeeded in setting up a joint supply commission.

In spite of this success, however, Monnet's career between the wars was not outstandingly successful. He was an official of the League of Nations; he advised various foreign governments on economic and financial matters, notably Poland, Rumania and

China; he worked for a number of international business corporations; he made a short and inconclusive venture into French politics, and he continued to look after the interests of his own family firm. Only with the worsening of international relations and the prospect of imminent war did he rediscover his essential role. In 1938 he carried out several official missions for the French government in the United States which were mainly concerned with French rearmament and with the purchase of American aircraft. With the declaration of war in September, 1939, Monnet was given the task, at his own request, of co-ordinating the British and French economic war efforts and he created, and then presided over, a whole network of Anglo-French committees. He was the principal Anglo-French official, and as such he played a vital part in the proposal for a complete union of France and Britain, which was put forward during the military crisis which culminated in the fall of France in June, 1940.

It was typical of Monnet that although he was in London in June, 1940, he did not align himself with General de Gaulle. Possibly, like many Frenchmen, he had his doubts about de Gaulle. Probably, given his understanding of technical matters, he was convinced that the most important country in the world was the United States and that it was there that the destiny of France would be resolved. Therefore he served Roosevelt in Washington, and when de Gaulle established his government in Algiers after the Anglo-American invasion of North Africa, Monnet played a part in facilitating relations between the French and the Americans. He now appeared as an expert in economic matters and his ideas for the economic reorganization of liberated France were particularly welcome. Two points were outstanding. One was that before 1939 France was economically backward and very far from using all her economic potential, the other was that French statesmen and the French public had been notably ignorant in economic matters. Therefore it was important for there to be technical control.

It so happened too that Monnet's position corresponded well to a political difficulty. In the circumstances of post-war France there was no possibility of having a completely free economy; nor was the majority of the population in favour of a Communist or Socialist state which would be one of rigid economic control. Therefore Monnet's form of economic planning was welcome. His was a planning which was rational rather than dogmatic, indicative rather than totalitarian, consultative rather than dictatorial. It was based on the idea that certain objectives should be discerned and designated. Then, meeting together, the government officials, the owners of industry and the employers, the trade unions and the independent experts, could agree on how these objectives could be realized. Thus it was that Monnet became the chief planner of the French economy, the *Commissaire au Plan*, and he brought together a number of economists, officials, engineers, technicians, with whom he was to work regularly over many years.

It is certain that for Monnet the French plan was only a part of a whole. All his experience had shown him that the future lay with international organizations. A traditional idealism, perhaps going back to Aristide Briand (although he was cynical about all politicians), caused him to regard the various European nationalisms as the cause of wars and the curse of the modern world. A more specific economic understanding caused him to believe that all the problems which were facing France, whether of food production, raw materials, capital investment, international currency, prices or trade, were best dealt with in a framework of several European countries. He sought, in the first instance, to discuss the British and French plans for economic recovery and to envisage the possibility of a pooling of their resources. Unlike Briand he believed that it was through discussion of technical details, usually between the technicians of the different countries, meeting not so much as the representatives of their various countries but rather as people with particular knowledge, that the greater principles of collaboration could be identified and attained. In spite of this hope relations between England and France failed to develop precisely because of a number of technical details.

It was therefore rather to Franco-German relations that Monnet turned his attention. In any case, the development of the so-called "cold war" had highlighted the necessity of some agreement concerning the country which lay between France and Soviet Russia. For Monnet the cold-war crisis provided the opportunity of creating both a European mentality and European institutions, out of which there could emerge further ideas of European unity and international co-operation. In April, 1950, therefore, he proposed to the French government that the whole of the coal and steel production of France and West Germany should be placed under a common High Authority, and that other countries of Europe could, if they wished, join their coal and steel production to this same Authority. Like most of Monnet's ideas, this was not original, and a number of other people had talked about the possibilities of such an arrangement. But Monnet's timing was precise. Economically, such an arrangement would affect the future of France and of all other associating countries, at a moment when they were emerging from the post-war crisis. Politically, here was the establishment of an authority rather than the free-run of capitalist enterprise. Psychologically, here was the shock of a Franco-German agreement only five years after the war. Internationally, here was the reassertion of European strength and activity, in opposition to Soviet Russia and independently of the United States of America.

Monnet succeeded in persuading the French government to accept this plan. This meant, in Monnet's mind, the beginning of action. In June, 1950, the governments of France, Italy, West Germany and the three governments of Holland, Belgium and Luxembourg expressed their willingness to negotiate on the basis of the French proposals. Great Britain issued a statement refusing to negotiate on such terms, and referred to the "Six-power communiqué" of the others. This was the beginning of the Six.

In the autumn of 1950, Monnet turned his attention to the question of European defence, for the eventuality of war with Soviet Russia. His solution was as might be expected. He feared the nationalism that could emerge from individual states rearming; he resented the economic wastage which a country such as France would suffer if rearming alone; he suspected that America might tire of defending Europe; he saw the opportunity which co-operation in matters of defence would provide for greater European union. Based upon memoranda written by Monnet and his team, a European Defence Community treaty was worked out. After the final acceptance of the European Coal and Steel Community by the Six in April, 1951, by the Spring of 1952 the Six had also initialled a treaty for a European Defence Community which provided for a European army, under the control of a European Defence Minister and jointly financed and equipped. This was a considerable step towards western European unity. But it was less fortunate than the proposal for a Coal and Steel Pool. Not only did Great Britain once again refuse to have anything to do with it, but political difficulties prevented successive French governments from seeking parliamentary ratification. By 1954 it had to be abandoned.

In the meantime Monnet had become President of the European

Aristide Briand (*right*), eleven times Prime Minister of France in the years before, during, and after the First World War, was one of the earliest and most forceful advocates of European federation.

A politician of a very different stamp was General Charles de Gaulle, who in May, 1940, escaped to England and raised the flag of the "Free French". This photograph shows him reviewing in England a contingent of French troops. When Paris was liberated in 1944 the French made it abundantly clear that de Gaulle was the man of their choice, but in January, 1946, he retired from politics. In 1958, when the army in Algeria revolted, the nation turned to him again. He de-colonized France's possessions in Africa, and created the Fifth Republic. The twentieth-century saviour of France was also a firm believer in a united Europe.

At first a traditionalist Pablo Picasso developed through the years a number of highly individual styles, which art historians have found it useful to speak of as his Cubist period, his "blue" period and his "pink", and many more. During the Spanish Civil War he took the republican side, and his *Guernica* (below) represents the tragedy of the internecine conflict as a nightmare of horrifying character.

Since 1939 he has resided mainly in France, and above he is seen working in his studio at Vallauris.

Coal and Steel Community High Authority, with his headquarters in Luxembourg. The first meeting was held in August, 1952, and from this time onwards, the group of French, Germans, Italians, Dutch, Belgians and Luxembourgers who were under his leadership began to make a reality of their co-operation. As he wished, they saw the Community's problems not according to a national viewpoint, but as problems in which they had a common interest. But although Monnet was determined that "the common market" in coal and steel should succeed, he was also determined that this limited community should expand into something greater. He wanted to join the adhesion of Great Britain to the High Authority, and he wanted to extend the Community to more than coal and steel.

Monnet was showing that he had many qualities. He was patient; he had a great mastery of technical detail; his memoranda were carefully written and re-written; his acquaintances were numerous and he had a mass of important contacts throughout Europe. He was ready to accept a minor success, without insisting upon his original schemes, and when Britain accepted to become associated with the High Authority, but not a full member, in 1954, he readily accepted this as a step forward.

But Monnet realized that it was necessary to give a new impulse to the European movement. In November, 1954, he announced that he was not seeking to be re-elected to his office as President of the European Coal and Steel Community since he wished to possess all his freedom in order to take part in the construction of European unity. Europe was now becoming prosperous; the danger of war seemed to be receding; the institutions which had been intended as first steps to a greater unity had not played their expected role. It was necessary to start again.

In the spring of 1955, under the influence of Monnet, the Belgian government proposed that the Six should consider the extension of the Coal and Steel Community to cover energy and transport, and the establishment of new organizations for atomic energy and employment insurance. A conference held in Messina, in June, 1955 set up a committee to examine various proposals, and Monnet left Luxembourg in order to lead an unofficial action committee for the United States of Europe. Various European events, such as the Suez crisis and the Soviet intervention in Hungary in 1956, or the Soviet launching of its first Sputnik in 1957, helped to hurry on the work of the unofficial committee, presided over by Paul-Henri

Spaak. Eventually a treaty, creating a European Economic Community, was presented to the representatives of the Six in Rome in March, 1957, which was accepted and later ratified by the various parliaments. But no one has ever doubted the importance of Monnet's action committee in forcing the pace and influencing the whole political community of Europe.

After the success of the Treaty of Rome, Monnet's committee continued to work towards a number of particular objectives. He wanted Great Britain to enter the Community; he hoped for the establishment of some meaningful association between a united Europe and the United States; he believed that Europe should move forward from the economic arrangements of the Treaty of Rome, towards a real political unity. He found many obstacles in his way, notably the hesitation of British statesmen and the particular view of Europe as a collection of nation-states which General de Gaulle imposed upon France and France's allies. But Monnet's persistence paid once again. By 1972 he could see Europe moving in the direction he had always hoped for.

ROBERT SCHUMAN

IT WOULD not be correct to consider those statesmen who were important in the emergence of a united Europe, without giving some place to Robert Schuman. In many ways this quiet, shy, simple bachelor was a very unusual person to play a prominent role in French politics. He was born in Metz in 1886 and therefore had been brought up in territory which had been annexed to Germany; during the Second World War he had been made a prisoner by the Germans and had escaped from them. He was profoundly attached to Lorraine and he was highly respected in Metz, where his political situation was secure. But he spoke German fluently; he found it easy to negotiate with Germans; it was natural that he should be sympathetic to any project for reconciling France and Germany and he felt politically strong enough to be able to make such an attempt.

He was also a profoundly religious man, often tempted to enter a monastery. Certainly he felt the need to make some progress towards establishing a just peace in Europe. Doubtless he was influenced by various religious organizations which had already been active in France during the German occupation, and which preached both internationalism and anti-Communism. He had become associated with the new political party, the *Mouvement*

Républicain Populaire, a Catholic Progressive Party which had emerged out of the resistance movement, and he had rapidly become a minister in various post-liberation governments.

In the spring of 1950, having been Prime Minister, he was Foreign Minister in the government presided over by a fellow M.R.P., Georges Bidault. Perhaps it was not surprising that when he was given a copy of Jean Monnet's proposal to set up a coal and steel pool in western Europe (which he received through his personal assistant, a close associate of Monnet) he decided to accept it. But it was important that Schuman should have been a very determined man, since he never wavered in his support for this proposal, and it was also important that he should have been a very skilful politician, since it was by no means easy to persuade the French government to accept this policy.

As Schuman, possibly advised by Monnet, saw it, there were three problems which had to be surmounted at the same time. The one was to ensure that the Germans should not turn the proposals down, and therefore, in the utmost secrecy Schuman sent a special emissary to Dr Adenauer. The other was to gain American support, and Schuman profited from an unexpected visit to Paris from the American Secretary of State, Dean Acheson, to explain the idea and gain his approval. The third was to get the authorization of the French Cabinet. On the morning of 9 May when the Cabinet was already meeting, Schuman received a telephone call from Bonn which gave him Dr Adenauer's agreement. Then, speaking rapidly and in a rather dull voice he presented the plan to the Cabinet. Only two of them had had any foreknowledge. The Prime Minister was cynical, but did not think it worth opposing. Other ministers probably did not understand the significance of what was being proposed. But when the Cabinet had given Schuman authority to proceed, he took the dramatic step of announcing the project from the Quai d'Orsay that very afternoon. In this way the Schuman plan was launched.

There are those who refuse to see this as a success story. Fundamental to their idea is the fact that the British government was annoyed at having been left out of the French government's consultations, and therefore they argue that the whole development of European union was falsified from the start. But Schuman, whilst recognizing British difficulties, was very careful to make his position clear to the British Government, and it is unlikely that there was any real misunderstanding when the British government rejected all attempts to make them accept the principles of negotiation.

When the question of European defence came up, Schuman was hostile to any simple rearmament of Germany, such as the Americans had proposed, and any creation of German divisions within the terms of the North American Treaty Organization. It was therefore for practical reasons that Schuman accepted the idea of a European Defence Community, but once he had accepted the idea then he wanted quick action. He became one of the most devoted and committed members of the Defence Community Treaty in France. As the situation evolved and the Defence Community was eventually rejected in France, this tended to reduce his acceptibility in French political circles. Even when he returned to power in 1955 it was not thought possible for him to be Foreign Minister, and he became Minister of Justice. The left-wing had always attacked him because they accused him of being too Catholic, too capitalist, and too German. The right wing suspected his idealism and his readiness to accept international solutions. With the coming of the Gaullist Republic in 1958 his political role was ended.

It has already been pointed out that Robert Schuman was an unusual figure in French politics. At the same time he was very typical of the M.R.P. and their approach to foreign affairs. The main contribution of the Fourth Republic (1946–1958) was in the realm of foreign policy and was the product of the centre parties. They sought for French security by creating European organizations. The problem of a weak and politically divided France would be overcome if France was an integral part of a prosperous and progressive Europe. These ideals were well expressed by the idealistic and shrewd Robert Schuman.

CHARLES DE GAULLE

(1890–1970)

CHARLES DE GAULLE will be among the better known of great Europeans who figure in this book. It was only in April, 1969, that he abandoned the Presidency of the Fifth Republic as a result of defeat in a referendum on regionalism. He died in 1970 unexpectedly from a heart attack one evening as he was sitting down to play patience. He had been for long a disturbing and invigorating factor in world politics. Outside of France, his policies at times aroused resentment, but equally he was admired. Indeed it was difficult not to admire him even when he was most difficult to understand. Stalin, whom de Gaulle met in Moscow at the end of 1944, had said, "De Gaulle is a simple man". This is both true and untrue. De Gaulle was a very special kind of nationalist leader, with far more in him than the man Stalin thought he had summed up. But he was, as Alexander Werth has pointed out, one of the few "monolithic" characters in French politics.

He entered the stage of world politics when, a relatively little known Brigadier-general, he made his celebrated broadcast from London on 18 June, 1940. He called upon Frenchmen to fight on. A new French Government, formed in the last hours of military defeat, had asked Hitler for an armistice. De Gaulle at that time had no political ambitions, and his motive was the same which led a few Frenchmen then, and many more later, to create the Resistance—an outraged sense of honour and anger at France's defeat. De Gaulle had one other motive, which he held to clearly: to ensure that France had not accepted defeat and would continue in the war. For him Pétain's France was not the real France. This led de Gaulle into political action. He was unknown outside his own country and he had hoped that well-known politicians and generals would lead a Free French movement. This did not happen and, on the contrary, some of the important French personalities who were in London in June, 1940, wanted de Gaulle to serve as an auxiliary of the British. Most of these people, including the well-known writer André Maurois, left London for Washington. So de Gaulle created

Free France, and stood with a handful of men and women against the government of his own country.

Although fortified by Churchill's backing, de Gaulle at first suffered more checks than successes. But by the end of 1942, if not earlier, the support which de Gaulle was receiving from the Resistance in France and from French Africa made it clear that, when the war was won, he would be the only leader acceptable to the French. During the war, however, particularly after 1942, one of the causes of tension between de Gaulle and the Allied leaders, Churchill and Roosevelt, was the refusal of Roosevelt to recognize that de Gaulle did, in fact, represent the French people. It would have saved the Allies considerable stress if this had not been the case. Already, from their prisons or their enforced residences in unoccupied France, Leon Blum, the Socialist leader, Edouard Herriot, the President of the former Chamber and the leader of the Radicals, and Jouhaux, the trade-union leader, had communicated the view to Churchill and Roosevelt that only de Gaulle after victory would be the acceptable leader of France. The non-Communist Resistance had recognized Free France; and the Communists, who since the invasion of Russia formed a powerful new element of the Resistance, had sent delegates to London. Roosevelt was not impressed by this. From 1940, indeed, he had disliked Churchill's backing of Free France which, he felt, damaged the aid the United States was giving the British cause by maintaining an influence with Marshal Pétain and the Vichy government.

Roosevelt disliked de Gaulle, and from the beginning considered him a bigot and a military demagogue, full of personal ambition. After their first meeting at Casablanca, which had none of the storms which sometimes arose between Churchill and de Gaulle, the dislike was mutual. Roosevelt said to his intimates of de Gaulle, "That man thinks he is Joan of Arc". However, as Churchill remarked in a different spirit to that of Roosevelt, there was a good deal in the remark.

In the history of Europe, the importance of Joan of Arc was to have inspired the French people to end their divisions and to drive the English out of France. She expressed French national feeling in a form which was at once royal and popular. The feeling she created dwarfed the insensate quarrels between Armagnacs and Burgundians. There is a paradox about the French. The idea of France has always been capable of appealing to Frenchmen from the days of Philippe Auguste and Saint Louis. But, as de Gaulle points out in his war memoirs, the dispersive elements deeply engrained in the character of the French have frequently in the course of history sapped the authority of the state. It was so in the 'thirties when French politics, and therefore national policy, was torn between the Right, which hated the Republic, and at first secretly, then openly, sided with Mussolini or Hitler as authoritarians—and the Communists. Between these violent forces, the short-lived governments of coalition were rendered weak, and lost the respect of the nation.

In her time a girl of nineteen played, thanks to her voices, the part of unifier; and five hundred years later so did de Gaulle. Both were able to do it because they stood above the quarrels of their time. De Gaulle was a soldier and a man of action, but he was also an intellectual who had studied the history of France with passionate care. He probably did not possess the virtues of the wisest politicians—as Churchill also remarked, but he had a perception of history. He had a magnificent long-term vision, and at short-term manoeuvring he was adept. But he lacked what can be called middle-term vision, that which implies an aptitude to compromise and negotiate. To understand de Gaulle, it is necessary to understand his family background, to begin at the beginning in fact.

On the first page of his war memoirs, de Gaulle states that his father and mother were both intransigent patriots, and that from his earliest days he had a special feeling about his country. France seemed to him like a princess of legend or a madonna on a fresco. "I had by instinct the impression that Providence had created her for the greatest achievements, and that when mediocrity had marked her acts or gestures I had the sensation of an absurd anomaly imputable to the faults of the French but not to the genius of the Country. The positive side of my mind convinced me that France is only herself when in the front rank . . . that our country such as she is, among others, such as they are, must, under peril of mortal danger, aim high and hold herself upright. In brief, in my view, France cannot be France without grandeur."

Charles de Gaulle was born in November, 1890. Both his father's and mother's families belonged to the upper-middle class with a strong Catholic, military and, in the case of the de Gaulle's, intellectual background. His grandfather was a well-known historian; one of his uncles was a botanist, the other an expert in Celtic literature and language. His father, a Royalist, taught in a fashionable Catholic college in Paris. Jean de Gaulle had a great influence on his children, though neither de Gaulle nor his brothers were Royalists—they belonged to the generation which came of age in 1914 and had rallied to the Republic. Both his parents recognized in Charles, the second son, qualities which they thought would lead him to great things. They built up in him a great self-confidence and pride which, however, was never shown in public except in the form of reserve and silence. When Charles de Gaulle did his military service, his commanding officer excused himself to de Gaulle's father for not having given him, Charles, a stripe. "What would be the point of making a corporal out of a young man who already considers himself the Constable of France," he said.

De Gaulle was an excellent classical scholar and his aptitude for history quite remarkable. He seemed fitted to follow an intellectual profession. Indeed as the author of the war memoirs, de Gaulle is assured of a place in the history of French literature. However, with the full backing of his father, he chose the Army. In the 1914 war he was mentioned three times in Army Orders before being wounded and taken prisoner at Verdun. It was in a prisoner-of-war establishment for officers who had tried to escape that de Gaulle largely composed a book on the danger of military influence on the civil authorities in war-time Germany. De Gaulle's subsequent military career was helped by Marshal Pétain under whom he had served. He was devoted to the Army; in 1932 he was considered so able an officer that he was made Secretary to the National Defence Council. However, his advocacy of the creation of a French armoured force on the lines of the Panzer divisions which Hitler was building, an advocacy shared by Paul Reynaud, did him no good with his superiors. Gamelin, who liked him, called him a "philosopher"; Weygand, who did not, "a journalist".

At the age of forty-nine, when war broke out, Colonel de Gaulle commanded a tank brigade behind the Maginot line. In mid-May, with the German armoured divisions racing towards the sea, de Gaulle was given command of an embryo-armoured division. He led the only two offensive operations during the battle of France; both, after some initial success, failed for lack of resources, but de Gaulle was noted as an able commander. On 5 June, when it was clear France risked complete defeat, the then Prime Minister, Paul Reynaud, brought de Gaulle into his re-shuffled government as Under Secretary of War. De Gaulle was a Minister for only eleven days. During this time he won the confidence of Churchill who saw in him a resolute enemy of the Nazis.

The impressions which de Gaulle made on many different kinds of men during the war years reveal not only the de Gaulle of that time, but the President of the Fifth Republic who, with such Machiavellian skill, managed to dupe the French Army and a large part of the nation over his Algerian policy and, from 1958 onwards, to astonish and perturb the world. Churchill laid his finger on the essential, de Gaulle's unconscious identification of his actions with his country, from which he derived his authority to over-rule and over-ride men actuated by lower interests. "I always recognized in him," wrote Churchill, "the spirit and conception which, across the pages of history, the word France would ever proclaim. I understood and admired, whilst I resented, his arrogant demeanour. Here he was—a refugee, an exile from his country under sentence of death ... the Germans had conquered his country. He had no foothold anywhere. Never mind, he defied all. Always, even when he was behaving worst, he seemed to express the personality of France, a great nation with all its pride, authority and ambition."

De Gaulle was a soldier; he was also a man of long-range views, an intellectual concerned above all with history. Emmanuel d'Astier de la Vigerie, one of the first Resistance leaders to come to London—transported by a British submarine in 1941—viewed the General with some suspicion, but afterwards became his friend. He writes at that time: "He remains a mystery to me, the man whose only motive force is an historical idea, the greatness of France, and for whom this greatness of France is a road that replaces all other roads—those of God, of men, of progress and all idealogies.... How often I have regretted not to have known him before, during those days of June and July, 1940, when he begot the France shaped in his own image.... He was like a Hero of Plutarch who was seeking his place in history and had not found it yet."

Soldier and intellectual—but, above all, a man of vocation. Two men whose attitudes to life, politics and de Gaulle were in no way similar, stressed that de Gaulle's peculiar elevation of mind was characteristic of neither soldier nor intellectual, but rather of a priest. Alexander Werth said that de Gaulle was not, in the ordinary sense, cold or lacking in human feeling. It was that his alleged inhumanity was a warm inhumanity, like that of a great Prince of the Church. André Malraux, who became one of the General's few intimates, writes of their first meeting: "I did not come away with an impression of formality, but of a singular distance not only between him and myself, but also between what he was saying and what he was. I had already experienced this intense presence which words did not express. It was neither with soldiers, nor politicians nor artists—it was with certain men of religion whose words, affable and banal, seemed to have no relation to their interior life."

Perhaps these impressions were all derived from great occasions. In private life de Gaulle had nothing remotely resembling the megalomania of some great men. He was rather cynical, pessimistic and outspoken about the defects of other people. He was exceptionally courteous and also devoted to his wife and family. Malraux was to write later that the only difference between the public General de Gaulle and the private one was that the latter did not talk of public affairs.

When Paris was liberated in 1944 the French made it abundantly clear that de Gaulle was the man of their choice. "The French," wrote General Catroux, the only four-star general to join de Gaulle in the early days, "have had in the course of their history many saviours, but only one who, by his solitary effort, had reversed her destiny!" It was from this saving of France's honour, from having enabled France in 1945 to take a place among the victorious nations, that de Gaulle derived his sense of "legitimacy".

In January, 1946, two months after the French Chamber had accepted him as head of the first elected government after the war, he suddenly retired from politics because he believed that the political parties would not accept his policies. He wrote in his war memoirs of this event: "Every Frenchman, no matter what his political tendency, had the feeling that the General carried away with him something permanent, primordial and necessary which he incarnated through history. . . . In the leader now cast aside, they continued to see the designated holder of sovereignty, a last recourse in time of stress." Abstract words, with a strong content of myth. But the myth persisted; and in 1958 when the army in Algeria revolted against the government, there was no one but de Gaulle by whom the Republic could be saved.

So de Gaulle after his great triumph in 1944 had a second apotheosis when at the age of sixty-eight he was called on by President Coty and the leaders of the French Chamber to save France from civil war or, more likely, a military take-over by the French army. "Between you and the Seine, there is only de Gaulle", said Bidault to a Deputy who was bemoaning the need to recall the General. From 1958 to 1962 de Gaulle's task was as difficult, and more personally dangerous, than during the war. He took four years to get peace in Algeria, having to break slowly, and with many ruses, the unwillingness of the French army to allow Algerian independence and the hostility not only from the French *colons* but from a large sector of political opinion found in all parties which held to the myth that Algeria was a part of France.

He had to face in 1961 another revolt of the French army. It was fairly easily crushed because de Gaulle had the courage to tell the conscripts in the army not to obey the commands of disloyal generals and colonels. But he had to use many times what d'Astier de la Vigerie called his three weapons—secrecy, prestige and cunning. He has been reproached by his enemies for not, after 1959, taking the army into his confidence and telling them what his real goal was—to withdraw from Algeria in the higher interests of France. But he judged that the situation in the army and among the French Algerians was too explosive, and who can say he was wrong or that any other man at that time could have carried through the task? During his withdrawal from politics between 1946 and 1958, de Gaulle had thought a lot about world affairs and realized that there was no resisting the winds of change or fighting nationalism in Indo-China or Algeria. He had been in touch, during the years of exile, with men such as Bourguiba of Tunisia, the two Kings of Morocco and many African leaders. As soon as he came back in 1958, he de-colonized all France's possessions in Africa. As a result of this new Algeria, and as a result of de Gaulle's defence of the national interests of the new nations against the two super-powers, the Soviet Union and the United States, de Gaulle became a great name in Africa, Asia and Latin America; and France the most popular, or the least disliked, of all the affluent nations of the Third World.

Over Algeria de Gaulle, with his superior intuition, knew that a vast majority of the French nation, though a silent majority, wanted peace however obstinately and passionately many politicians considered that Algeria was French. To govern is to choose; to choose wisely is to make a choice based on the tide of world opinion, which de Gaulle had listened to just as, during the Second World War, he had studied every fragment of information which reached London about the attitudes of the French.

The third "hard" achievement of the General was to re-model the French constitution, as he had wanted to do in 1945, to give the executive greater stability and the President greater powers. The mandate to do this he made a condition of his return to power. The politicians did not like it, but thought that de Gaulle was impatient, as well as old, and would certainly retire after Algeria was settled. In the eyes of most Frenchmen, even non-Gaullists, the constitution of the Fifth Republic, a sort of hybrid between parliamentary democracy and a Presidential regime, has served France well, and preserved her from those enfeebling, constant changes of government which typified the Third and Fourth Republics; they feel it ought to be preserved. Others, however, think, and thought at the time, that danger lay in the increased powers of the President who, unlike the President of the United States, has the power to dissolve Parliament. The Socialist leader Guy Mollet, with whom de Gaulle always remained on friendly terms, criticized de Gaulle for getting rid of M. Michel Debré, the Prime Minister from 1959 to 1962, and appointing a man with no parliamentary record—M. Georges Pompidou. He saw in this personal choice, and he was right, the sign that de Gaulle, as President, was ceasing to be the arbiter between political forces and becoming the source of all national policies. Over saving the country in 1940 and over de-colonization, you have rendered magnificent service, said Mollet in effect. He continued by asserting that whilst de Gaulle himself was there, he was not worried, but he was very worried about what would happen after him. You can spoil your record, said Mollet.

Nobody doubted that de Gaulle, in his own way, was essentially a democrat and would never dream of using force to keep himself in power. This had been shown explicitly in 1946 when he had retired voluntarily at a time when everyone knew that he could have called on the Army had he wanted to. In 1965 de Gaulle stood for re-election as President and had to go to a second ballot. "Some people say I am a dictator. Have you ever heard of a dictator going to a second ballot?" Of course, there was something abnormal about de Gaulle's position as Head of State. He was a kind of Republican monarch. His feeling that pomp and ceremony should surround the President was not in accord with Republican manners, nor were his constant visits abroad and to the French departments. But at the beginning of his "reign", the prestige of the politicians and of parliament was so low, as a result of the confusion and inefficiency of the Fourth Republic, that nothing could be done about de Gaulle's style of governing. Besides de

Gaulle always had a consensus behind his major policies at least until 1967, when a public opinion poll showed that 70 per cent of the French approved of his foreign policy. The consensus were not always from the same people. Thus the Right and the Gaullists approved of the French *force de frappe*, whilst the Gaullists and the Left approved of his rapprochement with the Soviet Union and his anti-Americanism.

After 1967, his governing became less successful. In pursuit of what he considered the "noble" aims of France, the regime had neglected social policies on many of which de Gaulle had progressive ideas but had paid too little attention to carrying them out. "The events of May"—the revolt of the students which at its beginning had had widespread support from public opinion, and then the workers' strikes—dealt de Gaulle's prestige a blow from which it never recovered, even though at the last moment the General, by a master-stroke of dramatic action, had ended the crisis. Damaging too to his prestige was the Soviet invasion of Czechoslovakia. Even the attitude of de Gaulle to Israel before and after the Arab-Israel war in 1967 was much criticized in France. Over Quebec, when the ageing General was led astray by his enthusiasm for French nationalism, it is doubtful if his actions had the approval of the majority of the nation. But he never lost the at least nominal allegiance of the Gaullists, nor the widespread respect of the nation.

The twentieth-century saviour of France had the task not only of restoring the power of the state, but of guiding France in a post-war world dominated by the super-powers. Stalin was right in seeing de Gaulle as simple in the sense that the man whose main policy was to fight "the double hegemonies of the Soviet Union and the United States", remained fundamentally a nationalist. Whilst being willing to agree that if the two super-powers fought each other, France would be on the side of democracy, and therefore, remaining inside the Atlantic Alliance, de Gaulle progressively removed French forces from NATO and opted out of the Western bloc.

He strongly opposed American policy in Latin America, Indo-China and the Middle East. In this he aroused the sympathy not only of the Third World, but of many Europeans, by no means all of the Left. The French accepted his anti-Americanism warmly, but on the part of the unthinking, because it implied to them that if there were to be a third world war France would remain out of it.

A further guarantee was the French nuclear force which, though relatively insignificant, had a sting which, in de Gaulle's view, increased the respect felt for France. But opting out of the Western bloc implied that France, without the co-operation of the affluent nations of western Europe and North America, could not sufficiently back her efforts at influencing and helping the Third World. To have accepted help, in de Gaulle's view, implied subordination and, between great nations, "the iron rule of states is that nothing is given for nothing". So de Gaulle's attempt at restoring France's world influence as the leader of a group of under-developed or semi-developed countries whose independence was threatened, in one way or another, by the Americans or the Russians, was not without a psychological attraction which benefited France, but basically it had at times a resemblance to Don Quixote tilting at windmills.

De Gaulle was the first European statesman to perceive that after the war the nations of Europe would have to collaborate, and he envisaged as early as 1943 when in Algiers the formation of a group of nations whose arteries were the North Sea, the Rhine and the Mediterranean. But all his views in the post-war period expressed the feeling that France must be the physical and moral centre of such a group. "Europe will not be made unless France takes the lead", he said in 1950. But he condemned the building of European economic institutions in the fifties as a "meli-melo". He viewed the gradual coming into being of the Common Market as a development which would lead to the subordination of the nations of Europe to a group of international technocrats. But, in 1958 when he had returned to power, he honoured France's signature to the Rome Treaty. He perceived that France could gain economically from belonging to the Common Market, that she would be enabled to get her way over basic economic issues, and at once he said that the goal was "an imposing confederation of States". De Gaulle expanded the reconciliation between France and West Germany, begun by Robert Schuman and Adenauer, and his relation with Adenauer was of the warmest kind. When, in 1962, he paid a State visit to West Germany, he was given a tumultuous welcome. Thousands of Germans thought they were greeting in de Gaulle the first President of a united Europe.

In 1961, when de Gaulle and Harold Macmillan met, the latter said to him: "Let us bring Europe together, my dear friend. There are three men who can do it—you, Adenauer and I. If, while the three of us are still alive and in power, we let this historic opportunity pass us by, God knows if and when and to whom it will ever present itself again." "These words," wrote de Gaulle in *Memoirs of Hope*, "touched a sympathetic chord in me." But was not Britain too closely linked, still, with the United States? In 1963, after the British-American Nassau agreement, de Gaulle thought this was so. He vetoed Britain's entry into the Common Market. From that moment, the chance of making a political Europe, an imposing confederation, passed away. Neither Holland, nor Italy, nor West Germany would go any length, politically, without Britain.

In spite of de Gaulle's two successes which have about them an heroic quality—the epic wartime struggle and, in 1958, the de-colonization of Algeria—his career has a tragic element. The first tragedy was old age. Yet even in 1968 he was still remarkably buoyant. To the last, though bewildered at first by the strength of the student-worker revolt, he could re-cast his thinking and he recognized that the confused aspirations of the young needed to be satisfied. He was, however, too old to give a lasting impetus to the policies of participation and regionalism which he put forward in June, 1968. Although his ideas were paid lip-service to by his successor, President Georges Pompidou, the radical changes in society which de Gaulle advocated have not been proceeded with. In the words of Allan Hartley in a remarkable work entitled *Gaullism:* "The Gaullism which survived de Gaulle, the great party of the Right which is his incongruous monument, is but one example of the paradox of history which has so often decreed that a swan's egg should hatch some different, less noble, but ultimately more edible egg."

De Gaulle in his later years—perhaps from 1963 onwards when he rejected the negotiation and compromise by which Britain could have helped to create a European confederation—is bound to appear something of an anachronism. He pursued his own mono-logue with history, but the French people, not only rebellious youth but many conservative members of the Gaullist party of govern-ment, were no longer inclined to accept policies emerging from the monologue of a great man. Under de Gaulle France achieved, at moments, a more dynamic form of national unity than she had ever known. For de Gaulle himself, the real tragedy may have been that he knew he would have no successor who would con-tinue to preserve this national unity. Was not this inevitable in a man whose whole career had been one of struggling against daunting difficulties and conceiving vast projects. Nations in the last resort aspire not to glory, but to peace and prosperity.

Yet if the whole of de Gaulle's career has a certain tragic element, his outstanding achievements assure him of a permanent place in history. Even over the making of Europe it would be wrong to consider that the overall effect of de Gaulle on the union of western Europe—still to be achieved—was negative. De Gaulle created among Europeans the perception of the need for independence; and so important in its time was this, and so strong his influence, that posterity is likely to number him among the Fathers of Europe.

INDEX

INDEX